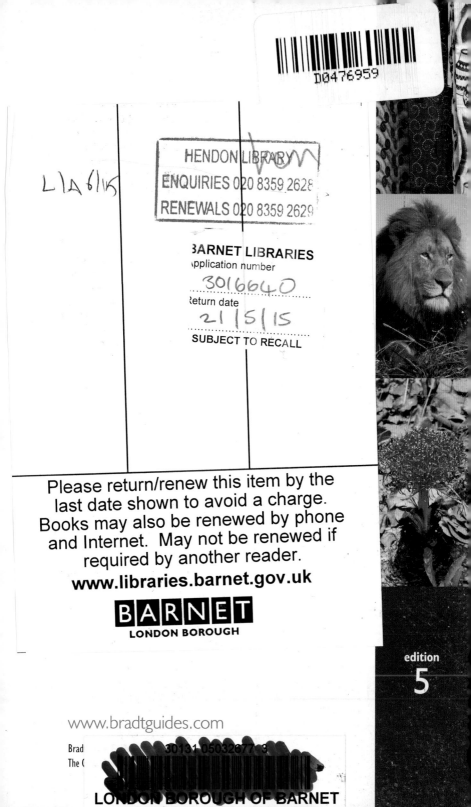

edition
5

www.bradtguides.com

Brad
The (

Zambia
Don't
miss...

Birdlife
Zambia is a superb birding
destination, with 757
different species – including
the grey-crowned crane
(SS) page 32

Victoria Falls
The spectacular Victoria Falls
are 1,688m wide and average
just over 100m in height
(SS) page 192

National Parks
Lower Zambezi
National Park is just
one of 20 national
parks in Zambia
(AZ) page 35

Shiwa Ng'andu
Shiwa Ng'andu is one of
the subcontinent's most
extraordinary memorials
to British colonial rule
(TH) page 316

Wildlife
Zambia's native fauna
comprises classic big
game found throughout
east and southern Africa,
as well as endemic
subspecies such as
Thornicroft's giraffe
(AZ) page 527

left — The Royal Livingstone Express offers an unusual vantage point for spotting wildlife in Mosi-oa-Tunya National Park (BH) page 196

below — Reed houses in Barotseland, where some aspects of life have altered relatively little since pre-colonial times (TH) page 478

bottom — The Ngonye Falls were formed by a similar process to Victoria Falls, with erosion taking advantage of cracks in the area's basalt rock (TH) page 475 above   Many homes boast traditional patterns, but this colourful house in Northern Province is unusual (TH) page 345

right   Children on a pontoon travelling across the Kafue River, east of Chirundu (TH) page 231

below   Fisherman with traps, Bangweulu Wetlands; the wetlands are often described as one of Africa's last great wilderness areas (SS) page 337 *above* One of Zambia's biggest attractions is its walking safaris, which are among the best in Africa (AZ) page 111

left The horseriding trip at Shiwa Ng'andu to the 'View of Angels' is a particularly attractive excursion (CM) page 322

below left The Zambezi, below Victoria Falls, is one of the world's most renowned stretches of river for white-water rafting (SS) page 203

AUTHOR

Chris McIntyre went to Africa in 1987, after reading physics at Queen's College, Oxford. He taught with VSO in Zimbabwe for almost three years and travelled around extensively, mostly with a backpack. In 1990 he co-authored the UK's first guide to Namibia and Botswana, published by Bradt, before spending three years as a shipbroker in London.

Since then, Chris has concentrated on what he enjoys most: Africa. He wrote the first guidebook to Zambia for Bradt in 1996, the first edition of their Namibia guide in 1998, a new Botswana guide in 2003, and co-authored a guide to Zanzibar in 2006. Whilst keeping these guidebooks up to date, he is also managing director of Expert Africa – a specialist tour operator that organises high-quality trips throughout Africa for individual travellers from around the world. It probably sends more travellers on safaris to Zambia than any other company.

Chris maintains a keen interest in development and conservation issues, acting as advisor to various NGOs and projects associated with Africa. He is a Fellow of the Royal Geographical Society and contributes photographs and articles to various publications, including *The Times*, *Wanderlust*, *BBC Wildlife* and *Travel Africa*. Now based in west London, Chris and his wife, Susan, still regularly travel and research in Africa. Chris can usually be contacted by email on chris.mcintyre@expertafrica.com.

PUBLISHER'S FOREWORD *Hilary Bradt*

When this book was first published, an American bookseller wrote to tell me that it was '… the most comprehensive and well-organised book of the bunch and I also believe it is one of the best travel books ever published.'
Over the years, Chris has expanded his guide in line with continuing developments in Zambia's tourism. This ensures that both first-time visitors and those who have a long familiarity with the country will find insightful comments about all that is new in the context of the detailed background text that is the hallmark of the book.

Fifth edition published January 2012   First published 1996

Bradt Travel Guides Ltd, IDC House, The Vale, Chalfont St Peter, Bucks SL9 9RZ, England
www.bradtguides.com
Published in the USA by The Globe Pequot Press Inc,
PO Box 480, Guilford, Connecticut 06437-0480

Text copyright © 2012 Chris McIntyre
Maps copyright © 2012 Bradt Travel Guides Ltd
Photographs copyright © 2012 Individual photographers (see below)

ISBN: 978 1 84162 373 3

British Library Cataloguing in Publication Data
A catalogue record for this book is available from the British Library

Photographs Maruska Adye (MA), Mark Boulton/BIOS photo/SpecialistStock (MB/B/SpS), Paul Goldstein (PG), Bob Hayne (BH), Tricia Hayne (TH), Chris McIntyre (CM), Per-Gunnar Ostby/OSF/SpecialistStock (PGO/OSF/SpS), Philip Perry/FLPA (PP/FLPA), Malcolm Schuyl/FLPA (MS/FLPA), Chris & Tilde Stuart/FLPA (C&TS/FLPA), Sunset/FLPA (S/FLPA), SuperStock (SS), Ariadne Van Zandbergen (AZ)
Front cover Leopard *Panthera pardus* (PG)
Back cover Elephant encounter on a canoe trip, Lower Zambezi National Park (AZ)
Title page Lion *Panthera leo* (AZ), *Chitenjes* (TH), Blood lily *Scadoxus multiflorus* (TH)

Illustrations Annabel Milne
Maps David McCutcheon
Colour map Relief map bases by Nick Rowland FRGS

Typeset from the author's disk by Wakewing, High Wycombe
Production managed by Jellyfish Print Solutions; printed and bound in India

Major Contributors

This book, just as much as the previous editions, has been a team effort, and many have devoted their energy to it. Largest amongst the contributions to this fifth edition are those from the following.

Tricia and Bob Hayne updated much of the text for this edition, having worked extensively on the previous two editions, and helped Chris to update his other guides to Botswana, Namibia and Zanzibar. Formerly editorial director of Bradt Travel Guides, Tricia is now a freelance travel writer, and a member of the British Guild of Travel Writers. When not getting lost in Zambia, she and Bob are more likely to be found toting backpacks on long-distance hikes.

Eleanor Dunkels' love of travel started with three months' marine research off Tanzania's Pemba Island and a further six months travelling in southern Africa. During her summers, whilst reading history at Newcastle University, she made time for trips to Asia and Central America, but the African bug had bitten. So, after another year exploring east Africa, she joined Expert Africa where she now specialises in Zambia, Tanzania, Rwanda and Mozambique.

Nick Hobbs was born in England and raised in South Africa, where his love for exploring remote wilderness areas was fostered. While reading zoology at university, he worked on various projects in Botswana, culminating in a guide's course in the Okavango Delta. Following an MSc at the University of Leeds, he joined Expert Africa, initially specialising in Botswana. He updated the Livingstone section for this edition.

UPDATES WEBSITE AND FEEDBACK REQUEST

If you have any comments, queries, grumbles, insights, news or other feedback please contact us on ☏ 01753 893444 or e info@bradtguides.com with a copy to the author, e chris.mcintyre@expertafrica.com. Alternatively you can add a review of the book to www.bradtguides.com or Amazon.

Periodically our authors post travel updates and reader feedback on the Bradt website. Check www.bradtguides.com/guidebook-updates for any news.

LIST OF MAPS

MAP GRID REFERENCES

Gridlines have been added to the maps of Lusaka, Livingstone, Kitwe, Ndola and Chingola, to allow easy location of sites. Map grid references are given in square brackets in the relevant text, with the page number followed by the grid co-ordinates, eg: [130 D4].

Contents

Acknowledgements

The fifth edition of this book has been built on the first four – and, like those, has been a team effort. For this edition (and in many cases for help with several earlier editions, too), we would particularly like to thank Tom and Viviane Heinecken; Charlie and Jo Harvey; Mark Harvey; Mike and Lari Merrett; the Wilderness team in Kafue and Livingstone; Edjan, Linda, Jacques and Tyrone at Mukambi; John and Carol Coppinger and Remote Africa's team – especially Alex for getting us out of the river; Derek, Jules and Izzy from Shenton Safaris; Andy and the team from Bushcamps; Chris Liebenberg and the Chongwe team; Riccardo at Kanyemba; and Grant and the team from Chiawa. We also owe a debt of gratitude to Evans Muhanga and Jammy Silumesi at the Zambia Tourism Board for kindly providing a vehicle for one of our research trips.

Several people dropped everything to check various sections of the text, or kindly provided bits of the jigsaw. These include the Voyagers' team in the Copperbelt, especially Nicky Duncan-Anderson and Grant Gatchell (who generously kept us on the road, too); VSO volunteer Robert Wootton in Mazabuka; Craig Zytkow at Ndole Bay Lodge; Claire Powell at Thorn Tree Safaris; and in Lusaka, Margot Bham. Thanks, too, to Heather Chalcraft, for her help, and for kindly allowing us access to information from *The Lowdown*.

Many others went out of their way to help with the research for earlier books, including Judi Helmholz and Arthur Sonnenberg in Livingstone; Christina (Gid), Abraham and the NCS crew; Jo and Robin Pope at RPS; Babette and Phil Berry at Kuyenda; Bryan Jackson for great walking, and pulling my Land Rover through a few rivers; Lynn, Pete and Paul Fisher; Charlie Rae; Pete Leonard, who kindly shared information from his encyclopaedic Zambian bird atlas; and Philip Briggs, for the kind use of his writings on Nyika and as the basis for the wildlife appendix.

Zambia's top birding expert, Bob Stjernstedt (see page 208), kindly reviewed the birding comments, making a number of very helpful additions and contributions. Ilse Mwanza's help over the years has been invaluable. And I still owe huge thanks to John Coppinger, not only for unstinting hospitality, but also for his time and many emails in the past about the Luangwa's history, wildlife and environment.

Many readers of earlier editions have helped with their news and views, and countless Expert Africa travellers have generously provided valuable feedback on their trips. These have given me hundreds of extra pairs of eyes and ears in Zambia every year – constantly updating me on the latest news and views of the various camps, lodges and offbeat corners. We couldn't list everyone here if we tried; most will, I hope, forgive me for not mentioning them. However, for extensive contributions I remain indebted to Dave and Louise Armstrong; Sue Grainger and Peter Dolby, Val and Bob Leyland, Harvey Linehan, Roger Marston, Vikki Threlfall, Eric and Mieke Van den Broele; and Larry Barham and Mary Earnshaw for their archaeological expertise. For this fifth edition we've also appreciated feedback from Marisca Bruinooge, Jackie Hadel, Laura Hampson, Kieron Humphrey, Bill McLelland, Heinz Papenheim, Rob Rowlands, Jeff Snijders, Mieke Symoens and family, Nick Thomas, Maina van der Zwan and Syrah van Son.

Colleagues at Expert Africa – especially Claire Scott, Eleanor Dunkels and Lucy Copson – know the country so well themselves that without their help with news and research, and support from them and the whole team there, I'd be unable to continue writing these guides.

Bradt's whole team have, as ever, been superb – including Sally Brock, David McCutcheon and Elspeth Beidas. That which is good and correct owes much to their care and attention; errors and omissions are my own.

Finally my love and thanks to Susie, for company on the road, generous help in writing, map-making and proofing, and for continuous good humour over many years and many books.

AUTHOR STORY

In 1995 I crossed the Zambezi with trepidation. I left behind me prosperous Zimbabwe, which I knew well; I'd lived in the rural areas there for nearly three years. Ahead was the unknown: Zambia. I had been able to find little about the country's attractions, and I expected problems, but backpacking around I found kindness and friendliness in a great country. I marvelled at the Victoria Falls; ventured into the national parks; canoed on the Zambezi; and dined under the stars. The result was the first travel guide to Zambia. Since then, I have returned often, initially with my backpack, but latterly driving a 4x4 and occasionally taking to the air. With Zambia's more inaccessible places within reach, I explored further, discovering hidden waterfalls, private reserves, the colonial extravagance of Shiwa Ng'andu, and the superb birding of Liuwa Plain.

Over the years, I have grown to love the country and have been lucky enough to share it with the visitors that I send there. In updating this guide for the fifth edition, my hope is that you, too, will find it by turns spectacular, challenging and intriguing.

Introduction

Zambia may be becoming increasingly well known, yet the country still retains its essence: that authentic feeling of a wilderness which is wild, beautiful and slightly unpredictable. For those in the know, it remains *the* place for walking safaris. In its three main safari areas – the Luangwa Valley, the Lower Zambezi and northern Kafue – you'll find top, owner-run camps, superb game and some of the continent's best guides. In all of these you'll see few other visitors; most Zambian camps are still tiny and remote. You'll travel around using small, open-sided 4x4s seeing few, if any, other vehicles. Throughout Africa there are khaki-uniformed chauffeurs who drive through the bush, but here you still find expert guides to trust with your life.

In 1999, I introduced the second edition of this guide with the comment that Zambia was a country for the cognoscenti, and especially those who knew about walking safaris – it wasn't a place for everyone. Ten years later, I was forced to reassess. A lot has changed in the intervening years and the options for visitors have broadened. Zambia now offers more than simply superb bushcamps: there is increasing variety – from cultural offerings to family-friendly safaris and luxury lodges. Transport is becoming much easier: internal flights make more areas accessible, whilst old Africa hands are starting to make mini-expeditions here in self-contained 4x4s. National parks that had been written off are coming back to life, as pioneers open up original camps in more offbeat areas. Levels of both quality and choice have generally increased.

Meanwhile, new places to stay and new areas to visit are starting up outside the old, established circuits. Gradually, the rest of this huge country (twice the size of Zimbabwe) is opening up, and its less famous attractions are coming to light. Many of these lesser-known areas are gems. Consider Kafue National Park: this is a wilderness area the size of Wales, yet it receives only a scattering of visitors. The far south of this park is ideal not only for adventurers equipped to camp, but also for visitors to a handful of rustic safari camps. It is less than a day's drive from the busy hub of Livingstone, yet most of its bush tracks were, until the last few years, becoming overgrown.

In the centre of Zambia lies the huge Lake Bangweulu, surrounded by the swamp that defeated Livingstone – his heart is buried nearby. This land of islands and waterways is a permanent wetland, home to the rare shoebill stork and an endemic species of antelope, the black lechwe. It's now easy to fly here, and the proximity of other destinations makes it more attractive: Kasanka National Park and Mutinondo Wilderness are both close by. So, also, is Shiwa Ng'andu, which remains one of the subcontinent's most extraordinary memorials to British colonial rule. Here an English aristocrat carved out a utopian estate from the untamed bush, whilst helping Zambia to achieve its own independence. Although Africa gradually defeated his dream, Shiwa, like Zambia, has been re-invented –

and now tells a new story of how sheer determination can re-shape a place in the wilderness into a world-class attraction for a handful of fortunate visitors.

Far to the west, Liuwa Plain National Park is the venue for one of Africa's last great wildlife migrations: blue wildebeest in their thousands, plus zebra, tsessebe and buffalo, all converging on a vast open plain for the rains. Liuwa is one of the most amazing reserves that I've ever visited in Africa, yet it receives only a few hundred visitors per year. Getting there still requires an expedition, but even this is changing as it is rapidly put on the map by massive investment.

Surrounding Liuwa, in the remote west of the country, is the ancient Lozi kingdom of Barotscland, where the landscape has changed little since Livingstone's day. The rich cultural heritage of a monarch and his people survived colonialism almost unscathed. Their seasonal rhythm is still followed, as the whole kingdom moves by boat from the rich floodplains to higher ground in February or March, making one great, grand traditional flotilla. Now the maps and GPS locations in this guide will enable you to navigate around these areas, and explore a very lovely and remote region that's been largely unvisited by travellers.

Zambia is an amazing country if you can get to its heart. Its government encourages tourism, and foreign exchange is desperately needed to alleviate the poverty of many of its people. But for such logic, this guide might have remained unwritten. Many would prefer Zambia to stay as it is – a favourite place to visit, with superb wildlife, fascinating culture, few other visitors, and Zambians who still treat travellers with kindness and hospitality.

So now, having committed more of Zambia's secrets to paper, I again ask those who use this guide to do so with respect. Zambia's wild areas need great care to preserve them. Local cultures are easily eroded by a visitor's lack of sensitivity, and hospitality once abused is seldom offered again. Enjoy – but be a thoughtful visitor, for the country's sake.

USEFUL INFORMATION

NOTE ON DATUM FOR GPS CO-ORDINATES For all the GPS co-ordinates in this book, note that the datum used is WGS 84 – and you must set your receiver accordingly before copying in any of these co-ordinates.

All GPS co-ordinates in this book have been expressed as degrees, minutes, and decimal fractions of a minute. For further details see page 58.

NOTE ON ACCOMMODATION LISTINGS Where a small group of lodges or hotels come under the same umbrella organisation within a similar area, these have been grouped together. For ease of recognition, the typography used for the 'parent' lodge is as for other lodges, but subsidiaries within the group are noted in small capital letters, with a grey symbol. For example:

🏠 **Kafunta**
🏠 ISLAND BUSHCAMP

Part One

GENERAL INFORMATION

ZAMBIA AT A GLANCE

Location Landlocked in the tropics at the northern edge of the region referred to as 'southern Africa'

Size 752,610km²

Climate December–April hot and wet, with torrential downpours in the afternoon; May–August dry, and fairly cool; September–November dry, but progressively hotter.

Status Republic

Population 13,046,508 (2010)

Population growth per year 2.4% (2011 est)

Life expectancy at birth 46 years

Capital Lusaka (population 2,198,916, 2010)

Other main towns Livingstone, Kitwe, Ndola, Kabwe

Economy Minerals (principally copper and cobalt), agriculture, hydro-electricity, tourism

Natural resources Copper, cobalt, gemstones

GDP US$15.69 billion (2010)

GDP growth rate 7%

Currency Kwacha (Kw)

Rate of exchange £1 = Kw7,954, US$1 = Kw4,970, €1 = Kw6,992, ZAR1 = Kw697 (September 2011)

Language English, numerous ethnic languages

Religion Christianity, Islam, indigenous beliefs

International telephone code +260

Time GMT +2

Electricity 220v, delivered at 50Hz; British-style plugs with three square pins

Weights and measures Metric

Flag Bright green background; panel lower right of three vertical bands of red, black and orange, surmounted by an orange eagle in flight.

Motto 'One Zambia, One Nation'

Public holidays 1 January, Youth Day (March), Good Friday, Holy Saturday, 1 May, 25 May, Heroes' Day (July), Unity Day (July), Farmers' Day (August), Independence Day (end October), 25–6 December. See pages 42–3.

Tourist board www.zambiatourism.com

History, Politics and Economy

HISTORY

ZAMBIA'S EARLIEST INHABITANTS Palaeontologists looking for evidence of the first ancestors of the human race have excavated a number of sites in Zambia. The earliest remains yet identified are stone tools dated to about two million years ago recovered from gravel deposits in the Luangwa Valley and probably also from Victoria Falls. It is thought that these probably belong to the *Homo erectus* species, whose hand-axes in Ethiopia have been dated to 1.75 million years. These were hunter-gatherer people, who could use fire, make tools, and had probably developed some simple speech.

Experts divide the Stone Age into the middle, early and late Stone Ages. The transition from early to middle Stone-Age technology – which is indicated by a larger range of stone tools often adapted for particular uses, and signs that these people had a greater mastery of their environment – was probably in progress around 300,000 years ago in Zambia, based on recent excavations near Lusaka and at Kalambo Falls near Mbala.

The famous 'Broken Hill Man' lived around this time. His skull and other bones and stone artefacts were unearthed from about 20m underground during mining operations near Kabwe in 1921. He has been described as being from a species called *Homo rhodesiensis*, but is more generally attributed to *Homo heidelbergensis*, the common ancestor of *Homo sapiens* in Africa, and of the Neanderthals in Europe. (His name comes from the fact that Kabwe's old name was Broken Hill.)

The late Stone Age in Zambia is normally characterised by a distinctive tradition of geometric rock art; by the use of composite tools, those made of wood and/or bone and/or stone used together; and by the presence of a revolutionary invention: the bow and arrow. This first appeared in Zambia about 25,000 years ago. Skeletons found around the Kafue Flats area indicate that some of these late Stone-Age hunters had a close physical resemblance to the modern San/Bushmen people, whose culture, relying on a late Stone-Age level of technology, survived intact in the Kalahari Desert until the middle of the 20th century.

THE IRON AGE Around 3000BC, late Stone-Age hunter-gatherer groups in Ethiopia, and elsewhere in north and west Africa, started to keep domestic animals, sow seeds and harvest the produce: they were among the world's first farmers.

By around 1000BC these new pastoral practices had spread south into the equatorial forests of what is now the Democratic Republic of Congo (DRC), to around Lake Victoria, and into the northern area of the Great Rift Valley, in northern Tanzania. However, agriculture did not spread south into the rest of central/southern Africa immediately. Only when the technology, and the tools, of iron-working became known did the practices start their relentless expansion southwards.

3

The spread of agriculture and Iron-Age culture seems to have been rapid. It was brought south by Africans who were taller and heavier than the existing small inhabitants. The ancestors of the San/Bushmen people, with their simple Stone-Age technology and hunter-gatherer existence, just could not compete with these Iron-Age farmers, who became the ancestors of virtually all the modern black Africans in southern Africa.

This major migration occurred around the first few centuries AD, and since then the San/Bushmen of southern Africa have gradually been either assimilated into the migrant groups, or effectively pushed into areas which could not be farmed. Thus the older Stone-Age cultures persisted in the forests of the north and east of Zambia – which were more difficult to cultivate – much longer than they survived in the south of the country.

MORE IMMIGRANTS By the 4th or 5th century AD, Iron-Age farmers had settled throughout much of southern Africa. As well as iron-working technology, they brought with them pottery, the remains of which are used by archaeologists to work out the migrations of various different groups of these Bantu settlers. These migrations continued, and the distribution of pottery styles suggests that the groups moved around within the subcontinent: this was much more complex than a simple north–south influx.

THE ORIGINS OF TRADE In burial sites dating from the latter half of the first millennium, occasional 'foreign' objects start to occur: the odd cowrie shell, or copper bangles in an area where there is no copper. This indicates that some small-scale bartering with neighbouring villages was beginning to take place.

In the first half of the second millennium, the pace and extent of this trade increased significantly. Gold objects appear (as well as the more common copper, iron and ivory) and shells from the Indian Ocean. The frequency of these indicates that trade was gradually developing. We know from European historical sources that Muslim traders (of Arab or possibly African origin) were venturing into the heart of Africa by around AD1400, and thus trade routes were being established.

As trade started, so the second millennium also saw the development of wealth and social structures within the tribes. The evidence for this is a number of burial sites that stand out for the quantity and quality of the goods that were buried with the dead person. One famous site, at Ngombe Ilede, near the confluence of the Lusitu and Zambezi rivers, was occupied regularly over many centuries. There is evidence that its inhabitants traded from the 14th century with people further south, in Zimbabwe, exporting gold down the Zambezi via traders coming from the Indian Ocean. Indications of cotton-weaving have also been found there, and several copper crosses unearthed are so similar that they may have been used as a simple form of currency – valuable to both the local people and traders from outside.

By the middle of the second millennium, a number of separate cultures seem to have formed in Zambia. Many practised trade, and a few clearly excelled at it. Most were starting to develop social structures within the group, with some enjoying more status and wealth than others.

THE CHIEFS From around the middle of the second millennium, there is little good archaeological evidence that can be accurately dated. However, sources for the events of this period in Zambia's history are the oral histories of Zambia's people, as well as their current languages and social traditions. The similarities and differences between the modern Zambian languages can be extrapolated by linguistic experts to point to the existence of about nine different root languages, which probably existed in Zambia in the 15th century.

The latter half of the second millennium AD saw the first chiefs, and hence kingdoms, emerge from Zambia's dispersed clans. The title 'chief' can be applied to anyone from a village headman to a god-like king. However, this was an era of increasing trade, when the groups with the largest resources and armies dominated local disputes. Thus it made sense for various clans to group together into tribes, under the rule of a single individual, or chief.

One of the oldest groups is thought to have been that of the Chewa people, led by the Undi, who came to the Luangwa area from the southern side of Lake Malawi in the 16th century. By the end of that century the Ng'andu clan (clan of the crocodile) established a kingdom amongst the Bemba people. These lived mostly in woodland areas, practising simple slash-and-burn types of agriculture. Perhaps because of the poverty of their lifestyle, they later earned a reputation as warriors for their raids on neighbouring tribes.

In the latter part of the 17th century the first recorded Lozi king (or Litunga, as he is known) is thought to have settled near Kalabo, in the west of Zambia, starting a powerful dynasty which lasts to the present day. Early in the 18th century Mwata Kazemba established a kingdom around the southern end of Lake Mweru in the Luapula Valley.

THE GROWTH OF TRADE As various cohesive kingdoms developed, their courts served as centres of trade, and their chiefs had the resources to initiate trade with other communities. Foodstuffs, iron, copper, salt, cotton, cloth, tobacco, baskets, pottery and many other items were traded within Zambia, between the various tribes.

From around the 14th century, Zambia had a trickle of trade with non-Africans: mostly Muslims exporting gold through the east coast of Africa. (This trade had started as early as the 10th century on the Limpopo River, south of Zimbabwe's gold-fields.) However, by the early 17th century the Muslims had been supplanted by the Portuguese, and by the latter half of the 17th century these Portuguese merchants were operating out of Mozambique, trading gold, ivory and copper with Zambia.

Trade with the outside world escalated during the 18th century, as more and more tribes became involved, and more foreigners came to the table. Some chiefs started to barter their commodities for weapons, in attempts to gain advantage over their neighbours. Those vanquished in local conflicts were certainly used as sources of slaves – an increasingly valuable trading commodity. These and other factors increased the pressure on Zambians to trade, and the influx of foreign traders made the picture more complex still.

By the early 19th century, both traders and slavers were visiting Zambia with increasing frequency. These were responding to the increasing consumer demands of newly industrialised Europe and America. More trade routes were opening up, not just through Mozambique and Angola, but also to the north and south. Internal conflicts were increasing, as both the means to conduct these, and the incentives for victory, grew.

WESTERN REQUIREMENTS During the 19th century, the West (western Europe and North America) had traded with the native Africans to obtain what they wanted – commodities and slave labour – without having to go to the trouble of ruling parts of the continent. However, as the century progressed, and the West became more industrialised, it needed these things in greater quantities than the existing tribal structures in Africa could supply. Further, there was demand for materials that could be produced in Africa, like cotton and rubber, but which required Western production methods.

Given that the West wanted a wider range and greater quantity of cheaper raw materials, the obvious solution was to control the means of supply. African political organisation was widely regarded as primitive, and not capable of providing complex and sustained trade. Inward investment would also be needed, but would be forthcoming only if white enterprises were safe from African interference. Hence the solution to Western requirements was to bring Africa, and the Africans, under European rule.

Another reason for considering the acquisition of African territory was that the world was shrinking. There were no inhabitable continents left to discover. Staking a nation's claim to large chunks of Africa seemed prudent to most of the Western powers of the time, and growing competition for these areas meant they could always be traded for one another at a later date.

LIVINGSTONE'S CONTRIBUTION David Livingstone's *Missionary Travels and Researches in South Africa* excited great interest in England. This account of his journeys across southern Africa in the 1840s and '50s had all the appeal that undersea or space exploration has for us now. Further, it captured the imagination of the British public, allowing them to take pride in their country's exploration of Africa, based on the exploits of an explorer who seemed to be the epitome of bravery and righteous religious zeal.

Livingstone had set out with the conviction that if Africans could see their material and physical well-being improved – probably by learning European ways, and earning a living from export crops – then they would be ripe for conversion to Christianity. He was strongly opposed to slavery, but sure that this would disappear when Africans became more self-sufficient through trade.

In fact Livingstone was almost totally unsuccessful in his own aims, failing to set up any successful trading missions, or even to convert many Africans permanently to Christianity. However, his travels opened up areas north of the Limpopo for later British missionaries, and by 1887 British mission stations were established in Zambia and southern Malawi.

THE SCRAMBLE FOR AFRICA British foreign policy in southern Africa had always revolved around the Cape Colony, which was seen as vital to British interests in India and the Indian Ocean. Africa to the north of the Cape Colony had largely been ignored. The Boers were on the whole left to their farming in the Transvaal area, and posed no threat to the colony.

However, Germany annexed South West Africa (now Namibia) in 1884, prompting British fears that they might try to link up with the Boers. Thus, to drive a wedge through the middle of these territories, the British negotiated an alliance with Khama, a powerful Tswana king, and proclaimed as theirs the Protectorate of Bechuanaland – the forerunner of modern Botswana.

Soon after, in 1886, the Boers discovered large gold deposits in the Witwatersrand (around Johannesburg). The influx of money from this boosted the Boer farmers, who expanded their interests to the north, making a treaty with Khama's enemy, the powerful Lobengula. This in turn prompted the British to look beyond the Limpopo, and to back the territorial aspirations of a millionaire British businessman, Cecil Rhodes. By 1888 Rhodes, a partner in the De Beers consortium, had control of the lucrative diamond-mining industry in Kimberley, South Africa. He was hungry for power, and dreamt of linking the Cape to Cairo with land under British control.

His wealth enabled Rhodes to buy sole rights to mine minerals in Lobengula's territory. Thence he persuaded the British government to grant his company – the British South Africa Company – the licence to stake claims to African territory with the authority of the British government. In 1889 Rhodes sent out several expeditions to the chiefs in the area now comprising Zimbabwe, Zambia and Malawi, to make treaties. These granted British 'protection and aid' in return for sole rights to minerals in the chiefs' territories, and assurances that they would not make treaties with any other foreign powers. This effective strategy was greatly helped by the existing British influence from the missions, which were already established in many of the regions. By 1891 the British had secured these areas (through Rhodes's British South Africa Company) from the other European powers, and confirmed their boundaries in treaties with the neighbouring colonial powers.

By the closing years of the 19th century, Zambia – or Northern Rhodesia as it was called – was clearly under British rule. However, this had little impact until local administrations were set up, and taxes started to be collected.

THE MINES In the early years of the 20th century, Rhodes's British South Africa Company did little in Northern Rhodesia. Its minerals were not nearly as accessible or valuable as those in Southern Rhodesia, and little protection or aid actually materialised. It became viewed by the colonials as a source of cheap labour for the mines of South Africa and Southern Rhodesia.

To facilitate this, taxes were introduced for the local people, which effectively forced them to come into the cash economy. Virtually the only way for them to do this was to find work in one of the mines further south. By 1910 a railway linked the mine at Kimberley, in South Africa, with Victoria Falls and beyond, making long-distance travel in the subcontinent more practical.

Meanwhile the cost of administering and defending the company's interests was rising, and in 1923 Southern Rhodesia became self-governing. In 1924 the British Colonial Office took over administration of Northern Rhodesia from the British South Africa Company, though the mining rights remained with the Company. The Colonial Office then set up a legislative council to advise on the government of the province, though only a few of its members came from outside the administration.

Shortly afterwards, in 1928, huge deposits of copper were located below the basin of the upper Kafue, under what is now known as the Copperbelt. Over the next decade or so these were developed into a number of large copper mines, working rich, deep deposits of copper. World War II demanded increased production of base metals, and by 1945 Northern Rhodesia was producing 12% of the non-communist world's copper. This scale of production required large labour forces. The skilled workers were mostly of European origin, often from South Africa's mines, whilst the unskilled workers came from all over Northern Rhodesia.

Wages and conditions were very poor for the unskilled miners, who were treated as migrant workers and expected to go home to their permanent villages every year or so to 'recover'. Death rates among them were high. Further, the drain of men to work the mines inevitably destabilised the villages, and poverty and malnutrition were common in the rural areas.

WELFARE ASSOCIATIONS As early as 1929 welfare associations had formed in several of the territory's southern towns, aimed at giving black Africans a voice and trying to defend their interests. These associations were often started by teachers or clerks, the more educated members of the communities. They were small at first, far too small to mount any effective challenge to the establishment, but they did succeed in raising awareness amongst the Africans, all of whom were being exploited.

In 1935 the African mineworkers first organised themselves to strike over their pay and conditions. By 1942 the towns of the African labourers in the Copperbelt were forming their own welfare associations, and by 1949 some of these had joined together as the Northern Rhodesian African Mineworkers' Union. This had been officially recognised by the colonial government as being the equal of any union for white workers. In 1952 the union showed its muscle with a successful and peaceful three-week strike, resulting in substantial wage increases.

The unions remain a force in Zambia, especially in the state sector. In February 2004, a coalition of unions organised the country's first national strike in 16 years, protesting against tax hikes and wage freezes which were being imposed on government employees.

CENTRAL AFRICAN FEDERATION The tiny European population in Northern Rhodesia was, on the whole, worried by the growth of the power of black African mineworkers. Most of the white people wanted to break free from colonial rule, so that they could control the pace and direction of political change. They also resented the loss of vast revenues from the mines, which went directly to the British government and the British South Africa Company, without much benefit for Northern Rhodesia.

During the 1930s and 1940s the settlers' representation on Northern Rhodesia's Legislative Council was gradually increased, and calls for self-rule became more insistent. As early as 1936 Stewart Gore-Browne (founder of Shiwa Ng'andu; see *Chapter 13*, page 316) had proposed a scheme for a Central African Federation, with an eye to Britain's future (or lack of one) in Africa. This view gained ground in London, where the government was increasingly anxious to distance itself from African problems.

In 1948 the South African Nationalist Party came to power in South Africa, on a tide of Afrikaner support. The historical enmity between the Afrikaners and the British in South Africa led the British colonials in Southern and Northern Rhodesia to look to themselves for their own future, rather than their neighbours in South Africa. In 1953 their pressure was rewarded and Southern and Northern Rhodesia were formally joined with Nyasaland (which is now Malawi), to become the independent Central African Federation.

The formation of the Federation did little to help the whites in Northern Rhodesia, though it was strongly opposed by the blacks, who feared that they would then lose more of their land to white settlers. Earlier, in 1948, the Federation of African Societies – an umbrella group of welfare associations – changed its name at an annual general meeting into an overtly political Northern Rhodesian Congress. This had branches in the mining towns and the rural areas, and provided a base upon which a black political culture could be based. A few years later, it was renamed as the Northern Rhodesia African National Congress.

INDEPENDENCE Despite the Federation, Northern Rhodesia actually remained under the control of the Colonial Office. Further, the administration of the Federation was so biased towards Southern Rhodesia that the revenues from its mines simply flowed there, instead of to Britain. Thus though the Federation promised much, it delivered few of the settlers' wishes in Northern Rhodesia.

A small core of increasingly skilled African mineworkers gained better pay and conditions, whilst poverty was rife in the rest of the country. By the 1950s small improvements were being made in the provision of education for black Zambians, but widespread neglect had demonstrated to most that whites did not want blacks as their political or social equals. Thus black politics began to focus on another goal: independence.

In 1958 elections were held, and about 25,000 blacks were allowed to vote. The Northern Rhodesia African National Congress was divided about whether to participate or not, and eventually this issue split the party. Kenneth Kaunda, the radical secretary general, and others founded the Zambia African National Congress (ZANC). This was soon banned, and Kaunda was jailed during a state of emergency.

Finally, in 1960, Kaunda was released from jail, and greeted as a national hero. He took control of a splinter party, the United National Independence Party (UNIP), and after a short campaign of civil disobedience forced the Colonial Office to hold universal elections. In October of 1962, these confirmed a large majority for UNIP. In 1963 the Federation broke up, and in 1964 elections based on universal adult suffrage gave UNIP a commanding majority. On 24 October 1964 Zambia became independent, with Kenneth Kaunda as its president.

ZAMBIA UNDER KAUNDA President Kenneth Kaunda (usually known as just 'KK') took over a country whose income was controlled by the state of the world copper market, and whose trade routes were entirely dependent upon Southern Rhodesia, South Africa and Mozambique. He also inherited a Kw50 million national debt from the colonial era, and a populace which was largely unskilled and uneducated. (At independence, there were fewer than one hundred Zambians with university degrees, and fewer than a thousand who had completed secondary school.)

In 1965, shortly after Zambia's independence, Southern Rhodesia made a Unilateral Declaration of Independence (UDI). This propelled Zambia's southern neighbour further along the path of white rule that South Africa had adopted. Sanctions were then applied to Rhodesia by the rest of the world. Given that most of Zambia's trade passed through Rhodesia, these had very negative effects on the country's economy.

As the black people of Rhodesia, South Africa and South West Africa (Namibia) started their liberation struggles, Kaunda naturally wanted to support them. Zambia became a haven for political refugees, and a base for black independence movements. However ideologically sound this approach was, it was costly and did not endear Zambia to its economically dominant white-ruled neighbours. As the apartheid government in South Africa began a policy of destabilising the black-ruled countries around the subcontinent, so civil wars and unrest became the norm in Mozambique and Angola, squeezing Zambia's trade routes further.

The late 1960s and early 1970s saw Zambia try to drastically reduce its trade with the south. Simultaneously it worked to increase its links with Tanzania – which was largely beyond the reach of South Africa's efforts to destabilise. With the help of China, Tanzania and Zambia built excellent road and rail links from the heart of Zambia to Dar es Salaam, on the Indian Ocean. However, as a trading partner Tanzania was no match for the efficiency of South Africa, and Zambia's economy remained sluggish.

During these difficult years Zambia's debt grew steadily. The government's large revenues from copper were used in efforts to reduce the country's dependence on its southern neighbours, and to improve standards of living for the majority of Zambians. Education was expanded on a large scale, government departments were enlarged to provide employment, and food subsidies maintained the peace of the large urban population. Kaunda followed Julius Nyerere's example in Tanzania in many ways, with a number of socialist policies woven into his own (much promoted) philosophy of 'humanism'.

In retrospect, perhaps Kaunda's biggest mistake was that he failed to use the large revenues from copper either to reduce the national debt, or to diversify Zambia's export base – but his choices were not easy.

By 1969, the Zambian government was receiving about three-quarters of the profits made by the mining industries in taxes and duties. Because of this, they were reluctant to invest further. With the stated aim of encouraging expansion in the industry and investment in new mines, the government started to reform the ownership of the copper mines. A referendum was held on the subject and the government took control of mining rights throughout the country. It then bought a 51% share in each of the mines, which was paid for out of the government's own dividends in the companies over the coming years. Thus began ZCCM (Zambia Consolidated Copper Mines).

In the early 1970s, the world copper price fell dramatically. Simultaneously the cost of imports (especially oil) rose, the world economy slumped and the interest rates on Zambia's debt increased. These factors highlighted the fundamental weaknesses of Zambia's economy, which had been established to suit the colonial powers rather than the country's citizens.

The drop in the price of copper crippled Zambia's economy. Efforts to stabilise the world copper price – through a cartel of copper-producing countries, similar to the oil-producing OPEC countries – failed. The government borrowed more money, betting on a recovery in copper prices that never materialised.

In the 1970s and 1980s Kaunda's government became increasingly intertwined with the International Monetary Fund (IMF) in the search for a solution to the country's debt. None was found. Short-term fixes just made things worse, and the country's finances deteriorated. The West did give Zambia aid, but mostly for specific projects that usually had strings attached. What Zambia most needed was help with the enormous interest payments that it was required to make to the West.

Various recovery plans, often instituted by the IMF, were tried. In 1986 food subsidies were sharply withdrawn, starting with breakfast meal, one of the country's staple foods. This hit the poor hardest, and major riots broke out before subsidies were hastily re-introduced to restore calm. In 1988 Zambia applied to the United Nations for the status of 'least-developed nation' in the hope of obtaining greater international assistance. It was rejected. By the end of the decade Zambia's economy was in tatters. The official exchange rate bore little relation to the currency's actual worth, and inflation was rampant. Zambia was one of the world's poorest countries, with a chronic debt problem, a weak currency and at times very high inflation. A reputation for corruption, reaching to the highest levels of the government, did little to encourage help from richer nations.

Despite Kaunda's many failures with the economy, his policies did encourage the development of some home-grown industries to produce goods which could replace previously imported items. It also created systems for mass education, which were almost entirely absent when he came to power.

THE EARLY 1990S These economic problems, and the lack of obvious material benefits for the majority of Zambians, gradually fomented opposition. UNIP's tendency to become authoritarian in its demands for unity also led to unrest. Kaunda's rule was finally challenged successfully by the capitalist Movement for Multiparty Democracy (MMD) led by Frederick Chiluba. This received widespread support during the late 1980s, on a platform of liberalisation and anti-corruption measures.

Kaunda agreed to an election, apparently certain that he would win. In the event, UNIP was resoundingly defeated by the MMD (16% to 84%), and Chiluba became Zambia's second elected president, in November 1991. Kaunda accepted the results, at least at face value. However, he later claimed that the elections were unfair because many of Zambia's older people, whom he regarded as his natural constituency, didn't vote. He continued to head UNIP until 2000, and he still lives in Zambia – which, in itself, is a rare and encouraging co-existence in the volatile world of modern African politics.

When elected, Frederick Chiluba faced enormous economic problems, which he attempted to tackle. He succeeded in liberalising and privatising much of the economy, resulting in a freely floating market for the kwacha, and policies to attract inward investment. However, in 1995 the country's debt stood at US$6.25 billion, and debt service payments were some 40% of the gross national product – equivalent to about US$600/£400 per capita per annum. Zambia owed US$3.1 billion to the World Bank and the IMF alone.

Initially Chiluba gained the confidence of Western donors when he came to power in 1991. However, his reforms were long term, and much of their success depended on the continued willingness of international donors to help him. Many allege that corruption grew during his time in power.

Certainly the general attitude of Zambians towards visitors changed under Chiluba: Zambia became a more welcoming country than it was under Kaunda's reign. Tourism began to be recognised as a direct and helpful source of jobs and foreign currency, and the climate of suspicion prevailing in Kaunda's Zambia was replaced with a warmer welcome.

THE LATE 1990S Presidential elections were held in 1996. However, using his enormous majority, Chiluba changed the constitution to include a clause that 'no person born of non-Zambian parents can be president'. Kenneth Kaunda, as is well known, was born of Malawian parents, and so this was a clear move to exclude him from running for the office. It was not the only such move, and caused endless furore.

As head of UNIP, KK called for all UNIP candidates to boycott the elections, believing that they could not be fair. In the event, several UNIP candidates split off and stood as independent candidates, but the overall result was another resounding win for Chiluba. (MMD won about 132 of 150 seats.) It's widely thought that he would have won anyhow, even in a fair election, so it seems a pity that he resorted to dubious tactics to achieve the victory.

With poetic justice, it later transpired that Chiluba himself was of illegitimate birth and uncertain national origin. *The Post* newspaper claimed to have researched and verified that his own parents were of DRC/Zairean descent, which led to a long-running persecution of the paper by the government for 'being disrespectful' and 'insulting' the president – both of which are punishable offences in Zambia. (Travellers take note!)

THE COUP At the end of October 1997, a small group of soldiers briefly took over the state-run radio station. They were led by Stephen Lungu, the self-styled 'Captain Solo', who claimed to represent the 'National Redemption Council'. (Neither he nor the council had been heard of before.) He announced that the group had launched 'Operation Born-again' and ousted the MMD government and Chiluba, saying later in a short broadcast that he had seen 'an angel and the message was that the Government had to be overthrown'.

Although this group transpired to have been little more than a few drunken soldiers, Chiluba used the incident as an excuse to institute a state of emergency for five months. He detained more than 70 civilians and soldiers, including opposition leaders and the former president, KK. Some detainees claimed that torture was used during interrogations, allegations which were later substantiated by the government's own human rights commission headed by Supreme Court judge, Lombe Chibesakunda. The clampdown by the state attracted heavy criticism from human rights groups and affected the international donor community's willingness to release funds for debt relief.

A year later the case against many was dropped for lack of evidence, and some sued the state for wrongful arrest. In 2003, a further ten soldiers were freed, but the remaining 44 were convicted and sentenced to death. However, within a couple of months the president had commuted the sentences to between ten and 20 years of hard labour, stating that he would not sign a death warrant during his tenure of office.

THE END OF CHILUBA'S REGIME Overall, many regarded President Chiluba's presidency as a disappointment, although, looking at conditions in neighbouring Zaire and Zimbabwe, most agreed that the situation in Zambia could have been much worse. Chiluba avoided any military involvement in the conflict in neighbouring Democratic Republic of Congo (DRC) – which had already sucked in Zimbabwe, Angola, Namibia, Chad, Uganda and Rwanda – and instead played a high-profile role in brokering various peace talks.

However, he continued KK's habit of regularly reshuffling ministers (thus ensuring that none developed their own power base), was slow to take decisions and proved unable to control corruption. Despite vowing that he would stand by the constitution, he tried his best to arrange a third term for himself. It was only tremendous pressure from the people, and from within the MMD, that forced him to step down in 2001.

THE 21ST CENTURY In 2001 the MMD's candidate and Chiluba's chosen successor, Levy Patrick Mwanawasa, was narrowly declared the victor with just 29% of the vote, but the elections were criticised by international observers, and three of the opposition parties challenged the results in the High Court. A lawyer by profession, Mwanawasa was almost universally respected for his integrity. With his mandate of 'Continuity with Change', he launched an anti-corruption campaign which resulted in the prosecution of Chiluba, and many of the ex-president's supporters. Yet despite the allegations of misappropriating some US$500,000 of government funds, Chiluba was finally cleared of all charges in 2009. He died on 18 June 2011.

Mwanawasa himself was re-elected in 2006 with a rather more convincing 43% of the vote, but he died from a stroke in August 2008. His vice-president, Rupiah Banda, took over the reins – albeit with a similarly shaky mandate – but it was not to last. On 20 September 2011, following a fiercely contested and at times violent election, the MMD met defeat at the hands of the Patriotic Front (PF), led by the charismatic Michael Sata. The 74-year-old Sata, nicknamed King Cobra, has significant experience, having served with both UNIP and the MMD before setting up the PF in 2001. Indeed, he was only narrowly defeated in the 2008 presidential by-election. The failure of the MMD to hold on to power is in part due to Sata himself, a more colourful character than his presidential adversary, but other factors include a public reaction against the state-controlled section of the media and increasing concern at the perceived lack of benefit to Zambia from the privatised mining industry.

On a less consequential note, keep your eye open for political slogans when you travel. I once saw one in Livingstone encouraging people to vote for women with the slogan, 'A government without women is like a pot on one stone.' This is, of course, immediately intelligible to any Zambian who cooks on an open fire.

GOVERNMENT

The chief of state and the head of government is the president, who appoints cabinet ministers from members of the National Assembly, a chamber of 150 elected representatives. Elections are held every four years, with all Zambian citizens of 18 years and over eligible to vote in a first-past-the-post system.

The country is divided into nine provinces for administrative purposes: Central, Copperbelt, Eastern, Luapula, Lusaka, Northern, North-Western, Southern and Western.

The judicial system was set up according to a British model, based on English common law and customary law. Legislative acts receive judicial review in an ad hoc constitutional council.

ECONOMY

Despite recent improvements in the economy and the write-off of most external debt, Zambia remains one of the world's poorest countries. Nevertheless, continued investment in the mining industry, and an increase in the output and value of both

ADMINISTRATIVE AREAS

N

Bradt

0 ——— 200km
0 ——— 100 miles

NORTHERN
Kasama •

Mansa •
LUAPULA

Solwezi •

NORTH-
WESTERN

Ndola •
COPPERBELT

Chipata •
EASTERN

CENTRAL
Kabwe •

• Mongu

LUSAKA
Lusaka ■

WESTERN

SOUTHERN

Livingstone •

KEY
- - - - - - - Provincial boundary
CENTRAL   Province
• Mansa   Provincial capital

copper and cobalt in recent years has brought considerable economic dividends. In the agricultural sector, good maize harvests in 2003, 2005 and 2010 have given an added boost to the economy. As a result, exports – largely to Switzerland, China, South Africa, the DRC and the UAE – rose by 67% in 2010 to US$7.2 billion, and GDP was up by 7%, compared with 6.3% in 2009 and 5.7% in 2008. Inflation has been brought largely under control, too, falling to single digits in 2006 and standing at around 8% in 2011.

Zambia's recent economic history has been a bumpy ride. In the mid-1990s, prospects looked good. GDP growth was about 6.5%; inflation was down to 24% (from 187% in 1993); a decline in manufacturing had been reversed; non-traditional exports were expanding at a rate of 33% a year; and the privatisation programme was being hailed as one of Africa's most successful. Even the kwacha had been stabilised and a surge in foreign investment was being reported.

By 1998, however, the reversal of Zambia's economic fortunes was stark. GDP growth was minimal, manufacturing output was again in a downturn, and inflation was slowly rising. While the breakdown in the privatisation of Zambia Consolidated Copper Mines (ZCCM) was a major cause of this reversal (see *Copper*, under *Zambia's mining industry*, below), part of the problem stemmed from the coup attempt in late 1997. On both counts, Western donors withheld aid to Zambia.

A year later, when the signs improved, aid and debt relief were again forthcoming, and there was optimism that Zambia's economy could continue to improve. Privatisation of the government-owned copper mines relieved the government from covering mammoth losses generated by the industry and greatly improved the chances for copper mining to return to profitability and spur economic growth.

THE BURDEN OF DEBT   For years, Zambia was visibly crippled by its burden of debt. At around US$500 per person, the country had one of the highest levels of per-capita debt in the world, but a GNI (gross national income) of only around US$340 per capita. About two-thirds of all Zambians lived on less than US$1 per day.

For most of the 1990s, Zambia followed a programme of economic reforms largely dictated by the IMF and World Bank. This scheme, known as the Enhanced Structural Adjustment Facility (ESAF), allowed the world's poorest nations to pay lower interest rates on the money that they owed. In 1995, with assistance from ESAF, Zambia embarked on a series of far-reaching reforms. These centred on trade liberalisation, deregulation and exchange-rate reform. Pivotal to the whole programme was a greater role for the private sector, and the sale of state-owned enterprises, thus encouraging direct foreign investment. The Zambia Privatisation Agency (ZPA), now the Zambia Development Agency, was set up to oversee privatisation.

Having largely followed the dictates of the IMF and World Bank, Zambia found itself in the 'good books' of its donors. However the social consequences were onerous: rising unemployment, increased prices for basic necessities (including the staple mealie-meal) and cuts in healthcare and education. All of these tended to foster an increase in social unrest.

By the late 1990s, Zambia's annual debt repayments were equivalent to about a third of the value of its exports of goods and services. To put this in perspective, Zambia was spending five times more on its interest repayments than it did on education, and three times as much as on healthcare. The consequences were clear: literacy declined and the percentage of infant deaths doubled from 1992 to 1999. Despite this, Zambia managed to remain current on its debt-service payments and even to clear some of its arrears – although such commitments were clearly a major constraint on economic development. Zambia relied on foreign donors for 35% of its budget, but for every dollar Zambia received in aid, it repaid US$3 to service its debt.

Debt write-offs and HIPC status In 1999, the Finnish government announced that it was writing off US$7.5 million of Zambia's debt, and the IMF decided to give Zambia a much-needed boost with US$14 million of its new US$349-million ESAF loan. Also, the World Bank promised US$65 million, despite continuing problems in selling the mines. These were crucial signals to other donors, and on 16 April of the same year the Paris Club agreed to write off US$670 million of Zambian debt, and restructure the repayments of about US$330 million of the rest. Another major step towards helping the country was to confer on Zambia the status of highly indebted poor country (HIPC), which would open the door to the World Bank and other donors relieving more of the debt.

Optimists hoped that these payments would mark the start of concerted efforts by the international community to alleviate Zambia's crippling debt, and that moves to liberalise Zambia's economy would bear fruit. However this optimism was tempered with more realism. Though Zambia had taken most of the economic medicine prescribed for it, trade liberalisation was tough on the country in the short term. A report by the World Development Movement, *Zambia: Condemned to Debt* (see *Appendix 3*, page 535), accused the IMF-backed reforms of being undemocratic and unfair and of undermining development – as well as of being counter-productive and unsuccessful. In 2003 the donors' 'Balance of Payment support' was frozen, on account of the country's weak fiscal management and inability to institute a new Poverty Reduction and Growth Facility strategy (PRGF) proposed by the IMF. Successful implementation of this PRGF strategy was one of the crucial milestone indicators needed by the IMF and World Bank before Zambia could reach the 'completion point' under the HIPC initiative that would trigger debt relief. Meanwhile, Zambia's debt repayments continued to cripple the economy.

In 2005, it was agreed at the G8 summit to write off US$40 billion of debt owed by 18 of the worlds HIPCs, of which Zambia was one. Following a write-off of US$7 billion, the country was left with a residual external debt of US$500 million. The Zambian government pledged to invest the proceeds in health and education, and in 2006 restored free health care to those living in rural areas. The government continues to borrow, however, and in 2010, the country's external debt stood at US$1.2 billion.

STRUCTURE OF THE ECONOMY Zambia's economy is totally dependent upon its mining sector, and particularly its copper mines, although agriculture, industry and tourism all make their contribution, and the government is committed to diversification. The country's high, well-watered plateau means that it has about 40% of southern Africa's water resources. Hydro-electric schemes, which provide most of the country's power, make it self-sufficient in energy, and Zambia already exports power to neighbouring countries.

Zambia's mining industry Mining as a whole accounts for around 85% of Zambia's export earnings and about 11% of its GDP, a figure that is anticipated to rise to 20% by 2015. Significant investment in recent years from countries as diverse as Brazil, South Africa and – most importantly – China has resulted from a combination of high copper prices and changes in regulations that have attracted considerable overseas interest in the sector.

Copper is easily the country's most important natural resource, with cobalt second; it also has considerable reserves of silver and selenium, as well as small but significant quantities of other minerals and gemstones.

Copper Zambia has large, high-quality deposits of copper ore, and is the world's seventh-largest producer of copper – employing over 12 million people. In 2010, production grew by over 17% to reach 819,159 tonnes, with a figure of 900,000 tonnes predicted for 2011. This compares with an output of around 700,000 tonnes recorded in the late 1970s. The opening of several new mines is a reflection of the high copper prices on the world market, running at an all-time high of US$9,660 a tonne at the end of 2010, and has contributed to a boom in Zambia's industrial heartland, the Copperbelt region.

Before 2000, all the mines were controlled by the parastatal Zambia Consolidated Copper Mines (ZCCM), which had long been viewed as the jewel of Zambia's economic crown. Of these, Nchanga and Nkana mines alone accounted for 65% of Zambia's total copper production. However, disuse and mismanagement caused Zambia's mines to degenerate, and by the late 1990s they were recording losses of around US$15–20 million per month. In 2000 they were eventually privatised, and bought by a consortium led by Anglo American. Ironically, the mines originally belonged to Anglo American before they were nationalised.

Cobalt Zambia is the world's second-largest producer of cobalt, currently producing around 4,000 tonnes per annum of this valuable, strategic metal: some 20% of the world's total production. It is usually produced as a by-product of copper or nickel mines. Indeed, in one Zambian deal, a private mining company that was granted rights to extract cobalt and copper from Nkana's slag heap estimated that this still contained about 56,000 tonnes of cobalt and 86,000 tonnes of copper.

Coal Zambia's main coal mine is the former state-owned open-pit mine at Maamba, near Lake Kariba. In 2009, a controlling share in the mine was bought by a Singapore-based company, who announced investment of US$108 million. As a result, it is estimated that production will return to around 360,000 tonnes a year, following a dip to just 8,000 tonnes in 2006. In recent years industrial unrest has bedevilled both this and the nearby Collum Mine, which, in 2010, hit the headlines when the Chinese management opened fire on protesting workers.

Other mineral resources Zambia has natural resources of amethyst, fluorite, feldspar, gypsum, aquamarine, lead, zinc, tin and gold – as well as a variety of gemstones. All are on a small scale, and few are being commercially exploited. An exception is emeralds, which are said to be among the highest quality in the world. However, although these are being mined on a small scale to the order of about US$200 million per year, about half are thought to be smuggled out of the country, so the real amounts remain uncertain. It has been estimated that if the resources were properly managed, the gemstone industry as a whole could be worth as much as US$600 million per year.

Other industrial sectors Zambia's manufacturing industry is focused primarily on construction, chemicals, textiles and fertiliser production, and accounts for about 34% of its GDP. The domestic market, though, is small, and high costs mean that the sector isn't very competitive regionally. Nevertheless, products such as cement and tobacco are performing relatively well – with exports of these, together with other non-traditional exports (NTEs), including agriculture, up from 19% in 2006 to 23% in 2009. The government aims to increase this contribution to around 30% by 2015.

Agriculture Agriculture accounts for less than 20% of Zambia's GDP, but employs perhaps 70% of its workforce. Although most farming is still done by small-scale subsistence farmers, large commercial farms are becoming more important, often financed by private investors. Zambia's varied topography encourages a wide diversity in the crops cultivated. The main commercial crops are maize (the staple food for most people), sugar, tobacco, cotton and coffee, with sorghum, rice, peanuts, soya beans, sunflowers and cassava also grown, and cattle, goats, beef and eggs produced. Following a series of excellent maize harvests in the last decade, the country recorded a 25% increase in production in 2010.

Tourism Zambia has the (arguable) benefit of a late-developing tourism industry, which should allow it to learn from the mistakes of others. Hopes for the development of tourism lie firmly with the private sector, and the government is happy for private investors to buy into the industry. Since the mid-1990s tourism has been expanding very steadily – which is by far the best way for a tourism industry to move if it is to stay on a sustainable basis – and increasingly there is a focus on the development that tourism can bring to local communities.

Until around 2000, Zambia's annual visitor influx could still probably have been counted in the low thousands. Then came political turmoil in Zimbabwe, which resulted in the rapid demise of that country's tourism industry. Livingstone, meanwhile, has experienced significant developments in its tourist infrastructure (albeit not without considerable pressure for unsustainable development from some sectors). As a result, the town has taken on the mantle of regional tourism capital, formerly held by its neighbour, the Zimbabwean town of Victoria Falls.

While tourism remains one of Zambia's least-developed sectors, generating an estimated 4% of GDP in recent years, arguably it holds the greatest potential. In 2007, the number of tourists rose by 17% over the previous year to 805,050.

The praises of Zambia's national parks are sung elsewhere in this book, but here it's worth noting that the country's best camps command prices (and standards) to match their equivalents in Tanzania, Zimbabwe or Botswana. What's more, Zambia still has vast tracts of pristine wilderness, which is exactly what is needed for new safari destinations. Most importantly, visitors to Africa realise that top wildlife guides, like those found in Zambia, are few and far between.

2

People and Culture

POPULATION OVERVIEW

Zambia's 2010 census puts the country's population at just over 13 million, some two-thirds of whom live below the poverty line. The vast majority of people are of black African (Bantu) descent, though there are significant communities whose ancestors came from Europe and India. Zambia is a large country, and its population density – around 17 people per square kilometre – is relatively low: just over half that of Zimbabwe, or about a quarter of the population density of Kenya. According to the United Nations, about 52% of the population is under 18 years of age, and the population growth rate is about 2.6% per annum. Some 71% of those above age 15 are literate.

Zambia's urban population is about 39% of the total, with the capital, Lusaka, home to almost 17% of the country's population. A further 1.9 million live in the Copperbelt Province, predominantly in the main towns of Kitwe, Ndola, Chingola and Mufulira. Thus, the rural areas generally have a low population density, and the country retains large tracts of wilderness.

Statistics indicate that although infant mortality is still nearly 9%, the average life expectancy for a Zambian has risen to 46 years. This is at least in part due to the decline in incidence of HIV/AIDS: it is estimated that the number of people between the ages of 15 and 49 who are affected by AIDS fell to around 13.5% in 2010.

However, the statistics say nothing of the warmth that the sensitive visitor can encounter. If you venture into the rural areas, take a local bus, or try to hitchhike with the locals; you will often find that Zambians are curious about you. Chat to them openly, as fellow travellers, and you will find most Zambians to be delightful. They will be pleased to assist you where they can, and as keen to help you learn about them and their country as they are interested in your lifestyle and what brings you to Zambia.

ETHNIC GROUPS

AFRICAN LANGUAGE GROUPS English is the official language in Zambia, and most urban Zambians speak it fluently. In rural areas it is used less, though only in truly remote settlements will you encounter problems communicating in English.

The main vernacular languages are Bemba, Kaonde, Lozi, Lunda, Luvale, Nyanja and Tonga – though more than 72 different languages and dialects are spoken in the country. Of these, the most widely recognised and understood are Nyanja and Bemba. For basic words and phrases, see *Appendix 2*, page 532.

Below are detailed some of the major language groups, arranged alphabetically. This is only a rough guide to the languages and dialects of Zambia's people. Although these different language groupings do loosely correspond to what many describe as

Zambia's tribes, the distinctions are blurred further by the natural linguistic ability of most Zambians. Whilst it is normal to speak English plus one local language, many Zambians will speak a number of local languages fluently.

When the colonial powers carved up Africa, the divisions between the countries bore only a passing resemblance to the traditional areas of these various ethnic groups. Thus many of the groups here are split between several countries. Note that the estimates of populations quoted below are based on surveys done during the 1980s, and average estimated population growth rates since then.

Bemba Bemba is the first language of about two and a quarter million Zambians: almost a quarter of the country's population. It is spoken in the rural areas of northern Zambia, from the Luapula River eastwards to Mpika, Kasama and beyond.

A NOTE ON 'TRIBES'

The people of Africa are often viewed, from abroad, as belonging to a multitude of culturally and linguistically distinct tribes – which are often portrayed as being at odds with each other. Whilst there is certainly an enormous variety of different ethnic groups in Africa, most are closely related to their neighbours in terms of language, beliefs and way of life. Modern historians eschew the simplistic tag of 'tribes', noting that such groupings change with time.

Sometimes the word tribe is used to describe a group of people who all speak the same language; it may be used to mean those who follow a particular leader or to refer to all the inhabitants of a certain area at a given time. In any case, tribe is a vague word which is used differently for different purposes. The term 'clan' (blood relations) is a smaller, more precisely defined, unit – though rather too precise for our broad discussions here.

Certainly, at any given time, groups of people or clans who share similar language and cultural beliefs do band together and often, in time, develop 'tribal' identities. However, it is wrong to then extrapolate and assume that their ancestors will have had the same groupings and allegiances centuries ago.

In Africa, as elsewhere in the world, history is recorded by the winners. Here the winners, the ruling class, may be the descendants of a small group of intruders who achieved dominance over a larger, long-established community. Over the years, the history of that ruling class usually becomes regarded as the history of the whole community, or tribe. Two 'tribes' have thus become one, with one history – which will reflect the origins of that small group of intruders, and not the ancestors of the majority of the current tribe.

Zambia is typical of a large African country. Currently historians and linguistics experts can identify at least 16 major cultural groupings, and more than 72 different languages and dialects are spoken in the country. As you will see, there are cultural differences between the people in different parts of the country. However, these are no more pronounced than those between the states of the USA, or the different regions of the (relatively tiny) UK.

There continues to be lots of inter-marriage and mixing of these peoples and cultures – perhaps more so than in the past, due to the efficiency of modern transport systems. Generally, there is very little friction between these communities (whose boundaries, as we have said, are indistinct) and Zambia's various peoples live peacefully together.

Map labels:
- 0 — 200km / 0 — 100 miles
- N — Bradt
- Mbala
- Nchelenge
- MAMBWE-LUNGU
- Nkonde
- NYIKA
- BEMBA
- Kasama
- Isoka
- Chama
- Mansa
- TUMBUKA
- Mpika
- Lundazi
- Mwinilunga
- LUNDA
- Solwezi
- NDOLA
- NYANJA
- LUNDA
- Chizela
- BEMBA
- Serenje
- BEMBA
- SENGA
- Chipata
- Zambezi
- LUCHAZI
- Kasempa
- LUVALE
- Kabompo
- KAONDE
- Petauke
- Katete
- Lukulu
- NSENGA
- MBUNDA
- NKOYA
- Kabwe
- Kaoma
- Mumbwa
- Kalabo
- MBWELA
- LUSAKA
- Mongu
- Luangwa
- LOZI
- LUYANA
- Namwala
- MASHI
- LOZI
- TONGA
- Sesheke
- LOZI
- LOZI
- LIVINGSTONE
- LANGUAGES

People and Culture ETHNIC GROUPS

2

Because people from these areas were the original workers in the mines of the Copperbelt, Bemba has subsequently achieved the status of *lingua franca* in the major urban areas of the Copperbelt and Lusaka.

It is recognised for administration and education purposes within Zambia, whilst outside its borders Bemba is also spoken by over 150,000 people in the Democratic Republic of Congo, and around 37,000 in Tanzania.

Kaonde Kaonde-speakers live mostly around the northern side of Kafue National Park, centring on the area around Kasempa, and extending southeast as far as Mumbwa. They are one of Zambia's larger language groups, and probably number about 200,000.

Lozi There are about 500,000 Lozi-speakers in Zambia, concentrated in the Western and Southern provinces, around Barotseland and Livingstone. The centre of Lozi culture is the rich agricultural floodplain around the Upper Zambezi River – and it is here that the Kuomboka (see *Festivals*, page 24) takes place each year.

Luchazi This language has only a small number of speakers, perhaps 70,000 in the west of Zambia – less than 1% of the country's population. There are thought to be a similar number of Luchazi-speaking people in Angola.

Lunda Not to be confused with Luunda, which is a dialect of Bemba, Lunda is the first language of about 230,000 Zambians and is spoken in areas of the Copperbelt, as well as nearby DRC and Angola. It is officially taught in primary schools, and can occasionally be heard on the radio or seen in newspapers in the area.

Luvale Luvale is an important language in Angola, where it is spoken by almost one million people. In Zambia there are only about 215,000 people whose first language is Luvale, and they live in the North-Western and Western provinces.

Luyana The Luyana-speaking people are a small group, perhaps numbering 130,000 in total. Their language has not been well documented, though it is spoken in Zambia, Angola, Namibia and also Botswana. In Zambia it is found almost exclusively in the Western Province.

Mambwe-Lungu These are other languages that need further study – so far they appear to differ from each other only slightly, as dialects would. In total about 280,000 Zambians count them as their first language – about 3% of the population. Their stronghold is in the northeast of the Northern Province, south of Lake Tanganyika. As you might expect, they are also spoken in Tanzania.

Mashi Mashi seems to be spoken by only a tiny number of Zambians, perhaps only 25,000 people, who are often nomadic within a southwestern area of the Western Province. Little has been documented about this language – though it has been noted that virtually all the native speakers of Mashi follow traditional religious practices, rather than the more recently introduced Christian beliefs.

Mbunda The first language of about 130,000 Zambians, Mbunda is spoken in the north of Barotseland and the northern side of western Zambia – as well as in Angola.

Nkoya-Mbwela Nkoya and Mbwela are two closely related languages. Mbwela is often referred to as a dialect of Nkoya, though here we have grouped them together as equals. They also have only a tiny number of speakers – around 80,000 people – who are found around the Mankoya area, in Zambia's Western and Southern provinces.

Nsenga There are thought to be over 330,000 people speaking Nsenga as their first language, of whom the vast majority live in Zambia. These are clustered around the area of Petauke – near to the borders with Zimbabwe and Mozambique, across which the language is also spoken.

Nyanja Nyanja is the Bantu language most often encountered by visitors in Zambia. It is widely used in much of the country, including the key cities of Lusaka and Livingstone. Nyanja is sometimes described as not being a language *per se*, but rather a common skill enabling people of varying tribes living in eastern, central and southern parts of Zambia and Malawi to communicate without following the strict grammar of specific local languages. In other words, like Swahili and other 'universal' languages, Nyanja is something of a *lingua franca* for Zambia.

Nyanja is certainly the official language of the police, and is widely used for administrative and educational purposes. About a million Zambians use Nyanja as their first language – mostly in the eastern and central areas of the country – and there may be double that number using the language in Malawi. Then there are around 330,000 Nyanja-speakers in Zimbabwe, and perhaps 500,000 in Mozambique. A total of approaching four million people in the subcontinent speak Nyanja as a first language.

Nyika Also known as Nyiha, or more precisely as Chi-Nyika, Nyika is spoken most widely in Tanzania, and also in Malawi. In Zambia it is used around the Isoka and Chama areas, across to the Malawi border. (It is closely related to the language known as Ichi-Lambya in Tanzania and Malawi.)

Tonga Tonga is the language of a small minority of Zimbabweans, many of whom were displaced south by the creation of Lake Kariba (see page 219). However, in Zambia it is the first language of around one million people, about 11% of the country's population, and is widely used in the media. Tonga is distributed throughout the south of the country, with its highest concentration in the middle Zambezi Valley.

Tumbuka Zambia has about 430,000 people who speak Tumbuka as a first language, mostly living on the eastern side of the country. Outside Zambia many Tumbuka-speakers live in Malawi and Tanzania, bringing the total number to about two million.

OTHER ETHNIC GROUPS

White Zambians There are a small number of white Zambians, very different from the expat community (see below) who are often white but simply working in the country on a temporary basis. Many white Zambians will trace their families back to colonial immigrants who came over during British rule, but most will regard themselves as Zambian rather than, say, British. This is generally an affluent group of people, and many of the country's businesses and especially the safari companies, are owned and run by white Zambians.

Asian Zambians Like the white Zambians, many people of Asian origin came here during the colonial period. When the British ruled African colonies like Zambia as well as India, there was movement of labour from Asia to Africa. Now, like the white Zambians, this is generally an affluent group. On the whole, Zambians of Asian descent retain a very strong sense of Asian identity and culture, and many are traders or own small shops.

Expatriates Distinct from Zambians, there is a large expat community in Zambia. These foreigners usually come to Zambia for two or three years, to work on short-term contracts, often for either multi-national companies or aid agencies. Most are highly skilled individuals who come to share their knowledge with Zambian colleagues – often teaching skills that are in short supply in Zambia.

In the 1990s there was a migration of trained Zambian teachers and lecturers to neighbouring countries, where they are paid better, but this has now stabilised.

RELIGION

It has been estimated that there are some 200 different Christian churches in Zambia, of which the most active in the community is considered to be the Catholic Church. However, as in many other sub-Saharan African countries, many people will also subscribe to some traditional African religious practices and beliefs.

EDUCATION

In theory, primary education has been free to all children in Zambia since 2002, and statistics suggest that all children do indeed go to school. In practice, however, this is only half the story. Parents still need to find the means to pay for school uniform and books and pencils, or their children will be turned away, and the 'voluntary contribution' so beloved of state schools in the West becomes a crippling burden to impoverished Zambian families. An annual 'fee' of Kw50,000 (US$10.50/£6.50) for each primary-age child is not unusual, with penalties levied, for instance, if a parent fails to turn up at a school meeting. At secondary level, fees are around Kw200,000 (US$42/£26). And this in a country where the minimum wage is just US$90/£60 a month.

Typically, primary schools are run on a shift pattern, with children spending three hours in the classroom each day; the first are in school at 07.00, finishing at 10.00, when the next group starts. The secondary school day normally runs from 07.00 to 13.00. There are also 'basic' schools, which serve a wider age range than primary in areas where there is no secondary school. Class sizes are large, frequently exceeding the expected norm of 45 children, and lessons are often disrupted by strike action on the part of the teachers.

Zambia's first university was established in Lusaka as recently as 1966, shortly after independence, and has since been joined by two more, both in the north of the country: one in Kitwe, and a second in Luanshya.

FESTIVALS

Zambia has several major cultural festivals which, on the whole, are rarely seen by visitors. If you can get to any, then you will find them to be very genuine occasions, where ceremonies are performed for the benefit of the local people and the participants, and not for the odd tourist who is watching.

Cultural celebrations were strongly encouraged during Kenneth Kaunda's reign, as he favoured people being aware of their cultural origins. 'A country without culture is like a body without a head', was one of his phrases. Thus during the 1980s one group after another 'discovered' old traditional festivals. Most are now large local events, partly cultural but also part political rally, religious gathering and sports event.

Bear in mind that, like most celebrations worldwide, these are often accompanied by the large-scale consumption of alcohol. To see these festivals properly, and to appreciate them, you will need a good guide: someone who understands the rituals, can explain their significance, and can instruct you on how you should behave. After all, how would you feel about a passing Zambian traveller who arrives, with curiosity, at your sibling's wedding (a small festival), in the hope of being invited to the private reception?

Photographers will find superb opportunities at such colourful events, but should behave with sensitivity. *Before* you brandish your camera, remember to ask permission from anyone who might take offence.

THE KUOMBOKA The most famous of Zambia's ceremonies takes place in the Western Province. It used to be around February or March, often on a Thursday, just before full moon. The precise date would be known only a week or so in advance, as it was decided upon by the Lozi king. Now that the ceremony attracts more visitors, it is usually held at Easter, though if water levels are not high enough, it will not take place at all.

The Lozi kingdom is closely associated with the fertile plains around the Upper Zambezi River. When dry, this well-defined area affords good grazing for livestock, and its rich alluvial soil is ideal for cultivation. It contrasts with the sparse surrounding woodland, growing on poor soil typical of the rest of western Zambia. So for much of the year, these plains support a dense population of subsistence farms.

However, towards the end of the rains, the Zambezi's water levels rise. The plains then become floodplains, and the settlements gradually become islands. The people must leave them for the higher ground, at the margins of the floodplain. This retreat from the advancing waters – known as the Kuomboka – is traditionally led by the king himself, the Litunga, from his dry-season abode at Lealui, in the middle of the plain. He retreats with his court to his high-water residence, at Limulunga, on the eastern margins of the floodplain.

The Litunga's departure is heralded by the beating of three huge old royal war drums – Mundili, Munanga and Kanaono. These continue to summon the people from miles around until the drums themselves are loaded aboard the royal barge, the *nalikwanda*, a very large wooden canoe built around the turn of the century and painted with vertical black-and-white stripes. The royal barge is then paddled and punted along by 96 polers, each sporting a skirt of animal skins and a white vest. Their scarlet hats are surmounted by tufts of fur taken from the mane of unfortunate lions.

The royal barge is guided by a couple of 'scout' barges, painted white, which search out the right channels for the royal barge. Behind it comes the Litunga's wife, the Moyo, in her own barge, followed by local dignitaries, various attendants, many of the Litunga's subjects, and the odd visitor lucky enough to be in the area at the right time. The journey takes most of the day, and the flotilla is accompanied by an impromptu orchestra of local musicians.

John Reader's excellent book, *Africa: A Biography of the Continent* (see *Appendix 3*, page 535), comments:

> When the Litunga boards the *nalikwanda* at Lealui he customarily wears a light European-style suit, a pearl-grey frock coat and a trilby hat; when he leaves the barge at Limulunga he is dressed in a splendid uniform of dark-blue serge ornately embroidered with gold braid, with matching cockade hat complete with a white plume of egret feathers.

In fact, Chapter 47 of this book contains the fascinating story of some of the first Europeans to see the original Kuomboka, and the sad narration of the gradual European subjugation of the Lozi kingdom. It also includes details of the Litunga's trip to London, in 1902, for the coronation of King Edward VII. It was here that the problem arose of what the Litunga should wear. Reader reports:

> By happy coincidence, the king [Edward VII] took a particular interest in uniforms; he was an expert on the subject and is even said to have made a hobby of designing uniforms. Doubtless the king had approved the design of the new uniforms with which Britain's ambassadors had recently been issued. Certainly he was aware that the introduction of these new outfits had created a redundant stock of the old style, which were richly adorned with gold braid. Lewanika [the Litunga] should be attired in one of those, the king ordained. And thus the Litunga acquired the uniform which has become part of the Kuomboka tradition. Not an admiral's uniform, as is often reported, but a surplus dress uniform of a Victorian ambassador; not a gift from Queen Victoria, but the suggestion of her son ...

When the royal barge finally arrives at Limulunga, the Litunga steps ashore in the ambassador's uniform to spend an evening of feasting and celebrations, with much eating, drinking, music and traditional dancing.

LIKUMBI LYA MIZE The Luvale people of western Zambia have an annual 'fair' type of celebration, which takes place for four or five days towards the end of August.

'*Likumbi Lya Mize*' means 'Mize day' and the event is held at the palace of the senior chief – at Mize, about 7km west of Zambezi. This provides an opportunity for the people to see their senior chief, watch the popular Makishi dancers, and generally have a good time. There is also lots of eating and drinking, plus people in traditional dress, displays of local crafts, and singing.

MUTOMBOKO (also Umutomboko) This is nothing to do with the Kuomboka, described above. It is an annual two-day celebration, performed during the last weekend of July, whereby the paramount chief celebrates the arrival of the Luunda people, the 'crossing of the river'. It is held in a specially prepared arena, close to the Ng'ona River, at Mwansabombwe.

On the first day the chief, covered in white powder, receives tributes of food and drink from his subjects – the cause for much feasting and celebration by all. On the second day an animal (often a goat) is slaughtered and the highlight is the chief's dance with his sword. See also page 373.

SHIMUNENGA This traditional gathering is held on the weekend of a full moon, in September or October, at Maala on the Kafue Flats – about 40km west of Namwala. Then the Ila people (whose language is closely related to Tonga) gather together, driving cattle across the Kafue River to higher ground. It used to be a lechwe hunt, but that is now forbidden.

THE NC'WALA On 24 February there is a festival to celebrate the first fruit, at Mutenguleni village, near Chipata. This large celebration was recently revived, after 80 years of not being practised. It consists of two parts. Firstly the chief tastes the first fruit of the land – usually sugarcane, maize and pumpkins. Secondly there is the ritual rebirth of the king (involving the king being locked up in his house) and the blessing of the fruit – which consists of a fairly gory spearing of a black bull whose blood the king has to drink. It's all accompanied by traditional dancing and beer-drinking.

OTHER FESTIVALS The above list of festivals is by no means exhaustive; others include:

Kufukwila A May celebration led by the chief of the Kaonde people, held in the Solwezi area of northwestern Zambia.

Kulamba Also a thanksgiving ceremony for the Chewa people, held in August. It's held in the Katete Province, in eastern Zambia, and here you'll be able to see lots of fascinating Nyao (secret society) dancers.

Lukuni Luzwa Buuka A celebration of past conquests by the Toka people in the Southern Province, usually held in August.

Lwiinda A ceremony celebrated by Chief Mokuni, of the Toka Leya people near Livingstone, around February. The people honour their ancestors and offer sacrifices for rain.

Malaila A ceremony to honour past chiefs, held in July by the Kunda people. (This is currently celebrated by Chieftainess Nsefu, near Mfuwe in the Luangwa Valley.)

Tuwimba A thanksgiving festival, in October, for the Nsenga people.

3

The Natural Environment

PHYSICAL ENVIRONMENT

TOPOGRAPHY Zambia lies landlocked between the Tropic of Capricorn and the Equator, far from both the Atlantic and the Pacific oceans. It is at the northern edge of the region referred to as 'southern Africa', while sharing many similarities with its neighbours in east and central Africa. Shaped like a giant butterfly, it covers about 752,610km², slightly smaller than the UK and France combined, and slightly larger than California plus Nevada. In comparison with its neighbours, it is almost double the size of Zimbabwe, but only two-thirds that of South Africa.

Most of the country is part of the high, undulating plateau that forms the backbone of the African continent. Typically, it has an altitude of between 1,000m and 1,600m, deeply incised by the great valleys of the Zambezi, the Kafue, the Luangwa and the Luapula that lie below 500m.

There are several large lakes on Zambia's borders: Tanganyika and Mweru in the north, and the manmade Kariba in the south. Lake Bangweulu, and its swamps and floodplain, dominate a large area of the interior.

GEOLOGY Zambia's oldest rocks, known as the Basement Complex, were laid down at an early stage in the pre-Cambrian era – as long as 2,000 million years ago. These were extensively eroded and covered by sediments which now form the Katanga system of rocks, dating from around 1,000 to 620 million years ago. These are what we now see near the surface in most of northeast and central Zambia, and they contain the important mineral deposits of the Copperbelt. Later still, from about 300 to 150 million years ago, the karoo system of sedimentary rocks was deposited: sandstones, mudstones, conglomerates and even coal. Towards the end of this era, molten rock seeped up through cracks in the crust, and covered areas of western Zambia in layers of basalt – the rock that is seen cut away by the Zambezi River in the gorges below Victoria Falls.

About 150 million years ago, during the Jurassic era of the dinosaurs, Africa was still part of Gondwana – a super-continent which included South America, India, Australasia and Antarctica. Since then Zambia's highlands have been eroded down from an original altitude of over 1,800m (Nyika Plateau is still at this altitude) to their present lower levels.

Very recently, perhaps only a few million years ago, the subcontinent had a dry phase. Then the sands from the Kalahari Desert blew far across southern Africa, covering much of western Zambia with a layer of Kalahari sand – as becomes abundantly clear the moment you try to drive in the region.

CLIMATE Situated squarely in the tropics, Zambia gets a lot of strong sunlight, though the intense heat normally associated with the tropics is moderated in most

KEY

Isohyets show mean annual rainfall in **mm** (*in*) $\underset{(31.5)}{\underline{800}}$

N

Bradt

Tanganyika

Mweru

Mwilunga ○ **1400** (55.1)

○Solwezi

1300 (51.2)

○ Nchelenge
1500 (59.1)

1400 (55.1)

○ Mbala

1300 (51.2)

Kasama ○

Isoka ○

Mansa ○

1200 (47.2)

Chama ○

1200 (47.2)

Mpika ○

900 (35.4)

○ Lundazi

1100 (43.3)

1000 (39.4)

○ Serenje

Chipata ○

1000 (39.4)

NDOLA ●

Kasempa ○

1200 (47.2)

○ Zambezi

1100 (43.3)

1000 (39.4)

Kaoma

Kabwe ○

○ Mumbwa

Mongu ○

900 (35.4)

LUSAKA ■

800 (31.5)

Seseke ○

Kariba

LIVINGSTONE ●

0 ———— 200km
0 ———— 100 miles

RAINFALL

places by the country's altitude and its rainfall. The climate is generally moderate; only in the great valleys does it feel oppressive. It can be summarised broadly into three periods: from December to April it is hot and wet, with torrential downpours often in the late afternoon; from May to August it is dry, and becomes increasingly cool; and from September to November it remains dry, but gets progressively hotter.

This follows a similar pattern to that in most of southern Africa, with rainfall when the sun is near its zenith from November to April. The precise timing and

CLIMATE STATISTICS: LUSAKA

	Temp °C		Temp °F		Humidity %		Rainfall
	max	min	max	min	am	pm	mm
Jan	26	17	78	62	84	71	231
Feb	26	17	78	62	85	80	191
Mar	26	17	78	62	83	56	142
Apr	26	15	78	59	71	47	18
May	25	12	77	52	59	37	3
Jun	23	10	73	50	56	32	0
Jul	23	9	73	48	54	28	0
Aug	25	12	77	53	46	26	0
Sep	29	15	84	59	41	19	0
Oct	31	18	87	64	39	23	15
Nov	29	18	84	64	57	46	91
Dec	27	17	80	62	76	61	150

duration of this is determined by the interplay of three airstreams: the moist 'Congo' air-mass, the northeastern monsoon winds, and the southeastern trade winds. The water-bearing air is the Congo air-mass, which normally brings rain when it moves south into Zambia from central Africa. This means that the northern areas, around Lakes Tanganyika and Mweru, receive the first rainfall – often in late October or November. This belt of rain will then work south, arriving in southern Zambia by the end of November or the start of December.

As the sun's intensity reduces, the Congo air-mass moves back north, leaving southern Zambia dry by around late March, and the north by late April or May. Most areas receive their heaviest rainfall in January, though some of the most northerly have two peaks: one in December and one in March. This twin-peak cycle is more characteristic of central and eastern Africa. The heaviest total rainfall is found in the north, and the lightest in the south. It's worth adding a caveat here. Zambia, as elsewhere, is experiencing fluctuations in its traditional weather patterns, so while the traditional pattern remains a good guide, be prepared for variations from the norm.

Lusaka's climate statistics (see box opposite) are typical of the pleasant climate found in the higher areas of southern and central Zambia. The lower-lying valleys, including the Luangwa and Lower Zambezi, follow the same broad pattern but are considerably hotter throughout the year. In October, which is universally the hottest month, temperatures there often reach over 45°C in the shade.

FLORA AND FAUNA

Zambia has many large national parks and game management areas (GMAs) where conservation and sustainable utilisation of the native wildlife are encouraged.

Miombo woodland – a mixture of grassland dotted with trees and shrubs – makes up about 70% of Zambia's natural environment, with *mopane* woodland dominating the lower-lying areas. The native fauna is classic big game found throughout east and southern Africa. Amongst the predators, leopard do exceptionally well here; lion are common but cheetah are not. Wild dog are uncommon, though seem to have increased in numbers in recent years, and there are many smaller predators. Zambia's antelope are especially interesting for the range of subspecies that have evolved. Giraffe, wildebeest, waterbuck and, especially, lechwe are notable for this – each having subspecies endemic to the country.

With rich vegetation and lots of water, Zambia has a great variety of both resident and migrant birds, over 750 species in total. Wetland and swamp areas attract some specialised waterfowl, and Zambia is on the edge of the range for both southern African and east African species.

FLORA As with animals, each species of plant has its favourite conditions. External factors determine where each species thrives, and where it will perish. These include temperature, light, water, soil type, nutrients, and what other species of plants and animals live in the same area. Species with similar needs are often found together, in communities which are characteristic of that particular environment. Zambia has a number of different such communities, or typical 'vegetation types', within its borders – each of which is distinct from the others. The more common include:

Woodlands Where they haven't been destroyed or degraded by people, woodlands cover the vast majority of Zambia, with miombo being especially common. Because the canopies of the trees in a woodland area don't interlock, you'll generally find them lighter and more open than the country's relatively few forested areas. The main types of woodland are:

Miombo woodland Without human intervention, the natural vegetation of most of Zambia (about 70%) is miombo woodland and its associated *dambos* (see below). This exists on Zambia's main plateau and its adjacent escarpments, where the acid soils are not particularly fertile and have often been leached of minerals by the water run-off.

Miombo woodland consists of a mosaic of large wooded areas and smaller, more open spaces dotted with clumps of trees and shrubs. The woodland is broadleafed and deciduous (though just how deciduous depends on the available water), and the tree canopies generally don't interlock. The dominant trees are *Brachystegia*, *Julbernardia* and *Isoberlinia* species – most of which are at least partially fire-resistant. There is more variation of species in miombo than in mopane woodland, but despite this it is often known simply as 'brachystegia woodland'. The ground cover is also generally less sparse here than in mopane areas.

Mopane woodland The dominant tree here is the remarkably adaptable mopane, *Colophospermum mopane*, which is sometimes known as the butterfly tree because of the shape of its leaves. It is very tolerant of poorly drained or alkaline soils, and those with a high clay content. This tolerance results in the mopane having a wide range of distribution throughout southern Africa; in Zambia it occurs mainly in the hotter, drier, lower parts of the country, including the Luangwa and Zambezi valleys.

Mopane trees can attain a height of 25m, especially if growing on rich, alluvial soils. These are often called cathedral mopane, for their height and the graceful arch of their branches. However, shorter trees are more common in areas that are poor in nutrients, or have suffered extensive fire damage. Stunted mopane will form a low scrub, perhaps only 5m tall. All mopane trees are semi-deciduous. The leaves turn beautiful shades of yellow and red before falling between August and October, depending on their proximity to water (the closer the water, the later the leaves fall). Fresh new leaves start unfurling from late October.

Ground cover in mopane woodland is usually sparse, just thin grasses, herbs and the occasional bush. The trees themselves are an important source of food for game, as the leaves have a high nutritional value – rich in protein and phosphorus – which is favoured by browsers and is retained even after they have fallen from the trees. Mopane forests support large populations of rodents, including tree squirrels, *Peraxerus cepapi*, which are so typical of these areas that they are known as 'mopane squirrels'.

Munga woodland The word 'munga' means thorn, and this is the thorny woodland which occurs when open grassland has been invaded by trees and shrubs – normally because of some disturbance like cultivation, fire or overgrazing. *Acacia*, *Terminalia* (bearing single-winged seeds) and *Combretum* (bearing seeds with four or five wings) are the dominant species, but many others can be present. Munga occurs mainly in the southern parts of Zambia.

Forests In most equatorial areas further north in Africa, where rainfall is higher, forests are the norm. However, there are a few specific ecological niches in Zambia where you will find forests – distinguished from woodlands by their interlocking canopy. These are:

Teak forest In a few areas of western and southwestern Zambia (including the southern part of Kafue National Park), the Zambezi teak, *Baikaea plurijuga*, forms dry semi-evergreen forests on a base of Kalahari sand. This species is not fire-resistant, so these stands occur only where slash-and-burn cultivation methods have never been used. Below the tall teak is normally a dense, deciduous thicket of vegetation usually referred to as *mutemwa*, interspersed with sparse grasses and herbs in the shadier spots of the forest floor.

Moist evergreen forest In areas of higher rainfall (mostly in the north of Zambia), and near rivers, streams, lakes and swamps, where a tree's roots have permanent access to water, dense evergreen forests are found. Many species occur, and this lush vegetation is characterised by having three levels: a canopy of tall trees, a sub-level of smaller trees and bushes, and a variety of ground-level vegetation. In effect, the environment is so good for plants that they have adapted to exploit the light from every sunbeam.

This type of forest is prevalent in the far north of the country, especially in the Mwinilunga area. However, three more localised environments can give rise to moist evergreen forests in other areas of the country.

Riparian forests (often called riverine forests) are very common. They line many of Zambia's major rivers and are found in most of the national parks. Typical trees and shrubs here include ebony (*Diospyros mespiliformis*), mangosteen (*Garcinia livingstonei*), wild gardenia (*Gardenia volkensii*), sausage tree (*Kigelia africana*), Natal mahogany (*Trichilia emetica*) and various species of figs. But walk away from the river, and you'll find riparian species thinning out rapidly.

Montane forests are found on the lower slopes of mountains, where the rainfall is high. The Zambian slopes of Nyika Plateau are probably the best example of this kind of vegetation.

Finally **swamp** forest occurs near to some of Zambia's permanent swamps. Kasanka National Park probably has the country's best, and most accessible, examples of this.

Grasslands and open areas

Dambo A 'dambo' is a shallow grass depression, or small valley, that is either permanently or seasonally waterlogged. It corresponds closely to what is known as a 'vlei' in other parts of the subcontinent. These open, verdant dips in the landscape often appear in the midst of miombo woodlands and support no bushes or trees. In higher valleys amongst hills, they sometimes form the sources of streams and rivers. Because of their permanent dampness, they are rich in species of grasses, herbs and flowering plants, like orchids – and are excellent grazing (if a little exposed) for antelope. Their margins are usually thickly vegetated by grasses, herbs and smaller shrubs.

Pan Though not an environment for rich vegetation, a pan is a shallow, seasonal pool of water with no permanent streams leading into or out of it. The bush is full of small pans in the rainy season, most of which will dry up soon after the rains cease. Sometimes there's only a fine distinction between a pan and a dambo.

Floodplain Floodplains are the low-lying grasslands on the edges of rivers, streams, lakes and swamps that are seasonally inundated by floods. Zambia has some huge areas of floodplain, most obviously beside the Kafue River, in the Barotseland area around the Zambezi, and south of the permanent Bangweulu Swamps. These often contain no trees or bushes, just a low carpet of grass species that can tolerate being submerged for part of the year. In the midst of some floodplains, like the Busanga Plains, you'll find isolated small 'islands' of trees and bushes, slightly raised above the surrounding grasslands.

Montane grassland More common in other areas of Africa, montane grassland occurs on mountain slopes at higher altitudes where the precipitation is heavy and the climate cool. Zambia's best examples of this are on Nyika Plateau, and here you'll find many species of flora and fauna that occur nowhere else in Zambia.

FAUNA See also *Appendix 1*, page 515, for an introductory field guide to some of Zambia's larger animals.

Mammals Zambia's large mammals are typical of the savanna areas of east and (especially) southern Africa. The large predators here are lion, leopard, cheetah, wild dog and spotted hyena, although cheetah and wild dog are relatively uncommon.

Elephant and buffalo occur in large herds in protected national parks, and in small, furtive family groups where poaching is a problem. Black rhino were probably, sadly, extinct in Zambia until they were re-introduced into North Luangwa National Park in 2003. There are also white rhino in the small, well-protected, Mosi-oa-Tunya National Park at Livingstone, re-introduced from South Africa.

Antelope are well represented, with puku and impala numerically dominant in the drier areas. There are several interesting, endemic subspecies found in Zambia, including the Angolan and Thornicroft's giraffe, Cookson's wildebeest, Crawshay's zebra, and two unusual subspecies of lechwe – the black and the Kafue lechwe – which occur in very large numbers in some of the country's bigger marshy areas.

Because Zambia is a wet country, with numerous marshy areas, its natural vegetation is lush and capable of supporting a high density of game. The country has a natural advantage over drier areas, and this accounts for the sheer volume of big game to be found in its better parks.

Birds Much of Zambia is still covered by original, undisturbed natural vegetation, and hunting is not a significant factor for most of the country's birds. Thus, with a range of verdant and natural habitats, Zambia is a superb birding destination, with 757 different species recorded by 2010. The Zambian Ornithological Society has a checklist on their website (*www.wattledcrane.com*), and – in partnership with BirdLife International – has designated a total of 42 'important bird areas' (IBAs), covering 14% of the country. For details, see Peter Leonard's *Important Bird Areas in Zambia, Appendix 3*, page 538).

Whilst the animal species differ only occasionally from the 'normal' species found in southern Africa, the birds are a much more varied mix of those species found in southern, eastern and even central Africa. The obvious celebrity is the ungainly shoebill stork, which breeds in the Bangweulu Swamps, and only one or two other places in central Africa. A lesser-known attraction is Chaplin's barbet, Zambia's only endemic bird species, found in southern Zambia around the south side of Kafue National Park. However, there are many other unusual, rare and beautifully coloured species that attract enthusiasts to Zambia, from the collared barbet to the black-cheeked lovebird, Heuglin's robin and Schalow's turaco.

In addition to its resident bird species, Zambia receives many migrants. In September and October the Palaearctic migrants (those that come from the northern hemisphere – normally Europe) appear, and they remain until around

April or May. This is also the peak time to see the intra-African migrants, which come from further north in Africa.

The rains from December to April see an explosion in the availability of most birds' food: seeds, fruits and insects. Hence this is the prime time for birds to nest, even if it is also the most difficult time to visit the more remote areas of the country.

FIELD GUIDES Finding good, detailed field guides to plants, animals and birds in Zambia is becoming much easier. There are now very comprehensive guides on the flora and fauna of southern Africa, which remain invaluable in Zambia. However, for total coverage there are also many smaller guides, published in Zambia by the Wildlife and Environmental Conservation Society of Zambia (see page 50), covering snakes, trees, wild flowers, birds and the like, and ideal for general game viewing and birdwatching. There's even a comprehensive guide to the Zambian bird species that have been excluded from the southern Africa guides, and – at the other end of the scale – a heavy but very comprehensive guide to the birds of sub-Saharan Africa. (See *Appendix 3*, page 536, for more details.)

CONSERVATION

A great deal has been written about the conservation of animals in Africa, much of it over-simplistic and intentionally emotive. As an informed visitor you are in the unique position of being able to see some of the issues at first hand, and to appreciate the perspectives of local people. So abandon your preconceptions, and start by considering the complexities of the issues involved. Here I shall try to develop a few ideas common to most current thinking on conservation, ideas to which the rest of the book only briefly alludes.

First, conservation must be taken within its widest sense if it is to have meaning. Saving animals is of minimal use if the whole environment is degraded, so we must consider conserving whole areas and ecosystems, not just the odd isolated species.

Observe that land is regarded as an asset by most societies in Africa, as it is elsewhere. To 'save' the land for the animals, and use it merely for the recreation of a few privileged foreign tourists, is a recipe for huge social problems – especially if the local people remain excluded from benefit and in poverty. Local people have hunted animals for food for centuries. They have always killed game that threatened them, or ruined their crops. If we now try to protect animals in populated areas without addressing the concerns of the people, then our efforts will fail.

The only pragmatic way to conserve Zambia's wild areas is to see the development of the local people, and the conservation of the animals and the environment, as interlinked goals.

In the long term, one will not work without the other. Conservation without development leads to resentful locals who will happily, and frequently, shoot, trap and kill animals. Development without conservation will simply repeat the mistakes that most developed countries have already made: it will lay waste a beautiful land and kill off its natural heritage. Look at the tiny areas of undisturbed natural vegetation that survive in the UK, the USA or Japan. See how unsuccessful we in the northern hemisphere have been at long-term conservation over the past 500 years.

As an aside, the local people in Zambia are sometimes wrongly accused of being the only agents of degradation. Many would like to see 'poachers' shot on sight, and slash-and-burn agriculture banned. But observe the importation of tropical hardwoods by the West to see the problems that our demands place on the natural environment in the developing world.

In conserving some of Zambia's natural areas and assisting the development of its people, the international community has a vital role to play. It could effectively encourage the Zambian government to practise sustainable long-term strategies, rather than grasping for the short-term fixes which politicians seem universally to prefer. But such solutions must have the backing of the people themselves, or they will fall apart when the foreign aid budgets eventually wane.

In practice, to get this backing from the local communities it is not enough for a conservation strategy to be compatible with development. Most Zambians are more concerned about where they live, what they can eat and how they will survive, than they are about the lives of small, obscure species of antelope that taste good when roasted.

To succeed in Africa, conservation must not only be compatible with development, it must actually promote it. It must actively help the local people to improve their own standard of living. If that situation can be reached, then local communities can be mobilised behind long-term conservation initiatives.

Governments are the same. As Luangwa's late conservationist Norman Carr once commented, 'governments won't conserve an impala just because it is pretty'. But they will work to save it if they can see that it is worth more to them alive than dead.

The best strategies tried so far on the continent attempt to find lucrative and sustainable ways to use the land. They then plough much of the revenue back into the surrounding local communities. Once the local communities see revenue from conservation being used to help them improve their lives – to build houses, clinics and schools, and to offer paid employment – then such schemes rapidly get their backing and support.

FIRE! *Tricia Hayne*

Somewhere – at any given time of the year – part of Zambia burns. Sometimes these are forest fires, spontaneously setting the bush alight as they have for millennia. Often, however, they are set deliberately. The reasons for this are many and varied, and not all are negative; fire is considered a mixed blessing by both agriculturalists and conservationists.

At worst, fires are set by poachers, or even traditional hunters, to drive animals out into the open. Subsistence farmers, too, employ destructive slash-and-burn techniques in order to create new plots of agricultural land from scrub or forest. More positively, in conservation areas, fire is an important tool in the armoury. Burning off the old grass before it is totally dry, for example, encourages the growth of new sweet shoots, which in turn attract grazers such as wildebeest. At a more local level, villagers will often set fire to long grass to create an open space around houses or to clear paths, thus discouraging rats and snakes. And sometimes controlled fires may be used to clear an area in order to create a firebreak as an insurance against greater damage.

Many of the tree species that make up the classic miombo woodland which covers large tracts of Zambia have evolved over time to become at least partially fire-resistant – and this in turn may help to explain their dominance in areas where fires are a regular part of the annual cycle. Other miombo species, however, as well as numerous indigenous trees such as mopane and teak, exhibit no such resistance. Thus, while the benefits are there, the risk of fire resulting in long-term environmental damage is a real threat.

Carefully planned, sustainable tourism is one solution that can work effectively. For success, the local communities must see that the visitors pay because they want the wildlife. Thus, they reason that the existence of wildlife directly improves their income, and they will strive to conserve it.

It isn't enough for people to see that the wildlife helps the government to get richer; that won't dissuade a local hunter from shooting a duiker for dinner. However, if he is directly benefiting from the visitors, who come to see the animals, then he has a vested interest in saving that duiker.

It matters little to the Zambian people, or ultimately to wildlife species, whether these visitors come to shoot the wildlife with a camera or with a gun. The vital issue is whether the hunting is done on a sustainable basis (ie: only a few of the oldest 'trophy' animals are shot each year, so that the size of the animal population remains largely unaffected).

Photographers may claim the moral high ground, but should remember that hunters pay far more for their privileges. Hunting operations generate large revenues from few guests, who demand minimal infrastructure and so cause little impact on the land. Photographic operations need more visitors to generate the same revenue, and so generally cause greater negative effects on the country.

The Zambian body responsible for conservation is the National Heritage Conservation Commission (NHCC), whose headquarters is in Livingstone. The commission publishes a biannual magazine, *Zambia Heritage*.

NATIONAL PARKS AND GMAS A considerable area of Zambia is protected by national parks. Of these, the latest to be gazetted is the area around Ngonye Falls, on the Upper Zambezi, while the addition of Lusaka National Park close to the capital will add further protection in a more urban area. These parks are designated for photographic visitors; here no hunting is allowed. Around the parks are large areas designated as game management areas (GMAs). Within these are villages and hence small-scale farms, and hunting is (at least in theory) controlled and practised sustainably. Both local and overseas hunters use the GMAs, and the latter usually pay handsomely for the privilege.

Integral to this model is that the GMAs provide a buffer between the pristine national park and the land outside where uncontrolled hunting is allowed. This should serve to protect the national park's animals from incursions by poachers, whilst the park acts as a large gene pool and species reservoir for the GMA.

The theory of GMAs is good, but their administration has many practical difficulties. In some of them hunting by the local people has been uncontrolled, and in a few much of the game has been wiped out – resulting in no income from the wildlife, and so more pressure to hunt unsustainably. Many have projects that aim to reverse this trend, to regenerate their game resources and then set the communities off on a sustainable path. However, much more work needs to be done if a long-term effect is to be felt across the country.

Both national parks and GMAs are the responsibility of the Zambia Wildlife Authority (ZAWA, *www.zawa.org.zm*), which replaced the National Parks and Wildlife Service several years ago, and has more autonomy and greater financial independence than its predecessor. One of the most recent conservation initiatives in Zambia is the establishment by ZAWA of community partnership parks (CPPs), the first of which is in the Bangweulu Wetlands. Broadly, these are owned by the local community rather than by the state, and will be managed by a partner within the private sector in cooperation with ZAWA.

KEY

1. Mweru Wantipa
2. Sumbu
3. Lusenga Plain
4. Nyika Plateau
5. Isangano
6. North Luangwa
7. Luambe
8. Lukusuzi
9. South Luangwa
10. Lavushi Manda
11. Kasanka
12. Lower Zambezi
13. Blue Lagoon
14. Lochinvar
15. Kafue
16. West Lunga
17. Liuwa Plain
18. Sioma Ngwezi
19. Mosi-oa-Tunya
20. Ngonye Falls

TOURISM Zambia lies in the heart of sub-Saharan Africa. To the northeast lie the 'original' safari areas of east Africa: Kenya and Tanzania. Some of their best parks are now rather crowded, though their wildlife spectacles are still on a grand scale. South of Zambia are the more subtle attractions of Zimbabwe, Botswana and Namibia. Each country draws its own type of wildlife enthusiasts, and all have an element of wilderness that can seem difficult to find in east Africa today.

All have embraced tourism in different ways. Zambia is fortunate in having addressed this question later than the others, with the chance to learn from the mistakes of its neighbours. It is hoped that sustainable tourism can be a saviour of Zambia's economy as well as its wildlife, though there is a long way to go before tourism contributes a sizeable slice of the country's revenue.

Nevertheless, tourism is helping Zambia – both in economic terms and with conservation. It is providing employment and bringing foreign exchange into the country, which gives the politicians a reason to support the preservation of the parks. Increasingly Zambia's small-scale safari operators have mobilised themselves behind local development objectives, and in recent years we're seeing very positive initiatives for tourism to help development and sustainable land use, both inside and outside of Zambia's national parks.

The visitor on an expensive safari is generally, by his or her mere presence, making a financial contribution to development and conservation in Zambia. See pages 81–2 for ways in which you can support small local charities which directly help the people of Zambia. When on safari, one very simple thing that you can do to help is to ask your safari operator:

- Besides employment, how do local people benefit from this camp?
- How much of this camp's revenue goes directly back to the local people?
- What are you doing to help the people living near this reserve?
- How much control do the local people have over what goes on in the area where these safaris operate?

If more visitors did this, it would make a huge difference.

If all safari operators felt that the majority of their clients wanted them to be involved with community development, then they would rapidly get involved. That said, most operators do have programmes to help their local communities. They've already realised that the mass of Zambian people must benefit more (and more directly) from tourism if conservation is going to be successful in Zambia.

HUNTING Big-game hunting, where visiting hunters pay large amounts to kill trophy animals, is practised on a number of private ranches and hunting areas. It is also a valuable source of revenue in the long term for people living in the country's GMAs. In some this is already working, whilst in others development agencies, including the World Wide Fund for Nature (WWF), are working to start up sustainable schemes.

Poaching After tales of government corruption and complicity with poachers, those travellers who have not ventured into Zambia can be forgiven for asking, 'Is there any game left in Zambia?' The answer is a definitive 'Yes'.

The 1970s and especially the 1980s saw rampant hunting in the GMAs, and considerable poaching of Zambia's national parks – partly small-scale hunting for food by local people, and partly large commercial poaching operations. The government reaction to this was a mixture of indifference and, allegedly, complicity.

The only national park with an appreciable number of foreign visitors, South Luangwa, was effectively defended from all but the most persistent infiltrations of specialist rhino-poachers. Other parks were, to various extents, neglected. Most still suffer from the results of that past neglect even now.

However, various parks and GMAs are now, once again, being developed for visitors. With that development comes a reason to protect the parks (as well as a financial motivation – see pages 34–5). Kafue's game populations are almost back to normal, as are those in the Lower Zambezi National Park. Both Kasanka and North Luangwa are being effectively protected with the help of two very different private conservation initiatives, Liuwa Plain has embraced that model, and others are likely to follow suit. The WWF has long been working hard to help the local people earn an income from the sustainable utilisation of wildlife around the Bangweulu Swamps. Camps are opening up along the upper reaches of the Zambezi.

So the message from Zambia is upbeat. The main parks have excellent game populations and many more are gradually recovering. Unlike much of Africa, Zambia has not generally been ravaged by overgrazing, and so even the parks that have suffered from poaching have usually retained their natural vegetation in pristine condition. This gives hope that good game populations can be re-established, and that large tracts of Zambia will once again be returned to their natural state.

4

Planning and Preparation

Tourists generally come to Zambia in small numbers, and for the most part restrict themselves to a few of the main towns and national parks. Away from these centres, visitors are regarded with mild curiosity and often shown great warmth and hospitality. Zambia is a genuinely friendly country which (perhaps Lusaka excepted) has not yet had enough bad experiences of visitors to lower its opinion of them.

Zambia's attitude to tourism has changed considerably over the past few years, and visitors are now generally seen as good for the country because they spend valuable foreign currency and create employment. Tourism is helping both Zambia's economy and – by making a major contribution to the preservation of the national parks – its conservation policy.

WHEN TO GO AND HIGHLIGHTS

WEATHER See the section on *Climate*, pages 27–9, for a detailed description of the weather that can be expected, and note that Zambia's rainy season occurs around December to April (slightly different every year).

Dry season Many of Zambia's tourists come during the dry season, with the peak being August to early October. Zambia's small camps and lodges ensure that it never feels busy, even when everywhere is full. Others visit early or late in the season – May to July or November – because the camps are quieter and often costs are lower. The dry season (May to November), when you are unlikely to meet rain and can expect clear blue skies, is the easiest time to travel. It is ideal if this is your first trip to Africa, or if seeing lots of big game is top of your wish list.

June to August are the coolest months, then from September onwards the heat gradually builds up. Note, though, that where the altitude is relatively low – like the Luangwa, the Lower Zambezi Valley or Lake Tanganyika – the temperature is always higher. These places, especially, can get very hot towards the end of October, and occasions of over 40°C in the shade in the middle of the day have earned October the tag of 'suicide month' amongst the locals.

November is a variable month, but many days can be cooler than October, as the gathering clouds shield the earth from the sun. On some days these bring welcome showers; on others they simply build, and with them come tension and humidity. It's always an interesting month.

Wet season A small but increasing number of visitors come during what's known as the 'emerald season', from December to April. While the likelihood of rain means that this isn't for everybody, it remains a fascinating time of year to visit. The camps that open then will often be quiet for days. Their rates can be much lower, and they're often far more flexible about bringing children on safari.

At this time of year, the days can vary enormously from one to the next. Even within a day, skies will often change from sunny to cloudy within minutes and then back again. Downpours are usually heavy and short, and often in the late afternoon. Even in the lower valleys, temperatures are pleasant, rising to only around 30°C, and the nights only slightly cooler (typically down to perhaps 15°C). You will need a good waterproof for the rainy season, but it seldom rains for long enough to really stop you doing anything. Except travelling on bush roads …

TRAVELLING Travelling around Zambia in the dry season often has its challenges – but in the wet season it's a totally different game. Most untarred roads become quagmires; many are completely impassable. The rivers swell to bursting, often beyond, as their surging brown waters undermine trees and carry them downstream like Pooh-sticks. Streams that were ankle-deep in October become potential rafting challenges. Many rural areas are cut off for a few months, so getting anywhere away from the main routes can be tricky.

However, if you are planning to fly into a national park for a safari, you'll find that only a few camps remain open. The South Luangwa has a network of all-weather roads for driving safaris. If you've often been to Africa in the dry season, then this is a fascinating time to visit – like being introduced to a different side of an old friend.

VEGETATION During the wet season, the foliage runs wild. The distinctive oxbow lagoons of the Luangwa and Lower Zambezi fill, while trees everywhere are deeply green. The open sandy plains become verdant meadows, often with shallow pools of water. It's a time of renewal, when a gentler light dapples Zambia's huge forests and areas of bush.

When the rains end, the leaves gradually dry and many eventually drop. More greys and browns appear, and good shade becomes harder to find. Eventually, by late September and October, most plants look dry and parched, coloured from straw-yellow to shrivelled brown.

GAME From the point of view of most herbivores, the wet season is a much more pleasant time. Those in national parks live in enormous salad bowls, with convenient pools of water nearby. It's a good time to have their young and eat themselves into good condition. Val and Bob Leyland were the first visitors for whom I ever organised a trip during the rains. On returning, they commented that 'having [previously] visited Africa last dry season, there's something special about seeing all the animals when they aren't struggling with thirst and a lack of vegetation … It gives a sense of luxuriance which isn't there in the dry season.'

Visiting South Luangwa in the wet season you will see game, but probably less of it. On my last trip during the rains I went on two night drives. On the first we saw a good range of antelope (including some wonderful sightings of young animals), a few elephant and buffalo and a leopard at the end of the evening. The next we found a hyena on a kill, and later followed three lionesses hunting for several hours. The birding was consistently phenomenal, far better than during the dry season.

However, if game viewing is your priority, or this is one of your first trips to Africa, then the animals are much easier to spot when it's dry, as no thick vegetation obscures the view. Further, they are forced to congregate at well-known water points, like rivers, where they can be observed. Many more tracks are navigable in the bush, and so more areas can be explored by vehicle. So if you want to see large numbers of animals, then do come to Zambia in the dry season – and later rather than earlier if possible.

A few specific animal highlights include:

- **February–May** Most of the herbivores are in their best condition, having fed well on the lush vegetation.
- **May–August** Leopard are generally easier to see, as they come out more during the twilight hours. Later in the year they often come out later in the evening, waiting until it is cool.
- **September–October** Buffalo groups tend to amalgamate into larger, more spectacular herds. (They splinter again just before the rains.) Lion sightings become more frequent, as they spend more time near the limited remaining water sources.
- **October–December** Crocodiles are nesting, so are found on or near exposed sandbanks.
- **November** The great wildebeest gathering masses on Liuwa Plain, in western Zambia. It's still accessible by 4x4 at this time of year, but you'll need a small expedition to witness it.
- **November–March** Baby warthogs and impala start to appear in November, followed by most of the mammals that calve sometime during the rainy season.

BIRDLIFE The birdlife in Zambia is certainly best when the foliage is most dense, and the insects are thriving: in the wet season. Then many resident birds are nesting and in their bright, breeding plumage. This coincides to a large extent with the 'summer' period, from around October to March, when the Palaearctic migrants from the northern hemisphere are seen. Certainly in terms of waterbirds – storks, herons, ducks, geese and the smaller waders – the rainy season (and just after) is an infinitely better time to visit.

The birding calendar's highlights include:

- **March–July** Large breeding colonies of storks and herons gather to breed. The only sites I know are in the Nsefu Sector of the South Luangwa National Park.
- **August–October** 'Fishing parties' of herons, egrets and storks will arrive at pools as they dry up, to feed on the stranded fish.
- **September–November** Carmine bee-eaters form large nesting colonies in the soft sand of vertical riverbanks.
- **October–November** Pennant-winged nightjars are in resplendent breeding plumage.
- **November–April** Most of the weavers are in breeding plumage.
- **February–April** Fire-crowned bishop birds, yellow-billed storks and the spectacular paradise whydahs have their breeding plumage on display.
- **April–June** Resident African skimmers are nesting.

PHOTOGRAPHY I find the light clearest and most spectacular during the rainy season. Then the rains have washed the dust from the air, and the bright sunlight can contrast wonderfully with dark storm clouds. The vegetation's also greener and brighter, and the animals and birds often in better condition. However, it will rain occasionally when you're trying to take shots, and the long periods of flat, grey light through clouds can be very disappointing. Sometimes it can seem as if you're waiting for the gods to grant you just a few minutes of stunning light, between the clouds.

A more practical time is probably just after the rains, around April to June, when at least you are less likely to be interrupted by a shower.

The dry season's light is reliably good, if not quite as inspirational as that found during the rains. You are unlikely to encounter any clouds, and will get better sightings of game to photograph. Do try to shoot in the first and last few hours of the day, when the sun is low in the sky. During the rest of the day use a filter (perhaps a polariser) to guard against the sheer strength of the light leaving you with a film full of washed-out shots.

WALKING SAFARIS For safe and interesting walking, you need the foliage to be low so that you can see through the surrounding bush as easily as possible. This means that the dry season is certainly the best time for walking. Walking in the wet season, through shoulder-high grass, is possible – but I'd only go with a very experienced guide and it is harder than during the dry season. My favourite months for walking are June to September, as October can get hot on longer walks.

FISHING The best times to fish in Zambia depend on the area. In the north, on Lake Tanganyika, the rainy season is ideal, between November and March, but in most other areas of the country much of that period is off limits for fishing. On Zambia's great rivers, such as the Zambezi, Kafue and Luangwa, fishing is at its best when the waters are clear. This usually happens from around May to June and lasts until the end of November. Although it is cold during those months the fish are there and will usually fall to bait and spinner, and even fly.

There is a ban on fishing during the months of December to February in all Zambian waters, with the exception of Lake Tanganyika, Lake Kariba, and private dams.

_i_ TOURIST INFORMATION

The Zambia Tourism Board (\ 0211 229087; e ztb@zambiatourism.org.zm, info@ zambiatourism.org.zm; www.zambiatourism.com) offers consumer and general information, and visa advice to potential travellers. It has a good website, and three offices overseas:

South Africa 570 Ziervogel St, Hatfield, Pretoria; \ +27 12 326 1847/1854; e tourism@ zambiapretoria.net, zambiatourism@iburst.co.za
UK 2 Palace Gate, London W8 5NG; \ 020 7589 6655; e ztblondon@aol.com

USA 2419 Massachusetts Av, NW Washington, DC 20008; \ +1 202 265 9717; e zntbusa@ aol.com

For details of other websites offering tourist information, see page 538.

PUBLIC HOLIDAYS

Aside from the private lodges and large hotels, much of Zambia effectively shuts down on public holidays. Independent travellers in particular may need to plan ahead, especially in terms of changing money and finding fuel.

New Year's Day	1 January
Youth Day	around 11–13 March
Good Friday	around March/April

Holy Saturday	day following Good Friday
Labour Day	1 May
Africa Freedom Day	25 May
Heroes' Day	first Monday of July
Unity Day	first Tuesday of July
Farmers' Day	first Monday of August
Independence Day	24 October (plus a holiday on the nearest Monday)
Christmas Day	25 December
Boxing Day	26 December

ORGANISING A SAFARI

Most visitors who come to Zambia for few weeks' safari stay at some of the small safari camps. Combinations of time in the Kafue, the Luangwa Valley, the Lower Zambezi and a few days around Victoria Falls would be typical.

WHEN TO BOOK If you have favourite camps, or a tight schedule, then book as far ahead as you can; eight to ten months in advance is perfect. Bear in mind that most camps are small, and thus easily filled. They organise their logistics with military precision and so finding space at short notice, especially in the busier months, can be tricky. (The exception to this rule is usually the rainy season.)

If you are looking to travel in the next few months, then one or two of your chosen camps may be full; you'll have to accept alternatives.

HOW MUCH? Safaris in Zambia are not cheap. Expect to pay US$4,000/£2,600 per person sharing per week, plus international airfares. This would include a few of your internal transfers or flights, camp transfers, meals, activities, laundry, park fees and even drinks.

HOW TO BOOK It's best to arrange everything together, using a reliable, independent tour operator. Many operators sell trips to Zambia, but few know the country well. Insist on dealing directly with someone who does. Zambia is changing fast, so up-to-date local knowledge is vital in putting together a trip that runs smoothly and suits you. Make sure that whoever you book with is bonded, so your money is protected if they go broke. If you're unsure, pay with a credit card. Never book a trip from someone who hasn't spent time there – you are asking for problems. Ask the person you're dealing with specifically, 'Have you been to this camp or place?'

Booking directly with most Zambian camps is easily possible; the camps are the easy bit. Once they are organised, you need to piece together the jigsaw puzzle of transfers, internal flights and stopovers to link them into your trip. Without local knowledge, this can be tricky – and you will have little recourse if anything goes wrong.

European, US and local operators usually work on commission for the trips that they sell, which is deducted from the basic cost that the visitor pays. Thus you should end up paying the same whether you book through an overseas operator, or talk directly to a camp in Zambia.

Perhaps because of the UK's historical links, or the high number of British safari-goers, there seems to be more competition amongst UK tour operators than elsewhere. Hence they've a reputation for being generally cheaper than US operators for the same trips.

TOUR OPERATORS Zambia is something of a touchstone for tour operators to southern Africa: those who know Zambia well are the small core of Africa specialists. Most operators can send you to Cape Town with ease. But ask them where to visit in Zambia, and you'll rapidly sort those that know southern Africa from those that haven't got a clue.

Don't let anyone convince you that there are only three first-class safari camps in Zambia, as it's rubbish. If your operator doesn't know most of the camps in this book – and offer a wide choice to suit you – then use one that does.

Here I must, as the author, admit a personal interest in the tour-operating business. I run the UK operator Expert Africa (see below), which is currently the leading operator to Zambia, and also organises trips for travellers to Africa from all over the world (especially America). Booking your trip with us (or, indeed, some other tour operators) will always cost you the same as or less than if you contacted Zambia's camps directly – plus you have the benefit of independent advice, full financial protection, and experts to make the arrangements for you. Expert Africa has probably the most comprehensive choice of the best Zambian lodges, camps and destinations available anywhere. In Zambia our safaris are completely flexible, depending on where you want to go. They start at about US$4,000/£2,000 per person for a week, including flights from London, accommodation, meals and game activities.

For a fair comparison, international tour operators featuring Zambia include the following. (Tour operators based in Zambia are listed in the relevant chapters.)

UK

Aardvark Safaris RBL Hse, Ordnance Rd, Tidworth, Hants SP9 7QD; ☎ 01980 849160; e mail@aardvarksafaris.com; www.aardvarksafaris.com. Small, reliable upmarket safari specialist to Africa, Mauritius & Seychelles. Also has US office.

Abercrombie & Kent St George's Hse, Ambrose St, Cheltenham, Glos GL50 3LG; ☎ 0845 218 2202; e info@abercrombiekent.co.uk; www.abercrombiekent.co.uk. Worldwide individual & group holidays to upmarket destinations with upmarket price tags.

Acacia Adventure Holidays 23a Craven Terr, London W2 3QH; ☎ 020 7706 4700; e info@acacia-africa.com; www.acacia-africa.com. Adventure holidays & overland/camping safaris throughout Africa.

Africa Explorer 5 Strand on the Green, London W4 3PQ; ☎ 020 8987 8742; e john@africa-explorer.co.uk; www.africa-explorer.co.uk. Tiny but knowledgeable company run by the jovial John Haycock.

Africa Travel New Premier Hse, 150 Southampton Row, London WC1B 5AL; ☎ 0845 450 1520; e info@africatravel.co.uk; www.africatravel.co.uk. General operator offering trips across Africa & the Indian Ocean.

Audley Travel New Mill, New Mill La, Witney, Oxon OX29 9SX; ☎ 01993 838500; e info@audleytravel.com; www.audleytravel.com. Large tailormade operator offering trips worldwide from Burma to New Zealand, including Africa.

Cazenove & Loyd Imperial Studios, 3–11 Imperial Rd, London SW6 2AG; ☎ 020 7384 2332; e info@cazloyd.com; www.cazloyd.com. Top-end tailormade operator with worldwide options, including Africa.

Expert Africa Upper Sq, Old Isleworth, Middx TW7 7BJ; ☎ 020 8232 9777; e info@expertafrica.com; www.expertafrica.com. Specialists to southern & east Africa & Seychelles; the UK's main operators to Zambia, with a wide range of unusual options – run by this book's author.

Gane & Marshall Aldenham, 2 Deer Park La, Tavistock, Devon PL19 9HD; ☎ 01822 600600; e info@ganeandmarshall.com; www.ganeandmarshall.co.uk. Tailormade operator featuring Africa, Mauritius, Seychelles & Oman.

Hartley's Safaris The Old Chapel, Chapel La, Hackthorn, Lincs LN2 3PN; ☎ 01673 861600; e info@hartleys-safaris.co.uk; www.hartleys-safaris.co.uk. Long-established tailormade specialists to east & southern Africa & Indian Ocean islands.

Journeys by Design 36 Park Cres, Brighton BN2 3HB; ☎ 01273 623790; e maddy@journeysbydesign. com; www.journeysbydesign.co.uk. Small tailormade operator (ground arrangements only) featuring east & southern Africa.

Nomad African Travel 14 Sharpes Hill, Barrow, Bury St Edmunds, Suffolk IP29 5BY; ☎ 01284 810101; e nomadat@onetel.com; www. nomadafricantravel.co.uk. Small UK operator specialising in set guided tours, with tailormade options.

Okavango Tours & Safaris White Lion Hse, 64A Highgate High St, London N6 5HX; ☎ 020 8347 4030; e info@okavango.com; www. okavango.com. Tailormade specialists to Africa & Indian Ocean islands, with a good knowledge of Zambia.

Original Travel 1b The Village, 101 Amies St, London SW11 2JW; ☎ 020 7591 0300; e info@ originaltravel.co.uk; www.originaltravel.co.uk. Upmarket holidays to several destinations, including Africa.

Safari Consultants Africa Hse, 2 Cornard Mills, Mill Tye, Great Cornard, Suffolk CO10 0GW; ☎ 01787 888590; e info@safariconsultantuk. com; www.safari-consultants.co.uk. Long-established tailormade specialists to east & southern Africa, & Indian Ocean islands, with a good knowledge of Zambia.

Safari Drive The Trainer's Office, Windy Hollow, Sheepdrove, Lambourn, Berks RG17 7XA; ☎ 01488

71140; e info@safaridrive.com; www.safaridrive. com. African operator specialising in self-drive trips in 4x4s.

Scott Dunn World 12 Fovant Mews, Noyna Rd, London SW17 7PH; ☎ 020 8682 5070; e africa@ scottdunn.com; www.scottdunn.com. Worldwide coverage (everywhere except North America), with a tailormade programme to Zambia.

Steppes Africa 51 Castle St, Cirencester, Glos GL7 1QD; ☎ 01285 880980; e enquiry@ steppestravel.co.uk; www.steppesafrica.co.uk. Upmarket tailormade operators to destinations worldwide.

Tribes Travel 12 The Business Centre, Earl Soham, Woodbridge, Suffolk IP13 7SA; ☎ 01728 685971; e bradt@tribes.co.uk; www.tribes. co.uk. Worldwide travel on fair-trade principles; particularly strong on cultural trips.

Wildlife Worldwide Long Barn Sth, Sutton Manor Farm, Bishop's Sutton, Alresford, Hants SO24 0AA; ☎ 0845 130 6982; e sales@ wildlifeworldwide.com; www.wildlifeworldwide. com. Worldwide operator offering tailormade & small-group wildlife holidays.

Zambezi Safari & Travel Company Africa Hse, Poundwell St, Modbury, Devon PL21 0QJ; ☎ 01548 830059; e info@zambezi.com; www. zambezi.com. Specialist safari planners with offices in Zimbabwe & UK, concentrating on small, owner-run operators throughout Africa.

France and Italy
Il Diamante Via 1 Nievo 25, 10153 Turin; ☎ 011 229 32 40; e info@ildiamante.com; www. ildiamante.com

Makila Voyages 4 place de Valois, 75001 Paris; ☎ 01 42 96 80 00; e info@makila.fr; www. makila.fr

USA
Africa Adventure Company 5353 N Federal Highway, Suite 300, Fort Lauderdale, FL 33308, USA; ☎ 954 491 8877, 1 800 882 9453; e safari@ africanadventure.com; www.africa-adventure.com

Adventure Center 1311 63rd St, Suite 200, Emeryville, CA 94608; ☎ 800 228 8747; www. adventurecenter.com

Geographic Expeditions 1008 General Kennedy Av, San Francisco, CA 94129-0902; ☎ 800 777 8183; www.geoex.com

OAT ☎ 1 800 493 6824; www.oattravel.com. Typically OAT takes over entire camps for a minimum of a year. They tend to appeal to more mature US-based clients who travel in groups of 16 with highly structured activities at rock-bottom prices.

Australia and New Zealand
The Classic Safari Company 109 Queen St, Woollahra, NSW 2025, Australia; ☎ 612 9327 0666; www.classicsafaricompany.com.au

Expert Africa 216 Havelock Rd, Hastings 4122, New Zealand; ☎ 06 870 6252; e info@ expertafrica.com; www.expertafrica.com

SUGGESTED ITINERARIES Those backpacking and driving themselves around Zambia need time but have great flexibility, and part of the adventure of such a trip is having no itinerary. However, most visitors have a much shorter time available.

Fly-in trips If you're flying in, then getting your itinerary right and arranging it carefully in advance is important. For most visitors to Zambia, the four main areas of attraction are the Luangwa Valley, Kafue National Park, the Lower Zambezi

NOTES FOR DISABLED TRAVELLERS   *Gordon Rattray (www.able-travel.com)*

Although Zambia's tourism infrastructure is developing fast, proper facilities for people with mobility problems are still rare. But don't let this put you off; depending on your ability and sense of adventure, most obstacles are surmountable and Africans are used to finding solutions for practical problems: if you need help, you will receive it.

PLANNING AND BOOKING Most mainstream operators listed in this guide (pages 44–5) will listen to your needs and try to create an itinerary suitable for you. Two operators specialised in catering to disabled travellers work in Zambia (see below). For the more independent traveller, it is possible to limit potential surprises by contacting local operators and establishments by email in advance.

ACCOMMODATION Lusaka's Southern Sun Ridgeway (page 129) has one adapted room. In Livingstone, the Zambezi Sun (page 179) and the Royal Livingstone (page 178) have roll-in showers and bathroom grab-rails, and the less pricey Zigzag Guesthouse (page 168) has fairly wide doorways and level access around the complex. I have yet to hear of completely accessible accommodation in any of Zambia's national parks.

TRANSPORT
Air travel Both Lusaka and Livingstone international airports have assistance, wheelchairs and aisle chairs for those who need help entering or leaving the aircraft. Livingstone also has accessible toilets and at the time of writing this feature is part of Lusaka's current 'five-year plan'.

Buses and trains There is no effective legislation in Zambia to facilitate disabled travellers' journeys by public transport; therefore, if you cannot walk at all then both of these options are going to be difficult. You will need to ask for help from fellow passengers to lift you to your seat, it will often be crowded and it is unlikely that there will be an accessible toilet.

By car Distances are great and roads are often bumpy, so if you are prone to skin damage you need to take extra care. Place your own pressure-relieving cushion on top of (or instead of) the original car seat and if necessary, pad around knees and elbows.
   If you're not sticking to the main roads, you will need to use a 4x4 vehicle, which will be higher than a normal car making transfers more difficult. Drivers/guides are normally happy to help, but are not trained in this skill, so you must thoroughly explain your needs and always stay in control of the situation.

Valley and Livingstone. All these parks are worth visiting for a week (less than three nights in a park is really too short), and there's often a slight saving if you spend at least a week exclusively with one operator. For most people, a visit to Livingstone takes two to three nights.

When designing a trip, bear in mind that:

* Keen walkers would usually include the Luangwa, and some of the smaller 'walking bushcamps' in their trip.

In Livingstone, Hemingways (see *Specialist operators*, below) can provide wheelchair accessible transfers.

HEALTH AND INSURANCE Doctors will know about 'everyday' illnesses, but you must understand and be able to explain your own particular medical requirements. Zambian hospitals and pharmacies are often basic, so it is wise to take as much essential medication and equipment as possible with you, and it is advisable to pack this in your hand luggage during flights in case your main luggage gets lost. Zambia can be hot; if this is a problem for you then try to book accommodation with fans or air conditioning. A useful cooling aid is a plant-spray bottle.

Travel insurance can be purchased in the UK from Age UK (0845 600 3348; www.ageuk.org.uk), who have no upper age limit, and Free Spirit (0845 230 5000; www.free-spirit.com), who cater for people with pre-existing medical conditions. Most insurance companies will insure disabled travellers, but it is essential that they are made aware of your disability.

SECURITY For anyone following the usual security precautions (pages 98–100) the chances of robbery are greatly reduced. In fact, as a disabled person I often feel more 'noticed' when in public places, and therefore a less attractive target for thieves. But the opposite may also apply, so do stay aware of where your bags are and who is around you, especially during car transfers and similar activities.

SPECIALIST OPERATORS
Hemingways +260 0213 323097; m +260 977 866492/870232; e info@hemingwayszambia.com; www.hemingwayszambia.com. Livingstone-based operator offering transfers using wheelchair-accessible vehicle. See page 164.
Endeavour Safaris 23 Lark Cres, Table View, 7441 Cape Town, South Africa +27 (0)21 556 6114; m +27 (0)73 206 7733; e info@endeavour-safaris.com; www.endeavour-safaris.com. Specialists in Botswana, South Africa & Namibia who also cover Livingstone.

FURTHER INFORMATION My new guide, *Access Africa – Safaris for People with Limited Mobility* (see *Appendix 3*, page 538), is packed with useful advice and resources for disabled adventure travellers, and covers the Livingstone area in detail.

www.able-travel.com Regularly updated with both worldwide and country-specific information.
www.apparelyzed.com Dedicated to spinal injury, but containing information that those with other disabilities will find useful. It also hosts a hugely popular forum.
www.globalaccessnews.com Searchable database of disability travel information.
www.rollingrains.com Searchable website advocating disability travel.

- For the variety offered by water-based activities, it's good to visit the Lower Zambezi or the Kafue.
- If you want to visit North Luangwa, then first spend a few days in the South Park, then perhaps 3–5 nights in North Luangwa.
- Shiwa Ng'andu works really well for 3–4 nights, ideally as part of a trip that passes through South Luangwa (the closest place for flights is Mfuwe).
- Kasanka, Bangweulu and Shiwa Ng'andu work well together, usually in that sequence.

Some combinations that work well are:

Short trips
- 7 nights South Luangwa, or Lower Zambezi, or Kafue
- 2–3 nights Livingstone plus 5–6 nights Kafue, or vice versa

Slightly longer trips
- 5–6 nights South Luangwa plus 4 nights North Luangwa
- 5–6 nights South Luangwa plus 3–4 nights Shiwa Ng'andu
- 5–6 nights Kafue plus 4 nights Lower Zambezi
- 5–6 nights Kafue or Lower Zambezi or South Luangwa, plus 2–3 nights Livingstone

Two weeks If you've got about two weeks, then the obvious option is to devote a week each to two of the main three parks. Alternatively, for something a bit more offbeat, consider:

- 3 nights Kasanka, 3 nights Bangweulu (especially green season), 4 nights Shiwa Ng'andu, 4 nights South Luangwa

4x4 trips If you're an experienced Africa hand, driving in your own self-contained vehicle in the dry season, then the choices are much wider. All such trips are long; they're effectively mini-expeditions. The country is your oyster, but there are two obvious routes, and a third that's rather more offbeat, each taking at least three weeks:

Western circuit Livingstone – Upper Zambezi – Mongu – Liuwa Plain – Mongu – Lukulu – Kafue (from northern tip right through to southern tip) – Livingstone

Eastern circuit Lusaka – Kasanka – Lake Waka Waka – Bangweulu – Mutinondo Wilderness – Shiwa Ng'andu – transit through North Luangwa – Luambe – South Luangwa – Lusaka

Northern circuit This suggestion, perhaps for those who have already visited some of the country's highlights, could take you north, visiting some of the lesser-known waterfalls and the Lake Tanganyika area: Lusaka – Kasanka – Bangweulu – Luapula River – Sumbu National Park – Kasama – Shiwa Ng'andu – Mutinondo Wilderness – Lusaka.

NATIONAL PARKS
Head office Almost all of Zambia's national parks fall under the control of the Zambia Wildlife Authority – known simply as ZAWA (*Private Bag 1, Chilanga;*

✎ *0211 278129, 278366, 279080;* e *info@zawa.org.zm; www.zawa.org.zm*). They set the rules and administer the parks from their head office, about 20km south of Lusaka. If you want to do anything unusual, such as filming or some form of research, then we'd suggest that you first discuss your ideas with the staff at Chilanga.

Park entry fees Most organised trips include park entry fees in their costs, but if you are travelling on your own then you must pay these directly, either at one of the ZAWA offices or at the park gates themselves – or, occasionally, at individual lodges themselves. Park offices are normally open 06.00 to 18.00. When paying your fees, you will need to state the gate from which you will be leaving the park. This is ostensibly for security reasons – though don't bank on anyone coming to find you if you come unstuck.

Park fees are officially payable per day (06.00–18.00), rather than per 24 hours, but the ZAWA head office acknowledges that those staying overnight have until 08.00 the following morning to leave the park without paying that day's park fees. However, if you are staying overnight and leaving any later than that, then you will have to pay for two days, as well as the overnight levy. There is a scale of entry fees, with additional charges for taking a vehicle into the parks, and for staying overnight. Fees vary, not just between parks, but according to the visitor, with international visitors paying significantly higher rates than those from southern Africa (SADC), who in turn pay more than Zambian citizens. Current ZAWA fees for international visitors are as follows, per person, per day:

South Luangwa	US$25 (self drive US$30)
Lower Zambezi	US$25 (self drive US$30)
North Luangwa	US$20 (self drive US$25)
Kafue	US$20
Liuwa Plain	US$40
Luambe	US$15
Mosi-oa-Tunya	US$10 (self drive US$15)
Blue Lagoon, Kasanka, Lochinvar, Sumbu	US$10
Other parks	US$5

The fee for taking a vehicle (up to 3 tonnes/50 hp) into the parks is the same in all cases: US$15 per day, or Kw15,300 for a Zambian-registered vehicle (which includes local hire cars). In most parks, an additional bed levy of around US$10 is charged per person per night, a fee that is almost always included in the rates at individual lodges. For campers, however, there is a camping levy of US$5 that is payable at the park gate, on top of any campsite rates.

All park fees are payable in cash – US dollars or kwacha – and you are strongly advised to have the correct money as change can be a problem. Do check the documentation carefully, and retain all receipts as these may be required both at lodges and at your exit gate.

Guides For more adventurous trips to remote parks, hire a game scout from the nearest camp to act as your guide – or, better, arrange this in advance through ZAWA. For around US$30 per day, this can be an inexpensive way to get a local guide who may be able to add a whole new dimension to your trip. It can also save wasted driving time, and probably personal anguish over navigational puzzles. Nowadays, guides normally have their own tents and food.

WECSZ The Wildlife and Environmental Conservation Society of Zambia (*4435 Kumoyo Rd, off Los Angeles Bd, Lusaka;* ✆ *0211 251630;* e *wecsz@coppernet.zm; www.conservationzambia.org;* ⏱ *08.00–17.00 Mon–Fri; membership Kw80,000 pp/ year*) supports environmental education and awareness in Zambia. It sponsors various conservation activities, organises monthly talks for Lusaka members, and runs innovative children's clubs, like the Chongololo and Chipembele conservation clubs, and the related Chongololo Club of the Air (broadcast on Radio 2 each Sunday). It also publishes a number of good, inexpensive field guides specific to Zambia (see *Appendix 3*, page 536).

The WECSZ owns three very simple camps in the national parks: Kafwala and Chibila camps in Kafue, and the Wildlife Camp at Mfuwe. They are managed by others, but some of the revenue still comes back to the society. All are for members only, and may be booked either in writing or in person at the Lusaka office. The society's books can also be bought in Lusaka or at one of the bookshops in town, as can its bi-annual magazine, *Black Lechwe* (*Kw20,000 per issue; free to members*), which is well written with plenty of interesting articles.

GETTING THERE

BY AIR However you get to the subcontinent, if you don't fly directly to Lusaka then do book your flight to Africa and any scheduled internal links between countries (eg: Nairobi–Lusaka or Johannesburg–Lusaka flights) at the same time. Booking the whole trip together is almost certain to save you money. Sometimes the airline taking you to Africa will have cheap regional flights within Africa; for example Johannesburg–Lusaka with British Airways is usually much cheaper if booked with a BA flight from London to Johannesburg, than it is if booked alone. At other times the tour operator you book through will have special deals if you book all the flights with them. And most importantly, if you book all your flights together then you'll be sure to get connecting ones, so you have the best schedule possible.

A US$25 **departure tax** is levied on all international flights. While this is almost always pre-paid on your ticket nowadays, it might be wise to ensure that you have sufficient US dollars in cash as a precaution; credit cards are not accepted. There is also a new US$5 **security tax**, which has to be paid at the airport on departure, usually as you pass through security on your way to check in.

From Europe The only direct flights to Zambia from Europe are run by British Airways (BA; *www.britishairways.com*), which operates three flights a week from London Heathrow. Various other airlines have connecting flights to Lusaka, usually through Nairobi, Addis Ababa or Johannesburg, but only BA flies direct.

These routes are mainly for business traffic and pre-booked holidays; finding cheap tickets online is usually difficult (if not impossible). Expect to pay about £750–850/US$1,200–1,360 for a return flight. Tour operators usually have access to slightly cheaper seats, but you will only be able to buy these if you are buying a complete holiday from them. (This often makes sense; see *Tour operators*, pages 44–5.)

If you want a cheap flight, but don't mind spending longer travelling, then consider using one of the nearby regional centres and connecting through to Zambia (see *From within Africa*, below). It used to be cheaper to fly to Harare than to Lusaka, but there is no longer any advantage in taking that route. Johannesburg is certainly the busiest airport on the subcontinent, and most of the world's larger airlines have flights there, or at least connections. Other options include flying via Malawi, Dar es Salaam, Nairobi or Addis Ababa.

From within Africa Several operators have regular flights linking regional cities with both Lusaka and other Zambian towns. From Johannesburg (JNB), South African Airways (SAA; *www.flysaa.com*) flies into Lusaka (LUN), Livingstone (LVI) and Ndola (NLA), and BA's subsidiary Comair (*www.comair.co.za*) covers Lusaka and Livingstone. Low-cost airlines are breaking into the market, with 1-time (*www.1time.co.za*) operating five flights a week between Jo'burg and Livingstone.

The only Zambian operator within the region is Zambezi Airlines (*www. flyzambezi.com*), which connects Lusaka (and Ndola) with Johannesburg, Dar es Salaam (DAR) and Harare (HRE). Plans to expand, including a flight between Livingstone and Cape Town (CPT), are under consideration.

Among the larger airlines, Kenya Airways (*www.kenya-airways.com*) have daily flights from Dar es Salaam, Nairobi (NBO) and Lilongwe (LLW) to Lusaka, codesharing with KLM, while Ethiopian Airlines (*www.ethiopianairlines.com*) has daily flights between Addis Ababa (ADD) and Lusaka. (It's worth noting that Ethiopia is one of the few African countries from which the US government allows direct flights to and from the USA.) Between April and October, Air Malawi (*www. airmalawi.com*) has five flights a week to Lusaka from Blantyre (BLZ), three of them via Lilongwe.

From North America If you are coming from the US, you will probably need to stop in London or Johannesburg to make connections to Zambia. There are no direct flights. Booking everything in the US may not save you money; investigate the flight prices in comparison with those available in London. Increasingly visitors from America are discovering that UK operators offer better-value safaris than their competitors in America. So consider buying a cheap ticket across the Atlantic, and then organising your Zambian trip through a reliable UK operator.

OVERLAND Most overland border posts open from about 06.00 to 18.00, although this is less rigidly adhered to at the smaller, more remote posts. The paperwork required can be lengthy and time consuming, so allow plenty of time – and in some cases, such as at Kazungula, several hours.

To/from South Africa or Namibia The South African Intercape Mainliner (*www. intercape.co.za*) has a regular bus between Windhoek and Livingstone/Victoria Falls.

CR Holdings (m *0979 476479, 0966 768279*) operates a service between Livingstone and Johannesburg every day except Monday, and between Lusaka and Johannesburg via Chirundu except on Friday.

For self drivers, there is a high-level bridge across the Zambezi at Sesheke (see *Chapter 15, page 469*).

To/from Zimbabwe Zambia's greatest flow of visitors comes from Zimbabwe, over the Livingstone–Victoria Falls border. Many visitors come for just a day trip and locals come to shop, so this is usually a very relaxed and swift border crossing. The crossings over the Kariba Dam and at Chirundu are also straightforward, and the latter is especially good for hitchhiking on long-distance lorries, which ply the route from Harare to Lusaka.

To/from Botswana Despite their territories only meeting at a point, Botswana does have one border crossing with Zambia: a reliable if somewhat chaotic ferry across the Zambezi linking Kazungula with the corner of Botswana, which costs about US$25.

To/from Angola Certain areas of Angola are still not regarded as safe to visit, so do check with the Foreign and Commonwealth Office (*www.fco.gov.uk*) if you're planning to use this route. The easiest border post with Angola is near Chavuma, northwest of Zambezi town. Elsewhere in western Zambia there is a danger of accidentally wandering into Angola, as the border has few markings.

To/from Democratic Republic of Congo (formerly Zaire) There are numerous crossings between Zambia and the DRC, especially around the Copperbelt. Otherwise there is a good track leading into DRC reached via Mwinilunga and Ikelenge. However, the DRC remains an unstable and potentially dangerous place to visit; you should check on the latest security situations before crossing the border, and be careful not to stray across by accident if you're in the Copperbelt region or heading east near Mkushi.

To/from Tanzania Many visitors from Tanzania enter Zambia by ferryboat across Lake Tanganyika into Mpulungu. The main alternative is the land border, either by road crossing or by Tanzania Zambia Railway Authority (TAZARA) train, crossing east of Tunduma. See *Chapter 13*, and the section on *Kapiri Mposhi* (pages 394–6), for more details of TAZARA's important rail link between Zambia and Dar es Salaam. There should also be good hitchhiking opportunities as there are plenty of long-distance lorries plying the route, as well as Zambian drivers picking up Japanese cars in Dar es Salaam.

To/from Malawi The main crossing between Zambia and Malawi is east of Chipata. This would also be the swiftest way to reach the Nyika Plateau, as the roads in Malawi are better than those to Nyika in Zambia.

To/from Mozambique There is a land crossing between Zambia and Mozambique south of Katete, which itself is southwest of Chipata, though this is not often used. A more common route would be via Malawi or Zimbabwe.

RED TAPE

VISAS AND ENTRY REQUIREMENTS Zambia's visa rules appear, on reading them, to be very complex, so it is probably essential to ask at your nearest Zambian embassy or high commission (*www.zambiaimmigration.gov.zm* or *www.zambiatourism.com/welcome.htm*), as they will know the latest news and how the rules are generally being interpreted.

Most visitors, including nationals of Great Britain and the USA, require a visa to enter Zambia. The old Zambian visa-waiver scheme was abolished in January 2008 and replaced by a fixed fee: currently US$50 for single entry and US$80 for a double entry, regardless of nationality. However, those staying for less than 24 hours – for example *en route* to Botswana – pay just US$20.

Most visas can be obtained on arrival at border posts (including international airports), or overseas at your local Zambian diplomatic mission, but applications for multiple-entry visas (*also US$80 pp*) must be made in advance at the nearest Zambian embassy or high commission (see below). You must have at least six months left on your passport, and at least three blank pages. You may also be asked to show an onward ticket, or at least demonstrate that you can support yourself as you pass through the country (credit cards are invaluable), but this is unusual.

In the 1980s, during KK's rule, visitors were routinely treated with suspicion but nowadays the prevailing attitude amongst both the government and the people is very welcoming. Visitors are seen as good for the country because they spend valuable foreign currency; if you look respectable you should not have any difficulty entering Zambia.

Given this logic, and the conservative nature of local Zambian customs, the converse is also true. If you're dressed very untidily and look as if you have no money when entering via an overland border, then you may be questioned as to how you will be funding your trip. Dressing respectably in Zambia is not only courteous, but will also make your life easier.

Visa extensions Visas can be extended by personal application to the Immigration Office in Lusaka (*Kent Bldg, Haile Selassie Rd;* \ *0211 251725/252659/252831/ 254393;* e *immighq@zamnet.zm; www.zambiaimmigration.gov.zm*). You'll need two completed application forms (each with a passport photo), a valid passport and proof of sufficient funds to cover your stay. If it's a business application then you'll also need an explanatory letter with some good reasons. Your application will take at least three working days to process.

Zambia's diplomatic missions abroad The following is a selection of Zambia's embassies and high commissions. For a complete list, see www.zambiatourism. com/travel/listings/zambianmissionsabroad.htm. For foreign embassies in Zambia, see *Chapter 7, Lusaka*, page 148.

Angola (embassy) PO Box 1496, Luanda; \ 0222 447491; e zamemblua@netangola.com

Belgium (embassy) 469 Av Molière, 1050 Brussels; \ 02 343 5649; www.zebru.org,

Botswana (high commission) PO Box 362, Gaborone; \ 0395 351951; e zamhico@work. co.bw

Canada (high commission) 151 Slater St, Suite 205, Ottawa, Ontario K1P 5H3; \ 0613 232 4400; e zhc.ottawa@bellnet.ca; www. zambiahighcommission.ca

Democratic Republic of Congo (embassy) BP 1144, Kinshasa; \ 0819 999437; e ambazambia@ic.cd

Ethiopia (embassy) PO Box 1909, Addis Ababa; \ 011 371 1302; e zam.emb@ethionet.et

France (embassy) 18 Av de Tourville, 75007 Paris; \ 01 56 88 12 70; e zambiansparis@ wanadoo.fr

Germany (embassy) Axelspringerstr 54A, 10117 Berlin; \ 030 206 2940; www.sambia-botschaft.de

Italy (embassy) Via Ennio Quirino Visconti 8, 00193 Rome; \ 0636 006903/002590/088824; www.zambianembassy.it

Kenya (high commission) PO Box 48741, Nairobi; \ 02 724796/724799/724850 e zambiacom@swiftkenya.com

Malawi (high commission) PO Box 30138, Lilongwe 3; \ 01 772635/772590; e zambiahighcom@sdnp.org.mw

Mozambique (high commission) PO Box 4655, Maputo; \ 021 492452; e zhcmmap@tvcabo. co.mz

Namibia (high commission) PO Box 22882, Windhoek; \ 061 327610–1; e zahico@iway.na

South Africa (high commission) PO Box 12234, Pretoria; \ 012 326 1847/1854; www. zambiapretoria.net

Sweden (embassy) Gardsvagen 18, Box 3056, 169 03 Solna; \ 08 679 99040; www. zambiaembassy.se

Tanzania (high commission) PO Box 2525, Dar es Salaam; \ 022 211 2977; e zambia@tanz.net

UK (high commission) 2 Palace Gate, London W8 5NG; \ 020 7589 6655, 7581 2142; www. zhcl.org.uk

USA (embassy) 2419 Massachusetts Av NW, Washington, DC 20008; \ 202 265 9717–9; www.zambiaembassy.org

Zimbabwe (embassy) PO Box 4698, Harare; \ 04 773782; e zambiae@mweb.co.zw

This depends on how you intend to travel and exactly where you are going. If you are flying in for a short safari holiday then you need not pack too ruthlessly – provided that you stay within your weight allowance. However, note that smaller, privately chartered planes may specify a maximum weight of 10–12kg for hold luggage, which must be packed in a soft, squashable bag. Once you see the stowage spaces in a small charter plane, you'll understand the importance of not bringing along large or solid suitcases.

If you are backpacking then weight becomes much more important, and minimising it becomes an art form. Each extra item must be questioned: is its benefit worth its weight?

If you have your own vehicle then neither weight nor bulk will be as vital, and you will have a lot more freedom to bring what you like. Here are some general guidelines.

CLOTHING For most days all you will want is light, loose-fitting cotton clothing. Pure cotton, or at least a cotton-rich mix, is cooler and more absorbent than synthetic materials, making it more comfortable in the heat. A squashable hat and a robust pair of sunglasses with a high UV-absorption are essential.

ONE DREAM THAT DIDN'T COME TRUE

Before you read this tale, it must be emphasised that the overwhelming majority of lodges and their owners in Zambia are honest and reliable, with a real commitment to good practice and responsible tourism. The events described below refer to an extreme exception, rather than the rule. Dave and Louise tell me it's a true account, and only the names have been changed.

The story begins in 1990, when a young English couple – Dave and Louise – fell in love with Africa on holiday. Nothing unusual there. Further trips heightened their affection, until the two were dreaming of swapping their England life for a new life in Africa. Neither being doctors, engineers or teachers – the professions needed most in Africa – their chances of employment seemed meagre. Until, that is, they met Stuart.

Stuart was a South African with fingers in many pies, including the construction of a safari camp. He didn't have time to supervise this, but – with their qualifications in business, finance and management, and with David also a professional chef – it seemed that Louise and David were the answer to his prayers, and vice versa. Before long, the pair had taken a year off, with a view to a permanent move if things worked out, packed their bags and flown to Zambia to oversee the building work. With qualified local builders, the couple's lack of knowledge of construction didn't seem to be a problem.

Initially, Dave and Louise had agreed to work for free, with a view to managing the camp when it was finished. Stuart promised that they would be provided with a 4x4, radio communication, a weapon, food, fuel and a tent at the camp/construction site. However, when the pair were finally dumped at the camp, 90km from the nearest town, things began to look a little less rosy. A few days after arriving, the owners of a nearby lodge warned them that Stuart was not a man to be trusted.

True, they were in the heart of Africa, in an idyllic spot overlooking the Zambezi with an abundance of the local fauna, including elephants, hippos, hyenas, lions,

For men, shorts (not too short) are fine in the bush, but long trousers are more socially acceptable in the towns and rural villages. (You will rarely see a respectable black Zambian man wearing shorts outside a safari camp.) For women, a knee-length skirt or culottes are ideal. Zambia's dress code is generally conservative: a woman wearing revealing clothing in town implies that she is a woman of ill repute, whilst untidy clothing suggests a poor person, of low social standing. On a practical note, women may want to consider a sports bra for safaris in bumpy game-drive vehicles.

These rules are redundant at safari camps, where dress is casual, and designed to keep you cool and protect skin from the sun. Green, khaki and dust-brown cotton is *de rigueur* at the more serious camps (especially those offering walking trips) and amongst visitors out to demonstrate how well they know the ropes. The same cognoscenti are usually to be found wearing old and well-worn items, rather than anything straight out of the box; charity shops in the UK can be a great source of safari wear! At the less serious camps you'll see a smattering of brighter-coloured clothes amongst many dull bush colours, the former usually worn by first-time visitors who are less familiar with the bush.

No matter what your plans, you'll need something warmer, such as a thick fleece, for evenings during the cooler winter months – roughly from April until August. And in the rainy season, don't forget an umbrella if you want to avoid getting drenched; a waterproof jacket, while occasionally useful, is rarely up to the task.

leopards, snakes and even the odd poacher for company. However, the promised vehicle, weapon and radio communication all failed to materialise, and the allowance to pay for their upkeep proved entirely inadequate. They were not even given enough to cover the cost of the building materials, or to buy sufficient food. Trips back to the city to see Stuart proved fruitless – he always seemed to be 'away on business'.

Though their dreams were crumbling, Dave and Louise remained determined, and resourceful. They set up an impromptu campsite to raise cash, and with the income generated they bought food to supplement the fish that Dave caught from the Zambezi.

Details were sketchy, but what Louise and Dave found out about Stuart wasn't proving positive. It involved allegations of smuggling: cobalt, diamonds and even ivory was mentioned. Stuart appeared to be using three different aliases, each with a different passport. The final straw came when a group of besuited heavies arrived at the camp, demanding money for their involvement with the 'big bwana' – Stuart's nickname. Dave and Louise successfully sent them away, but next time the couple visited Lusaka, they were arrested at a roadblock and had their visas revoked. It seemed that Stuart was behind this too. The pair were now visa-less and without work permits. They eventually fled Zambia, poorer, perhaps more cynical – but infinitely wiser.

Looking back, Dave doesn't regret the experience. He's philosophical, preferring to concentrate more on the positive aspects of the whole farrago, and the opportunity it gave them to live in the wilds of the world's most beautiful continent. Their decision to leave their jobs merely for a year proved to be a good one, and as Dave wrote at the end of his letter: 'I sincerely hope that our experience will act as some kind of warning to anyone else who is looking for the same dream.'

Note that washing is done daily at virtually all camps, so few changes of clothes are necessary.

FOOTWEAR If you plan to do much walking, either on safari or with a backpack, then lightweight walking boots (with ankle support if possible) are essential. This is mainly because the bush is not always smooth and even, and anything that minimises the chance of a twisted ankle is worthwhile. Secondly, for the nervous, it will reduce still further the minute chance of being bitten by a snake, or other creepy-crawly, whilst walking.

Because of the heat, take the lightest pair of boots you can find – preferably canvas, or a breathable material such as Gore-tex. Leather boots are too hot in October, but thin single-skin leather is bearable for walking in July and August. Never bring a new pair, or boots that aren't completely worn in. Always pack several pairs of thin socks – two thin pairs of socks are more comfortable than one thick pair, and will help to prevent blisters.

CAMPING EQUIPMENT If you are on an organised safari, then even a simple bushcamp will mean walk-in chalets with linen, mosquito nets and probably an en-suite shower and toilet. However, if you're planning any camping, then note that little equipment is available in Zambia, and see *Camping equipment* (pages 108–9) for ideas of what to take.

ELECTRICAL ITEMS The local voltage is 220V, delivered at 50Hz. Sockets fit plugs with three square pins, like the current design in the UK. Even the most remote safari camp nowadays can usually arrange for you to charge a camera battery, but if this is important, do make sure to check facilities in advance.

OTHER USEFUL ITEMS Obviously no list is comprehensive; only travelling will teach you what you need, and what you can do without. Here are a few of my own favourites and essentials, just to jog your memory.

For visitors embarking on an organised safari, camps will have most things but useful items include:

- Sunblock and lipsalve – for vital protection from the sun
- Binoculars – totally essential for game viewing
- A small pocket torch (see *Camping equipment*, page 109)
- 'Leatherman' tool – never go into the bush without one, but always pack it in your check-in bag; never in your hand luggage
- A small water bottle, especially on flights (see *Camping equipment*, page 109)
- Electrical insulating tape – remarkably useful for general repairs
- Camera – long lenses are vital for good shots of animals
- Basic sewing kit – with at least some really strong thread for repairs
- Cheap waterproof watch (leave expensive ones, and jewellery, at home)
- Couple of paperback novels
- Large plastic 'bin-liner' (garbage) bags, for protecting luggage from dust
- Simple medical kit (pages 87–8) and insect repellent

And for those driving or backpacking, useful extras are:

- Concentrated, biodegradable washing powder
- Long-life candles – as Zambian candles are often soft, and burn quickly

- Nylon 'paracord' – bring at least 20m for emergencies and washing lines
- Hand-held GPS navigation system, for expeditions to remote areas
- Good compass and a whistle
- More comprehensive medical kit

WHAT NOT TO TAKE There are several things worth leaving behind. Firstly, avoid anything which looks military. Leave all your camouflage patterns at home; wearing them anywhere in Africa is asking for trouble. You are very likely to be stopped by the genuine military, or at least the police, who will assume that you are a member of some militia – and question exactly what you are doing in Zambia. Few will believe that this is a fashion statement elsewhere in the world.

Secondly, even if you're going on the most expensive of safaris, leave any jewellery that you don't usually wear all day, every day, at home. It'll take a load off your mind not to have to worry about its security.

MAPS AND NAVIGATION

MAPS For general purposes, there are several reasonable road maps of Zambia, of which the best is currently the 1:1,500,000 sheet published in Germany by **Ilona HupeVerlag**, and widely available at bookshops in Lusaka. In addition to good road and topographical detail, it features fuel stations, campsites and GPS co-ordinates – though the last (and the distances) aren't always entirely reliable. There are also inset overview maps of Lusaka and Livingstone, and the major national parks.

Other commercially produced maps, available both in Zambia and overseas, include those published by International Travel Maps, Globetrotter (New Holland), both at 1:1,500,000, and Macmillan (1:2,200,000). The **International Travel Map** shows contours and the parks, with surrounding text boxes covering topics from wildlife to Zambia's history and geography. Road detail is good, with many of the pontoons (flat, open-sided ferry boats) carefully marked, though coverage of the main points of tourist interest is less detailed. The illustrated **Globetrotter** map incorporates several regional and national park maps at a larger scale, as well as town plans of Livingstone and Lusaka, and climate charts. The smaller-scale **Macmillan** map is less detailed, but better at marking the points of interest for visitors, and on the reverse are many excellent 'inset' maps of the main parks, plus plans of Lusaka and Livingstone.

For **more detail**, Zambia has an excellent range of 'Ordnance Survey'-type maps available cheaply in Lusaka, from the Ministry of Lands in Mulungushi House (see page 125). A wide range of maps is kept here, including the useful 1:250,000 series, a number of town plans, some 'tourist' maps of the parks – including an excellent 1989 map of South Luangwa's landscape and vegetation – and many more detailed maps of selected areas. Some are always out of print, and many are out of date – but you can usually find at least some sort of map to cover most areas. If you are planning to drive yourself around, then buy the maps for your trip at the start.

Navigation by any of these maps becomes more difficult as your location becomes more remote, when expecting any of them to be entirely accurate is unrealistic. Thus if you're heading into the wilds, get what maps you can and compare them with reality as you go.

Many overland travellers with a GPS (see below) would be lost – sometimes quite literally – without **Tracks4Africa** (*www.tracks4africa.com*), a digital mapping software package that covers the whole continent. More prescriptively, **Open Africa**

4

(*www.openafrica.org/country/zambia*) is an NGO which promotes a selection of routes across the continent, including six in Zambia.

GPS SYSTEMS If you are heading into one of the more remote parks in your own vehicle, then consider investing in a small GPS: a global positioning system. These can fix your latitude, longitude and elevation to within about 100m, using 24 American military satellites which constantly pass in the skies overhead. They will work anywhere on the globe.

The cost of commercial units has been around £100/US$160 in Europe or the USA for some time, although their features are continuing to improve as the technology matures. Even the less expensive models will store 'waypoints', so you can build up an electronic picture of an area, as well as working out basic latitude, longitude and elevation. So, for example, you can store the position of your campsite and the nearest road, making it easier to be reasonably sure of navigating back without simply retracing your steps. This can be invaluable in remote areas with lots of bush and no signposts, but it comes with a warning: a GPS takes no account of bends in the road, or indeed of natural hazards, so both directional arrows and distances may appear to be misleading at times.

Although a GPS may help you to recognise your minor errors before they are amplified into major problems, note that it is no substitute for good map work and navigation. Try not to rely on it too much, or you will be unable to cope if it fails, and always have a back-up plan in case it stops working. Note, too, that all these units use lots of battery power, so bring spares with you and/or a cigarette-lighter adaptor.

GPS positions in this book You'll note that I've given almost all of the GPS locations in this book a six-digit name. These were simply the names that I assigned to them in my system, as I recorded them, and I've used them throughout for ease of reference. All GPS co-ordinates have been expressed as degrees, minutes, and decimal fractions of a minute.

I hope that their inclusion may enable more adventurous and experienced readers to venture safely out to Zambia's lesser-known corners, although my points don't remove the need to take up-to-date local advice on safety and conditions.

Important note For all the GPS co-ordinates in this book, note that the datum used is WGS 84; you must set your receiver accordingly before copying in any of these co-ordinates. Many maps in Zambia used the ARC 1950 datum – so you should expect a slight discrepancy between points estimated from such maps, and your GPS unit.

PHOTOGRAPHY AND OPTICS

Don't expect to find any reasonably priced or reasonably available optical equipment in Zambia – so bring everything that you will need with you. For technical tips and equipment, see pages 60–1.

CAMERA INSURANCE Most travel insurance policies are poor at covering valuables, including cameras. If you are taking valuable camera equipment abroad, then include it in your house insurance policy, or cover it separately with a specialist.

BINOCULARS For a safari holiday, especially if you are doing much walking, a good pair of binoculars is essential. They will bring you far more enjoyment than a camera, as they make the difference between merely seeing an animal or bird at a distance, and being able to observe its markings, movements and moods closely. Do bring one pair per person; one between two is just not enough.

There are two styles: the small 'pocket' binoculars, perhaps 10–12cm long, which account for most modern sales, and the larger, heavier styles, double or triple that size, which have been manufactured for years. Both vary widely in cost and quality. If you are buying a pair, then consider getting the larger style. The smaller ones are fine for spotting animals; but are difficult to hold steady, and very tiring to use for extensive periods. You will only realise this when you are out on safari, by which time it is too late.

Around 8 x 30 is an ideal size for field observations, as most people need some form of rest, or tripod, to hold the larger 10 x 50 models steady. Get the best-quality ones you can for your money. The cheapest will be about £40/US$60, but to get a reasonable level of quality spend at least £250/US$400. If you use binoculars regularly, as against for just one holiday, then try to stretch your budget above the £500/US$900 barrier. Once you do this, makes like Swarovski, Zeiss and Leica, which are considerably better than cheaper models, come within reach – and will hugely enhance your experience of viewing wildlife.

$ MONEY AND BUDGETING

CURRENCY Zambia's unit of currency is the kwacha (Kw). Theoretically each kwacha is divided into 100 ngwee, although one ngwee is now worth so little that these subdivisions are never used. Almost all currency comes in the form of notes; the smallest denomination is in fact a coin, worth Kw50, but it is extremely rare. Locals frequently refer to 'thousand' as 'pin' – hence 'five pin', meaning '5,000 kwacha'.

Over the years, the kwacha has been devaluing steadily, in line with the country's inflation rate, but in recent years the rate of devaluation has slowed and it has become more stable. The old practices of strict exchange control and unrealistic exchange rates have gone – as has the black market for currency that these policies created.

EXCHANGE RATES Inflation has varied enormously since at least 1989, but at last seems to be coming under control. In December 2000 it was quoted as being around 30%, but by mid-2007 the underlying rate of inflation was down to a more manageable 9–11%. (See box on page 62 for more on this.) As the kwacha has strengthened, hotels and lodges have been expected to quote their prices in kwacha, rather than the US dollar which was preferred until recently. So while in recent years it has been easier to plan a trip to Zambia in US dollars, and previous editions of this guide quoted prices in US dollars, this is no longer necessary. Thus most of the prices in this guide are given in kwacha. Those that are given in US dollars are usually for lodges whose clientele comes primarily from overseas.

Where sterling and US dollar equivalents are given in this guide, I have assumed a notional rate of around £1 for Kw7,500, or US$1 for Kw4,500.

In September 2011 exchange rates against the kwacha were:

£1	= Kw7,954
US$1	= Kw4,970
€1	= Kw6,992
ZAR1	= Kw697

BUDGETING Zambia is not a cheap country to visit, especially if you want to see some of the national parks. This isn't because of high park fees: on the contrary,

US$5–40/£3.50–25 per day is reasonable by African standards. Rather, costs are high because most safari camps are small and seasonal, and their supply logistics are difficult and costly. However, you do generally get what you pay for: camps in remote locations and pristine environments tend to set very high standards.

To make up a trip using such camps, which are the easiest and most practical way for visitors to Zambia, budget for an all-inclusive cost of about US$400–800/£265–530 per person per day when staying in a camp. Internal flights cost varying amounts, but US$180/£100 per leg would be a good approximation.

At the other end of the spectrum, if you travel through Zambia on local buses, camping and staying in the occasional local (sometimes seedy) resthouse, then Zambia is not expensive. A budget of US$40–60/£20–30 per day for food, accommodation and transport would suffice. However, most backpackers who undertake such trips

DIGITAL PHOTOGRAPHIC TIPS *Ariadne Van Zandbergen*

EQUIPMENT Although with some thought and an eye for composition you can take reasonable photos with a 'point-and-shoot' camera, you need an SLR camera if you are at all serious about photography. Modern SLRs tend to be very clever, with automatic programmes for almost every possible situation, but remember that these programmes are limited in the sense that the camera cannot think, but only make calculations. Every starting amateur photographer should read a photographic manual for beginners and get to grips with such basics as the relationship between aperture and shutter speed.

Always buy the best lens you can afford. The lens determines the quality of your photo more than the camera body. Fixed fast lenses are ideal, but very costly. A zoom lens makes it easier to change composition without changing lenses the whole time. If you carry only one lens, a 28–70mm (digital 17–55mm) or similar zoom should be ideal. For a second lens, a lightweight 80–200mm or 70–300mm (digital 55–200mm) or similar will be excellent for candid shots and varying your composition. Wildlife photography will be very frustrating if you don't have at least a 300mm lens. For a small loss of quality, tele-converters are a cheap and compact way to increase magnification: a 300 lens with a 1.4x converter becomes 420mm, and with a 2x it becomes 600mm. Note, however, that 1.4x and 2x tele-converters reduce the speed of your lens by 1.4 and 2 stops respectively.

For wildlife photography from a safari vehicle, a solid beanbag, which you can make yourself very cheaply, will be necessary to avoid blurred images, and is more useful than a tripod. A clamp with a tripod head screwed on to it can be attached to the vehicle as well. Modern dedicated flash units are easy to use; aside from the obvious need to flash when you photograph at night, you can improve a lot of photos in difficult 'high contrast' or very dull light with some fill-in flash. It pays to have a proper flash unit as opposed to a built-in camera flash.

DIGITAL/FILM Digital photography is now the preference of most amateur and professional photographers, with the resolution of digital cameras improving the whole time. For ordinary prints a six-megapixel camera is fine. For better results and the possibility to enlarge images and for professional reproduction, higher resolution is available up to 16 megapixels.

Memory space is important. The number of pictures you can fit on a memory card depends on the quality you choose. Calculate in advance how many pictures you can fit on a card and either take enough cards to last for your trip, or take are simply 'in transit' between Malawi and Zimbabwe. They see little of Zambia's wildlife or its national parks, missing out on even its cheaper attractions.

If you have your own rugged 4x4 with equipment *and* the experience to use it, then you will be able to camp and cook for yourself, which can cut costs for four people down to around US$30–40/£20–26 per person per day including camping and park fees, but excluding fuel (which is expensive in Zambia). However, to hire such a vehicle and supply it with fuel would cost upwards of another US$60/£40 per person per day.

The cost of food depends heavily on where you buy it, as well as what you buy. If you can shop in Lusaka for your camping supplies then you will save money and have a wider choice than elsewhere. Imported foods are inevitably more expensive than locally produced items. If you are sensible, then US$12–25/£8–16 per day

a storage drive on to which you can download the content. A laptop gives the advantage that you can see your pictures properly at the end of each day and edit and delete rejects, but a storage device is lighter and less bulky. These drives come in different capacities up to 80GB.

Bear in mind that digital camera batteries, computers and other storage devices need charging, so make sure you have all the chargers, cables and converters with you. Most hotels have charging points, but do enquire about this in advance. When camping you might have to rely on charging from the car battery; a spare battery is invaluable.

If you are shooting film, 100 to 200 ISO print film and 50 to 100 ISO slide film are ideal. Low ISO film is slow but fine grained and gives the best colour saturation, but will need more light, so support in the form of a tripod or monopod is important. You can also bring a few 'fast' 400 ISO films for low-light situations where a tripod or flash is no option.

DUST AND HEAT Dust and heat are often a problem. Keep your equipment in a sealed bag, stow films in an airtight container (eg: a small cooler bag) and avoid exposing equipment and film to the sun. Digital cameras are prone to collecting dust particles on the sensor which results in spots on the image. The dirt mostly enters the camera when changing lenses, so be careful when doing this. To some extent photos can be 'cleaned' up afterwards in Photoshop, but this is time-consuming. You can have your camera sensor professionally cleaned, or you can do this yourself with special brushes and swabs made for the purpose, but note that touching the sensor might cause damage and should only be done with the greatest care.

PROTOCOL In some countries, it is unacceptable to photograph local people without permission, and many people will refuse to pose or will ask for a donation. In such circumstances, don't try to sneak photographs as you might get yourself into trouble. Even the most willing subject will often pose stiffly when a camera is pointed at them; relax them by making a joke, and take a few shots in quick succession to improve the odds of capturing a natural pose.

Ariadne Van Zandbergen is a professional travel and wildlife photographer specialising in Africa. She runs The Africa Image Library. For photo requests, visit www.africaimagelibrary.co.za or contact her on ariadne@hixnet.co.za.

EXCHANGE RATES 1995–2011

Although the kwacha has stabilised in recent years, its rates against the US dollar and UK pound have varied greatly over the last decade or so, providing an interesting context to the present economic climate. Rough trends have been as follows:

Date	To US$	To British £	To SA rand	To euro
1995: July	925	1,480	255	–
1996: July	1,270	1,970	289	–
1997: July	1,310	2,180	287	–
1998: July	1,945	3,200	310	–
1999: July	2,500	4,000	415	2,630
2000: July	3,083	4,656	448	2,710
2001: July	3,585	5,208	453	2,480
2002: July	4,720	7,340	470	4,690
2003: July	4,930	8,020	655	5,600
2004: July	4,775	8,800	785	5,870
2007: July	3,978	8,081	560	5,453
2011: July	4,880	7,725	707	6,788

would provide the supplies for a good, varied diet, including the odd treat. In any event, it will be cheaper than eating out.

In Lusaka and the main cities the bigger hotels are about US$200–325/£135–215 for a double room, whilst a good guesthouse will cost around US$65–100/£45–65. Camping at organised sites on the outskirts of the cities is, again, a good bet if you have the equipment and transport. It will cost from around US$5/£3 per person per night.

Restaurant meals in the towns are still relatively inexpensive, although costs have risen in recent years: expect to pay US$15–30/£10–20 for a good evening meal, including a local beer or two. Imported beers are more expensive than local beer (which is perfectly adequate), and South African wines are more costly again. European wines and spirits, as you might expect, are ridiculously priced (and so make excellent gifts if you are visiting someone here). You will pay well over US$100/£55 for a bottle of champagne in Lusaka!

Finally, do be aware that prices in Zambia – as anywhere else – can and do rise, as can VAT (which is currently 16%). Rates quoted in this guide were correct at the time of research in 2011, but many will change during the life of the guide, so please do be sensitive to any increases.

HOW TO TAKE YOUR MONEY Although both US dollars and UK pounds sterling are easily changed at a bank, in practice US dollars are far more useful to the visitor. You will normally need to have US dollars in cash to pay for visas at the border, for any tax due at the airport, and for all national parks' fees. Sometimes you can pay for the larger hotels and other services in US dollars (small-denomination notes) too, although this becomes less common away from the bigger towns.

If you're going to more offbeat locations, you increasingly need kwacha – although in case of need, some places will accept cash in low denominations of US dollars. If you're driving yourself, it is crucial that you allow sufficient cash (in kwacha) to pay for fuel; credit cards and US dollars will not be accepted.

I travel with mostly US$1, US$5, US$10 and US$20 bills (and a few £10 or £20 notes). Because of the risk of forgeries, people are sometimes suspicious of larger-denomination notes; conversely, some places offer a lower exchange rate for smaller-denomination notes. US$100 and even US$50 bills are often rejected in shops and even some banks.

In the Western Province near the Namibian border, South African rand are occasionally accepted; elsewhere they're virtually useless.

Most of the larger hotels and shops, and some safari camps, accept the major **credit and debit cards** (Visa and MasterCard), but bear in mind that a 3–5% commission may be levied, so be sure to enquire, prior to using your card, about any charges. Don't expect to be able to pay park fees by card.

It is advisable to take at least two cards, ideally a Visa and a MasterCard, and note that many banks will accept Visa but not MasterCards. Do remember to notify your bank of your travel plans in advance of departure, in case of any attempted fraud (and thus a block on your account) while you're travelling.

Some travellers still prefer to take some of their money as **travellers' cheques**. While these may be preferable from a security point of view, as they are refundable if stolen, they are less flexible, and cannot be used as cash as they are in the USA. (Note that Amex travellers' cheques are not always welcomed, and their charge cards are seldom of use in Zambia.)

CHANGING MONEY AND BANKING If you need to change foreign currency, receive bank drafts, or do any other relatively complex financial transactions, then banks in the larger cities (ideally Lusaka) are your best option, though almost all banks will exchange US dollars. For the most part, banking hours are around 08.30 to 15.30, Monday to Friday, although in smaller towns they may close earlier, or be open only on certain days. A few of the bigger banks also open around 09.00 to 11.00 on Saturdays, a policy that is spreading nationwide.

ATMs are widely available in the major towns, but outside of these, they are not the norm. Even where they do exist, they are not entirely reliable, so carry plenty of cash as back up. At a number of banks (including Barclays, Standard Chartered and Stanbic) you can use European debit cards bearing the Maestro or Visa logo to withdraw up to Kw2,000,000 per day.

If you are changing money at one of the main banks, in Lusaka or Livingstone, then there is minimal difference in the rates between travellers' cheques and pounds sterling or US dollars in cash. If you use a bureau de change, you'll usually get better rates for cash.

The once relatively wide 'black market' in foreign currency, with US dollars worth much more if changed surreptitiously with a shady (and illegal) street dealer rather than at a bank. was effectively wiped out when financial reforms enabled the kwacha to float at a free-market rate. Now the shady characters on the street who hiss 'Change money' as you pass are more likely to be conmen relying on sleight of hand than genuine money-changers. Give them a very wide berth.

TIPPING Tipping is a difficult and contentious topic – worth thinking about carefully. While I'm told that it's illegal in Zambia, it is practised widely, and is often expected, especially in restaurants, though the amounts are generally moderate. Read the section on *Local payments* in *Chapter 6*, page 116, and realise that thoughtlessly tipping too much is just as bad as tipping too little.

Ask locally what's appropriate; here I can give only rough guidance. Helpers with baggage might expect Kw1,000–2,000/US$0.25–0.50, someone looking after your car around Kw1,500–2,500/US$0.30–0.50, depending on the time you're away, whilst sorting out a problem with a reservation would be Kw4,500–12,000/US$1–2.50. Restaurants will often add an automatic service charge to the bill, in which case an additional tip is not usually given. If they do not do this, then 10% would certainly be appreciated if the service was good. Tipping a taxi driver is not normally expected.

At safari camps, tipping is not obligatory despite the assumption from some visitors that it is. If a guide has given you really good service then a tip of about US$5–8 per day per guest would be a generous reflection of this. If the service hasn't been that good, then don't tip.

Always tip at the end of your stay, not at the end of each day or activity. Do not tip after every game drive. This leads to the guides only trying hard when they know there's a tip at the end of the morning. Such camps aren't pleasant to visit and this isn't the way to encourage top-quality guiding. It's best to wait until the end of your stay, and then give what you feel is appropriate in one lump sum.

However, before you do this find out if tips go into one box for all of the camp staff, or if the guides are treated differently. Ask the managers as you're about to leave. Then ensure that your tip reflects this – with perhaps as much again divided between the rest of the staff.

GETTING AROUND

BY AIR For those who want to fly internally in Zambia, the number of possibilities is increasing. Although only Proflight operates a scheduled service, offering internet booking with payment by credit card, several other local companies provide very reliable charters. None of the others is featured on any of the global flight reservations systems, so outside of Zambia (and even inside sometimes) most travel agents won't have a clue about the intricacies of Zambia's internal flights. You are strongly advised to book your internal flights through an experienced tour operator, who uses them regularly. (As an aside, this means that if the airline goes bust the tour operator loses money; you don't.) If you want to arrange something whilst you are in Zambia, or need to get in touch with an airline in a hurry, see the contact details below and on page 122.

The services that I have encountered are high-quality operations, so you need have few worries about safety. On the whole, the smaller charter operations are very reliable, and more flexible for individual passengers, than the larger airlines.

However, if you book an internal flight a long time in advance, be aware that its timings (and indeed existence) may change. Cancellation at short notice is unlikely, though taking a philosophical attitude towards this possibility would be wise. A good operator will always be able to make a back-up plan for you.

Note that internal flights are subject to both a US$8 **departure tax** and a new US$3 **security tax**.

There are an increasing number of scheduled internal flights offered by Proflight (see below), but for other destinations you will have to **charter** your own plane. This isn't for the backpacker's budget, but if you plan to stay at private safari camps then short charters may be within your price range.

It's possible to charter planes seating up to 12 passengers. Costs vary according to the size of plane. You can expect to pay around US$2.10 per kilometre for a single-engine plane seating 3–5 passengers; US$2.6/km for a twin-engine plane for 4–5 people; US$3/km for a pressurised twin-turbine plane seating 6–7, or US$4/km for 7–12 passengers. Use these figures as a rough guide only, as the rates fluctuate

ONE-WAY FLYING DISTANCES (KM)

	Bangweulu	Kafue	Kalabo	Kasanka	Livingstone	Zambezi	Lusaka	Mfuwe	Nchila	Shiwa Ng'andu
Bangweulu		490	885	70	810	410	435	235	650	185
Kafue (Lunga)	490		405	465	410	385	255	610	400	670
Kalabo	885	405		865	455	750	610	1,015	450	1,070
Kasanka	70	465	865		760	350	380	195	670	220
Livingstone	810	410	455	760		480	390	840	750	980
Zambezi (Jeki)	410	385	750	350	480		140	365	750	545
Lusaka	435	255	610	380	390	140		455	635	600
Mfuwe	235	610	1,015	195	840	365	455		860	230
Nchila	650	400	450	670	750	750	635	860		810
Shiwa Ng'andu	185	670	1,070	220	980	545	600	230	810	

significantly according to the route travelled, the individual companies and the (increasingly high) price of fuel. When making your calculations, remember to include any mileage to/from the aircraft's base, and when booking remember that tour operators who book these trips every day will be given much better rates that individuals interested in a one-off charter. And if you do decide to charter, it's important to be aware that there is a maximum luggage allowance of 12kg per person (15kg on Proflight), to be carried in soft bags only.

For rough one-way distances, in kilometres, see box above.

Scheduled airlines

Proflight 0211 845944/5; m 0977 335563; e reservations@proflight-zambia.com; www. flyzambia.com. Proflight has regular scheduled flights linking Lusaka with the Lower Zambezi (US$90–150), Mfuwe (US$90–250) & Livingstone (US$83–250), all pp one way. Other destinations are Ndola (US$116–320 return), Solwezi, Mansa, Kasama, Chipata & – from 2011 – Mongu. In Jul 2011 they introduced seasonal flights 3 times a week to the Lower Zambezi from Mfuwe & Livingstone.

Charter airlines

Avocet Air Link 0211 236437, airport 0211 233422, after hrs 0211 264866; m 0977 770502; e avocet@zamnet.zm; www. avocet-charters.com. Operates twin-engine Cessna 400 planes out of Lusaka.
Ngwazi Air Charters 0211 840477, 271196; m 0966 657001, 0968 269169; e resngwaziair@ iconnect.zm, johnngwaziair@iconnect.zm; www. ngwaziaircharters.com
Proflight In addition to its scheduled service, Proflight (see above) operates charter flights nationwide.

Royal Air Charters m 0979 143928; e operations@royalaircharters.com; www. zam-ads.com/royal-air-charters. A new company linked to Royal Zambezi Lodge on the Lower Zambezi.
Sky Trails 0216 245268; m 0977 740899/790500, 0979 206337; e reservations@ skytrailszambia.com; www.skytrailszambia.com. Originally specialising in northern & eastern Zambia, Sky Trails now has a Lusaka base, too. As experts in wildlife aerial surveys & anti-poaching work, they have high-wing aircraft that offer

good views. Rates in their sgl-engine C206, taking 4–5 passengers, are US$2.20/km, which works out at Lusaka–Kasanka US$1,620, or Mfuwe–Shiwa Ng'andu US$1,020. For an extra 10% (making it particularly good value), there's the option of a twin-engine C337.

Wilderness Air 0211 271051; m 0978 770484; e reservations@sefofane.co.zm; www. sefofane.com. Operates all of Wilderness Safaris' flights & private charters into various lodges across Zambia & neighbouring countries.

BY RAIL There are two totally separate rail systems in Zambia: ordinary trains and TAZARA (Tanzania Zambia Railway Authority) trains. Zambia's **ordinary rail network** was privatised in 2003 and is now run by RSZ (Railway Systems of Zambia) on a 20-year contract – but the system is currently worse than ever. Trains run on only one line, linking Livingstone with Kitwe in the Copperbelt via Lusaka. They're painfully slow, and rarely used by travellers – one local described the journey as 'like signing a death warrant'! If you have lots of patience, and a few good books, then try them by all means – just remember to take plenty to eat and drink for the journey as nothing is available on board.

In contrast, the **TAZARA** service is very popular with backpackers. It connects Kapiri Mposhi with the Indian Ocean, at Dar es Salaam in Tanzania. This is a reliable international transport link which normally runs to time and is by far the fastest way between Zambia and Tanzania with the exception of flying. See *Kapiri Mposhi* in *Chapter 13*, pages 395–6, for details of this useful service.

For rail aficionados, there's an occasional third option in the form of the luxury train operated by the South African Rovos Rail (*+27 12 315 8242*; e *reservations@ rovos.co.za; www.rovos.com*) between Cape Town and Dar es Salaam. It's a 14-day journey, crossing into Zambia at the Victoria Falls Bridge near Livingstone, and joining the TAZARA line at Kapiri Mposhi before entering Tanzania. Prices start from around US$9,000 per person sharing.

BY BUS AND COACH Zambia's **local buses** are cheap, frequent and a great way to meet local people, although they can also be crowded, uncomfortable and noisy. In other words they are similar to any other local buses in Africa, and travel on them has both its joys and its frustrations. In the main bus stations, there are essentially two different kinds: the smaller minibuses, and the longer, larger 'normal' buses. Both will serve the same destinations, but the smaller ones tend to go faster and stop less. They may also be a little more comfortable. Their larger relatives will take longer to fill up before they leave the bus station (because few buses ever leave before they are full), and then go slower and stop at more places. For the smaller, faster buses there is usually a premium of about 20% on top of the price. Be aware, too, that even buses said to be running to a timetable may not depart until they are full, so check carefully what service you can expect – and ideally take a look at the bus on which you'll be travelling too. A broken windscreen hints at poor overall maintenance.

Then there are a few **postbuses** which operate between the post offices in the main towns, taking both mailbags and passengers as they go. These conform to a more fixed schedule, and standards have improved in recent years. Tickets are booked in advance at the nearest post office. For details, see pages 124–5.

Various luxury **coach services** connect most major towns and the smaller towns in between. See individual chapters for details of those that are running at the time of writing.

BY TAXI Taxis are common and very convenient in Lusaka, Livingstone and the main towns of the Copperbelt, and are starting to appear in smaller towns; Tom

Kok reports that even Kaoma has several taxis. (Elsewhere they are uncommon or don't formally exist.) They can be hailed in the street, though foreign travellers may be best advised to book one through a reliable source or through your hotel. Meters are non-existent, but all drivers should have typed sheets of the 'minimum' rates to and from various local places – though charges can be higher if their customers appear affluent. Rates should always be agreed before getting into the vehicle. If you are unsure of the route then rates per kilometre, or per hour, are easy to negotiate.

BY POSTBOAT Rather like the postbuses, postboats used to operate on the Upper Zambezi and the waters of Lake Bangweulu during the rainy season, transporting cargo, passengers and even vehicles. However, this service has now been subcontracted, with information sketchy and none too reliable, even at the individual ports themselves. For the most part it's best to ask advice locally.

DRIVING Driving in Zambia is on the left, based on the UK's model. However, the standard of driving is generally poor, matched only by the quality of the roads. Most roads in the cities, and the major arteries connecting these, are tar. These vary from silky-smooth recently laid roads, to pot-holed routes that test the driver's skill at negotiating a 'slalom course' of deep holes, whilst avoiding the oncoming traffic that's doing the same. Inconveniently, the smooth kind of road often changes into the holed variety without warning, so speeding on even the good tar is a dangerous occupation. Hitting a pot-hole at 40–60km/h will probably just blow a tyre; any faster and you risk damaging the suspension, or even rolling the vehicle.

As an additional hazard, even the tar roads are narrow by Western standards, often with steep sides designed to drain off water during the rains. As a result, it's all too easy, faced with a sharp bend or an oncoming lorry, to veer off the road, a fact borne out by the regular sight of a truck lying on its side in the ditch, or to damage the sump of the vehicle. Finally, watch out for speed humps that may occur without warning, even on major roads. You often find these at the entrance and exit of a town (Kapiri Mposhi, for example), but also sometimes as you approach a level crossing.

Away from the main arteries the roads are gravel or just dirt and usually badly maintained. During the dry season these will often need a high-clearance vehicle: a 4x4 is useful here, but not vital. (The exceptions are areas of western Zambia standing on Kalahari sand, which always require 4x4.) During the wet season Zambia's gravel roads are less forgiving, and they vary from being strictly for 4x4s to being impassable for any form of vehicle. Travel on anything except the tar roads is very difficult during the rains. For more details, and particularly if you intend to hire a vehicle, read the important section on driving in *Chapter 6*, pages 101–7.

Speed limits are 120km/h on main roads and 50km/h in towns, but there are significant local variations, particularly in the approach roads to Lusaka, where they tend to be strictly enforced. Beware of speed humps, often without warning, at the approach to a town, in both directions.

All vehicles should carry two warning triangles for use in case of an accident or breakdown (although you'll often see brushwood laid out on the road at strategic intervals to warn of an accident or breakdown). They should also display reflective tape: white at the front, and red at the rear. Failure to comply with these regulations may result in a fine.

Police (and immigration) roadblocks are an occupational hazard of driving, and you can expect to be stopped regularly. They are usually indicated in advance by oil drums or traffic cones placed in the middle of the road, but some are very poorly marked, so keep an eye out for them, and do stop! Note that most overseas visitors

4

Distances in kilometres (approx)

Note that distances between towns are only one part of the equation when calculating travelling times. More important are the type of road (tar, gravel, dirt), and the conditions, both of which must be taken into consideration.

	Chipata	Chirundu	Kapiri Mposhi	Kasama	Kitwe	Livingstone	Lusaka	Mansa	Mbereshi	Mongu	Mpika	Mporokoso	Mpulungu	Mwinilunga	Sesheke	Solwezi
Chirundu	695															
Kapiri Mposhi	780	346														
Kasama	1475	996	644													
Kitwe	990	498	150	796												
Livingstone	1080	608	682	1332	834											
Lusaka	560	136	210	860	362	472										
Mansa	1400	926	650	350	800	1262	790									
Mbereshi	1600	1126	850	386	1000	1462	990	200								
Mongu	1210	760	834	1484	986	525	624	1414	1614							
Mpika	1269	839	493	221	643	1175	703	559	759	1327						
Mporokoso	1635	1156	804	160	954	1492	1020	307	181	1644	381					
Mpulungu	1679	1210	864	210	1014	1576	1074	517	560	1698	431	370				
Mwinilunga	1470	1020	674	1324	501	1356	884	1324	1524	780	1167	1478	1538			
Sesheke	1260	741	872	1522	1024	190	662	1452	1652	335	1311	1682	1736	1115		
Solwezi	1210	744	398	1042	225	1080	608	1048	1248	896	891	1202	1262	292	1231	
Zambezi	1650	1156	810	1454	658	1150	1020	1460	1660	625	1303	1614	1674	396	960	515

can drive on a national licence for up to 90 days, and that both drink driving and driving using a mobile phone when at the wheel are illegal. For more on this subject, see *Chapter 6*, pages 102–3.

Fuel Availability of fuel can be a problem, so it is important to top up whenever you can rather than to let the tank run low. Not only are fuel stations thin on the ground outside of major centres, but supplies can be erratic, so that at any given time unleaded petrol, for example, may be difficult to find throughout the country.

The price of fuel is extremely high by southern African standards, a reflection of high government taxes, which account for over 50% of the price. Despite the country's distance from the nearest port, transportation is less of an issue: crude oil is brought by pipeline from Dar es Salaam to Ndola, where it is refined then distributed both within Zambia and to the DRC. Thus the country's cheapest fuel is in Ndola, but it varies quite significantly according to the part of the country, and from one fuel station to another. In summer 2011, the price of petrol in Lusaka and Livingstone was around Kw8,647/US$1.92 a litre, with diesel at Kw7,958/US$1.77. (As an indication of potential difference, the price of diesel in the Western Province at the same time was heading for Kw9,000 a litre/US$2.)

Vehicle hire With difficult roads, which seem to vanish completely in some of the more remote areas, driving around Zambia away from the main arteries is not easy. The big car-hire firms do have franchises in Lusaka, but most concentrate on businesspeople who need transport around the city. Even now, some will insist that foreigners hiring cars also hire a chauffeur, and only the specialists are geared up for visitors in search of recreation.

Hiring a 2WD A mid-range model like a Ford Mondeo from, say, Europcar (*www. europcarzambia.com*) will cost around US$180/£120 per day with fully comprehensive insurance, 100km 'free' per day, and a 63¢/42p charge per kilometre after that. While this is an improvement on rates even a few years ago, just add up the distances on a map and you'll realise that it still isn't viable for most trips. Further, a standard saloon vehicle just wouldn't stand up to the pot-holes found on most of the main highways, never mind the state of the dirt tracks beyond, so for exploring beyond the major towns you'll be needing either a high-clearance 2WD or – better – a 4x4.

See *Car hire* in the chapters on Lusaka (page 127), Livingstone (page 164), and the Copperbelt (pages 397, 409 and 412) for contact details of the various car-hire agencies.

Hiring a 4x4 Until recently, it wasn't possible to hire reliable 4x4 vehicles in Zambia so the only option was to bring them in from outside, or arrange for a safari company to take you around on a mobile safari. However, this has changed, and there are now a few options within Zambia itself. All the same, it's important to realise that self-drive trips around Zambia are not for the inexperienced; I think that they're suitable only for those who have previously taken several in Africa, including at least one self-drive 4x4 trip (a 4x4 trip around Botswana makes a perfect precursor). And if you have any doubts, read the box *Lessons in bush travel* on pages 272–3, then think hard about what you're planning. Bear in mind, too, that self-drive trips are expensive; it can often be cheaper to fly between major cities before collecting a vehicle.

There are a few obvious candidates; the best choice depends on the route you're taking.

Safari Drive (see page 45) If you're thinking of a trip just around the eastern side of Zambia, then this UK-based company has a small fleet of Land Rover Defender 110 & Puma vehicles available out of Lilongwe in Malawi, for about US$300–330/£200–220 per day. All come extremely well equipped with sturdy kit for bush camping, including long-range fuel tanks, rooftop tents, portable fridges & satellite phone, as well as the relevant paperwork to take them across the border into Zambia.

Hemingways See page 164

Limo Hire Zambia 0211 278628; m 0977 743145; e limohirezambia@gmail.com; www. limohire-zambia.com. From its base south of Lusaka, this company offers a wide range of vehicles, including 4x4 Toyota Land Cruisers with rooftop tents. Reports suggest that equipment is adequate if sometimes a little tired.

Voyagers 0212 617062, 620604; e carrental@voyagerszambia.com; www.voyagerszambia.com/safveh.htm. Based in Ndola, but with offices in Lusaka, Livingstone & elsewhere in the Copperbelt (& also at the airports), Voyagers have fully equipped Ford 4x4s complete with long-range fuel tank, rooftop tents, cooking equipment, fridge & linen, all designed to fit into the vehicle. Also available are fully equipped camper vans: Toyota Land Cruisers with a sleeping/dining area behind the driver's cab. Base rates are US$230 & US$188 per day respectively, including VAT, fully comprehensive insurance & 200km. It's an efficient operation with particularly helpful staff. If provided with a rough itinerary, they will also advise on the state of the roads (& thus the type of vehicle required), & can book accommodation *en route*.

HITCHHIKING
Hitchhiking is a practical way to get around Zambia – especially in the more remote areas. Most of Zambia's poorer citizens hitchhike, and view buses as just a different form of vehicle. Either way, lifts are normally paid for.

MOTORING ACCIDENTS

If you drive carefully in Zambia, during the day, and stick to the speed limits and sensible speeds (maximum 100–120km/h on good tar, much less on gravel or pot-holed tar), then you should never have an accident here. However, animals and people (especially cyclists) on the road can be a nightmare, so don't be shy about using your horn a lot, and well in advance, particularly in busy towns.

If you're unfortunate enough to be involved in an accident, you need to think clearly. If you've hit a dog, a goat or a chicken, then you do not have to stop. It would be courteous to compensate the owner – although you may end up in a heated situation which becomes very difficult. If you hit a wild animal, you should report it to the local ZAWA office, or police station. Always check the vehicle, too; if you have hit a goat, for example, the impact could damage the coolant system and cause a leak.

If you hit a person, then the accident must be reported. Your natural instinct will be to stop – but most Zambians will tell you that you should not to do so, for fear of being seriously assaulted by friends or relatives of the injured person. That said, if the person is injured then you may be able to help to get him or her to hospital. I've never had to make this choice, and hope I never have to. (Should you be in this situation, and decide to help, do remember to wear plastic gloves and glasses to minimise the risk of HIV infection, and don't attempt mouth-to-mouth resuscitation without a protective mask.) In any case, you must go directly to the nearest police station, or police roadblock. If a death has occurred then you will be expected to hand over your passport to the police.

In order to make an insurance claim in Zambia you will need to obtain a police report, for which you'll be expected to pay.

Hitching has the great advantage of allowing you to talk one-to-one with a whole variety of people, from local businesspeople and expats, to truck drivers and farmers. Sometimes you will be crammed in the back of a windy pick-up with a dozen people and as many animals, while occasionally you will be comfortably seated in the back of a plush Mercedes, satisfying the driver's curiosity as to why you are in Zambia at all. It is simply the best way to get to know the country, through the eyes of its people, though it is not for the lazy or those pressed for time.

Waiting times can be long, even on the main routes, and getting a good lift can take six or eight hours. Generally, on such occasions, the problem is not that lots of potential vehicles refuse to take you. The truth is that there are sometimes very few people going your way with space to spare. If you are in a hurry then combining hitchhiking with taking the odd bus can be a quicker and more pragmatic way to travel.

The essentials for successful hitching in Zambia include a relatively neat, conservative set of clothes, without which you will be ignored by some of the more comfortable lifts available. A good ear for listening and a relaxed line in conversation are also assets, which spring naturally from taking an interest in the lives of the people that you meet. Finally, you must always carry a few litres of water and some food with you, both for standing beside the road, and for lifts where you can't stop for food.

Dangers of drink driving Unfortunately, drinking and driving is common in Zambia. It is more frequent in the afternoon/evening, and towards the end of the month when people are paid. Accepting a lift with someone who is drunk, or drinking and (simultaneously) driving, is foolish. Occasionally your driver will start drinking on the way, in which case you would be wise to start working out how to disembark politely.

An excuse for an exit, which I used on one occasion, was to claim that some close family member was killed whilst being driven by someone who had been drinking. Thus I had a real problem with the whole idea, and had even promised a surviving relative that I would never do the same … hence my overriding need to leave at the next reasonable town/village/stop. This gave me an opportunity to encourage the driver not to drink any more; and when that failed (which it did), it provided an excuse for me to disembark swiftly. Putting the blame on my own psychological problems avoided blaming the driver too much, which might have caused a difficult scene.

Safety of hitchhiking Notwithstanding the occasional drunk driver, Zambia is generally a safe place to hitchhike for a robust male traveller, or a couple travelling together. It is safer than the UK, and considerably safer than the USA; but hitchhiking still cannot be recommended for single women, or even two women travelling together. This is not because of any known horror stories, but because non-Zambian women, especially white women, hitching would evoke intense curiosity amongst the local people. Local people might view their hitching as asking for trouble, whilst some would associate them with the 'promiscuous' behaviour of white women seen on imported films and television programmes. The risk seems too high. Stick to buses.

ACCOMMODATION

Zambia boasts the full range of accommodation, from top-class safari lodges and international hotels to simple guesthouses and campsites, with an equally diverse range of standards and prices. Pricing can appear complex at first, since many of the better establishments have a two- or even three-tier structure. Typically, there will be two rates: one for local visitors, the other for international guests. In some cases, the 'local' rate will be further divided into Zambian citizens and Zambian residents; in others, these two may be lumped together, but a further category introduced: visitors from within southern Africa.

Prices quoted in this guide are for the most part international rates – those payable by visitors from Europe, America and other Western countries. While prices were correct at the time of research, inevitably many will rise during the life of the guide.

HOTELS Traditionally, hotels in Zambia have tended to fall into two categories, all geared to the business market: large concrete blocks with pretensions to an 'international' standard, or small, run-down places catering to Zambians who are not very particular about quality. They're a very uninspiring bunch on the whole, and most visitors spend as little time in them as possible. Things started to change when Sun International opened two hotels near Victoria Falls in Livingstone in 2001, and since then other investors have seized the initiative. The South African Protea chain is gradually increasing its presence in Zambia, while a couple of new places in Solwezi have set an entirely new standard for the region.

The larger hotels are restricted to Lusaka, Livingstone and the Copperbelt. They generally have clean modern rooms, good communications and all the facilities that international businesspeople expect, although standards in the Copperbelt are more variable. Their prices (generally fixed) reflect this, at around US$200–325/£135–215 for a double room, or at least US$120–195/£80–130 for a single. Most still have little to distinguish them from each other, and are pretty soulless.

Zambia's smaller and cheaper hotels vary tremendously, but very few are good and many seem over-priced.

GUESTHOUSES In the last few years Zambia's larger towns, and especially Lusaka, have seen a proliferation of small guesthouses of varying quality spring up throughout the more spacious suburbs. These are not very practical if you need a courtesy bus to the airport, room service, or a telephone beside your bed – but they are often full of character and can be good value. Expect them to cost US$$65–100/£45–65 for a double room, or upwards of US$40–60/£25–45 for a single. Typically rates will include a continental breakfast, which is usually just a roll or a couple of slices of bread and a cup of tea, but could be a substantial meal complete with eggs.

GOVERNMENT RESTHOUSES These are dotted around the country in virtually every small town: a very useful option for the stranded backpacker. The town or district council usually runs them and, although a few have degenerated into brothels, others are adequate for a brief overnight stop. Most have rooms with private facilities that are normally clean (as are the sheets), though rarely spotless or in mint condition.

LODGES AND BUSHCAMPS Zambia's lodges and bushcamps are a match for the best in Africa. As befits a destination for visitors who take their game viewing and birdwatching seriously, the camps are very comfortable but concentrate on good guiding rather than luxury *per se*. En-suite showers and toilets are almost universal, the accommodation is fairly spacious, the organisation smooth and food invariably good to excellent. However, a few forget that their reputations are won and lost by the standards of their individual guides.

Aside from a few larger lodges, you can usually expect a maximum of ten to 18 guests, and close personal care. But beware: if you seek a safari for its image, wanting to sleep late and then be pampered in the bush; or expect to dine from silverware and sip from cut-glass goblets ... then perhaps Zambia isn't for you after all.

✖ FOOD AND DRINK

FOOD Zambia's native cuisine is based on *nshima*, a cooked porridge made from ground maize. (In Zimbabwe this is *sadza*, in South Africa *mealie-pap*.) This is usually made thin, perhaps with sugar, for breakfast, then eaten thicker – the consistency of mashed potatoes – for lunch and dinner. For these main meals it will normally be accompanied by some spicy relish, perhaps made of meat and tomatoes, or dried fish. Do taste this at some stage when visiting. Safari camps will often prepare it if requested, and it is always available in small restaurants in the towns. Often these will have only three items on the menu: nshima and chicken; nshima and meat; and nshima and fish – and they can be very good.

Camps, hotels and lodges that cater to overseas visitors will serve a very international fare, and the quality of food prepared in the most remote bushcamps amazes visitors. Coming to Zambia on safari your biggest problem with food is likely to be the temptation to eat too much.

If you are driving yourself around and plan to cook, then get most of your supplies in Lusaka or one of the larger towns. Supermarkets have revolutionised what's available, and really have all that you will need. In the smaller towns, supplies are usually limited to products that are popular locally. These include bread, flour,

---

RESTAURANT PRICE CODES

Price codes are based on the average cost of a main course, which usually exclude VAT (currently 16%) and service of around 10%. For specialities such as seafood, you can expect to pay considerably more.

$$$$$	£12+; US$20+; Kw90,000+
$$$$	£9.50–12; US$14–20; Kw70,000–90,000
$$$	£6–9.50; US$9–14; Kw45,000–70,000
$$	£4–6; US$6–9; Kw30,000–45,000
$	under £4; under US$6; under Kw30,000

November typically marks the beginning of the rainy season in Zambia. The first rains bring vast swarms of termites out of their nests to find mates and reproduce. Termites are a once-a-year delicacy not to be missed for culinary adventurers. And capturing them is half the fun!

Termites are attracted to light, so it's easiest to catch them when they are swarming around in the evening. Get a large bowl and fill it with water. Catch live termites with your hand as they fly around and drop them into the water (which keeps them from flying or crawling out). Or you can wait until the morning and collect them off the ground after they have dropped their wings (then you don't have to pull the wings off yourself). Gather as many as you need, live ones only.

PREPARATION Remove any wings from termites and throw wings away. Place wingless termites in a colander or bowl and rinse them under running water. Heat a frying pan with a dash of cooking oil until sizzling temperature. Drop in live termites and sauté until they are crisp and golden brown (about one minute). Add salt to taste. Serve in a bowl as you would peanuts. *Bon appétit*!

rice, soups and various tinned vegetables, meats and fish, though locally grown produce such as tomatoes, bananas or sweet potatoes will be available in season. This is fine for nutrition, but you may get bored with the selection in a week or two.

DRINK

Alcohol Like most countries in the region, Zambia has two distinct beer types: clear and opaque. Most visitors and more affluent Zambians drink the **clear beers**, which are similar to European lagers and always served chilled. Mosi, Castle and Rhino are the lagers brewed by South African Breweries' Zambian subsidiaries. They are widely available and usually good. There is one craft brewery in Zambia which makes Dr Livingstone's Lager, Zikomo Copper Ale, Safari Stout and Baobab White, which is brewed with the fruit from the baobab tree.

Note that all beer produced in Zambia has a deposit on its bottles, like those of soft drinks. If you want to avoid this, buy cans instead. The contents will cost about US$1/Kw4,500 from a supermarket, or upwards of US$2.45/Kw11,000 in a hotel bar or restaurant. Imported lagers such as Windhoek, Holsten and Amstel will cost considerably more than this.

Less-affluent Zambians usually opt for some form of the **opaque beer** (sometimes called *chibuku*, after the market-leading brand). This is a commercial version of traditional beer, usually brewed from maize and/or sorghum. It's a sour, porridge-like brew, an acquired taste, and is much cheaper than lager. Locals will sometimes buy a bucket of it, and then pass this around a circle of drinkers. It would be unusual for a visitor to drink this, so try some and amuse your Zambian companions. Remember, though, that traditional opaque beer changes flavour as it ferments and you can often ask for 'fresh beer' or 'strong beer'. If you aren't sure about the bar's hygiene standards, stick to the pre-packaged brands of opaque beer like Chibuku, Chinika, Golden, Chipolopolo or Mukango.

Soft drinks Soft drinks are available everywhere, which is fortunate when the temperatures are high. Choices are often limited, though the ubiquitous Coca-

Cola is usually there at around US$1.10/Kw5,000 – perhaps a little cheaper in a supermarket, and a little more in a decent café. Diet drinks are rarely seen in the rural areas – which is no surprise for a country where malnutrition is a problem.

Until recently, all soft drinks were sold in glass bottles, though increasingly plastic bottles are in use. If you're faced with glass, try to buy up at least one actual bottle (per person) in a city before you go travelling: it will be invaluable. Because of the cost of bottle production, and the deposit system (typically around US$0.30/Kw1,500 per bottle), you will often be unable to buy full bottles of soft drinks in rural areas without swapping them for empty ones in return. The alternative is to stand and drink the contents where you buy a drink, and leave the empty behind you. This is fine, but can be inconvenient if you have just dashed in for a drink while your bus stops for a few minutes.

Water Water in the main towns is usually purified, provided there are no shortages of chlorine, breakdowns or other mishaps. The locals drink it, and are used to the relatively innocuous bugs that it may harbour. If you are in the country for a long time, then it may be worth acclimatising yourself to it – though be prepared for some days spent near a toilet. However, if you are in Zambia for just a few weeks, then try to drink only bottled, boiled or treated water in town – otherwise you will get stomach upsets. Bottled water can be bought almost anywhere, although if you want it cold you may often find it's frozen! Expect to pay around US$0.60/Kw2,500 for a half-litre in a supermarket, more in a smaller outlet or garage.

Out in the bush, most of the camps and lodges use water from boreholes. These underground sources vary in quality, but are normally free from bugs so the water is perfectly safe to drink. Sometimes it is sweet, at other times a little alkaline or salty. Ask locally if it is suitable for an unacclimatised visitor to drink, then take their advice.

🛒 SHOPPING

CURIOS Zambia's best bargains are handicrafts: carvings and baskets made locally. The curio stall near Victoria Falls close to the Zimbabwean border has a good selection, but prices are lower if you buy away from tourist areas, in Lusaka (try Kabwata Cultural Centre, pages 151–2), or at some of the roadside stalls.

Wherever you buy handicrafts, don't be afraid to bargain gently. Expect an eventual reduction of about a quarter of the original asking price and always be polite and good-humoured. After all, a few cents will probably make more difference to the person with whom you are bargaining than it will mean to you.

Note that you will often see carvings on sale in the larger stalls which have been imported from Kenya, Tanzania, DRC and Zimbabwe. Assume that they would be cheaper if purchased in their countries of origin, and try to buy something Zambian as a memento of your trip.

Occasionally you will be offered 'precious' stones to buy – rough diamonds, emeralds and the like. Expert geologists may spot the occasional genuine article amongst hoards of fakes, but most mere mortals will end up being conned. Stick to the carvings if you want a bargain.

For a more practical and much cheaper souvenir get a *chitenje* for about Kw30,000–40,000 – there are shops in the smallest of towns. You will see these 2m-long sections of brightly patterned cotton cloth everywhere, often wrapped around local women. Whilst travelling use them as towels, sarongs, picnic mats or – as the locals do – simply swathed over your normal clothes to keep them clean. When back home, you

4

can cut the material into clothes, or use them as wall-coverings or tablecloths. Either way, you will have brought a splash of truly African colour back home with you.

Imports and exports There is no problem in exporting normal curios, but you will need an official export permit from the Department of National Parks to take out any game trophies. Visitors are urged to support the letter and the spirit of the CITES bans on endangered species, including the ban on the international trade in ivory. This has certainly helped to reduce ivory poaching, so don't undermine it by buying ivory souvenirs here. In any case, you will probably have big problems when you try to import them back into your home country.

SUPPLIES Since 1996, Zambia's shops have emerged from a retailing time-warp, where cramped corner shops had the monopoly. Until then, most of the country's residents were innocent of consumer-friendly hypermarkets where wide, ergonomically designed aisles are lined with endless choice. Then, in 1996, Shoprite/Checkers arrived, promoting a largely alien practice of high-volume, low-margin superstores using good levels of pay to reward honest employees. This rocked Lusaka's existing, mainly Asian, shop-owning community who had always gone for the high-margin corner-shop approach. Rumours were rife of the ways in which Shoprite's arrival was resisted, and even blocked by the capital's existing business community. Now, though, Shoprite has found a very solid footing, with stores in most of Zambia's major towns that are normally the best and cheapest places to shop for supplies.

However, all is not rosy. To many it seems that while the state is dismantling many of its own monopolies, the private sector is being allowed to generate new ones. Many aggressive South African companies, from Shoprite to Game, and HI-FI to Electric City, have moved into Zambia and started to dominate it, causing resentment from local businesspeople. Critics say the success of these is down to South Africa's policy of lucrative tax breaks, which effectively subsidise exports. They fear that by allowing these new companies to build monopolies, local entrepreneurs are losing out. They point to the import bills generated by such stores, which often source more of their stock from outside Zambia than from inside. However, supporters cite the increased availability of goods, and the small Zambian businesses that are improving their standards and starting to supply these stores.

Whatever the arguments, you can now buy most things in Zambia (and in kwacha) at a price, and if you have the money then this will seem like a good thing. Perhaps the best advice for the careful visitor is to try to buy Zambian products wherever possible, for the sake of the local economy.

COMMUNICATIONS AND MEDIA

POST The post is neither cheap nor fast, though it is fairly reliable for letters and postcards. Currently it costs Kw4,050 to send a letter to the UK, or Kw4,950 to the US, while a postcard costs Kw2,500 to either destination. It's worth noting that Zambia has some lovely stamps for sale, a favourite of stamp collectors.

The best way to send mail quickly within Zambia is via EMS (Expedited Mail Service), a reasonably priced service where letters are hand delivered (no postbox mail). It is also available to overseas destinations and is generally less expensive than a courier company. For express mail services, there are several choices, some of which also offer phone, fax and internet as well. With any you can send letters, parcels and small packets to destinations within Zambia and worldwide. This is costly but reliable. If you need important documents sent from overseas, couriers such as DHL or FedEx (see pages 147 and 189 for contact details in Lusaka and Livingstone) are the quickest way to be assured of them reaching you safely. Packages take about a week from Europe or the USA.

Post offices in large towns are normally open Monday to Friday, 08.00–17.00, Saturday 08.00–12.30, but you can expect shorter hours in more out-of-the-way places.

TELEPHONE The Zambian telephone system, operated by Zamtel, is overloaded and has difficulty coping, despite an overhaul in 2007 and its more-recent privatisation. It is still common for companies to have several different numbers, although increasingly both business and personal users rely on mobile phones.

Payphones, as you might expect, are increasingly rare. Although the old payphones have given way to cardphones, these are increasingly hard to find, and those that remain are none too reliable. In theory, phonecards are available from Zamtel offices and other outlets from around Kw10,000 initially, but are then rechargeable by buying scratchcards in units from Kw10,000 to Kw100,000. You can dial internationally from these, and there is no time limit placed on their use.

Telephone codes To dial into the country from abroad, the international access code for Zambia is +260. From inside Zambia, you dial 00 to get an international line, then the country's access code (eg: 44 for the UK, or 1 for the USA).

Since 2007, there has been a single access code – 021 – for the whole country. As a result, all telephone numbers changed to combine the new access code with the original regional code. Each of these covers a large region of the country, broadly incorporating the following towns:

0211   Central: Chilanga, Chirundu, Chisamba, Chongwe, Kafue, Luangwa, Lusaka, Mumbwa, Namalundu Gorge, Siavonga

0212   Copperbelt and Luapula: Chililabombwe, Chingola, Itimpi, Kalulushi, Kawambwa, Kitwe, Luanshya, Mansa, Masaiti, Mufulira, Mwense, Nchelenge, Ndola, Samfya

0213	South-central: Choma, Gwembe, Itezhi-Tezhi, Kalomo, Kazungula, Livingstone, Maamba, Mazabuka, Monze, Namwala, Pemba, Zimba
0214	Northeast: Chambeshi, Chinsali, Isoka, Kasama, Luwingu, Mbala, Mpika, Mporokoso, Mpulungu, Mungwi, Nakonde
0215	North-central: Chibombo, Kabwe, Kapiri Mposhi, Mkushi, Serenje
0216	East: Chadiza, Chama, Chipata, Katete, Lundazi, Mfuwe, Nyimba, Petauke
0217	West: Kalabo, Kaoma, Lukulu, Mongu, Senanga
0218	Northwest: Kabompo, Kasempa, Mufumbwe, Mwinilunga, Solwezi, Zambezi

When dialling from a landline within the same area, there is no need to dial the code. However, if – like most Zambians – you're using a mobile phone, then you *will* need to include the code.

Mobile phones The use of mobile phones, or 'cells' as they're usually called in Zambia, has grown very rapidly to counter the problems with the country's still-unreliable landline network. Coverage is surprisingly widespread, although in rural areas you can expect it to be patchy at best, or non-existent. The major networks are Airtel (formerly Celtel, then Zain), and MTN, as well as the state-owned Zamtel. All Zambian mobile-phone numbers are prefaced 09, and consist of ten digits.

Top-up cards for each of the mobile networks are available in even the smallest towns, or from touts at major road junctions. If you're in the Livingstone area, be careful of picking up Zimbabwean networks, as prices may be based on official Zimbabwean exchange rates, and hence be much more expensive than their Zambian equivalents.

If you're planning to use your own mobile phone in Zambia, it's almost certainly going to be cheaper to buy a local SIM card for the duration of your visit. Expect to pay around Kw7,000 (about £1/US$1.50), plus talk-time cards – available from Kw3,000. As elsewhere, there are numerous packages, some – such as a family package – with cheaper evening calls, so do ask before you buy. Whatever you select, call charges to other Zambian mobiles are exceptionally reasonable by Western standards, and international texts shouldn't break the bank either.

Email and the internet Despite considerable issues with speed and outdated hardware, the email community in Zambia is quite large – although far fewer people have access to the internet. Many email subscribers are linked by satellite telephone systems in order to avoid the telephone problems, but access remains difficult. If you're emailing someone in Zambia and don't get a reply within 48 hours, it would be wise to re-send the email. There are fairly reliable and high-speed internet cafés in Lusaka and many of the bigger towns.

MEDIA
The press The main daily papers are *The Post* (*www.postzambia.com*), which is privately owned and fairly independent, and the *Times of Zambia* (*www.times.co.zm*) and the *Daily Mail*, both of which are owned by the government. The *Financial Mail* is part of the *Daily Mail*, as are the *Sunday Mail* and the *Sunday Times*. On the whole, *The Post* is the most outspoken and interesting paper. It's well worth having a look at the various websites before you go; some of the stories can be fascinating.

There are also several weekly papers, including the *National Mirror, Monitor* and *Mail & Guardian*, which despite its independent status tends to be strongly pro-government. There are also a few good monthlies, including *Mining Mail*, and the indispensable Lusaka-based guide, *The Lowdown*.

Zambia claims to have a free press, and most issues are debated openly. However, when the more sensitive ones are skirted around, only *The Post* tries to take a more investigative approach. Often this is respected, but see Zambia's most recent history in *The late 1990s* in *Chapter 1*, page 11, for an example of an incident when the authorities were less than respectful in their approach.

Various publications are targeted directly at the visitor. Of these, *Travel Zambia* (*www.travelzambiamag.com*), is published annually but available more frequently online. The bi-monthly *Zambian Traveller* (*www.thezambiantraveller.com*) is distributed through hotels and lodges in Zambia as well as being available to download. It features a range of articles covering everything from mining and conservation to hotel reviews. There's also *Zambezi Traveller* (*www.zambezitraveller.com*), a tourist newspaper with a strong environmental bent.

Radio and television Radio is limited, as Zambia National Broadcasting Corporation (ZNBC) runs three channels which are all used as government communication tools: Radio 1, Radio 2 and Radio 4. (Radio 4 used to be the rather fun Radio Mulungushi, until it was swallowed up.)

There is some good news though, as in the cities – especially Lusaka – you'll find smaller commercial stations. The obvious one is Radio Phoenix, which broadcasts popular music and Zambian news, though it's worth scanning the airwaves. Outside of the large cities, you'll find little, although those with short-wave radios can always seek the BBC World Service, the Voice of America and Radio Canada.

The public television stations are also run by ZNBC, broadcasting during the week from midday through to midnight, with programmes at weekends starting at around 07.00. They stick to the official party line on most issues, but do tune in – some of their panel debates can be fascinating. Most hotels with in-room televisions subscribe to satellite channels, often including BBC World, CNN and/or the South African cable network, M-Net, with its multitude of sports and movie channels.

CULTURAL GUIDELINES

Comments here are intended to be a general guide, just a few examples of how to travel more sensitively. They should not be viewed as blueprints for perfect Zambian etiquette. Cultural sensitivity is a state of mind, not a checklist of behaviour – so here we can only hope to give the sensitive traveller a few pointers in the right direction.

When we travel, we are all in danger of leaving negative impressions with local people. It is easily done – by snapping that picture quickly, whilst the subject is not looking; by dressing scantily, offending local sensitivities; by just brushing aside the feelings of local people, with the high-handed superiority of a rich Westerner. These things are easy to do, in the click of a shutter, or flash of a dollar bill.

You will get the most representative view of Zambia if you cause as little disturbance to the local people as possible. You will never blend in perfectly when you travel – your mere presence there, as an observer, will always change the local events slightly. However, if you try to fit in and show respect for local culture and attitudes, then you may manage to leave positive feelings behind you.

One of the easiest, and most important, ways to do this is with **greetings**. African societies are rarely as rushed as Western ones. When you first talk to someone, you should greet them leisurely.

So, for example, if you enter a bus station and want some help, do not just ask outright, 'Where is the bus to ...' That would be rude. Instead you will have a better reception (and better chance of good advice) by saying:

4

Traveller: 'Good afternoon.'
Zambian: 'Good afternoon.'
Traveller: 'How are you?'
Zambian: 'I am fine, how are you?'
Traveller: 'I am fine, thank you.' (*Pause*) 'Do you know where the bus to ...'

This goes for approaching anyone – always greet them first. For a better reception still, learn these phrases of greeting in the local language (see pages 532–4). English-speakers are often lazy about learning languages, and, whilst most Zambians understand English, a greeting given in an appropriate local language will be received with delight. It implies that you are making an effort to learn a little of their language and culture, which is always appreciated.

Occasionally, in the town or city, you may be approached by someone who doesn't greet you. Instead s/he tries immediately to sell you something, or even hassle you in some way. These people have learned that foreigners aren't used to greetings, and so have adapted their approach accordingly. An effective way to dodge their attentions is to reply to their questions with a formal greeting, and then politely – but firmly – refuse their offer. This is surprisingly effective.

Another part of the normal greeting ritual is **handshaking**. As elsewhere, you would not normally shake a shop-owner's hand, but you would shake hands with someone to whom you are introduced. Get some practice when you arrive; there is a gentle, three-part handshake used in southern Africa which is easily learnt.

Your **clothing** is an area that can easily give offence. Most Zambians frown upon skimpy or revealing clothing, especially when worn by women. Shorts are fine for walking safaris, otherwise dress conservatively and avoid short shorts, especially in the more rural areas. Respectable locals will wear long trousers (men) or long skirts (women).

Homosexuality is illegal in Zambia, although no-one – as far as I know – has ever been prosecuted, and same-sex relationships have never been a problem for guests in safari camps. While it's not at all unusual in traditional societies to see two men – or two women – casually holding hands, public **displays of affection** between two people (gay or straight) may create tension and are best avoided.

Photography is a tricky business. Most Zambians will be only too happy to be photographed – provided you ask their permission first. Sign language is fine for this question: just point at your camera, shrug your shoulders, and look quizzical. The problem is that then everyone will smile for you, producing the type of 'posed' photograph that you may not want. However, stay around and chat for five or ten minutes more, and people will get used to your presence, stop posing, and you will get more natural shots of them (a camera with a quiet shutter is a help). Note that special care is needed with photography near government buildings, bridges and similar sites of strategic importance. You must ask permission before photographing anything here, or you risk people thinking that you are a spy.

If you're **seeking directions**, don't be afraid to stop and ask. Most people will be polite and keen to help – so keen that some will answer 'Yes' to questions if they think that this is what you want to hear. So try to avoid asking leading questions. For example, 'Yes' would often be the typical answer to the question, 'Does this road lead to ...?' And in a sense the respondent is probably correct – it will get you there. It's just that it may not be the quickest or shortest way. To avoid misunderstandings, it is often better to ask open-ended questions like, 'Where does this road go to?' or 'How do I drive to ...?'

The specific examples above can only be taken so far – they are general by their very nature. But wherever you find yourself, if you are polite and considerate to the Zambians you meet, then you will rarely encounter any cultural problems. Watch how they behave and, if you have any doubts about how you should act, then ask someone quietly. They will seldom tell you outright that you are being rude, but they will usually give you good advice on how to make your behaviour more acceptable.

TRAVELLING POSITIVELY

If you ask locally you'll often find projects that need your support. Many lodges and camps also assist with community or wildlife projects, and will be able to suggest a good use for donations. Alternatively, there are several ideas below. All welcome donations – so make a resolution now to help at least one of them as an integral part of the cost of your trip.

HELPING ZAMBIA'S POORER COMMUNITIES Visiting Zambia, especially the rural agricultural areas and the towns, many visitors are struck by the poverty and wish to help. Giving to beggars and those in need on the street is one way. It will alleviate your feelings of guilt, and perhaps some of the immediate suffering, but it is not a long-term solution.

There are ways in which you can make a positive contribution, but they require more effort than throwing a few coins to someone on the street.

CHIN (Children in Need Network) 1799/13 Nchenja Rd, Northmead, Lusaka; 0211 227160; e chin@zamnet.zm; www.chin.org.zm. A group of non-governmental organisations, community-based groups & government departments working with children in need. Their website will give you some idea of the scale of the help required.

Habitat for Humanity 4652 Addis Ababa Dr, Rhodes Park, Lusaka; 0211 251087; e hfhzam@ zamnet.zm; www.habitatzam.org.zm. This is a non-profit, Christian NGO trying to solve the housing problems of the poor. Since 1984 they have built over 2,150 houses in different projects throughout the country, using largely volunteer labour. Families pay back the loan over a 10yr period into a revolving fund, enabling more houses to be built in the same community.

Zambia National Association of the Physically Handicapped (ZNAPH) 5 Cheetah Rd, Kabulonga, Lusaka; 0211 268088; www. add.org.uk. Supported by the UK-based ADD International, ZNAPH has branches in most Zambian towns. The charity runs workshops teaching practical skills such as carpentry & tailoring.

ZOCS (Zambia Open Community Schools) 20 Tito Rd, Rhodes Park, Lusaka; 0211 253841/3; e zocs2008@gmail.com; www.zocs. org.zm. My favourite project, ZOCS provides a basic education to young Zambians who could not otherwise afford school at all. Education is vital for Zambia's future, while in the present it gives children some hope. Deaths from AIDS have left increasing numbers of orphans, many of whom end up on the streets. This project is making a difference on a local level, helping communities to organise their own schools.

ENVIRONMENT AND WILDLIFE Of the numerous worthwhile conservation initiatives in Zambia, these two are involved in areas most visited by tourists – so seem particularly apt. Both are committed to working with the local community and wildlife authorities to promote the conservation and sustainable use of the area's natural resources through a programme of environmental protection, education and community development.

Conservation Lower Zambezi (CLZ)
0975 615149; e clz@iwayafrica.com; www.conservationlowerzambezi.net. See page 236.

South Luangwa Conservation Society (SLCS) 0216 246069; m 0979 180452; e rachel@slcszambia.org; www.slcszambia.org. See page 266.

VOLUNTEERING Zambia, like many African countries, hasn't been slow to take advantage of the upsurge in volunteering holidays. To set the ball rolling, contact The Book Bus (*64–66 Market Pl, Warwick CV34 4SD, UK;* 01926 411122; e info@thebookbus.org; www.thebookbus.org), which takes volunteers to help operate their mobile library and storytelling service.

Meanwhile there are many pitfalls for unwary volunteers, so be sure to do your homework – especially if you are trying to get involved with a local community. An excellent place to start is www.ethicalvolunteering.org, which also has a downloadable pamphlet entitled *The Ethical Volunteering Guide*. Some of the many issues to consider include:

- For every bona fide organisation there will be others who are willing to take your cash without delivering on their side of the deal.
- Try to be realistic about what your skills are; they will probably define what you can usefully contribute. Zambian communities don't need unskilled hobbyists; they need professionals. To teach skills properly takes years of volunteering, not weeks. (How long did *you* take to learn those skills?) So, for example, if you're not a qualified teacher or builder in your home country, then don't expect to be let loose to do any teaching or building in Zambia.
- Most volunteers will learn much more than the members of the communities that they come to 'help'; be aware of this when you describe who is helping whom.
- Make sure that what you are doing isn't effectively taking away a job from a local person.

Time in Zambia will do you lots of good; make sure it's not to the detriment of your hosts.

5

Health and Safety

There is always great danger in writing about health and safety for the uninitiated visitor. It is all too easy to become paranoid about exotic diseases that you may catch, and all too easy to start distrusting everybody you meet as a potential thief – falling into an unjustified us-and-them attitude towards the people of the country you are visiting.

As a comparison, imagine an equivalent section in a guidebook to a Western country – there would be a list of possible diseases and advice on the risk of theft and mugging. Many Western cities are very dangerous, but with time we learn how to assess the risks, accepting almost subconsciously what we can and cannot do.

It is important to strike the right balance: to avoid being either excessively cautious or too relaxed about your health and your safety. With experience, you will find the balance that best fits you and the country you are visiting.

✚ HEALTH *with Dr Jane Wilson-Howarth and Dr Felicity Nicholson*

BEFORE YOU GO

Travel insurance Visitors to Zambia must take out a comprehensive **medical insurance policy** to cover them for emergencies, including the cost of evacuation to another country within the region. Such policies come with an emergency number (often on a reverse-charge/call-collect basis). You would be wise to memorise this – or indelibly tattoo it in as many places as possible on your baggage.

Personal-effects insurance is also a sensible precaution, but check the policy's fine print before you leave home. Often, in even the best policies, you will find a limit per item, or per claim – which can be well below the cost of a replacement. If you need to list your valuables separately, then do so comprehensively. Check that receipts are not required for claims if you do not have them, and that the excess that you have to pay on every claim is reasonable.

Annual travel policies can be excellent value if you travel a lot, and some of the larger credit-card companies offer excellent deals. However, often it is better to get your valuables named and insured for travel using your home contents insurance. These year-round policies will try harder to settle your claim fairly as they want your business in the long term.

Immunisations Having a full set of immunisations takes time, normally at least six weeks, although some protection can be had by visiting your doctor as late as a few days before you travel. Ideally, see your doctor or travel clinic (see below) early on to establish an inoculation timetable.

Legal requirements As of 2011, Zambia is still not to be considered a **yellow fever** endemic area, and at the time of writing no vaccinations were required by those entering or leaving the country. That said, the South African authorities periodically change their views, and have gone through times when they insist that visitors passing through South Africa *en route* from (or even to) Zambia must have a yellow fever certificate. So it is important to check the latest situation well in advance of departure, and again just before you leave.

Irrespective of this, there may be times when visiting the north or west of the country when immunisation might be worth considering for health reasons, rather than just for the immigration authorities. Yellow fever vaccination is not suitable for everyone so it is important to seek expert medical advice at least ten days before your trip. Assuming that immunisation is suitable for you, one vaccination is required, and must be administered at least ten days before departure for the certificate to be valid; it then lasts for ten years.

Recommended precautions Preparations to ensure a healthy trip to Zambia require checks on your immunisation status: it is wise to be up to date on **tetanus**, **polio** and **diphtheria** (now given as an all-in-one vaccine, Revaxis, that lasts for ten years), and hepatitis A. Immunisations against meningococcus and rabies may also be recommended. Immunisation against cholera is not usually required for trips to Zambia.

Hepatitis A vaccine (Havrix Monodose or Avaxim) comprises two injections given about a year apart. The course costs about £100, but may be available on the NHS; it protects for 25 years and can be administered even close to the time of departure. **Hepatitis B** vaccination is recommended for those working in a medical setting or with children, and should be considered for longer trips (four weeks or more). That said, any visitor should consider having the vaccine as it is possible to contract the disease through accidental exposure or cross-contamination from unsterilised blood products. For the best protection, three injections are needed. If time is short, these can be given over a three-week period for those aged 16 or over. Longer schedules give more sustained protection so are preferable if time allows – and must be used in those under 16. Hepatitis A vaccine can also be given to those over 15 as a combination with hepatitis B as 'Twinrix', though two doses are needed at least seven days apart to be effective for the hepatitis A component, and three doses are needed for the hepatitis B.

The newer injectable **typhoid** vaccines (eg: Typhim Vi) last for three years and are about 85% effective. Oral capsules (Vivotif) may also be available for those aged six and over. A dose of three capsules over five days lasts for approximately three years but may be less effective than the injectable forms. **Meningitis** vaccine containing strains A, C, W and Y may be recommended, especially for trips of more than four weeks (see *Meningitis*, page 95).

Vaccination against **rabies** is now recommended for all visitors as there is an international shortage of rabies immunoglobulin (RIG), which is essential if you have not had three doses of vaccine before you travel (see *Rabies*, pages 95–6). Ideally three injections are taken over a minimum of 21 days, though even taking one or two doses of vaccine may be better than none at all as in some circumstances it may mean that RIG is not needed. Contrary to popular belief these vaccinations are relatively painless.

Experts differ over whether a BCG vaccination against **tuberculosis** (TB) is useful in adults: discuss this with your travel clinic.

In addition to the various vaccinations recommended above, it is important that you should be properly protected against malaria. For detailed advice see below.

Ideally you should visit your own doctor or a specialist travel clinic (see below) to discuss your requirements if possible at least eight weeks before you plan to travel.

Malaria Malaria is the most dangerous disease in Africa, and one of the greatest risks to the traveller. It occurs throughout Zambia, all the year round, so it is essential that you take all possible precautions against it.

Malaria prevention Prophylaxis regimes aim to infuse your bloodstream with drugs that inhibit and kill the malaria parasites which are injected into you by a biting mosquito. This is why you must start to take the drugs *before* you arrive in a malarial area – so that they are established in your bloodstream from day one. Unfortunately, malaria parasites continually adapt to the drugs used to combat them, so the recommended regimes must adapt and change in order to remain effective. None is 100% effective, and all require time to kill the parasites – so unless there is a medical indication for stopping, it is important to complete the course after leaving the area as directed (usually one to four weeks depending on the regime). Falciparum (cerebral) malaria is the most common in Africa, and usually fatal if untreated, so it is worth your while trying to avoid it.

Seek current advice on the best antimalarials to take: usually mefloquine, Malarone or doxycycline. If mefloquine (Lariam) is suggested, start this two and a half weeks (three doses) before departure to check that it suits you; stop it immediately if it seems to cause depression or anxiety, visual or hearing disturbances, severe headaches, fits or changes in heart rhythm. Side effects such as nightmares or dizziness are not medical reasons for stopping unless they are sufficiently debilitating or annoying. Anyone who has been treated for depression or psychiatric problems, has diabetes controlled by oral therapy or who is epileptic (or who has suffered fits in the past) or has a close blood relative who is epileptic, should avoid mefloquine.

In the past doctors were nervous about prescribing mefloquine to pregnant women, but experience has shown that it is relatively safe and certainly safer than the risk of malaria. That said, there are other issues, so if you are travelling to Zambia while pregnant, seek expert advice before departure.

Malarone (proguanil and atovaquone) is as effective as mefloquine. It has the advantage of having few side effects and need only be continued for one week after returning. However, it is expensive and because of this tends to be reserved for shorter trips. Malarone may not be suitable for everybody, so take advice from a doctor. The licence in the UK has been extended for up to three months' use and a paediatric form of tablet is also available, prescribed on a weight basis.

A third alternative is the antibiotic doxycycline (100mg daily). Like Malarone it can be started one to two days before arrival. Unlike mefloquine, it may also be used in travellers with epilepsy, although certain anti-epileptic medication may make it less effective. In perhaps 1–3% of people there is the possibility of allergic skin reactions developing in sunlight; the drug should be stopped if this happens. It is also unsuitable in pregnancy or for children under 12 years.

Chloroquine and proguanil are no longer considered to be effective enough for Zambia but may be considered as a last resort if nothing else is deemed suitable.

All tablets should be taken with or after the evening meal, washed down with plenty of fluid and, with the exception of Malarone (see above), continued for four weeks after leaving.

Despite all these precautions, it is important to be aware that no anti-malarial drug is 100% protective, although those on prophylactics who are unlucky enough to catch malaria are less likely to get rapidly into serious trouble. In addition to taking anti-malarials, it is therefore important to avoid mosquito bites between dusk and dawn (see *Avoiding insect bites*, pages 91–2).

There is unfortunately the occasional traveller who prefers to 'acquire resistance' to malaria rather than take preventative tablets, or who takes homeopathic prophylactics thinking these are effective against a killer disease. Homeopathy theory dictates treating like with like so there is no place for prophylaxis or immunisation in a well person; bone fide homeopaths do not advocate it. Travellers to Africa cannot acquire any effective resistance to malaria, and those who don't make use of prophylactic drugs risk their life in a manner that is both foolish and unnecessary.

TRAVEL CLINICS AND HEALTH INFORMATION A full list of current travel clinic websites worldwide is available on www.istm.org. For other journey preparation information, consult www.nathnac.org/ds/map_world.aspx. Information about various medications may be found on www.netdoctor.co.uk/travel.

UK

Berkeley Travel Clinic 32 Berkeley St, London W1J 8EL (near Green Park tube station); ☎ 020 7629 6233; ⊕ 10.00–18.00 Mon–Fri; 10.00–15.00 Sat

Edinburgh Travel Health Clinic 14 East Preston St, Newington, Edinburgh EH8 9QA; ☎ 0131 667 1030; www.edinburghtravelhealthclinic.co.uk; ⊕ 09.00–19.00 Mon–Wed, 09.00–18.00 Thu & Fri. Travel vaccinations & advice on all aspects of malaria prevention. All current UK prescribed anti-malaria tablets in stock.

Fleet Street Travel Clinic 29 Fleet St, London EC4Y 1AA; ☎ 020 7353 5678; e info@fleetstreetclinic.com; www.fleetstreetclinic.com; ⊕ 08.45–17.30 Mon–Fri. Injections, travel products & latest advice.

Hospital for Tropical Diseases Travel Clinic Mortimer Market Bldg, Capper St (off Tottenham Ct Rd), London WC1E 6AU; ☎ 020 7387 4411; www.thehtd.org; ⊕ 13.00–17.00 Wed & 09.00–13.00 Fri. Consultations are by appointment only & are only offered to those with more complex problems. Check the website for inclusions. Runs a Travellers' Healthline Advisory Service (☎ 020 7950 7799) for country-specific information & health hazards. Also stocks nets, water purification equipment & personal protection measures. Travellers who have returned from the tropics & are unwell, with fever or bloody diarrhoea, can attend the walk-in emergency clinic at the hospital without an appointment.

InterHealth Travel Clinic 111 Westminster Bridge Rd, London SE1 7HR; ☎ 020 7902 9000; e info@interhealth.org.uk; www.interhealth.org.uk; ⊕ 08.30–17.30 Mon–Fri. Competitively priced, one-stop travel health service by appointment only.

MASTA (Medical Advisory Service for Travellers Abroad) At the London School of Hygiene & Tropical Medicine, Keppel St, London WC1E 7HT; ☎ 09068 224100 (premium-line number, charged at 60p/minute); e enquiries@masta.org ; www.masta-travel-health.com. For a fee, they will provide an individually tailored health brief, with up-to-date information on how to stay healthy, inoculations & what to take.

MASTA pre-travel clinics ☎ 01276 685040; www.masta-travel-health.com/travel-clinic.aspx. Call or check the website for the nearest; there are currently 50 in Britain. They also sell malaria prophylaxis, memory cards, treatment kits, bednets, net treatment kits, etc.

NHS travel websites www.fitfortravel.nhs.uk or www.fitfortravel.scot.nhs.uk . Provide country-by-country advice on immunisation & malaria prevention, plus details of recent developments, & a list of relevant health organisations.

Nomad Travel Clinics Flagship store: 3–4 Wellington Terr, Turnpike La, London N8 0PX; ☎ 020 8889 7014; e turnpike@nomadtravel.co.uk; www.nomadtravel.co.uk; walk in or appointments ⊕ 09.15–17.00 daily, late night Thu. See website for clinics in west & central London, Bristol, Southampton & Manchester. As well as dispensing health advice, Nomad stocks mosquito nets & other anti-bug devices, & an excellent range of adventure travel gear. Runs a Travel Health Advice line on ☎ 0906 863 3414.

Trailfinders Immunisation Centre 194 Kensington High St, London W8 7RG; ☎ 020 7938 3999; www.trailfinders.com/travelessentials/travelclinic.htm; ⊕ 09.00–17.00 Mon, Tue, Wed

& Fri, 09.00–18.00 Thu, 10.00–17.15 Sat. No appointment necessary.

The Travel Clinic Ltd, Cambridge 41 Hills Rd, Cambridge CB2 1NT; ✆ 01223 367362; e enquiries@travelclinic.ltd.uk; www. travelcliniccambridge.co.uk; � 10.00–16.00 Mon, Tue & Sat, 12.00–19.00 Wed & Thu, 11.00–18.00 Fri

Irish Republic

Tropical Medical Bureau 54 Grafton St, Dublin 2; ✆ 01 2715200; e graftonstreet@tmb.ie; www. tmb.ie; ⏱ until 20.00 Mon–Fri & Sat mornings.

USA

Centers for Disease Control 1600 Clifton Rd, Atlanta, GA 30333; ✆ 800 232 4636 or 800 232 6348; e cdcinfo@cdc.gov; www.cdc.gov/travel. The central source of travel information in the USA. Each summer they publish the invaluable Health Information for International Travel.

Canada

IAMAT Suite 10, 1287 St Clair St West, Toronto, Ontario M6E 1B8; ✆ 416 652 0137; www.iamat. org

Australia and New Zealand

TMVC (Travel Doctors Group) ✆ 1300 65 88 44; www.tmvc.com.au. 30 clinics in Australia & New Zealand, including: *Auckland* Canterbury Arcade, 174 Queen St, Auckland 1010, New Zealand; ✆ (64) 9 373 3531; e auckland@ traveldoctor.co.nz; *Brisbane* 75a Astor Terr, Spring Hill, Brisbane, QLD 4000, Australia; ✆ 07 3815 6900; e brisbane@traveldoctor.com.au;

South Africa

SAA-Netcare Travel Clinics ✆ 011 802 0059; e travelinfo@netcare.co.za; www.travelclinic. co.za. 11 clinics throughout South Africa.

The Travel Clinic Ltd, Ipswich Gilmour Piper, 10 Fonnereau Rd, Ipswich IP1 3JP; ✆ 01223 367362; ⏱ 09.00–19.00 Wed, 09.00–13.00 Sat
Travelpharm www.travelpharm.com. The Travelpharm website offers up-to-date guidance on travel-related health & has a range of medications available through their online mini-pharmacy.

For other clinic locations, & useful information specific to tropical destinations, check their website.

IAMAT (International Association for Medical Assistance to Travelers) 1623 Military Rd #279, Niagara Falls, NY 14304-1745; ✆ 716 754 4883; e info@iamat.org; www. iamat.org. A non-profit organisation with free membership that provides lists of English-speaking doctors abroad.

TMVC Suite 314, 1030 W Georgia St, Vancouver, BC V6E 2Y3; ✆ 604 681 5656; e vancouver@tmvc. com; www.tmvc.com. One-stop medical clinic for all your international travel health & vaccination needs.

Melbourne 393 Little Bourke St, Melbourne, Vic 3000, Australia; ✆ (03) 9935 8100; e melbourne@traveldoctor.com.au; *Sydney* 428 George St, Sydney, NSW 2000, Australia; ✆ (02) 9221 7133; e sydney@traveldoctor.com.au
IAMAT 206 Papanui Rd, Christchurch 5, New Zealand; www.iamat.org

TMVC NHC Health Centre, cnr Beyers Naude & Waugh Northcliff; ✆ 0861 300 911; e info@ traveldoctor.co.za; www.traveldoctor.co.za. Consult the website for clinic locations.

MEDICAL KIT Pharmacies in the main towns in Zambia generally have good supplies of medicines, but away from these you will find very little. If you're venturing deep into the wilds, then you should take with you anything that you expect to need. If you are on an organised trip, an overlanding truck, or staying at hotels, lodges or safari camps, then you will not need much, as these establishments normally have comprehensive emergency kits. In that case, just a small personal medical kit might include:

- alcohol-based hand rub or bar of soap in plastic box
- antiseptic, eg: iodine or potassium permanganate (don't take antiseptic cream)
- aspirin or paracetamol
- blister plasters (if you plan any serious walking)
- condoms or femidoms and contraceptive pills
- impregnated bednet or permethrin spray
- insect repellent
- lipsalve (ideally containing a sunscreen)
- malaria prophylaxis
- antihistamine tablets
- Micropore tape (for closing small cuts – and invaluable for blisters)
- moisturising cream
- sticking plaster (a roll is more versatile than pre-shaped plasters)
- sunscreen

However, if you are likely to end up in very remote situations, then you should also consider taking the following – and know how to use them:

- antibiotic eye drops, for sore, 'gritty', stuck-together eyes (conjunctivitis)
- a good medical manual (see *Appendix 3*, page 538).
- antibiotics: ciprofloxacin or norfloxacin, for severe diarrhoea
- burns dressings (burns are a common problem for campers)
- injection swabs, sterile needles and syringes
- lint, sterile bandage and safety pins
- malaria diagnostic kits (5) and a digital thermometer (for those going to remote areas)
- steristrips or butterfly closures
- strong painkiller (eg: codeine phosphate – also use for bad diarrhoea)
- tinidazole for giardia or amoebic dysentery (see below for regime)
- tweezers (perhaps those on a Swiss army knife)
- water purification equipment (2% tincture of iodine and dropper is ideal)
- oral rehydration sachets

If you wear glasses, bring a spare pair. Similarly those who wear contact lenses should bring spare ones, also a pair of glasses in case the dust proves too much for the lenses. If you take regular medication (including contraceptive pills) then bring a large supply with you – much easier than hunting for your usual brand in Zambia. Equally, it's worth having a dental check-up before you go, as you could be several painful days from the nearest dentist.

IN ZAMBIA
Hospitals and dentists Zambia's public-health system is overstretched and under-funded, presenting a risk of coming away with something worse than you had when you arrived. In the main cities – Lusaka, Livingstone and the Copperbelt – there are better-funded private hospitals that cater for both affluent Zambians and expats/diplomatic staff. These are much better, and will accept payment from genuine travel health insurance schemes.

For situations that are more serious, and may require immediate evacuation, **Speciality Emergency Services MedRescue (SES;** 🖃 *0211 273302-7, 212663-4;* 📱 *0977 770302-5;* 📧 *med@zamnet.zm; www.ses-zambia.com*) operates throughout Zambia, with bases in Lusaka, Livingstone and Kitwe. If offers ambulances and in-patient care, as well as emergency cover. SES can also arrange short-term insurance cover for visitors, either prior to arriving in Zambia or at their local offices. Most tour operators, and many lodges, include SES cover in their rates, but it's important to have good travel insurance – costs for evacuation are extremely high.

Pharmacies Pharmacies in main towns have a basic range of medicines, often at considerably lower prices than in their Western counterparts; they also stock malaria-test kits. That said, not all of these outlets are reliable, so stick to one that has been recommended.

As you might expect, specific brands are often unavailable, so bring with you all that you will need, as well as a repeat prescription for anything that you might run

---

LONG-HAUL FLIGHTS, CLOTS AND DVT   *Dr Felicity Nicholson*

Any prolonged immobility, including travel by land or air, can result in deep-vein thrombosis (DVT) with the risk of embolus to the lungs. Certain factors can increase the risk and these include:

* Having a previous clot or a close relative with a history
* Being over 40, with increased risk in over 80s
* Recent major operation or varicose-veins surgery
* Cancer
* Stroke
* Heart disease
* Obesity
* Pregnancy
* Hormone therapy
* Heavy smoking
* Severe varicose veins
* Being very tall (over 6ft/1.8m) or short (under 5ft/1.5m)

A deep-vein thrombosis causes painful swelling and redness of the calf or sometimes the thigh. It is only dangerous if a clot travels to the lungs (pulmonary embolus). Symptoms of a pulmonary embolus (PE) – which commonly start three to ten days after a long flight – include chest pain, shortness of breath, and sometimes coughing up small amounts of blood. Anyone who thinks that they might have a DVT needs to see a doctor immediately.

PREVENTION OF DVT
* Keep mobile before and during the flight; move around every couple of hours
* Drink plenty of fluids during the flight
* Avoid taking sleeping pills and excessive tea, coffee and alcohol
* Consider wearing flight socks or support stockings (see *www.legshealth.com*)

If you think you are at increased risk of a clot, ask your doctor if it is safe to travel.

out of. Outside of the main centres, you will be lucky to find anything other than very basic medical supplies. Thus you should carry a very comprehensive medical kit if you are planning to head off independently into the wilds.

Staying healthy Rural Zambia is often not a healthy place to be. However, visitors using the better hotels, lodges and camps are unlikely to encounter any serious problems. The standards of hygiene in even the most remote bushcamps are generally at least as good as you will find at home.

The major dangers in Zambia are car accidents (especially likely if you drive at night) and sunburn. Both can also be very serious, yet both are within the power of the visitor to avoid.

The following is general advice, applicable to travelling anywhere, including Zambia.

Food and storage Throughout the world, most health problems encountered by travellers are contracted by eating contaminated food or drinking unclean water. If you are staying in safari camps or lodges, or eating in restaurants, then you are unlikely to have problems in Zambia.

However, if you are backpacking and cooking for yourself, or relying on local food, then you need to take more care. Tins, packets and fresh green vegetables (when you can find them) are least likely to cause problems – provided that clean water has been used in preparing the meal. In Zambia's hot climate, keeping meat or animal products unrefrigerated for more than a few hours is asking for trouble.

Water and purification Whilst piped water in the major towns is unlikely to harbour any serious pathogens, it will almost certainly cause upset stomachs for overseas visitors. In more rural areas, the water will generally have had less treatment, and therefore will be even more likely to cause problems. Hence, as a general rule, ensure that all water used for drinking or washing food in Zambia is purified.

To purify water yourself, first filter out any suspended solids, perhaps passing the water through a piece of closely woven cloth, or something similar. Then bring it to the boil, or sterilise it chemically. Boiling is much more effective, provided that you have the fuel available.

Tablets sold for purification are based on chlorine dioxide. Iodine is no longer recommended for use and is not sold in the UK and the rest of Europe as there have been concerns over its safety.

Heat and sun Heatstroke, heat exhaustion and sunburn are often problems for travellers to Zambia, despite being easy to prevent. To avoid them, you need to remember that your body is under stress and make allowances for it. First, take things gently; you are on holiday, after all. Next, keep your fluid and salt levels high: lots of water and soft drinks, but go easy on the caffeine and alcohol. Third, dress to keep cool with loose-fitting, thin garments – preferably of cotton, linen or silk. Finally, beware of the sun. Hats and long-sleeved shirts are essential. If you must expose your skin to the sun, then use sunblocks and high-factor sunscreens (the sun is so strong that you will still get a tan). Be especially careful of exposure in the middle of the day and of sun reflected off water, and wear a T-shirt and lots of waterproof suncream (at least SPF15) when swimming. The glare and the dust can be hard on the eyes, too, so bring UV-protecting sunglasses and, perhaps, a soothing eyebath.

Prickly heat A fine pimply rash on the trunk is likely to be heat rash; cool showers, dabbing dry and talc will help. Treat the problem by slowing down to a relaxed schedule, wearing only loose, baggy, 100%-cotton clothes and sleeping naked under a fan; if it's bad you may need to check into an air-conditioned hotel room for a while.

Eye problems Bacterial conjunctivitis (pink eye) is a common infection in Africa; people who wear contact lenses are most open to this irritating problem. The eyes feel sore and gritty and they will often be stuck together in the mornings. They will need treatment with antibiotic drops or ointment. Lesser eye irritation should settle with bathing in salt water and keeping the eyes shaded. If an insect flies into your eye, extract it with great care, ensuring you do not crush or damage it otherwise you may get a nastily inflamed eye from toxins secreted by the creature. Small elongated red-and-black blister beetles carry warning colouration to tell you not to crush them anywhere against your skin.

Skin infections Any mosquito bite or small nick in the skin gives an opportunity for bacteria to foil the body's usually excellent defences; it will surprise many travellers how quickly skin infections start in warm humid climates and it is essential to clean and cover even the slightest wound. Creams are not as effective as a good drying antiseptic such as dilute iodine, potassium permanganate (a few crystals in half a cup of water) or crystal (or gentian) violet. One of these should be available in most towns. If the wound starts to throb, or becomes red and the redness starts to spread, or the wound oozes, and especially if you develop a fever, antibiotics will probably be needed: flucloxacillin (250mg four times a day) or cloxacillin (500mg four times a day). For those allergic to penicillin, erythromycin (500mg twice a day) for five days should help. See a doctor if the symptoms do not start to improve within 48 hours.

Fungal infections also get a hold easily in hot, moist climates so wear 100%-cotton socks and underwear and shower frequently. An itchy rash in the groin or flaking between the toes is likely to be a fungal infection. This needs treatment with an antifungal cream such as Canesten (clotrimazole); if this is not available try Whitfield's ointment (compound benzoic acid ointment) or crystal violet (although this will turn you purple!).

Avoiding insect bites The most dangerous biting insects in parts of Zambia are **mosquitoes**, because they can transmit malaria, yellow fever and a host of other diseases.

Research has shown that using a mosquito net over your bed, and covering up exposed skin (by wearing long-sleeved shirts, and tucking trousers into socks) in the evening, are the most effective steps towards preventing bites. Bednet treatment kits are available from travel clinics; these prevent mosquitoes biting through a net if you roll against it in your sleep, and also make old and holey nets protective. Mosquito coils and chemical insect repellents will help, and sleeping in a stream of moving air, such as under a fan, or in an air-conditioned room, will help to reduce your chances of being bitten.

DEET (diethyltoluamide) is the active ingredient in many repellents (Repel have an excellent range), with the current recommended strength being 50–55%. It will dissolve some plastics and synthetic materials, and may irritate sensitive skin, so you need to be careful. An alternative to this is to use Bug Guards – wrist and ankle bands containing 100% DEET in capsule form. The capsules break on movement, but the chemical never touches the skin. One pack contains four bands, which when used, last for two weeks. Mosquito nets, socks and even cravats can be impregnated and used to deter insects from biting. Eating large quantities of garlic, or cream of tartar, or taking yeast tablets, are said to deter some biting insects, although the evidence is anecdotal – and the garlic may affect your social life.

Mosquitoes and many other insects are attracted to light. If you are camping, never put a lamp near the opening of your tent, or you will have a swarm of biters waiting to join you when you retire. In hotel rooms, be aware that the longer your light is on, the greater the number of insects sharing your accommodation.

Aside from avoiding mosquito bites between dusk and dawn, which will protect you from elephantiasis and a range of nasty insect-borne viruses, as well as malaria (see pages 85–6), it is important to take precautions against other insect bites. During the day, if you are pushing through scrubby country it is wise to wear long, loose (preferably 100%-cotton) clothes; this will keep off both ticks and tsetse flies, and day-biting *Aedes* mosquitoes which may spread viral fevers.

Tsetse flies hurt when they bite. They thrive in broad-leaved woodland across Zambia but are highly localised. They are also said to be attracted to the colour blue and moving vehicles. Locals will advise on where they are a problem and where they transmit sleeping sickness.

Minute pestilential biting **blackflies** spread river blindness in some parts of Africa between 19°N and 17°S; the disease is caught close to fast-flowing rivers since flies breed there and the larvae live in rapids. The flies bite during the day but long trousers tucked into socks will help keep them off. Citronella-based natural repellents (eg: Mosi-guard) do not work against them.

Tumbu flies or putsi, often called mango flies, are a problem where the climate is hot and humid. The adult fly lays her eggs on the soil or on drying laundry and when the eggs come into contact with human flesh (when you put on clothes or lie on a bed) they hatch and bury themselves under the skin. Here they form a crop of 'boils' each with a maggot inside. Smear a little Vaseline over the hole, and they will push their noses out to breathe. It may be possible to squeeze them out but it depends if they are ready, since the larvae have spines that help them to hold on.

In putsi areas either dry your clothes and sheets within a screened house, or dry them in direct sunshine until they are crisp, or iron them.

Jiggers, or sandfleas, are another flesh-feaster, which can be best avoided by wearing shoes. They latch on if you walk barefoot in contaminated places, and set up home under the skin of the foot, usually at the side of a toenail where they cause a painful, boil-like swelling. They need picking out by a local expert.

Snakes, spiders and scorpions ... Encounters with aggressive snakes, angry spiders or vindictive scorpions are more common in horror films than in Zambia. Most snakes will flee at the mere vibrations of a human footstep whilst spiders are far more interested in flies than people. You will have to seek out scorpions if you wish to see one. If you are careful about where you place your hands and feet, especially after dark, then there should be no problems. You are less likely to get bitten or stung if you wear stout shoes and long trousers. Simple precautions include not putting on boots without shaking them empty first, and always checking the back of your backpack before putting it on.

Snakes do bite occasionally, and you ought to know the standard first-aid treatment. First, and most importantly, *don't panic*. Most snakes are harmless and even venomous species will only dispense venom in about half of their bites.

If bitten, you are unlikely to have received venom; keeping this fact in mind may help you to stay calm.

Even in the worst of these cases, the victim has hours or days to get to help, and not a matter of minutes. He/she should be kept calm, with no exertions to pump venom around the blood system, whilst being taken rapidly to the nearest medical help. The area of the bite should be washed to remove any venom from the skin, and the bitten limb should be immobilised. Paracetamol may be used as a painkiller, but never use aspirin because it may cause internal bleeding.

Most first-aid techniques do more harm than good: cutting into the wound is harmful and tourniquets are dangerous; suction and electrical inactivation devices do not work. The only effective treatment is antivenom. In case of a bite, which you fear may be both serious and venomous then:

- Try to keep calm. It is likely that no venom has been dispensed.
- Stop movement of the bitten limb by applying a splint.
- If you have a crêpe bandage, wrap it around the whole limb (eg: all the way from the toes to the thigh), as tight as you would for a sprained ankle or a muscle pull.
- Keep the bitten limb *below* heart height to slow spread of any venom.
- Evacuate the victim to a hospital that has antivenom.
- *Never* give aspirin. You may offer paracetamol, which is safe.
- *Do not* apply ice packs.
- *Do not* apply potassium permanganate.

If the offending snake can be captured without any risk of someone else being bitten, take it to show the doctor. But beware, since even a decapitated head is able to dispense venom in a reflex bite.

When deep in the bush, heading for the nearest large farm or camp may be quicker than going to a town: it may have a supply of antivenom, or facilities to radio for help by plane.

DISEASES AND WHEN TO SEE A DOCTOR

Travellers' diarrhoea There are almost as many names for this as there are travellers' tales on the subject. Firstly, do resist the temptation to reach for the medical kit as soon as your stomach turns a little fluid. Most cases of travellers' diarrhoea will resolve themselves within 24–48 hours with no treatment at all. To speed up this process of acclimatisation, eat well but simply: avoid fats in favour of starches, and keep your fluid intake high. Bananas and papaya fruit are often claimed to be helpful. If you urgently need to stop the symptoms, for a long journey for example, then Lomotil, Imodium or another of the commercial anti-diarrhoea preparations will do the trick. They stop the symptoms, by paralysing the bowel, but will not cure the problem. They should be used only as a last resort and never if you have bad abdominal cramps with the diarrhoea.

If the diarrhoea persists for more than two days, or the stools contain blood, pus or slime, and/or you have a fever, you must seek medical advice. There are as many possible treatments as there are causes, and a proper diagnosis involves microscopic analysis of a stool sample, so go straight to your nearest hospital. The most important thing, especially in Zambia's climate, is to keep your fluid intake up. If it is not possible to reach medical help quickly then a dose of norfloxacin or ciprofloxacin repeated twice a day until reaching medical help may be appropriate (if you are planning to take an antibiotic with you, note that both norfloxacin and ciprofloxacin are available only on prescription in the UK). If the diarrhoea is greasy and bulky and is accompanied by sulphurous (eggy) burps the likely cause is giardia. This is best treated with tinidazole (four x 500mg in one dose, repeated seven days later if symptoms persist).

The body's absorption of fluids is assisted by adding small amounts of dissolved sugars, salts and minerals to the water. Sachets of oral rehydration salts give the perfect biochemical mix you need to replace what is pouring out of your bottom but they do not taste so nice. Any dilute mixture of sugar and salt in water will do you good so, if you like Coke or orange squash, drink that with a three-finger pinch of salt added to each glass. The ideal ratio is eight level teaspoons of sugar and one level teaspoon of salt dissolved in one litre of water. Palm syrup or honey make good substitutes for sugar, and including fresh citrus juice will not only improve the taste of these solutions, but also add valuable potassium.

Drink two large glasses after every bowel action, and more if you are thirsty. If you are not eating you need to drink three litres a day *plus* whatever you are sweating *and* the equivalent of what's going into the toilet. If you feel like eating, take a bland diet; heavy greasy foods will give you cramps.

If you are likely to be more than a few days from qualified medical help, then come equipped with a good health manual and the selection of antibiotics which it recommends. *Bugs, Bites & Bowels* by Dr Jane Wilson-Howarth (see *Appendix 3*, page 538) is excellent for this purpose.

Malaria You can still catch malaria even if you are taking anti-malarial drugs so you should do everything possible to avoid mosquito bites. Untreated malaria is likely to be fatal, but even strains resistant to prophylaxis respond well to prompt treatment. Because of this, your immediate priority upon displaying possible malaria symptoms – including a rapid rise in temperature (over 38°C), and any combination of a headache, flu-like aches and pains, a general sense of disorientation, and possibly even nausea and diarrhoea – is to establish whether you have malaria, ideally by visiting a clinic.

A definite diagnosis of malaria is normally possible only by examining a blood sample under the microscope. It is best to get the problem properly diagnosed if possible, so don't treat yourself if you can easily reach a hospital first. Even if you test negative, it would be wise to stay within reach of a laboratory until the symptoms clear up, and to test again after a day or two if they don't. It's worth noting that if you have a fever and the malaria test is negative, you may have typhoid or paratyphoid, which should also receive immediate treatment.

If (and only if) medical help is unavailable, then self-treatment is fairly safe, except for people who are pregnant or under 12 years of age. Should you be travelling to remote parts of Zambia, you would be wise to carry a course of treatment to cure malaria, and a rapid test kit. With malaria, it is normal enough to go from feeling healthy to having a high fever in the space of a few hours (and it is possible to die from falciparum malaria within 24 hours of the first symptoms). In such circumstances, assume that you have malaria and act accordingly – whatever risks are attached to taking an unnecessary cure are outweighed by the dangers of untreated malaria.

There is some division about the best treatment for malaria, but either Malarone or Coarthemeter are the current treatments of choice. Discuss your trip with a specialist at home or in Zambia.

Dengue fever This mosquito-borne disease – and other similar arboviruses – may mimic malaria but there is no prophylactic medication available to deal with it.

The mosquitoes that carry this virus bite during the daytime, so it is worth applying repellent if you see any mosquitoes around. Symptoms include strong headaches, rashes and excruciating joint and muscle pains and high fever. Dengue fever only lasts for a week or so and is not usually fatal. Complete rest and paracetamol are the usual treatment. Plenty of fluids also help. Some patients are given an intravenous drip to keep them from dehydrating. It is especially important to protect yourself if you have had dengue fever before. A second infection with a different strain can result in the potentially fatal dengue haemorrhagic fever.

Sexually transmitted diseases AIDS is spread in exactly the same way in Africa as it is at home, through body secretions, blood and blood products. The same goes for the dangerous hepatitis B. Both can be spread through sex.

Remember that the risks of sexually transmitted disease are high, whether you sleep with fellow travellers or locals. About 80% of HIV infections in British heterosexuals are acquired abroad. If you must indulge, use condoms or femidoms, which help reduce the risk of transmission. If you do have unprotected sex, visit a clinic as soon as possible; this should be within 24 hours, or no later than 72 hours, for post-exposure prophylaxis. And if you notice any genital ulcers or discharge, get treatment promptly.

Hepatitis This is a group of viral diseases which generally start with Coca-Cola-coloured urine and light-coloured stools. It progresses to fevers, weakness, jaundice (yellow skin and eyeballs) and abdominal pains caused by a severe inflammation of the liver. There are several forms, of which the two most common are typical of the rest: hepatitis A (or infectious hepatitis) and hepatitis B (or serum hepatitis).

Hepatitis A and hepatitis E, are spread by the faecal-oral route, that is by ingesting food or drink contaminated by excrement. They are avoided in the same ways you normally avoid stomach problems: by careful preparation of food and by drinking only clean water. But as there are now excellent vaccines against hepatitis A it is certainly worth getting inoculated before you travel (see *Recommended precautions*, page 84). In contrast, the more serious but rarer hepatitis B is spread in the same way as AIDS (by blood or body secretions), and is avoided the same way as one avoids AIDS. There is also a vaccine which protects against hepatitis B. In most cases with lots of bed rest and a good low-fat, no-alcohol diet most people recover within six months. If you are unlucky enough to contract hepatitis of any form, use your travel insurance to fly straight home.

Meningitis This is a particularly nasty disease as it can kill within hours of the first symptoms appearing. The tell-tale symptoms are a combination of a blinding headache (light sensitivity), a blotchy rash and a high fever. Immunisation with meningitis ACWY vaccine protects against the most serious bacterial forms of meningitis, but not against Group B for which there is no vaccine. Although other forms of meningitis (usually viral) exist, there are no vaccines for these. Local papers normally report localised outbreaks. A severe headache and fever should make you get to a doctor immediately. There are also other causes of headache and fever; one of which is typhoid, which occurs in travellers to Zambia. Seek medical help if you are ill for more than a few days.

Rabies Rabies is contracted when broken skin comes into contact with saliva from an infected animal. The disease is almost always fatal, but there is post-exposure treatment. It is possible to be immunised against rabies before you travel. You are advised to take this if you intend working with animals or you are travelling for four weeks or more to remote areas.

If you are bitten, scratched or licked over an open wound by any warm-blooded mammal, including ground squirrels and bats, clean and disinfect the wound thoroughly by scrubbing it with soap under running water for five minutes, and then flood it with local spirit or diluted iodine. This helps stop the rabies virus entering the body and will guard against wound infections, including tetanus.

Seek help immediately, ideally within 24 hours, though it is never too late, as the incubation period for rabies can be very long. Those who have not been immunised will need a full course of injections. The vast majority of travel health advisors including WHO recommend rabies immunoglobulin (RIG), but this product is expensive (around US$800) and is now very hard to come by – which is why pre-exposure vaccination is now recommended regardless of duration of stay. Tell the doctor if you have had pre-exposure vaccine, as this should change the treatment you receive. The later stages of the disease are horrendous – spasms, personality changes and hydrophobia (fear of water). Death from rabies is probably one of the worst ways to go.

Tickbite fever African ticks are not the rampant disease transmitters they are in the Americas, but they may spread tickbite fever and a few dangerous rarities in Zambia. Tickbite fever is a flu-like illness that can easily be treated with doxycycline, but as there can be some serious complications it is important to visit a doctor. It is most prevalent in Zambia between November and January.

Ticks should ideally be removed as soon as possible as leaving them on the body increases the chance of infection. They should be removed with special tick tweezers that can be bought in good travel shops. Failing that you can use your fingernails: grasp the tick as close to your body as possible and pull steadily and firmly away at right angles to your skin. The tick will then come away complete, as long as you do not jerk or twist. If possible douse the wound with alcohol (any spirit will do) or iodine. Irritants (eg: Olbas oil) or lit cigarettes are to be discouraged since they can cause the ticks to regurgitate and therefore increase the risk of disease. It is best to get a travelling companion to check you for ticks; if you are travelling with small children, remember to check their heads, and particularly behind the ears.

Spreading redness around the bite and/or fever and/or aching joints after a tick bite imply that you have an infection that requires antibiotic treatment, so seek advice.

Bilharzia or schistosomiasis Bilharzia is an insidious disease, contracted by coming into contact with contaminated water. It is caused by parasitic worms which live part of their lives in freshwater snails, and part of their lives in human bladders or intestines. A common indication of an infection is a localised itchy rash – where the parasites have burrowed through the skin – and later symptoms of a more advanced infection may include passing bloody urine. Bilharzia is readily treated by medication, and only serious if it remains untreated.

The only way to avoid infection completely is to stay away from any bodies of fresh water, which in Zambia includes Lake Kariba. Obviously this is restrictive, and would make your trip less enjoyable. More pragmatic advice is to avoid slow-moving or sluggish water, and ask local opinion on the bilharzia risk, as not all water is contaminated. Generally bilharzia snails do not inhabit fast-flowing water, and hence rivers are free of it. However, dams and standing water, especially in populated areas, are usually heavily contaminated. If you think you have been infected, don't worry about it – just get a test done on your return at least six weeks after your last possible exposure.

Avoiding bilharzia If you are bathing, swimming, paddling or wading in fresh water which you think may carry a bilharzia risk, try to get out of the water within ten minutes.

• Avoid bathing or paddling on shores within 200m of villages or places where people use the water a great deal, especially reedy shores or where there is lots of water weed.
• Dry off thoroughly with a towel; rub vigorously.
• If your bathing water comes from a risky source try to ensure that the water is taken from the lake in the early morning and stored snail-free, otherwise it should be filtered or Dettol or Cresol added.
• Bathing early in the morning is safer than bathing in the last half of the day.
• Cover yourself with DEET insect repellent before swimming: it may offer some protection.

Sleeping sickness or trypanosomiasis
This is really a cattle disease, which is rarely caught by people. It is spread by bites from the distinctive tsetse fly – which is slightly larger than a housefly, and has pointed mouth-parts designed for sucking blood. The bite is painful. These flies are easily spotted as they bite during the day, and have distinctive wings which cross into a scissor shape when they are resting. Note that not all tsetses carry the disease.

Prevention is easier than cure, so avoid being bitten by covering up, and applying chemical insect repellents. Avoid wearing dark colours, especially blue, since these are favoured by the flies.

Tsetse bites are nasty, and the vast majority will swell up and turn red – that is a normal allergic reaction to any bite. However, if the bite develops into a boil-like swelling after five or more days, and a fever starts two or three weeks later, then seek immediate medical treatment to avert permanent damage to your central nervous system. The name 'sleeping sickness' refers to a daytime drowsiness which is characteristic of the later stages of the disease.

Because this is a rare complaint, most doctors in the West are unfamiliar with it. If you think that you may have been infected, draw their attention to the possibility. Treatment is straightforward, once a correct diagnosis has been made.

RETURNING HOME
Many tropical diseases have a long incubation period, and it is possible to develop symptoms weeks after returning home (this is why it is important to keep taking anti-malaria prophylaxis for the prescribed duration after you leave a malarial zone). If you do get ill after you return home, be certain to tell your doctor where you have been. Alert him/her to any diseases that you may have been exposed to. Several people die from malaria in the UK every year because victims do not seek medical help promptly or their doctors are not familiar with the symptoms, and so are slow to make a correct diagnosis. Milder forms of malaria may take up to a year to reveal themselves, but serious (falciparum) malaria will usually become apparent within three to six months, and can start as early as one week into a malarial area.

If problems persist, get a check-up at one of the hospitals that specialise in tropical diseases: the Hospital for Tropical Diseases in the UK (page 86), or the Centers for Disease Control in the USA (page 87). Note that to visit such a hospital in the UK, you need a letter of referral from your doctor.

5

SAFETY

Zambia is not a dangerous country. If you are travelling on an all-inclusive trip and staying at lodges and hotels, then problems of personal safety are exceedingly rare. There will always be someone on hand to help you. Even if you are travelling on local transport, perhaps on a low budget, you will not be attacked randomly just for the sake of it. A difficult situation is most likely to occur if you have made yourself an obvious target for thieves, perhaps by walking around, or driving an expensive 4x4, in town at night. The answer then is to capitulate completely and give them what they want, and cash in on your travel insurance. Heroics are not a good idea.

The British Foreign and Commonwealth Office currently advises caution when travelling in rural parts of the country bordering the Democratic Republic of Congo (DRC), especially after dark, a reflection of ongoing cross-border raids. The advice does not relate to main roads, or to towns along the routes, including those between Kapiri Mposhi and Serenje, Serenje and Mansa, and the main routes through the Copperbelt. However, those proposing to travel north from Ndola to Mufulira should be cautious.

For women travellers, especially those travelling alone, it is doubly important to learn the local attitudes, and how to behave acceptably. This takes some practice, and a certain confidence. You will often be the centre of attention but, by developing conversational techniques to avert over-enthusiastic male attention, you should be perfectly safe. Making friends of the local women is one way to help avoid such problems.

THEFT Theft is a problem in Zambia's urban areas. Given that a large section of the population is living below the poverty line and without any paid work, it is surprising

SAFETY FOR WOMEN TRAVELLERS   *Janice Booth*

When attention becomes intrusive, it can help if you are wearing a wedding ring and have photos of 'your' husband and children, even if they are someone else's. A good reason to give for not being with them is that you have to travel in connection with your job – biology, zoology, geography, or whatever. (But not journalism – that's risky.)

Pay attention to local etiquette, and to speaking, dressing and moving reasonably decorously. Look at how the local women dress, and try not to expose parts of yourself that they keep covered. Think about body language. In much of southern Africa direct eye-contact with a man will be seen as a 'come-on'; sunglasses are helpful here.

Don't be afraid to explain clearly – but pleasantly rather than as a put-down – that you aren't in the market for whatever distractions are on offer. Remember that you are probably as much of a novelty to the local people as they are to you; and the fact that you are travelling abroad alone gives them the message that you are free and adventurous. But don't imagine that a Lothario lurks under every bush: many approaches stem from genuine friendliness or curiosity, and a brush-off in such cases doesn't do much for the image of travellers in general.

Take sensible precautions against theft and attack – try to cover all the risks before you encounter them – and then relax and enjoy your trip. You'll meet far more kindness than villainy.

that the problem is not worse. Despite Lusaka's reputation, in my experience theft is no more of an issue here than it is in Harare – while the centre of Johannesburg is significantly more dangerous than either. However, car jacking is on the increase, so it is wise to take sensible precautions to protect your vehicle – and you.

How to avoid it Thieves in the bigger cities usually work in groups – choosing their targets carefully. These will be people who look vulnerable and who have items worth stealing. To avoid being robbed, try not to fit into either category – and certainly not into both. Observing a few basic rules, especially during your first few weeks in Zambia's cities, will drastically reduce your chances of becoming a target. After that you should have learnt your own way of assessing the risks, and avoiding thefts. Until then:

- Try not to carry anything of value around with you.
- If you must carry cash, then use a concealed money-belt for your main supply – keeping smaller change separately and to hand.
- Try not to walk around alone. Move in groups. Take taxis instead.
- Try not to look too foreign. Blend in to the local scene as well as you can. Act like a streetwise expat rather than a tourist, if you can. (Conspicuously carrying a local newspaper may help with this.)
- Rucksacks and large, new bags are bad. If you must carry a bag, choose an old battered one. Around town, a local plastic carrier bag is ideal.
- Move confidently and look as if you know exactly what you are doing, and where you are going. Lost foreigners make the easiest targets.
- Never walk around at night – that is asking for trouble.

If you have a vehicle then don't leave anything in it, and avoid leaving it parked outside in a city. One person should always stay with it, as vehicle thefts are common, even in broad daylight. Armed gangs doing American-style vehicle hijacks are on the increase, though still rare – and their most likely targets are new 4x4 vehicles. When driving in urban areas, and especially at night, keep the doors locked, and ensure that you're not using a mobile phone within easy reach of a passer-by. Scams to get you to stop include faking an accident, so be on the alert. And if you are held up then just surrender: you have little choice if you want to live.

Reporting thefts to the police If you are the victim of a theft then report it to the police – they ought to know. Also try to get a copy of the report, or at least a reference number on an official-looking piece of paper, as this will help you to claim on your insurance policy when you return home. Some insurance companies won't act without it. But remember that reporting anything in a police station can take a long time, and do not expect any speedy arrests for a small case of pick-pocketing.

ARREST To get arrested in Zambia, a foreigner will normally have to try quite hard. During the Kaunda regime, when the state was paranoid about spies, every tourist's camera became a reason for suspicion and arrest. Fortunately that attitude has now vanished, though as a precaution you should still ask for permission to photograph near bridges or military installations. This simple courtesy costs you nothing, and may avoid a problem later.

One excellent way to get arrested in Zambia is to try to smuggle drugs across its borders, or to try to buy them from 'pushers'. Drug offences carry penalties at least as stiff as those you will find at home – and the jails are a lot less pleasant.

Zambia's police are not forbidden to use entrapment techniques or 'sting' operations to catch criminals. Buying, selling or using drugs in Zambia is just not worth the risk.

Failing this, arguing with any policeman or army official – and getting angry into the bargain – is a sure way to get arrested. It is essential to control your temper and stay relaxed when dealing with Zambia's officials. Not only will you gain respect, and hence help your cause, but also you will avoid being forced to cool off for a night in the cells.

If you are careless enough to be arrested, you will often only be asked a few questions. If the police are suspicious of you, then how you handle the situation will determine whether you are kept for a matter of hours or for days. Be patient, helpful, good-humoured and as truthful as possible. Never lose your temper; it will only aggravate the situation. Avoid any hint of arrogance. If things are going badly after half a day or so, then start firmly, but politely, to insist on seeing someone in higher authority. As a last resort you do, at least in theory, have the right to contact your embassy or consulate, though the finer points of your civil liberties may be overlooked by an irate local police chief.

BRIBERY Bribery is a fact of life in Zambia, though it is a difficult subject to write about. If you're visiting on an organised holiday, then it's unlikely to become an issue – you'll not come across any expectation of bribes. However, independent travellers ought to think about the issue before they arrive, as they are more likely to encounter the problem, and there are many different points of view on how to deal with it.

Some argue that it is present already, as an unavoidable way of life, and so must be accepted by the practical traveller. They view using bribery as simply practising one of the local customs. Others regard paying bribes as an unacceptable step towards condoning an immoral practice; thus any bribe should be flatly refused, and requests to make them never acceded to.

Whichever school of thought you favour, bribery is an issue in Zambia that you may need to consider. It is not as widespread, or on the same scale, as countries further north – but on a low level is not uncommon. A large 'tip' is often expected for a favour, and acceptance of small fines from police for traffic offences often avoids proceedings which may appear deliberately time-consuming. Many pragmatic travellers will only use a bribe as a very last resort, and only then when it has been asked for repeatedly.

Never attempt to bribe someone unsubtly, or use the word 'bribe'. If the person involved hasn't already dropped numerous broad hints to you that money is required, then offering it would be a great insult. Further, even if bribes are being asked for, an eagerness to offer will encourage any person you are dealing with to increase their price.

Never simply say, 'Here's some dollars, now will you do it?' Better is to agree, reluctantly, to pay the 'on-the-spot-fine' that was requested; or to gradually accept the need for the extra 'administration fee' that was demanded; or to finally agree to help to cover the 'time and trouble' involved ... provided that the problem can be overcome.

6

In the Wilds

🚗 DRIVING

Driving around Zambia isn't for the novice, or the unprepared. Long stretches of the tarred roads are extensively pot-holed, most of the secondary gravel roads are in very poor repair, and many areas rely on bush tracks maintained only by the passage of vehicles. If you plan on exploring in the more rural areas, and remote parks, then you will need at least two sturdy, fully equipped 4x4 vehicles. It says something of the roads in general that until very recently most of Zambia's car-hire companies would rent vehicles only if you took a local driver – and even then only for use in towns.

Those planning to drive themselves around Zambia should read this section in conjunction with the general details on driving in *Chapter 4*, pages 67–70.

EQUIPMENT AND PREPARATIONS

Fuel and fuel consumption Petrol and diesel are available in most of the towns (see page 69), but elsewhere diesel is generally more widely available. Although shortages are relatively rare, they do still occur – especially in the more remote west – and you'll need to be prepared for them. For travel into the bush in particular you will need long-range fuel tanks, and/or a large stock of filled jerrycans. It is essential to plan your fuel requirements well in advance, and to carry more than you expect to need.

Remember that using the vehicle's 4x4 capability, especially in low-ratio gears, will significantly increase your fuel consumption. Similarly, the cool comfort of a vehicle's air conditioning will burn your fuel reserves swiftly.

Spares Zambia's garages do not generally have a comprehensive stock of vehicle spares – though bush mechanics can effect the most amazing short-term repairs, with remarkably basic tools and raw materials. Spares for the more common makes are easiest to find, so most basic Land Rover and Toyota 4x4 parts are available somewhere in Lusaka, at a price. If you are arriving in Zambia with a foreign vehicle, it is best to bring as many spares as you can, though be aware that you could be charged import duty. Spares for both Toyota and Ford are available in Lusaka and Kitwe, Southern Cross in Lusaka and Chingola stock Mercedes and Jeep parts. For more general spares, there are branches of Autoworld in several major cities, including Lusaka and Ndola,

Navigation See the section on *Maps and navigation* in *Chapter 4*, pages 57–8, for detailed comments, but there are good maps available – and for this there's no alternative to visiting the Surveyor General's office in Mulungushi House, in Lusaka. You should seriously consider taking a GPS system if you are heading off the main roads in the more remote areas of the country.

COPING WITH ZAMBIA'S ROADS

Tar roads Many of Zambia's tar roads are excellent, and a programme of tarring is gradually extending these good sections. However, within them there are occasional patches of pot-holes. These often occur in small groups, making some short stretches of tar very slow going indeed. If you are unlucky, or foolish, enough to hit one of these sections after speeding along a smooth stretch of tar, then you are likely to blow at least one tyre and in danger of a serious accident. For this reason, if for no other, even tar roads that look good are worth treating with caution. It is wiser never to exceed about 80km/h.

At the beginning of the rainy season, in October and November, take particular care. During the dry season there can be a considerable build up of diesel and oil on tar roads, so after the first rains water tends to lie on this layer and can create a surface akin to black ice.

Strip roads Occasionally there are roads where the sealed tar surface is only wide enough for one vehicle. This becomes a problem when you meet another vehicle travelling in the opposite direction … on the same stretch of tar. Then local practice

POLICE ROADBLOCKS

Often in Zambia you'll come across a police or immigration roadblock. You'll find them on all the main roads around the larger towns, and randomly placed on other tar roads and arteries also. It's vital that you stop for them, and it'll speed your journey if you know how to deal with them. I usually slow down on my approach, turn off any music or air conditioning, take off my sunglasses and roll down my window. Then greet the officer with a broad smile and a traditional greeting, or at least a polite 'Good morning, how are you?' (See *Cultural guidelines* in *Chapter 4*, pages 79–81, for more on these.)

Foreigners will often be waved through. Sometimes you'll be asked a few questions – typically about where you are going and what you are doing. Keep your answers simple, honest and clear. You may be asked to test your lights, or indicators, or to show your insurance or identification, so it's important to have your passport, driving licence and vehicle documentation to hand. Answer politely with good humour and keep cool.

Like any country, Zambia has occasional radar traps, and there are rules of the road; if you contravene these, then you may be fined. If so, then it's best to fill out the official forms, pay the official fine as swiftly as possible, and keep the receipt. Fines vary from Kw18,000 for driving without a seatbelt to Kw65,000 for speeding.

SPURIOUS CHARGES The vast majority of roadblocks are fair and friendly, but occasionally you may find one where the officers are really looking to levy a fine. This is rare, but it happens! Then the officers will either find a problem, or make one up, to try to get you to pay an on-the-spot fine – and they won't be using official forms.

Some of their favourite excuses may be the finer, real or fictitious, points of the law of the road. These might include claiming that you haven't got two six-inch white strips of reflective tape on your front bumper, or two in red on the back bumper; or that you should have two steel triangles (a favourite is to fine people with plastic ones!) and make sure they are easy to get at; or that your reversing lights don't work. Another ploy is to charge a fine, but one that's lower than it is to wait until the last possible moment before you steer left, driving with two wheels on the gravel adjacent to the tar, and two on the tar. Usually, the vehicle coming in the opposite direction will do the same, and after passing each other both vehicles veer back on to the tar. If you are unused to this, then slow right down before you steer on to the gravel.

Gravel roads Gravel (or dirt) roads can be very deceptive. Even when they appear smooth, flat and fast (which is not often), they still do not give vehicles much traction. You will frequently put the car into small skids, and with practice at slower speeds you will learn how to deal with them. Gravel is a less forgiving surface on which to drive than tar. The rules and techniques for driving well are the same for both, but on tar you can get away with sloppy braking and cornering which would prove fatal on gravel.

Further, in Zambia you must always be prepared for the unexpected: an animal wandering onto the road, a rash of huge pot-holes, or an unexpected corner. So it is verging on insane to drive over about 60km/h on any of Zambia's gravel roads. Other basic driving hints include:

should be – if you're asked for, say, Kw20,000 for speeding, the likelihood is that no receipt will be forthcoming.

Whatever the charge, however unreasonable, it's vital that you keep your cool, take your time, and don't appear at all bothered. Act as if you've all the time in the world, keep smiling and stay helpful and cheerful. Never get angry; always keep it amiable. However, do politely insist on a few of Zambia's basic road laws:

- You should always, very pleasantly and politely, record the officer's name and number – I'd be casual about this – but make it clear that you have done it.
- Note that higher police officers and authorities try hard to stamp out this sort of corrupt behaviour. For this reason you should always find a way to report dodgy behaviour to a higher officer at the local station, though obviously don't imply that the officer(s) in question is doing anything wrong.
- You never need to give your car keys or licence to a police officer; they have the right to see your licence – but not to take it off you.
- If you are charged with anything, then you have the right to insist that the officer accompanies you to the local police station, to discuss the charge with his superior. So, basically, you say politely that you're happy to pay the fine … but you wish to do so at the local police station.
- Never threaten to 'report' an officer – but instead you might innocently insist that you need a receipt with a stamp – and you'll have to take it to the station for one, even after they let you go.
- Finally, I'd never admit to being late, or having to be anywhere too quickly; it's tantamount to admitting that you'll be willing to pay a bribe to get away faster.
- If you willingly pay bribes then your corruptness is perpetuating the practice. Don't do it.

Stick to these rules, take your time, remain patient and they'll eventually let you go – or at least the price of the 'fine' will reduce to being insignificant!

Slowing down If in any doubt about what lies ahead, always slow down. Road surfaces can vary enormously, so keep a constant lookout for pot-holes, ruts or patches of soft sand which could put you into an unexpected slide. If you do find the vehicle wandering having hit a corrugated section, always steer into the direction in which you are travelling.

Passing vehicles When passing other vehicles travelling in the opposite direction, always slow down to minimise both the damage that stone chippings will do to your windscreen, and the danger in driving through the other vehicle's dust cloud.

Using your gears In normal driving, a lower gear will give you more control over the car – so keep out of high 'cruising' gears. Rather stick with third or fourth, and accept that your revs will be slightly higher than they normally are.

Cornering and braking Under ideal conditions, the brakes should only be applied when the car is travelling in a straight line. Braking whilst negotiating a corner is dangerous, so it is vital to slow down before you reach corners. Equally, it is better to slow down gradually, using a combination of gears and brakes, than to use the brakes alone. You are less likely to skid.

DRIVING AT NIGHT Never drive at night unless you have to. Both wild and domestic animals frequently spend the night by the side of busy roads, and will actually sleep on quieter ones. Tar roads are especially bad as the surface absorbs all the sun's heat by day, and then radiates it at night – making it a warm bed for passing animals. A high-speed collision with any animal, even a small one like a goat, will not only kill the animal, but also cause very severe damage to a vehicle, with potentially fatal consequences. A word of caution about other road users, too: there's a prevalence for both drivers and pedestrians to be under the influence of alcohol at night. Finally, watch out for drivers with poorly maintained vehicles, who tend to drive between dawn and dusk to avoid contact with the police.

4X4 DRIVING TECHNIQUES You will need a high-clearance 4x4 to get anywhere in Zambia that's away from the main arteries. However, no vehicle can make up for an inexperienced driver – so ensure that you are confident of your vehicle's capabilities before you venture into the wilds with it. You really need extensive practice, with an expert on hand to advise you, before you'll have the first idea how to handle such a vehicle in difficult terrain. Finally, driving in convoy (preferably with some reasonably strong people) is an essential precaution in the more remote areas, in case one vehicle gets stuck or breaks down. Some of the more relevant techniques include:

Driving in sand If you're in a 4x4 and are really struggling in deep sand, then stop on the next fairly solid area that you come to. Lower your tyre pressure until there is a small bulge in the tyre walls (having first made sure that you have the means to re-inflate them when you reach solid roads again). A lower pressure will help your traction greatly, but increase the wear on your tyres. Pump them up again before you drive on a hard surface at speed, or the tyres will be badly damaged.

Where there are clear, deep-rutted tracks in the sand, don't fight the steering wheel – just relax and let your vehicle steer itself. Driving in the cool of the morning is easier than later in the day because when sand is cool it compacts better and is firmer. (When hot, the pockets of air between the sand grains expand and the sand becomes looser.)

If you do get stuck, despite these precautions, don't panic. Don't just rev the engine and spin the wheels – you'll only dig deeper. Instead stop. Relax and assess the situation. Now dig shallow ramps in front of all the wheels, reinforcing them with pieces of wood, vegetation, stones, material or anything else which will give the wheels better traction. Lighten the vehicle load (passengers out) and push. Don't let the engine revs die as you engage your lowest-ratio gear. That probably means using '4x4 low' rather than '4x4 high'. Use the clutch to ensure that the wheels don't spin wildly and dig themselves further into the sand.

Sometimes rocking the vehicle backwards and forwards will build up momentum to break you free. This can be done by the driver intermittently applying the clutch and/or by getting helpers who can push and pull the vehicle at the same frequency. Once the vehicle is moving, the golden rule of sand driving is to keep up the momentum: if you pause, you will sink and stop.

Navigation note Remember that your fuel consumption when driving in sand is much higher than on harder surfaces. Also, when navigating on sandy roads observe that your wheels slip and spin, and so your milometer will register a much greater distance than you have actually travelled. I've generally used a GPS to track distances for this book – not a vehicle's milometer.

Driving through high grass After the rains, many of Zambia's tracks are often knee-high in seeding grass. As your vehicle drives through, stems and especially seeds can build up in front of and inside the radiator, and get trapped in crevices underneath the chassis. This is a major problem in the less-visited areas of Kalahari sand. It's at its worst in March to June, after the rains, and in western Zambia and Kafue.

This causes a real danger of overheating (see below) and fire. First, the build-up of seeds and stems over the radiator insulates it. Thus, if you aren't watching your gauges, the engine's temperature can rocket. It will swiftly seize up and catch fire. Secondly, the grass build-up itself, if allowed to become too big, can catch fire due to its contact with the hot exhaust system, underneath the vehicle.

In addition to the obvious precaution of carrying a fire extinguisher, there are several strategies to minimise these dangers; best apply them all. Firstly, before you set out, buy a few square metres of the tightly woven window-meshing gauze material used in the windows of safari tents. Fix one large panel of this on the vehicle's bull-bars, well in front of the radiator grill. Fix another much closer to it, but still outside of the engine compartment. This should vastly reduce the number of seeds reaching your radiator.

Secondly, watch your vehicle's engine-temperature gauge like a hawk when you're travelling through areas of grassland.

Thirdly, stop every 10km or so (yes, really, that often) and check the radiator and the undercarriage for pockets of stems and seeds. Pay special attention to the hot areas of the exhaust pipe; you should not allow a build-up of flammable material there. Use a stick or piece of wire to clean these seeds and stems out before you set off.

When driving through the grass, take particular care to avoid hidden obstacles, which can inflict considerable damage to your vehicle. Watch out too, for bush fires, which can move rapidly and make some roads impassable for a while.

Driving in mud This is difficult, though the theory is the same as for sand: keep going and don't stop. That said, even the most experienced drivers get stuck. Many areas of Zambia (like large stretches of the Kafue, Luangwa and Lower Zambezi

6

valleys) have very fine soil known as 'black-cotton' soil, which becomes impassable when wet. This is why many of the camps close down for the rains, as the only way to get there would be to walk.

Mud can also have the same overheating effect as grass seed, so it's important to wash it away from the radiator once you stop.

Push-starting when stuck If you are unlucky enough to need to push-start your vehicle whilst it is stuck in sand or mud, there is a remedy. Raise up the drive wheels, and take off one of the tyres. Then wrap a length of rope around the hub and treat it like a spinning top: one person (or more) pulls the rope to make the axle spin, whilst the driver lifts the clutch, turns the ignition on, and engages a low gear to turn the engine over. This is a very difficult equivalent of a push-start, but it may be your only option.

On rocky terrain Have your tyre pressure higher than normal and move very slowly. If necessary, passengers should get out and guide you along the track to avoid scraping the undercarriage on the ground. This can be a very slow business, but often applies in some of Zambia's mountainous areas.

Crossing rivers The first thing to do is to stop and check the river. You must assess its depth, its substrate (type of riverbed) and its current flow; and determine the best route to drive across it. This is best done by wading across the river (whilst watching for hippos and crocodiles, if necessary). Beware of water that's too deep for your vehicle, or the very real possibility of being swept away by a fast current and a slippery substrate.

If everything is OK then select your lowest gear ratio and drive through the water at a slow but steady rate. Your vehicle's air intake must be above the level of the water to avoid your engine filling with water. It's not worth taking risks, so remember that a flooded river may subside to safer levels by the next morning.

Many rivers in Zambia have pontoon crossings capable of ferrying vehicles across. Traditionally these are hand-operated wooden platforms tied on top of buoyant empty oil cans and kept in line by steel cables stretched across the river. Nowadays, on the busier crossings, such structures are often motorised, with a steel superstructure, but in many cases the cables remain. The pontoons are usually manned by local people for either a large official charge (Kw56,000 per vehicle is fairly average) or – occasionally – a handsome tip. You need to take great care (everybody out, use first gear) when driving on and off these, and make sure that the pontoon is held tightly next to the bank on both occasions.

Overheating If the engine has overheated then the only option is to stop and turn it off. Don't open the radiator cap to refill it until the radiator is no longer hot to the touch. Even then, keep the engine running and the water circulating while you refill the radiator – otherwise you run the risk of cracking the hot metal by suddenly cooling it. Flicking droplets of water onto the outside of a running engine will cool it. And see *Driving through high grass* above.

DRIVING NEAR BIG GAME The only animals which are likely to pose a threat to vehicles are elephants – and generally only elephants which are familiar with vehicles. So, treat them with the greatest respect and don't 'push' them by trying to move ever closer. Letting them approach you is much safer, and they will feel far less threatened and more relaxed. Then, if the animals are calm, you can safely turn the engine off, sit quietly, and watch as they pass you by.

If you are unlucky, or foolish, enough to unexpectedly drive into the middle of a herd, then don't panic. Keep your movements, and those of the vehicle, slow and measured. Back off steadily. Don't be panicked, or overly intimidated, by a mock charge – this is just their way of frightening you away. Professionals will sometimes switch their engines off, but this is not for the faint-hearted.

▲ BUSH CAMPING

Many 'boy scout'-type manuals have been written on survival in the bush, usually by military veterans. If you are stranded with a convenient multi-purpose knife, then these useful tomes will describe how you can build a shelter from branches, catch passing animals for food, and signal to the inevitable rescue planes which are combing the globe looking for you – whilst avoiding the attentions of hostile forces.

In Zambia, bush camping is usually less about survival than comfort. You're likely to have much more than the knife: probably at least a bulging backpack, if not a loaded 4x4. Thus the challenge is not to camp and survive, it is to camp and be as comfortable as possible. With practice you'll learn how, but a few hints may be useful for the less experienced.

WHERE YOU CAN CAMP In frequently visited national parks, there are designated campsites that you should use, as directed by the local game scouts. Elsewhere the rules are less obvious, though it is normal to ask the scouts, and get their permission, for any site that you have in mind.

Outside of the parks, you should ask the local landowner, or village head, if they are happy for you to camp on their property. If you explain patiently and politely what you want, then you are unlikely to meet anything but warm hospitality from most rural Zambians. They will normally be as fascinated with your way of life as you are with theirs. Company by your campfire is virtually assured.

CHOOSING A SITE Only experience will teach you how to choose a good site for pitching a tent, but a few points may help you avoid a lot of problems:

* Avoid camping on what looks like a path through the bush, however indistinct. It may be a well-used game trail.
* Beware of camping in dry riverbeds: dangerous flash floods can arrive with little or no warning.
* In marshy areas camp on higher ground to avoid cold, damp mists in the morning and evening.
* Camp a reasonable distance from water: near enough to walk to it, but far enough to avoid animals which arrive to drink.
* If a lightning storm is likely, make sure that your tent is not the highest thing around.
* Finally, choose a site which is as flat as possible – you will find sleeping much easier.

CAMPFIRES Campfires can create a great atmosphere and warm you on a cold evening, but they can also be damaging to the environment and leave unsightly piles of ash and blackened stones. Deforestation is a major concern in much of the developing world, including parts of Zambia, so if you do light a fire then use wood as the locals do: sparingly. If you have a vehicle, consider buying firewood in advance from people who sell it at the roadside.

If you collect it yourself, then take only dead wood, nothing living. Never just pick up a log: always roll it over first, checking carefully for snakes or scorpions.

Experienced campers build small, highly efficient fires by using a few large stones to absorb, contain and reflect the heat, and gradually feeding just a few thick logs into the centre to burn. Cooking pots can be balanced on the stones, or at the point where the logs meet and burn. Other campers will use a small trench, lined with rocks, to similar effect. Either technique takes practice, but is worth perfecting. Whichever you do, bury the ashes, take any rubbish with you when you leave, and make the site look as if you had never been there.

Don't expect an unattended fire to frighten away wild animals – that works in Hollywood, but not in Africa. A campfire may help your feelings of insecurity, but lion and hyena will disregard it with stupefying nonchalance.

Finally, do be hospitable to any locals who appear. Despite your efforts to seek permission for your camp, you may effectively be staying in their back gardens.

USING A TENT (OR NOT) Whether to use a tent or to sleep in the open is a personal choice, dependent upon where you are. In an area where there are predators around (specifically lion and hyena) then you should use a tent – and sleep *completely* inside it, as a protruding leg may seem like a tasty takeaway to a hungry hyena. This is especially true at organised campsites, where the local animals are so used to humans that they have lost much of their inherent fear of man.

Outside game areas, you will be fine sleeping in the open, or preferably under a mosquito net, with just the stars of the African sky above you. On the practical side, sleeping under a tree will reduce the morning dew that settles on your sleeping bag. If your vehicle has a large, flat roof then sleeping on this will provide you with peace of mind, and a star-filled outlook. (Hiring a vehicle with a built-in rooftop tent would seem like a perfect solution, until you want to take a drive whilst leaving your camp intact.)

CAMPING EQUIPMENT If you are taking an organised safari, you will not need any camping equipment at all. However, for those travelling independently very little kit is available in Zambia. So buy high-quality equipment beforehand as it will save you a lot of time and trouble once you arrive. Here are a few comments on various essentials.

Tent During the rains a good tent is essential in order to stay dry. Even during the dry season one is useful if there are lion or hyena around. If backpacking, invest in a high-quality, lightweight tent. Mosquito-netting ventilation panels, allowing a good flow of air, are essential. (Just a corner of mesh at the top of the tent is not enough for comfort.) Don't go for a tent that's small; it may feel cosy at home, but will be hot and claustrophobic in the heat.

I have been using the same Spacepacker tent, manufactured by Robert Saunders Ltd (*Five Oaks Lane, Chigwell, Essex IG7 4QP, UK; www.robertsaunders.co.uk*) for over ten years. It's a dome tent with fine mesh doors on either side which allow a through draught, making all the difference when temperatures are high. The alternative to a good tent is a mosquito net, which is fine unless it is raining or you are in a big game area.

Sleeping bag A lightweight, 'three-season' sleeping bag is ideal for Zambia, unless you are heading up to the Nyika Plateau in winter where the nights freeze. Down is preferable to synthetic fillings for most of the year, as it packs smaller, is lighter, and feels more luxurious to sleep in. However, when down gets wet it loses its efficiency, so bring a good synthetic bag if you are likely to encounter much rain.

Ground mat A ground mat of some sort is essential. It keeps you warm and comfortable, and it protects the tent's groundsheet from rough or stony ground. (Do put it underneath the tent!) Closed cell foam mats are widely available outside Zambia, so buy one before you arrive. The better mats cost double or treble the price of the cheaper ones, but are stronger, thicker and warmer – well worth the investment. Therm-a-Rests, the combination air-mattress and foam mats, are strong, durable and also worth the investment – but take a puncture repair kit with you just in case of problems.

Sheet sleeping bag Thin, pure-cotton sheet sleeping bags (eg: YHA design) are small, light and very useful. They are easily washed and so are normally used like a sheet, inside a sleeping bag, to keep it clean. They can, of course, be used on their own when your main sleeping bag is too hot.

Stove 'Trangia'-type stoves, which burn methylated spirits, are simple to use, light, and cheap to run. They come complete with a set of light aluminium pans and a very useful all-purpose handle. Often you'll be able to cook on a fire with the pans, but it's nice to have the option of making a brew in a few minutes while you set up camp. Methylated spirits is cheap and widely available, even in the rural areas, but bring a tough (purpose-made) fuel container with you as the bottles in which it is sold will soon crack and spill all over your belongings.

Petrol- and kerosene-burning stoves are undoubtedly efficient on fuel and powerful – but invariably temperamental and messy. Gas stoves use pressurised canisters, which are not allowed on aircraft and are difficult to buy in Zambia.

Torch (flashlight) This should be on every visitor's packing list. Find one that's small and tough, preferably water- and dust-proof. Head-mounted torches leave your hands free (useful when cooking or mending the car) but some people find them bulky and uncomfortable to wear. The small, strong and super-bright torches (eg: Maglites) are excellent, but their bulbs are difficult to buy in Zambia. Bring several spares with you.

Those with vehicles will find that a strong spotlight, powered by the car's battery (perhaps through the socket for the cigarette lighter), is invaluable for impromptu lighting.

Water containers For everyday use, a small two-litre water bottle is invaluable, however you are travelling. If you're thinking of camping, you should also consider a strong, collapsible water-bag – perhaps 5–10 litres in size – which will reduce the number of trips that you need to make from your camp to the water source. (Ten litres of water weighs 10kg.) Drivers will want to carry a number of large containers of water, especially if venturing into the Kalahari sand in western Zambia, where good surface water is not common.

See *Planning and preparation*, pages 56–7, for a memory-jogging list of other useful items to pack.

ANIMAL DANGERS FOR CAMPERS Camping in Africa is really very safe, though you may not think so from reading this. If you have a major problem whilst camping, it will probably be because you did something stupid, or because you forgot to take a few simple precautions. Here are a few general basics, applicable to anywhere in Africa and not just Zambia.

Large animals Big game will not bother you if you are in a tent – provided that you do not attract its attention, or panic it. Elephants will gently tiptoe through your guy ropes whilst you sleep, without even nudging your tent. However, if you wake up and make a noise, startling them, they are far more likely to panic and step on your tent. Similarly, scavengers will quietly wander round, smelling your evening meal in the air, without any intention of harming you. Bear the following precautions in mind:

* Remember to use the toilet before going to bed, and avoid getting up in the night if possible.
* Scrupulously clean everything used for food that might smell good to scavengers. Put these utensils in a vehicle if possible, suspend them from a tree, or pack them away in a rucksack inside the tent.
* Do not keep any smelly foodstuffs, like meat or citrus fruit, in your tent. Their smells may attract unwanted attention.
* Do not leave anything outside that could be picked up – like bags, pots, pans, etc. Hyenas, amongst others, will take anything. (They have been known to crunch a camera's lens, and eat it.)
* If you are likely to wake in the night, then leave the tent's zips a few centimetres open at the top, enabling you to take a quiet peek outside.

Creepy-crawlies As you set up camp, clear stones or logs out of your way with great caution: underneath will be great hiding places for snakes and scorpions. Long moist grass is ideal territory for snakes, and dry, dusty, rocky places are classic sites for scorpions.

If you are sleeping in the open, it is not unknown to wake and find a snake lying next to you in the morning. Don't panic: your warmth has just attracted it to you. You will not be bitten if you gently edge away without making any sudden movements. (This is one good argument for using at least a mosquito net!)

Before you put on your shoes, shake them out. Similarly, check the back of your backpack before you slip it on. Just a curious spider, in either, could inflict a painful bite.

☀ WALKING IN THE BUSH

Walking in the African bush is a totally different sensation from driving through it. You may start off a little unready – perhaps even sleepy – for an early morning walk, but swiftly your mind will awake. There are no noises except the wildlife, and you. So every noise that isn't caused by you must be an animal, or a bird, or an insect. Every smell and every rustle has a story to tell, if you can understand it.

With time, patience and a good guide you can learn to smell the presence of elephants, and hear when a predator alarms impala. You can use ox-peckers to lead you to buffalo, or vultures to help you locate a kill. Tracks will record the passage of animals in the sand, telling what passed by, how long ago and in which direction.

Eventually your gaze becomes alert to the slightest movement, your ears aware of every sound. This is safari at its best: a live, sharp, spine-tingling experience that's hard to beat and very addictive. Be careful: watching game from a vehicle will never be the same again for you.

WALKING TRAILS AND SAFARIS One of Zambia's biggest attractions is its walking safaris, which can justly claim to be amongst the best in Africa. The concept was pioneered here, in the Luangwa Valley, by the late Norman Carr. He also founded Nsefu Camp and Kapani Lodge, and trained several of the valley's best guides. It was he who first operated walking safaris for photographic guests, as opposed to hunters. The Luangwa still has a strong tradition of walking – which, in itself, fosters excellent walking guides. Several of the camps are dedicated to walking safaris, and guiding standards are generally very high.

One of the reasons behind the valley's success is the stringent tests that a guide must pass before he, or she, will be allowed to take clients into the bush. Walking guides have the hardest tests to pass; there is a less demanding exam for guides who conduct safaris from vehicles.

The second major reason for excellence is Zambia's policy of having a safari guide and an armed game scout accompany every walking safari. These groups are limited (by park rules) to a maximum of seven guests, and there's normally a tea-bearer (carrying drinks and refreshments) as well as the guide and armed scout.

If a problem arises with an aggressive animal, then the guide looks after the visitors – telling them exactly what to do – whilst the scout keeps his sights trained on the animal, just in case a shot is necessary. Fortunately such drastic measures are needed only rarely. This system of two guides means that Zambia's walks are very safe. Few shots are ever fired, and I can't remember hearing of an animal (or a person) ever being injured.

Contrast this with other African countries where a single guide (who may, or may not, be armed) watches out for the game *and* takes care of the visitors at the same time. The Zambian way is far better.

Etiquette for walking safaris If you plan to walk then avoid wearing any bright, unnatural colours, especially white. Dark, muted shades are best; greens, browns and khaki are ideal. Hats are essential, as is sunblock. Even a short walk will last for two hours, and there's no vehicle to which you can retreat if you get too hot.

Binoculars should be immediately accessible – one pair per person – ideally in dust-proof cases strapped to your belt. Cameras too, if you decide to bring any, as they are of little use buried at the bottom of a camera bag. Heavy tripods or long lenses are a nightmare to lug around, so leave them behind if you can (and accept, philosophically, that you may miss shots).

Walkers see the most when walking in silent single file. This doesn't mean that you can't stop to whisper a question to the guide; just that idle chatter will reduce your powers of observation, and make you even more visible to the animals (who will usually flee when they sense you).

With regard to safety, your guide will always brief you in detail before you set off. S/he will outline possible dangers, and what to do in the unlikely event of them materialising. Listen carefully: this is vital.

Face-to-face animal encounters Whether you are on an organised walking safari, on your own hike, or just walking from the car to your tent in the bush, it is not unlikely that you will come across some of Africa's larger animals at close quarters. Invariably, the danger is much less than you imagine, and a few basic guidelines will enable you to cope effectively with most situations.

First of all, don't panic. Console yourself with the fact that animals are not normally interested in people. You are not their normal food, or their predator. If you do not annoy or threaten them, you will be left alone.

If you are walking to look for animals, then remember that this is their environment and not yours. Animals have evolved in the bush, and their senses are far better attuned to it than yours. To be on less unequal terms, remain alert and try to spot them from a distance. This gives you the option of approaching carefully, or staying well clear.

Finally, the advice of a good guide is far more valuable than the simplistic comments noted here. Animals, like people, are all different. So whilst we can generalise here and say how the 'average' animal will behave, the one that's glaring at you over a small bush may have had a really bad day, and be feeling much grumpier than normal.

That said, here are a few general comments on how to deal with some potentially dangerous situations.

Buffalo This is probably the continent's most dangerous animal to hikers, but there is a difference between the old males, often encountered on their own or in small groups, and large breeding herds.

The former are easily surprised. If they hear or smell something amiss, they will charge without provocation – motivated by a fear that something is sneaking up on them. Buffalo have an excellent sense of smell, but fortunately they are short-sighted. Avoid a charge by quickly climbing the nearest tree, or by side-stepping at the last minute. If adopting the latter, more risky, technique then stand motionless until the last possible moment, as the buffalo may well miss you anyhow.

The large breeding herds can be treated in a totally different manner. If you approach them in the open, they will often flee. Sometimes though, in areas often used for walking safaris, they will stand and watch, moving aside to allow you to pass through the middle of the herd.

Neither encounter is for the faint-hearted or inexperienced, so steer clear of these dangerous animals wherever possible.

Black rhino If you are both exceptionally lucky to find a black rhino, and then unlucky enough to be charged by it, use the same tactics as you would for a buffalo: tree climbing or dodging at the last second. (It is amazing how even the least athletic walker will swiftly scale the nearest tree when faced with a charging rhino.)

Elephant Normally elephants are a problem only if you disturb a mother with a calf, or approach a male in musth (state of arousal). So keep well away from these. Lone bulls can usually be approached quite closely when feeding. If you get too close to any elephant it will scare you off with a 'mock charge': head up, perhaps shaking – ears flapping – trumpeting. Lots of sound and fury. This is intended to be frightening, and it is. But it is just a warning and no cause for panic. Just freeze to assess the elephant's intentions, then back off slowly.

When elephants really mean business, they will put their ears back, their head down, and charge directly at you without stopping. This is known as a 'full charge'. There is no easy way to avoid the charge of an angry elephant, so take a hint from the warning and back off very slowly as soon as you encounter a mock charge. Don't run. If you are the object of a full charge, then you have no choice but to run – preferably round an anthill, up a tall tree, or wherever.

Lion Tracking lion can be one of the most exhilarating parts of a walking safari. Sadly, they will normally flee before you even get close to them. However, it can be a problem if you come across a large pride unexpectedly. Lion are well camouflaged;

it is easy to find yourself next to one before you realise it. If you had been listening, you would probably have heard a warning growl about 20m ago. Now it is too late.

The best plan is to stop, and back off slowly, but confidently. If you are in a small group, then stick together. *Never* run from a big cat. First, they are always faster than you are. Secondly, running will just convince them that you are frightened prey, and worth chasing. As a last resort, if they seem too inquisitive and follow as you back off, then stop. Call their bluff. Pretend that you are not afraid and make loud, deep, confident noises: shout at them, bang something. But do not run.

John Coppinger, one of Luangwa's most experienced guides, adds that every single compromising experience that he has had with lion on foot has been either with a female with cubs, or with a mating pair, when the males can get very aggressive. You have been warned.

Leopard Leopard are very seldom seen, and would normally flee from the most timid of lone hikers. However, if injured, or surprised, then they are very powerful, dangerous cats. Conventional wisdom is scarce, but never stare straight into the leopard's eyes, or it will regard this as a threat display. (The same is said, by some, to be true with lion.) Better to look away slightly, at a nearby bush, or even at its tail. Then back off slowly, facing the direction of the cat and showing as little terror as you can. As with lion – loud, deep, confident noises are a last line of defence. Never run from a leopard.

Hippo Hippo are fabled to account for more deaths in Africa than any other animal (ignoring the mosquito). Having been attacked and capsized by a hippo whilst in a dugout canoe, I find this very easy to believe, but see *Appendix 1* (page 526) for an alternative comment on this. Visitors are most likely to encounter hippo in the water, when paddling a canoe (see *Canoeing*, below) or fishing. However, as they spend half their time grazing on land, they will sometimes be encountered out of the water. Away from the water, out of their comforting lagoons, hippos are even more dangerous. If they see you, they will flee towards the water – so the golden rule is never to get between a hippo and its escape route to deep water. Given that a hippo will outrun you on land, standing motionless is probably your best line of defence.

Snakes These are really not the great danger that people imagine. Most flee when they feel the vibrations of footsteps; only a few will stay still. The puff adder is responsible for more cases of snakebite than any other venomous snake in Zambia because, when approached, it will simply puff itself up and hiss as a warning, rather than slither away. This makes it essential to always watch where you place your feet when walking in the bush.

Similarly, there are a couple of arboreal (tree-dwelling) species which may be taken by surprise if you carelessly grab vegetation as you walk. So don't.

Spitting cobras are also encountered occasionally, which will aim for your eyes and spit with accuracy. If one of these rears up in front of you, then turn away and avert your eyes. If the spittle reaches your eyes, you must wash them out *immediately* and thoroughly with whatever liquid comes to hand. water, milk, even urine if that's the only liquid that you can quickly produce.

⅄ CANOEING

The Zambezi – both above the Victoria Falls and from Kariba to Mozambique – is in constant use for canoeing trips. Paddling along this beautiful, tropical river is as much a part of Zambia's safari scene in the Lower Zambezi as are open-top Land Rovers. Generally you either canoe along the river for a set number of days, stopping each night at a different place, or paddle for a short stretch from one of the camps – as an alternative activity to a walk or a game drive.

Rather than traditional *mekoro* (dug-out canoes, singular *mokoro*), most operators use large, two- or three-person Canadian-style fibreglass canoes. Three-person canoes usually have a guide in the back of each, while two-person canoes are often paddled in 'convoy' with a guide in just one of the boats. Less confident (or lazier) paddlers might prefer to have a guide in their own canoe, while the more energetic usually want to have the boat to themselves.

ZAMBEZI CANOE GUIDES Most of the Zambezi's specialist canoeing operations are run by large companies on a very commercial basis. On these you can expect to join a party of about seven canoes, one of which will contain a guide. S/he should know the stretch of river well and will canoe along it regularly. The actual distances completed on the two-/three-night trips are quite short. All the trips run downstream and a day's canoeing could actually be completed in just three hours with a modicum of fitness and technique.

Like other guides, the 'river guides' must possess a professional licence in order to be allowed to take paying guests canoeing. Note that only a few of the best river guides also hold licences as general professional guides (ie: are licensed to lead walking safaris). These all-rounders generally have a far deeper understanding of the environment and the game than those who are only 'river guides'.

However, their greater skill commands a higher wage – and so they are usually found in the smaller, more upmarket operations. Given the inexperience of some of the river guides, I would always be willing to pay the extra. Although the safety record of river trips is good, accidents do happen occasionally.

THE MAIN DANGERS
Hippo Hippos are strictly vegetarians, and will usually attack a canoe only if they feel threatened. The standard avoidance technique is first of all to let them know that you are there. If in doubt, bang your paddle on the side of the canoe a few times (most novice canoeists will do this constantly anyhow).

During the day, hippopotami will congregate in the deeper areas of the river. The odd ones in shallow water – where they feel less secure – will head for the deeper places as soon as they are aware of a nearby canoe. Avoiding hippos then becomes a fairly simple case of steering around the deeper areas, where the pods will make their presence obvious. This is where experience, and knowing every bend of the river, becomes useful. Problems arise when canoes inadvertently stray over a pod of hippos, or when a canoe cuts a hippo off from its path of retreat into deeper water. Either is dangerous, as hippos will overturn canoes without a second thought, biting them and their occupants. Once in this situation, there are no easy remedies. So – avoid it in the first place.

Crocodiles Crocodiles may have sharp teeth and look prehistoric, but are rarely a danger to a canoeist while in the boat, although the larger, wilier animals can pose a serious threat. If you find yourself in the water, the situation is considerably worse. Then the more you struggle and the more waves you create, the more you will attract their unwelcome attentions. There is a major problem when canoes are overturned by hippos – then you must get out of the water as soon as possible, either into another canoe or onto the bank.

When a crocodile attacks an animal, it will try to disable it, normally by getting a firm, biting grip, submerging, and performing a long, fast barrel-roll. This will disorient the prey, drown it, and probably twist off the limb that has been bitten. In this dire situation, your best line of defence is probably to stab the reptile in its eyes with anything sharp that you have. Alternatively, if you can lift up its tongue and let the water into its lungs whilst it is underwater, then a crocodile will start to drown and will release its prey.

Jo Pope reports that a man survived an attack in the Zambezi when a crocodile grabbed his arm and started to spin backwards into deep water. The man wrapped his legs around the crocodile, to spin with it and avoid having his arm twisted off. As this happened, he tried to poke his thumb into its eyes, but with no effect. Finally he put his free arm into the crocodile's mouth, and opened up the beast's throat. This worked. The crocodile left him and he survived with only a damaged arm. Understandably, anecdotes about tried and tested methods of escape are rare.

MINIMUM IMPACT

When you visit, drive through, or camp in an area and have 'minimum impact' this means that that area is left in the same condition as – or better than – when you entered it. Whilst most visitors view minimum impact as being desirable, spend time to consider the ways in which we contribute to environmental degradation, and how these can be avoided.

DRIVING Use your vehicle responsibly. If there's a road, or a track, then don't go off it – the environment will suffer. Driving off-road can leave a multitude of tracks that detract from the 'wilderness' feeling for subsequent visitors. Equally, don't speed through towns or villages: remember the danger to local children, and the amount of dust you'll cause.

HYGIENE Use toilets if they are provided, even if they are basic longdrop loos with questionable cleanliness. If there are no toilets, then human excrement should always be buried well away from paths, or groundwater, and any tissue used should be burnt and then buried.

If you use rivers or lakes to wash, then soap yourself near the bank, using a pan for scooping water from the river – making sure that no soap finds its way back into the water. Use biodegradable soap. Sand makes an excellent pan-scrub, even if you have no water to spare.

RUBBISH Biodegradable rubbish can be burnt and buried with the campfire ashes. Don't just leave it lying around: it will look very unsightly and spoil the place for those who come after you.

Bring along some plastic bags with which to remove the rest of your rubbish, and dump it at the next town. Items that will not burn, like tin cans, are best cleaned and squashed for easy carrying. If there are bins, then use them, but also consider when they will next be emptied, and if local animals will rummage through them first. Carrying out all your own rubbish may still be the sensible option.

HOST COMMUNITIES Whilst the rules for reducing impact on the environment have been understood and followed by responsible travellers for years, the effects of tourism on local people have only recently been considered. Many tourists believe it is their right, for example, to take intrusive photos of local people – and even become angry if the local people object. They refer to higher prices being charged to tourists as a rip-off, without considering the hand-to-mouth existence of those selling these products or services. They deplore child beggars, then hand out sweets or pens to local children with outstretched hands.

Our behaviour towards 'the locals' needs to be considered in terms of their culture, with the knowledge that we are the uninvited visitors. We visit to enjoy ourselves, but this should not be at the expense of local people. Read *Cultural guidelines*, pages 79–81, and aim to leave the local communities better off after your visit.

LOCAL PAYMENTS If you spend time with any of Zambia's poorer local people, perhaps camping in the bush or getting involved with one of the community-run projects, then take great care with any payments that you make.

First, note that most people like to spend their earnings on what *they* choose. This means that trying to pay for services with beads, food, old clothes or anything else instead of money isn't appreciated. Ask yourself how you'd like to be paid, and you'll understand this point.

Second, find out the normal cost of what you are buying. Most community campsites will have a standard price for a pitch and, if applicable, an hour's guided activity, or whatever. Find this out before you sleep there, or accept the offer of a walk. It is then important that you pay about that amount for the service rendered – no less, and not too much more.

As most people realise, if you try to pay less you'll get into trouble – as you would at home. However, many do not realise that if they generously pay a lot more, this can be equally damaging. Local rates of pay in rural areas can be very low, and a careless visitor can easily pay disproportionately large sums. Where this happens, local jobs can lose their value overnight. (Imagine working hard to become a game scout, only to learn that a tourist has given your friend the equivalent of your whole month's wages for just a few hours guiding. What incentive is there for you to carry on with your regular job?)

If you want to give more – for good service, a super guide, or just because you want to help – then either buy some locally made produce (at the going rate) or donate money to one of the organisations working to improve the lot of Zambia's most disadvantaged (see *Travelling positively*, page 81).

Part Two

THE GUIDE

Voyagers

THE ZAMBIAN EXPERTS

Voyagers is Zambia's number one travel agency and car hire company, offering a service that is inspired by people with firsthand knowledge of Zambia. Convenient and tailored to suit individual requests, visitors travelling with us will experience the best Zambia has to offer.

Voyagers holds the franchise for Europcar in Zambia. We have an impressive fleet, including camper vans and buses, which allows us to cater to all your requirements. We also offer a professional chauffeur service.

Our offices are strategically located throughout Zambia. Should you require any advice or assistance we will be only too willing to help.

Get in touch with the Zambian experts today...

AWARDED **BEST AGENT SOUTHERN AFRICA & INDIAN OCEAN ISLANDS** - SAA TOURISM AWARD 2010/11

LUSAKA	e lusaka@voyagerszambia.com	t +260 211 253064-5/082-4
NDOLA	e ndola@voyagerszambia.com	t +260 212 621333-8
CHINGOLA	e chingola@voyagerszambia.com	t +260 212 311642/722/312195
KITWE	e kitwe@voyagerszambia.com	t +260 212 225056/229102-3

www.voyagerszambia.com

7

Lusaka

Despite the assertions of the tourist board, Lusaka is still not high on Zambia's list of major attractions. Its wide, tree-lined boulevards can be pleasant, but as the city grows the traffic is increasingly chaotic and many of the suburbs are sprawling and dirty. However, Lusaka is no worse than London, New York or any number of other big cities. Like them, it has a fascination because it is unmistakably cosmopolitan, alive and kicking. Now home to almost one in five of Zambia's people, it has a discernible heartbeat which smaller or more sanitised cities lack. So if you go to Zambia with an interest in meeting a cross-section of its people, Lusaka should figure on your itinerary.

In my experience, the city's former bad reputation has been exaggerated. Walking around at night is stupid and potentially dangerous, and during the day pickpockets will strike if you keep valuables obvious or accessible – as they will in any big city. However, as Lusaka has grown and security measures have increased, especially around the growing number of malls, the perceived risks at least have lessened. Visitors to Lusaka who allow their paranoia to elevate the city's dangers to the dizzy heights of Lagos are deluding themselves. It isn't that dangerous, if you are careful.

HISTORY

Lusaka's status as a capital city dates only from 1935. Until then, the capital of Northern Rhodesia had been Livingstone, but as the country's mines were developed it was felt that the town was too far away from the industrial heartland in the Copperbelt.

The site of the new capital was chosen both for its central location and for its position high on a plateau, resulting in a relatively cool climate. There was already a permanent settlement here: Lusaka owes its establishment to construction of the railway at the beginning of the 20th century, when a camp was needed for the workers. The decision to site the new state buildings on the ridge a couple of kilometres to the east of the railway was linked to the frequency with which the lower-lying land was flooded during the rains. While it was anticipated that Lusaka's heart would eventually shift east, the capital remained firmly divided, with its spacious new administrative area contrasting with the bustle of the business area focused on Cairo Road. Now commercial developments have combined with increasing levels of affluence to shift the focus once again – blurring the traditional divides and opening up new areas both close to the centre and out towards the suburbs.

GETTING THERE AND AWAY

BY AIR Lusaka (airline code LUN) is reasonably well served by international flights. Currently British Airways is the main intercontinental airline connecting

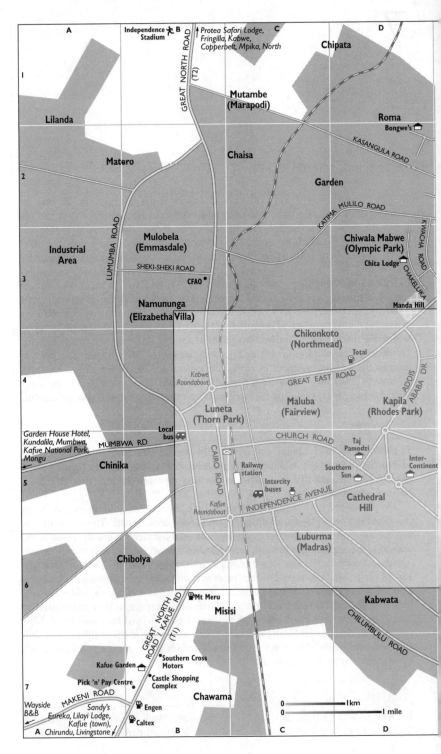

A   **B**   **C**   **D**

Independence ⚥ **B**   ↑ *Protea Safari Lodge,*
Stadium   *Fringilla, Kabwe,*
    Copperbelt, Mpika, North   **C**

Chipata

I

Lilanda

Mutambe
(Marapodi)

Roma
Bongwe's 🏠

KASANGULA ROAD

Matero

Chaisa

2

Garden

KATIMA MULILO ROAD

Industrial
Area

Mulobela
(Emmasdale)

Chiwala Mabwe
(Olympic Park)

Chita Lodge 🏠

SHEKI-SHEKI ROAD

3

CFAO •

Manda Hill

Namununga
(Elizabetha Villa)

Chikonkoto
(Northmead)

Total ⛽

Kabwe
Roundabout

GREAT EAST ROAD

ADDIS ABABA DR

4

Luneta
(Thorn Park)

Maluba
(Fairview)

Kapila
(Rhodes Park)

Garden House Hotel,
Kundalila, Mumbwa,
Kafue National Park,
Mongu

Local 🚌
bus

MUMBWA RD

CHURCH ROAD

Taj
Pamodzi 🏠

Inter-
Continent

Chinika

Railway
station 🏢

Southern
Sun 🏠

5

CAIRO ROAD

Intercity
buses 🚌

INDEPENDENCE AVENUE

Cathedral
Hill

Kafue
Roundabout

Luburma
(Madras)

Chibolya

6

Kabwata

Mt Meru 🏠

Misisi

CHILUMBULU ROAD

GREAT NORTH ROAD / KAFUE RD (T1)

• Southern Cross
Motors

Kafue Garden 🏠

• Castle Shopping
Complex

Pick 'n' Pay Centre •

7

Wayside
B&B

🚌 Engen

Chawama

MAKENI ROAD

🚌 Caltex

Sandy's
Eureka, Lilayi Lodge,
Kafue (town),
Chirundu, Livingstone

| 0 | | 1 km |
| 0 | | 1 mile |

A   **B**   **C**   **D**

E   F   G   H

I

NGWEZI RD

La Revolución ✕

Ngombe

LUKANGA

Kalundu

ZAMBEZI

IBALA ROAD

LUSIWASI

NANESHILA

Mwambula

Reed Mat

Chelston, Airport
Pioneer Camp,
Chipata, Mfuwe,
South Luangwa NP

2

Juls

Mwambula

Mika

GREAT EAST ROAD (T4)

Comfort
Lodge

*Munali
Roundabout*

Great East

Radisson

GREAT EAST ROAD

Golfview

Ody's

*Acacia
Park*

Munali

Arcades

BP Protea

• University
of Zambia

KALINGALINGA ROAD

▶ Chainama Hills
Golf Course

3

(T4) ✕ Sichuan

THABO MBEKI RD

Showgrounds

NANGWENYA ROAD

Kalingalinga

Mutendere

Total

4

ALICK NKHATA ROAD

Total

• Air Force base

HAILE SELASSIE
AVENUE

Kabulonga

SABLE ROAD

Lusaka Trust
Hospital

5

tal

LOS ANGELES BOULEVARD

Lusaka
Golf
▶ Club

Muskaan
✕

Dutch
Reform ✝

KABULONGA ROAD

8 Reedbuck

REEDBUCK

Dil, US Embassy

BP

Ridgeway

• State House

Kabulonga
Shopping centre

CHINDO ROAD

LAKE ROAD

⊞ Hospital

pages 130–1

LEOPARDS HILL ROAD

Serenity

Belvedere

6

Cemetery

BURMA ROAD

INDEPENDENCE AVENUE

CHINDO RD

Kaingo

Crossroads

Engen

LAKE RD

Woodlands

BP

LEOPARDS

Woodlands

7

Libala

CHILUMBULU ROAD

N

Bradt

*Kilimanjaro,
Adventure City,
Jackal & Hide,
LZNP (4x4 only)*

E   F   G   H

Europe direct with Zambia, but other carriers are possible if you use Nairobi or Johannesburg as gateways to the continent. See *Planning and Preparation*, page 50, for more details of the best fares to Zambia, and pages 64–6 for local airlines, and general comments on getting around the country by air.

International airlines Airlines represented in Lusaka include:

✈ **Air Botswana** ✆0211 227739/40, 227285; www.airbotswana.co.bw
✈ **Air Malawi** ✆0211 228120/1; www.airmalawi.com
✈ **British Airways** ✆0211 254444; www.britishairways.com
✈ **Ethiopian Airline** ✆0211 236401/235761; www.ethiopianairlines.com
✈ **Kenya Airways/KLM** ✆0211 228908/228886, airport✆0211 271042; www.kenya-airways.com

✈ **South African Airways** ✆0211 254350; airport✆0211 271101; www.flysaa.com
✈ **TAAG-Angolan Airways** ✆0211 222401/ 221684
✈ **Zambezi Airlines Airport** ✆0211 256735/ 271226/271149/271160, InterContinental Hotel ✆0211 250329, Downtown Shopping Centre ✆0211 234180; e reservations@flyzambezi.com; www.flyzambezi.com.

Local airlines and charter companies The charter companies and local airlines based in Lusaka have had a chequered past, with companies forming and disappearing with monotonous regularity. The current contenders – of which Proflight are by far the largest and most organised – wisely stick mainly to domestic routes. For details of these and other operators, see *Chapter 4, Planning and preparation*, pages 65–6.

Lusaka Airport The airport is well signposted, if isolated, 25km east of the city's major hotels, off the Great East Road. Transport there is either by shuttle bus from one of the big hotels (Taj Pamodzi, InterContinental or Southern Sun Ridgeway), or via the Platinum Shuttle (m *0979 069571, 0966 249299*) or by private taxi. The Platinum service runs up to six times a day between the airport and the Golfview, Arcades, Southern Sun Ridgeway and downtown Lusaka, with one-way fares at Kw50,000 per person. This slightly undercuts the hotel shuttles which cost about US$20 per person one way, while a taxi for the same journey should cost around US$40 for up to four passengers (though this is the route for which the drivers will charge most imaginatively). At weekends, the journey takes only about 20 minutes, but during the week – and especially at peak periods – you should allow at least double that time because of the traffic. If you're driving yourself, note that the speed limit between Lusaka and the airport is 80km/h, rising to 100km/h, and there are frequent speed traps. Parking at the airport costs Kw5,000 per day, though rates are higher in the secure area, where you'll need to book.

In addition to offices for all the main airlines, facilities at the airport include a post office, and desks for the major car-hire companies: Avis and Voyagers (representing Europcar). There are also two banks, one with a 24-hour ATM, and a couple of gift shops.

In the departure lounge upstairs it's well worth the cost of a drink to take advantage of the comfortable seating in the bar/café. Also on hand are a duty-free shop and several gift shops – including an outlet for Tribal Textiles.

BY BUS
Long-distance coaches and buses Zambia's buses fall broadly into two categories. Comfortable, long-distance coaches, often with air conditioning, ply the

longer routes, operating to a timetable and generally keeping good time. Rather less well-maintained vehicles may cover the same ground, but may wait until they're full before leaving. Both now operate out of the **Intercity Bus Terminal** [130 B5]on the western side of Dedan Kimathi Road, near the railway station. It's a noisy, bustling station sheltering under a large purpose-built roof, and the place to catch a bus to virtually any of Zambia's provincial or district capitals, even those that are quite isolated such as Nakonde or Kashikishi.

Locals are paranoid about thieves who frequent the area, so expect warnings about safety. It is certainly not a place to go idly strolling at night, or to display your valuables, but if you keep your wits about you, and keep a firm eye on your belongings, then you should have no problems. Be aware, though, that ticket touts can be quite aggressive in their bid for your custom, so be firm if you haven't made up your mind.

Despite the apparent confusion that greets you, there is some order to the terminal's chaos. The buses sitting in bays are grouped roughly by their eventual destinations, as indicated on the boards displayed next to the driver. If you can't see the name you want, then ask someone – most people will go out of their way to help, and the staff on the 24-hour information desk (☏ 0211 226676) are usually very helpful. While in theory you can phone for details of buses, in practice it's far better to turn up in person.

Coach operators tend to come and go, so it's best to ask around the city's travel agents or at the bus station itself for the latest news, including details of services to South Africa. Carriers include the well-recommended Mazhandu Family Buses (m 0977 805064; www.mazhandubuses.com), which accept online reservations, and Juldan Motors (m 0955 776315; e juldans@zamnet.zm). CR buses (☏ 0211 288427), RPS (☏ 0211 235550) and Euro-Africa are also major operators, but there are numerous regional variations, some better than others. The first departures tend to be early in the morning, around 05.00, and are fairly punctual; it's advisable to be there half an hour ahead of the listed departure time. The best are well maintained and comfortable, with air conditioning and on-board toilet, and they tend to reach their destinations in good time – albeit sometimes at high speed.

For some (but not all) long-distance buses, you will need to buy a **ticket** at the terminus in advance. There are often different prices for any given place, depending on the company, the standard of the bus, and the speed of service, and the cost of a return ticket may differ from that of the outward journey. Expect about a 20% premium for the better companies. Tickets are on sale the day beforehand, and the buses run to a timetable – in theory. In reality, many buses may not leave until they are full, which can take hours. If this is the case, try to avoid paying until the bus has started on its way, as you may want to swap buses if another appears to be filling faster and hence is likely to depart earlier.

Buses to some destinations leave frequently, others weekly – according to demand. The best way to find out is to go to the bus station and ask. There are regular services between Lusaka and Livingstone, and Lusaka and the Copperbelt, as well as east to Chipata. Just a few of the many options, with approximate one-way fares (which can vary considerably), include:

To/from Livingstone Several buses a day run between Livingstone and Lusaka, some of them fast, modern coaches which run to a timetable. The journey takes about six hours, and a ticket costs up to Kw115,000, depending on the speed and standard of service. There is also usually at least one operator running fast, air-conditioned coaches between Livingstone and Kitwe, via Lusaka. Operators change regularly, so ask locally before you travel. The best is Mazhandu, but others include CR, Shalom and Booker.

To/from the Copperbelt and beyond Several buses a day, mostly in the morning and early afternoon, head from Lusaka to Kitwe via Kabwe, Kapiri Mposhi and Ndola, taking approximately six hours. Some services then continue on to Chingola and Solwezi. Approximately Kw55,000 to Kapiri Mposhi, Kw65,000 to Ndola, Kw70,000 to Kitwe.

To Chipata Up to eight buses a day. Reliable operators are Johabbee & Kobs, departing at 06.00 and 07.00 daily. Kw130,000 one way.

To Kashikishi Via Kabwe, Kapiri Mposhi, Serenje, Samfya, Mansa and Nchelenge; also to Kawambwa. Bus operators include Juldan Motors and Germins. Five buses a day, departing around 16.00. Serenje Kw110,000, Mansa Kw150,000, Kashikishi Kw180,000.

To Mongu Normally eight buses per day, at 09.30 and 13.30. Kw100,000.

To Mpulungu Four buses a day via Kasama and Mbala. Operators include the recommended Juldan Motors. Depart around 16.00. Kw180,000.

To Sesheke Departures at 06.30 and 19.30 with Mazhandu and CR. Kw105,000–125,000.

A few **international buses** also leave from here, travelling to Johannesburg, Harare, Lilongwe and Blantyre in Malawi, and Dar es Salaam.

Postbuses The post office has continued to expand its scheduled passenger bus service, on which vehicles stop only at post offices. These run to a timetable, so are generally quicker than the normal buses, and less crowded; some are brand-new vehicles. Tickets are available from the bus station in Lusaka, just behind the main post office on Cairo Road [130 B4]. Those from Lusaka to Ndola or Livingstone may be bought on the day of departure, but all others must be pre-booked either in Lusaka or at local post offices where the buses stop, ideally two to three days before departure. Postbuses stop only at post offices; you cannot hail them from the roadside.

Services currently run on the following routes, returning to Lusaka the following day. Fares quoted here are for the full journey; if you alight at a town *en route*, fares are reduced proportionately.

Lusaka to Chipata Lusaka – Petauke – Sinda – Katete – Nyimba – Luangwa – Chipata. Depart Tuesday, Thursday and Saturday at 07.00, arriving in Chipata at 14.00. Kw90,000 one way.

Lusaka to Ndola Lusaka – Kabwe – Kapiri Mposhi – Ndola. Depart Monday to Saturday at 07.00, 07.30, 08.00, 13.00, and also 14.00 Tuesday, Thursday and Saturday. Kw50,000 one way.

Lusaka to Kasama Lusaka – Mkushi – Serenje – Mpika – Kasama. Depart Monday, Wednesday and Friday at 06.30, arriving at Kasama at 17.00. Kw110,000 one way.

Lusaka to Livingstone Lusaka – Mazabuka – Monze – Chisikesi – Pemba – Batoka/Choma – Kalomo – Livingstone. Depart Monday, Wednesday and Friday at 09.30, returning Tuesday, Thursday and Saturday at 09.30. Outward bound tickets are Kw90,000; return tickets to Lusaka Kw70,000.

Ndola to Livingstone via Lusaka Depart Monday, Wednesday and Friday at 05.00. Kw140,000 one way.

BY TRAIN Ordinary passenger trains connect Lusaka with Livingstone, and with Kitwe in the Copperbelt, but for most travellers they are far too slow and totally impractical.

Trains to Livingstone leave Lusaka at 00.30 on Monday and Friday, arriving in Livingstone 24 hours later. The return train arrives back in Lusaka at midnight. Heading north, trains to Kitwe leave Lusaka at 14.00 on Tuesday and Saturday, reaching Kitwe the next day at 14.30. Fares are Kw40,000 to Livingstone and K32,000 to Kitwe, so at least it's cheap.

The regular, efficient TAZARA trains to Tanzania are different. They leave from Kapiri Mposhi, not Lusaka (see pages 395–6 for details), but tickets are also available with rather less hassle in Lusaka at Tazara House ([130 B5] *Independence Av; www.tazarasite.com;* ⊕ *07.30–16.30 Mon–Fri*); the entrance gate is on Dedan Kimathi Road. The current timetable is usually displayed on a noticeboard outside, to the left of the door, but if not, take a look in the hall on the second floor.

DRIVING FROM LIVINGSTONE For details of getting to Lusaka by road from Livingstone, see *Chapter 9*, pages 213–19.

ORIENTATION

Lusaka is very spread out, so get hold of a good map when you first arrive (see *Maps*, below). Its business heart is the axis of Cairo Road, which runs roughly north–south. This is about six lanes of traffic wide, 4km long, and has a useful pedestrian island which runs like a spine down its centre. Parallel to Cairo Road, to the west, is Chachacha Road – a terminus for numerous local minibuses and home to the lively Central Market, while west again, on Lumumba Road, is the larger New City Market.

Completely separate, about 2km to the east, is the much larger, more diffuse 'Government Area'. It is linked to Cairo Road by Independence Avenue, and centres on the areas of Cathedral Hill and Ridgeway. Here you will find the established big international-standard hotels, government departments and embassies set in a lot more space. It has a different atmosphere from the bustle of Cairo Road: the quiet and official air that you often find in diplomatic or administrative corners of capitals around the world. Then, a little further east again, you'll find the modern shopping malls at Manda Hill and the Arcades, both situated on the Great East Road.

MAPS A limited selection of Zambia's most commonly used maps can be found at one of the city's bookshops (see page 145), which – more importantly – also sell the recommended street atlas of Lusaka and Livingstone published by Streetwise at Kw35,000.

Detailed maps covering the whole of Zambia can be bought cheaply from the main government map office at the Ministry of Lands (*basement of Mulungushi Hse, cnr Independence Av & Nationalist Rd;* ⊕ *08.30–12.00, 14.00–16.30 Mon–Fri*). Prices are around Kw20,000–30,000 per map. Aside from the normal 'Ordnance

Survey'-type maps, special tourist maps are available on request. To see what's in stock, browse through the maps in the entrance area before choosing. The detailed street map of Lusaka held by the office has now been superseded by commercial mapping, but for trips venturing beyond Lusaka, and particularly off the main roads, you'll simply have to come here and buy up a selection of the 1:250,000 series, or for serious expeditions, the more detailed 1:50,000 sheets. They're generally very good, though their information is inevitably dated.

GETTING AROUND

If you don't have your own vehicle you'll probably need to use taxis, and/or the small minibuses that ply between the outer suburbs/townships and the centre. If you are careful, then these are very useful and quite safe. The other possibility is to hire a car with a driver – which is the norm – then the driver can act as a convenient guide for a short trip. As the number of vehicles on the road has increased, traffic congestion has become a major problem, especially in the mornings and evenings. Pick your journey times carefully.

BY TAXI Lusaka's taxis were traditionally small, decrepit Datsuns, held together by remarkable roadside mechanics and lots of improvisation; today, however, they are largely rather less run-down Toyota Corollas. The licensed ones are light blue and white in colour, with a large number painted on their side, but even these have no meters. When taking a taxi, you should agree a rate for the journey before you get into the vehicle; expect to pay around Kw3,250 per kilometre. If you know roughly what it should cost, then most drivers recognise this and don't try to overcharge. As a last resort when bargaining, all licensed taxis should have a rate-sheet, giving the 'standard' prices for waiting time and various common journeys – though drivers will not admit to having one if the bargaining is going their way. Typical fares are:

Kw25,000	between Ridgeway (international hotels) and Manda Hill/ Arcades
Kw25,000	between Ridgeway and Cairo Road
Kw100,000	between the airport and Ridgeway
Kw30,000–40,000	between the centre of town (bus station) and the inner suburbs
Kw30,000	per hour of additional waiting time

If you need a vehicle all day, then consider hiring a taxi with its driver. Start by making a clear deal to pay by the hour or the kilometre, and record the time or the mileage reading. Around Kw30,000 per hour, or Kw3,250 per kilometre, is fair, though a tough negotiator would pay less. Drivers inevitably change, but there's one consistent taxi service that can be booked by phone:

Dial a Cab m 0966 222222, 0977 773937

BY MINIBUS These are the packed transport that the city's poorer commuters use to travel between the outer, satellite suburbs and the centre of town. The blue-and-white vehicles dominate the local traffic scene, fanning out from their bases at City Market [130 A4] and the Kulima Tower on Freedom Way [130 A4], both to the west of Cairo Road, or Downtown – to the south by the Kafue roundabout [130 B5]. The buses are all privately owned, and cover many different routes, so competition between them is fierce. Minibuses are an especially good way to reach the farther-flung suburbs, or to get a lift along one of the main routes out to a good hitching spot. Fares are relatively low, reflecting the cramped seating and general lack of timetable – for the most part, buses leave town only when they are full. There is a minimum fare of Kw2,500.You can expect to pay around Kw3,000 for a journey between Cairo Road and the international hotels, or Kw4,000 to Manda Hill. Minibuses usually have regular stops, but if you're lucky they can sometimes just be flagged down if they're not full.

CAR HIRE See *Vehicle hire* in *Chapter 4*, pages 69–70, for advice and a guide to typical rates. Lusaka's car-hire companies cater more for businesspeople visiting the city than for tourists. Some offer only chauffeur-driven vehicles, and will usually only have time-and-mileage rates rather than the 'unlimited-mileage' rates normally expected by those hiring cars for fly-drive trips. (Which makes sense as you'd have to be insane to hire a 2WD for a fly-drive trip around Zambia.) The larger companies, including some offering 4x4 hire, are:

African Tracks 155 Kabulonga Rd (next to Dil restaurant); 0211 840579; m 0955 755154, 0966 755154, 0977 399551; e saul@milomax. co.za. 4x4 bus transfers & safaris.

Avis Airport 0211 271020; 24hr emergency m 0977 434495; e avis@zamnet.zm; www.avisworld.com. Min age 23.

Juls Car Hire 5507 Libala Rd, Kalundu; 0211 292979/293972; e juls.travel@travelport. co.zm; www.julsafrica.com. Minibuses & 4x4s only, either self drive or chauffeur-driven.

Limo Hire 21 Lilayi Rd; 0211 278628; m 0977 743145; e limohirezambia@gmail.com; www.limohire-zambia.com

Voyagers/Europcar 6941 Suez Rd; 0211 253064–5, airport 0211 253082–4; e lusaka@ voyagerszambia.com; www.voyagerszambia. com. Reliable franchisee for Europcar, with both 2WD & 4x4 vehicles, with or without a driver. For 4x4 hire, see page 70.

ZéDash Southern Sun Ridgeway; 0211 252385; m 0977 857891; e info@zedashtravel.com

DRIVING YOURSELF Traffic in and around Lusaka can be chaotic at the beginning and end of a working day, and accidents are not infrequent. Speed limits on the roads around the city are strictly enforced, with an on-the-spot fine of about Kw180,000 for infringements. Watch out for speed traps, especially along the Great East Road towards the airport where the limit gradually decreases from the initial 100 km/h. In the city centre, though, most drivers would be hard pushed to get anywhere near the urban limit of 50km/h.

Parking on the streets is not a good idea unless you leave someone trustworthy in charge of the vehicle. Far more sensible is to use one of the guarded private car parks. In the vicinity of Cairo Road, this means either the large free area at Central Park, or in front of Shoprite (Kw1,000/hr). Most hotels and guesthouses have secure parking, as do shopping complexes such as Manda Hill and Arcades, and many restaurants.

It is not advisable to drive at night in or around the city. Aside from the risk of car-jackings, you're likely to encounter vehicles without lights (especially around the time of the full moon), and even people sleeping on the warm tarmac, a hazard that's said to be particularly common on the Great North Road.

There are numerous fuel stations throughout the city and more springing up on every corner. Nowadays shortages of fuel are relatively rare.

WHERE TO STAY

There is an increasing level of choice between Lusaka's international hotels, with improving standards of service and design, although they can often be soulless.

You might ask yourself if you need to be near the centre, or can afford to stay beyond the suburbs, at somewhere like Lilayi, Pioneer, Protea Safari Lodge, or Chaminuka (see pages 138–40). These are more pleasant than being in town, but transport (with the exception of Pioneer, which is close to the airport) can be a costly issue. A good balance is to head for the new and – at present unique – Eight Reedbuck Hotel.

Those on a budget should choose their lodgings with care. Price is often a poor guide and the quality of the budget hotels and guesthouses varies considerably. Ask around if you can, as new places are opening all the time. If your budget is very tight then head for a backpackers' hostel or a campsite. Lusaka's cheap hostels are often seedy.

A word of warning: if you plan to make international phone calls from any hotel, find out their charges first, or – better – buy a local SIM card. Hotel phone bills can run into hundreds of dollars for just a few minutes.

TOP END $$$$–$$$$$ If you're passing through Lusaka, perhaps between flights, or are here for a few days' business, then the top international hotels may fit the bill. Three of these have been established in Lusaka's central area for many years, while a fourth – the Radisson – should be open by the end of 2011. The arrival on the scene of Lusaka's first boutique hotel opens up an entirely different option for those seeking something less corporate.

⌂ **Taj Pamodzi Hotel** [131 E4] (193 rooms) Addis Ababa Dr; 📞 0211 254455; e pamodzi. lusaka@tajhotels.com; www.tajhotels.com. The 5-star Pamodzi is a member of the Indian-owned Taj group of hotels, & the level of service is impressive. Its rooms have AC, bath/shower, DSTV, fridge/minibar, safe & phone. Some have a proper balcony, & those on the higher of the Pamodzi's 9 floors afford some fine views.

Downstairs, there's a spacious lobby, a comfortable lounge where soft piano music is played in the late afternoon, an open-plan bar with discreet sports TV & occasional live bands, cake & jewellery shops & a business centre; there's also WiFi access throughout – at a fee. The well-equipped fitness centre incorporates 2 squash courts, plus sauna, steam room, hair salon & spa; the gym is one of the best in town, popular with Lusaka's more affluent residents. Outside, lawns surround a good-size swimming pool under jacaranda trees. This is overlooked by an informal restaurant with a large terrace area, & the more formal Steak & Grills restaurant, open for dinner only with live music every night. A good, varied buffet b/fast is part of the deal, while dinner menus include some very good Indian dishes. I've often stayed here, & always found the staff to be courteous & helpful. **$$$$$**

⌂ **Radisson Blu Hotel** [121 E3] (145 rooms) Great East Rd; 📞 +27 (21) 431 2900; e info. lusaka@radissonblu.com; www.radissonblu.com/ hotel-lusaka. Opposite the Arcades, the stylish domes of the new Radisson are flanked by low-rise blocks of rooms & adorned by palm trees. Scheduled to open at the end of 2011, the hotel will have a restaurant, fitness centre, spa area, swimming pool & bar, plus function rooms & free WiFi throughout. **$$$$$**

⌂ **Hotel InterContinental** [131 F4] (204 rooms, 20 suites) Haile Selassie Av; 📞 0211 250000/250149/250661; e reservations@ interconti.com.zm; www.ichotelsgroup.com. This is the second of Lusaka's 5-star hotels, but when last visited, the staff were less than helpful & the standard of service seemed to have dropped again (after having temporarily improved). Rooms, which were renovated in 2007, are reasonably big, with enough space to include both a couch & a desk; you can expect an en-suite bath/shower, DSTV, fridge & phone. For meals there's the Savannah Grill & Restaurant, which has both a buffet & a daily à-la-carte menu served either indoors or on a pleasant covered terrace over the pool. More upmarket is the Olive Grove, a Mediterranean-style venue open Mon–Sat for dinner only. There's also a rather soulless bar, typical of those in large hotels.

The InterCon's lobby is a good meeting place, with huge windows looking out to the front & a café whose piano is sadly only for show. A display of masks in the lobby is complemented by other examples of African art, but otherwise it's largely anonymous. There are some smart gift shops, though, & the more active can take advantage of the hotel's gym & attendant health facilities, attractive oval swimming pool & floodlit tennis courts. There's also a 24hr business centre. **$$$$$**

🏠 **Eight Reedbuck Hotel** [121 H5] (10 suites) 8 Reedbuck Rd, Kabulonga; ⬳0211 264788/264733; e info@tribehotels.co.zm; www.tribehotels.co.zm. The anonymous façade belies the interior of this small place, whose personal & flexible approach justifies the title of Lusaka's first boutique hotel. It is the brainchild of Clive Shamwana, a genial & cosmopolitan Zambian who, after years of experience in the UK service industry, decided to open a small, quality guesthouse that felt authentically Zambian but where the needs of overseas travellers were understood. The result? A very Zambian place, with much more character than the big hotels.

Large, individual & fairly eclectically furnished, each suite is subtly furnished to reflect the name of a Zambian tribe. So, for example, the Lozi suite has a black-&-white striped theme, & is decorated with carvings & fabric art from western Zambia. Two are slightly larger & more expensive than the others, but all enjoy broadly similar facilities: satellite TV, a proper fridge, safe, tea-/coffee-making facilities, AC, an in-house phone & free WiFi access (albeit a little slow). Most have kingsize beds, & there's usually space for an extra child bed. The en-suite bathrooms, with shower & separate bath, are as different as the suites. Those on the ground floor have a glass roof above the shower – with bushes & trees around it outside – & some even have a jacuzzi. Smokers should ask for a ground-floor room with a private garden.

On the dinner menu, Zambian dishes are listed alongside those with a Zambian twist, but with an overseas palate in mind. Try *nyama ibisi*, for example: beef fillet seasoned with fresh herbs, drizzled with fresh chilli sauce, & served with a salad. The garden has several shaded sitting areas & a very big, clear & inviting swimming pool. They've even thought of transport, with their own driver, & a good relationship with a reliable taxi company. **$$$$$**

🏠 **Southern Sun Ridgeway** [131 E4] (155 rooms) Cnr Independence Av & Church Rd; ⬳0211 251666; e reservations@holidayinn. co.zm; www.holidayinn.co.zm. The former Holiday Inn is close to the InterCon, & though its rooms show little more imagination the service is friendly & the atmosphere more relaxed. Rooms are functional & clean with shower & bath, AC, phone, DSTV, razor plug, & tea-/coffee-making facilities. Beds are queensize double or twin.

On the ground floor there's the main Musuku restaurant, serving buffet lunch & dinner (*Kw130,000 & Kw150,00 respectively*) or à-la-carte meals from b/fast through to dinner. Alongside is McGinty's Irish Pub (⏰ 10.00– 23.00), which serves salads & more substantial pub grub against a backdrop of TV screens featuring an unrelenting diet of news & sport – a cool, dark retreat from the heat. However, instead of gazing into your pint here, try stepping outside into the central courtyard & studying the colony of masked weavers nesting in a tree over the ornamental pond, where a few small crocs bask on the sheltered rocks. The hotel also has an inviting pool set in its shady garden & an adjacent gym.

In front of the entrance you'll find offices of ZéDash car hire, South African Airways & Proflight, & there's a very useful Barclays ATM too. There's also a shop: books, curios, carvings & gemstones. **$$$$–$$$$$**

MID-RANGE $$$–$$$$ While one or two of Lusaka's mid-range hotels have been here for years, others of very different styles have capitalised on the rapidly growing business and conference market. The South African Protea chain have plans for a third hotel, Protea Hotel Mulungushi, also close to the Arcades.

🏠 **Golfview** [121 G3] (78 rooms, 5 apts) 10247 Great East Rd; ⬳0211 290718/ 290770/291490/291822/291858/291896;

e reservations@golfview-hotels.com; www. golfview-hotels.com. No longer part of the Cresta hotel group, the Golfview is well placed some

16km from the airport, & 13km from the city centre. While technically a 3-star establishment, its rates put it in a higher bracket. It's an earthy terracotta & cream complex with en-suite dbl & twin rooms of neutral décor with AC, minibar, tea/coffee facilities & a phone. Half have views over an attractive pool & the golf course, so do ask for one of these: rates are the same for all. New self-catering 3-bedroom apartments are ideal for families or long-stay visitors. If the entrance is rather soulless, this doesn't extend to the bar & traditional restaurant which overlook the pool, enclosing a small courtyard with umbrella shade. There's also a business centre. The hotel is affiliated to the adjacent Chainama Hills Golf Club, where residents can play free of charge except for club rental & caddy fees. **$$$$**

🏠 **Protea Hotel Lusaka** [121 E3] (100 rooms) Arcades, Great East Rd; 📞 0211 254664; e reservations@phlusaka.co.zm; www. proteahotels.com/lusaka. This long-promised new hotel & casino opened in 2008. With direct access to the Arcades, & a stone's throw from Acacia Park, the Protea is unique in Lusaka in being within a short stroll of shops, cafés & several good restaurants. Spacious dbl & twin rooms all have AC & come equipped with the standard business accoutrements, which here include DSTV, safe, hairdryer & free WiFi. While the entrance lobby – & the splash pool located on a small balcony – are rather uninspiring (why did they hide an attractive water feature behind the lift?), the restaurant & bar are pleasant, & the standard of service from a young team is impressive. Airport shuttle US$20 pp. **$$$$**

🏠 **Sandy's Lodge** [120 A7] (36 chalets) Kafue Rd; 📞 0211 278116; m 0966 713098; e lodge@sandyscreations.net; www. sandyscreations.net. Some 10km south of the Kafue roundabout, this smart new lodge opened in 2008. Its rooms are individual thatched chalets, built in neat rows running parallel to the main road; to minimise traffic noise, ask for a room at the back. Sliding double-glazed doors lead through to spacious, well-appointed bedrooms of neutral décor that tick all the corporate boxes: kingsize or twin beds, AC/heating, DSTV, kettle, minibar, desk, WiFi & a large en-suite bath & separate shower. The lodge is a good family option, too, with 5 family rooms (2 bedrooms & a sitting area), a children's menu,

baby pool, & access to the jungle gym at the adjacent garden centre. Arguably the greatest family draw, though, is a superb free-form swimming pool, for guests only, next to an impressive circular restaurant & bar with flat-screen TV that's open to residents & outsiders alike. The menu (**$$$–$$$$**) majors on grills with a few Thai & vegetarian options, & there's an extensive winelist. Airport transfer US$30 (max 4). **$$$$**

🏠 **Protea Hotel Cairo Road** [130 B4] (75 rooms) Cairo Rd; 📞 0211 238360; e reservations@phcairoroad.co.zm; www. proteahotels.com/cairoroad. While it won't win any prizes for design, the 7-storey Protea on Cairo Rd has certainly raised the standard for business hotels in the area, & has the bonus of some good views of the city from its top floors. Sgl, dbl or twin rooms & dbl suites are clean, smart & functional, & are kitted out in much the same way as its sister hotel above. The ground-floor restaurant is in the same mould – light & airy – & the internet centre (⏰ 08.00–22.00) has some of the best rates in town; there's also free WiFi. Crucially, the hotel has its own secure multi-storey car park. Airport shuttle US$20 pp. **$$$–$$$$**

🏠 **Chrismar Hotel** [131 H4] (47 rooms) Los Angeles Bd; 📞 0211 253036/253605; m 0969 893728, 0976 085553; e book@chrismarhotels. com; www.chrismarhotels.com. In extensive grounds next to the Lusaka Club, with secure parking, the Chrismar opened in 1999. If it's looking a little faded now, the staff remain friendly & helpful, though the rooms can be noisy at w/ends. Of these, the older ones – with carpeted floors, en-suite bath/shower & tea/coffee facilities – are rather small. Lighter & more spacious are 22 newer suites, with leopard-print covers & colourful African wall-hangings; these have a bath & shower, DSTV & AC. Some overlook the courtyard, others the swimming pool.

Outside a rather over-elaborate stone bridge leads across a fishpool with fountain, half hidden by an overgrown bamboo. Umbrella-shaded tables surround the large swimming pool with its own bar, next to the popular Cattleman's Grill (page 142), a favourite for meat-eaters & a w/end venue for live bands. Indoors, there's a calmer brasserie & a new lounge bar where cocktails are proving a hit with Lusaka's ladies. Fitness fanatics can use the gym, there's a children's play area, & guests have free WiFi for 2hrs each day. **$$$**

BUDGET $-$$$ Even 'budget' hotels and guesthouses aren't that cheap in Lusaka, but if you have upwards of Kw225,000 (US$50) per night to spend on a double room, then there is a choice within this range. However, many are used extensively for conferences and few shine. Most visitors prefer the city's smaller guesthouses, which are often much friendlier and start at the same kind of price, though the range is considerable. The last few years have seen a real boom in the numbers, and the quality, of such guesthouses throughout Zambia, but especially in Lusaka. Some are simply restaurants that offer a few rooms for guests as a legal convenience, others are dedicated entirely to their guests, with prices to match. A few are old favourites, but beware of the speed with which these open up and then close down again.

Centre and Cairo Road

Lusaka Hotel [130 B4] (77 rooms) Cairo Rd; 0211 229049/52; m 0977 640895; e lushotel@zamnet.zm; www.lusakahotel.com. Some decades ago the Lusaka Hotel was the only hotel in Lusaka, right at the centre of town. Now competition is fierce, not least from the newer Protea Hotel opposite, & the hotel has raised its game. While it remains rather dated in style, there's secure parking, a new entrance lobby, & all rooms have been upgraded. These now have simple tiled floors, AC, tea/coffee makers, TV, phone, fridge & en-suite shower; standard rooms are a little larger with bath & shower. Downstairs there's a bar, & the restaurant – whose menu includes traditional Zambian dishes – spills outside alongside a small swimming pool. **$$-$$$**

Fairview Hotel [130 C3] (31 rooms) Church Rd; 0211 222604/5, 239637; e reservationsfairview@yahoo.com; www.fairview.co.zm. Significantly cheaper than the Chrismar, & more central, the Fairview is a hotel training centre, so you can expect attentive service from its young personnel. En-suite rooms with heavy wooden bedsteads & ornate mirrors feel rather old-fashioned despite refurbishment in 2011, but they're spotlessly clean, & flat-screen TVs plus a fridge & tea/coffee facilities add a more modern touch. The public rooms include a terrace bar overlooking Church Rd, & a restaurant that serves traditional Zambian food at lunchtime during the week ($-$$) with a Western à-la-carte menu in the evenings. There's limited WiFi access & a small business centre with internet. Outside is a beer garden, & secure parking. **$$**

Longacres Lodge [131 G4] (58 rooms) Los Angeles Bd; 0211 254847; e longacreslodge@zamtel.zm; www.zambiahostels.com. This government-run establishment is often used for conferences, & is unique for its labyrinth of long corridors, some open to one side. Carpeted rooms are reasonably clean & have basic dbl or twin beds, with a TV, en-suite bath, & perhaps a dressing table or wardrobe; suites have a sitting area & fridge as well, with the option of linking rooms for families, & executive rooms boast AC. There's secure parking & an on-site restaurant. **$$**

Marble Inn [130 C3] (10 rooms) Makanta Cl; 0211 230617; e marbleinn@gmail.com. Next to Kuomboka Backpackers, this simple guesthouse is clean, pleasant & good value, though the lack of b/fast may deter some. Dbl rooms are tiled & light, with pine furniture, mosquito nets, fans, DSTV & en-suite showers. **$$** exc b/fast.

Ndeke Hotel [131 G4] (47 rooms) Chisidza Cres; 0211 251734; e gardengroup@zamtel.zm; www.gardengroupzambia.com. Hidden behind a high inner wall near the roundabout of Haile Selassie Av & Los Angeles Bd, the old Ndeke had a welcome facelift a few years back, its spacious entrance now enlivened by original artwork & wooden sculptures. Rooms are in a 2-storey terracotta-painted block at the back, some overlooking a good swimming pool. The newer ones have cane furniture & cream paintwork, but some of the older-style rooms remain too. (Rates are the same, so asking for a new room makes sense.) Most have TV & en-suite toilet & bath, but 4 sgls have en-suite showers, & share a toilet. At the front is a slightly sunken dining area with a lounge above, & outside is a courtyard. **$$**

Nena's Guest House [130 C2] (4 rooms) 126 Masansa Cl, Rhodes Pk; 0211 239541; m 0977 773213; e nenaguesthouse@zamnet.zm; www.nenaguesthouse.co.zm. Yugoslavian-born Nena opened her eponymous guesthouse &

restaurant in 2002. Clean, en-suite rooms with dbl or twin beds have DSTV & AC, while outside is a small camping area, with a couple of pre-erected tents. Guinea fowl & hens forage in the garden around a large pool with its own terrace & a nearby bar, & there's secure parking. The restaurant ($$$; ⏲ *06.00–09.00, 12.00–22.00*), open to allcomers, specialises in Yugoslav dishes, though service is on the slow side. On Fri evening & Sun lunch there's a spit roast. **$$** *Camping Kw25,000 pp.*

East towards the airport

🏠 **Chita Lodge** [120 D3] (14 rooms) 25 Chakeluka Rd; 🕿 0211 293779; e chitalodge@ microlink.zm; www.chita.co.zm. Stylish & professionally run, Chita Lodge opened in 2001 & is a great-value option: friendly, modern & very well looked after. To find it, turn left immediately after Manda Hill onto Kwacha Rd, take the 2nd left, then take the first right & it's on the left-hand side. Indoors, a wildlife theme is reflected in the décor & touches of original artwork. Spotless dbl & twin rooms are spacious, with smart tiled floors & comfy chairs; each has an en-suite shower or bath, phone, AC/heating, fridge, hot drinks facilities, DSTV, & a DVD. Ten rooms adjoin the main lodge with a further 4 in a separate complex about 100m down the road. The rooms here are newer & there's a small bar, which makes up for the distance from the main facilities.

The main lodge boasts secure parking, a crystal-clear swimming pool with soft grassy surround. There's a small dining area & bar with tables on a shaded terrace by the pool. The restaurant serves both light lunches & dinner, when the menu à-la-carte ranges from Indian dishes through traditional Zambian fare such as oxtail & fried bream to a range of grills ($$– $$$). This is without doubt one of Lusaka's best places to stay within this price range. **$$$**

🏠 **Comfort Lodge** [121 F2] (10 rooms) Great East Rd, Jesmondine; 🕿 0211 290314; e comfort_ lodge@iconnect.zm; www.comfort_lodge.com. Just east of the university, this light, airy lodge is marked by a bright yellow signboard & walls. From the comfy chairs in the lounge/reception to the dining area overlooking the pool with a thatched bar, it's a pleasant & relaxed place, if suffering a little from traffic noise. Rooms have

🏠 **Pearl Haven Inn** [131 F1] (8 rooms) Twikatane Rd, Rhodes Pk; 🕿 0211 252455; e pearl@zamnet.zm. Run by Malcolm Jhala, Pearl Haven is in a commercial residential area, 5mins' walk from Manda Hill. Dominating the front, a thatched bar on stilts towers over a good-size swimming pool. Behind is a restaurant, then back again are the rooms. These are extraordinarily ornate, with floral curtains & heavy carved furniture, & come with an en-suite bath & shower, AC, satellite TV, fridge, minibar, tea & coffee facilities & direct-dial phone. **$$**

DSTV, AC, en-suite bath or shower, fridge & kettle; more interestingly, wrought-iron furniture is adorned with leopard-print fabrics & paintings of horses grace every wall. There's an à-la-carte menu for lunch & dinner ($$–$$$) & a salon on site if you need a haircut. **$$$**

🏠 **Juls Guesthouse** [121 E2] (17 rooms, 5 apts) 5508 Lusiwasi Rd, Kalundu; 🕿 0211 292979/293972; e juls.travel@travelport. co.zm; www.julsafrica.com. In a quiet residential area, Juls's self-catering apartments & en-suite rooms are mostly let to long-stay visitors such as NGO staff. To find it, take the 2nd left after the Arcades roundabout, then turn right. Simple, modern rooms, with twin beds & stone floors are a pleasant change from most of Lusaka's guesthouses; all have AC, & 'executive' rooms have phones. There are 3 spacious lounges with satellite TV, while outside is a well-kept garden & shaded terrace with braai area, plus a swimming pool & sauna. There's also a floodlit tennis court & a pool table. Home-cooked meals ($$$–$$$$) are available by arrangement. Owner Julie Limpic runs the adjacent travel agency, too (page 150).**$$$**

🏠 **Mika Lodge** [121 F2] (29 rooms) 106 Central St, Jesmondine; 🕿 0211 291557/291494; e mika@coppernet.zm. Opened in 2007, Mika Lodge is on the cnr of 1st St. The juxtaposition of cool, tiled entrance with heavy armchairs & arrangements of fresh flowers suggests a modern approach tempered with tradition – a reflection of the lodge as a whole. Each cream-painted room, with tiled floor & dbl bed, has a good desk, AC, TV, WiFi (for your own computer) & en-suite shower. There's a bright, modern restaurant ($$–$$$) with funky chairs & roses on the tables. The atmosphere is one of businesslike efficiency: definitely more of a small hotel than a guesthouse but very good value & immaculately maintained. **$$$**

🏠 **Reed Mat Lodge**   [121 F2] (15 rooms, 5 chalets) 9718 5th St, Munali; ✆ 0211 293426; m 0977 7854768, 9180339; e info@ reedmatlodge.com; www.reedmatlodge.com. This Zambian-run lodge with a strong cultural ethic is about 15mins from the airport. Rooms, either en suite or with shared facilities, are set in attractive gardens & decorated with local crafts. Two lounges have DSTV, & WiFi access is on hand. Children are particularly welcome, with cots & play equipment available, & there's a new 8-bed private chalet with 2 bedrooms & its own lounge. Home-cooked meals are served in the restaurant, or guests can use the kitchen themselves. Outside is a pool – in the shape of the African continent! – & secure parking. **$$–$$$**

🏠 **Great East Hotel**   [121 G2] (31 rooms) Great East Rd; ✆ 0211 294139; e greasthotel@ yahoo.com, greasthotel@zambia.co.zm. On the south side of the Great East Rd, about 7km from the city centre, this basic but very friendly

hotel has a 1980s' motel feel. Rooms, each with table & chairs, fan, & DSTV, are quite spacious & clean although very dated – especially for the price. In most, a picture window takes up one wall, & the en-suite facilities have baths rather than showers. Dinner is available. **$$**

🏠 **Mwambula Garden Lodge**   [121 F2] (9 rooms) Mwambula Rd; ✆ 0211 292826; m 0977 897020, 0979 343229; e mwambulagardenlodge@yahoo.com; www. mwambulagardenlodgezambia.com. Beyond the unprepossessing entrance & the garden gnomes, you'll find a friendly welcome at this small guesthouse. Turn north off the Great East Rd just before the Munali roundabout, then take the first left; it's on the right. Attractive gardens with an enormous stand of bamboo & a pool form the focus of the lodge, whose best rooms overlook the garden. These are L-shaped, with heavy wooden furniture, TVs, fans & mosi nets, & adequate en-suite showers. Wicker chairs on the veranda make for a peaceful place to relax – peaceful, that is, except on the occasional BBQ night, open to allcomers. **$$**

Southeast: Kabulonga and Leopards Hill

🏠 **Kilimanjaro Country Lodge**   [121 H7] (8 rooms) Leopards Hill Rd; ✆ 0211 250527/ 255830; m 0975 838461; e info@ kilimanjarozambia.com; www. kilimanjarozambia.com. In a tranquil, relatively rural spot next to the café of the same name, this new lodge opened in 2009, & will have 18 rooms by 2012. To get there, follow Leopards Hill Rd southeast for 7.5km, & it's signposted on the right. At a flat US$80 per room, including b/fast, free transfers to the airport (30mins) & Manda Hill, & free WiFi access (by 2012), it's clear that it means business. Dbl, twin & family en-suite rooms are divided across 3 buildings, each with a communal tea station. Embroidered bedding, quirky tables & beaded lampshades add a touch of individuality, while pleasant lawned gardens give plenty of space for children to run around, to play badminton, or simply to relax. With the on-site café offering b/fast, lunch & dinner, this could be a good option for the first or last night of a safari, too. **$$$**

🏠 **Belvedere Lodge**   [121 G6] (21 rooms) Leopards Hill Rd; ✆ 0211 251761; e enquiries@

zambiahostels.com; www.zambiahostels.com. On the east side of the city, close to Kabulonga shopping centre, the government-run Belvedere has en-suite rooms with bath or shower. They're small & uninspiring, but reasonably modern & clean, each with a fan, mosquito nets, fridge & TV. There's also a restaurant & separate bar. **$$**

🏠 **Serenity Lodge**   [121 G6] (8 rooms, cottage) 2 Leopards Hill Rd, Kabulonga; ✆ 0211 262182; m 0955 195500; e serenity@coppernet. zm. Opened in 2001, Serenity is a 2-storey lodge with large, clean, carpeted rooms, albeit rather randomly furnished. Rooms also boast DSTV, a kettle, AC, fridge, phone & en-suite bath or shower (or both). A 2-bedroom cottage provides further choice. There's a small, neat dining room, WiFi access, a pool, & a tennis court that's seen better days. **$$**

🏠 **Kaingo Lodge**   [121 G6] (6 rooms) 35D Leopards La, Kabulonga; ✆ 0211 263231; e kaingo@zamtel.zm. This well-kept & personal guesthouse, deep in the suburbs, has been run by Jesmine & David Thompson since 1998, & offers exceptionally good value. To find it, turn right off

Leopards Hill Rd onto Leopards La, just before the Crossroads complex. A little way down here there's an alley on the right, & Kaingo is the first gate on the right; the sign is very small.

Kaingo is popular with business visitors & NGO personnel sent to Zambia for short postings, but works equally well for just a night or 2. Each room is individual, but all are en suite with dbl beds (& space for another sgl), AC or fan, WiFi access, fridge & TV. There's a comfy TV lounge & honesty bar, & all meals are available. A big draw is the mature garden, set around a large swimming pool with attendant fountains & a swim-up bar. **$**

South along the Kafue Road

⌂ **Wayside B&B** [120 A7] (8 rooms) 40 Makeni Rd; 0211 272736; m 0966 765184; e wayside@iconnect.zm; www.wayside-guesthouse.com. This oasis of calm has been run with flair & attention to detail by Beverley Horn since 1998. Take the Kafue Rd for about 4.5km, go past the Castle shopping complex, then turn right onto Makeni Rd at the traffic lights, almost opposite Caltex; Wayside is on the left after about 2km.

A row of en-suite rooms, each with a covered porch & proper table & chairs outside, fronts a beautiful garden, while another 3 are tucked away in a separate cottage, 2 of them linked by a fully equipped kitchen/dining room & private garden. Solid wood furniture, Zambian wall-hangings & curtains of local fabric give a sense of place; amenities include a fan, fridge, tea/coffee facilities, safe, DSTV & free WiFi. Rates are the same for all, but 2 larger rooms have a small study, & 2 of those in the cottage have AC. B/fast (& dinner on request) are served in a cosy dining room, while a separate room offers a large TV, DVD player, dining table, comfy chairs & small library, ideal for groups or families to get together. Luggage can be stored for those heading out of town for a few days. Gardening is Beverley's passion, & it shows – in the flowers & shrubs, the well-tended lawns, the walled garden encompassing a sparkling pool & bar, & the tranquil parkland area beyond, woven with paths & big enough for jogging should you be so inclined. It all adds up to one of Lusaka's best B&Bs. **$$$**

⌂ **Kafue Road Garden Hotel** [120 B7] (23 rooms) Kafue Rd, Makeni; 0211 274987; e gardengroup@zamtel.zm; www.gardengroupzambia.com. Some 3km south of the Kafue roundabout, this old-style hotel is simple but clean. To find it, turn right just after the Castle shopping centre, then double back on a rough track & turn immediately left. The bare corridors & gardens are shortly to be adorned with paintings & sculptures by local artists, with work available for sale. Rooms are large & quite plush, equipped with en-suite shower or bath, TV, fridge, kettle & fan. Snacks & full meals are served in the restaurant, & there's the occasional braai. **$$**

West towards Mumbwa & Kafue National Park

⌂ **Garden House Hotel** [120 A5] (65 rooms) Mumbwa Rd; 0211 213004; e gardengroup@zamtel.zm; www.gardengroupzambia.com. About 6km west of the city, this is well situated if you arrive late from Kafue National Park. The institutional feel of the corridors is relieved by plenty of original Zambian artwork on the walls. Dbl or twin rooms have DSTV, fridge, en-suite shower or bath, & either a fan or AC. The restaurant caters for all meals, & there's a pool in the otherwise unadorned gardens. The hotel is noteworthy as the place where the MMD political party was started in 1990. **$$**

HOSTELS AND CAMPING If you're visiting on a tight budget, then look towards one of the campsites on the edge of town, which are surprisingly attractive, or one of the backpackers' hostels in the centre. Excellent camping is also available at Pioneer Camp, just east of the airport (see page 138), and – rather more basic – at Fringilla Farm Lodge (see page 390).

⌂ **Bongwe's Barn 'n' Guesthouse** [120 D2] (8 rooms) 305 Ngwezi Rd, Roma; m 0978 164038, 0976 012590; e thebarn@bongwesafaris.com; www.bongwesafaris.com/

barn. This converted barn, opened in summer 2011, is 2.8km from Arcades, & is the Lusaka base of the safari company of the same name. Self styled 'cheap & cheerful' it comes with en-suite dbl & family rooms, as well as dbls & twins sharing ablutions. A bar with pool table & TV, a pub grub menu & a pool add to the package. They can arrange onward travel & activities, have WiFi access, & will do your laundry too. Airport transfers are free to safari clients; taxi around US$35. **$$**

⚐ Eureka [120 A7] (camping, 4 A-frames, 13 chalets, 5-bed cottage, 26 dorm beds) Kafue Rd; ☎ 0211 272351/278110; e eureka@zamnet.zm; www.eurekacamp.com. Lusaka's best campsite is on a private farm within a game area, owned & run since 1992 by Henry & Doreen van Blerk, & all protected by an electric fence. Expect to see the ghostly stripes of zebra by moonlight, or to be woken by impala browsing the trees.

The site is clearly signposted on the eastern side of Kafue Rd, opposite Baobab College, about 10km south of the Kafue Rd roundabout. For campers, there's an extensive area of beautiful lawn under trees, with electric hook-ups available. If you don't fancy camping, consider a simple thatched A-frame chalet, with 2 or 3 beds, sharing well-kept toilets & showers with the campers. More privacy comes with the en-suite 2- or 3-bed chalets, which are worth booking in advance. There's also a 5-bed cottage with toilet & shower, & a large, 6-room bunkhouse aimed primarily at school groups.

Most people bring their own food, but you can get b/fast, good burgers & pies at the bar, as well as fresh meat for the braai, wood & charcoal. Here you'll also find easy chairs, a dartboard, pool table & DSTV. A fenced swimming pool & a volleyball court offer more active pastimes.

Eureka has maintained its position as the city's best place for budget travellers. If you don't have a vehicle, take a Chilanga bus from Kulima Tower bus station [130 A4] & ask to be dropped at Eureka; the fare is about Kw5,000. To return to town, just wait for a minibus outside the gates. A taxi from the bus station will cost about Kw50,000 pp. *Camping US$7 pp (overlanders & backpackers US$3.50 pp); A-frame US$40/45 2-bed/3-bed; chalet US$55/70 2-bed/3-bed; cottage US$100; dorm bed US$20 pp.*

⌂ Kuomboka Backpackers [130 C3] (13 rooms, 30 dorm beds) 9965 Makanta Cl; ☎ 0211 222450; m 0977 777324, 0979 862514; e ashrafkaaz@gmail.com. Easy-going, modern & clean, Kuomboka was taken over in Jun 2011. Although it's all rather cramped, facilities are good: a small curio shop; an equally small outside bar & TV; a guest kitchen; & a dining area with a new menu planned – or order a takeaway from the nearby Mahak (page 143). Dbl & trpl rooms share a bath & toilet (trpls have a fan & facilities to make hot drinks), & there are 3 10-bed dorms. Despite the name, it's as popular with the volunteer market as with backpackers. *Kw150,000 dbl; dorm bed Kw50,000.*

⌂ Lusaka Backpackers [130 C3] (26 dorm beds, 4 dbl rooms, 2 cabins, chalet, 2 safari tents) 161 Mulombwa Cl, off Bwinjimfumo Rd; ☎ 0211 222257; e info@chachachasafaris.com; www.chachachasafaris.com. A large wall map of Zambia sets the tone for the former Chachacha, which gained a new name & a new owner in 2010. It's a relaxed, slightly rambling place, long established on the backpacker circuit, though parts of it could do with a facelift. A taxi from the bus station (or to Manda Hill) will cost about Kw20,000, or from the airport around US$30 (up to 3 people).

Clean dorms have 6 or 8 beds, while for a little more privacy there are private rooms in the main house, or in rather jaded cabins or an A-frame chalet in the garden. Cheaper are twin-bedded tents. All showers & toilets are communal, there are safes to store your valuables, & there's WiFi access (*Kw5,000/ ½hr*).

The kitchen is kitted out with hotplates, a fridge & various cooking utensils, but if you don't want to cook for yourself, a set meal (around Kw35,000) is usually available each evening, as is b/fast (*Kw25,000*). The outside bar with pool table & small pool is a good place to discuss travels or just put the world to rights. If you're planning to explore beyond Lusaka, they can organise a number of trips within Zambia & will store your backpack free of charge. *Dorm bed US$12; cabin/A-frame chalet US$30; tent US$15.*

⌂ Lusaka Backpackers II [130 D3] (5 rooms) Omelo Mumbwa Rd; contact Lusaka Backpackers above. An offshoot of Lusaka Backpackers, this converted house (yet to be named!) is scheduled to open in 2011. Its aim? To offer no-frills rooms – 3 en-suite dbls & 2 sgls sharing a bathroom –

at affordable rates: US$50 & US$20 respectively. Continental b/fast will be included, but for anything more substantial there's Chit Chat café down the road. Guests will be able to use other amenities at the main backpackers. **$**

🏠 **Pioneer Camp** See below for details of this popular campsite, which now offers smart chalets too.

🏠 **YWCA** [121 F7] Nationalist Rd; 📞 0211 252726; e ywcalskb@iconnect.zm. Opposite the

University Teaching Hospital, the YWCA accepts both men for short stays, & women as long as required. Small, very basic rooms (2 en suite) are set around pleasant gardens, but the communal cooking, washing & toilet facilities are none too clean. There's a restaurant for simple meals. With the hospital's morgue across the street, you can expect plenty of noise when mourners collect their dead in the early mornings. *Kw75,000–180,000.*

LODGES OUTSIDE TOWN If you've more than a night and want somewhere to relax away from the city, then try one of these. All have lots of space and are set in large areas of greenery, often stocked with game. Because of this, they are out of the centre, so communications can be less easy. Also, because they are smaller, most of them organise transfers to/from the airport (or the city) on an individual basis, and this is reflected in their rates or in transfer charges. However, for an extended stay all are very pleasant and worth seeking out. Listing them by area:

North and northeast

🏠 **Chaminuka Lodge** (30 suites) 📞 0211 840883–4; e information@chaminuka.com, reservations@chaminuka.com; www.chaminuka. com. Chaminuka is about 50km northeast of town, close to the airport. Many guests are effectively in transit, & the lodge usually provides transfers; it also caters for day visitors. From the airport, it is 28km along a gravel road, a ½hr drive, or slightly longer during the rains, when you will need a 4x4. To find it, head towards the airport, go under the arch, then turn left straight after the police roadblock; the lodge is signposted. Once the private home of one of Lusaka's most affluent citizens, the lodge stands atop a small rise overlooking Lake Chitoka. This is one of 4 small, manmade lakes in the 100km² Chaminuka Nature Reserve, which has a variety of different woodland & savanna habitats, lots of wetlands, & plenty of game. Buffalo, lion & hyena are kept in their own fenced enclosures.

Chaminuka is said to house the country's largest collection of traditional & contemporary Zambian art. From a spacious lounge, adorned with original art & leather sofas, large sliding glass doors lead onto a wide terrace. It's all very grand; some would say soulless. Around the main building are square, red-brick chalets, with en-suite facilities & lots of space. Rooms have solid wood queen- or kingsize beds, TVs, phones, AC & patio doors onto the surrounding lawns; some interconnect to make family rooms.

There are a few *insakas* (small lounges), a dining room, a small library including a section on African history & a TV, & a snooker room (with full-size table). Outside are 2 swimming pools, with adjacent terrace, table tennis, tennis court & a new spa with sauna & jacuzzi. Activities are flexible. In addition to 4x4 game drives, walks, birdwatching & fishing sorties on the lakes, horseriding is available for all levels. Airport transfer US$50 pp return. *US$288 pp sharing FBA, inc drinks/house wine & tours. Day visitor US$132 inc b/fast, activities & use of all facilities.*

🏠 **Fringilla Farm Lodge** (46 rooms, 5 chalets, 2 flats, 2 houses, camping) Great North Rd, Chisamba; 📞 0211 213885/214364; e fringill@zamnet.zm; www.fringillalodge.com. Situated about 50km north of Lusaka towards Kabwe. See page 390.

🏠 **Pioneer Camp** (13 chalets, cottage, camping) Palabana Rd; m 0966 432700/731420; e info@pioneercampzambia.com; www. pioneercampzambia.com. The emphasis at the popular Pioneer, which was taken over in 2008 by Paul Barnes, has moved towards that of a safari lodge, although campers remain welcome & the atmosphere is still friendly & relaxed. Pioneer is about a ½hr drive from the centre of Lusaka or – crucially – a similar distance from the airport. To get there, drive east on the Great East Rd, then turn right 1km after the turn-off to the airport, just after the roadblock. It's a further 5km from there on (sometimes very uneven) gravel roads, & is clearly signposted. If you don't have transport, take a minibus from Manda Hill to Chelston, by the water tower (approx Kw2,800), then take a taxi for about Kw45,000. If the owners are going into town, they're happy to offer a free lift; otherwise, a taxi to town or the airport costs Kw100,000 (up to 4 people).

Pioneer has 2 basic chalets, a couple of 3-bed thatched chalets sharing a toilet & shower; 2 family chalets of a similar standard with their own facilities; a large, self-contained 2-bedroom cottage sleeping up to 6; & 7 twin 'luxury' chalets, located on the edge of the site & facing east to catch the sunrise. These last are a cut above the others: spacious & well designed, each with an en-suite bathroom; one is built of natural stone under high thatch, cool & dark, with a toilet & stone bath discreetly tucked behind a solid screen of the same material. There is also a large grassy campsite with plenty of shade, a clean ablution block, & a small, fenced pool – all in about 12ha of woodland surrounded by a discreet electric fence, beyond which is a 6km walking trail. The camp's rural location means that you'll wake to the sound of Heuglin's robin rather than the blare of a horn.

The large, thatched bar area is the focus for a real mix of travellers, which makes for plenty of interesting conversation. There are comfy chairs aplenty, & a small satellite TV. Snacks & meals are on hand, with a full b/fast (*around US$5*), & dinner (*US$10*). Fridge/freezer space is available, as are laundry facilities. With its rural location close to the airport, Pioneer is a good choice for the first or last night of a safari holiday. *'Safari' chalet US$140 pp sharing B&B, or US$155 DBB, inc airport transfers; 3-bed chalet US$30 pp B&B. Cottage US$150 (6 people, exc b/fast). Camping Kw30,000 pp.*

🏠 **Protea Hotel Safari Lodge** (60 rooms) Chisamba; 📞 0211 212843−6; e reservations@phsafarilodge.co.zm; www.proteahotels.com/safarilodge. The recently enlarged Protea stands in a 12km² private game reserve of rolling bush about 45km north of Lusaka. To get there, take the Great North Rd for about 38km, then turn right & follow the signs for a further 7km along a recently graded track.

A large, curved, thatched roof shelters the lounge, bar & a deceptively spacious restaurant that manages to remain quite intimate. The food is good, popular amongst Lusaka's more affluent residents for the buffet Sun lunch (*all you can eat Kw180,000*); at other times there's either a buffet or an à-la-carte menu. In one corner there's a business centre with 2 computers & a printer; in another, a comfy sofa & chairs. A smaller 'sister' building hosts a cosy bar with plenty of seating for relaxing with a beer in hand. The lodge has free WiFi throughout.

The original bedrooms are stunning: high, thatched ceilings, lots of style & space, & views across the lawns from a private veranda. All have en-suite bathrooms with marble tops, bath & separate (powerful) shower, as well as phones, tea/coffee makers, safes & DSTV. Mosi nets cover the kingsize dbls or twins. Larger suites or family rooms are constructed in pairs, each with 2 bunks in a separate area, & with the option of interlinking the rooms as required. These are more conventional but still very comfortable, their colourful headboards & mirror frames embellished with zany African patterns.

Outside, beautiful herbaceous borders surround a figure-of-8 swimming pool & a network of lawns. Beyond lies a wilderness area, including a lake (in the rainy season), which is home to a wide range of wildlife. I've watched a memorable flock of Abdim's stork during the wet season here, but the grass was too high (& lunch too good) to go out searching for game, though you'd expect to find zebra, warthogs, reedbuck, puku, kudu & impala amongst other common game. More surprising is the presence of Lichtenstein's hartebeest, tsessebe, oribi, sable, Kafue lechwe, eland & sitatunga. Clearly it's worth exploring during the dry season, either on a game drive (*Kw25,000 pp*) or by quadbike (Kw100,000 pp), or on one of 2 short walking trails. A large lion enclosure houses 4 resident lions, 2 males & 2 females, while even more prominent are various antelope that have been hand reared, including a bushbuck, Safari, with her foals. Finally, there is a 23-year-old elephant named Imphamvu, who is occasionally seen on drives. If she seems friendly it's because she was rescued & brought up in the Luangwa by John Coppinger of Remote Africa Safaris. After attempts to release her back into the wild failed, she finally ended up at Protea. Now she's a star attraction, though guests should of course keep their distance. **$$$$**

West of Lusaka

⌂ **Kundalila Lodge** (6 chalets) Windmill Farm, Mumbwa Rd; m 0977 772471; e liz@ cookeafricansafaris.com; www.kundalilalodge. com. ⊕ 15°23'29,98'S, 28°03'38,26'E. Owned & run by the Cooke family, Kundalila lies 28km west of Lusaka, on the right just past Farmers Bar & the turning for Nampundwe. It's a tranquil place, its thatched en-suite chalets with twin or kingsize beds set among lawns in mature gardens on the family farm. Evening meals are available on request, served in the thatched *lapa* where there's also a convivial bar. Farm walks, game & fishing trips & market visits can be arranged with advance notice. Airport transfers US$40 pp (min 2 people). **$$$**

South of Lusaka

⌂ **Lilayi Lodge** (12 rondavels) ☎0211 840435; m 0955 045883/7; e lilayireservations@ lilayi.com; www.lilayi.com. If you can arrange the transport, then Lilayi is the most pleasant, & the best value, of the more upmarket options close to Lusaka. The lodge is on a 600ha farm, criss-crossed with game-viewing roads. To get there, head south from the Kafue roundabout at the end of Cairo Rd for about 11km. Turn left at the signpost,right at the T-junction (where the police training college is in front of you), then immediately left; this leads straight to the lodge, which is about 9km off the main road.

Lilayi means 'place of rest', & the name is apt: cool green lawns are dotted with comfortable, well-furnished brick rondavels. Half of these are suites, with a bedroom, spacious lounge, & en-suite bath, shower & toilet; the others have 2 en-suite bedrooms off a small, shared lounge.

The main building has a spacious bar & restaurant overlooking a large pool, plus an upstairs lounge. The à-la-carte menu (**$$$**) includes daily specials such as venison, & is sometimes complemented by an outdoor braai.

The farm has been well stocked with most of Zambia's antelope, including some of the less common species like roan, defassa waterbuck, tsessebe & giraffe, & boasts a good range of bird species. So if you failed to sight something in one of the parks, walk around here for a few hours before you leave or ask to be taken on a game drive or guided walk (*free to overnight guests; non residents Kw30,000 pp*). For experienced riders, horseriding is an option, by prior arrangement (*US$30 pp/hr; hard hats available*). There are also facilities for badminton & volleyball, & a small curio shop. *US$190–250 dbl DBB.*

✗ WHERE TO EAT

The gradual evolution that was Lusaka's eating scene has speeded up in the last couple of years as the two main shopping malls vie for business. Manda Hill is arguably the best place to go for fast food, with the likes of Nandos and Subway among other imports jostling for position – though Cairo Road and the various fuel stations offer their own variations.

For more classy fare, the Arcades and adjacent Acacia Park are the better bet, but there are several more individual restaurants dotted around the city that are well worth seeking out.

With quite a high turnover of restaurants, it's inevitable that my recommendations are soon obsolete, so ask around for what's new, or buy a copy of *The Lowdown* for the best of the latest restaurants. Do remember that menu prices are frequently quoted without VAT (currently 16%) and service (10%).

If you're on a tight budget, then you will want to buy supplies from the shopping centres and cater for yourself. See *Shopping: food and supplies* (page 145) for details of these. Some of the supermarkets, such as Spar in the Arcades, serve ready-made dishes at lunchtime, catering for the local office trade. The surprising lack of street-food stalls is the result of a controversial policy introduced in 1999 banning all vendors from the streets of the city.

CAFÉS, PUBS AND LIGHT MEALS

Chit Chat [130 D3] 5A Omelo Mumbwa Rd; m 0977 774481; ⊕ 08.30–22.00 Tue–Sat, 08.30–16.30 Mon. No longer the trendy place of yore, Chit Chat retains a pleasant garden & sheltered terrace, & friendly if slow service. Burgers & samosas are reasonable, & b/fast is served. $

Kilimanjaro Café [121 H7] Leopards Hill Rd; ☎ 0211 250527; ⊕ 07.00–22.00 daily. It's worth the trek to Kilimanjaro's new location out of town (see Kilimanjaro Country Lodge, page 135, for directions). With its hallmark colourful crafts, WiFi access & well-equipped play area, it's fun, spacious & very child friendly. Tables spill onto a wide veranda fronted by grassland dotted with trees. The menu was being 'upgraded' when we visited, but with b/fast, coffee & cakes, salads & light lunches, or burgers, steaks & curry, there's already something for any time of day. $–$$$

La Mimosa [121 E3] Arcades; ☎ 0211 257264; ⊕ 07.30–22.30. Consistently popular, this conventional coffee shop with sports TV spills out onto the pavement under umbrellas.

As well as b/fasts, baguettes, crêpes & salads, it serves good coffee – including decaffeinated choices. $

Mint Café [121 E3] Arcades; m 0965 900800; ⊕ 08.00–20.00 Sun–Thu, 08.00–22.00 Fri/Sat. This stylish little café is bright, modern & minimalist. Stop for a variety of light meals such as salads, wraps & sandwiches as well as smoothies & fresh juices – or head for its more grown-up sibling, Mint Lounge. $–$$

Vasilis [131 F1] Manda Hill; ⊕ 08.00–19.30 daily. Coffee & cakes or pizza & baguettes – it's all at this modern café-cum-bakery with tables inside & out. $

Zebra Crossings [131 F1] Ababa Hse, Twikatane Rd; ☎ 0211 257148; ⊕ 09.00–17.00 Mon–Fri, 09.00–14.00 Sat. A seasonal menu with salads, soups, daily specials & lots of veggie options have marked out this open-sided venue as a lunchtime favourite. Come for coffee & cakes, too, & check out the artwork from Ababa House's latest exhibition (page 146) that adorn the café. It's creative, colourful & child friendly (& there's a WiFi hotspot too). $$–$$$

RESTAURANTS In recent years, the number and variety of restaurants in Lusaka has all but exploded, with almost every ethnic cuisine catered for (frequently in the same venue), and a range of standards to match. If you're looking for somewhere special, then a consensus of informed opinion gives Lusaka's top spots for foodies as Marlin's and Rhapsody's. That said, the competition is hotting up with the opening of four new restaurants at Acacia Park, a short stroll from the Arcades, each with tables both inside and on a balcony with an incongruous backdrop of palm trees and bank buildings.

The Showgrounds, near Manda Hill on the Great East Road [131 G1], is worth an evening visit in its own right, when its restaurants and bars come to life.

For competent but unimaginative food, the big **hotels** – the InterCon, Taj Pamodzi and Southern Ridgeway – all have their own restaurants. The Taj Pamodzi also does a good line in Indian cuisine, with a popular Indian buffet on Friday nights. The location and generally good service of these hotels make them an easy option for visitors, but there are more interesting alternatives within relatively easy reach.

Nobody walks in Lusaka at night, so unless you're staying at the Protea Arcades (with direct access to the restaurants at Arcades and Acacia Park), you'll need either to dine at your hotel or take a taxi. In this case, arrange with your driver to collect you at the end of the evening as well. For those with their own vehicle, most restaurants and shopping complexes offer secure or guarded parking. In most places, it's perfectly acceptable to take your own wine, although you may be charged corkage of around Kw30,000 in the more upmarket establishments. Finally, do remember that restaurants can get very busy, so at the classier places – especially on Friday and Saturday nights – it's wise to book.

✖ **Plates** [121 E3] Acacia Park; ☎0211 841015; www.plateszambia.com; ⊕ 12.00–22.00 Mon–Thu, 12.00–24.00 Fri/Sat. Gaining a reputation for serious food, albeit at relatively high prices, Plates offers quite a formal environment. Alongside the standard steaks, specials such as pan-fried herb-crusted chicken with new potatoes & spicy rocket salad should get the tastebuds stirring. $$$–$$$$$

✖ **Rhapsody's** [121 E3] Arcades; ☎021 256705/6; www.rhapsodys.co.za; ⊕ 12.00–late. With its large circular bar, varnished brickwork, & blue & terracotta décor, Rhapsody's is often buzzing – especially on Fri nights. The restaurant, set slightly higher than the bar, is fronted by a covered courtyard that is popular at lunchtime, when there's a separate menu. Evening options range through steaks, salads, fish & veggie dishes, with sufficient innovation (such as chicken wrapped with bacon, peppers & chillis) to lift it above Lusaka's norm. No shorts allowed after 18.00. Booking advised; credit cards accepted. $$$–$$$$$

✖ **Le Triumph Dolphin** [130 D2] Paseli Rd, Northmead; ☎0211 292133; m 0977 774954; ⊕ 11.00–15.00 &18.00–late Mon–Sat. Old favourites belting out on the sound system contrast with Le Triumph's slightly sleezy atmosphere. Service is good, & the food's not bad either – especially the steaks. Creole dishes & (pricey) seafood are specialities. If karaoke's not your thing, come on a Monday or before 21.00. $$$–$$$$$

✖ **Chicago's** [131 F1] Manda Hill; ⊕ 09.00–22.00, bar 16.00–late. Al Capone wouldn't look out of place at this dark & trendy venue, Lusaka's take on gangsterland. In the food stakes, it offers all the standards, plus an unlikely sushi menu. It's also a popular late-night drinking den. $$$–$$$$

✖ **La Gondola** [121 E3] Arcades; ☎0211 250280; ⊕ 12.00–22.00 daily. All things Italian can be found here, including pasta & good pizzas – plus more standard fare of wraps & steaks. $$$–$$$$

✖ **Ocean Basket** [121 E3] Arcades; m 0977 755368. A branch of the popular South African fish chain that's gradually making inroads across southern Africa. The ambience is diner rather than dinner. $$$–$$$$

✖ **Cattleman's Grill** [131 H4] Chrismar Hotel, Los Angeles Bd; ☎0211 253036/253605; ⊕ daily.

Strictly for carnivores, this thatched outdoor restaurant has African friezes decorating the walls. Fri & Sat nights are particularly busy, with regular live bands. $$$

✖ **Chang Thai** [121 E3] Acacia Park; ☎0975 835999; ⊕ 12.00–15.00, 18.00–22.30 daily. An unlikely find in Lusaka, Chang Thai is at its best in the evening when soft lighting & candles illuminate the warmth of the interior. The food is surprisingly good, the staff efficient & friendly, & there's a takeaway service too. $$$

✖ **Dil Restaurant** [121 H5] 153 Ibex Hill Rd; ☎0211 262391/262691. This is sometimes cited as Lusaka's best restaurant for high-quality Indian food (& some Chinese dishes). The food is good, but it's not cheap. $$$

✖ **Dong Fang** [131 G4] Dunduza Chisidza Ct, Longacres; ☎0211 254328. Set in a red-brick colonial building in a quiet area of the city, this pleasant restaurant offers large portions of traditional Chinese fare. $$$

✖ **Gerritz** [131 E2] 26 Chaholi Rd, Rhodes Pk; ☎0211 253639; www.gerritzrestaurant.com; ⊕ 12.00–21.00 Mon–Fri, 12.00–16.00 Sun; closed Sat. This German restaurant is owned & run by the eponymous chef, who serves reliable & original dishes from a mixed menu. The atmosphere is casual, with regular theme evenings usually advertised in *The Lowdown*. $$$

✖ **Marlin's** [131 G4] Lusaka Club, nr cnr of Los Angeles Bd & Haile Selassie Av, Longacres; ☎0211 252206. At the back of the old sports club, this apparently uninspiring place serves some of the best (& best-value) food in town. The sizeable pepper steaks are renowned (ask for a 'lady's steak' if you're not up for it), or try the superb crab tom yam soup. Salads, chow meins & stir fries are always good, & the service is professional & discreet. Booking is essential. $$$

✖ **Mike's Kitchen** [121 E3] Arcades; m 0968 315444; ⊕ 11.00–21.30 Sun–Thu, 11.00–22.30 Fri/Sat. With booths, red-&-white checked floors & a menu like a glossy magazine, Mike's is an all-American diner. Classic chicken, grills & burgers share the menu with more esoteric offerings: snails, sweet-&-sour pork, schnitzel, & South African favourites such as boerwors. There's a great selection of milkshakes, but service is very slow. $$$

✗ Muskaan [121 G5] Kabulonga Rd; ☎ 0211 265976. Muskaan's Indian cuisine is rated highly by locals both for quality & value for money. Also at Chindo Rd; ☎ 0211 262078. $$$

✗ News Café [121 E3] Acacia Park; m 0977 774020; www.newscafe.co.za. The South African chain may be familiar to those in transit at Johannesburg airport, but it's created quite a stir in Lusaka. With paninis, tramezzinis & a whole lot more, it's all quite informal, but that doesn't seem to deter the in crowd. $$$

✗ Sichuan [121 E3] Showgrounds, Great East Rd; ☎ 0211 253842. One of countless Chinese restaurants in the city – & recommended, if a little hard to find. Once inside the large warehouse building, however, you'll find good-value authentic Chinese food. $$-$$$$

✗ Times Café [121 E3] Arcades; ☎ 0211 258017; ⊕ 11.00 till very late Mon–Sat. A generally younger crowd heads for this minimalist but loud sports bar offering eat-in or takeaway snacks, steaks, grills & salads. $$-$$$$

✗ Mint Lounge [121 E3] Acacia Park; ☎ 0975 071505. Lusaka's buzzword for healthy eating, Mint Lounge is a great lunchtime venue, & a good

spot for sundowners, though less inviting in the evening. Informal, cool & with inside & outside seating, it's a must for salads, wraps, cakes or a late b/fast. $$-$$$

✗ O'Hagans [121 G7] Woodlands; ☎ 0211 255555; ⊕ 10.30–late, last food orders 22.30; occasional happy hours. The popular O'Hagans moved every last table & beer tap to its new suburban home – & you'd hardly know the difference. The menu boasts a range of specials from Irish boxty to eisbein, but if it's the staples you're craving, never fear: main meals of fish & chips or steaks continue to dominate, & they still do their half & full portions of salads. $$-$$$

✗ La Revolución [121 E2] 254/18 Zambezi Rd, Roma; m 0977 966035; ⊕ 12.00–late daily. With *banditos* on the outer walls & gardens & fountains in a courtyard setting, this Mexican-themed place attracts expats & hip Zambians alike. Come for traditional Mexican food, or themed salsa or ladies' nights, & stay for beer & cocktails. Fri night is particularly busy. $$-$$$

✗ Mahak [130 C2] 61 Great East Rd; ☎ 0211 229002. A great Indian restaurant, where an all-you-can-eat vegetable thali offers amazing value for money. $

ENTERTAINMENT AND NIGHTLIFE

BARS AND NIGHTCLUBS The period that a nightclub remains in fashion, and hence remains in business, is even shorter than the life of most restaurants, so recommendations in this section will, by their very nature, be out of date quickly. It's better to ask the locals about the best places, and follow their suggestions. Always be mindful of your safety: don't take much cash to a club with you, and don't linger anywhere that feels uncomfortable.

Consistently popular are the bars at **O'Hagans** and **Rhapsody's**, which open till late and attract a mixed, fairly upmarket crowd. More clubby in style is **Chicago's** at Manda Hill, while a younger, more local clientele is to be found at the **Times Café**. See above for details of these.

For live music, there's a nightly band at the Steaks & Grills restaurant at the **Taj Pamodzi** [131 E4]. Otherwise you'll need to be in town on a Friday or Saturday night, when there are bands at the Chrismar's **Cattleman's Grill** [131 H4]. The lively and easy-going **Frog** [130 C3] *Kabelenga Rd;* ☎ *0211 225756;* ⊕ *Mon–Thu 10.00–23.00, Fri–Sat 10.00–late)* usually has a disco on Friday nights and live bands on Saturdays (*entrance Kw5,000–10,000*), but salsa nights are on the menu, too, & you can mop up the drink with nshima & beef, goat or chicken. If karaoke's your thing, head straight for **Le Triumph Dolphin** (see above) after 21.00, any night except Monday.

Several popular clubs are found around **Northmead** shopping centre [130 D1]. Be warned, though, that there is a security problem at night, so go with a local, and don't even think about taking a vehicle or anything valuable. **Zenon** is a crowded, no-smoking disco, from where the crowds tend to move on to **The Lounge**. There's dancing at **Room 101** by the casino in the Arcades ([121 E3] *entry Kw50,000*), or – further out – at **Chez Ntemba**, behind the Kamwala Market ([130 B5] *entry Kw50,000 Fri/Sat*), which has a small cover charge and plays mainly rumba. The bar is good and on Friday and Saturday nights partying continues until dawn – but there's no food available. Along the Kafue Road, there's also **The Tube** [120 B7] *nr Castle shopping complex; entry free*) and, a little further south, in the Makeni area, the **Majestic Casino** has a heavily used pool table.

ENTERTAINMENT Lusaka at last has a permanent cinema ([121 E3] *Arcades*; ☏ *0211 256719*) in the form of a modern five-screen multiplex. Films are mostly fairly up to date, and tickets cost Kw28,000, or half price from Monday to Thursday.

The Lusaka Playhouse, opposite the Southern Sun Ridgeway and Taj Pamodzi hotels in the centre of town [131 E4], features a variety of local theatrical productions. For details, check the current edition of *The Lowdown*, or just turn up to see what's on. Note, though, that parking in the area isn't great, so you'd be well advised to leave your vehicle in the car park of the Southern Sun.

If the city is hosting a concert, the most likely venue is the Mulungushi International Conference Centre, which is situated opposite the Arcades [121 E3], out towards the airport.

SHOPPING

Lusaka's main shopping centre used to be Cairo Road which, before 1996, was full of small, cramped private trader's shops where it was very difficult to find the right place to buy what you wanted. Then Shoprite opened its flagship store in the centre, followed shortly afterwards by the city's first shopping mall. Since then, the city's shopping opportunities have marched on apace, and shops along the Cairo Road have become increasingly restricted.

The complex at **Manda Hill** [131 F1], on the Great East Road, revolutionised shopping in Lusaka when it was first opened. Modern and clean, with plenty of parking and a conspicuous security presence, it's the preferred place to shop for both visitors and many local people. Following recent expansion, it now offers two-storey parking and feels exactly like any shopping mall in the West. Come on a Saturday afternoon and you'll see Lusaka's fashionistas seeking out the latest trends alongside mothers doing the week's grocery shopping and plenty of young men wandering around looking cool.

A stone's throw to the east, on the other side of the road, the **Arcades** complex [121 E3] has more of an entertainments and restaurant bias, but it still offers a range of shops, including music and video stores and a SuperSpar supermarket. There's also a filling station and round-the-clock guarded parking for up to 750 vehicles.

In the wealthier suburbs, smaller shopping complexes include **Crossroads** at Leopards Hill [121 H6], the new **Woodlands** shopping centre [121 G7], and the more established **Kabulonga** [121 G5]. With the opening of the new **Pick 'n' Pay Centre** [120 B7] at Makeni, there'll be another option to the south, too. Nevertheless, Lusaka's traditional, vibrant markets (pages 150–1) continue to thrive, and are well worth a visit if you have the time.

Shops at Lusaka's malls are usually open Monday to Friday, from around 09.00 to 18.00, but on Saturday and Sunday most shops close earlier, especially on Sunday when midday or early afternoon is the norm. Shops elsewhere in the city are usually closed on a Sunday.

FOOD AND SUPPLIES Most of Lusaka's visitors now stick to one of the large **supermarkets**, which are just like any found in Europe or America. The original Shoprite [130 B4], on the eastern side of Cairo Road, with guarded parking (*Kw1,000*) was their pioneering store in Zambia. Now, however, such supermarkets have proliferated, first at Manda Hill, then at the Arcades, and more recently with the new Pick 'n' Pay at Woodlands. There are smaller (but still sizeable) supermarkets elsewhere, too. Of these, Melissa minimarket [130 D1] *Great East Rd, Northmead*) is one of the best. It isn't cheap compared with its larger rivals, but several delis and a bakery or two have sprung up around it, and opposite it is a small craft market. There's another branch at Kabulonga shopping centre [121 G5] *cnr Kabulonga & Chindo rds*). Also out that way is Crossroads mall [121 H6] *Leopards Hill Rd*), which has a large SuperSpar among other offerings. For those staying to the south of the city, perhaps at Eureka, there's Spar at Downtown [130 B5] by the Kafue Road roundabout, the Castle supermarket [120 B7], and a little beyond this the new Pick 'n' Pay Centre.

If you're buying in bulk, head for the Shoprite Wholesale Outlet on the Kafue Road [130 B6], about 1km south of the Cairo Road roundabout. You don't need to purchase vast quantities, though buying just one or two of something is not usually allowed.

Fresh fruit and vegetables can of course be picked up from one of the local markets (see pages 150–1), as well as from various street-sellers.

BOOKS AND MUSIC

Book Cellar [131 F1] Manda Hill; ☎ 0211 255475/6. Stocks books on Zambia, wildlife, plus new novels, maps & reference books of all kinds.
Bookworld [131 F1] Manda Hill; [130 A3] Cairo Rd; [121 G5] Kabulonga; [121 H6] Crossroads; ☎ 0211 255470. This is the place for a wider range of literary interests, including Zambian literature & poetry.
Planet Books [121 E3] Arcades; ☎ 0211 256715. Similar stock to the Book Cellar.
Sounds [121 E3] Arcades & [121 H6] Crossroads. A reasonable selection of music CDs.

CAMPING & OUTDOOR EQUIPMENT
Most of the basic outdoor equipment can be found at Game ([131 F1] *Manda Hill*), but for gas canisters you could also try the Mica hardware store ([121 E3] *Arcades*), or possibly Shoprite ([130 B4] *Cairo Rd*). For fishing tackle and a range of outdoor essentials, there's Tackle & Pet Haven at Manda Hill [131 F1].

CAR SPARES
See pages 147–8.

CRAFTS, CURIOS AND GIFTS
For typical African carvings, basketware and curios, you probably won't get better value or a wider selection than at Kabwata Cultural Centre, on Burma Road ([131 E7], page 151), although there's a good range of baskets at the shop in the National Museum [130 C5]. Every Sunday a regular curio market is held at the Arcades [121 E3], or you could try the small craft market at the back of the outdoor market at Northmead [130 D1], opposite Melissa minimarket (park at the supermarket), which sells some good malachite bracelets, necklaces and a wide selection of carvings.

Specialist shops afford the opportunity to browse at leisure, without the hassle of bargaining. Or how about combining retail therapy with lunch? Try Ababa House [131 F1] or Kilimanjaro Café [121 H7]. The expensive shops at the InterContinental, Taj Pamodzi and Southern Sun Ridgeway hotels showcase gems and jewellery, though don't expect any bargains; Jagoda might be a better bet.

For a much cheaper souvenir in the form of a *chitenje* (page 75), try one of the smaller local shops such as Safique, or take a trip to one of the markets (pages 150–1). Even if you come away empty-handed, you'll have seen a far more authentic side to Zambian shopping culture than that offered by upmarket shops.

Ababa House [131 F1] Twikatane Rd; 0211 257148; m 0977 742457; ⊕ 09.00–17.00 Mon–Fri, 09.00–14.00 Sat. In a converted private house, Serena Ansley showcases the work of over 80 artists & craftworkers, from AIDS orphans & the Malambo Women's co-operative at Monze to professionals. Much of their work is very affordable – & transportable. Browsing through the pottery, sculptures, furniture, jewellery, textiles & more makes for a very enjoyable hour or so, particularly if combined with coffee or lunch in the Zebra Crossings café. An outlet for wickedly delicious homemade chocolates is an added bonus. And if further incentive is required, there's also a hair salon specialising in Western styles! An art exhibition is held at 17.30 on the 1st Thu of each month, with snacks & a cash bar; the month's art is then displayed in the café.

Jackal & Hide [121 H7] Sugarbush Farm, Leopards Hill Rd; 0211 213841; m 0977 874771; e gillie@tribaltextiles.co.zm; www. jackalandhide.net; ⊕ 08.00–12.30 Mon–Sat, 14.00–16.30 Mon–Fri. Hand-crafted leather handbags from Kw350,000 may not be cheap, but they are unusual, & designs can be made up to order. Find it 10.4km beyond Crossroads.

Jagoda [130 D3] 1 Luano Rd; 0211 220814; www.jagodagems.com

Kilimanjaro Café [121 H7] Leopards Hill Rd; 0211 250527. Inject some fun into your shopping at this out-of-town café, which is decked out with a colourful array of toys, carvings, paintings & gorgeous patchwork textiles, all for sale. For directions, see Kilimanjaro Country Lodge, page 135.

Kubu Crafts [131 F1] Manda Hill; 0211 256644. Prices at this established craft emporium are lower than in the past – but this comes hand in hand with a drop in quality.

Safique [130 B5] Independence Av; 0211 228449. Next to Tazara House, this fabric emporium is a great place to pick up a good-quality *chitenje*, though bargaining isn't part of the deal.

PHARMACIES These are dotted all over the city. Recommended are:

Jubilee Chemist 0211 255556/7, 265331/238216. Branches at Cairo Rd [130 A4], Manda Hill [131 F1], Crossroads [121 H6] & Kabulonga [121 G5]

Link 0211 231124. Branches at Manda Hill [131 F1], Arcades [121 E3] & Woodlands [121 G7]. More expensive than Jubilee, but arguably with better stock.

PHOTOGRAPHIC SUPPLIES
Phoenix Photographics [130 B4] Cairo Rd; 0211 221916; [131 F1] Manda Hill; 0211 255469; ⊕ 10.00–14.00 daily. Don't expect to find a great range, though they do stock film, & can arrange camera repairs.

BANKS AND CHANGING MONEY

BANKS Although many of the main banks have their head offices along Cairo Road, more useful for most visitors are their branches at Manda Hill, the Arcades and almost all other shopping complexes, where security is far better than on Cairo Road. Most of these have ATMs, so obtaining cash is usually straightforward. There is also a well-guarded Barclays ATM at the Southern Sun Ridgeway.

CHANGING MONEY Use a bank or bureau de change to change money wherever possible; otherwise stick to a hotel – though these generally offer poor rates of exchange, or charge steep commissions.

Be aware, too, that counterfeit US$100 and Kw50,000 notes are in circulation. Wherever you change money, don't forget to take some ID with you.

When changing travellers' cheques, you may – somewhat controversially – need to take the 'proof of purchase' slip that you were given when you bought the cheques.

Bureaux de change While Cairo Road remains the stronghold of Lusaka's bureaux de change, usually with the best rates, they are now to be found in shopping complexes across the city, including in the Spar supermarket at the Arcades [121 E3]. With the slight decrease in rates comes a conspicuous improvement in security. There is also a bureau de change upstairs at the main post office on Cairo Road ([130 B4] ☉ *08.00–17.00 Mon–Fri, 08.00–12.00 Sat*). Bureaux de change usually deal only with cash and will not exchange travellers' cheques.

COMMUNICATIONS

INTERNET Lusaka may not have quite the proliferation of internet cafés as other African capitals, but there are certainly several around. Start with the various shopping malls – Manda Hill, Arcades, Woodlands, Crossroads and Northmead all have this facility. Be warned that you'll often be faced with outdated hardware, so even the simplest email can take a significant time to write and send. Most of the better hotels and several cafés and guesthouses now offer wireless internet access, often free of charge, and some have business centres with internet facilities, too. As with internet cafés, connections can be erratic and the service is often slow.

POST AND TELEPHONE Lusaka's busy main **post office** is in the centre of Cairo Road, [130 B4]. The main hall on the ground floor has a row of assistants in cubicles – above which the occupant's responsibilities are detailed. If you're just looking for stamps, it's probably quicker to go to one of the smaller post offices around the city.

Both the main post office and the one at Ridgeway have a philatelic counter for purchasing Zambia's colourful stamps, including first-day issues and blocks. Upstairs you will find a bureau de change where rates are on a par with those of the banks.

The major **mobile-phone** providers have countless branches throughout the city. Top-up cards are easily available in shops and from street vendors at major road junctions.

COURIERS If you need to send something valuable then do not trust the postal service; a courier is by far the best way. The main couriers in Lusaka are:

DHL (Zambia) ☎0211 229768; www.dhl.co.zm
FedEx ☎0211 252189; www.fedex.com
Mercury Express/UPS ☎0211 257361/4; www.ups.com

Skynet Couriers ☎0211 224047; www.skynet.net

OTHER PRACTICALITIES

CAR REPAIRS AND SPARES Repairs used to be difficult to arrange as spare parts were in poor supply, but this has changed considerably. One of the most highly recommended places for car repairs in general is Brian Vermaak at **World of Wheels** (☎ *0211 227256*). Specialists include:

CFAO [120 B3] Sheki-Sheki Rd; 0211 243112/240167. The local Nissan dealer.
Southern Cross Motors [120 B7] Kafue Rd; 0211 214287/8, 214778/80. Mercedes, Jeep & Mitsubishi.

Toyota [130 A2] Cairo Rd; 0211 228228/ 229109. The main Toyota centre for parts, sales & service.

For **spares and tyres** in general, try:

Autoworld [130 A5] Freedom Way; 0211 223207, 237716/9; www.autoworldzm.com. The new outlet at Woodlands [121 G7] also handles basic repairs.

Impala Service Station [130 A2] Great North Rd; 0211 238275/238284. Just north of the Kabwe roundabout at the end of Cairo Rd.
TS Tyre Services [121 E3] opp Arcades; 0211 290142; [130 A3] Cairo Rd 0211 235901

EMBASSIES AND HIGH COMMISSIONS IN LUSAKA

The following is a selection of Lusaka's diplomatic missions in Lusaka. For a complete list, see www.zambiatourism.com/travel/listings/foreign or look in the front of the telephone directory.

E Angola (embassy) 6660 Mumana Rd, Olympia Pk Ext; 0211 290346/291142/292595
E Botswana (high commission) 5201 Pandit Nehru Rd; 0211 250019/250555
E Canada (high commission) 5119 United Nations Av; 0211 250833; www.canadainternational.gc.ca
E Denmark (embassy) 5219 Haile Selassie Av; 0211 254277; www.amblusaka.um.dk
E DRC (Zaire) (embassy) 1124 Parirenyatwa Rd ; 0211 213343/229044–5
E Finland (embassy) Haile Selassie Av (opp Ndeke Hse), Longacres; 0211 251988/252026; www.finland.org.zm
E France (embassy) 74 Independence Av; 0211 251322/251340; www.ambafrance-zm.org
E Germany (embassy) 5209 United Nations Av; 0211 250644/251259/251262; www.zambiaembassy.de
E India (high commission) 1 Pandit Nehru Rd; 0211 253006/253158–60; www.hcizambia.com
E Ireland (embassy) 6663 Katima Mulilo Rd, Olympia Pk Ext; 0211 290482/291124/ 292288; www.embassyofireland.co.zm
E Italy (embassy) 5211 Embassy Pk, Diplomatic Triangle; 0211 250755/250781/ 250783; www.amblusaka.esteri.it
E Kenya (high commission) 5207 United Nations Av; 0211 250722/250742/250751; www.kenyamission.org.zm

E Malawi (high commission) Bishops Rd, Kabulonga; 0211 265764/9
E Mozambique (embassy) 9592 Kacha Rd, Northmead; 0211 220333/239135
E Namibia (high commission) 6968 Kabanga Rd, Rhodes Pk; 0211 250968/252250
E Netherlands (embassy) 5208 United Nations Av; 0211 253819/253590/253994; www.netherlandsembassy.org.zm
E Nigeria (high commission) 5203 United Nations Av; 0211 253177/263265/263268
E Norway (high commission) cnr Birdcage Wk, Haile Selassie Av; 0211 252188/252625; www.norway.org.zm
E Portugal (embassy) 23 Yotam Muleya Rd, Woodlands; 0211 253720/260296
E South Africa (high commission) D26 Cheetah Rd, Kabulonga; 0211 260999
E Sweden (embassy) Haile Selassie Av; 0211 251711; www.swedenabroad.com
E Tanzania (high commission) Ujamaa Hse, 5200 United Nations Av; 0211 253220/2–4; ⊕ for visas 08.00–12.00 only.
E UK (high commission) 5210 Independence Av; 0211 423200; http://ukinzambia.fco.gov.uk
E US (embassy) Kabulonga Rd, Ibex Hill; 0211 357000; http://zambia.usembassy.gov
E Zimbabwe (high commission) Haile Selassie Av; 0211 254006/12/16

EMERGENCIES

For a serious medical condition, see *Chapter 5, Health and Safety*, pages 93–7, and don't hesitate to use the emergency number given with your medical insurance. As a failsafe, many adventure/safari companies, lodges and camps also subscribe to an emergency medical evacuation service. Good travel insurances will also cover you for use of their service, although authorisation for this in an emergency can take time. Their regional offices are:

✚ **Health International/Medical Air Rescue Service (MARS)** ☎0211 236644/231175–6

✚ **Specialty Emergency Services MedRescue (SES)** Emergency ☎0211 212663/4; general ☎0211 273302–7; m 0977 770302/5; e med@ zamnet.zm; www.ses-zambia.com

For less life-threatening conditions, either your embassy or hotel should be able to recommend a doctor. The government-run **University Teaching Hospital** ([131 G6] *Nationalist Rd;* ☎0211 254113) has a department for emergencies, but it is sadly overstretched and best avoided if possible.

A sick foreign traveller will usually be accepted by one of the well-equipped clinics used by the city's more affluent residents without too many questions being asked at first, though proof of comprehensive medical insurance will make this all the more speedy. Some are affiliated to specific insurance companies, so it would be wise to check this first if you can.

✚ **Al-Shifa Health Centre** [131 F1] 8238 Nangwenya Rd; ☎0211 253338/254819
✚ **Care for Business (CFB)** [131 F2] 4192 Addis Ababa Dr; ☎0211 252917; m 0979 700100; www.cfbmedic.com.zm
✚ **Corpmed Clinic** [130 B3] 3236 Cairo Rd (behind Barclays Business Centre); ☎0211 222612/226983; www.corpmedzambia.com

✚ **Fairview Hospital** [130 D4] Chilubi Rd; ☎0211 373000; www.medicare-zambia.com. New private hospital opened in Feb 2011.
✚ **Lusaka Trust Hospital** [121 H5] 2191 Nsumbu Rd, Woodlands; ☎0211 252190/253481/254702. 24hr service.
✚ **Mum's Care Clinic** [130 B2] Gt East Rd; ☎0211 237915. Despite the name, this is a general clinic, rather than a specialist maternity unit.

RELIGIOUS SERVICES Lusaka is well served both for churches and mosques. The city's Anglican Cathedral of the Holy Cross is close to the international hotels in the Ridgeway district [131 E4]. Regular services are held here every Sunday at 08.00, 10.00 and 17.00, while those on weekdays vary; for details, see the noticeboard outside the church. The Catholic Cathedral is off Kumoyo Road [131 G4].

TRAVEL AGENTS There's no shortage of travel agents in the capital, but attentive and efficient service isn't as common, and at present only a few, such as Voyagers, are used to the demands of overseas clients. In addition, many have their own favourite properties or trips, and will recommend those, regardless of what would suit you best.

Most safari arrangements are best made as far in advance as possible. Unless you are travelling totally independently (driving or hiking, and camping everywhere), you should ideally book with a good specialist tour operator before you leave home (see pages 44–5). This will also give you added consumer protection, and recourse from home if things go wrong. By booking ahead, you also have the best chance of getting into the places you want to visit.

If you do choose to book locally, try one of Lusaka's better travel agents – or one for which you have a reliable personal recommendation. Several readers have been defrauded by rogue Zambia-based travel agents in recent years, so always pay by credit card as it will give your money some degree of protection.

AAA Travel Zambia [131 F1] Ababa Hse, Twikatane Rd; m 0977 060651; e info@ aaatravelzambia.com. Linked to the South African AAA Travel, & agents for Mukambi Safari Lodge.
Bush Buzz [131 G1] 10 Nangwenya Rd; 0211 265893/256992; e info@bush-buzz.com; www.bush-buzz.com
Juls [121 E2] 5507 Libala Rd, Kalundu; 0211 292979/293972; e juls.travel@travelport.co.zm; www.julsafrica.com

The Travel Shop [121 E3] Arcades; 0211 250893/257772; [131 F1] Manda Hill; 0211 257856/7; e travelshop@microlink.zm, silverlinetravel@microlink.zm; www.travelshopzambia.com
Voyagers [131 E4] Suez Rd (100m from Southern Sun Ridgeway); 0211 253064–5; e travel@voyagerszambia.com; www.voyagerszambia.com

FURTHER INFORMATION

There are few really useful sources of information about Lusaka, except for the excellent monthly *The Lowdown* (*www.lowdown.co.zm*). Each issue of this super booklet approaches 100 pages in length and has independent reviews of restaurants, topical articles, letters and occasional travel features, and a sprinkling of humour. At Kw7,000 per issue, you can't afford not to buy a copy if you see one – even if you're only passing through the capital. Seek them out at hotels, supermarkets, service stations, craft and bookshops in Lusaka and Shoprite outlets across the country.

SPORT AND ACTIVITIES

The bigger **hotels** have their own fitness suites, featuring gyms, saunas and spas, as well as one or two very good private pools. The **municipal swimming pool** ([131 G2] *Nangwenya Rd; admission around Kw10,000*), near the International School, is Olympic size and is usually open between October and April.

Lusaka has all the normal sports clubs, including the **rugby** club at the Showgrounds, and **golf** clubs both at Longacres [121 F5] and at Chainama [121 G3], towards the airport.

The National Sports Development Centre in the Showgrounds [131 G1] has the city's cheapest and best **squash** courts (glass-backed), as well as **tennis** courts and a bar.

WHAT TO SEE AND DO

Perhaps the most fun to be had around town is simply people-watching, and talking with those who live here. From the poor street vendors (when the police haven't chased them away!) to taxi drivers and the aid-agency expats in the larger hotels, you'll find that people are usually happy to chat. They will comment freely on politics and the issues of the day, and probably ask you how you view things as a foreigner.

These conversations can be fascinating, but be mindful that there aren't debating points to be earned, just new points of view to learn. Try not to expound your prejudices and you'll have much longer and more interesting conversations. Other ways to spend your time in Lusaka include:

MARKETS AND BAZAARS Several of the markets (⊕ *06.00–18.00 Mon–Sat*) are fascinating to wander around, but pay attention to your safety and don't take anything valuable with you. Think twice before wandering around with a backpack, which is inviting theft, and if you have a safe place to leave your money-belt, then don't take that either.

Most of the market stalls concentrate on vegetables and fresh and dried fish, plus new and second-hand clothes. There'll be plenty of others, though, selling everything from baskets to tobacco, bicycle parts to an assortment of hardware. Of particular interest may be the traditional-healer stalls, tinsmiths and furniture makers.

The more relaxed of the two main markets for visitors is **Kamwala Market** on Independence Avenue [130 B5]; if you're heading west, it's just before the railway on the left-hand side of the road. Stalls here are predominantly owned by the city's Chinese and Lebanese communities, and have a reputation for poor quality, though the difference between this and other markets is none too clear to the casual observer.

On the western side of Cairo Road, the **New City Market** – widely known as 'Soweto' Market although the location and name were changed some years ago – is on Lumumba Road [130 A4], which in itself is lined with street vendors peddling their wares. This is the city's biggest market, lively and interesting – it's even popular with adventurous expats on Saturday mornings. Here in particular it's important to dress down for a visit, and don't even think of taking those valuables with you.

There are two other large markets in the centre, both smaller than the New City Market. The **Central Market** is near the Kulima Tower on Chachacha Road [130 A4], and **Comesa** (or Luburma) Market is off Independence Avenue near the Kafue Road fly-over bridge [130 A5]. Comesa is the preserve of traders from across the region, importing goods from Botswana, Zimbabwe, Namibia, Mozambique and Angola. In all of these you'll find clothing donated by charities from the West, with shoes piled up in great heaps. This trade, known as *salaula*, has badly affected Zambia's indigenous clothes industry – which previously thrived on the production and sale of printed cotton fabrics, like the common *chitenjes*. This is why *salaula*'s long-term value as a form of aid is hotly debated.

Many visitors will find the Sunday **street market** at the Arcades ([121 E3] ⊕ *10.00–17.00*) less daunting, though bargaining here is as important as in the bigger markets.

Somewhat different in character is the genteel bazaar held on the last Saturday of each month at the **Dutch Reform Church** ([121 G5] *Kabulonga Rd; ⊕ 08.00–14.00; entry Kw3,000 pp*). It's a good place for gifts and crafts, from jewellery to handmade clothing and carvings from all over central Africa. It's also a friendly and relaxed place to have coffee and cakes, to savour Chinese and Indian snacks, or to find good biltong.

MUSEUMS AND CULTURE

Kabwata Cultural Centre ([131 E7] Burma Rd; ⊕ *07.00–18.00*) The rondavels of the Kabwata Cultural Village are all that remain of 300 similar huts, which were built in the 1930s and '40s by the colonial government to house Lusaka's black labour force. They were designed with just one room, to house single men whose families were expected to remain in the rural areas rather than become permanent urban settlers.

Between 1971 and '73 the government demolished most of the huts to construct the flats now seen nearby. Fortunately, in 1974, 43 rondavels were saved and turned into a 'cultural centre' with the aim of preserving the country's cultural heritage. Today, many of the rondavels house artists from all over Zambia, who live and work here. In addition to wood- and stone-carvers, you'll find jewellery and other crafts, much of it the work of a women's co-operative based at the centre, as well as some interesting textiles. Sadly, though, with little money spent on it, the centre isn't in a great state of repair, and plans to upgrade and revitalise it have so far come to nothing. Nevertheless, it is probably the city's best spot for buying hand-carved crafts and curios. Large wooden hippos are cheaper than equivalent carvings at the craft centre near Victoria Falls in Livingstone.

National Museum ([130 C5] *Independence Av;* ⊕ *09.00–16.30 daily, exc Christmas & New Year's Day; entry US$5/3 adult/child; no photography*) Lusaka National Museum officially opened its doors to the public in October 1996, more than ten years after its inception. It was to have been part of the UNIP Party complex on Independence Avenue but, after Kaunda's electoral defeat in 1991, the plans came to naught and the complex remained an unfinished eyesore until the government stepped in.

The museum houses several galleries on two storeys, and is well worth a visit. Upstairs is the museum proper, currently in the throes of a major and ongoing reorganisation, subject to securing appropriate funding. The eventual aim is to focus individually on Zambia's history, rural culture and urban culture, with a separate children's corner. Already there's a life-size rural village complete with rondavels and model people, set against a painted mural, all depicting traditional village life. It's well thought out and executed, and bodes well for the future. A section on urban culture was nearing completion in 2011.

For now, the rest of the museum has sections devoted to archaeology and ethnography, political and social history, and an area where artwork by children is displayed. Of these, the ethnography section is probably the most interesting, with exhibits of the material culture of various Zambian ethnic groups, including musical instruments, pottery and basket work, and a popular display of artefacts relating to witchcraft and initiation ceremonies. Don't miss the display of masks, particularly the Makishi masks of the North-Western Province. By contrast, the archaeology section is very small, essentially showing only a cast of 'Broken Hill Man', Zambia's contribution to early hominid finds. The political-history displays feature colonial, independence-era and present-day leaders, with the emphasis on Kaunda's liberation struggle.

On the ground floor, work by contemporary Zambian painters and sculptors is displayed around the walls, while in the central area a handful of traders have jewellery and clothes for sale. This is also where short-term exhibitions take place, as well as occasional special functions like book launches or film premieres (for details check the local press). Students of Zambian history will find the small library useful, but visitors may be more likely to head for the well-stocked shop selling a good range of baskets and other crafts, and a few relevant books. There's also a simple snack bar.

Freedom Statue ([130 C5] *Independence Av*) This memorial to fallen freedom fighters is just west of the National Museum. The statue, of a man breaking his chains, symbolises Zambia's liberation from the colonial yoke.

Presidents' Park ([131 F5] *Independence Av*) This small new memorial is being created to honour two of Zambia's recent presidents: Levy Patrick Mwanawasa, who died in 2008, and his predecessor in office, Frederick Chiluba, who died in 2011. It's ironic that the two men, once united within the MMD party, and now reunited, should have ended their lives in conflict when Mwanawasa brought a corruption case against his former colleague and president that was to last six bitter years. For details, see *Chapter 1, History.*

Henry Tayali Visual Arts Centre ([131 G1] m *0977 531335;* e *VAC@zamnet.zm;* ⊕ *10.00–17.00 Mon–Fri, 10.00–16.00 Sat*) In the middle of the Agricultural Showgrounds, opposite Manda Hill, this interesting art gallery has permanent as well as changing exhibitions of contemporary Zambian art. Items on display are for sale, at prices negotiated with the artist. The centre is probably the best place in Lusaka from which to buy paintings, and sometimes carvings and sculptures. Note, though, that opening hours can be somewhat erratic.

Namwande Art Gallery (*Leopards Hill Rd;* m *0977 750694;* ⊕ *closed Mon*) Those interested in Zambian painting and sculpture might also try this gallery, which is about 15km southeast of Lusaka centre, just past the American School. Expect oil paintings by prominent Zambian artists as well as watercolours, wood and stone carvings, and some delicate ceramics by over 150 Zambian practitioners. There are also pieces from other African artists.

The Showgrounds ([131 G1] *Great East Rd*) Known more formally as the Agricultural Society Showgrounds, this enclosed area is just past Manda Hill. Once a year, its network of roads fills to overflowing with visitors to stalls and displays for an annual exhibition of many aspects of Zambian industry and commerce. For most of the rest of the year it's reduced to an eclectic mix of restaurants, bars and businesses, from Barclays Bank to a canine vet and a primary school to fast-food outlets. Note that many of its entrances and exits close around sunset.

Township and city tours Lusaka Township Tours (m *0977 651675/584232/ 343907;* e *zebracitytours@gmail.com; tour US$20 pp*) is a registered youth enterprise run by a group of local guys from the Garden Compound: Taonga Tembo, Tobias Tembo and Chisanga Chomba. Their two-hour township tours cover various aspects of Zambian daily life and culture, and incorporate both clinics and local breweries. They're fun and informative, and come well recommended. They also offer city tours of Lusaka. For more informatio, check out their page on Facebook.

OUTSIDE THE CITY
Adventure City ([121 H7] *off Leopards Hill Rd;* m *0966 767631;* ⊕ *09.00–14.45 Tue–Sun; entry Kw35,000/20,000 adult/child*) Located bout 9km down Leopards Hill Road, Adventure City is clearly signposted a further 2km down a bumpy track to the left. Very popular with children and families, its main attractions are the swimming pools and waterslides, but there is also plenty of play equipment, from sandpits to trampolines. For little ones, Jungle Monkeys is a great place to let off steam, under supervision, while for adults, a bar is set well away from the rest of the complex. With attractively landscaped gardens, this is also a good spot for a family picnic.

Kalimba Reptile Park (✆ *0211 213272;* m *0977 623788;* ⊕ *09.00–17.00 Mon–Fri, 09.00–18.00 Sat/Sun; entry Kw25,000/15,000 adult/child under 14*) This well-established park has good displays of crocodiles, snakes, chameleons and tortoises, including the rare African slender-nosed crocodile, *Crocodilus cataphractus*. These occur from the DRC to west Africa, but are endangered because of the degradation of their habitat and because they are hunted for food in the DRC. In Zambia, *C. cataphractus* are found only in the Luapula River system, where they were (erroneously) thought to be extinct until recently.

Kalimba also has fishing ponds for anglers, stocked with bream, as well as crazy golf, a children's playground and a volleyball court. Drinks and snacks are available, with croc-burgers – derived from farmed animals – a major attraction.

To get there, head out of town on the Great East Road, then turn left onto District Road at the Caltex station, about 1km before the Chelston water tower. Follow this road, the D564, for about 11km to a T-junction, turn right and the park is about 1km later on the right. (There's also an alternative access road that's clearly signposted from the airport.)

Munda Wanga Wildlife Park & Sanctuary (*Kafue Rd, Chilanga;* \ *0211 278614/278529;* e *sanctuary@zamnet.zm; www.mundawanga.com;* ⊕ *08.00–17.00 daily; entry Kw25,000/15,000 adult/child*) About 20 minutes' drive south of the city, Munda Wanga's botanical gardens and wildlife sanctuary are now firmly back on the map. To get there, follow the Kafue Road south for about 15km (and watch your speed – there's a limit of 80km/h along this road). The park, with its bright red gates, is on the right. For visitors without transport, take a local bus from the Kulima Tower depot on Freedom Way ([130 A4] *Kw5,000 one way*).

The park's history has been depressing, but since privatisation in 1998, both the sanctuary and the botanical gardens have been revitalised with the help of volunteer workers. Now, environmental education is the watchword, with the aim of helping Lusaka's citizens (and the wider public) to understand and appreciate the importance of their natural heritage. There's an educational centre for local schoolchildren, many of whom will not have seen these animals in their natural habitat. For visitors who have no time to travel to one of the national parks, this is one way to see the wide variety of Zambian fauna at close quarters.

Local sponsors have helped to achieve the park's aim to specialise in native Zambian species, for which specialist environments have been created. In the wetlands area, the Kafue lechwe shares space with the puku, while impala are clearly visible in the grassland zone – and waterbuck move between the two. Predators, which include a cheetah, three wild dogs and six lions, are housed in large, natural enclosures. Phoenix, the park's appealing young elephant, sadly died following release into the Kafue National Park.

On Friday–Sunday and public holidays, feeding time at 14.00 is particularly popular – and it's suggested that you should arrive at 12.00 to take full advantage of this. There's also a bird sanctuary that's home to illegally traded or damaged birds, such as African grey parrots and black kites.

Alongside the animal park, the botanical gardens have been redeveloped with an interpretation centre. The work of young Zambian sculptors – all for sale – is displayed in a natural setting in the gardens, which are a super venue for a picnic (drinks and snacks are available) or a laze in the sun. Children, though, are likely to head for the recreational village, with its swimming pool and waterslide. Nearby is a licensed bar where lunch is served.

Lusaka National Park Some 15km southeast of the city, along Leopards Hill Road, this new conservation area has been designated close to a zone earmarked for commercial development. The 70km² site, which has over the years suffered from both deforestation and poaching, will be larger than Livingstone's Mosi-oa-Tunya National Park.

A public-private partnership with ZAWA, it is anticipated that the park will initially be stocked with herbivores such as wildebeest, hartebeest, sable antelope, zebra and bushbuck. The introduction of species such as lion and white rhino are also under consideration.

Visitor facilities are expected to include a lodge, campsite, restaurant, picnic areas and self-drive game loops. In the long term, it is possible that horseriding, boat cruises, canoeing, fishing and cultural exhibitions may also be offered.

However, despite assurances that the park would be open to the public early in 2011, work is way behind schedule. According to the Ministry of Tourism, the area has been fenced, and the translocation of animals has begun, but progress is slow, and there is no new date for opening.

8

Livingstone and the Victoria Falls

Livingstone is probably better oriented towards visitors than any other corner of Zambia. In spite of this, visitors travelling north from Zimbabwe are attracted simply by the Victoria Falls. Until relatively recently the town of Livingstone often remained unseen. In the past, some have even viewed it with suspicion, being bigger and less well known than the small Zimbabwean town which shares the name of the waterfall. As a result of Zimbabwe's recent political instability, however, Livingstone has developed rapidly over the last decade or so. Indeed, the town now plays host to a number of tour operators and lodge owners who cut their teeth across the border – so Zimbabwe's loss is very much Livingstone's gain.

The Zambian and Zimbabwean sides offer different views of the Falls, and if you have time it is worth seeing both sides to appreciate the whole waterfall. It's worth noting, though, that at present Livingstone is the preferred destination for most people visiting the Victoria Falls. Historians might note that most adventure activities like rafting, bungee jumping and microlighting originally started on the Zambian side of the Falls, before being taken over by more commercial Zimbabwean companies.

HISTORY

We can be sure that the Falls were well known to the native peoples of southern Africa well before any European 'discovered' them. After the San/Bushmen hunter-gatherers, the Toka Leya people inhabited the area, and it was probably they who christened the Falls Shongwe. Later, the Ndebele knew the Falls as the aManza Thunqayo, and after that the Makololo referred to them as Mosi-oa-Tunya.

However, their first written description comes to us from Dr David Livingstone, who approached them in November 1855 from the west – from Linyanti, along the Chobe and Zambezi rivers. Livingstone already knew of their existence from the locals, and wrote:

> I resolved on the following day to visit the Falls of Victoria, called by the natives Mosioatunya, or more anciently Shongwe. Of these we had often heard since we came into the country: indeed one of the questions asked by Sebituane [the chief of the Makololo tribe] travelling was, 'Have you the smoke that sounds in your country?' They did not go near enough to examine them, but, viewing them with awe at a distance, said, in reference to the vapour and noise, 'Mosi oa tunya' (smoke does sound there). It was previously called Shongwe, the meaning of which I could not ascertain. The word for a 'pot' resembles this, and it may mean a seething cauldron; but I am not certain of it.

SOUTHERN ZAMBIA

Livingstone continues to describe the river above the Falls, its islands and their lush vegetation, before making his most famous comment about sightseeing angels, now abused and misquoted by those who write tourist brochures to the area:

> Some trees resemble the great spreading oak, others assume the character of our own elms and chestnuts; but no one can imagine the beauty of the view from anything witnessed in England. It had never been seen before by European eyes; but scenes so lovely must have been gazed upon by angels in their flight. The only want felt is that of mountains in the background. The Falls are bounded on three sides by ridges 300 or 400 feet in height, which are covered in forest, with the red soil appearing amongst the trees. When about half a mile from the Falls, I left the canoe by which we had come down this far, and embarked in a lighter one, with men well acquainted with the rapids, who, by passing down the centre of the stream in the eddies and still places caused by many jutting rocks, brought me to an island situated in the middle of the river, on the edge of the lip over which the water rolls.
>
> From the autobiographical *Journeys in South Africa*

Those who bemoan the area's emphasis on tourism should note that there must have been sightseeing boat trips ever since David Livingstone came this way.

Being the most eastern point reachable by boat from the Chobe or Upper Zambezi rivers, the area of the Falls was a natural place for European settlement. Soon more traders, hunters and missionaries came into the area, and by the late 1800s a small European settlement had formed around a ferry crossing called the Old Drift, about 10km upstream from the Falls. However, this was built on low-lying marshy ground near the river, buzzing with mosquitoes, so malaria took many lives.

By 1905 the spectacular Victoria Falls Bridge had been completed, linking the copper deposits of the Copperbelt and the coal deposits at Wankie (now Hwange) with a railway line. This, and malaria, encouraged the settlers to transfer to a site on higher ground, next to the railway line at a place called Constitution Hill. It became the centre of present-day Livingstone, and many of its original buildings are still standing. A small cemetery, the poignant remains of Old Drift, can still be made out on the northern bank of the Zambezi within the Mosi-oa-Tunya National Park.

In 1911 Livingstone became the capital of Northern Rhodesia (now Zambia), which it remained until 1935, when the administration was transferred to Lusaka.

GEOLOGY

The Falls are, geologically speaking, probably a very recent formation. About a million years ago, the Zambezi's course is thought to have been down a wide valley over a plateau dating from the karoo period, until it met the Middle Zambezi rift – where the Matetsi River mouth is now.

Here it fell about 250m over an escarpment. However, that fast-falling water would have eroded the lip of the waterfall and gouged out a deeper channel within the basalt rock of the escarpment plateau – and so the original Falls steadily retreated upstream. These channels tended to follow some existing fissure – a crack or weakness, formed when the lava first cooled at the end of the karoo period. At around the Batoka Gorge these fissures naturally run east–west in the rock, parallel to the course of the valley.

By around the Middle Pleistocene period, between 35,000 and 40,000 years ago, this process had formed the Batoka Gorge, carving it out to within about 90km of the present Falls.

However, as water eroded away the lip of the Falls, its valley gradually turned north, until it was almost at right angles to the basalt faultlines which run east–west. Then the water began to erode the fissures and turn them into walls of rock stretching across the valley, perpendicular to it, over which gushed broad curtains of water.

Once such a wall had formed, the water would wear down the rock until it found a faultline behind the wall, along which the water would erode and cause the rock subsequently to collapse. Thus the new faultline would become the wall of the new Falls, behind the old one. This process resulted in the eight gorges that now form the river's slalom course after it has passed over the present Falls. Each gorge was once a great waterfall.

Today, on the eastern side of the Devil's Cataract, you can see this pattern starting again. The water is eroding away the rock of another faultline, behind the line of the present Falls, which geologists expect will form a new waterfall a few thousand years from now.

LIVINGSTONE

GETTING THERE AND AWAY
By air Livingstone's international airport, code LVI (↖ *0213 321153/323322*), is just 5km northwest of the town centre on Airport Road. A US$2 million programme of upgrading and redevelopment is in hand to include extending the airport runway to accommodate flights direct from Europe; completion is tentatively planned for April 2012.

As it stands, the airport has pleasant waiting rooms, airline offices, a bank (⊕ *08.00–16.00 Mon–Fri, 08.15–14.30 Sat*) with ATM, a post office, several car-hire kiosks and a desk for Bushtracks Africa. You can also buy sundries such as sweets and postcards, and there are curio shops for last-minute purchases. If you're after extra security for your luggage, there's a wrapping service for US$10 per bag.

A simple snack bar (⊕ *08.00–18.00 daily*) serves substantial local dishes, but once you've passed through passport control, neither the bar nor the small 'private' lounge (*entry US$15 pp, inc unlimited drinks*) offers anything more substantial than snacks. As if in recompense, though, there's now a duty-free shop and a couple more curio outlets, including Kubu Crafts.

Airlines The airport is served by a number of scheduled airlines and charter companies.

International airlines Both Comair and South African Airways have daily flights between Johannesburg and Livingstone, typically departing Johannesburg mid morning, and returning early afternoon; the flight time is around 1½ hours. New to the route is the low-cost 1time which, with flight schedules running slightly earlier, operates every day except Tuesday and Saturday. One-way fares between Livingstone and Johannesburg are from around US$140 with 1time, or US$240 with the traditional airlines.

In June 2011, Zambezi Airlines introduced a tri-weekly service between Cape Town and Livingstone. Flights leave Cape Town on Monday, Wednesday and Friday, and return Tuesday, Thursday and Sunday.

✈ **1time Airline** ↖ 0213 322744; m 0976 487202; www.1time.co.za

✈ **British Airways/Comair** ↖ 0213 322827; www.comair.co.za

LIVINGSTONE & VICTORIA FALLS

↑ Lusaka

Livingstone Airport

AIRPORT ROAD

GREAT NORTH ROAD

LUSAKA ROAD

pages 162–3

HILLCREST

NORTH END

MARAMBA

LIVINGSTONE

MALOTA

DAMBWA NORTH

LIBUYU

Riverside lodges, Simonga, Kazungula, Sesheke, west

NAKATINDI ROAD

FALLS VIEW

Park gate

KASHITU

in special use only

Railway station

LINDA

DAMBWA

Zigzag

Bushtracks

Maramba

Mosi-oa-Tunya National Park

Old Drift Cemetery

Fallsway Lodge

Protea

Arts Café

Falls Park shopping centre

ZAMBIA

Bushfront Lodge

Game Park gate

Chrismar

(ROYAL MILE)

SICHANGO RD

Vuma

Reptile Park

Livingstone Safari Lodge

Zambezi

The Boat Club
African Queen
The Waterfront

Batoka Sky/
LVI's Adventure

Siloka Island

David Livingstone Safari Lodge

Maramba River Lodge

United Air

N

Bradt

Picnic site

Stanley Safari Lodge

ZIMBABWE

Mukuni village

VICTORIA FALLS

Baobab tree

Entrance gate

Victoria Falls (waterfall)

Airstrip

Entrance to Falls/ curio market

page 193

VICTORIA FALLS ROAD

Gorge swing

Mosi-oa-Tunya National Park

Songwe

Songwe village,
Taita Falcon

Zambezi

0 — 2km
0 — 1 mile

↓ Hwange, Bulawayo

✈ **South African Airways** ✆ 0213 323031–3; www.flysaa.com

✈ **Zambezi Airlines** ✆ 0211 257606; www. flyzambezi.com.

Internal and charter airlines Of the charter companies that fly into Livingstone, the following have offices in the town. Remember that luggage must be carried in soft bags, and is usually restricted to 12kg per person.

✈ **Proflight** ✆ 0213 324745; e reservations@ proflight-zambia.com; www.flyzambia.com. A reliable company offering scheduled & charter flights, including links between Livingstone & the Lower Zambezi. Flights are scheduled to connect to international flights whenever possible.

✈ **Wilderness Air** ✆ 0211 271051; m 0978 770484 (24hr); e reservations@sefofane.co.zm; www.wilderness-air.com. Operates all of Wilderness Safaris' flights into various lodges across Zambia & neighbouring countries. Private flights can be booked directly.

By bus Although the main bus terminus is on the corner of Akapelwa Street and Mosi-oa-Tunya Road, opposite Barclays Bank, one of the town's most reliable companies is currently Mazhandu Family Bus Services, which is based in front of the Hungry Lion. Some buses also leave from around the post office, and others from Town Market.

Buses gather in the early morning, most heading towards Lusaka. This trip takes around six to seven hours, depending on the company, with a one-way fare costing Kw65,000–75,000 (fares on buses from Lusaka are slightly more expensive at around Kw85,000). Ticket prices for some companies may be lower, but check out the state of the bus first; a cracked windscreen doesn't instil much confidence.

If you want to go west to Kazungula or Sesheke your best bet is to board the daily Mazhandu Family Bus that goes to Mongu via both towns.

Expect the first buses to leave at around 05.00, with others to follow according to demand (and note that music played may be at ear-splitting levels). Tickets can usually be bought on the bus, but when demand is high – especially early in the morning, when touts are around – bus stations can be chaotic, so it's wise to buy tickets the day before. It's also advisable to be at the bus station at least half an hour before departure, since buses may leave early if they're full.

🚌 **Bookers Express** [162 B2] Buses to Lusaka from the same location as Mazhandu. Prices are lower (Kw60,000 one way), but standards do not compare.

🚌 **CR Carriers** [162 B1] ✆ 0211 288425; m 0977 861063. An established company but with very mixed standards. 5–6 buses a day to Lusaka between 05.00 & 20.00 from the corner of Mosi-oa-Tunya Rd & Akapelwa St, opposite Barclays Bank. There are also onward services to Ndola (4–5hrs) & Kitwe (5–6hrs).

🚌 **Germins** [162 B2] m 0977 545992. Operates from Town Centre Market with the 1st departure at 06.00 & the last at 20.00.

🚌 **Mazhandu Family Bus Services** [162 B2] m 0977 805064; e panga@zamnet.zm; www. mazhandubuses.com. Livingstone's most reliable bus company operates from outside the Hungry Lion. Regular daily departures to Lusaka start at 06.00, with the last bus at 20.30. Services also run to Kazungula (Kw30,000) & on to Sesheke (Kw55,000) with buses at 05.00, 14.00 (Kazungula only) & 13.30. On 'business class' buses (09.00 daily), which have AC, fares from Lusaka are Kw110,000, against the economy fare of Kw80,000.

🚌 **Shalom** [162 B2] m 0976 209885. Operates from Town Centre Market, with the 1st bus to Lusaka at 06.30, & the last at 22.00.

In addition to these, **Intercape Mainliner** (*www.intercape.co.za*) runs a return service from Windhoek in Namibia to Livingstone and on to Victoria Falls town.

Buses arrive in Livingstone at South End Travel, next to Barclays Bank [162 B1]. Tickets must be booked in advance, either online or at the Intercape Mainliner offices in Windhoek. Prices start from around US$75 one way.

By train The railway station ([163 D7] *reservations* \ *0213 321001, ext 36*) is well signposted about 1km south of the town centre on the way to the Falls, on the eastern side of Mosi-oa-Tunya Road. However, most trains nowadays are geared to freight, and travelling by train from Livingstone is rarely viable. If you're not to be put off, there are in theory two passenger trains a week (Monday and Friday) to Lusaka, but check with the railway station to see if any trains are operating, and beware: this is the slowest and most unreliable method of transport between the two cities. Even the cheap fare is unlikely to make up for the very lengthy journey and the delays that are commonplace *en route*.

Driving west Those heading west, into Namibia's Caprivi Strip, Botswana or western Zambia, should take the Nakatindi Road – signposted as the M10 – past the lodges by the river. After about 70km this comes to the Zambezi River at Kazungula – where Namibia, Botswana, Zimbabwe and Zambia all meet at a notional point. Here you can continue northwest within Zambia to Sesheke, or take the ferry across the Zambezi into Botswana, near Kasane.

GETTING AROUND

Orientation Livingstone town itself is fairly compact and surrounded by several small township suburbs, sprawling out from its centre. Much bigger than the Zimbabwean town of Victoria Falls, on the other side of the river, the town has two main business areas concentrated along the all-important Mosi-oa-Tunya Road. Sections of this are lined with classic colonial buildings with corrugated-iron roofs and wide wooden verandas, some restored and others in a state of disrepair.

The larger and busier central business district begins atop a small hill just past the museum, while in the lower part of town is a smaller but growing retail area known as '217'. Developments further south have introduced a new shopping area between Livingstone and the Falls. Navigation is easy, even without a map, though signposts are often missing or may point to establishments no longer in existence.

Drive north out of the city, and the main street leading to the capital becomes Lusaka Road. Head south for about 10km and you reach the Zambezi River and the Victoria Falls themselves, and the border post to cross into Zimbabwe via Victoria Falls Bridge. Many visitors choose to stay close to the Falls at one of Sun International's two hotels, but there are now several new options on this side of town.

Travel west from town on the M10 Nakatindi Road and you'll find yourself driving parallel to the north bank of the Zambezi upstream towards Kazungula and the ferry to Botswana. Signposts to the left point to small, exclusive lodges perched at picturesque spots on the river's bank.

A good street atlas covering both Livingstone and Lusaka is published by Streetwise and is available locally.

By taxi or with a tour operator Livingstone town is small enough to walk around, as is the Falls area. However if you are travelling between the two, or going to the airport, or in a hurry, then use one of the plentiful – if battered – light-blue taxis that congregate near the old Shoprite at the main taxi stand [162 B2] or on Mosi-oa-Tunya Road opposite the craft market in the park [162 E3]. All taxis are supposed to carry a fare chart, though you will be lucky to see one. A taxi between

LIVINGSTONE

NORTH END

162

town and either the Falls or the airport will cost around Kw40,000–45,000/US$9–10 for up to four passengers. A taxi out to the riverside lodges will cost from around Kw70,000/US$15, depending on the location; some are a considerable distance from town. Competition amongst taxi drivers can be fierce, so be sure to negotiate for the best deal and agree on the price in advance.

While you can negotiate to hire a taxi for the day to take you around town, to the Falls and to outlying areas, you'll have a more informative trip with one of the licensed and more knowledgeable tour operators. For details, see pages 190–2.

By bus Minibuses run to the Falls from the Town Centre Market in the centre of Livingstone throughout the day, departing when they are full. Expect to pay around Kw7,000 for the ten-minute journey.

Driving yourself Driving in Livingstone is pretty straightforward, though watch out for the none-too-subtle speed humps along Mosi-oa-Tunya Road.

Most lodges and hotels in and around Livingstone have secure parking, as do many restaurants. If you're parking on the street in town, you're likely to come across any number of volunteers to look after your car or to wash it for you. There's nothing organised about this, and you're under no obligation to accept their help, but if you're prepared to trust someone then – in spite of considerable protestations to the contrary – a tip of about Kw1,500–2,500/US$0.30–0.50 should be about right, depending on the length of time you're away.

There are several 24-hour fuel stations on the main Mosi-oa-Tunya Road. At the time of research in 2011, the price of diesel was Kw7,954 per litre, with unleaded at Kw8,647.

Car hire If you don't have a vehicle and wish to explore the area at your own pace, you can hire a car with or without a driver – the former can even be a cheaper option. Alternatively, you can rent a 4x4 with full kit if you wish to do a self-drive safari.

For a very special occasion, what about a restored 1939 Rolls Royce, complete with liveried chauffeur? It's available through Bushtracks (see page 191) for both transfers and excursions, perhaps with a picnic from the Royal Livingstone Hotel.

🚗 **Hemingways** 0213 323097; m 0977 866492, 870232; e info@hemingwayszambia.com; www.hemingwayszambia.com. Specialist vehicle hire, with or without a driver, for day tours, or transfers or independent safaris. Vehicles include disabled-accessible transport in the form of a 16-seater VW minibus with Ratcliffe wheelchair lift. Self-drive Toyota Hilux double-cab vehicles are fully equipped for camping, including rooftop tents, long-range fuel tanks & fridge.

🚗 **Thunderbird Investments** [163 D7] Mosi-oa-Tunya Rd; 0213 320331; e thunderbird@microlink.zm; ⏰ 08.00–20.30 Mon–Sat, 13.00–20.30 Sun. Well signposted north of the railway station, Thunderbird rents cars, 4x4s & minibuses, & can arrange taxis, other transport & tours. It also has an internet café (Kw150/min) & business centre.

🚗 **Voyagers** [map 159] 0213 322753; m 0978 778991; e carrental@voyagerszambia.com, livingstoneairport@voyagerszambia.com; www.voyagerszambia.com, www.europcarzambia.com. From its base at the airport, Voyagers Rentals is the franchisee for Europcar, with self-drive & chauffeur-driven vehicles in all price ranges & styles. They can also arrange trips throughout the region, including transfers from Kazungula & into Botswana, Zimbabwe & Namibia.

By bicycle Guided bike tours can be arranged with Cliff Sitwala (m *0978 171547, 0977 747837*; e *localcowboy@yahoo.com*) – widely known as 'Cowboy Cliff' – who also offers bike hire. Prices for a half day guided tour are around US$25 per person; options include riverside rides to the Falls, market and village tours and a visit to the small school that he's built from the proceeds of his bike business.

You can also rent bikes from Jollyboys. A word of warning, though: there have been reports of individual cyclists being mugged, so it's wise to go with a group.

WHERE TO STAY Since the late 1990s, Livingstone has experienced a boom in tourism and now offers a great variety of places to stay for all types of travellers and budgets. Whereas accommodation used to be of widely varying standards, now you will find excellent choices in all price ranges, with many providing the service, standards and amenities that international visitors have come to expect. If the choice is overwhelming, knowing the options in advance will make finding the right place much easier. Most of the larger establishments accept credit cards.

Along the Zambezi River, numerous bush lodges occupy lovely situations, some close enough to enjoy the attractions and activities of the Falls, others further upstream and more remote. Closer to town, and to the Falls, an increasing number of upmarket hotels, some on the river, and others in a more urban setting, offer Western creature comforts. At the cheaper end of the market, staying in a guesthouse or in-town lodge, where you may meet African travellers or volunteers from overseas, can add a multi-cultural dimension to your visit, while backpacker accommodation tends to cater strictly to the international budget traveller.

In town
Hotels Hotels in Livingstone itself are still relatively spread out, with some in town, and others on the road south towards the Falls. Establishments listed here are roughly in order of price.

Protea Hotel Livingstone [map 159] (80 rooms, 13 apts) Mosi-oa-Tunya Rd; \0213 324630; e reservations@phlivingstone. co.zm; www.proteahotels.com. About 0.5km south of the railway, & adjacent to Falls Park shopping centre, this surprisingly elegant hotel opened in 2008. From the entrance, flanked by giant pots overflowing with water, a wide tiled lobby, with a formal restaurant to one side, leads in turn through to a courtyard. Here, there's a rectangular swimming pool with its own bar & plenty of loungers. Dark-wood furniture & classic styling define the rooms, some of which face the courtyard. Each features a kingsize bed, or 2 of queen size, making them suitable for up to 2 adults & 2 children. In the en-suite bathroom, some have a bath & shower, others just a shower. AC, safes, tea-/coffee-making facilities, satellite TV & a phone complete the picture. The hotel has its own activity centre, while for the more work orientated, there are conference facilities, free WiFi access & a business centre. There's also a secure car park. **$$$$**

Fallsway Lodge [map 159] (17 rooms) \0213 324545/324646/324747; e fallswaylodge@microlink.zm; www. fallswaylodge.co.zm. Located south of the town, opposite the Protea, Fallsway opened its doors in Jul 2008, with an additional 24 rooms still to be added. It's a mid-market place, with lawned gardens & a swimming pool that has a children's area. Single, twin, dbl & family rooms, all en suite, are classified as 'small' or 'large'. They're modern & clean, with AC, DSTV, fridge, kettle, safe & phone. The marble-floored restaurant overlooks the garden & serves local & Western cuisine, though guests can also cater for themselves. 2-for-1 cocktails are served in the bar on Wed & Fri, 19.00–20.00. As well as having WiFi hot spots, the hotel has a room where guests can surf the internet for 30mins without charge. **$$$**

Kaazmein Lodge [162 G3] (32 rooms, camping) Maina Soko; \0213 322244; m 0955 32 2244, 0977 77 7324; e kaazmein@microlink. zm; www.kaazmeinlodge.com. Whatever you may think of this lodge, opened in 2007, it's certainly different. Set in some 8ha, it features a series of manmade lakes, complete with artificial islands & bridges over narrow streams, & the go ahead has been given to introduce small game into the grounds. At its heart is a huge, 2-storey domed structure which houses both a restaurant & conference facilities. There is a bar across the lake, near to a blue thatched gazebo set up like a bandstand for seating, & a pool table a short walk away. Accommodation is set well apart from this area, with rooms built either in 2-storey blocks with fans & fridges, or in a separate block where they have AC & a TV but no fans. All are en suite, with décor on the ornate side. Budget travellers can camp & have their own ablution block. Finally, there's a pool & secure parking. Rates have fallen considerably since the lodge was first opened. **$$$** *Camping US$10 pp.*

🏠 **Ngolide Lodge** [163 D8] (16 rooms) 110 Mosi-oa-Tunya Rd; ☎0213 321091/2; e ngolide@gmail.com; www.ngolidelodge. com. On the south side of town, as the main road leaves Livingstone for the Falls, this thatched lodge fronted by small gardens has a secure car park. It's actually more of a mini-hotel than a lodge, well built & compact, if a bit dark. Small but comfortable rooms under high thatch lead off a central quadrangle. Decorated with ethnic fabrics, each has polished floors, a stone or tiled bathroom, twin or dbl beds with mosi nets, AC, tea/coffee maker, safe & satellite TV; some also have a fridge. There is a licensed bar & the Indian restaurant, tucked away at the back, is among the best in Livingstone. There's WiFi access across the whole site. **$$$**

🏠 **Wasawange Lodge** [162 D3] (22 rooms, 2 apts) Airport Rd; ☎0213 324066/324078;

e waslodge@zamnet.zm. Situated 2km from the town centre & the same distance from the airport, Wasawange Lodge is a comfortable small hotel with a rather austere reception area & a few ethnic touches. Its spacious dbl & twin rooms are individual rondavels with en-suite facilities, AC, a fridge/minibar, in-room coffee/tea, mosquito repellent & satellite TV. Clean & well serviced, they have high wooden ceilings, large mirrors & rugs to cover nice stone floors. The place has a good restaurant, bar, swimming pool & sauna, & its conference rooms are popular with business visitors. Transfers & all activities can be arranged. **$$$**

🏠 **New Fairmount Hotel & Casino** [162 E3] (104 rooms) Mosi-oa-Tunya Rd; ☎0213 320723/8, 322630, 320075; e nfhc@zamnet.zm; www.newfairmounthotel.com. In the centre of town, between Mose & Mwela streets, this large old hotel of Moorish design in sparkling white plaster was once the town's focal point, & remains good value. En-suite rooms – ranging from 'singles' (with a dbl bed) to executive suites – are clean & traditional in style, with AC, fridge, kettle, satellite TV & even a DVD/video player. These are set around white-painted concrete courtyards at the back, where there's a swimming pool (open to non-residents) & plenty of shady seating. The hotel has an air-conditioned restaurant serving Zambian & international dishes, plus a casino & nightclub, both popular at w/ends. A desk for Bwaato Adventures occupies a corner of the cavernous entrance lobby where WiFi is also available to guests (*Kw26,000/2 days*). In front is ample covered parking under the watchful eye of 24hr security. **$–$$**

Guesthouses Even the most unobservant visitor in Livingstone can't help but notice the multitude of signs pointing to guesthouses all over town, but standards vary immensely. Many are new to tourism and others cater to the local market rather than to overseas visitors. One thing is for certain: the Western image of a guesthouse – a charming and personal B&B – is not to be found here … yet. Rather, a 'guesthouse' can be anything from a basic hostel to a quasi mini-hotel. Some are old, converted homes with smallish rooms, limited facilities and lower prices; others are newly constructed with restaurant, bar, pool, air conditioning and other mod-cons, and priced accordingly. Interior decoration leans either towards the basic and functional, perhaps with the odd ethnic touch, or tends to be overblown, with an abundance of velvet, chrome and multi-patterned fabrics. Inevitably new places crop up all the time so it's worth looking around to see what catches your eye and which location suits you best; there are numerous options around the water tower to the north of town, and several along the road to the airport, too. Always ask to see the room and facilities before booking in, as there's no shortage of choice. Options here are listed alphabetically.

⌂ **Chanters Lodge** [162 E1] (12 rooms) Lukulu Cres; ✆0213 3323412; e richardchanter@ gmail.com; www.chanters-livingstone.com. Run by former Lusaka hotelier Richard Chanter, Chanters was one of the first guesthouses in Livingstone. It stands in a leafy residential area off Obote Av, some 2km to the north of town. Lukulu Cres is the 4th right turn & is well signposted.

Comfortable en-suite rooms – some with bath & shower, others with just a shower or bath – vary in size from 'singles' (with a dbl bed) to family accommodation, but all have AC, satellite TV, fridge & WiFi. The public rooms are pleasant, with tables & chairs extending onto a patio & garden at the back around a small pool. There's also secure parking. The restaurant (page 182) is open all day until 21.30. **$$**

⌂ **Green Tree Lodge** [162 A3] (5 chalets, camping) 2015 Kombe Dr; ✆0213 322631; m 0977 630159; e greentreelodge@ livingstonezambia.com; www. greentreelodgezambia.com. Individual en-suite chalets with secure parking alongside make this an attractive proposition for the self driver. The chalets are set among fruit trees, & each boasts dbl or twin beds, AC, fridge, TV, WiFi & kettle, as well as its own veranda. It's also possible to camp on the grass, close to the pool & bar, where meals are available. **$$** *Camping US$6 pp.*

⌂ **Guest Mate Inn** [162 F2] (10 rooms) 387 Obote Av; ✆0213 323939; m 0977 777520; e guestmate@microlink.zm. This simple guesthouse ('Arrive as a guest, leave as a friend!') has en-suite dbl & family rooms, half in the main house, & the others – newer, smaller & carpeted – at the back. AC, satellite TV, WiFi access & free use of the internet are all here & there are plans to construct a pool in 2011. **$$** *inc cont b/fast.*

⌂ **Limbo Lodge** (12 chalets) 205/206 Lusaka Rd; ✆0213 322096; m 0955 78 0330, 0977 88 1567; e limbolodge@zamnet.zm; www. limbolodge.com. A tranquil option in a lovely garden, Limbo offers warm hospitality & good value. You'll find it 100m to the right of the road heading north out of town. Each of its thatched chalets houses 2 rooms, which can interconnect

to form a family room. All are en suite, with ethnic décor, mosi nets, minibar, coffee/tea facilities, satellite TV & AC. In addition, there's a restaurant & bar, a swimming pool, & a brand new conference room, as well as secure parking. **$$**

⌂ **Namel's Guest Lodge** (9 rooms) Lusaka Rd; ✆0213 324274; e namelslodge@zamnet. zm; www.namelslodge.com. From the centre of town, head towards Lusaka up the main road. At the top of the hill, just past the water tower, are several guesthouses, including Namel's, set back from the road on the left. It's about a 20min walk from town. This pleasant guesthouse offers carpeted en-suite rooms all equipped with AC, mosquito nets, a safe, coffee/tea facilities, fridge & satellite TV. There's a swimming pool with an outside bar, & 24hr security in the ample parking area. Namel's caters to business travellers, but is also a good choice for couples & families with their own transport. Rooms at the back are the best & quietest. There's a lunch & dinner menu, or self-catering facilities are available for a nominal charge. **$$**

⌂ **Nokenu Guest Lodge** (15 rooms) 1575 Kanini Cres, off Lusaka Rd; ✆0213 324507; e wchiyesu@yahoo.com. This new addition to Livingstone's guesthouse portfolio, close to Namel's, underwent extensive renovations & expansion in early 2011 & now has a swimming pool & a restaurant serving local & European cuisine. The older rooms, inside the house, have dbl beds & are clean & comfortable, if a little dark. Some are en suite while others share. Newer rooms, situated around a courtyard at the back of the house, have AC, satellite TV & a fridge, & all are en suite. **$**

⌂ **Rite Inn** [162 E3] (10 rooms) 301 Mose St; ✆0213 323264; e riteinn@zamnet.zm. In a small, secure courtyard within walking distance of town, Rite Inn has clean, attractive rooms that are among the nicest we've seen. Both twin or dbl rooms, & a family room decorated in an African motif have tiled bathrooms, AC, fridges, coffee/tea service, digital safes & satellite TVs. These & the reception area are adjacent to a sparkling swimming pool, surrounded by a large tiled patio. The street-side carport is patrolled around the clock, or you can park inside the courtyard on request. There is a small bar & restaurant. **$$**

🏠 **Southern Comfort Lodge** (8 rooms) 75 Lusaka Rd; ☎ 0213 323103; m 0977 88 2962; e sclodge@zamnet.zm; www.southerncomfortlodge.com. Situated just beyond the water tower, close to Namel's & Wane's, Southern Comfort feels more like a hotel than a guesthouse. A large & spacious main building with decorative floor tiles leads to well-sized rooms with fans, fridges & satellite TV. Each is en suite with a creatively tiled bathroom. There's a rather flamboyant lounge & a dining area. Parking is inside a walled gate. **$$**

🏠 **Wane Guest Lodge** (7 rooms, house) Lusaka Rd; ☎ 0213 324058; m 0977 881536; e wangull@zamnet.zm. Another lodge on 'guesthouse row'; look for the sign on the main road & the name on the entrance gate. The en-suite bedrooms & separate, self-catering family house (sleeping 5) are clean & well-appointed. Each has AC, a bath, satellite TV, telephone, fridge & tea/coffee station. As well as a full restaurant (*Kw45,000*) & bar, serving international & Zambian dishes, there's 24hr room service, a small pool & round-the-clock security. **$$**

🏠 **Zambezi Ultima Guesthouse** [162 E2] (14 rooms) 36 Likute Way; ☎ 0213 323534. Situated on a large plot in the residential section of town, this guesthouse has dbl & twin rooms,

& 2 suites that can be used for families – all painted in the same colour as Livingstone's blue taxis. Even so, the newer en-suite rooms in the garden area are nice enough & the hotel has a pool & an outside bar, dining room, satellite TV, & kitchen facilities. All rooms are en suite with AC & mosi nets. **$$**

🏠 **Zigzag** [map 159] (12 rooms) Industrial Rd; ☎ 0213 322814; m 0977 681741; e zigzag@microlink.zm, www.zigzagzambia.com. Signposted down a side road off Mosi-oa-Tunya Rd, near the railway crossing, Zigzag is on the edge of town & has secure parking. From its origins as a coffee house, restaurant & craft market (see page 184), it has expanded to include a block of twin, dbl & family rooms in its 0.5ha garden complex. These are nicely furnished with AC, tiled bathrooms & ethnic décor, & there's a lounge with satellite TV. The leafy, shaded garden houses an enticing pool & a children's play area with swings & a jungle gym. **$$**

🏠 **Likute Guesthouse** [162 E3] (14 rooms) 62 Likute Way; ☎ 0213 323661; m 0977 60 3971, 0977 80 6510; e likuteguest@zamnet.zm. This clean & welcoming guesthouse is conveniently located in a small walled complex behind the Fairmount Hotel. En-suite rooms have AC, mosi nets, satellite TV, kettle & fridge, & there's a pleasant lounge. The staff are friendly, meals are available on request & there's secure parking. **$**

Backpackers For the budget-minded, nothing beats Livingstone's popular backpackers' hostels. Generally clean, convenient and cheap, they are ideal for independent travellers – but can be crowded at times. As a one-stop shop, they offer shared and private rooms, camping, booking agency, restaurant, bar, kitchen, laundry, pool and even a built-in social life.

🏠 **Fawlty Towers** [163 D6] (34 dorm beds, 15 rooms, camping) 216 Mosi-oa-Tunya Rd; ☎ 0213 323432; e ahorizon@zamnet.zm; www.adventure-africa.com. Just south of the turn-off to Nakatindi/Kazungula Rd, you can't miss this popular international backpackers' place, which was refurbished in 2011. Look for the colourful wrought-iron burglar bars shaped like rising suns. Enter through the large gates covered by straw mats, & you come to the reception & lounge with satellite TV & free internet facilities. Upstairs in the main building are 4 dorms sleeping 6, 1 sleeping 4, & both a trpl & a twin

room, all sharing toilets & showers. There's also a reading lounge, self-catering kitchen & dining room serving a full English b/fast for about US$4. Behind the main building, you'll find a spacious private garden shaded by mango trees & coloured with bougainvillea where lawns fringe an inviting pool. Campers on the lawns share clean toilets & showers. Also in the garden area are a further 6-bed dorm, plus 2 twins & a dbl, all sharing showers & toilets; & – in a separate complex, 8 twin, 7 dbls & 2 4-bed en-suite rooms. There is also a 2nd communal kitchen (all accessories provided). Everything is neat & clean, all rooms come with mosi nets, desk fans & bed linen, & showers have hot & cold running water. Tea & coffee are on hand all day, & free pancakes are offered poolside each afternoon. There's even a laundry service at US$10 per bag. Fawlty Towers is quiet, secure, well run & tremendously convenient for the centre of Livingstone. They offer free transport & transfers to Victoria Falls daily at 10.00. To help with organising your stay there's also an in-house booking office (☉ 07.30–16.30 Mon–Fri, 07.30–13.00 Sat). **$–$$** exc b/fast. Dorm bed US$12; camping US$6 pp.

🏠 **Jollyboys Backpackers** [163 C5] (13 en suite chalets, 10 with shared ablutions, 50 dorm beds, camping) 34 Kanyanta Rd; ☎ 0213 324229/322086; e jollybs@zamnet.zm; www. backpackzambia.com. The ever-popular Jollyboys occupies a tree-shaded site just behind the museum, a 2-min walk from the town centre. Owner-operated & managed by the helpful & friendly Kim, Sue & John, its reputation as the quintessential backpackers' lodge remains undimmed.

The main facilities are set within a large, central thatched courtyard, with the dorms, reception area & ablutions around the perimeter, as well as 11 en-suite twin & dbl rooms with AC & mosi nets. Mixed dorms (bring your own bedding or pay a deposit to use theirs) come with 4 beds, 8 beds (& AC!), or – the cheapest – 16 beds, all with fans & sharing a good-sized toilet & shower block with endless hot water. In the back garden are 2-bed A-frame thatched chalets & some camping space, both sharing ablution facilities.

In the middle of the 'quad' is a wonderful sunken lounge with firepit & pillows – a perfect spot to chill out, read & meet fellow travellers. Above is a wooden deck from which you can see the spray from the Falls. A pool table, table tennis & sitting area are also under cover looking out to an enticing rock swimming pool, lawns & gardens. Adjacent are the open-plan bar with satellite TV, & the restaurant, where you can enjoy a home-cooked meal at reasonable prices. There's also a separate self-catering kitchen. Internet/email is on site (Kw3,000/15min), bikes can be hired (US$5/10 ½/full day), & there's a laundry service, book exchange (Kw2,000 per book, with proceeds to charity), secure parking & short- & long-term

baggage storage. There's also a free pick-up service from the airport, by arrangement. Kim & Sue offer friendly, first-hand advice on what to see & do; there are free lifts to the Falls at 10.00 daily, & they can book any & all activities. The atmosphere is relaxed & unpretentious, if busy, & with the bar shut by 23.00 noise isn't a major issue. **$–$$**, exc b/fast. 4/8/16-bed dorm US$12/10/8 pp, camping US$6 pp.

🏠 **Jollyboys Camp** [163 E6] (24 dorm beds, 9 en suite rooms, 6 twin chalets, camping) 80 Chipembi Rd; ☎ 0213 324756; e jollycamp@ backpackzambia.com; www.backpackzambia. com. This offshoot of Jollyboys, owned & run by the same people, is close to the golf course, less than 10mins' walk to the centre of town. It has all the hallmark offerings of its well-known parent, but with a greater focus on family accommodation. This comes in the form of twin & dbl en-suite rooms, including a family room, 6 twin chalets, & 4- & 6-bed dorms with shared ablutions. For campers, there are spaces both for tents & – with power points, water & lights – for 4x4 vehicles with rooftop tents. All guests can use the bar, self-catering kitchen, braai facilities, internet/email, short- & long-term baggage storage, secure off-street parking, swimming pool, table tennis, & free pick up from the airport. Evenings around the firepit offer the chance to mull over the day's activities, kids are catered for with their own jungle gym. **$–$$** exc b/fast. Dorm bed US$10; camping US$5 pp.

🏃 **Jungle Junction** Bovu Island; m 0978 725282; e stay@junglejunction.info; www. junglejunction.net. The return of the riverside Jungle Junction to the Livingstone scene will please a lot of backpackers in particular. For details, see page 176.

🏠 **Livingstone Backpackers** [163 D5] (72 dorm beds, camping) 559 Makambo Rd; ☎ 0213 324730; e ahorizon@zamnet.zm; www.livingstonebackpackers.com. Affiliated to Fawlty Towers, this hostel to the south of Town Market opened in 2009. Budget accommodation comes in the form of mixed dorms with 4 beds in each. The hostel also has a cabana bar, a climbing wall, pool & activity centre. There is no internet access but guests may use the free facility at Fawlty Towers. There are free transfers to the Falls daily at 10.00. Dorm bed US$8; camping US$5 pp.

8

Beside the Zambezi: Upriver Livingstone's riverside lodges are for the most part spread along the shores of the Zambezi leading west from the town off Nakatindi Road. As well as the more exclusive lodges, there are now a few more accessible offerings further upstream, including a couple of campsites. The following are listed from east to west.

⌂ **Toka Leya** (12 tented chalets) Contact Wilderness Safaris, page 431. Set within the national park, some 5km from Livingstone, Toka Leya's khaki-coloured canvas, natural wood decking & walkways defined by rope handrails, blends into the riverine environment. Although each tented chalet faces the river, some lie well back, glimpsing the water through the trees rather than affording a panoramic view. From wide wooden verandas, boasting a table, chairs & wicker chaises longues, glass sliding doors lead through to the bedroom. Here, 4-poster dbl or twin beds flanked by smart table lamps are enveloped by mosi nets; there's also a desk, a couple of comfy chairs, plus AC/heating, fan, & a hairdryer. At the back are a roomy dressing area, twin basins, separate toilet & shower, & a further outside shower. (3 family rooms have an entirely separate twin room at the back, too.) It's airy & spacious but not cavernous, with Persian-style rugs & brightly coloured lamps enlivening an otherwise neutral décor.

The understated style runs through to the main lounge & restaurant area, segmented into 'rooms' by squashy sofas, with linking walkways to a bar, tree-shaded deck & sheltered firepit – where there is regular evening entertainment. Nearby, wicker sunloungers surround a small infinity pool, & by the river is a simple spa, a relaxing spot with 2 rooms for massages, manicures, body wraps & more. Dinner is often taken at a group table, though it can be served privately on your own deck, & there are individual tables during the day. Particularly popular at lunchtime is pizza, freshly prepared out of a wood-fired oven. There's also free WiFi throughout the camp.

Boat trips from the lodge's jetty, 2hr game drives & 1½hr birding/nature walks are all possible, as are trips to the Falls, museum & market; most other activities can be booked. Environmental issues are high on the agenda, with a filtration system for drinking water, solar geysers for hot water, & a worm farm for kitchen waste; guests can even plant a tree as part of a project to replace lost specimens along the river. *US$421/*

567 pp sharing/sgl FB, inc local drinks, laundry, 2 activities/day, exc spa treatments. ⊕ *All year.*

⌂ **Sussi & Chuma** (12 chalets, 2 houses) Contact Sanctuary Retreats, page 269. Named after the Zambian bearers who carried David Livingstone's body from Zambia to Dar es Salaam after his death, Sussi & Chuma lies within the national park, just 10mins' drive from Livingstone. Although built in 2001, it has since been fully refurbished.

If you've a yearning to act out a fantasy of living in a tree house, this could be your chance. Set amongst riverine forest, Sussi's large, almost circular chalets are set quite high up on wooden platforms overlooking the Zambezi. Large glass doors open out onto a sizeable balcony with comfortable chairs. Décor is minimalist, almost stark, but very comfortable, with natural fabrics, dark wooden floors, & a walk-in mosquito net around the bed(s). Thoughtful touches include AC, a safe, intercom system, & an area with minibar & kettle. Next to the bedroom are a basin, shower & bath with a view; only the toilet is private. The ultimate in privacy comes with the 2-bedroom Chuma houses, each with en-suite bathrooms, a private plunge pool, & a chef & butler.

Raised walkways connect the chalets to a large 2-storey thatched central area, which mirrors the circular design of the rooms. Upstairs, a sitting room with comfortable sofas & a bar have views over the river. Below, the dining area extends onto a circular deck where meals may be taken with other guests, or individually, as you prefer. The lodge has its own wine cellar, but can order specific wines on request. A short walkway leads to a sheltered bend of the river, the location of an infinity pool & a sundowner deck with firepits. Spa treatments are available using Africology products, also sold in the gift shop. Guests have the use of a laptop computer, & parts of the lodge offer WiFi reception.

Activities include game drives or boat cruises at sunrise & sunset, fishing, a village tour, & visits to the Falls. *US$565–695 pp sharing FB, inc local drinks, laundry, 2 guided activities/day. House*

US$2,295–3,080 per night. Children under 9 in houses only. ☺ *all year.*

⌂ **Thorntree River Lodge** (9 chalets) 📞 0213 327480; reservations: +27 31 310 3333; e ceres@threecities.co.za; www.thorntreelodge. net. Thorntree is 15km from the Falls on private land within the broader confines of the national park, about 10mins' drive from town & clearly signposted. Brick-under-thatch chalets line the riverbank, each with electricity, en-suite bath, small riverside veranda & simple but attractive interiors; most also feature an outdoor bath or shower. There are also 2 well-appointed honeymoon suites with open sides.

The comfortable bar, lounge & dining area has a riverside deck from which you can watch elephants moving between the islands in the Zambezi. A figure-of-8 swimming pool lies next to a thatched spa with a jacuzzi, plus steam & massage rooms – the latter overlooking a waterhole where buffalo, elephant, hippo, waterbuck & bushbuck come to drink from time to time.

Set a little way along the river (though entirely separate from the lodge) is a thatched boma with ethnic decoration, the base for SafPar's elephant-back safaris where guests can meet the resident herd. River cruises are operated from the lodge, & numerous other activities offered (see Safari Par Excellence, page 192). *US$320–403 pp sharing FB, inc 1 activity/day (sunset cruise, game drive or Falls tour), exc VAT, drinks, transfers & US$10 pp/day park fee.*

⌂ **No Name Camp** (6 rooms; camping) m 0977 820919/632001; e nonamecamp@ yahoo.com. While this congenial German-owned camp is neither on the river, nor in the same class as the surrounding lodges, it does offer camping, & en-suite rooms at a reasonable rate, & is popular with self drivers. You can't miss the Trabant at the front, a rooftop tent acting as a noticeboard for up-to-date specials & deals offered at the lodge. Inside, the dark, stone-built reception, bar & dining area are decidedly reminiscent of a Bierkeller. **$$**. *Camping Kw30,000 pp.*

⌂ **Bushbuck River House** (6 rooms, camping) Contact Nomad African Travel, page 45. Situated 16km from town, Bushbuck lies just outside the national park. Take the first left after No Name Camp, cross the railway, turn sharp

left following the railway line back, then turn towards the river for about 1km. A traditional thatched farmhouse, it's in a quiet spot with good river views & reportedly excellent home-cooked meals, & is more affordable than most in this location. The main house has 5 en-suite rooms; a 6th, in the orchard with bush & river views, uses outside ablutions. Both camping & self catering are further options. Relax in the attractive poolside boma, watch the river from a high viewing platform, or chill in the lounge with DSTV, including Sky Sports. *£49 pp sharing HB; orchard £25 pp room only; camping £7 pp; whole house £360/night self catering (min 3 nights).*

⌂ **The River Club** (10 chalets) 📞 0213 327457; m 0977 892179; e riverclub@ wilderness.co.za; www.theriverclubafrica.com, www.wilderness-safaris.com; for reservations, contact your tour operator. Perched on a rise beside the Zambezi, the River Club – with a distinctly colonial atmosphere, & the décor & service to match – was opened in 1997. It's an exclusive & intimate lodge, set in securely fenced grounds, where organic vegetables are grown, & where there's also a helipad. Most guests are transferred from Livingstone by boat, a scenic 10min ride. For drivers, the turning off Nakatindi Rd is clearly signposted.

Large, thatched chalets are built on stilts amidst indigenous riverside trees, with stunning views over the Zambezi below. All boast teak furniture & quality fabrics, though the beautifully polished floors tend to be slippery, so be careful. Creature comforts include duvets, AC/heating, a ceiling fan inside the canopied mosquito nets, a fridge, international electric sockets, a hairdryer & a digital safe. In most, the main bathroom with claw-foot tub is on a lower level, with a 2nd basin & loo by the bedroom. Of similarly high standard are 3 suites, all on one level with their own decks & private pools. Two of these have gardens with sunloungers in front, & of these, one is a wheelchair-friendly room; both are ideal for honeymooners. The 3rd, a family suite, has a kingsize bed, & a separate twin room.

The colonial style runs through to the main building, with magnificent river views from its wide verandas. Here you can enjoy traditional afternoon tea or, cocktail in hand, watch the sun slip beneath the horizon. Inside are the reception, a small gift shop, cloakrooms, a formal dining room (with a magnificent teak table), a comfortable lounge, a massive double-sided fireplace & a well-stocked library. Antiques, colonial pictures & many decorator touches add to the Edwardian ambience, while WiFi access throughout brings a touch of the 21st century. Meals are elegant affairs featuring pre-set dinner menus that change daily. Typically guests dine together, but individual tables can be arranged, & for absolute privacy there's a classy riverside 'gazebo'. Opposite the main building, & built in the same style, is a 'summerhouse', ideal for small groups with its own lounge & dining table, plus a snooker room with AC & a small library.

Overlooking the river is a stunning infinity pool surrounded by sunloungers shaded by over-sized umbrellas. Walkways, illuminated at night, cross the sweeping lawns, while palms, brightly coloured bougainvillaea & gardens complete the picture. Croquet, boules & bush golf are on hand, & for the more active, there's an all-weather tennis court & a 2.5km nature-walk/running track around the 20ha property. A wellness centre provides the perfect venue for massages & other treatments, while below is a small gym, with a sauna & jacuzzi. Included in the rates are a choice of fishing, sundowner boat trips, game-park drives, Falls visits, & trips to a local village. All other activities can be booked direct from the lodge. *US$421/572 pp sharing/sgl FBA.* ☉ *all year.*

⌂ **Tongabezi** (5 cottages, 6 houses) ☎0213 327450/68; ℮ reservations@tongabezi.com; www. tongabezi.com. Set on a sweeping bend of the Zambezi, 15km west of the town centre, Tongabezi opened in the 1990s & remains one of the most exclusive lodges on the north side of the Zambezi. Its setting is matched by excellent service from a team of first-class local staff.

Overlooking the river are beautiful & tastefully decorated thatched cottages with kingsize or twin beds, large tiled en-suite bathrooms with river-view bathtubs, & private sitting areas. Even more exclusive are the individually designed houses with one side completely open to the river: the Bird House, the Tree House, the Dog House & the Honeymoon House (once cited as 'worth getting married for'). Each has a kingsize bed & impressive en-suite bathroom with inviting tub. The fully enclosed Nut House has large folding french doors & its own infinity plunge pool at the top of the cliff.

Then, tucked away from the river in its own private enclosure, is the newly renovated Garden Cottage. Ideal for families or 2 couples sharing, it comprises 3 separate buildings – 2 en-suite dbl rooms & a lounge with fireplace & french windows – set in a rough horseshoe around a private plunge pool with decking; perfect for outdoor dining. Each of Tongabezi's houses is carefully secluded from its neighbours, & has the services of a dedicated private valet.

A riverside thatched boma, shaded by ebony trees hung with trailing creepers, incorporates the bar, dining room & 2 intimate lounge areas, 1 with a fireplace. Right on the river with stunning views – especially from its upper storey – is the aptly named Look Out. With comfy chairs, a small library, desks, a computer with internet access & even a private dining area (which must be pre-booked), it's an attractive place to relax. Further relaxation comes in the form of in-room massages, manicures & pedicures. There's a good swimming pool, too, set against a rock wall under a tumbling waterfall, with sunloungers on a large wooden deck over the Zambezi.

Towards sunset, everyone gathers outside around a roaring campfire for sundowners & hors d'oeuvres. Meals are sumptuous affairs, cooked to a high standard & served on the riverside deck, in the dining room, or even in your own cottage. By special arrangement & when the water isn't too high, couples can dine under the stars on Tongabezi's floating 'sampan', with each course hand delivered by canoe – a romantic & memorable occasion.

The lodge's ethos is confirmed by its school, Tujatane, run for around 160 children of Tongabezi staff & from local villages. School visits are popular with guests, & many contribute to the school & the children's future education.

Guided sunrise & sunset boat trips from the lodge's jetty, canoeing, birdwatching trips, fishing, game drives (to Mosi-oa-Tunya National Park), island picnics, village visits, shopping excursions, museum tours & gorge walks are all included (exc park fees & museum entrance). Mountain bikes are available to visit Simonga village & explore the surrounding area. With advance notice, & at extra cost, guests may also sleep on Sindabezi Island (see below), or have a meal on Livingstone Island (see page 195), beside the Falls. *Cottage US$485/580, house*

US$590/685, Nut House US$695/790, all pp sharing, low/high season (Nov–May/Jun–Oct), FBA, inc local drinks, laundry, levies, exc transfers, park fees. 40% sgl suppt high season, no children under 7.

🏠 **Sindabezi Island** (5 chalets) Contact via Tongabezi, above. A short, 2km boat (or canoe) trip downstream from Tongabezi, Sindabezi Island offers barefoot luxury on an island retreat, just a stone's throw across the water from Zimbabwe's Zambezi National Park. Rebuilt in 2009, it is claimed to be the most environmentally friendly property on the river, with all waste water recycled & hot water from solar geysers. Its individually designed en-suite chalets are carefully spaced around the shore of the sandy island for maximum privacy. With solid wood furniture & copper basins, these are beautifully appointed; 2 – designated for honeymooners – have outdoor baths, & one even has its own beach. All are raised on decks & are open on 3 sides, with canvas roll-down walls for protection from the elements. There's a campfire for relaxing over a drink, & a deck high in the ebony trees offers a cool retreat, with commanding views of the river. A relaxed open-sided dining area with teak decking is just one of the settings for meals prepared by the island's own chef. While the rooms now have subtle battery lighting, paraffin lanterns maintain the sense of remoteness. Elephants & hippos are frequent visitors here & game is often sighted on the river banks. With your own guide, you can explore the river & surrounding islands by boat or canoe, or go walking, fishing & birdwatching, as well as take part in all activities run at Tongabezi itself. *Chalet US$430/490, honeymoon chalet US$465/555, both pp sharing low/high season (Nov–May/Jun–Oct) FBA, inc drinks, laundry, transfers to/from island. 4 or more people booking together can reserve the whole island for their exclusive use (max US$550/600 pp).*

🏠 **Tangala House** (sleeps up to 8) e ben@ tongabezi.com, or contact via Tongabezi, above. Right on the Zambezi about 1km from Tongabezi, this luxury private house is worth considering for families (not least because it's well protected against insects), or for those seeking a greater degree of privacy & freedom than is possible in a lodge. Accommodation for 4–8 people is in 4 en-suite bedrooms. Of these, 3 – including a twin, a

dbl & a larger master suite – overlook the river; the 4th has a garden view. Beautifully furnished & equipped living & dining areas lead out onto a large swimming pool overlooking the Zambezi, with views in both directions. The house is available either for rental only, or on a FB basis but without activities, or FBA as at Tongabezi, but with a chef, waiters, housekeeping staff, pool attendant, private guide & even a trained nanny provided, plus private use of vehicles & boats. *US$650 pp, inc use of boat & vehicle, & friendly dogs; children under 14 US$325 pp. Min 4 adults, 3 nights.*

🏠 **Natural Mystic Lodge** (10 chalets) 📞 0213 327436; m 0977 408024; e nmlodge@zamnet.zm; www. naturalmysticlodge.com. The statue at the entrance to Natural Mystic, of Namatama (Mother Earth) with her water pot, depicts the philosophy that underpins this lodge: that the source of life comes from the earth. The low-lying, often wet site, some 20km from Livingstone, is crossed by a walkway with strategic points from which visitors can watch visiting hippos or the occasional elephant. Sadly, though, it was looking rather unkempt when visited in 2011, the walkways were warped & the lodge looked in need of a revamp. Its simple thatched chalets are grouped close together, 4 of them fronting the river (although you can see the river only when the door is open). With 2 double beds & a floor fan in each, they're quite cramped. Some have a bath & shower, others just a shower, & all have a small porch area.

The lodge's best feature is a large decked bar/ restaurant area (*dinner Kw100,000*), right on the river & open to non-residents. There's also a small swimming pool with stone surround, & a lounge with satellite TV. River cruises, game drives & other tours/activities can be organised, as can fishing (*rod hire US$10/day*). **$$$$** *Extra guest US$30 (max 4); 20% discount for Peace Corps & VSO volunteers.*

🏠 **Chundukwa River Lodge** (5 chalets, 1 cottage) 📞 0213 327452; m 0977 781215; e chundukwa@gmail.com, chundukwa@zamnet. zm; www.chundukwariverlodge.com. Situated 23km from Livingstone, Chundukwa's en-suite, twin or dbl chalets are raised on stilts about 3m off the ground & reached via raised walkways. All are well spaced along the river, with the stilts partly submerged when it's in full flow. At the edge of the lodge is a self-contained cottage that sleeps 4 adults & 2 children & has its own swimming pool: perfect for families. In the thatched main area are the bar & dining area; the lodge prides itself on the quality of its home-cooked food. In keeping with the theme this area is open plan with views across the river to Chundu Island & Zimbabwe's Zambezi National Park beyond. Chundukwa is also the home of the Livingstone Polocrosse Club (page 200), evidenced by the pitches (& the horses) next to the entrance road. Horseriding can be arranged (*2hr horse trail around US$55*) for both novices & more experienced riders. Other activities, too, can be organised through the lodge. **$$$$**

🏠 **Waterberry Zambezi Lodge** (7 chalets) 📞 0213 327455; enquiries +44 (0)1379 783392; e reservations@waterberrylodge.com; www. waterberrylodge.com. About 35mins' drive from Livingstone, Waterberry Lodge was fully refurbished in 2011. It's an understated place, set in a secluded position on the banks of the Zambezi, with a lagoon at the back that makes a good focus for bird & nature walks. Although the site is open, & frequented by hippos, children are welcome – but parents need to exercise a degree of caution. Polished concrete floors (which are nicer than they sound) & significant use of natural materials characterise the buildings, from dbl, twin or family thatched chalets to the 2-storey main lodge. Rooms all have en-suite bathrooms, fans & mosi nets. Most are grouped around the main building & swimming pool, but 2 larger rooms are set further back, with a private deck over the lagoon, & a secluded honeymoon suite sits at the river's edge (at time of research, when the Zambezi was at its highest, water was virtually lapping at its door).

The 2-storey central building has a dining area & ground-floor terrace, while upstairs the main bar & lounge are open under deep thatch, with magnificent views over the river & Zambezi National Park beyond. Here there is plenty of seating, a few reference books, & a well-stocked bar. Meals – tailored to fit around individual activities – are served in the dining area, on the sundeck, or on the terrace overlooking the pool, & there are island picnics & traditional bush dinners, too.

Activities offered are very flexible ranging from sunset & daytime cruises to birding, fishing, a tour of the Falls, & village & market visits, as well as – more unusually – a wilderness awareness course & photographic workshops. *US$250 pp FB, inc laundry, sunset cruise, airport transfer, exc bar drinks.*

🏠 **Kubu Cabins** (6 cabins, 1 villa, camping) 📞 0213 327227; m 0974 543439; e reservations@kubucabins.com; www. kubucabins.com. Following nearly a decade of disrepair, Kubu Cabins has recently been given a new lease of life. About 20mins' drive from Livingstone, & signposted from the road, it's under the same ownership as the neighbouring Camp Nkwazi, a short walk upstream. Facilities there can be used by guests at Kubu Cabins, too. As well as 4 small twin-bedded chalets under A-frame thatched roofs with bathrooms at the rear, Kubu has a larger family unit that sleeps 6, & the 'doll house' – a characterful 2-storey building sleeping 4 that wouldn't look out of place in a fairytale. For those wanting a touch more space there is the 'Villa' which sleeps 6 in 3 rooms: 1 with bunks; the others with queensize beds. Both the cabins & the Villa have basic but fully stocked kitchenettes, with utensils & the use of a good-sized fridge, but only the family cabin & the Villa have stoves. There is also a large campsite. *Cabin US$125; camping US$10.*

🏠 **Camp Nkwazi** (10 chalets, camping); 📞 0213 327227; m 0973 048830; e reservations@campnkwazi.com; www. campnkwazi.com. Shaded by riverine forest on the banks of the Zambezi, Camp Nkwazi was heading for completion in 2011, together with a restaurant & separate reception area. Its en-suite chalets are well spaced out, some with a river view & others overlooking a lagoon at the rear of camp. Each stands slightly elevated off the ground & has canvas walls on wooden frames. Across from the lagoon several camping areas have been cut out of the thick bush, but retaining plenty of privacy. This is certainly one of the better-designed campsites in the area. Smaller pitches for 3 or 4 vehicles & larger areas for overlanders each have their own ablution blocks, & electricity is being installed. Boat trips are offered on site, & the camp can book activities in town or at the Falls. *US$100 pp self catering; camping US$20 pp.*

🏠 **Islands of Siankaba** (6 chalets, 1 honeymoon/VIP chalet)〉0213 327490; m 0977 791241; e info@siankaba.net; www. siankaba.com; reservations 〉0211 260279; m 0977 720530. Siankaba is an exclusive lodge that offers considerable attention to detail & superb cuisine. It is 35km from Livingstone, followed by a 7km track through open bush & a 5-min boat ride. The mood is set as you leave the jetty with its small gift shop & chug along a peaceful back channel of the Zambezi before joining the main river. Shortly upstream, Siankaba lies on 2 separate islands linked by suspension bridges (great fun to walk across). On one, spacious chalets reached along raised wooden walkways nestle like bird hides among the trees that overhang the banks, their decks an ideal place to watch the river in complete privacy. In contrast to the half-canvas walls & roof, everything about the accommodation oozes luxury & comfort. Polished teak furniture sits on polished teak floors, offset by thick oriental rugs. Stately comfortable beds with an integral ceiling fan are hung like 4-posters with pristine white mosquito nets, & good reading lights complement the otherwise subdued lighting. Set on a platform to the rear are a regal claw-footed bathtub & twin pedestal basins with views towards the river, as well as a modern shower & separate toilet. Tucked discreetly away, a safe & fridge are almost incidental. For even greater luxury or privacy, the honeymoon/VIP chalet boasts its own deck with views across the river & loungers in the shade of a pergola, as well as a minibar, games compendium, 'his & hers' aromatherapy bath products & reference bookcase. Private meals can be set up on the deck & b/fast in bed is offered as standard.

The adjacent island serves as the epicentre of the camp. Here you'll find the spacious restaurant & comfortable bar/lounge area, with natural décor & tables out on the terrace for al-fresco dining. Among the trees is a secluded pool with stylish sunloungers, & running round the island is a 1.5km nature trail. Activities include a sundowner cruise, birding & fishing excursions, & a mokoro trip among the islands. Sustainably sourced bamboo mountain bikes are supplied for guests' use, & village walks – taking in a visit to the local school & returning by mokoro – are popular, too. The school, Mandia, is a

government-run establishment that – along with other community projects like tree planting & a clinic – is supported by a trust fund operated by the lodge. *Chalet US$425/510; honeymoon chalet US$480/570, all pp sharing/sgl FB, inc drinks, transfers to/from Livingstone airport, & their own activities. No children under 12.*

🏠 **Royal Chundu Zambezi River Lodge** (10 chalets) lodge 〉0213 327060; reservations: 〉+27 41 407 1000; e reservations@ mantiscollection.com; www.royalchundu.com. Following a complete rebuild, Royal Chundu re-emerged in 2010, polished & manicured & very firmly upmarket. About 63km from Livingstone, or just over 1hr's drive from the Falls, it's on a peaceful, wooded stretch of the river, visited by just the occasional canoeist from the nearby village, & a haven for birds.

Solid thatched chalets are tantalisingly close to the river, raised on low stilts & enfolded by waterberry & water-pear trees, yet with 180° views from smart wooden decks. Inside, all-round mosi nets envelop the kingsize bed & side tables, fronted by comfortable chairs & glazed wooden doors that concertina open. Twin showers, twin basins, a separate toilet & bidet, dressing area, safe, AC, room service – it's all here, just like a 5-star hotel.

At the heart of the lodge, linked to the chalets by wide wooden walkways, a large, sparkling infinity pool overlooks the river, bordered by neat lawns & with shaded day beds for R&R. B/fast is usually served on the expansive deck, while dinner may be either in the firelit boma – perhaps with entertainment from the local villagers – or in the formal dining room, complete with fireplace & polished silver, where everything from cigars to (very pricey) fine wines is on hand.

There's a large, open-sided lounge/bar next door, with plenty of books (including railway memorabilia belonging to owner Hugh O'Mahoney's father), squashy sofas & coffee tables, while above – carefully shielded for noise – are a TV lounge, small library & computer room, with more comfy chairs. (There's also WiFi throughout – but no mobile phone coverage.) A new floating riverside spa has added a further level of luxury to this already swanky lodge.

The lodge has good links with the local village, which guests can visit, & where many of the items in the curio shop are made. Other activities (at extra cost) include boat cruises, fishing, canoeing, bush walks & mountain biking. While it's too far from the Falls for easy access, the lodge operates full-day trips combining the Falls with lunch on Livingstone Island & an evening on the *Royal Livingstone Express. US$390 pp FB, inc sundowner cruise.*

🏠 **Katombora Island Lodge** (4 suites) Contact via Royal Chundu, above. Just a short boat trip upstream of Royal Chundu, its exclusive sister-lodge is set on its own 1km² private wooded island, overlooking the Katombora Rapids. It is staffed with its own chef & guide, & equipped with a boat, ensuring that activities, too, are exclusive. Standards are on a par with those at the main lodge, but the suites here are even closer to the river & boast a wider frontage, with an outdoor, lamplit bath on the deck, a shower that's open on 2 sides, & a more spacious sitting area to one side of the room. The main building incorporates 2 colonial-style lounges with contemporary comforts & a fireplace each side, & a dining area for full silver-service dinners. Boma dinners are an alternative option, with b/fast usually taken on the deck, where a small infinity pool looks across to Zimbabwe. A 3–4km nature trail takes in the huge jackalberries, baobab trees & python creepers that characterise the island, or you can participate in any activities offered by the main lodge. *US$490 pp FB, inc sundowner cruise.*

🏕 **Jungle Junction** (4 chalets, 4 huts, 5 tents, camping) Bovu Island; m 0978 725282; e stay@junglejunction.info; www.junglejunction.net. About 1hr's drive from Livingstone, this popular backpackers' hang out re-opened a couple of years ago. Just a 10min mokoro ride from shore, its launch site is suitable only for 4x4s & can be difficult to find; it isn't signposted. With this & the lack of mobile-phone reception, it's best to book in advance.

Facilities are still rustic, but the setting is splendid: indigenous shade trees, sandy beaches & sweeping river views. Large, reed-walled chalets are built on stilts with wood floors, mesh windows, mosi nets & a veranda with river views. Smaller 'fisherman's huts' (2 double, 2 twins with mattresses on the ground, encircled by mosi nets), also with raised wood floors, are simple A-frame structures without walls, windows or doors. There are also small walk-in tents in the campsite, with mattresses on the floor, gauze windows & zip doors. All of these share basic ablutions (flush loos & hot showers) with the campsite. Here, there's plenty of space to pitch a tent on the sandy shore, & there's a kitchen with utensils, charcoal & essentials provided. There is no electricity, though a generator heats water & powers the fridges, & a solar power system is available for recharging batteries.

The barefoot bar with its river views is undoubtedly the most popular place to hang out in camp, & in the adjacent library, books line shelves made of mekoro. The restaurant serves the standard fare of sandwiches & steaks etc or traditional Zambian meals (🕑 *all day; full b/fast or lunch US$7; dinner to US$12).* A small shop sells curios & basic essentials, but it's better to bring your own food if you plan to cook.

A one-off charge of US$25 pp covers activities for the duration of your stay. These include fishing, nature walks, village/school visits & trips taking you hippo watching or to a secluded swimming spot. Think twice before venturing into crocodile-infested waters, though, no matter how safe it is deemed; crocs quickly become habituated to people & may lurk in the shadows. Fashioning your own fishing rod out of a reed pole is quite novel, or you can hire tackle (*approx US$15/day).* Transfers & all boat activities are by mokoro, which are fun but potentially perilous. *Hut US$20 pp; chalet US$30/125 pp room only/FB, inc return transfers. Camping US$10 per tent per night.*

Game park, Falls and Gorge environs

The development by Sun International of a prime spot close to the Falls has introduced a whole new style of accommodation to Livingstone. Other accommodation to the south of town has in recent years been augmented by lodges built away from the river, affording the advantages of open bush but without the high prices associated with a riverside location. Many of the following are actually much closer to the Falls than those situated on the upper river to the west of Livingstone, and are listed as if heading south from Livingstone towards the Falls, then out towards the gorges.

🏠 **Chrismar Hotel** [map 159] (109 rooms) Sichango Rd; 📞0213 323141; e booklvn@ chrismarhotels.com; www.chrismarhotels.com. Opened in 2005, this mid-market hotel near the entrance to the national park is well thought out & offers good value for money. While it is not on the river, its bush setting is enhanced by numerous fountains & water features, including the largest swimming pool in town, complete with a bar in the middle. Dbl & twin rooms, in a range of styles up to executive suites, are set around spacious grounds, & wouldn't disgrace a hotel of far better quality – despite the faux-fur fabrics. An interesting design feature is a window between the bedroom & en-suite bathroom, which boasts a shower & jacuzzi bath, while cool tiled floors, AC, TV, WiFi access, a safe, hairdryer & a fridge are all important extras. As you'd expect, there are a couple of restaurants, as well as an activity centre, with a gym & conference centre the most recent additions. **$$$$**

🏠 **The Bushfront Lodge** [map 159] (14 chalets, camping) Sichango Rd; 📞0213 322446; reservations 📞0213 320607; e bushfront@safpar. com; www.safpar.com. The former Nyala Lodge, now owned & operated by SafPar, is about 5km from town, bordering the national park. It is set a few kilometres upriver from the Falls among indigenous vegetation with abundant birdlife. Thatched chalets have en-suite bathrooms with potted plants – & some with rock walls with water cascading off a small ledge that serves as the shower tap. For campers there are 3 individual pitches with modern ablutions & a braai area. The main lodge area is well designed & maintained, with satellite TV, a large bar/ lounge & a restaurant. All meals are served here, & snacks are always available. Guests can relax by the small pool or explore Livingstone – all activities can be booked at the lodge. **$$$** *Camping US$10 pp.*

🏠 **The Zambezi Waterfront** [map 159] (21 rooms, 24 tents, camping) off Sichango Rd; 📞0213 320606/7; m 0977 434143; e waterfront@safpar.com; www.safpar.net. This large, secure & affordable riverside complex, within the unfenced area of Mosi-oa-Tunya National Park, incorporates a range of facilities on a beautiful spot, one of the best places to view the sunset over the Zambezi. The main thatch- &-pole building, wi*h a great view over the river,

contains the reception, booking office, internet café & a small souvenir shop. A spacious restaurant & teak bar (with satellite TV) both have plenty of seating indoors & out. Outside, amongst palm trees, is a sunken pool surrounded by teak decking, with lounge chairs overlooking the river. Eight large A-frame thatched chalets house individual rooms that are comfortable, light & airy, with teak furniture, quality fabrics & ethnic touches. At ground level are individual en-suite dbl or twin rooms with a patio, & river or garden views. The upper level comprises larger suites with a queen bed, separate lounge area, good-size bathroom, & deck offering sweeping river views. Also up here are spacious family rooms with 4 sgl beds & a deck, overlooking the garden.

Beyond the main building is the Adventure Village with a large natural-style rock pool, another bar & a thatched auditorium where daily activity briefings are given & rafting videos are shown in the evening, accompanied by a BBQ. In the gardens here, permanent tents are perched on wooden platforms, each with 2 beds with bedding & linen (or bring your own). Nearby ablutions are clean & spacious, with flush toilets & hot & cold showers. Further along, a separate grassed camping area has its own ablutions, BBQ & washing-up area; taking about 75 campers, it gets pretty noisy when it's busy with overland trucks.

The Waterfront is SafPar's one-stop shop, where their own Adventure Centre offers a full range of activities & excursions, many that they operate themselves (see page 192). Among these are 2 boats offering b/fast, lunch or sunset cruises (*US$55 pp inc snacks, unlimited drinks & park fees*) from the Waterfront's own jetty. The more upmarket *Mambushi* takes 25 passengers max, while the larger *Makumbi* offers more of a 'booze cruise'. *Chalet room* **$$$$** *Tent US$30 pp; camping US$10 pp.*

🏠 **David Livingstone Safari Lodge & Spa** [map 159] (77 rooms) 📞0213 324601; e res1@dlslandspa.com;www.dlslandspa.com. Opened in 2008, this efficient, 4-star hotel under steep thatch makes the most of its wide river frontage. The entrance lobby, restaurants, rooms & even a good-sized infinity pool command excellent views of the river, where the *Lady Livingstone* (see page 196) awaits passengers to cruise along the Zambezi. Huge basketwork lampshades & wooden sculptures dominate the décor, conveying a strong sense of Africa. Concrete walkways with rustic pole railings lead across the sprawling site to tastefully appointed rooms, each furnished in dark wood with AC, large, flat-screen TV, safe & walk-in mosi nets (helpfully encompassing bedside lights & a phone). Glazed folding doors lead to a small balcony with a couple of chairs, while behind lies a modern bathroom with separate toilet & shower. Two rooms are specifically designed for paraplegics, while 5 suites each have a lounge/bar area & a private jacuzzi. There's WiFi throughout, & a helpful laptop-loan scheme means that guests can email home without resorting to a soulless business centre. In addition to the 1st-floor Kalai Restaurant & the Ujiji bar, a waterside terrace serves drinks, snacks & light lunches (food, drinks & services are subject to 10% service charge). Other facilities include the highly exclusive spa, a gym, gift shop, & activity centre. **$$$$$** *inc 1 activity/day (sunset cruise or Vic Falls tour).*

🏠 **Maramba River Lodge** [map 159] (9 chalets, 16 tents, camping) 0213 324189; e maramba@zamnet.zm; www.maramba-zambia.com. This well-established lodge & campsite, founded in 1991, lies 4km from the Falls, down a short, bumpy track just south of Livingstone Reptile Park. Situated within the national park on the banks of the Maramba River, it is a real oasis in the bush, with green lawns & mature trees, hippos, elephants & birds aplenty. The owners live on site with their children, & the lodge is excellent for families & individuals, with an activity booking office, pool, children's play area, craft shop, fully licensed riverside bar & simple restaurant.

There are 4 types of accommodation. The thatched en-suite chalets (with 2 or 4 beds) are bright & airy, in a pretty location under mopane & mahogany trees. Each has treated mosquito nets & ceiling fans. 6 spacious (Landela) tents combine lodge comfort with the pleasures of camping. They are en suite (with tiled bathroom & open-air shower) & have handcrafted furniture, including a dbl & a sgl bed under walk-in mosi nets & a small veranda. Simpler accommodation comes in the form of 10 twin-bedded safari tents under thatch, with chairs, clothes storage, electricity & en-suite facilities. The small campsite is very popular, so it's wise to book in

advance; campers share an ablution block with hot showers & laundry facilities. **$$$** *Camping US$10 pp, & US$3 per vehicle if power required. US$180 dbl B&B inc morning & afternoon tea.*

🏠 **Livingstone Safari Lodge** [map 159] (9 chalets, camping) m 0955 832168, 0977 403881; e livingstone-lodge@microlink.zm; www.livingstonebushlodge.com. This rambling 'love-it-or-hate-it' lodge (emphatically not to be confused with David Livingstone Safari Lodge!) is set amid 8.5ha of open bush near the Maramba River, on a securely fenced site 6km from the centre of Livingstone, & a similar distance from the Falls. To get there, follow Mosi-oa-Tunya Rd towards the Falls, & turn left after the Reptile Park. From here, take the 1st left-hand track, then it's clearly signposted, almost 1.5km on a level sandy road.

The lodge's laid-back approach is epitomised by its eccentric Dutch owner, Tjisse Kamstra, a fount of local knowledge, stories & forthright views whose commitment to Livingstone includes supporting several orphaned children. A motley family of dogs, chickens & ducks greets the newly arrived. The rustic bar includes a pool table & braai area, & guests are welcome to try the xylophones & drums that are temptingly displayed on the terrace (though musicians are brought in on request: dinner with entertainment costs around US$12–15).

Asphalt paths link the main building to some decidedly quirky en-suite chalets dotted around the grounds. Secluded & cooled by a through breeze, most have high thatched roofs & colourful stencilled walls, mosquito nets, coffee/tea facilities, & private verandas. Some have 2 dbl beds; others have a 2nd upstairs bedroom with bunk beds. Campers can choose from 2 pitches with private showers & toilets, or the main campsite, which has electric hook-ups & plenty of water points. Ablution & laundry facilities are tiled & clean, with hot & cold showers. A large, secluded swimming pool is set away from all buildings. **$$$** *Camping US$6/12 pp standard/en-suite.*

🏠 **Royal Livingstone** [map 193] (173 rooms) Mosi-oa-Tunya Rd; 0213 321122; reservations +27 11 780 7800; e crobook@za.suninternational.com; www.suninternational.com. Opened in 2001, this opulent 5-star hotel situated in extensive grounds is owned by the

South African Sun International group. If its broad, low, white frontage is rather disappointing at first glance, inside all is spacious & elegant, with an old-world attention to detail & service. Step outside onto extensive verandas, where sweeping lawns lead to an unparalleled frontage along the Zambezi, the 'smoke' from the Falls rising tantalisingly close. A 15-min walk along the river brings you to the Falls themselves via the direct access point that is the preserve of the two Sun International hotels, or guests can be escorted by porters in pith helmets on one of the hotel's 'club cars' (golf-cart style). The hotel is in the national park; zebra, impala & giraffe are often seen grazing in the grounds.

All rooms have twin or kingsize beds & are fitted with AC, satellite TV, radio, blu-ray DVD player, minibar, safe & phone; 2 rooms are fully equipped for the disabled. Tasteful & comfortable, if on the small side, each room has its own private balcony, & benefits from the services of a butler. Should all this not be sufficient, there are also 4 suites.

Meals are served either in the excellent à-la-carte restaurant (page 181), or outside on the veranda, while for a special occasion private candlelit dinners on the lawns can be arranged at extra cost. The long, wood-panelled bar has a relaxed, colonial air. Elsewhere on the property is an African boma, crafted in the traditional Zambian manner with seating for up to 350 people, with a smaller riverside boma for special functions (including weddings) & small groups. A grand swimming pool overlooks the Zambezi, surrounded by sunloungers. This is a great spot to relax, as are the massage tents along the riverfront (massage approx US$122 pp; manicures, pedicures & facials also available). The concierge can organise activities, from whitewater rafting & horseriding to game drives or a trip on the *Royal Livingstone Express*. The hotel has its own helipad.

Considerably more expensive than the adjacent Zambezi Sun, the Royal Livingstone caters for a very different market – those seeking traditional standards of décor & service in a truly gracious setting. If you'd like to indulge without the high price of accommodation, consider sundowners on their magnificent riverside deck, or a highly civilised afternoon tea in the lounge (about US$20 pp). **$$$$$**

🏠 **Zambezi Sun** [map 193] (212 rooms) 393 Mosi-oa-Tunya Rd; 🔌0213 321122; reservations 🔌+27 11 780 7800; e intmark@sunint.co.za; www.suninternational.com. This is the lively 3-star sibling of the Royal Livingstone, & what a contrast. Crenellated walls are more reminiscent of a north African mosque than of southern Africa, their deep desert red contrasting with the Zambian sky. Vervet monkeys, the bane of the staff, cavort through the colourful grounds as if through a children's playground. Although it's close to the Falls, there are no views of the river, though balconies overlook the extensive lawns from each of the rooms. Well designed, if rather compact, the rooms are very comfortable – the standard of a good international business hotel – but with considerably more flashes of colour & individuality. Each has AC, satellite TV, safe & phone, with a bath & shower en suite. 2 rooms are adapted for paraplegics.

In addition to the extensive buffet restaurant (*US$37 pp*), there's a relaxed al-fresco grill beside the pool that snakes through the grounds, or – adjacent to The Falls activity centre – both Squire's Grillhouse & a simple café. In the dry season, traditional meals are occasionally served in the boma, accompanied by dancing (*US$40 pp*). If you want something more formal, you can always book into the posh restaurant next door. You can use the Royal's spa, too – although on-site massages can be organised here. The complex also includes a children's club & playground, & business & conference centres. Ultimately, though, everything hinges on the location. Just a few hundred metres' walk from the lip of the Falls & the curio market, & with unrestricted access, the hotel's position is unbeatable. **$$$$$**

🏠 **Stanley Safari Lodge** [map 159] (10 cottages) Reservations 🔌+27 72 170 8879; lodge emergency m 0967 848615; e reservations@stanleysafaris.com; www. stanleysafaris.com. This Belgian-owned luxury lodge, opened in 2002, has sweeping views down towards the Zambezi & the Falls in the distance, & is best suited as a place to chill out, relax & unwind. Advance reservations are essential, with almost all clients arriving by air & collected at the airport. Should you be driving yourself, turn east off the main road to the Falls almost opposite the Royal Livingstone & continue past a large baobab on your right, bearing sharp right after 500m, then following the road towards Mukuni village for a further 2km. The turning (⊕ 17°54' 1.45 S, 25°53' 39.32 E) is on the rise of a hill, on the left, just after the sign for Munali Farm.

The lodge is set behind a high electric fence, but once inside all is calm & spacious. Large, fairly formal gardens with a central pool face west towards the Zambezi. The main building is a beautifully designed thatched affair with an open-aspect lounge, bar & dining area, & the 'map room' (with a laptop & free WiFi) deserves to be popular with guests. Above is a further sitting area, while below, a wine cellar allows candlelit tastings of a range of South African, French & Italian wines. Permutations for serving dinner are many – including the option of a dining table *in* the infinity pool!

Six stylish open 'cottages', each slightly different but most with a view, are built in a half-moon shape, with kingsize or twin beds, a 'loo with a view' & an outside shower & bath. The honeymoon suite has its own plunge pool & fireplace, & those with children will love the family room, with a shallow paddling pool, & a bucket shower set outside around a tree, giving younger children the opportunity to experience in safety the fun of living in the bush. There are also 2 'colonial' suites, entirely enclosed with doors & windows, a lounge with fireplace, a covered terrace & private plunge pool. One of these is suitable for families, with 2 en-suite bedrooms.

Throughout, the décor is both stylish & comfortable, with good use of wood, stone & natural fabrics, & plenty of space. *Cottage US$370/490–470/650 pp sharing/sgl; open suite US$410/530–550/730; closed suite 470/590–610/790, all FBA, inc local drinks, laundry, transfers to Livingstone airport.*

🏠 **Taita Falcon Lodge** (7 chalets, camping) lodge ☎ 0213 327046, reservations ☎ 0213 321850; e taita-falcon@microlink.zm; www. taitafalcon.com. ⊕ 17°58.879'S, 25°54.654'E. Perched on the very edge of Batoka Gorge, with the raging waters below, Taita's view is breathtaking to say the least. It is a 45-min drive from Livingstone, for which you'll need a high-clearance vehicle, & a 4x4 during the rains. The lodge has its own helipad, but drivers should follow the main road from town towards the Falls, take the well-signposted left turn opposite

the entrance to the Royal Livingstone, then go right at the baobab tree. From here, follow the signs for about ½hr along 11km of long, winding track, passing through Songwe village.

The lodge is named after the rare Taita falcon that frequents cliffs & gorges, especially in the Zambezi Valley – & this area is one of the best in Africa for spotting them. They are small (less than 30cm long) with cream to brown underparts – no bars or markings – & a strong, fast style of flight. Look for them especially in the evenings, perhaps trying to catch swallows or bats on the wing. Verreaux's (black) eagles, peregrine falcons & many other raptors & small birds are also resident, numbering among the 234 bird species recorded here.

Run by Faan & Anmarie Fourie, the lodge is pleasant & informal surrounded by indigenous gardens & with personable service. Its en-suite chalets are constructed of stone, timber & reeds under thatch. Rebuilt & enlarged a few years ago, they retain their rustic idiosyncrasy, with pull-down rush 'windows', a simple sliding door, & locally made beds, tables & chairs. With a shower, basin & toilet at the back, & a separate outside shower in a garden area at the front, they're open in design, but entirely private. Two can be made up as family rooms, sleeping up to 5; the rest are dbls or trpls. Electricity is from a generator.

Narrow pathways, accessible by wheelchair, weave through the bush parallel to the cliff, linking the chalets to the bar & restaurant. In front of the bar, overlooking the gorge & Rapids 16 & 17, downstream of the Falls, is a great place both to spot birds & to watch the rafters down below. That said, & although the chalets are set back from the precipice, I'd be wary of letting children run wild here. There's a nice small pool for a dip, encompassed by a tiled patio with adjacent small lawn.

A couple of kilometres from the lodge is a small campsite with 3 pitches, set well apart with their own ablution blocks but with no river view. Campers can use the lodge's bar & restaurant if they book in advance, but not the pool.

Included in some of the lodge rates are a tour of Songwe village & one of 4 activities: a game drive, a sunset cruise, a town tour, or a visit to the Falls. Other activities include guided bush & bird walks, hiking trails in & around the gorge (equipped hikers can do 2–3-day hikes) & fishing (for the fit – it's a steep walk!). Taita Falcon Lodge is a relaxing place in a remote spot – albeit only 12km from the Falls. Adrenalin junkies, though, could feel cut off from the epicentre of things. *US$275–295 pp FB, inc airport transfers; US$375–395 pp sharing FB, inc local drinks, 1 activity/day, airport transfers. Self-drive rates on request. Camping US$15 pp.*

✗ WHERE TO EAT

Takeaways and fast food There are several takeaways in town, including Wonderbake, one of the best and most popular, plus Kaazmein across the road near the post office [162 A2], and the Hungry Lion on the corner with Mutelo Street [162 B2]. For a few thousand kwacha, these serve the usual fare of pre-packaged chips, burgers, samosas, sandwiches and soft drinks. All are in the centre of town, along Mosi-oa-Tunya Road. Falls Park shopping centre [map 159] is a useful source of fast food, too, with branches of Steers and Debonair's Pizza along one side and sharing an outside seating area. Most are open every day until around 21.00.

Wonderbake [162 B1] Mosi-oa-Tunya Rd, next to Rite Pub & Grill; ⏱ 08.00–21.00 Mon–Sat, 08.00–20.00 Sun. One of the few places in the area with WiFi, this is a convenient location for a quick snack & a great spot to rendezvous, though it's often crowded. Expect fresh bread, samosas & pies, drinks, chicken, cakes, sandwiches & ice cream; plus espressos & cappuccinos should you need a jolt of caffeine. $

Yapa Z Sports Café [162 E4] Muwela St; ⏱ 10.00–22.00. While there is a basic café & takeaway here, serving the likes of chicken & chips, most punters come for the large TV screens set in a dark but cavernous sports bar, where you can get soft drinks & beer. $

Restaurants In the last decade, several independent restaurants have opened up in Livingstone, offering a wider variety (Indian, Chinese, seafood, etc) than the hotels at fairly decent prices. Don't expect to find haute cuisine, as food tends more towards standard pub fare and sustenance rather than fine dining. Here's a small selection of the current favourites, though it's also worth remembering restaurants in those hotels that are not listed, which often cater to foreign tastes and may have more to offer, albeit at higher prices.

✗ **Royal Livingstone** [map 193] Mosi-oa-Tunya Rd; ☎ 0213 321122. Sun's flagship hotel has a fabulous restaurant with surprisingly reasonable prices, particularly when compared with the Zambezi Sun next door. The setting is lovely – old-world elegance & comfort – the service excellent, & the food the best in town. However, be sure to book in advance; if the hotel is full they don't take outside reservations. If you feel like a bit of refined luxury, try the very genteel afternoon tea (about US$22), with sandwiches & cakes – though be warned: vervet monkeys might try to steal your food. $$$$$
✗ **Zambezi Sun** [map 193] Mosi-oa-Tunya Rd; ☎ 0213 321122. The buffet dinner here is wide ranging with a selection of grilled kebabs, burgers, omelettes to order, salads & desserts, though at US$45 pp it's not cheap. Alternatively, there's an al-fresco grill located alongside the entertainment area at the pool, ideal for light lunches & snacks. Tables are set inside & out around a large pool, & the atmosphere is lively, especially in the afternoons. When there's live music, it's good value for an evening out, but don't expect cordon bleu standards. Within the same complex are Squire's (see below) & a small café serving drinks & snacks. $$$$$
✗ **Squire's Grillhouse & Action Bar** [map 193] The Falls, Mosi-oa-Tunya Rd; ☎ 0213 323351; ⏱ 12.00–22.00 daily. This branch of the South African restaurant chain next to the Zambezi Sun serves decent but standard fare, mostly grilled meat, chicken & fish, as well as burgers. It's on the expensive side, & the beer is extortionate, but they do have some better-value lunch specials. The unprepossessing location is a drawback, & there's noise from the road, but the service is friendly & efficient. $$$–$$$$

✕ The Zambezi Waterfront [map 159] Sichango Rd; ☎ 0213 320606/7. The magnificent setting of SafPar's riverside complex makes this a good place to dine. You can enjoy b/fast, lunch or dinner (or a snack) overlooking the Zambezi at affordable prices. The food is good & plentiful with the usual variety of chicken dishes, burgers & chips, soups, sandwiches & daily specials served by friendly staff. There is also a full bar. While it is out of town, it's the kind of place you might go for a meal & stay for hours to savour the riverside ambience. $$$–$$$$

✕ The Arts Café [map 159] 1878/B Mosi-oa-Tunya Rd; ☎ 0213 323346; m 0977 371700; www.lipaf.org. The home of the Livingstone Performing Arts Foundation (Lipaf) has a bright & airy restaurant that offers both indoor &

outdoor dining & a traditional Zambian menu. There are also a few specials such as crocodile steak or fried mopane worms for the more adventurous palate. Meals are reasonably priced & music nights are held regularly with those dining in the restaurant exempt from the Kw10,000 cover charge. $$$

✕ Chanters [162 E1] Lukulu Cres; ☎ 0213 323412; www.chanters-livingstone.com; ☉ 07.00–21.30 daily. Chanters has a varied & comprehensive menu, with a good selection of fish as well as local specialities such as braised oxtail & a range of pasta & vegetarian dishes. The food is good, & the garden setting attractive. $$$

✕ Ocean Basket [163 D6] 82 Mosi-oa-Tunya Rd; ☎ 0213 321274; www.oceanbasket.com;

THE LEGACY OF LIVINGSTONE'S JEWISH COMMUNITY *Peter Jones*

Among the earliest white settlers north of the Zambezi were many Jews from the Baltic states of Lithuania and Latvia, then part of the Russian empire. From the 1880s onwards, they came in large numbers to the goldfields of South Africa, both as economic migrants, and as refugees fleeing religious and political persecution. Some more adventurous souls, including Elie and Harry Susman, moved on north to Bulawayo and then, attracted by the cattle stocks of Barotseland, crossed the Zambezi shortly before the Cape-to-Cairo railway reached the Victoria Falls in 1904.

Jewish traders played an important role at the Old Drift on the Zambezi river bank and then in the new town of Livingstone, which was laid out in 1905. A Hebrew Congregation was established in 1910 and the foundation stone of the synagogue was laid in 1928. In the late 1930s, Livingstone's Jewish population was reinforced by a new influx of German Jewish refugees from Nazism. Then, during World War II, there was an even larger influx of Polish, and mainly Christian, refugees.

After the war, Indian traders began to replace their Jewish counterparts in the retail trade, but Jewish businesses branched out into the development of secondary industry. The Susman Brothers & Wulfsohn group either took over or established both Zambezi Saw Mills, with its famous railway, and Zambia Textiles, while the Tow Brothers established an iron foundry. The most prominent Jewish families in the town were the related Susmans and Grills, and the Kopelowitzes.

While there is no longer a Jewish presence in the town, their influence can be seen in its colonial architecture. It was, for example, the Grill family who built the remarkable **Capitol Cinema** [162 B1] on Mosi-oa-Tunya Road in the early 1930s. (This was fully renovated in 2009, but sadly its new lease of life was short, and it has once more closed.) Others places of interest that can be visited include:

• The **Synagogue** on Likute Way (formerly Highway), now the Church of Christ. The first synagogue in Northern Rhodesia, its foundation stone was laid by Eli Susman in 1928. The church elders are very happy to open the doors to

⌚ 12.00–22.00 daily. A branch of the South African chain, this fish restaurant is located in a restored historical building near the junction of Kazungula Rd. If you have a hankering for fish or prawns in this landlocked country, this is the place. They even do good sushi. Set inside a large secure courtyard with sprawling lawn & ample parking, it offers dining either inside or out on the wide veranda. Staff are efficient & very friendly & the food, served in large frying pans, is good. $$–$$$$$

✗ **Armadillo Oriental & Grills** [162 F3] 48 Mosi-oa-Tunya Rd; ☎ 0213 324781; ⌚ 09.00–midnight daily. This imposing new restaurant near the New Fairmount Hotel is popular for both Indian & Continental cuisine, as well as burgers & steaks. Meals are served on a wide terrace overlooking the road, or in the cool, tiled interior, & there is a popular bar next door. $$–$$$

✗ **Ngolide Lodge's Indian Restaurant** [163 D8] 110 Mosi-oa-Tunya Rd; ☎ 0213 321091/2; ⌚ 07.00–10.00, 12.30–14.00, 18.15–22.00. One of the better places to eat in town, this small Indian restaurant, also known as Kamuza, is tucked away at the back of Ngolide Lodge. On offer are a variety of dishes, from fish masalla to kadai chicken & loads of veggie options; you can also order a takeaway. As it only has a few tables & is very popular, do book in advance. $$–$$$

✗ **O'Driscoll's** [163 D6] Mosi-oa-Tunya Rd (behind Fawlty Towers); ☎ 0213 323432; ⌚ 11.00–22.00 daily. Popular with both visitors & local tour operators, who come to unwind

allow you to look inside. The 'Sefer Torah' was removed to Lusaka when one of the last Jewish families, the Iljons, left the area in 1972. Nickie Iljon's name still adorns the building that housed his shop on Mutelo Street, formerly Codrington Street.

- The **clock** at the Livingstone Museum, donated by the Susman brothers in 1951 to commemorate the 50th anniversary of their arrival north of the Zambezi.
- **Stanley House,** on the main Mosi-oa-Tunya Road next to the Capitol Cinema, which housed the elegant stores of the wealthy Harry Sossen, who was married to Bella Grill.
- The **Zambezi Saw Mills** office in the industrial area, now the Railway Museum. In the cabinet it is still possible to read the guards' reports which show that bales of cloth belonging to Susman Brothers & Wulfsohn, and destined for their Western and North-Western Province stores, were pilfered at various intervals!
- The **old cemetery** on the outskirts of town, which incorporates a small walled-off section for the Jewish community.

Less visible, but no less interesting, is the history behind two roads. Susman Drive, now called Kapufi Avenue, was originally named after Eli Susman and all the good work that he did for the community. And the town's central crossroads was once known to the locals as 'Ficks, Flax and Aufochs' corner after the three shops at the intersection. Sam Fix was a tailor, Flax ran a haberdashery and the Aufochs family had a trading store on the opposite corner. After independence, Mainway and Sackville Street became Mosi-oa-Tunya Road and Akapelwa Street respectively.

Further information on the Jewish community in Zambia can be found in Hugh Macmillan and Frank Shapiro's *Zion In Africa: the Jews of Zambia* and Macmillan's *An African Trading Empire: the story of Susman Brothers & Wulfsohn, 1901–2005* (see *Appendix 3*, page 535).

after a hard day's rafting, touring or guiding, the former Hippos was fully refurbished in 2011. Expect an unpretentious bar with a distinctly Irish feel & Guinness behind the bar. Tables are set under a gigantic thatched roof & an open-plan main area with cushioned seating. And there's satellite TV for when the bar's namesake (Bryan O'Driscoll, the Irish Rugby Union captain) is in action. $$–$$$

✕ Old Drift Restaurant & Bar [163 G6] Livingstone Royal Golf & Country Club; \ 0213 323052; m 0978 170791; ⊕ 08.00–22.00 daily. The à-la-carte restaurant & bar in the golf club's colonial-style clubhouse has a beautiful setting overlooking the course. Excellent food is served throughout the day, with pizzas, sandwiches, burgers, steaks & samosas at lunch. Dinners are more extravagant & slightly more expensive but good value overall. There are free snacks & happy-hour prices 17.30–18.30 every Fri. $$–$$$

✕ Olga's [163 D6] Nakatindi Rd; \ 0213 324160; www.olgasproject.com; ⊕ 07.00–23.00 daily. Close to the Catholic church, this is the place for pizzas cooked in a traditional wood-fired oven, as well as pasta dishes & salads. A thatched eating area incorporates crafts & furniture made by members of the Local Youth Community Training Centre & a school for disadvantaged youngsters, with profits from the restaurant fed back to the centre. There's also en-suite accommodation planned for the future. $$–$$$

✕ Zigzag [map 159] Industrial Rd; \ 0213 322814; ⊕ 07.00–21.00 Sun–Wed, 07.00–23.00 Thu–Sat. Zigzag is a welcome respite from the hustle & bustle of town. Large & inviting, with shady guava, lemon & mango trees, it's a popular place for an extensive b/fast, coffee & cakes, lunch, or an evening meal. There's also a children's menu, a range of desserts & milkshakes, & a fully licensed bar. There's also an enticing pool with grassy surround, a changing area & a children's play area, useful if you want to keep the kids entertained as you sip your cappuccino, or surf the net courtesy of free WiFi access. $$–$$$

✕ The Spot [163 D7] 125 Mosi-oa-Tunya Rd; m 0978 170791; ⊕ 11.00–late Tue–Sat, 11.00–15.00 Sun. Funky, rustic & recommended, this light & breezy bar & restaurant is set in a

colonial rail worker's house, decorated with traditional masks & ornaments. Popular with locals & tourists alike, it serves both traditional & Western dishes & has a licensed bar. There's indoor & outdoor seating & a children's play area in the pleasant shaded gardens. $$

✕ Rite Pub & Grill [162 B1] Mosi-oa-Tunya Rd; ⊕ 08.00–24.00. Diagonally opposite Barclays Bank, this is a pleasant enough place to stop for lunch, dinner or a drink. Inside, individual booths with their own thatched roof are a bit on the dark side, but nevertheless cosy, while next door is the more relaxed covered area of Eat Rite. A fairly standard menu includes pizza & chips, & there's a full bar. $–$$$

✕ Da Fusion [162 B2] Mosi-oa-Tunya Rd; \ 0213 322259; ⊕ 08.00–midnight. Opposite the post office, this is a small, family-run restaurant & takeaway. Come here for good curries, naan bread, samosas & tandoori chicken, as well as Zambian dishes such as *nkoro* stew & fried *nkuku* (chicken). It is pleasantly air-conditioned, & popular with impecunious backpackers. $–$$

✕ Fez Bar [163 D6] Mosi-oa-Tunya Rd; m 0978 667555; ⊕ 09.00–23.00 daily. This popular evening hang-out was re-opening in a new location next to The Spot in late summer 2011. If you have a taste for tequila & dancing into the early hours, this is the place to be, with its impressive pop-art murals, sunken couches & outside seating. There's a large-screen satellite TV & even DJs at the w/end. Mexican food, standard fare of chicken, steaks & chips, & their 'famous' burger (generally considered to be the best in Livingstone) are all available. $–$$

✕ Laughing Dragon [162 A1] John Hunt Way; \ 0213 322555; ⊕ 11.00–23.00 daily. Set behind the museum, Laughing Dragon serves authentic Szechuan Chinese food, has a full alcohol licence & also does takeaways. The menu depends on what's available in Livingstone that day, but the food is good, & the quantities generous. Their chow mein is delicious, & one reliable correspondent described the deep-fried oyster mushrooms as 'too yummy for words'. $–$$

✕ Mukamba/Ann's Steak House [162 D4] 97 John Hunt Way. Down the road from Jollyboys, this is a great place to chill out with some cheap Zambian food & drinks, often accompanied by live, local music. $–$$

ENTERTAINMENT AND NIGHTLIFE Livingstone's **nightlife** centres largely around dancing and drinking, although the bars at various restaurants offer a pleasant atmosphere if you simply want to relax and chat. For sundowners, join the crowd at the Zambezi Waterfront [map 159], overlooking the river. The Fez Bar [163 D6] is a lively venue most nights – a favourite hangout for local expats letting off steam after a tough day looking after visitors. Other popular options are Da Fusion [162 B2] and Mukamba [162 D4].

For live music, there's a band at the Zambezi Sun [map 159] most evenings and at weekends, and at the Rite Pub [162 B1] at weekends only. Mukamba often features live local bands, too. Traditional dancing can be seen at The Waterfront, though you'll need to check times and dates with them.

Those in search of dancing should try Eat Rite's open-air disco on Kapondo Street, which later moonlights as a nightclub – Steprite Sounds. A cover charge is made when there's a band playing. The New Fairmount Hotel [162 E3] has the dark and popular Club Fairmount (\ *0213 320723; ⊕ normally 20.00–04.00 Thu–Sat, but phone to confirm*), that's generally jam-packed at weekends, as well as a casino (⊕ *07.00–midnight daily*). And there's also Chez N'temba [162 B2], just off Mosi-oa-Tunya Road beyond the Hungry Lion. In all of these places, the music is loud, you can dance until you drop and, because they can become very rowdy later in the evenings, it's advisable to venture out in a group.

SHOPPING With both the Falls Park shopping centre [map 159] and the newly built Mosi-oa-Tunya Square ([163 D6] commonly referred to as the 'Shoprite Centre'), options for shopping in Livingstone have improved considerably in recent years. There are also a couple of markets, and several shops along the main Mosi-oa-Tunya Road. Opening hours are usually around 09.00–17.00 Monday to Friday, and Saturday mornings, unless otherwise stated.

Food and drink Although you can find most things in Livingstone, you may still have to visit several shops, and imported gourmet items are harder to come by and expensive.

Of the **supermarkets**, the new branch of Shoprite ([163 D6] *Mosi-oa-Tunya Sq; ⊕ 08.00–20.00 daily*) has upstaged the sadly diminished Spar Super Store ([map 159] *Falls Park*), and is now the place of choice for those in the know. (The original Shoprite on Kapondo Street is an entirely different affair, so don't get them confused!)

For somewhere less corporate, there's Mini Market ([162 B1] *Mosi-oa-Tunya Rd, across from post office*), which stocks a good supply of fresh fruit and vegetables in addition to the basics. If it's just **meat** you're after, cross Mosi-oa-Tunya Road to Pama Meats for a selection of beef, poultry and pork, or try Shopper's Butchery ([162 B1] *John Hunt Way, behind post office*). Wonderbake [162 B1] sells good fresh-baked **bread** and pastries.

For fruit and vegetables, try the Zambian open-air **markets**. Positioned around town, these have fresh tomatoes, onions and other basic fruits and vegetables, and are generally cheaper than the supermarkets.

Books and magazines Bookworld ([163 D6] *Mosi-oa-Tunya Sq;* \ *0213 321414; ⊕ 09.00–18.00 Mon–Fri, 09.00–17.00 Sat, 09.00–13.00 Sun*) has the best stock in Livingstone and also sells stationery, games and the like. Alternatively, several of the curio shops stock wildlife reference books and regional travel guides. Jollyboys (see page 169) has a book-exchange system, as do many other places to stay in town. Current magazines may be harder to come by. Your best bet is the Spar at Falls Park [map 159] or Shoprite at Mosi-oa-Tunya Sq [163 D6] – though be warned, magazines are expensive and tend to be several months old, so be sure to check the issue date. Oddly, the street vendors in front of the Capitol Theatre [162 B1] often have more recent ones at much lower prices, but this is very hit or miss.

Clothes You can pick up clothing essentials at the PEP store ([162 B2] *Mosi-oa-Tunya Rd, opposite Zanaco*), or at Power Sales, a few doors down from the same bank, though you'll need to be selective. There are also plenty of shops selling a hotchpotch of stuff that includes assorted clothing, mostly from China – so it can become rather a mission (or adventure) to find what you seek. For more fashionable wear try the clothing stores at Falls Park shopping centre [map 159] or at the Zambezi Sun [map 193], though these will be pricier. For shoes, there's Bata, by Barclays Bank [162 B1], though both the selection and sizes are rather limited.

Despite its shortcomings on fashion, Livingstone is a great place to find African wear – brightly coloured shirts, skirts and dresses, some complete with matching caps or headscarves – and garments can often be made to order with a few days' notice. *Chitenje*, the colourful lengths of traditional African cloth, can be found at most of the small Indian shops on the main road and on Kuta Way, parallel to the main road, or at any of the local markets (see page 198). Clothes can be made up at Emmah's Wear (see below) from your own fabrics or theirs.

Crafts, curios and gifts If you like bargaining and have lots of patience, then try one of the craft markets (see page 198), either in town or next to the Falls. Alternatively, look out for the informal craft market in the car park at Falls Park shopping centre [map 159], where curio vendors lay out their goods on a more ad hoc basis.

If time isn't on your side, or you don't fancy the hassle of bargaining, one of the following might suit you much better.

Arts Café [map 159] See page 182. The base for the Livingstone Performing Arts Foundation & with an excellent restaurant serving local dishes, this is also a curio shop. The quality of items on offer is good & there's a great variety of genuine local handicrafts, without any pressure to buy. There are workshops each afternoon where local artisans are ready to help you create your own basket, woodcarving or anything else you'd like to try.

Bobbili Gems [163 D6] Mosi-oa-Tunya Sq; ℡ 0213 323210; m 0976 446240; ⊕ 09.00–18.00. If bling is your thing, look no further. Bobbili Gems designs its own jewellery – necklaces, earrings & other items – much of it fashioned from Zambian silver, beads, semi-precious stones & gemstones. Friendly staff are on hand to answer your questions & help you find that special souvenir, or the resident artisan will work with you to create your own signature piece. There is also a smaller store at the airport for last-minute gifts.

Emmah's Wear [163 D7] 121 Mosi-oa-Tunya Rd; ℡ 0213 322254; ⊕ 08.00–17.00 Mon–Fri, 08.00–12.30 Sat. Just north of the railway station, Emmah's can tailor-make anything from clothing to tablecloths, quickly & affordably. Bring your own fabric (bought at a local market or an Indian shop in town) or choose one at their shop, & expect to pay from Kw45,000 for a simple skirt. There's also a small craft shop here.

Kubu Crafts Livingstone Airport & The Falls, Mosi-oa-Tunya Rd [map 193]; ℡ 0213 320230; www.kubucrafts.com. Although the flagship store of Livingstone's most established curio shop has now closed, 2 smaller branches remain. Though they're very tourist orientated, crafts from all over Africa – textiles, wood carvings, pottery, metal sculptures & more – afford plenty of choice, & browsing is hassle free.

Livingstone Trading Company [map 193] The Falls, Mosi-oa-Tunya Rd; ℡ 0213 323864; ⊕ 08.00–18.00 daily. Next to the Zambezi

Sun, this is a good option for everything from children's & ladies' clothes to books, cards & basic toiletries.

Museum Curio Shop & Art Gallery [163 A2] Livingstone Museum. The museum's curio shop showcases Zambian handicrafts & basketware. A wide selection of Zambian paintings & other art by local artists is for sale – everything from wildlife to people to abstract.

The Shop that Thunders [map 193] Victoria Falls entrance; e theshopthatthunders@zamnet. zm. Next to the information centre on the Zambian side of the Falls, this shop stocks the usual collection of souvenirs & memorabilia – wall-hangings, basketware, carvings, postcards & gifts. It's convenient if you're at the Falls &

doesn't involve the haggling required at the adjacent curio market. They also sell cool drinks & snacks.

The Whole in the Wall [163 D6] 217 area, next to Fawlty Towers; ☎0213 324189; e tambao@zamnet.zm. This small but well-outfitted shop has a good variety of innovative, locally produced souvenirs, tending towards smaller & easy-to-carry items like wire animals, keyrings, postcards, maps, T-shirts, handicrafts & gifts.

Women in Mining [map 193] The Falls, Mosi-oa-Tunya Rd; ⊕ 08.00–18.00 daily. If it's gemstones or jewellery you're after, this shop linked to the Association of Zambian Women in Mining (AZWIM) could be the place.

Pharmacies For cosmetics, toiletries or medicines there are five good pharmacies stocking a selection of items including insect repellents, beauty products, suncreams, medical supplies, baby supplies, batteries, film and more. Each has a trained pharmacist, who can also offer advice on medications and fill prescriptions. Otherwise, the Spar Super Store in Falls Park shopping centre [map 159] and Shoprite in Mosi-oa-Tunya Square [163 D6] sell a variety of beauty products and the basics.

Health & Glow Pharmacy [163 D6] Mosi-oa-Tunya Rd; ☎0213 322249; ⊕ 08.00–18.30 Mon–Fri, 08.00–14.00 Sat, 09.30–13.00 Sun. Next to Fawlty Towers & opposite Shoprite, these well-stocked shops have helpful, knowledgeable staff.

HK Pharmacy & Photo Studio [162 B1] Mosi-oa-Tunya Rd, next to Capitol Theatre; ☎0213 324296; ⊕ 08.30–19.00 Mon–Fri, 08.00–14.00 Sat. Get your prescriptions filled & photos digitally printed at the same time. They also have a wide selection of beauty products.

L F Moore Chemists [162 C1] 133 Akapelwa St; ☎0213 321640; ⊕ 08.00–18.00 Mon–Fri,

08.00–13.00 Sat, 09.30–12.30 Sun/public holidays. Established in 1936, L F Moore is a Livingstone institution. It remains one of the best-stocked chemists in town, with friendly staff who will go out of their way to help.

Link Pharmacy [163 D6] Mosi-oa-Tunya Sq; ☎0213 324222; ⊕ 09.00–18.00 Mon–Fri, 09.00–17.00 Sat, 09.00–13.00 Sun. If this well-stocked chemist doesn't have what you want, they can usually get it from their Lusaka store.

Musamu Chemist [162 B1] 141A, cnr Kuta Way & Zambezi St; ☎0213 323226; after hours m 0979 276839; ⊕ 08.00–20.00 Mon–Fri, 08.00–18.00 Sat, 09.00–13.00 Sun

Other supplies Basic **camera supplies** can be found at the various chemists (see above), but a better bet is Konica Photo Express ([162 C1] *Mosi-oa-Tunya Rd, nr Airport Rd*), which offers one-hour photo processing, enlargements and passport photos, and stocks film and related supplies. Also recommended are the convenient HK Photo Studio ([162 E4] *nr Capitol Theatre*), and Kodak Express ([162 E4] *Liso Hse, next to Finance Bank*).

For cassette tapes and DVDs of popular **music**, including many African selections, try Zimbabwe or Town Centre Market at the bottom of Kapondo Street [163 B2]. They have a wide selection of cheap (probably bootlegged) cassette tapes, DVDs and videos. Follow your ears for blaring music and you'll find a kiosk selling tapes! Often goods will be brought direct to you from one of the many roving salesmen in town selling cassettes, DVDs and other sundries. A more recent alternative is Sounds ([163 D6] *Mosi-oa-Tunya Sq*).

If you have **computer** trouble, Falcon Technologies ([map 159] *Linda Rd, past Zigzag;* 0213 322676; m 0977 747707) offers repair and service and also sells new and used computers.

BANKS AND CHANGING MONEY Livingstone has several major banks and various bureaux de change dotted throughout town. Most of the banks have ATMs, for which you'll generally need a Visa card rather than MasterCard. More convenient, but with the least favourable exchange rate, is to change money at a hotel or lodge.

Unless you are very savvy or very desperate, avoid the freelance 'money-changers' who tend to congregate around the Capitol Theatre and at the border. No matter how carefully you watch, they always take advantage of unsuspecting (and even suspicious) tourists by short-changing them somehow.

The major **banks** are situated around the post office area, parallel to the main Mosi-oa-Tunya Road [162 D4]. Typically they open Monday to Friday 08.00–14.00, and sometimes on Saturday mornings, but get there early if you want to avoid long queues. The spacious air-conditioned interior and more private exchange facilities of Zanaco make it preferable to the generally crowded Barclays.

$ **Barclays** Mosi-oa-Tunya Rd; 0213 32114/5, 324196. Also small branch with ATM at The Falls [map 193].
$ **Finance** John Hunt Way; 0213 320121/2, 322951. The main branch has an ATM & Moneygram office; smaller branch at Mosi-oa-Tunya Sq [163 D6].

$ **Stanbic** Mosi-oa-Tunya Sq; 0213 324350/1
$ **Standard Chartered** 0213 321743/ 321745. Also at Falls Park, inc ATM [map 193].
$ **Zanaco** Cnr Mutelo St & Mosi-oa-Tunya Rd; 0213 321901/320171/320995.

Many of the **bureaux de change** are close to or opposite Barclays Bank, with others at Falls Park shopping centre. You can also exchange money at the post office, though rates are likely to be lower than at the private bureaux de change.

$ **Fx Africa** [162 B1] Mosi-oa-Tunya Rd, nr Capitol Theatre; 0213 320154; ⊕ 08.00–16.30 Mon–Fri, 08.00–11.30 Sat
$ **Zampost** [162 B1] Mosi-oa-Tunya Rd, in post office complex; 0213 322472; ⊕ 08.00–16.30 Mon–Fri, 08.00–12.30 Sat

$ **Zampost** [map 159] Falls Park; 0213 324797; ⊕ 09.00–12.30, 12.45–17.00 Mon–Fri, 08.00–12.30 Sat

COMMUNICATIONS

Internet Internet cafés have cropped up all around town, with one – Sparrow Enterprises ([162 B2] ⊕ *07.00–19.30 daily*) – near the post office and another at PostNet near the Capitol Theatre ([162 B1] ⊕ *08.00–18.00 Mon–Fri, 08.00–13.00 Sat*). Virtually all places of accommodation offer some kind of internet access, too, as does Thunderbird Investments [163 D7]. While rates are low and comparable, at around Kw150/minute, the standard of computers, speed and service varies; high-speed service in Livingstone is pretty rare. For those with a laptop, Wonderbake [162 B1] is a WiFi hot zone, so a good place for a cappuccino while you check your emails.

Post and courier You can't miss Livingstone's post office ([162 B2] ☎ *0213 21976;* ⏰ *08.00–12.00, 14.00–16.30 Mon–Fri, 08.00–12.30 Sat*) in the centre of town in a sprawling complex of banks and shops, adjacent to the main road.

DHL Mosi-oa-Tunya Hse; ☎ 0213 320979. Located on the bottom floor of this high-rise building.

FedEx John Hunt Way (opp St Andrew's Church); ☎ 0213 322742. In addition to the courier service, this is also an agent for Western Union.

PostNet Stanley Hse, Mosi-oa-Tunya Rd; ☎ 0213 200044. The new PostNet is an agent for DHL & Western Union, & offers internet access too.

Telephone If you can't make phone calls where you are staying, try one of the internet cafés or shops advertising a telephone service, such as PostNet [162 B1], or the post office itself [162 B2]. Next to the post office, adjacent to the postboxes, is a small office offering international phone and fax that is open throughout the day.

Many visitors will find it more convenient to purchase a local SIM card. Those for both Airtel and the state-owned Zamtel are easily obtainable from numerous outlets across town; look out for their signs at shopping malls and on Mosi-oa-Tunya Road, including next to Wonderbake. Expect to pay around Kw7,000 (£1/US$1.50) for a SIM card, with top-up cards available from Kw3,000.

OTHER PRACTICALITIES

Car repairs and spares The two biggest workshops in town are Foley's Africa (*Industrial Rd;* ☎ *0213 320888;* e *info@foleysafrica.com; www.foleysafrica.com*), which caters for Land Rovers; and Bennett Engineering, also known as Harry's workshop ([map 159] ☎ *0213 321611, 322380,* m *0978 308936;* e *hbennett@iconnect.zm*), opposite Falls Park. Bennett services most of the tour operators' vehicles in town and is your best bet for more serious problems.

For more basic repairs, contact Fallsway Motors ([163 D6] ☎ *0213 321049*) at the corner of Nakatindi Road, or Channa's Motors (*Mosi-oa-Tunya Rd;* ☎ *0213 320468*), just across the railway line. Their facilities are somewhat limited and service can be slow but they can often help get you moving again, barring major problems. For punctures and tyre repairs try the Total fuel station, on the right side of Mosi-oa-Tunya Road as you head up towards the centre of town [163 D5]. If it's parts or vehicle accessories that you need, the most central place is Autoworld ([162 A2] *Mosi-oa-Tunya Rd;* ☎ *0213 320264;* e *autoworld@zamtel.zm*), about 50m south of Barclays Bank.

Emergencies Medical facilities are limited in Livingstone, and the local hospitals are not up to the standard of those in the West, but in the event of an emergency contact:

✚ **SES** [162 E2] Speciality Emergency Services, cnr Likute Way & Obote Rd; ☎ 0213 322330; emergency control centre ☎ 0211 273302–7; m 0977 740306–8; e seslivingstone@zamnet.zm; www.ses-zambia.com. The local base is staffed with South African-trained paramedics.

Many tour operators are also affiliated to Medical Air Rescue Service (MARS; *http://medairescue.com*). For less serious medical assistance, the two Sun International hotels, Zambezi Sun and the Royal Livingstone, have a mini-clinic with nurse for their own guests. Alternatively, try one of the following:

✚ Dr Shafik's Hospital [162 G2] Katete Av; 📞0213 321130 (24hrs); 📱 0955/0966/0977 863000; 📧 shafikhosp@zamnet.zm
✚ Health Point (Dr Shanks) [162 D1] Mushili Way; 📱 0978 100666; 📧 shanks@zamnet.zm

✚ Southern Medical Centre [163 D5] Makambo Rd; 📞0213 323547/323786; 📱 0955 797577; 📧 sanjaysouthmed@gmail.com

Should you need an **optician**, head for Falls Park shopping centre [map 159] or try Sunbird Opticians ([162 B1] *Mosi-oa-Tunya Rd, nr Barclays Bank*). For pharmacies, see page 187.

Laundry and dry cleaning Facilities are available at all of the larger lodges and hotels and – for a fee – at the lower end of the scale too. Alternatively, there is a good service at Livingstone Dry Cleaners & Steam Laundry ([162 B1] *Mosi-oa-Tunya Rd, next to Pama Meats & opposite post office*).

Tourist information The Zambia Tourism Board ([163 A2] *Mosi-oa-Tunya Rd;* 📞 0213 321404/87; 📧 zntb@zambiatourism.org.zm; www.zambiatourism.com; ⏱ 08.00–17.00 Mon–Fri, 09.00–12.00 Sat), has an office at the tourist centre next to the Livingstone Museum, easily spotted for the two-seater plane outside. Here you can expect pleasant, friendly staff working with limited resources. You can pick up brochures and get referrals, but agents and tour operators (pages 190–2) are usually better geared to assist you with actual bookings.

Travel agents For international airline tickets and fares, your best choice is:

Southend Travel [162 E4] Liso Hse, nr Finance Bank, Mosi-oa-Tunya Rd; 📞0213 320773/ 320241/322128; 📧 southend@zamnet.zm; ⏱ 08.00–17.30 Mon–Fri, 08.00–13.00 Sat.

Agents for 1Time, Zambezi Airlines, British Airways & SAA, & able to advise on special air fares, & also for the Intercape Mainliner bus service (page 160).

WHAT TO SEE AND DO

The area around Victoria Falls has been a major crossroads for travellers for over a hundred years. From the early missionaries and traders, to the backpackers, overland trucks and package tourists of the last few decades – virtually everyone passing through the region from overseas has stopped here. Recently this has created a thriving tourism industry and, apart from simply marvelling at one of the world's greatest waterfalls, there are now lots of ways to occupy yourself for a few days. Some of these are easily booked after you arrive; one or two are better pre-arranged.

The past decade has witnessed a huge shift in the area's atmosphere. Visitors used to be from southern Africa, with perhaps the odd intrepid backpacker and the fortunate few who could afford an upmarket safari. Now the sheer volume of visitors to the Falls has increased massively. This increase, especially noticeable in the proportion of younger visitors, has fuelled the rise of more active, adventurous pursuits like white-water rafting, bungee jumping, river-boarding and other thrill-based pastimes.

A genteel cocktail at a luxury hotel is no longer the high point of a visit for most people. You are more likely to return home with vivid memories of the adrenalin rush of shooting rapids in a raft, or the buzz of accelerating head-first towards the Zambezi with only a piece of elastic to save you.

TOUR OPERATORS In a town where tourism is such big business, almost everyone – from hoteliers to car-hire companies to taxi firms – can handle bookings for individual activities. Those listed here are the specialists. For flight operators, see page 160.

Many companies offer **guided sightseeing tours** around Livingstone, including visits to traditional villages, local markets, museums, the Falls, game park and historical sites. While some activities can be organised without notice, others need to be pre-booked, so it's as well to be organised if you don't want to be disappointed. Rates almost always include transfers from your accommodation, within a reasonable radius.

If you are staying in one of the lodges, sightseeing tours for guests using their own guides and vehicles are generally included. Bushtracks Africa, Wild Side Tours & Safaris and Bwaato Adventures are popular operators, although there are many others (see below). Of these, Wild Side is run by people who have lived in Livingstone for years, and who understand the place well; it can personalise tours to suit individual requirements. Bwaato Adventures, operating here for several years, is also well positioned, while the larger Bushtracks runs set trips aimed largely at guests at many of the top hotels and lodges. Several other specialist operators have combined under the marketing umbrella of the Livingstone's Adventure Group, making a convenient one-stop shop for their activities. In all cases, trips are professionally run with competent guides. Most tours can be either stand-alone or in combination with others.

Abseil Zambia [163 D6] aka **The Zambezi Swing**; Fawlty Towers; \ 0213 321188; e theswing@zamnet.zm; www. thezambeziswing.com. Gorge swinging, abseiling, highwiring & rap-jumping activities at their site atop the 5th gorge on the Zambian side, some 5km from the Falls.

African Queen/African Princess [map 159] Contact Livingstone's Adventure. Two luxury catamarans operating b/fast, lunch & dinner trips.

Angle Zambia \ 0213 327489; m 0977 707829/586353; e anglezam@microlink.zm; www.zambezifishing.com. Half-day, full-day & multi-day fishing trips with experienced guides. Also owns Barotse Tiger Camp on the Barotse Floodplain (page 499).

Batoka Sky Adventures [map 159] Maramba Aerodrome, off Sichango Rd; \ 0213 320058; contact Livingstone's Adventure. Microlights & helicopters for scenic flights over the Falls, gorges, game park & upper river.

Bundu Adventures [map 159] Maramba River Lodge; \ 0213 324406/7; e info@ bunduadventures.com; www.bunduadventures. com. With a brand new activity centre at Maramba River Lodge, Bundu offers rafting, riverboarding, kayaking, canoeing & the new 'spray view' tour (Aug–Jan) which gives a unique perspective of the falls, from right beneath them.

Bushtracks Africa [map 159] Mosi-oa-Tunya Rd; \ 0213 323232; e victoriafalls@ bushtracksafrica.com; www.bushtracksafrica. com. One of the best & most reliable tour operators in Livingstone, Bushtracks is located just south of the railway station, where the railway line crosses the road. It's an effective one-stop shop for everything from game drives & river cruises to day trips to Botswana, as well as operating the *Royal Livingstone Express*.

Bwaato Adventures [162 E3] New Fairmount Hotel; \ 0213 324227; e bwaato@zamnet.zm. Alongside city, museum & village tours are guided birding trips & 3hr game ('rhino') walks, & there's also a walking & canoe combo.

Floating Skies m 0977 431427; e trl-blazers@ yahoo.com. In addition to various village & cultural tours, Floating Skies organise individual tours, including, for example, around the town's sites of Jewish interest. They also run week-long trips to Kafue & western Zambia.

Gwembe Safaris [map 159] Livingstone Reptile Park, Mosi-oa-Tunya Rd; \ 0213 321733, 321648; e gwemsaf@iconnect.zm; www. gwembesafaris.com. Booking agents, tour operators, & owners of the reptile park.

Kayak the Zambezi m 0971 565044; e kayak@thezambezi.com; www.thezambezi.com. The kayaking specialists for novice & experienced paddlers alike. Will help you plan day trips & longer expeditions as well as offering the latest craze (commercially speaking at least) at Rapid 11: river surfing (for experienced riders only).

Livingstone's Adventure [map 159] 4023 Sichango Rd; ☎ 0213 323567/321513/323589/ 323754; e reservations@livingstonesadventure. com; www.livingstonesadventure.com. This umbrella organisation with good insurance coverage groups together a variety of activities: the *African Queen*, Batoka Sky (helicopter & microlights), Livingstone Quad Company, Makora Quest (canoeing), Victoria Carriage Company (horseriding) & Victoria Falls River Safaris. Booking several trips attracts a discount. To experience the Zambezi from 2 angles, their 'combo' follows a river safari with a more sedate river cruise

Livingstone Quad Company [map 159] Maramba Aerodrome, off Sichango Rd; contact Livingstone's Adventure. Quadbike excursions either from the aerodrome on an 'eco-trail' or on a local 'village trail'.

Livingstone Walking Safaris [162 F1] 4 Nakambala La; ☎ 0213 322267; m 0977 450716, 0977 712496; e gecko@zamnet.zm. Guided walks in Mosi-oa-Tunya NP with ½-day activities taking in the usual walking safari or tracking the national park's star attraction – the resident white rhino.

Makora Quest ☎ 0213 320732; e quest@ iconnect.zm; www.victoriafallszambia.com, or contact Livingstone's Adventure. Livingstone's most established canoe operator, with extensive local knowledge & friendly service.

Nomad African Travel Zambia ☎ 0213 327769; m 0977 846164/755429; e nomad@ microlink.zm; www.nomadafricantravel.co.uk. Local transfers & booking service, plus guided, tailormade & self-drive safaris throughout southern Africa.

Raft Extreme 2 Maambo Way; ☎ 0213 324024/323929; e grotto@zamnet.zm. Caters predominantly for white-water rafting groups, with bookings from individuals if there's space.

Safari Par Excellence [map 159] Zambezi Waterfront & Activity Centre, Sichango Rd; ☎ 0213 320606/9; m 0977 434143; e zaminfo@safpar.com; www.safpar.com. One of Livingstone's larger tourism enterprises, 'SafPar' is a one-stop shop for everything you need. The company also operates the *Lady Livingstone* as well as the lion & elephant encounters at Thorntree.

Shearwater Adventures ☎ 0213 324231; e bungi@zamnet.zm; www.africanadrenalin.co.za. Bungee jumping, gorge swing & bridge slide.

Taonga Safaris [map 159] Sichango Rd, next to the Boat Club; ☎ 0213 322508; m 0977 878065; e taonga@zamnet.zm; www.thezambezi.com/ taonga. Booze cruises catering mainly to backpackers.

United Air Charters ☎ 0213 323095; e info@ uaczam.com; www.uaczam.com. Operates a fleet of helicopters for scenic & charter flights from its spectacular base on Baobab Ridge, to the east of Mosi-oa-Tunya Rd.

UTc [163 B2] Heritage Hse, 360s Mosi-oa-Tunya Rd; ☎ 0213 324413; m 0977 687063; e utczam@ zamnet.zm; www.utczambia.com. Offers guided tours & transfers, plus accommodation booking.

Victoria Carriage Co Contact Livingstone's Adventure. Horse-drawn carriage trips on Sun International property & horseriding in the bush near the Falls.

Victoria Falls River Safaris Contact Livingstone's Adventure. Aluminium 'safari' boats with shade, akin to the 4x4 of the river, can go far beyond the reach of conventional craft.

Wild Side Tours & Safaris [163 D7] 131 Mosi-oa-Tunya Rd; ☎ 0213 323726; e wild@ iconnect.zm. Located in a restored railway house in the 217 area; look for the big 'i' sign indicating tourist information. Owner operated, & one of Livingstone's long-time tour companies, Wild Side offers a full service including village & town tours, game drives, cultural tours, activities & transfers, as well as online accommodation booking.

VICTORIA FALLS The Falls are 1,688m wide and average just over 100m in height. Around 550 million litres (750 million during peak months) cascade over the lip every minute, making this one of the world's greatest waterfalls. Closer inspection shows that this immense curtain of water is interrupted by gaps, where small islands stand on the lip of the Falls. These effectively split the Falls into smaller waterfalls, which are known as (from west to east) the Devil's Cataract, the Main Falls, the Horseshoe Falls, the Rainbow Falls and the Eastern Cataract.

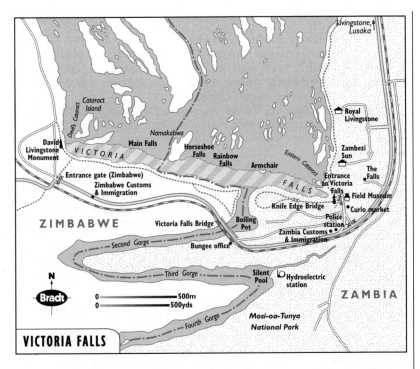

VICTORIA FALLS

Around the Falls is a genuinely important and interesting rainforest, with plant species (especially ferns) rarely found elsewhere in Zimbabwe or Zambia. These are sustained by the clouds of spray, which blanket the immediate vicinity of the Falls. You'll also find various monkeys and baboons here, whilst the lush canopy shelters Livingstone's lourie amongst other birds.

The flow, and hence the spray, is greatest just after the end of the rainy season – around March or April, depending upon the rains. It then decreases gradually until about December, when the rains in western Zambia will start to replenish the river. During low water, a light raincoat (available for rent on site) is very useful for wandering between the viewpoints on the Zimbabwean side, though it's not necessary in Zambia. However, in high water a raincoat is largely ineffective as the spray blows all around and soaks you in seconds. Anything that you want to keep dry must be wrapped in several layers of plastic or, even better, zip-lock plastic bags.

The Falls never seem the same twice, so try to visit several times, under different light conditions. At sunrise, both Danger Point and Knife-edge Point are fascinating – position yourself carefully to see your shadow in the mists, with three concentric rainbows appearing as halos. (Photographers will find polarising filters invaluable in capturing the rainbows on film, as the light from the rainbows at any time of day is polarised.)

Moonlight is another fascinating time, when the Falls take on an ethereal glow and the waters blend into one smooth mass which seems frozen over the rocks.

On the Zambian side (*entry US$20 pp, vehicle US$5; gate ⏰ 06.00–19.00 daily*), viewing the Falls could not be easier, and every season brings a reason to visit. For photographers, the area is best explored in the early morning, when the sun is still behind you and illuminates the Falls, or in the late afternoon when you may catch a stunning sunset. If you visit when the river is at its lowest, towards the end of the dry season, then the channels on the Zambian side may have dried up. Yet, while the Falls will be less spectacular then, their fascinating geology, normally obscured by spray, is revealed. In recent years, the diversion of water to generate power has been curtailed so the flow of water is more constant, and there is generally some water flowing over the edge on the Zambian side.

The main path leads along the cliff opposite the Falls, then across the swaying knife-edge bridge, via scenic points, photo stops and a good vantage point from which to watch bungee jumpers. This finishes at the farthest west of the Zambian viewpoints.

A third path descends right down to the water's edge at the Boiling Pot, which is used as a raft launch-site during the main rafting season. It is a beautiful (but steep) hike down, first navigating big cement steps, then through palm-fringed forest and finally scrambling over boulders, but well worth the long, hot climb back as long as you have good footwear. Take a picnic and relax by the river if you've time (and if you notice a smell of urine, it's probably from the monkeys!).

Viewing the Falls by moonlight (*US$25 pp*) is possible for four days at full moon, including two days before and one day after. Watch for a lunar rainbow at this time, too; it's an amazing sight. It's best not to go alone, as elephants occasionally wander about.

If you are touring on your own a helpful starting point is the small information centre or **field museum**, directly across from the Falls entrance, which provides a good overview of the origins of Victoria Falls. The museum is packed full of informative exhibits and interesting photos covering the area's fascinating geology, archaeology and history, complete with an excavation right in the middle. Knowledgeable guides are on hand to answer questions, or you can explore at your leisure. Snacks and cold drinks are available in the shop next door.

While you can easily explore on your own, most tour operators offer excellent guided tours of the Falls (both Zimbabwe and Zambia sides) and the surrounding area, either stand-alone or in combination with historical, cultural, game-viewing and other sightseeing tours. These are highly informative with professional guides offering detailed explanations of the formation of the Falls and gorges, the river, local history and flora and fauna. Tours cost around US$25–35 per person, including entrance fees.

From the Zimbabwean side (*entry US$20 pp; gate ⊕ summer 06.00–18.00, winter 06.30-18.00 daily*) Viewing the Falls is more regulated here. The entrance to the Falls can be reached via paths from the Victoria Falls Hotel, the Kingdom Hotel and just opposite Ilala Lodge. There is a small ticket booth and display at the entrance gate, which is a few hundred metres from the Zimbabwean border post. Tickets are valid for the whole day, so you can return for no extra cost during the same day. There's also a car park for self drivers too. Be prepared, however, for the mandatory hassle of generally pleasant but very persistent vendors and 'guides' along the way. Perhaps the easiest way to organise to see the Falls is through a tour operator, who will arrange visas and transfers as well as entry fees. Alternatively, make an afternoon of it and have tea at the Victoria Falls Hotel. Visiting in the afternoon, when the angle of the sun offers the best views, is ideal.

If you're planning to visit independently, allow at least half a day, and expect a fair delay at the border (⊕ 06.00–22.00). The cost of a **visa** depends on nationality. As an indication, US citizens pay US$30 for a single-entry visa; UK citizens US$55, and Canadians US$65.

Technically this area is within the Victoria Falls National Park – and you will find a map of the paths at the entrance. Start at the western end, by Livingstone's statue – inscribed with 'Explorer, Missionary and Liberator', and overlooking the Devil's Cataract.

Visiting the viewpoints in order, next is the Cataract View. If water levels are low, and the spray not too strong, after clambering down quite a steep stairway you will be greeted by views along the canyon of the Falls. Climbing back up, wander from one viewpoint to the next, eastwards, and you will eventually reach the slippery-smooth rocks at Danger Point.

Few of these viewpoints have anything more than brushwood fences and low railings to guard the edges – so going close to the edge is not for those with vertigo. Viewing the Falls by moonlight is possible by special arrangement.

LIVINGSTONE ISLAND (*Prices inc transfers & park fees: breakfast US$70; lunch US$125; afternoon tea US$100*) Livingstone Island (also known as Namakabwa Island) lies in the middle of the great waterfall, and is the island from which Dr Livingstone first viewed the Falls. Trips are run exclusively by Tongabezi (see page 172) between July and March (subject to water levels), with guests transferred to the island from the Royal Livingstone launch site by boat. There you'll have the opportunity to take in the scene – gazing over the edge, perhaps chancing a thrilling dip in the Devil's Pool right on the Falls edge, and having a gourmet meal in an exclusive setting. Several trips are offered daily; choose either morning (called 'breezer'), with a full English breakfast, gourmet lunch, or afternoon high tea with a full bar and hors d'oeuvres.

When the water's at its lowest, around October and November, you can sometimes walk across the top of the Falls, climbing over rocks, exploring pot-holes and crossing small streams along the way – it's even possible to swim at the very edge of the Falls at the right time of year. These activities are now permitted only if booked through Tongabezi. (Aside from the fact that the island is private, there is a risk of being stuck on top of the Falls should water levels unexpectedly rise. If you were to attempt the walk alone, you would almost certainly be turned back by ZAWA scouts.)

RIVER CRUISES Floating on the Upper Zambezi with a glass in one hand, and a pair of binoculars in the other, is still a pleasant way to watch the sun go down, even if nowadays booze-cruise boats operate round the clock (you can choose from breakfast, lunch, sunset or dinner cruises), and sometimes all congregate close together. Whatever type of boat you choose, taking a gentle look around the Zambezi's islands, surrounded by national parks on both sides of the river, is one of the region's highlights.

African Queen ([map 159] *US$55 pp b/fast, 2hr lunch or sunset cruise, inc open bar & canapés*) On the Zambian side, surely the most elegant and leisurely way to experience the river is aboard the *African Queen* or its sister boat, the *African Princess*. These old-style double-decker riverboats complete with gleaming brass cruise regally upriver from their dock on the aptly named but sadly dilapidated Royal Mile. (The name is derived directly from royalty, for it was from here that George VI and his entourage took a launch onto the river during their visit in 1947. Today it is known more prosaically as Sichonga Road.) In the rarified atmosphere on board, guests sip cocktails or soft drinks to the rhythmic accompaniment of xylophones, or marimba, that sound the vessel's imminent departure. As the boat makes its stately way upstream, you may spot the odd hippo, crocodile or elephant – or even, if you're very lucky, a white rhino – not to mention numerous birds. Such luxury doesn't come cheap, but the price includes an open bar (with a charge for premium and imported brands) and a substantial finger buffet. Lunch and dinner cruises are also available.

Lady Livingstone ([map 159] *SafPar Sunset US$60 pp, inc drinks & snacks, exc park fees US$10; b/fast cruise US$65; lunch cruise US$70 pp*) Taking 144 passengers on three decks, this newcomer based at David Livingstone Safari Lodge is similar in design and style to the *African Queen*, but with a twist. The bar is at one end of the boat, giving more room for passengers to circulate, and the choice of drinks is generally wider than on its rival. Snacks are served as three courses during the course of the cruise, ending with 'delicious chocolate truffles' & brownies. The most popular excursion is the 2–2½-hour sunset cruise, departing between 16.00 and 16.30, but there are also lunch and breakfast cruises.

Other boats (*US$40–45 pp; SafPar dinner cruise US$50*) On the Zambian side, smaller craft plying the same route are organised by Victoria Falls River Safaris, Safari Par Excellence and Taonga Safaris. All have an open bar and are generally popular with backpackers. Typically cruises last around 2½ hours. Away from the crowded waters near the Falls, Wild Side Tours & Safaris offers a more serene alternative, 25km upstream. Here you can cruise in solitude, taking in the scenery, prolific birdlife and wildlife along the banks of the Zambezi National Park. Hippos, elephants and crocodiles are commonly seen as well as waterbuck, bushbuck and even buffalo.

If you'd like to go further afield, try Victoria Falls River Safaris, whose propeller-free aluminium safari boats (*from US$75 pp plus US$10 park fees, min 2 passengers*) allow them to go both further and into shallower waters than most other craft.

FISHING EXCURSIONS (*Angle Zambia: US$125/255 ½/full day inc lunch; multi-day trips on request*) Among the angling fraternity, the Zambezi River is synonymous with great fishing for prized tigerfish and Zambezi bream. If you dream of hooking a 'tiger' then a memorable day on the river with a knowledgeable guide can help make it come true. Angle Zambia, with their excellent local knowledge and friendly, personalised service, is highly recommended. Owner-operated by Gerard and Viv Simpson, they run half- and full-day fishing trips on the Upper Zambezi, about 30km from Livingstone. Catering to both novice and experienced anglers as well as fly-fishermen, the company has three 6m aluminium boats complete with fish finders, sunshades and radio communications to their base. Trips include fishing tackle, boat hire, fuel, transfers, a qualified guide and refreshments.

ROYAL LIVINGSTONE EXPRESS (*Bushtracks; dep winter 17.30, summer 17.45 Wed & Sat, or other days if demand is high enough; US$175 pp, inc transfers, dinner & drinks; not recommended for children under 12*) The whistle of a steam loco rarely fails to stir a frisson of excitement, and Livingstone's foray into steam has proved a considerable success since its inaugural journey in late 2007. A joint venture between Bushtracks and Sun International, the train brings Zambia's railway history to life. It is pulled by one of two locomotives, the first of which – the 10th class *Princess of Mulobezi*, built in Glasgow in 1924 for Rhodesian Railways – until recently took pride of place in Livingstone's Railway Museum. Restored with meticulous attention to detail by Ben Costa, a Zimbabwean railway engineer with a passion for the iron horse, the locos and attendant wooden carriages are polished until they gleam. Many of the train's staff have the railways in their blood, some tracing their railway ancestry back three or more generations.

The train starts its 15km journey in a siding next to the Bushtracks office, getting up steam as it heads for Mosi-oa-Tunya National Park, past excited children and families gathering for the evening meal. Wine, beer and soft drinks are served in air-conditioned comfort, with a cash bar on board for those who prefer spirits.

Large windows, as well as an observation car, ensure good visibility for all, and – if elephant, buffalo or other game are spotted inside the national park – the train will sometimes stop for a better view. For a photo opportunity of the train itself, however, the best time is when it nears Sinde River Siding, when the loco is uncoupled, and passengers can disembark and watch as it is relocated to the other end of the train. An unhurried five-course dinner is served as night falls, prepared on board by chefs from the Royal Livingstone Hotel, and served by their staff in an atmosphere enhanced by soft lighting and classical music. As dessert arrives, a hiss of steam announces the train's departure for Livingstone, the rhythmic rock of the rails accompanying a final coffee and petit fours.

CULTURAL ATTRACTIONS AND TOURS

Museums Given its fascinating history, it is no surprise that Livingstone has several good museums. The main Livingstone Museum is the most important of these, and certainly one of the best in the country.

Tours (*1½hrs, inc entry fees & transfers, US$20 pp Bwaato Adventures to US$35 pp Bushtracks*) can be organised to visit the Livingstone Museum or the Railway Museum, or both. Although you can readily visit on your own, an organised tour is an easy alternative, especially as part of a full day's sightseeing trip, with transfer included.

Livingstone Museum ([163 B2] *Mosi-oa-Tunya Rd; US$5/2 adult/child.* ⊕ *09.00–16.30 daily*) In a prime position in the centre of town, Livingstone's main museum more than justifies a visit. To start with, there's an excellent three-dimensional map showing how the Zambezi River flows over Victoria Falls and downstream into the gorges, which puts everything into good perspective. Then there are exhibits on the Stone Age, and features on Zambian culture, politics, history, animals and traditional village life in the area. Watch out, too, for the 'History' exhibition – it's easily missed but, with a unique collection of David Livingstone's personal possessions, including many of his letters, it's a must.

The museum often has special exhibitions, of which the witchcraft one is especially interesting, if somewhat hair-raising. Sculpture and paintings by Zambian artists are also displayed and available for sale, as are local handicrafts and curios. The staff are friendly and knowledgeable and guided tours are included.

Railway Museum ([163 A8] *National Heritage Conservation Commission; Chishimba Falls Rd; US$15/7 pp adult/child;* ⊕ *08.00—16.30 daily*) This collection of beautifully preserved old steam locomotives and memorabilia, and displays on railway history, originally belonged to the artist David Shepherd. It celebrates the iron horse's history in Livingstone since the 3ft 6in narrow-gauge railway was built by the British in 1905. The museum lies on the site of the Zambezi Saw Mills, but sadly, a serious fire has taken its toll and the collection now is really more for extreme railway buffs. Fortunately, the 1922 10th Class 156 out of Glasgow that used to take pride of place has now been put to work hauling the *Royal Livingstone Express*.

Field Museum [map 193] Directly across from the entrance gate to Victoria Falls, next to the curio market, this is signed as an information centre, but is more of a small interpretation centre. It's well worth a visit for an understanding of the geology, archaeology and history of the Falls.

Markets Livingstone has many colourful local markets. In addition to the large and fascinating Maramba Market [162 G4], there is also Porters' Market, further north [162 G2]. For something smaller and closer to town, try Zimbabwe, Central or Town Centre Market (take your pick of the names!), down the road from Shoprite and next to the minibus station [163 B2].

At the heart of Livingstone's community, these markets offer everything from fresh produce to second-hand clothes (called *salaula*), from hand-fashioned metal pots to live chickens, from *chitenjes* (the traditional African cloth) to hand-crafted wood furniture and more. Several companies handle **market tours** (*Bwaato 2hrs US$20 pp; Bushtracks 1½hrs US$35 pp; Floating Skies inc town walk & traditional lunch US$40 pp*).

Craft markets Just inside the Zambian border, by the entrance to the Falls, is an outstanding curio market [map 193]. The carvers and traders come mostly from Mukuni village, though the goods come from as far as the Democratic Republic of Congo and Malawi. In town itself there's Mukuni Park Curio Market ([162 E3] ☉ *06.00–20.00 daily*), where local artisans, craftsmen and traders sell their wares from newly constructed permanent stalls along the edge of the park. Both of these are excellent places to buy wood and stone carvings, handicrafts, chessboards, masks, drums, malachite bangles, baskets and the like, and are open during daylight hours throughout the week. There are usually about 20 or 30 individual traders, laying their wares out separately, and competing with one another for your business. The best buys are *makenge* baskets (these come exclusively from Zambia's Western Province), malachite and heavy wood carvings: hippos, elephants, rhinos, giraffes and smaller statues, often made out of excellent-quality, heavy wood. However, do consider the ethics of encouraging any further exploitation of hardwoods. Note, too, that some wooden items, especially wooden salad bowls and tall giraffes, are prone to cracking once you get them home due to changes in climate, and that very rarely are 'antiques' sold at craft markets anything other than fakes. Unless you have the expertise to tell the difference, it's better to buy such artefacts from a reputable shop in town.

The curio markets are places to bargain hard, and you can expect to hear all sorts of prefabricated stories as to why you should pay more. When you start to pay, you will realise how sophisticated the traders are about their currency conversions, reminding you to double-check any exchange rates. Traders will accept most currencies and sometimes credit cards.

For something rather less demanding, there's an ad-hoc craft and curio market in the car park at the Falls Park shopping centre [map 159]. Buying items from street traders, however, is illegal, so stick to the designated markets.

Village visits (*Mukuni Village: Bushtracks US$35, SafPar US$45. Bwaato Paradise Island Village Tour 8hrs; US$90, inc transfers, lunch & refreshments*) While some of the lodges organise independent visits to local villages for their guests, there are also several organised trips to different locations. Most popular among these is **Mukuni village**, a settlement of over 6,000 Leya people to the east of the Falls. An organised tour here, lasting around 2½ hours, will give you a glimpse of how local people live and work in a traditional setting along with informative explanations.

You can visit local huts, view villagers at work, watch curio making and even sample traditional beer and food. However, Mukuni village, with its proximity to the Falls and popularity with tour operators, relies heavily on the tourist trade, so tends towards a commercial, rather than authentic, feel, with often relentless though friendly pressure to buy curios made there.

Some operators organise less commercial tours which involve clients going to smaller villages, perhaps visiting local markets to buy food which they then prepare in the village and eat with the locals while having some language lessons (and of course a walk around the village).

Further afield is **Songwe village**, about a 40-minute drive through the bush, and less commercial as it receives fewer tourists. The Livingstone Quad Company also offers guided quadbike excursions to villages and the bush (see page 209). Alternatively, if your heart is set on a more remote village off the beaten path and you have the time, Bwaato Adventures offer a day trip some 45km upriver to one of the rural villages along the Zambezi.

Simonga village (m *0977 870548; overnight Kw75,000 pp FBA, exc transport; day visitor Kw20,000;* ☉ *all day*) An alternative that's easily accessible for independent visitors, this traditional village some 15km from Livingstone has been welcoming day visitors since 2001, with three traditional huts renovated in 2011 for tourist accommodation. During a tour of the village, a guide will explain about daily life: culture, housing, agriculture, water supply and medical care. You can see the basic school, watch cultural performances and visit the traditional healer, as well as meet the head lady. For those staying overnight, traditional food is served at breakfast, lunch and dinner, and the village has its own water supply.

To get there from Livingstone, go to Mingongo station along the Kanzungula Road (*taxi around Kw10,000*), then hitchhike or take a minibus/taxi to the turn off for Simonga Basic School. The fare should be Kw5,000, though *mzungus* may be asked to pay double or more; stand firm! A taxi all the way from Livingstone will cost Kw30,000–40.000. In the village ask for Aston or the head lady, Inonge.

Historical tour of Livingstone (*Bushtracks 1½hrs US$35 pp; SafPar 2½hrs US$45 pp; Wild Side US$60/110 ½ /full day inc refreshments/lunch*)
Livingstone, the capital of Northern Rhodesia from 1907 to 1935, has a fascinating history marked by many old historical buildings and accented by colourful characters, intriguing tales and a once-vibrant social life. A guided historical tour through town – on foot and by vehicle – will trace the town's history from frontier town to modern-day tourist capital, including the first hospital, school, library, churches, sports clubs, shopping districts, the old North Western Hotel and other historical sites.

African heritage tour (*Bushtracks ½ day; US$100 pp, inc park fees & bottled water*)
Dubbed the 'Mists of Time' tour, this trip takes in the Victoria Falls and one of the local villages. In the hands of Russell Gammon, whose family history in Africa dates back to the 19th century, the aim is to bring these sites to life through the stories of those who have left their mark on Livingstone over the years.

Music and dance
The opportunity to see local dance theatre is offered by the Livingstone Performing Arts Foundation ([map 159] see *The Arts Café*, page 182, for contact details). The group's *Dancing Around Zambia* (*US$25*) is performed regularly and features traditional dancing and drumming in a celebration of Zambia's diverse cultures. They are also working on a new project based on a

Zambian fable. The enthusiastic performances are matched by a top-quality stage with seating for up to 80 people, and a restaurant/café next door. For details of performances and venues, contact them direct.

SPORTS AND SPAS Many of Livingstone's hotels and lodges have small gyms or even tennis courts for their guests to use, or trained massage therapists on hand, but some facilities are open to all, and are worthy of specific mention. Every couple of years, visitors might be surprised to witness the Oxford and Cambridge **Boat Race** on the Zambezi. The race takes place between alumni from the two prestigious universities and starts at the Zambezi Boat Club, near the Falls. The next event is planned for September 2012.

Polocrosse

Not surprisingly in a town with such a rich colonial history, horseriding is popular locally. Polocrosse is a fast-paced mix of polo and lacrosse that Zambia excels at, even participating in the 2011 World Cup in England. The home of the Livingstone Polocrosse Club is a little way out of town at Chundukwa Lodge (page 173). During the season, which runs from April to September, the sport attracts a good following locally.

Golf

The Livingstone Royal Golf and Country Club ([163 G6] ⟍ *0213 320440;* e *info@livingstonegolf.com; www.livingstonegolf.com; green fees US$15/30 9/18 holes; caddy fees US$5/18 holes; club hire (left- & right-handed) US$10*), established in 1908, was once a popular social and sports club, complete with tennis and lawn bowling. Re-opened in 2006, it is the second-oldest golf club in Zambia and designated as a national monument. To get to the club from the centre of town, turn onto Akapelwa Street, cross the railway line, turn left at the junction towards the central police station, and then immediately right. Follow the signs.

Once visited by royalty and the site of many tournaments, the club fell into a state of disrepair, but both the course and the clubhouse have now been fully renovated. The 18 holes of the par-72, 6,205m parkland-type golf course have been entirely re-landscaped, the fairways and greens replanted with Bermuda and hybrid Bermuda grass, respectively. The clubhouse itself was renovated with great care to preserve its teak woodwork and many historical features, and the result speaks for itself – a stunning colonial-style building with restaurant and bar, in a genteel setting in the heart of Livingstone.

The club also houses an excellent **gym and fitness centre** with personal trainer in residence. For the kids there are a trampoline, boules and a wooden climbing frame with swings. A training swimming pool was completed in 2009 and two lawn tennis courts are planned for the future. Both members and non-members are welcome to play a round of golf, enjoy a meal in the clubhouse, or simply relax, drink in hand, on its sweeping veranda.

Massages and pampering

When you are exhausted from all the sightseeing, shopping and other diversions, relief is only a phone call away.

Royal Spa [map 193] Royal Livingstone Hotel; ⟍ 0213 321121, ext 2546; e rlsalon@sunint.co.za; ⏱ 10.00–19.00 Mon–Fri, 08.00–19.00 Sat–Sun. If your idea of the ultimate massage is in a billowing white tent on the banks of the Zambezi with spray from the Falls & hippos as backdrop, then this is the place to go. It offers diverse riverside massages in stylish tented gazebos, each with 1 side open to the river & 2 massage beds. Such divine pampering isn't cheap: expect to pay upwards of US$122 pp. Also available within the salon itself are all the usual spa

services: manicures, pedicures, facials, waxing, basic hair care & beauty products, all catering to foreign visitors & priced accordingly.
David Livingstone Safari Lodge & Spa
[map 159] ☎0213 324601; e camelot@ dsllandspa.com; ☺ 09.00–20.00 daily. Up there with the best – & the most expensive.

Salon Namel [map 159] Falls Park; ☎0213 324272; e namelslodge@zamnet.zm. This more affordable salon offers hair & beauty care including massages, manicures, pedicures, facials, haircuts, etc. Despite the rather plain & uninspiring design, the services are generally good & offer value for money.

THRILLS AND SPILLS The Falls area is indisputably *the* adventure capital of southern Africa. There is an amazing and seemingly endless variety of ways to get your shot of adrenalin: white-water rafting, canoeing, bungee jumping, kayaking, abseiling, gorge swinging, riverboarding or simply a flight over the Falls.

None comes cheaply. Most are upwards of US$100 per activity, which adds up quickly. If you wish to do multiple activities, check out the many combination packages on offer. These can be slightly cheaper than booking individually. There are also choices of operator for most of these, so if you book locally, shop around to find something that suits you before you decide. Prices won't vary much, but you will find the true range of what's available. Whatever you plan, expect to sign an indemnity form before your activity starts.

On the Zambian side there is a single cable car at Rapid 25 to bring clients out of the gorge after rafting trips, with the cost included in the activity price.

Flight of Angels Named after Livingstone's famous comment, 'Flight of Angels' describes any sightseeing trip over the Falls by microlight or helicopter. This is a good way to get a feel for the geography of the area, and is surprisingly worthwhile if you really want to appreciate the Falls. If you're arriving from Kasane, or leaving for there, consider combining a sightseeing flight and an air transfer. Otherwise any of these trips can be readily booked by agents in the area.

Microlight ([map 159] *Batoka Sky Adventures US$135 pp/15 mins, US$270/½hr, inc transfers from Livingstone & Victoria Falls town; weight limit 110kg unless notified in advance*) This is a totally different experience from a light aircraft: essentially sightseeing from a propeller-powered armchair 500m above the ground; it's the closest you can come to soaring like a bird over the Falls.

Microlights take only one passenger plus the pilot. Because the passenger sits next to the propeller, cameras cannot be carried for safety reasons. However, for US$20 you can arrange to be photographed above the Falls from a camera fixed to the wing. Flights are operated out of Batoka Sky's Maramba Aerodrome and within five minutes are over the Zambezi. A 15-minute flight takes in a circle over the Falls and the islands in the river. The longer flight then continues upstream before crossing over the national park. Microlights are affected by the slightest turbulence, so if you book in advance, it's best to specify early morning or late afternoon, when conditions are ideal.

Helicopter (*Typically US$140/280 pp for 15/30 mins, inc transfers from either Livingstone or Victoria Falls*) This is the most expensive way to see the Falls, but it is tremendous fun. A 15-minute trip takes in the Falls and the national park, or for 30 minutes you will fly over the gorges below the Falls as well; at extra cost, you can stop in the gorge at Rapid 22, 'Bobo Camp', for a one- or two-hour picnic (min six people). Alternatively, if you plan to raft, riverboard or ride a jet boat, you can get an exhilarating lift out of the gorge by helicopter – at extra cost of course, but including a scenic flight over the Falls and Zambezi gorges. Flights are operated by United Air Charters, in four-, five- and six-seater helicopters from the aptly named Baobab Ridge just south of town, and Batoka Sky, based at the Maramba Aerodrome, in three-, four- or six-seater craft. All are designed to give each passenger a good view – though the front seats are on a first-come, first-served basis. Note that Batoka Sky will fly with just two people.

Bungee jumping (US$120 per jump; no refund if you change your mind; tandem jump US$155. Min age 14, but under-18s require attendance of parent or guardian & their signature on the indemnity form. Min/max client weight 40/140kg (88/308lb). ⊕ 9.30–17.00, or from 10.00 at high water due to spray from Falls) There's only one company organising bungee jumping: African Extreme, part of Shearwater Adventures and an offshoot of the original New Zealand pioneers, Kiwi Extreme. Solo or tandem, you jump from the middle of the main bridge between Zambia and Zimbabwe, where the Zambezi is 111m below you. It is among the highest commercial bungee jumps in the world, and not for the nervous.

You can book in advance, either direct or through a tour operator, or simply turn up at the bridge and pay there. There's a bar on site, and digital photos and videos of your jump are available.

Bridge walks (US$50/60 pp with/without lunch, min 2 people) There's no-one better positioned to show you the ins and outs – no, make that ups and downs – of the Victoria Falls Bridge than the bungee folks, whose intimate bridge knowledge will not only fascinate you but have you clambering around and underneath the bridge like a monkey. With safety harness on and accompanied by guide, you have the opportunity to explore the bridge's superstructure while hearing all about its construction and riveting history. While not as adrenalin-charged as bungee jumping, it's still bound to get your heart beating faster as you navigate your way high above the Zambezi.

Abseiling, high-wiring, gorge swing and slide (Abseil Zambia US$95/100 pp ½/full day, inc insurance, transfers & snacks. Gorge swing only US$70/60 dbl/sgl. Flying fox or cable slide only US$40. Shearwater Adventures swing/tandem swing US$120/190; slide/tandem slide US$35/50; 'big air experience' US$155) A very popular addition to the adventure menu is the Zambezi swing, a cable swing set across the gorge which, together with a 90m-high cable slide (flying fox), abseiling (rappelling) and 'rap' jumps (rappelling forwards) down the side of the gorge, offers daring fun for all ages. These are currently offered by both Abseil Zambia at the top of the fifth gorge on the Zambian side, and Shearwater Adventures from their site on the bridge (see above).

At Abseil Zambia, the swing is a fixed 135m cable spanning the gorge. Participants are harnessed to ropes attached to the cable's sliding pulley and, after stepping off the cliff face, experience a heart-stopping 53m, three-second free-fall, followed by an exhilarating pendulum-like swing across the gorge, accelerating up to 140km/h (with a pull of roughly 2.5 times gravity) for some two minutes before being lowered to the ground. Described by participants as 'even more thrilling than bungee jumping', it's definitely not for the faint-hearted, though participants as young as eight and as old as 76 have braved it. It's even possible to try it out in tandem.

A slightly tamer alternative is the high wire or flying fox, set on another static cable stretched across the gorge. With harness and pulley, you leap off a platform and 'fly' (slide) across the gorge some 90m above the ground. It can be done in either a sitting or a flying position, and is suitable for children.

Except for the flying fox, be prepared to hike some 30 minutes out of the gorge after each go.

A full day's activity allows you to go up, down and over the gorge to your heart's content. Lunch, beer and cool drinks are included and sundowners are offered. Videos or disks of your activities are available at extra cost. It's also possible to spend just a half day, or to do any activities on their own.

The site is 5km from the Falls. If you're driving yourself, turn off the main road to the Falls just before the Zambezi Sun, and follow the signposts.

Canoeing on the Upper Zambezi
(Canoeing US$100/110 ½/full day inc b/fast or lunch; overnight US$250, floating US$50, elephant encounter US$130; min age 12) Canoeing down the Upper Zambezi is a cool occupation on hot days, and the best way to explore the upper river, its islands and channels. Zimbabwe's Zambezi National Park stretches all along the western shore providing ample opportunity for game viewing, while lodges, farms, villages and bush dot the Zambian side as you head downstream to the upper reaches of the Mosi-oa-Tunya National Park. The silence of canoes makes them ideal for floating up to antelope drinking, elephants feeding or crocodiles basking. Birdlife is prolific – you may hear the cry of the African fish eagle or see pied kingfishers hover and dive. Hippos provide the excitement, and are treated with respect and given lots of space.

A variety of options is available, from half- to full-day excursions, combo canoeing and game drives, and even overnight camping trips with the evening spent under the stars. You'll find any of them generally relaxing, although paddling becomes a bit more strenuous if it's windy. All canoe trips are accompanied by a licensed river guide, and sometimes also a motorboat for additional safety. Canoes range from two-seater open-decked kayaks to inflatable 'crocodiles'.

There are some sections of choppy water if you'd like a little more excitement, though it's possible to avoid most of these easily if you wish. Trips concentrating on these shouldn't be confused with the white-water rafting beneath the Falls (see below).

For those who'd like the experience but don't want to paddle, canoe operators also run guided 'float' trips known as the Livingstone Drift on the Upper Zambezi. Participants can paddle when they feel like it or simply float downstream on a raft.

No prior canoeing experience is necessary, and once you are used to the water, the better guides will encourage you to concentrate on the wildlife. Lunch is typically served on an island. Trips are run by Makora Quest, Bundu Adventures and Safari Par Excellence, with the latter two also running float trips using rafts. At Tongabezi, canoeing for guests is included in the rates. SafPar offers an 'Elephant Encounter' trip combining a half-day canoeing safari, riverside brunch and an opportunity to interact with their elephants used for elephant-back safaris. A further option is a half-day's canoeing (or floating) followed by lunch and a drive in the game park.

White-water rafting
The Zambezi below the Falls is one of the world's most renowned stretches of white water. It was the venue for the 1995 World Rafting Championships, and rafting is now very big business here, with keen competition for tourist dollars. (About 50,000 people now go down the river every year, paying about US$120–145 each. You can do the sums.)

Experienced rafters grade rivers from I to VI, according to difficulty. Elsewhere in the world, a normal view of this scale would be:

- Class I   No rapids, flat water.
- Class II   Easy rapids, a float trip. No rafting experience required.
- Class III   Intermediate to advanced rapids. No rafting experience required.
- Class IV   Very difficult rapids. Prior rafting experience highly
                     recommended. No children.
- Class V   For experts only. High chance of flips or swims. No children or
                     beginners.
- Class VI   Impossible to run.

The rapids below the Falls are mostly graded IV and V. This isn't surprising when you realise that all the water coming slowly down the Zambezi's 1.7km width is being squeezed through rocky gorges that are often just 50–60m wide.

Fortunately for the rafting companies, most of the rapids here may be very large, but the vast majority of them are not 'technical' to run. This means that they don't need skill to manoeuvre the boat while it is within the rapids, they just require the rafts to be positioned properly before entering each rapid. Hence, despite the grading of these rapids, they allow absolute beginners into virtually all of the rafts. That said, you should think very carefully about committing yourself if you have no experience. Boats do flip over, and the consequences can be severe. It's also important to ensure that your chosen operator will give a thorough safety briefing before departure, explaining what to do in the event of a capsize.

High or low water, and which side of the river? Rafting is offered from both Zambia and Zimbabwe by a wide range of companies. Some, like SafPar, operate from both sides.

From July to January, when the water is low, full- or half-day trips leave from the Boiling Pot just below the Falls: a spectacular start to the day. (Trips departing from Zimbabwe leave from Rapid 4 at this time of year.) This period, when the river's waves and troughs (or 'drops') are more pronounced, is probably the best time to experience the Zambezi's full glory.

In high-water months (February to July), only half-day trips are offered, starting below Rapid 9 on both sides of the river. Note that when the river is highest its rapids may seem less dramatic, but it is more dangerous, due to the strong whirlpools and undercurrents. If the water is too high, rafting is suspended until it recedes to a safer level.

The trips A typical rafting trip will start with a briefing, covering safety/health issues, giving the plan for the day and answering any questions. Once you reach the 'put-in' at the river, you will be given a short safety/practice session to familiarise yourself with the raft and techniques that will be used to run the rapids. Half-day trips will run about half of the rapids, but a full day is needed to get through all the rapids from 1 to 25. Lunch and cool drinks are included. It's also possible to organise a multi-day trip of between one and five days with SafPar.

The climb up and out of the gorge at the end of the trip can be steep and tiring, especially in hot weather, but on the Zambian side, a cable car at Rapid 25 has made this a thing of the past – albeit at a price (though the cost of the lift is included in SafPar's rates). Alternatively, most companies offer a heli–raft combo, whereby you can opt to fly out instead at additional cost. Beyond the obvious advantage of 'taking the easy way out', the heli flight is an exhilarating end to an exciting day, zipping you out of the gorge with a bird's-eye view of the rapids you've just run and the Falls as well.

A trained river guide pilots every raft, but you need to decide whether you want to go in an oar boat or in a paddle boat. In an oar boat expect to cling on for dear life, and throw your weight around the raft on demand – but nothing more. Oar boats are generally easier and safer because you rely on the skills of the oarsmen to negotiate the rapids, and you can hang onto the raft at all times. Only occasionally will you have to 'highside' (throw your weight forward) when punching through a big wave.

In a paddle boat the participants provide the power by paddling, while a trained rafting guide positions the boat and yells out commands instructing you what to do. You'll have to listen, and also paddle like crazy through the rapids, remembering when and if you are supposed to be paddling. You can't just hang on! In paddle boats you are an active participant and thus are largely responsible for how successfully you run the rapids. The rafting guide calls commands and positions the boat, but then it's up to you. If your fellow paddlers are not up to it, then expect a difficult ride. Paddle boats have a higher tendency to flip and/or have 'swimmers' (someone thrown out of the boat).

Originally, only oar boats were run on the Zambezi. However, nowadays paddle boats have become more popular as rafting companies compete to outdo each other in offering the most exciting rides. There is, of course, a very fine line between striving to be more exciting, and actually becoming more dangerous.

With either option, remember that people often fall out and rafts do capsize. Despite this, safety records are usually cited as excellent. Serious injuries are said to be uncommon and fatalities rare.

Rafting operators (*US$135/145 pp ½/full day inc transfers & gorge lift or cable car at Rapid 25 if appropriate; min age 15*) All rafting companies offer broadly similar experiences. To gain a competitive edge, some now offer freebies like dinner and sundowners in their prices, so it's well worth asking around and comparing what's included, as this changes from time to time. The rapids are numbered from 1 to 25, starting from the Boiling Pot, so it's easy to make a rough comparison of the trips on offer.

Zambian operators include Bundu Adventures, Raft Extreme and Safari Par Excellence. Special options include breakfast, lunch, sundowners and barbecue dinner. All offer videos and photos of your trip at additional cost. A shorter, three-hour trip from rapids 1 to 7 is also available through Bundu Adventures, at US$115 per person.

In addition to day trips, there are four-day expeditions as far as the proposed Batoka Gorge Dam site, while seven-day expeditions reach the mouth of the Matetsi River. These offer more than the adrenalin of white water, and are the best way to see the remote Batoka Gorge, though trips are few and far between.

Riverboarding (*US$150 pp; riverboard & raft combo US$165–185 pp inc transfers, light b/fast, lunch & sundowner; min age 15*) For a more up-close and personal encounter with the Zambezi rapids, adrenalin junkies can try their hand at riverboarding (also known as boogie-boarding) or combo riverboarding and rafting. After donning your fins, lifejacket and helmet, you and your foam board (the size of a small surfboard) will have an opportunity to 'surf' the big waves of the Zambezi, after being taught basic skills in a calmer section of the river. A raft accompanies each trip and takes you downstream to the best spots of the day. Here you can try finding the best 'standing waves' where you can stay still and surf as the water rushes beneath you. Experts can stand, but most will surf on their stomachs. It's thrilling for the fit who swim strongly, but not for the faint of heart. Trips are offered by both Bundu Adventures and Safari Par Excellence.

White-water kayaking (*Kayak the Zambezi & Bundu Adventures; experienced kayakers US$80/120 pp ½/full day, inc lunch & transfers; tandem US$160 pp*) Yet another option for white-water enthusiasts is kayaking in the gorge. Those without experience can try tandem kayaking in Topolino Duo kayaks; a qualified guide sits in the back, piloting and manoeuvring the kayak through rapids, while you sit in front and assist with paddle power. In all cases you must be a confident swimmer; kayaks, smaller and lighter than rafts, may capsize in bigger rapids, and although your guide will attempt to right it by executing an 'Eskimo roll', you (and your guide) may have to swim the rest of the rapid.

There are also four-day courses for experienced kayakers and fully outfitted multi-day expeditions by special arrangement.

WILDLIFE ENCOUNTERS
Mosi-oa-Tunya National Park (*Park entry US$10 (self drive US$15) pp/day; vehicle US$15/day; guided game drive US$50 pp; game walk US$75 pp*) Much of the Zambian area around the Falls is protected within the Mosi-oa-Tunya National Park, until 2009 the smallest national park in Zambia, which now has a fenced off area of 66km². The original area, about half this size and known as 'the game park', lies in the middle, and this is where walks and game drives take place. The newer area stretches along the river in both directions. Visitors can also see the cemetery at Old Drift, the site of Livingstone's first settlement.

Getting there and around You can drive yourself around easily, or go with one of the many operators (page 190–2) who run 4x4 trips into the park. The three lodges inside the park – Toka Leya, Sussi & Chuma and Thorntree River Lodge – also offer their guests guided drives or walks from the lodge. There's even a luxury steam train, the *Royal Livingstone Express* (see pages 196–7). For the more adventurous there are three-hour walking safaris, led by licensed safari guides from Livingstone Walking Safaris (*US$70*) or Bwaato Adventures (*US$70–85 pp*). Beyond the excitement of tracking game on foot, these are an excellent way to learn about the flora and fauna. The best time to go for birds is early in the morning, but walks also take place in the afternoon.

Flora and fauna The park boasts tracts of riverine vegetation, dry mixed woodland and mopane trees. A few hours' driving could yield sightings of most of the common antelope and some fine giraffe, as well as buffalo, elephant and zebra. There is also the chance of spotting white rhino, of which four were imported from South Africa in 2008 – although three of their predecessors met their demise at the hands of poachers. Even wild dog are present: a pack recently crossed the river from Zimbabwe. There are, however, no lion, leopard or other cats present.

For birdlife, see below.

Birdwatching Birdwatching isn't normally regarded as an adrenalin sport, but with the outstanding avifauna to be found in and around the Falls, serious 'twitchers' might disagree.

Even the casual visitor with little interest will often see fish eagles, Egyptian geese, lots of kingfishers, numerous different bee-eaters, Hadeda and sacred ibis, and various other storks, egrets and herons. Meanwhile, avid twitchers will be seeking the more elusive birds like the rare Taita falcon, as Batoka Gorge is one of the best sites to look for them. Rock pratincoles have almost as restricted a distribution (just following the Zambezi), but can often be seen here balancing on boulders by the water's edge and hawking for insects, while African skimmers can be found nesting upon sandy shores of islands. Look in the riverine forest around the Falls and you may spot a collared palm thrush rummaging around; again, these are really quite rare birds recorded in only a few areas. In contrast, African finfoot occur throughout sub-Saharan Africa, but are always shy. They prefer slow water, overhung with leafy branches, and they find the upper sections of the Zambezi perfect, so are often seen there if you look when it's quiet. Back on land, keep an eye out for birds of prey; on a recent visit, a martial eagle was spotted surveying our early-morning walk from on high.

For many years, Bob Stjernstedt, known locally as 'Bob the Birder' (m 0978 169567; e birdingwithbob@gmail.com; www.birdingwithbob.com), has been one of Zambia's leading ornithologists. He is based in Livingstone and will still lead guided birdwatching excursions in the area for US$100/200 per person for a half/ full day (the latter includes lunch at Taita Falcon Lodge), based on a minimum of two people. Alternatively you can arrange a half-day trip with Cliff Sitwala (m 0978 171547; e localcowboy@yahoo.com), or with a member of the Zambian Ornithological Society, for US$50 per person.

Elephant riding (*SafPar: US$160 pp ½ day inc light snacks & drinks plus US$10 park fees; no children under 10*) Zambezi Elephant Trails, based at Thorntree River Lodge, offer the only elephant-back safaris in Zambia. Here you and your *nduna* (elephant guide) will ride African elephants through the bush and along the river in the upper reaches of the Mosi-oa-Tunya National Park, where you may encounter a variety of game. In addition to the hour-long ride, you will have a chance to interact with the elephants close up.

We are assured that all the elephants were originally orphaned, and are comfortable around people.

Horseriding and horse-drawn carriages (*Victoria Carriage Co; 2hr ride US$75; ½ day with lunch US$110*) Riding along the Zambezi and through the bush is a wonderful way to experience nature up close. You can choose from rides as short as a couple of hours to half-day trips with lunch along the river and/or through the bush in search of game. Trips for all levels are offered by the Victoria Carriage Company in the area by the Falls and national park. Hard hats are supplied.

More sedate transport comes in the form of Victorian horse-drawn carriages, which depart every half an hour from the Royal Livingstone and make a tour around the Sun International complex near the Falls.

Livingstone Reptile Park ([map 159] *Gwembe Safaris: entry US$10/7adult/ child.* ⊕ *All year*) Just to the south of Livingstone, the Reptile Park (still signposted 'Livingstone Crocodile Park') offers the opportunity to see some huge crocs at close quarters – from behind the safety of a chain-link fence or from covered walkways – and to get some great photographs. Well-informed and friendly guides offer explanations about the behaviour and history of the animals, and feeding times (usually early afternoon) are posted at the entrance. The park has a valuable educational role, with visiting groups from local schools and the wider community learning about these dangerous creatures, and in many cases developing a new-found respect for them. Picnic tables are set in the landscaped grounds and there's a café serving the park's signature 'Croc Bite'.

The park also features some of Zambia's snakes, housed in glass cages. It, hopefully, will be your only chance to see Africa's most dangerous snakes – black mamba, cobra,

THE ETHICS OF WALKING WITH LIONS

There are now several operations in Africa which offers visitors the opportunity to pay to touch, stroke and walk with baby lions. All cite their 'projects' as part of larger conservation initiatives to 'save lions', some with the backing of charities (often small charities, very closely linked with the projects). The problem with this for conservationists is two-fold: first, what happens to the cubs when they grow older; and second, are these projects really doing valuable conservation work?

WHAT HAPPENS TO ALL THE BABY LIONS? When lion cubs reach about 18 months old, they become too large and dangerous to be mixed with people. Lions typically live for about 16 years in the wild and up to 25 in captivity. If they have spent time as cubs mixing with people, then they cannot be released into an unfenced area, because sooner or later they'd probably come across local villagers – and with no fear of humans they'd be likely to kill.

Most of Africa's national parks and really wild areas are unfenced. It doesn't take much to do the maths and estimate the number of adult lions that each of these projects will produce every year. These will all need to be housed in fenced areas stocked with game for them to eat. Many conservationists claim that there just aren't enough such areas, and they point out that 'lions breed like rabbits' when given the right conditions.

Considerable controversy was stirred up by a *Sunday Times* article by Chris Haslam in February 2008 entitled 'African lion encounters: a bloody con'. This looked at one such operation and alleged that, once adult, the original lion cubs were likely to be used for 'canned hunting' on farms in South Africa. The paper was unable to prove that farms in South Africa which had received lions from the project in question had definitely used the lions for canned hunting, and hence issued a retraction. However, you only have to search the internet to realise that there's great debate over the ethics of such operations.

VALUABLE CONSERVATION? Many leading lion conservationists question if there is any conservation value at all in most of these projects.

They argue that habitat destruction and human encroachment are the real conservation issues that need to be addressed for conserving Africa's lions, and observe that there is little evidence of these commercial operations doing any meaningful work of this type. They also question the wisdom of randomly mixing lion populations, which risks introducing deleterious genes or diseases into established lion populations.

So I'd urge you to think carefully about the ethics of your actions and to try to look beyond the fine words of the commercial concerns involved. Your few hours of fun may come at a hefty price.

---

puff adder – up close and personal; you can even hold the 'safe' snakes to get a feel for them. There is also an activity centre here where visitors can book any of a wide range of activities or go on one of Gwembe's game drives in the Mosi-oa-Tunya National Park (in which case you get free entrance to the Reptile Park).

Walking with lions (*SafPar Lion Encounter: US$125 pp ½ day, inc transfers within Livingstone, b/fast or snacks, drinks; exc US$10 park fees; 1¼ hr walks at*

06.15 & 15.00; min age 15; min height 1.5m. Mukuni Big 5 Safaris: US$120 pp/½ day, inc transfers within Livingstone) For visitors, the appeal of this encounter is the opportunity to walk with lion cubs, which are bred specially for the programme. Clearly this is very appealing to some people and is also unusual. (See box opposite for more on the controversy surrounding this activity.) Mukuni also offers the chance to walk with cheetah and visit their 'research centre'.

Mabula Game Farm (+0212 608 324332; e *reservations@lodge.mabula.co.za; www.mabulacottage.com; US$90/1050 ½/full day*) In a bush setting, 40km north of Livingstone and clearly signposted 1km east of the main road, this game farm offers game drives, nature walks and horseriding. Don't expect to see anything too exciting here, although it's the site of an eland domestication project, but for puku, kudu and other antelope, it's a fairly safe bet. There's a bar, restaurant, and pool too – and limited accommodation in the form of two cottages and a campsite if you'd like to stay over.

OTHER ACTIVITIES
Quadbikes (*Eco Trail US$80; village trail US$140, inc transfers. Other destinations & tailormade trips also available*) Guided quadbike (four-wheel motorbike) excursions are operated by the Livingstone Quad Company. Choose from a one-hour 'eco-trail' at Batoka Land (starting at Maramba Aerodrome), consisting of 17ha in and around the unfenced portion of the national park, or a two-hour trip venturing out into the bush to explore African villages and the landscape by the Zambezi gorges. Participants are given an introduction and a chance to practise before heading out on the trail of their choice.

Segway tours (e *victoriafalls@bushtracksafrica.com; general tour US$35 or U$45 with sundowners*) If your idea of fun is to glide along laid-out trails to observe wildlife such as giraffe, baboons, zebra, impala and monkeys, this is for you. No experience is necessary, since coaches are on hand to teach the basics of riding the two-wheeled, stand-on segway. Operated by Bushtracks on Sun International property.

SAFARIS AROUND THE FALLS AREA
Livingstone is well placed for day-trip safaris, both in Zambia's Mosi-oa-Tunya National Park (see above) and in Victoria Falls and Zambezi national parks across the river in Zimbabwe.

If you are seeking a four- or five-day excursion from the Falls area, there are several superb game parks within easy reach. Some of the local operators (see pages 190–2) run trips from Livingstone, and for backpackers there are usually a few operators running buses or trucks to Windhoek, Maun or even Harare. Like cut-down overland trips, these often stop at parks on the way.

VICTORIA FALLS NATIONAL PARK, ZIMBABWE Like the northern side of the river, a good section of Zimbabwe's land around the Falls is protected – though only the rainforest area, criss-crossed by footpaths to viewing points, is actually fenced off. If you are feeling adventurous, then follow the riverbank upstream from Livingstone's statue. (If the gate is closed beyond the statue, then retrace your steps out of the entrance to the rainforest; and turn right, then right again, down Zambezi Drive, to reach the outside of that gate.)

This path runs next to Zambezi Drive for a while. After almost 2km, Zambezi Drive leaves the river and turns back towards town, passing a famous baobab tree called the Big Tree. From there the path continues for about 8km upstream until it reaches A'Zambezi River Lodge, just outside the gate to the Zambezi National Park. This is a very beautiful, wild walk but, despite its innocent air, you are as likely to meet hippo, elephant or buffalo here as in any other national park. So take great care as you admire the view across the river. You may also want to plan ahead and arrange a pick-up from A'Zambezi back into town, or alternatively just ask the hotel on arrival.

ZAMBEZI NATIONAL PARK, ZIMBABWE This park borders the Zambezi River, starting about 6km from Victoria Falls and extending about 40km upstream. You cannot walk here (without a professional guide), so you need a vehicle, but there are several Zimbabwean operators running morning and afternoon drives through the park who will collect you from any of the main hotels.

The park is actually bisected by the main road from Victoria Falls to Kazungula/Kasane (which has long been an unlikely, but favourite, spot for sightings of wild dogs). Better game viewing is to be had from the roads designed for it: the Zambezi River Drive, or the Chamabondo Drive.

The former is easily reached by driving out of town along Park Way, past the Elephant Hills Hotel and the Victoria Falls Safari Lodge. This road follows the river's course almost to the end of the park, and there are plenty of loop roads to explore away from the river.

The Chamabondo Drive has a separate entrance on the road to Bulawayo. Take a right turn just before the road crosses the Massive River, about 7km out of town. This leads past several pans and hides until it terminates at Nook Pan, from where you must retrace your steps as there are no loop roads.

The park has good populations of elephant, buffalo and antelope – especially notable are the graceful sable which thrive here. The riverfront is beautiful, lined with classic stands of tall winterthorn trees, *Acacia albida*. Note that when wet this park is often impossible to drive through in a 2WD, and when dry some of the roads remain in poor condition.

KAFUE NATIONAL PARK, ZAMBIA The southern side of Kafue is actually quite close to Livingstone, though the area is remote and relatively undeveloped. You will need either a couple of fully kitted 4x4s in convoy, or the help of a local operator. Game viewing in this part of the park is by vehicle and on foot from one of a handful of camps, several of which have good campsites. For details, see *Chapter 14*.

CHOBE NATIONAL PARK, BOTSWANA This is often suggested as a day trip from the Falls, but is really too far to be worthwhile. (You end up arriving after the best of the morning's game viewing is finished, and leaving before the afternoon cools down sufficiently for the game to re-appear!) However, the Chobe riverfront, around Serondela, probably has higher wildlife densities than any of the other parks mentioned here. So if you can cope with the sheer number of vehicles there, it may be worth a trip for a few days. Its luxurious lodges (and high park fees) mean that northern Chobe is always expensive.

In spite of that, day trips with some of the major operators are extremely popular. A typical trip with Wild Side (*US$160 pp*) will incorporate a game drive and lunch at one of the hotels. Bushtracks includes a morning riverboat on the Chobe River, with an afternoon game drive (*US$185 pp*), and Makora Quest even offers an excursion that also takes in Namibia's Kasai Wetlands followed by a game drive in Chobe Game Reserve, lunch, then a river cruise (*US$200 pp*). Longer trips are also available. Jollyboys offers a full-day excursion (*US$140 pp*) which includes all transfers, a light breakfast, lunch and a game drive and boat cruise along the river

There are regular transfers between Victoria Falls and Kasane (in Botswana, beside the park) which take around two hours. Then stay at Chobe Game Lodge or Chobe Chilwero – the only two lodges in that section of the park. Either can easily be arranged by a good tour operator before you arrive, or by a travel agent in Livingstone. The lodges in Kasane, outside the park, don't compare (though Impalila Island Lodge or Ichingo Chobe River Camp on the opposite bank of the river are little-known options that are both excellent value, and cheaper).

Alternatively, if you have a good 4x4 then you can drive yourself around and (advance reservations essential) camp at the basic, unfenced site at Ihaha. Take all your food and equipment with you, and watch for the baboons.

HWANGE NATIONAL PARK, ZIMBABWE Zimbabwe's flagship national park has three established public camps that provide excellent value, basic accommodation and camping. It also has several more basic camping spots at picnic sites.

Alternatively there are a few more expensive private lodges in the park, most of them towards the south side of the park's road network in an area of Kalahari sandveld.

CHIZARIRA NATIONAL PARK, ZIMBABWE One of Zimbabwe's wildest and least visited parks, Chizarira requires patience, lots of driving skill, and preferably a 4x4 – and that's just to get there. Most visitors fly in, or are taken by an operator, and because the land is rugged and remote much of the game viewing is on foot. You won't see the quantities of game this way that you see elsewhere, but the wilderness experience is excellent.

One main lodge operates, Chizarira Wilderness Lodge, and also a tented camp, Jedson's Safari Camp. Both are excellent. Alternatively, Leon Varley and his team run walking safaris here and have been doing so for years. They're another first-class operation.

KAZUMA PAN NATIONAL PARK, ZIMBABWE This small, little-visited national park borders Botswana between the Zambezi and Hwange national parks. Like Chizarira, it is used for walking safaris more than for driving, though the environment is very different. It consists of a huge, almost flat depression – a grass-covered pan surrounded by forests that are dominated by the familiar mopane and teak trees.

Only a few groups are allowed into the park at any time, each requiring a fully licensed walking guide – which effectively limits access to organised operators.

LAKE KARIBA & THE LOWER ZAMBEZI

9

Lake Kariba and the Lower Zambezi

Zambia's border with Zimbabwe is defined by the course of the Zambezi as it slowly meanders towards the Indian Ocean. Below the Victoria Falls, it flows east, sometimes northeast, and today's biggest features of this river are artificial: Lake Kariba, between Zambia and Zimbabwe, and Lake Cabora Bassa, in Mozambique.

Zambia's attractions on Lake Kariba are limited to a few islands in the lake, accessed from Sinazongwe, and perhaps Siavonga, which is a pleasant place to relax. Of the islands, Chete is large enough to be a credible wilderness destination with some good wildlife on it, but its lodge has been closed for some years. Chikanka, however, remains accessible to those on a mid-range budget.

Below the wall of Kariba Dam, the Zambezi continues through the hot, low-lying Lower Zambezi Valley amid some of the best game viewing in the country. On both sides of the river – Zambian and Zimbabwean – are important national parks. This is also the place to canoe down one of the world's great rivers, whilst game spotting and avoiding the hippos.

FROM LIVINGSTONE TO LUSAKA

(see also map *Southern Zambia*, page 156)
This main tar road is only 473km, but it seems longer. Despite its many sections that are faultlessly smooth, particularly as far as Mazabuka, there are some rough patches to negotiate, and speed humps in the towns, so allow about six or seven hours for the journey if you're driving yourself, and stick to a safe 80km/h or so. Better still, stop along the way and explore, making Choma's museum top of your list. If you've more time, then detour to Sinazongwe and on to one of Kariba's islands.

Those brave few hitchhikers will find it one of the easiest roads in the country: lots of towns, regularly spaced, and plenty of traffic. The buses are frequent if you get stuck.

Here I've arranged a few brief comments on what you'll find if you're heading towards Lusaka from Livingstone, with suggestions for places to stay *en route*.

ZIMBA Zimba is the first town reached from Livingstone, after about 76km. It's around 397km to Lusaka and really only notable for having a large local market close to the main road. Aside from a post office, a church and a few small shops, there's little else to detain you here.

🏠 Where to stay
⋀ Mabula Farm m 0977 866517. About halfway between Livingstone & Zimba there's a campsite & wildlife farm signposted to the east. For details, see *Chapter 8, Livingstone*, page 209.

KALOMO This small town, about 126km from Livingstone and 347km from Lusaka, marks the turn-off from the main road towards the Dumdumwenze gate into the southern section of Kafue National Park. The turning is clearly signposted. See *Chapter 14*, pages 444–5, for details of this route, and note that a 4x4 is essential to drive in the park.

The all-important **fuel** station (✪ KAFUEL 17°01.661'S, 26°29.271'E) is on the main road, just south of the Kafue turn-off. There are also branches of both Barclays and Finance **banks**, the former with an ATM, plus a district hospital, a chemist, and Catholic and Anglican churches. Should you need somewhere to stay, there's the **Kalomo Hotel** (↘ *0213 265231/265300*), set back from the main road, and a couple of small guesthouses.

Excursions from Kalomo

Administrator's House Some 6km from the tar road, between the centre of Kalomo and its main suburb/township, this national monument dates to around 1903–04. It was built for the Administrator of Northwestern Rhodesia, as appointed by the British South Africa Company. Then Kalomo was the 'capital' of the territory, and the house is said to be the first non-traditional brick house built in Northern Rhodesia. It is now occupied and so not open to the public but as you pass through Kalomo there's a small monument by the roadside to record this history.

Kalundu Mound About 3km north of Kalomo, on the main road, is a slightly raised mound (a matter of just a few metres) of earth through which the road passes. This marks the site of an Iron-Age village, and the mound is the accumulated debris of many centuries of occupation.

It was excavated in the late 1950s and early 1960s when the road was being built, and the archaeologists estimated that it might have been occupied as early as the 4th century AD, although it was certainly full of people from about AD800–1300. (Note that the occupants during this latter period are sometimes referred to by Zambian archaeologists as following the 'Kalomo Tradition'.)

CHOMA Choma (✪ 16°48.547'S, 26°59.302'E) is another small, friendly town, about 285km from Lusaka and 188km from Livingstone. The main road between the two, here called Livingstone Road, runs through the centre of the town, and on (or just off) it you'll find all the amenities of small-town life: shops, market, cafés, post office, internet facilities, a couple of fuel stations, and branches of several major banks, as well as a well-stocked Spar supermarket. Perhaps more surprisingly, there's a super little museum (see below).

Some 10km north of the town, the Tazimani Craft Shop offers an excellent range of locally made craft products and artwork. Further north, the occasional craft stall has been set up at the roadside by the charcoal sellers, and you'll also see local fishermen touting their catch by waving it aggressively in the face of passing cars.

Where to stay A recent boom in accommodation has resulted in over a hundred lodges and guesthouses in the Choma area. As well as those listed below, the following – with similar facilities – are also recommended: **Leon's Lodge** (*12 rooms;* ↘ *0213 220156;* m *0978 666008;* e *lettiz2002@yahoo.com;* **$$**); **Crystal Lodge** (*17 rooms;* m *0969 975098;* e *crestlinehospitality@yahoo.com;* **$**) behind Barclays Bank; and the budget **Majajomu Guest House** (*4 rooms;* m *0977 871206;* **$**). Out of town, consider Nkanga River Conservation Area (see opposite).

🏠 **Kozo Lodge** (41 chalets) `0213 225347, 0211 264933/266518; m 0977 619665/711890; e kozolodge@zamtel.zm; www.kozolodge. co.zm. About 5km south of Choma, Kozo Lodge is signposted to the east of the road, across the railway. Dbl & twin chalets of varying styles, all with satellite TV, nestle under deep thatch on a spacious, well-maintained site; most are en suite. With a bar, restaurant & takeaway service, it's well set up for drivers heading through on the main road. **$$**

🏠 **Mana Nest Lodge** (15 rooms) `0213 220846; m 0961 783890; e manalodge@ yahoo.com. Opened in 2011 under friendly management, Mana Nest provides en-suite dbl & twin rooms with DSTV, AC, fridges, filtered water & tea/coffee-making facilities. There's

a restaurant & bar, secure parking, & internet access. **$–$$**

🏠 **Racheal's Lodge** (20 rooms) `0213 220753; m 0978 428131; e rachealslodge@ yahoo.com. A popular lodge with rooms in a wide price range, Racheal's is 1km to the west at the southern end of town. Most dbl & twin rooms are en suite, & feature DSTV, fans/AC, filtered water, fridge & tea/coffee facilities. Internet is available, as are a restaurant, bar & secure parking. **$–$$**

🏠 **Kamuboola Lodge** (16 rooms) m 0964 274827, 0979 304886. Situated at the northern end of town, in a secure, pleasantly landscaped setting, Kamuboola offers en-suite dbl & twin rooms with DSTV & fans. There's also a restaurant & bar. **$** *exc b/fast.*

✗ **Where to eat** Tasty **snacks and meals** are served in the lovely grounds of the museum. Elsewhere, Wonderbake behind Spar serves excellent coffee and scones, and Spar itself sells takeaways. Hachis Restaurant offers a variety of good food – and the cleanest toilets in Zambia. **Evening meals** are available at most of the lodges as well as at the Sports Club and Golf Club – both situated on the northern approach to town. The New Choma Hotel provides an evening braai in the Sugar Hut bar which is good value.

What to see and do Choma's popular small **museum and crafts centre** (CMCC, `0213 220394; m 0979 323929; e cmcc@coppernet.zm; ⊕ 09.00–17.00 daily; admission US$2/1 adult/child*) is on the main road through town. In addition to a collection of regional artefacts, the centre focuses on contemporary crafts and – to a lesser extent – art, showcasing the work of rural craftspeople throughout the area, with a particular emphasis on basketry.

NKANGA RIVER CONSERVATION AREA About 5km north of Choma there's a signpost to Nkanga, 20km away – which is also easily reached on the new tarred road from Namwala. Here you'll find a conservation area that covers a number of local farms, and protects antelope including sable, eland, puku, hartebeest, wildebeest, kudu, tsessebe and many other species. The area is also one of Zambia's important bird areas (IBA), with a total of 439 species noted. These include Zambia's only endemic bird, Chaplin's barbet.

As it's a conservation area that sustainably manages its populations of native game, some trophy hunting is also conducted, though this does not interfere with the photographic visitors.

🏠 **Where to stay**

🏠 **Masuku Lodge** (6 rondavels) `0213 225225; m 0977 760756/532650; e masukulodge@gmail.com, masuku@zamnet. zm; www.masukulodgezambia.com. Located on a farm in the conservation area, about 25km from Choma, Masuku is owned by ex-

diplomat Bill Somerset & his wife, & comes well recommended. The lodge overlooks a *vlei* which has been dammed to provide a lake. Guests stay in thatched, en-suite rondavels with twin beds, & dine together in a central lounge/dining area. Much of the farm's game, including sable &

zebra, can be spotted in the immediate vicinity, where there are some good walks; game drives can also be arranged. *US$85/95/105 pp B&B/ DBB/FB.* ☺ *All year.*

🏠 **Nkanga River Conservation Area** (2 chalets, camping) ☏ 0213 225592; m 0977 863873/766260; e nansaibm@zamtel.zm; nansaibm@gmail.com. Within the conservation area are en-suite chalets at the farmhouse, where meals are served en famille. In a separate riverbank location is a basic campsite, the domain of bushbuck, Cape clawless otter & countless birds. There's a communal shelter here, with firewood & the facility for BBQs, plus cold showers, toilets & electric lights. Note that it can become cold by the river, especially May–Jul, & do bring mosquito protection. Game drives are available (*Kw400,000/vehicle, max 8, booking essential*), as are guided walks for game & birdwatching (*Kw30,000 pp/day*). Other activities include fishing for bream & barbel (*Kw60,000/ group inc basic equipment*). Nkanga also runs valuable educational bushcamps Apr–Oct for groups (min 14) of children aged 7–16, covering bush knowledge, skills & outdoor activities. *Lodge Kw380,000 pp FB inc laundry. Camping Kw30,000 pp.* ☺ *All year; advance booking essential.*

BATOKA Little more than a market-lined road with a small post office, Batoka is significant for visitors as the turn-off for Sinazongwe and Lake Kariba, which is signposted to the east of the road. It's almost the midway point between Livingstone (222km) and Lusaka (251km). This isn't a natural choice for somewhere to stop, but if you're stuck, then you could try **Batoka Lodge** to the west of the main road.

PEMBA Another small town, scarcely more than a dot on the map, Pemba is about 261km from Livingstone.

CHISEKESI The linear community of Chisekesi, 270km from Livingstone, boasts a useful fuel station. Just to the north is the **Mayfair Guesthouse**.

Chisekesi is the turn-off to Chipepo Harbour and some of the non-commercial Kariba islands, at a distance of 92km. This is one of the settlement areas of the Tonga people displaced when the dam was constructed (Siavonga/Lusitu is another).

After the dam was built, ZESCO was committed to restoring the road that connects Siavonga with Sinazongwe and southwest to Sianzovo with its amethyst mines and market, but this remains inconsistent and rough going in parts. (As an aside, stones are sold illegally here by Senegalese traders known as the Masenesene.) Beyond Sianzovo a rough road continues to Syagulula, where there's a women's basket-making co-operative that is the source of some of the baskets sold at Choma Museum, and on a further 15km to Devil's Gorge. You'll need some large-scale maps of the area, but the scenery is rewarding. A similarly poor road connects Sianzovo market back to Kalomo.

MONZE Monze (✪ 16°15.436'S, 27°28.588'E) is another small town with little of note except a fuel station (a second is temporarily closed).

🏠 **Where to stay**

🅰 **Moorings Campsite** (2 chalets, camping) ☏ 0213 255049; m 0979 869087; e enquiries@ mooringscampsite.com, tsavory@zamnet.zm; www.mooringscampsite.com. Clearly signposted to the east of the main road, about 11km north of Monze, this is probably the best place to camp between Livingstone & Lusaka. The campsite is set in a grassy field on Thea Savory's mixed 2,600ha farm, supplementing the income from cattle, maize & soya. The site is also well placed for Lochinvar National Park, about 2hrs' drive away. Do ask managers James & Kim about the area's birding potential; keen birders may spot Chaplin's barbet here.

Campers pull up alongside one of a number of thatched rondavels that are dotted about the field, each with electric light & space for a large open fire, with wood available. The ablution block is spotlessly clean & visitors may use the small kitchen – although Kim will do home-cooked meals on request. There are also small, brick-built chalets, & a large, airy bar area with plenty of chairs.

Visitors to the campsite are welcome to look around. Thea originally came to Monze from the Netherlands to work in the local hospital. Now she runs a medical clinic which is free for the farm's permanent workers & their families; other patients pay a small fee. The farm effectively has its own primary school, too, & partially funds secondary education.

Finally, there is the Malambo Women's Craft Centre where local women come to make quilts, cushion covers & other items for sale at both Ababa House & the Dutch Reform bazaar in Lusaka (see pages 145 & 151). The centre is also home to adult education classes, with English lessons followed by a topic such as cookery or gardening. It all adds up to so much more than a campsite so it's well worth breaking your journey. *Camping US$7 pp; chalets US$35/50 sgl/dbl.* ⊕ *All year.*

Excursions from Monze

Fort Monze About 16km to the west of the town is the site of Fort Monze, which was one of the first police posts established in Zambia by the colonial powers. (Access is now only possible in the dry season, and the track is in very poor condition. It's signposted from town.) This post was founded in 1898 by the British South Africa police, led by Major Harding, who was subsequently buried in the cemetery here. The post was demolished soon after, in 1903, by which time the colonial authorities had a much firmer grip on the country. Now all that's left is a rather neglected graveyard and a monument in the shape of a cross.

Lochinvar National Park Lochinvar National Park, northeast of Monze, has been designated as a wetland of international importance for its very special environment. It's about 48km from Monze, and if you have an equipped 4x4 and some time to explore, then it's well worth a visit. See pages 458–63 for details.

MAZABUKA This large, bustling, tree-lined town, 349km from Livingstone and 124km from Lusaka (✪ 15°51.489'S, 27°45.747'E), is at the centre of a very prosperous commercial-farming community. The huge Zambia Sugar company (locally referred to as the Nakambala Sugar Estates) dominates the area, and you'll see their fields of mono-culture sugarcane lining the main road either side of town.

🏠 **Where to stay** Although Mazabuka has a wide range of simple guesthouses there is little to choose between many of them. The larger and better-quality options are:

🏠 **Royal Laricio** (15 rooms) m 0977 825205; e claramuyund@yahoo.co.uk. This friendly lodge is signposted on the right, half way up the hill towards Lusaka. All rooms are en suite with DSTV, fridge & tea/coffee facilities. It has a bar, restaurant, relaxing garden & conference facilities. **$$**

🏠 **Tukale Lodge** (12 rooms) Nyati Rd; ☎ 0213 230014; m 0977 779078; e tukalebookings@gmail.com. Another friendly option with en-suite dbl & sgl rooms, all with DSTV, AC, fridge & tea/coffee facilities. Tukale has a restaurant, bar, garden, secure parking & WiFi. To find it, head towards Lusaka & turn left at the top of the hill opposite the golf club & radio station; Tukale is on the right after 50m. A 2nd Tukale Lodge nearby has 18 rooms & the same facilities. **$$**

🏠 **Golden Pillow** (8 rooms) Livingstone Rd; ☎ 0213 321026; e goldenpillowlodge@yahoo.co.uk. With en-suite rooms, AC, DSTV, fridge & tea/coffee facilities, this, too, is at the top of the hill – behind a small bus stop on the left as you travel to Lusaka. There is also a bar, restaurant & lounge with TV. **$–$$**

🏠 **Linga Longa** (7 rooms) Chachacha Rd; ☎ 0213 230784; m 0977 875808; e linga.longa@

yahoo.com. The bright-green walls of the welcoming Linga Longa are easily spotted on the left on Chachacha Rd; to find it, pass Shoprite on your left, go over a crossroads & take the 1st right. Rooms offer a mix of en suite, AC, DSTV & fridge, depending on the price. Outside is a spacious, shaded garden & secure parking. **$**

🏠 **Namusa Lodge** (7 rooms) Chachacha Rd; m 0977 835392, 0966 136353; jsumbwa@yahoo. com. Close to Linga Longa, Namusa has a bar & restaurant, & is adding more rooms & internet facilities. At present, 6 roms are en suite with DSTV, AC & fridge. **$**

✕ **Where to eat** Both the supermarkets have their own fast-food outlets and bakeries, and several other fast-food joints serve snacks and larger meals, too. In the town centre, **Pumuna's** restaurant offers a broader range and more substantial meals, and there is a branch of the pizza chain **Debonairs**.

Outside of town on the left as you head towards Livingstone is **Bethlehem Bakery**. Run by St Bakhita Catholic Church it makes fresh and tasty bread, rolls, pizza slices, focaccia, burgers, pies, chips, biscuits and drinks, with all profits used to support the most vulnerable communities in the area. There is also a small arts centre next to the bakery. In the other direction, around 8km north of Mazabuka, the **Pama pub** serves takeaway meals and pub food all day, and the on-site butchery sells fresh, good-quality meat from the Pama farm. Slightly more expensive and more upmarket is **Nakambala** restaurant, in the heart of the Zambia Sugar estate (just ask for directions to the main gate), which serves more Western-style meals.

Other practicalities Along with Choma, Mazabuka is the most developed of the towns between Livingstone and Lusaka. Aside from several **fuel** stations both in town and on the way out to Livingstone, it has branches of all the major **banks** with ATMs, and two reasonably fast and reliable **internet cafés** (Hustlers and Makwembo). There is a major branch of **Shoprite** in the centre of town, and the **Kontola Hypermarket** on the roundabout leading from the town towards Livingstone. A range of smaller shops includes a **pharmacy**.

Around Mazabuka
Mwanachingwala Conservation Area This conservation area on the Kafue Flats, some 25km north of Mazabuka, covers about 470km² beside the Kafue River, northeast of Lochinvar, and just south of the river. It combines land contributed by the local community of Chief Mwanachingwala, with some of the private commercial farms in the area, and is rich in birdlife. The area is also home to the Kafue lechwe and the shy sitatunga.

There are currently no facilities for visitors, but those who make the journey are welcome to walk, fish, or hire a mokoro to explore the area's hidden lagoons. Arrangements can also be made to meet Chief Mwanachingwala and to visit his village, or a large, semi-permanent fishing village.

For access, in the dry season only, you'll need a 4x4. Head south of Mazabuka towards Livingstone for around 5km, then turn right on Ghana Road, cross the Kaleya Stream, then after 3km or so take another right to Etebe School. A further 3–4km brings you to a turn off to Mamba Fishing Camp – you're then on the Kafue Flats.

In theory, information about the area is available at the municipal offices in Mazabuka, and this is where arrangements to visit should be made. (If you're heading south, turn left turn at the junction by Shoprite, and they're on the left.) However, there's no guarantee that the office will be staffed, so be prepared to ask around and allow plenty of time.

MAZABUKA TO LUSAKA The final stretch of the journey between Livingstone and Lusaka covers a distance of 131km. North of Mazabuka, the road surface has deteriorated significantly, so take particular care on this stretch. The road passes through the Munali Hills, where – 56km north of Mazabuka – there's a sign to **Munali Hills historic site**, a stone cairn 1km along the Munali Pass road commemorating Livingstone's passage through the hill pass that separates the Lusaka high plateau from the Kafue Flats. (Munali, meaning 'you have been' or 'you have passed through', was the nickname given to Livingstone.)

Further north, you come to the small town of **Kafue**, which is the turn-off to Chirundu and the Lower Zambezi, and Siavonga on Lake Kariba. Look out at the junction for roadside stalls selling baskets, from small decorative items to large linen numbers. For details of this road and the town itself, see *From Lusaka to Chirundu*, pages 231–2.

LAKE KARIBA

Lake Kariba was created by the construction of a huge dam, started in November 1956 and completed in June 1959. It was the largest dam of its time – 579m wide at its crest, 128m high, 13–26m thick – and designed to provide copious hydro-electric power for both Zimbabwe and Zambia. It was a huge undertaking that turned some 280km of the river into around 5,200km² of lake. It has six 100,000kW generators on the Zimbabwean side, and five on the Zambian side – although the electricity generated here is promptly sold to Zimbabwe. The total construction cost was £78 million.

In human terms, construction of the dam immediately displaced thousands of BaTonga villagers, on both sides of the border, and took the lives of 86 workers in the process – around 18 of whom are entombed within the dam's million cubic metres of cement. It has opened up new industries relying on the lake, just as it closed off many possibilities for exploiting the existing rich game areas in that section of the Zambezi Valley.

It inevitably drowned much wildlife, despite the efforts of Operation Noah to save and relocate some of the animals as the floodwaters rose. However, the lake is now home to rich fish and aquatic life, and several game reserves (and lodges) are thriving on its southern shores.

For the visitor, Zambia's side of the lake is less well developed than Zimbabwe's and lacks a national park. Only on its islands, Chete and Chikanka, will you find much game. However, the fishing is very good and the small resorts of Siavonga and Sinazongwe make pleasant places to relax, or to base yourself for outings onto the lake.

There is a commercial ferry in operation on the Zimbabwean side between Kariba and Milbibezi; otherwise the only way to go on the lake is to hire your own boat, or to visit one of the islands (see pages 226–7 and 230).

HEALTH AND SAFETY AROUND THE LAKE

Bilharzia Bilharzia is found in Lake Kariba, but only in certain parts. Unfortunately, it isn't possible to pinpoint its whereabouts exactly; but shallow, weedy areas that suit the host snail are likely to harbour the parasites, and you're unlikely to contract bilharzia whilst in deep water in the middle of the lake.

See *Chapter 5*, pages 96–7, for more detailed comments on this disease. Local people who engage in watersports consider it an occupational hazard, and are regularly treated to expel the parasites from their bodies (those who can afford the treatment, that is).

Animal dangers The lake contains good populations of crocodiles, and also a few hippos. Both conspire to make bathing and swimming near the shore unsafe. However, it is generally considered safe to take quick dips in the middle of the lake – often tempting, given Lake Kariba's high temperatures and humidity. The crocodiles have apparently not yet learned how to catch water-skiers.

SIAVONGA

Approaching Siavonga The road to Siavonga (⊕ 16°32.371'S, 28°42.545'E) leaves the main Lusaka–Chirundu road (see page 231) a few kilometres west of the Chirundu Bridge over the Zambezi. From that turn-off, it is some 71km of rolling road (excellent tarmac) to North Bank Guesthouse in Siavonga, mostly through areas of subsistence farming. From Lusaka to Siavonga takes around 2½ hours. The area is relatively densely populated, largely the result of 'forced migration' when the dam was built and entire villages, such as Lusitu (⊕ 16°08.050'S, 28°44.329'E), which now lies along this road, were relocated. You can expect animals wandering over the road, so drive slowly. While straight after the rains this makes an attractive drive, enhanced by some marvellous ancient baobabs, during a visit I made at the end of

---

THE TRAP　　*Heather Chalcraft*

According to legend, the name of Kariba should be *kariwa*, 'the trap', for long ago a lake behind the hills broke through and the violent torrent tore out the gorge; when the water subsided it left behind a massive stone slab, the *kariwa*, until it collapsed.

The real trapping of the river took place on 2 December 1958, when the peaceful course that the Zambezi had run for centuries was stopped in its stride. This was the day on which the gap in the wall was closed. Less than 100 years ago, the Kariba Gorge was considered an obstacle to river navigation, for in its 26km the river ran fast. In 1912, a district commissioner visiting from Southern Rhodesia (now Zimbabwe) reported on the potential dam site with a view to irrigation of the Zambezi Valley. Ten years later, it was suggested as a source of hydro-electric power but, as in 1912, there was no money available for this. By 1937 it was recognised that the potential of Zambia's copper mines could not be realised without cheap electrical power but it was only in 1951 that Kariba was recommended as a suitable site for the construction of a dam.

The project was dogged by controversy. A similar scheme had already been suggested on the Kafue River, but the experts backed Kariba as it was the bigger of the schemes. When the announcement was made in March 1955 that the dam was to be built at Kariba there was outrage north of the Zambezi where politicians called it the 'Great Betrayal'.

Finance for the dam, a total of £80 million, came from a variety of sources, including the World Bank, the Colonial Development Corporation, the British South Africa Company and the Rhodesian Federal Government. The closing date for tenders was 17 April 1956 and one tender arrived in Salisbury (now Harare) with only ten minutes to spare – the aircraft with the courier from Italy had been delayed due to a technical fault. Three months later, the main contract for the construction of the dam and south-bank power station was awarded to an Italian firm – Impresit South Africa – at a value of over £25 million. Another Italian-controlled firm, Rhodesia Power Lines, was awarded the contract for the transmission lines at a value of nearly £10 million. The British companies that had tendered for the job were outraged.

the dry season, the problems of erosion and overgrazing seemed especially bad. Numerous gullies cut through the powdery red soil, there was little green grazing to be seen anywhere, and even the goats were looking thin. It is, though, a good route for roadside stalls – selling baskets in a range of sizes, as well as numerous pieces of quartz, for which you'll need to be prepared to bargain very hard. (And be aware, too, that some of these 'gemstones' are broken pieces of insulation glass.)

About 15km after the turning off the main road, there's a track to the left (⊕ 16°07.948'S, 28°44.290'E) leading to Ngombe Ilede, 'the cow that is lying down', some 13km away. Now designated a national monument, the flat, square, sacred stone lies in a stark landscape devoid of all but baobabs. More details can be found in D W Phillipson's book, *National Monuments of Zambia* (see *Appendix 3*, page 537).

Nearing Siavonga, the road winds its way around the hills in steep spirals, affording some superb views, before finally dropping down into the town, on the edge of Lake Kariba.

Like Kariba, its Zimbabwean neighbour over the dam, Siavonga has a strange layout as the result of being built on the upper sections of three or four hills – the lake's artificially created shore. What started out as a camp for the builders working

One of the earliest contracts awarded, to Costain, was for the construction of Kariba township where those involved in the building of the dam would live for the duration. Original estimates were that the township would take two years to complete, but this was cut down by a third. Work went on for 18 hours a day, seven days a week, with temperatures sitting at 43°C at 22.00 and 32°C at 05.00. Fitters took to carrying tools in buckets of water to prevent them becoming too hot. Houses, from foundations to door locks, were being completed at the rate of three every two days. A bank was built from start to finish in nine days.

The building of the dam was an outstanding engineering feat. A great river which could in the space of a few hours become a raging torrent had to be tamed; the site was remote with no roads leading to or from it; the gorge in which they had to work was narrow; and the temperatures and humidity were high. In November 1956, the first skip of concrete, two tons of it, was poured. This was only the first of nearly three million tons used in the wall – enough to pave a road from Zambia to Russia. On 22 June 1959 the last skip of concrete was released on the curve of the wall by the federal prime minister, Sir Roy Welensky – ten months ahead of schedule despite the floods of 1957 and 1958 when the Zambezi did its best to fight man's intentions.

Meanwhile virgin bush was being cleared to the north for the transmission lines – a job which was started in 1955 and was to take four years. The trees, which would be covered with water, were being pulled down and work was commencing on the south-bank power station. For those who worked at Kariba, they needed no references or testimonials – they only had to say 'I worked at Kariba' and the job was theirs. But there were human tragedies too – a number of people lost their lives during the construction of the dam; some are still buried within the wall. Eight of Chief Chipepo's people who were forcibly being moved to higher ground were killed during violent clashes with the police. And the human tragedies continue for those displaced people …

First published in The Lowdown, *January 2004*

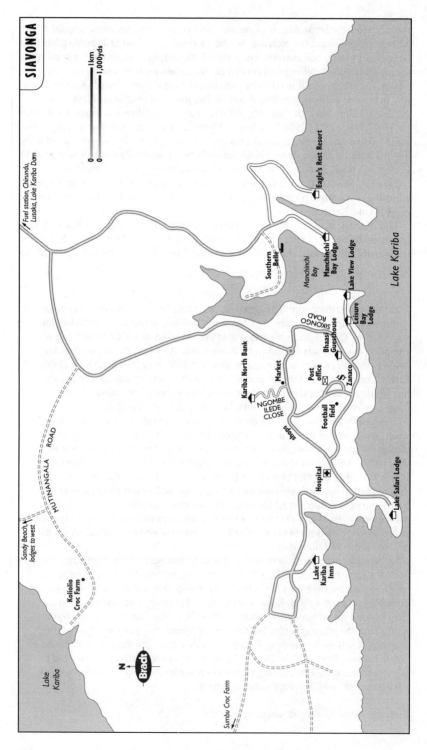

SIAVONGA

1km
1,000yds

Fuel station, Chirundu,
Lusaka, Lake Kariba Dam

Lake Kariba

Eagle's Rest Resort

Southern Belle

Manchinchi Bay

Manchinchi Bay Lodge

Lake View Lodge

SIKONGO ROAD

Bhaasi Guesthouse

Leisure Bay Lodge

Kariba North Bank

Market

NGOMBE ILEDE CLOSE

Post office

Zanaco

Football field

shops

Hospital

Lake Safari Lodge

MUTINANGALA ROAD

Sandy Beach,
lodges to west

Koliolio Croc Farm

Lake Kariba Inns

Lake Kariba

N

Bradt

Sumbu Croc Farm

222

on the dam in the 1950s eventually developed into a quiet holiday resort. There are a few things to do here, mainly focusing on the lake. The one thing that everyone should try is the local fresh fish (mainly *tilapia* bream) from the dam that is offered by all hotels and lodges.

Getting there and away Minibuses ply the route between here and Lusaka each day, costing Kw70,000 one way. Alternatively, you could take a minibus between Lusaka and Chirundu, then hitch from the junction.

Getting around The small town is quite spread out, and the roads curve incessantly, sticking to the sides of the hills on which the town is built. Each of the hotels is tucked away in a different little cove or inlet, and to get from one to another usually involves several kilometres of up-and-down, winding roads. So while you could walk everywhere, you'll find it much easier with your own transport.

Where to stay and eat Siavonga has a surprising amount of accommodation considering its size and relatively few attractions (though the lake itself is a powerful draw). The reason is its proximity to Lusaka – normally just 2½ hours' drive away – which makes it very convenient for conferences, the stock trade for almost all Siavonga's hotels. Because the town is used to the 'packaged' conference trade, check the rates for dinner, bed and breakfast, and full board – these are often good value, especially as there are no sparkling local restaurants to compete. On a quiet night, you can find a good bed at a reasonable price. Campers have less choice, but are well catered for at the refurbished Eagle's Rest, although those with their own transport could consider heading out to Sandy Beach. On the lake, the *Southern Belle* (see below) acts like a floating hotel, or there are boats for hire by the day or night (page 224).

On a practical note, the fact that this is predominantly a business area means that most of the hotels accept credit cards.

Lakeside

Lake Kariba Inns (46 rooms) 0211 253768/511249; m 0977 770480; e info@ karibainns.com; www.karibainns.com. With its pleasant gardens that afford good views, & a range of facilities, Lake Kariba Inns is arguably the best of Siavonga's options, though it's often full of convention participants, so it pays to book ahead. All rooms have en-suite shower, AC, & cable TV, while in executive rooms you can expect a small entrance hall, space for 2 children's beds if needed, & a veranda – some overlooking the lake. The food is good & the staff both efficient & attentive. As an added bonus, the hotel is introducing game on the adjacent hill, starting in 2011 with zebra, impala & puku.

The main building has a large bar, buffet restaurant, & the requisite pool, as well as a gym & sauna. Guests may use these & the pedal boats free of charge, but the new beauty salon overlooking the lake & other water-based activities, including fishing & boat trips, are extra. A steep set of stairs leads down to the water, many metres below, where the inn's boats – *Chipembere, Annelisa & Matusadona* (see page 227) – are usually moored. **$$$**

Lake Safari Lodge (60 rooms) 0211 511148; e info@lake-safari.com; www.lake-safari. com, www.lakesafari.com. This pleasant hotel is perched on a headland slightly above the water, & is a good choice for a few days by the lake.

Rooms, spread out between the main building & a slipway into the water, vary in size & quality, but all are en suite with AC, fridge, fan & – following a significant re-design – a view of the lake. Top in the view department, though, are the newest 'G' wing rooms, which boast jacuzzis & large, flat-screen TVs. By 2012 the simple rondavels will be gone, but the old *African Eagle* boat will be pulled up on land to provide budget accommodation.

For the energetic, the lodge has a gym, 2 excellent swimming pools & boating facilities that include cabin cruisers, speedboats & 'banana' boats. Inside, the bar is open most of the time, & popular with locals. The kitchen serves good food until late, including bream which the hotel farms itself. There's WiFi throughout, & the presence of conference guests justifies a business centre with internet. $$–$$$$

🏠 **Manchinchi Bay Lodge** (30 rooms) 📞 0211 232616/220220/511218/511283; 📱 0955 314119/849814, 0976 849814, 0977 757582, 0978 314119; 📧 info@manchinbaylodge.com; http://manchinbaylodge.com. In its heyday, this was Siavonga's plushest place, with the best gardens in town thanks to its extensive manicured lawns, shrubby borders, & a main swimming pool with an adjacent shallow one for children. Then standards slipped & the place went to seed, but now, thanks to a new owner, it seems to be getting back on track. The garden came first, the pool has been cleaned, & we understand that all the rooms have been refurbished. All have en-suite shower, AC, DSTV, kettle & a veranda with a view of the lake. With sundowner cruises as well, perhaps it's time to give the place another chance. $$$

🏠 **Leisure Bay Lodge** (20 rooms) 📞 0211 511136, Lusaka office 📞 0211 251734; 📧 gardengroup@zamtel.zm; www.gardengroupzambia.com. Nestled in a small cove with sandy beach & thatched umbrellas, Leisure Bay Lodge has a large patio restaurant & adjacent bar (with TV) which is often busy with locals – & is a good place to meet people. To the front, a recently built pool is a feature in itself, set in lawns right by the beach. Most of its small en-suite twin rooms overlook the lake, & all have AC. They're simple & clean – nicer than those at their sister hotels in Lusaka – yet still seem rather dingy. $$

In town

🏠 **Kariba North Bank Guesthouse** (9 rooms) 📞 0211 511197; 📧 karno@zamnet.zm. This pleasant guesthouse located high on a hill overlooking the town & lake was once for government staff only but is now open to the public; most of its clients are civil servants, business people & conference overspills. Rooms are very well appointed & spotlessly clean, each with a balcony, albeit with high walls so there

🏠 **Eagle's Rest Resort** (12 chalets, camping) 📞 0211 511168; 📱 0978 869126; 📧 eagles@siavonga-zambia.com; www.eaglesrestresort.com. Eagle's Rest is 10km from the Kariba Dam wall. To find it, turn left at the gate to Manchinchi Bay Lodge, & follow the winding road for about 1km. The only place in Siavonga itself to be geared more to tourists than to conferences, it has seen recent marked improvements. Each of its compact but renovated chalets has a dbl or twin beds, AC, fridge & en-suite shower & toilet, while outside is a sheltered area for preparing food, with a sink, & a BBQ overlooking the bay. The adjacent campsite is beautifully located & nicely maintained, with ablutions block & points for electricity & water. There's a modest restaurant/bar for b/fast, lunch & evening meals (*Kw40,000–80,000*), but much nicer is the lively thatched beach bar. With its pool & beach volleyball the place is popular with families, who can also do various watersports, canoe on the lake (*Kw60,000 pp*) or take part in sunset cruises (*Kw60,000 pp*), fishing trips (*from Kw450,000/4 people*); fishing tackle can be hired. For houseboat cruises on the *Bateleur* or *Mkwazi*, see page 227. *Chalet US$80 pp B&B; camping US$12 pp.*

🚢 **Southern Belle** (21 cabins) 📞 0211 511638/9; 📧 reservations@phsouthernbelle.zo.zm; www.proteahotels.com/southernbelle. The sweeping staircase from the central salon adds a touch of glamour to this large, 55m houseboat, based in Manchinchi Bay. Formerly in Zimbabwe, it was relaunched by Protea in Dec 2010 following a US$1 million refit. Dbl, twin & trpl en-suite cabins boast energy-efficient AC & satellite TV. With a separate restaurant, 2 bars, a conference room & a plunge pool with sunloungers on deck, it offers 2-night fixed-date cruises on the lake as well as group bookings & charters. Passengers can also take part in fishing trips, bush walks & cultural tours. *US$225–430/320–500 sgl/dbl FBA.*

is no view of the lake except from the suites. These, though, are huge, plush affairs with heavy drapes & heart-shaped beds – truly amazing! The kitchen's output is modest by comparison, offering typical government-guesthouse fare (chicken/beef/fish with rice/nshima/chips). $$$

🏠 **Bhaasi Guesthouse** 📱 0977 960526. This simple guesthouse has both en-suite rooms & those sharing facilities. $ *exc b/fast.*

Other places in town include the self-catering **Chimuthuzi Guesthouse** (❏ *0211 511381*), which is near the football field and has a difficult/rocky access; and the government-run **Lake View Lodge** (❏ *0211 511102/68*), which is usable at a pinch.

West of town Sandy Beach Safari Lodge is the most established lodge along the coast, but there are now several other options. To reach these, take the turning to the west about 2km north of Siavonga (✪ 16°24.290'S, 28°43.763'E). It's a very rough track, for which a high-clearance vehicle is essential, and a 4x4 in the rainy season. For the more westerly lodges, it's far easier to arrange a boat transfer with the lodge concerned than to drive yourself.

🏠 **Sandy Beach Safari Lodge** (8 rooms, camping) m 0955 824444, 0967 860739; e sandybeachzm@gmail.com, bookings@ sandybeachzambia.com; www. sandybeachzambia.com. ✪ 16°29.240'S, 28°39.874'E. It's a somewhat Bohemian affair, this lodge, about 16km from the turn off & set on a wide, red-sand beach with views south across the lake. German owner Herman & his nephew Alex share a decidedly laid-back approach. Come for the location, the tranquillity or perhaps to indulge in the multitude of activities (banana boats, canoeing, windsurfing, sailing, hiking trails, abseiling & even diving are on offer, depending on your experience), but don't expect any frills. A motley collection of chalets range from the basic to the simple, but all are adequate, some with en-suite shower, some with a fan, others with AC. Camping is possible, too, with campers using a shower & toilet in one of the rooms, or you can arrange to camp on Banana Island across the lake. Back on the beach, there's a convivial bar & restaurant serving all meals. **$$** exc b/fast (Kw35,000). Camping Kw30,000.

🏠 **Village Point** (4 chalets, 3 huts, camping) m 0979 523572/278676; e mail@village-point. com, nessylewis@yahoo.co.uk; http://village-point.com. Opened in 2007, this upmarket lodge run by Vanessa Hope is definitely geared to more hedonistic bush lovers. Set in 20ha on a peninsula in Lotri Bay, it is 40km west of Siavonga, or

30mins by speedboat. Tall chalets are perched above the lake with an open-fronted upper storey under thatch to make the most of the breeze – & the views. For the more budget minded, there's Mango Grove, designed in the style of a Zambian village, with both dbl-bedded huts & a larger one containing 4 beds. There's also a campsite, & tents can be hired. Dinner is served outside under the stars. To balance some excellent fishing, walking & birding opportunities, the lodge prides itself on its village tours & will in time be adding a spa. *Kw300,000 pp FB, exc drinks. Camping Kw20,000 pp, or Kw40,000 with hired tent.*

🏠 **Kotakota Hills** (4 chalets, 4 tents) m 0976 859830, 0977 553685; e info@kotakota. com; www.kota-kota.com. We have heard news of this upmarket lodge set in a private game reserve on the shore of the lake, about half way between Siavonga & Sinazongwe. There is a poor road to Chipepo from Chisekesi, but the lodge itself is usually accessed by ½hr boat transfer from Chipepo, or by air. The main area, of stone & thatch construction, sits right over the lake, while accommodation is a mix of similarly designed chalets sleeping up to 4, & safari tents set on high platforms. All are well appointed in a slightly rustic style, & all are en suite. On offer are game drives & walks, fishing, canoeing, village tours & beach dinners. *US$250 pp sharing FB inc 1 activity; exc bar, transfers.* ☉ All year.

Other practicalities Siavonga is quite a sleepy, relaxed place but it does have a **post office**, a few shops and a Zanaco **Bank** (☉ *08.15–14.30 Mon–Fri, 08.15–12.00 Sat*) with an ATM. These, together with the civic centre (which includes a police station and a courtroom), form the 'town centre' which is perched on one of the hills. The fuel station here has closed, but there are two options close to the turn-off to Siavonga from Lusaka.

For **shopping**, a simple supermarket and a bakery stock the basics, while fresh produce can be found at one of the town's two markets.

What to see and do Most of the activities in Siavonga revolve around the lake: boating, fishing and watersports (though note the comments on safety on pages 219–20).Visits to the dam wall are also possible. Overnight canoe trips into the used to be run by Vundu Adventures are no longer operating, though it's probably only a matter of time before another company fills the gap.

Watersports For windsurfing or waterskiing, try Lake Kariba Inns.

Lake/sundowner cruises Cruises are offered by Eagle's Rest and Lake Kariba Inns from around Kw60,000 per person.

Houseboats/fishing trips There are several options for hiring boats or pontoons (essentially floating platforms) in Siavonga (and Sinazongwe; see page 230) – especially through Lake Kariba Inns. For most you hire the whole boat, but there's also the *Southern Belle* (page 224), which accepts bookings from individuals, more like a floating hotel.

THE FOOD OF THE PAINTED WOMEN   *Heather Chalcraft*

Fishing for kapenta (*Limnothrissa miodon*) is an important commercial enterprise on Lake Kariba, giving a living to a significant number of people around the lake. It first came to the towns and cities of Zambia from Lake Tanganyika, although as early as 1860 the explorer Richard Burton had described the use of circular nets lowered from a canoe to catch fish attracted by the light of an *mbaula* (a wood-fired brazier). Today, kapenta rigs have enormous lights on the surface and are fitted with the same circular nets, although they are much larger, and the lights are lowered into the water. The lights attract the fish and, when there are sufficient numbers, the net is lifted to the surface with the catch.

The possibility of introducing kapenta into Lake Kariba was considered as early as 1956, although the first experimental attempts began in 1952. Under the supervision of Dr George Coulter, Senior Fisheries Officer in the then Northern Rhodesia, a brood of sardine fry of the genus *Limnothrissa* was netted near Mpulungu and placed into two galvanised-iron transport tanks. They all died within five hours. A second method, whereby the fry were caught in a large polythene net and placed in polythene bags, resulted in a greater survival rate, although mortality was still high. However, some individual fry survived and were growing beyond the maximum transportation size, so a trial run to Kariba of 350 fry was attempted. These were transported by road to Abercorn (now Mbala) Airport, by air to Kariba Airport and by road to the lakeshore.

At Kariba, 7½ hours after capture, 45% of the fry had survived. Half of these were introduced immediately to a lakeside storage dam where they all died within a few minutes, possibly because of a difference in water temperatures. The next day only 14 of the original 350 were still alive. These were placed in a keep-net in the lake where they lived and grew for more than three months until a storm wrecked the net and the fry escaped into the lake. Albeit accidentally, the first introduction of sardines to Lake Kariba had taken place.

But it was still not known whether they would find conditions suitable for breeding, nor which of the two species involved would be the better. Investigations were carried out and by September 1966 it was decided that

Bateleur (12 berth) Contact Eagle's Rest (page 224). A relatively large boat offering sunset cruises with a cash bar at Kw60,000 pp, as well as day & overnight trips sleeping up to 12 passengers. *Day trip Kw1,500,000 (up to 50 people); overnight Kw3,000,000 per night, plus Kw200,000 pp/day for catering.*

Chipembere Contact Lake Kariba Inns (page 223). A much simpler affair, *Chipembere* is little more than a flat pontoon, about 13m x 5m in size, with an engine at the back & flush toilet on board. Accommodating up to 30 passengers, it runs trips to the dam wall & the islands. Occasional booze cruises are run, with a cash bar, mainly over long w/ends (*Kw50,000 pp*). *Kw650,000 to dam wall; Kw670,000 to inc islands.*

Matusadona (6 berth) Contact Lake Kariba Inns (page 223). A proper houseboat, on which overnight cruises can be arranged, the *Matusadona* has 2 private cabins with bunks & one dbl cabin. There's a kitchen, bar & shower/toilet on board, & a shaded upper deck with a small plunge pool; you can sleep up here to keep cool. A small crew, including a chef, will normally accompany you, & a tender boat is brought along to allow forays to the shore. *US$500 per night, inc fuel, tender & fishing tackle.*

Visiting the dam Whilst you're here, take a walk over the dam wall (despite the border controls on each side) and perhaps even up to the observation point on the

Limnothrissa miodon, the larger, less specialised species, would be the one. *Limnothrissa miodon* was known to grow to 17cm in Lake Tanganyika and did not require such deep water for laying its eggs as the other species. Further experiments on the catching, handling, keeping and transportation of the sardines were undertaken until, in 1969, fish of varying sizes were caught in Lake Kariba and identified as kapenta, suggesting that they had not only survived but also bred in their new environment. The Kariba kapenta grew much smaller than the Tanganyika ones, reaching sexual maturity before a length of 5cm and rarely growing beyond 6cm.

The first attempts to catch the kapenta were made using banana boats, lights and scoop, and lift nets. The catches were not spectacular but large numbers of fish could be seen under the lights, and by the end of the first year some had been caught 64km east of Sinazongwe. It was not until 1976 that commercial fishing of kapenta started on the Rhodesian (Zimbabwean) side of the lake, followed by the Zambian side in the early 1980s, after Zimbabwe's independence. At night one can see the flickering lights across the dark waters of Lake Kariba. These are the fishing rigs at work. Catches are seasonal as during the summer months the kapenta move inshore to breed in protected bays. Commercial catches rise again after March when the adults return to open waters. However, if the rain has been poor, there is less food for them, which means poor harvests for fisherfolk (and for the fish and birds which feed on them).

But it is not only on Lake Kariba that man, fish and birds benefit from this 'silver gold'. These hardy little fish are sucked into the turbines and spewed into the stilling pool below the dam. They survive, only to fall prey to the hundreds of tern and kingfishers that are waiting for their dazed emergence at the dam's tailrace. Survivors have even made the 220km journey through a river devoid of plankton and infested with predators, to establish new shoals in Lake Cahora Bassa in Mozambique.

From an article first published in The Lowdown, *January 2004*

Zimbabwean side. In theory, if you leave your ID at the Zambian border post you are allowed to drive the 2km down to the dam wall and enjoy an east/west view of lake and gorges, huge spillgates, and Zam and Zim's power stations. Cars are not allowed to stop on the wall, which is for pedestrians only, but there is a place to park.

Across the border in Zimbabwe, there's an excellent little market at the Heights in Kariba, from where there are magnificent views of the lake. It's only a ten-minute drive, but with a Zimbabwean visa costing around US$50 for a single entry, is an expensive trip. The market is well known for its Nyaminyami sticks on which the river guardian is represented as a snake with its head at the top of the stick. The local carvers have become adept at carving intricate, interlinked rings and cages containing balls out of just one piece of wood. They're not cheap, but make great souvenirs.

Note that both Zimbabwe and Zambia are acutely aware of the vulnerability of the dam to damage or terrorist attack. So don't appear 'suspicious', and always ask before taking photographs – it may be just a wall to you, but it's of vital importance to them. There used to be morning tours available of the underground hydro-electric power station, so ask at the dam if these are still running.

Kapenta rig tour Kapenta are small, sardine-like fish, similar to whitebait, that were introduced on commercial grounds into Kariba in the 1960s (see box, pages 226–7). Since then, fishing for them has become an important new industry around the lake, in both Zimbabwe and Zambia. When dried, kapenta are tasty, high in protein, and very easy to transport: an ideal food in a country where poorer people often suffer from protein deficiency.

Look out over the lake at night and watch the fishing rigs use powerful lights to attract the fish into their deep nets. These are then brought back to shore in the early morning, sun-dried on open racks (easily smelled and seen), and packaged for sale. Short tours lasting a couple of hours in the early evening can be arranged to one of these rigs through the hotels in Siavonga, and you'll bring back fresh kapenta to eat.

Crocodile farms Siavonga boasts two private crocodile farms, both open to the public. At Kaliolio, located on the Mutinangala Road, the foreman most ably leads visitors around ('appreciation' appreciated). There's also Sumbu, situated past Lake Kariba Inns, but not signposted. Only the old/breeding crocs can be viewed here; the delicate youngsters are out of bounds (crocs are amazingly susceptible to disease). There's no guide around this place, though a worker might come running if he sees you.

SINAZONGWE Zambia's second small town on Lake Kariba is roughly equidistant between Livingstone and Siavonga. It is a typical small Zambian town, originally built as the fishing and administrative centre for the southern lakeshore area, and is used mainly as an outpost for kapenta fishing. Despite the town's location, its centre is actually up the hill away from the lake, with a couple of simple restaurants, a small hospital and the appropriately named Budget Guest House, while Sinazongwe post office is actually a couple of kilometres further inland, at Sinazeze.

When the lake was first flooded Sinazongwe was a much busier harbour, and even had the only lighthouse on the lake. Although its prosperity has faded somewhat, it is well placed to become the hub of operations for Zambian tourism to Lake Kariba, and its first campsite has now been developed into attractive self-catering chalets.

Getting there and away There's a good tar road from Batoka, signposted to Maamba Mines, on the main Lusaka–Livingstone road (30km northeast of Choma), to within 17km of Sinazongwe, and then the rest is a reasonable, all-weather gravel road. Hitching is certainly a possibility, and shouldn't be that difficult. Driving time to/from Lusaka is approximately four to five hours, or from Livingstone three to four hours.

By air Light aircraft charters from Lusaka cost around US$2,000 for a six-seater plane one way, or a little less if the aircraft is based in Livingstone. Sinazongwe lies almost directly beneath the flight-path between Livingstone and the Lower Zambezi National Park – between which there are occasional direct charter fights. Organising a seat on these would be tricky, so you must check with a knowledgeable tour operator.

Where to stay
Between them the two places in this area offer a wide range of accommodation suited to a variety of budgets.

Lakeview Lodge (3 chalets) m 0962 667752, 0976 667752; e reservations@lakeview-zambia.com, lakeviewzambia@gmail.com; www.lakeview-zambia.com. Clearly signposted about 1km from Sinazongwe, this tranquil lodge is an ideal place to unwind, with just reed cormorants & lizards for company. Overlooking the lake from their secluded, airy terraces are cream-painted chalets, simply furnished with 5 sgl beds, a low table & chairs, & en-suite shower, with ceiling fans to help out the breeze off the lake. Lawns lead down to the reed-fringed lakeshore, backed by large boulders that shelter a small sandy beach. There's an attractive dining room & trestle tables on the veranda, with stone pots & cooling ceiling fans. However, with new owners in 2011 there are plans to upgrade the rooms, as well as adding backpackers' accommodation, a fully licensed restaurant & bar, & a swimming pool with entertainment area. Activities will include fishing, sunset cruises, guided walks, & overnight camping on Chikanka Island. **$$**

Kariba Bush Club (2 houses, backpacker lodge, 4 chalets, camping) Siansowa; m 0979 493980; e info@karibabushclub.com; www.karibabushclub.com. Worth considering for a quiet couple of days, this complex is right on the lakeshore, over 60km from Sinazongwe. To get there, take the Maamba turn-off at Batoka, go past the Sinazongwe turn-off after Sinazeze & continue for about 30km on the tar, following the brown-&-white signs. About 4km before Maamba, at another signpost, take the good dirt road to the left. Follow this (& the signs) for about 30km to a security gate & on to the lodge (a total of 110km from Batoka).

At the heart of the club is the thatched Clubhouse standing among indigenous trees. This caters for backpackers & low-budget travellers, with 3 private rooms, a dormitory that sleeps 8, a 'honeymoon' chalet, & camping. All rooms have mosquito protection & fans. There are BBQ facilities & a self-catering kitchen, or you can dine in the restaurant on specialities such as crocodile & coconut curry, & lake bream. There's a lounge, a swimming pool & a bar with satellite TV (open till late), with a spectacular 200° view of the lake. A shop selling foodstuff, crafts, fishing tackle & basic amenities, plus an internet café, laundry, luggage storage & travel advice complete the package.

Baobab & Marula houses sleep 6 & 10 people respectively, so are ideal for families & groups of friends; both are fully equipped. Marula has 2 units: the main house (3 bedrooms, bathroom & toilet, kitchen, lounge with satellite TV, & verandas back & front), plus a 2-bedroom cottage with bathroom. Baobab has a kitchen, lounge, bathroom & 3 bedrooms – 2 twins & a dbl. There's a swimming pool which is partially shaded by some enormous trees, & the entire area is lawned to the lakeshore, making it cool during the hot months.

As well as sunset & dinner cruises (*US$25/40 pp*) & fishing (*US$35/70 pp ½/full day inc tackle*), there are tours of the large Zongwe crocodile farm (*US$20 pp*). *Marula US$350; Baobab US$275, both per night, self-catering; chalet US$85/110 pp B&B/FB; room US$30–35 dbl; dorm bed US$20 pp. Camping US$9 pp.*

Maaze Island Tented Camp (6 tents) Contact Kariba Bush Club. This self-catering camp, with en-suite tents, a main dining/lounge boma & a fully equipped kitchen, is on a private island overlooking a quiet bay. The island is stocked with various antelope (eland, kudu, defassa waterbuck, impala, reedbuck, zebra, wildebeest & warthog), as well as monkeys, baboons, hippos & crocodiles – & elephants have made their own way over. *US$45 pp self catering.*

Houseboats Although most houseboats are hired from Siavonga, Kariba Bush Club (above) runs group trips on the lake here.

🚤 *Eva* The smaller *Eva* sleeps up to 4 people in 2 cabins, with a lounge & kitchen, & dining area on the deck. *US$100/135 pp.*

🚤 *Kholisa* For larger groups, up to 30, there is the 13-cabin *Kholisa*, geared to a party crowd with a BBQ, music system & fishing tackle available. Most cabins have AC & en-suite facilities. *From US$70/100 pp self catering/FB.*

ISLANDS ON LAKE KARIBA Of the numerous islands on Lake Kariba, only two are currently inhabited, Chikanka and Maaze (see above); Chete has been closed for some years.

Chete Island

Chete is the largest island on the lake, and after a quick glance at the map you'll realise that it's much nearer to the Zimbabwean mainland (150m) than it is to Zambia (15km). This is because the border is defined as the deepest part of the Zambezi's old river course, not a line through the middle of the lake. In fact, the island lies just offshore from Zimbabwe's Chete Safari Area – so it's no surprise to learn that it's become recognised under Zambia's national parks system as a private wildlife reserve and bird sanctuary.

Chete is in a remote southern part of the lake, isolated except for the occasional twinkle from the nocturnal fishing of kapenta rigs in the distance. The island's game isn't tame, nor as dense as you'll find in the Luangwa or the better areas of the Kafue, but there is a sense of solitude and wilderness such as only a wild island like this can give. Its closest point of contact is really Sinazongwe, 17km away across Lake Kariba.

Much of the bigger game migrates to and fro between Zimbabwe and the island. This is especially true of the elephant bulls, but typically there's a resident breeding herd of around 80–100 elephants on the island. A pride of lion frequents the island, too, including a large male whose spore is often spotted following his strolls near the lodge in the early hours of the morning. Then there are perhaps half-a-dozen leopard, a herd of eland, and plenty of waterbuck, bushbuck, impala and some magnificent kudu. Not forgetting the many crocodile and hippo that surround the shores, and a wide variety of birds – some 378 species have been counted here and in the surrounding area. Vultures circle in the thermals over the high ground, and a solitary martial eagle may be spotted over the centre of the island, while lower down, numerous smaller birds come to the fore, including little bee-eaters and colourful blue waxbills.

Typically, a guided walk across the centre of the island takes around two hours. The landscape is very varied, similar in parts to Zimbabwe's Chizarira and Matusadonna national parks. Areas of dense cover, rugged interior woodlands and gorges contrast with lightly wooded clearings criss-crossed with game tracks; nearer the shore, the terrain opens up into expansive floodplains. There are no roads here, and now that the lodge is closed, the island is totally deserted.

Chikanka Island

Chikanka Island is now strictly an archipelago of three islands due to a rise in the level of the lake since it was formed. It lies about 8km from the Zambian mainland, 10km west–southwest of Chete and 18km southwest of Sinazongwe. Covering 240ha (2.4km²), it is smaller than Chete, and is also privately owned. The islands are mostly wooded, with mopane trees, marulas and the occasional baobab contrasting with the stark skeletons of drowned trees in the surrounding lake. Rock figs display their intricate root system; wild purple morning glory entwines its way through the waterplants along the shoreline, and dwarf plated lizards flash their brilliant blue tails as they dart among the rocks.

Chikanka has some plains game, including kudu, impala and bushbuck, and elephants occasionally visit too. Not surprisingly, there are also hippos and crocodiles around the shores, so it's not sensible to swim, but guided canoeing and game walks are offered. The channels between the islands boast a good variety of fish, including bream, tiger fish, Cornish jack and bottlenose.

🏠 **Where to stay**

🏠 **Chikanka Island Camp** (5 chalets) m 0962 667752, 0966 667752; e reservations@ lakeview-zambia.com, lakeviewzambia@gmail. com; www.lakeview-zambia.com. Reached by boat from Lakeview Lodge (page 229), & under the same ownership, Chikanka is a lovely spot to spend a night or two. A-frame chalets have been built on one of the islands, each in a peaceful & secluded spot on a low cliff, looking east over the lake towards Zimbabwe, so the view at dawn is truly memorable. Stone clad, with a Tonga-thatched roof, each chalet is gauzed to deter insects & is simply furnished with dbl beds (plus mosquito nets) & en-suite shower & toilet. Lighting is powered by a generator. There are also plans for overnight camping on the island for visitors to Lakeview Lodge. The large thatched dining area is fronted by a terrace that leads down to the lake, & a small paddling pool. *Kw400,000 pp FB (min 4 guests); drinks, transfers & fishing extra.*

FROM LUSAKA TO CHIRUNDU

Leaving Lusaka, you soon pass through the town of Kafue and, shortly before the busy turning to Livingstone, cross over the wide and slow Kafue River that is also heading to join the Zambezi. From here the road gradually, consistently and occasionally spectacularly, descends. It leaves the higher, cooler escarpment for the hot floor of the Zambezi Valley, before passing the turn-off to Siavonga and crossing the busy bridge at Chirundu into Zimbabwe.

This tar road is an important commercial artery, so is kept in reasonably good repair – though you can expect some outbreaks of pot-holes on the flatter sections south of Kafue. Between Kafue and Chirundu, lumbering trucks struggle to negotiate the steep, sharp bends, with breakdowns common and accidents all too frequent.

Occasional craft stalls set up on the side of the road sell carved wooden animals, drums, baskets and other mementos. The famous giraffe carvers have moved from their old spot near the turn-off to Lechwe Lodge and can now be found in thatched shelters near the point where the railway crosses the road. If you decide to buy, and you're flying home, remember that such carvings have to be put in the plane's hold, so make sure that they are very carefully packed.

KAFUE This straggling industrial town about 50km south of Lusaka is dominated by the Nitrogen Chemicals factory to the north, and lies close to the Norwegian-built hydro-electric dam on the Kafue River (see box, *Kafue River floods*, page 460). Kafue has a post office and a bus station, but more important for the visitor are two **banks** with ATMs, and the **fuel** stations: two in town, and a Total garage located towards Chirundu, just after the turn-off to Livingstone. Trips on the *Kafue Queen* (see below) offer the chance to explore the river.

Where to stay

Now that the excellent Lechwe Lodge has closed, options are limited to the rather mundane River Motel, a clutch of small guesthouses that predominantly serve the town's industries, and a relatively new community campsite.

House of Excellence Guesthouse
(12 rooms) m 0975 269671. In a quiet location yet just 200m from the main road, this pleasant new guesthouse is well signposted. Despite institutional corridors its clean, en-suite rooms are nicely kitted out with a fridge, kettle, AC & fan. There's a restaurant serving all meals, & a courtyard area with secure parking. **$$**

River Motel (48 rooms, 30 chalets, camping) Great North Rd; 0211 214139; m 0977 774613; e rivermotel@yahoo.com. About 5km south of Kafue, this large motel to the west of the main road is surprisingly good for a small-town hotel. Its relative prosperity is largely explained by the conference trade. En-suite rooms have a dbl or twin beds with simple wooden furniture, & a few have AC. Less attractive are slightly decrepit chalets with a small lounge, a bathroom with shower & bath,

& a kitchenette for which equipment can be supplied. Outside, is a limited space for camping. Facilities include a small gym, a good swimming pool & a cocktail bar; there is also a boat launch on the river. The restaurant serves buffet meals (Kw25,000–45,000); the staff are friendly; & the atmosphere is pleasant & relaxed. **$–$$**
Camping Kw50,000 pp.

Shingoma Campsite (chalets, camping) m 0955 813984, 0977 232949/232949; e finot@zamnet.zm. Working in co-operation with the *Kafue Queen* (see below), this riverside community site with hot showers has simple chalets & space for camping – with tent hire available at US$20/night. Camping rates include a river cruise, dinner, b/fast & a village tour. Access is by boat, so reservations are essential. Camping US$60 pp DBB; chalet US$65 pp plus transfers, self catering.

What to see and do

Launched in 2006, the colourful *Kafue Queen* (*contact via Shingoma Campsite, above; ⊕ departs 12.00 & 15.00 daily; Kw80,000 pp with cash bar; BBQ Kw35,000 pp*) offers the opportunity to explore the gorges of the Kafue River from a two-storey shaded pontoon boat that can take up to 100 passengers. The boat leaves its mooring just north of the bridge over the river, some 8km south of Kafue town, making its way downstream past a number of local villages and into the gorges. Aside from hippo and crocodile, wildlife along this stretch includes the Cape clawless otter, and the birding potential is excellent, with numerous species of kingfisher, as well as African fish eagles and black eagles. Each cruise lasts 2½–3 hours.

There are **fishing** (*Kw600,000/½day*) and **speedboat** (*Kw400,000/hr*) trips too, or visitors can picnic and fish from the bank at the jetty (*Kw10,000/day*), where there are thatched shelters & cold drinks.

Tours of the **Kafue Dam**, at the eastern end of the gorges, can occasionally be arranged with the Zambian electricity suppliers, ZESCO, which even has its own small lodge for both conference and individual visitors.

CHIRUNDU BORDER AREA

A few kilometres before Chirundu, just 500m after the turn-off to Siavonga and Kariba, is the Chirundu Forest Reserve – a small area around the road where the remnants of petrified trees can be seen strewn on the ground. There's a small parking spot on the right, where there may be baskets for sale, too.

The border post at Chirundu always seems to be busy with a constant stream of trucks going through, or at least waiting to go through. There's a BP garage here – though it hasn't had **fuel** for some years (the nearest supply is at Gwabi River

Lodge). There's a selection of basic **shops**, a Zanaco **Bank**, a **post office**, a good mission **hospital**, and a handful of **cheap lodgings**, including Chimpakasa Lodge and Dreamland Guesthouse. Chirundu is a promising place to look for a lift if you are hitchhiking, but otherwise there is a slightly seedy, unsafe feel typical of a town where many people come and go, but few ever stay.

Getting to the Lower Zambezi The unsignposted dirt road to Gwabi River Lodge and the Lower Zambezi branches east from the main road about 200–300m from the border. It's often clogged with parked trucks. To find it, pass the Manica Freight Company office, and turn left opposite the sign to the Zanaco Bank. After just over 5km you'll pass the sign for Zambezi Breezers, then a further 6.5km on is the Gwabi turn-off. From here, after another 2km, the road descends to the Kafue River. To reach Chiawa or anywhere beyond, the river currently has to be crossed on the pontoon, but rumours of a bridge to be built over the river are gaining momentum.

Where to stay

Zambezi Breezers (10 tented chalets, 7 rooms, camping) m 0977 628120, 0979 279468; e zambezibreezers@gmail.com; http://sites.google.com/site/zambezibreezers, www.zambezibreezers.com (under construction) (⊕ 15°59.112'S, 28°52.833'E). Right on the banks of the Zambezi River, this Dutch-owned camp is about 7km from Chirundu. To get there, follow the directions above, then turn right on to a good 2WD track for a further 2km. A taxi from Chirundu should cost around Kw60,000.

It's a wide, riverside site with lawned gardens & a small pool, backed by a large, open-fronted bar & restaurant with an à-la-carte menu ($$$) that ranges from toasties to fish & steak, veggie options to local dishes. Tented twin, dbl & family chalets on low wooden decks have been cleverly designed to give a wide river frontage, extra height to increase the flow of air, & mosi nets that curtain off the whole bedroom. All but 1 are en suite. Cheaper are basic twin rooms which share clean ablutions at the spacious, grassy campsite. It's all simple & unpretentious, but very well maintained & with mains electricity. Activities focus on fishing & game viewing by boat (US$60 ½day, plus fuel), with some rods & tackle for hire. Chalet US$75/140 sgl/dbl B&B; room US$40 exc b/fast; camping US$10 pp. ⊙ All year.

Gwabi River Lodge (8 chalets, 4 tents, camping) 0211 515078; m 0966 870222, 0979 650920; e gwabi@mwebafrica.com; www.gwabiriverlodge.com. This well-known small lodge, self styled 'the gateway to the Lower Zambezi', changed hands in 2011, & improvements are ongoing. Some 12km from

Chirundu, it is set in green lawns on the Kafue River, 3km from its confluence with the Zambezi. You'll find everything has its price here, from a bag of ice to use of the car park for non-residents (US$5/night) – but these prices are generally reasonable. Crucially for drivers, the lodge has a fuel station (petrol & diesel) & a small workshop for minor repairs, including tyres. For those without transport, there's a weekend shuttle from Lusaka (Fri–Sun), & boat transfers to other lodges along the river.

The en-suite chalets, already solidly built with stone floors, AC, mains electricity & DSTV, are being further upgraded in 2012. Camping – with your own kit or in pre-erected twin-bedded tents – is along the river, on a well-lit site with ablution block, braai & electric points, & nightly entertainment from a percussion band of painted reed frogs. There's a great pool, overlooking the river (some distance below) with superb sunset views from the terrace, & a cool bar with pool table & sports TV. A-la-carte menus incorporate everything from b/fast to sandwiches to steaks.

As well as boat cruises, river-based activities include fishing (boat hire US$60/115 ½/full day plus fuel), with rods & tackle available for hire, & canoeing (US$25/day per boat, & guide US$25/day). Overnight canoe trips of up to 3 nights can be organised. You can also rent speedboats. In the off season, fishing in the dams is a great treat for children. There are guided walks, too; the lodge is fenced & small game can be found on the property, while elephant & hippo are often seen from the river. US$55/65 pp sharing/sgl B&B; tent US$35 pp B&B; camping US$10 pp.

The Lower Zambezi Valley, from the Kariba Dam to the Mozambique border, has a formidable reputation for big game – leading UNESCO to designate part of the Zimbabwean side as a World Heritage Site. The Lower Zambezi National Park protects a large section of the Zambian side. Across the river, much of the Zimbabwean side is protected by either Mana Pools National Park or various safari areas. This makes for a very large area of the valley devoted to wildlife, and a terrific amount of the bigger game, notably elephants and buffalo, actually cross the river regularly.

However, take a look at a map of the Zambian bank and you'll realise that the land up to 55km east from the Kafue River (from Gwabi River Lodge) is not in the national park at all; the river defines the border with the Chiawa Game Management Area (GMA), which is owned by the operators within the area, obtained with permission from the chieftainess. Only to the east of the Chongwe River are you in the national park.

As you might expect, the game densities increase as you travel east, with the best game in the national park, and fewer animals on the privately owned land nearer to Chirundu. The situation is similar on the other bank of the river, in Zimbabwe, so if you want good game viewing then do get into the park if you can, or at least near to it.

GEOGRAPHY From Chirundu to the Mozambique border, the Zambezi descends 42m, from 371m to 329m above sea level, over a distance of over 150km. That very gentle gradient (about 1:3,500) explains why the Zambezi flows so slowly and spreads out across the wide valley, making such a gentle course for canoeing.

From the river, look either side of you into Zambia and Zimbabwe. In the distance you will spot the escarpment, if the heat haze doesn't obscure it. At around 1,200m high, it marks the confines of the Lower Zambezi Valley and the start of the higher, cooler territory beyond which is known as the 'highveld' in Zimbabwe.

The valley is a rift valley, similar to the Great Rift Valley of east Africa (though probably older), and it shares its genesis with the adjoining Luangwa Valley. The original sedimentary strata covering the whole area are part of the karoo system, sedimentary rocks laid down from about 300 to 175 million years ago. During this time, faulting occurred and volcanic material was injected into rifts in the existing sediments. One of these faults, the wide Zambezi Valley, can still be seen. In geologically recent times, the Zambezi has meandered across the wide valley floor, eroding the mineral-rich rocks into volcanic soils and depositing silts which have helped to make the valley so rich in vegetation and wildlife. These meanders have also left old watercourses and oxbow pools, which add to the area's attraction for game.

So look again from one side of the valley to the other. What you see is not a huge river valley: it is a rift in the earth's crust through which a huge river happens to be flowing.

FLORA AND FAUNA
Flora Most of the park, made up of higher ground on the sides and top of the escarpment, is thick bush – where game viewing is difficult. This is broadleafed miombo woodland, dominated by brachystegia, *julbernardia*, *combretum* and *terminalia* species. Fortunately, there's little permanent water here, so during the dry season the game concentrates on the flat alluvial plain by the river.

Acacia species and mopane dominate the vegetation on the richer soils of the valley floor, complemented by typical riverine trees like leadwood (*Combretum imberbe*), ebony (*Diospyros mespiliformis*), and various figs (*Ficus* species). Here the riverine landscape and vegetation are very distinctive: similar to the Luangwa Valley, but quite different from other parks in the subcontinent.

Perhaps it is the richness of the soils which allows the trees to grow so tall and strong, forming woodlands with carpets of grasses, and only limited thickets of shrubs to obscure the viewing of game. The acacia species include some superb specimens of the winterthorn (*Faidherbia albida*, which used to be known as *Acacia albida*), and the flat-topped umbrella thorn (*Acacia tortilis*). Both of these produce seedpods which the game love, the former looking like apple-rings, the latter being tightly spiralled seedpods which are very nutritious (19% protein, 26% carbohydrate, 5% minerals). It all results in a beautiful, lush landscape that can support a lot of game, and is excellent for the ease of viewing which it allows.

Mammals The Lower Zambezi has all the big game that you'd expect, with the exceptions of rhino (due to poaching), giraffe and cheetah. Buffalo and elephant are very common, and can often be seen grazing on the islands in the middle of the river, or swimming between Zimbabwe and Zambia. It is normally safe to get quite close by drifting quietly past these giants as they graze.

The antelope in the valley are dominated by large herds of impala, but good populations of kudu, waterbuck, bushbuck, zebra and the odd duiker or grysbok also occur. Giraffe are notable for their absence – in fact, there's no record of them ever having lived here.

Lion, leopard and spotted hyena are the major predators. There have long been plans to re-introduce cheetah but these have not yet come to fruition. On my first visit, back in 1995, lion were very visible, with one marvellous pride having in excess of 30 animals – and the game viewing has improved a lot since then. Many of the larger trees have branches that seem made-to-measure for leopards, which are sometimes seen on night drives, and increasingly during the day, too. There are also positive plans to re-introduce rhino into the park.

In the river, crocodile and hippo are always present, but look also for the large water monitor lizard, or *leguvaan*, and the entertaining Cape clawless otter, which both occur frequently though the latter are very seldom seen.

Birds Around 350 species of bird have been recorded in the valley. By the river you will find many varieties of water-loving birds like pied, giant, woodland, malachite and brown-hooded kingfishers, to name the more common of the species. Similarly, darters, cormorants, egrets and storks are common, and fish eagles are always to be found perching on high branches that overlook the river. Less common residents include ospreys, spoonbills and African skimmers, and it's rich in waders, both resident and migrant.

CONSERVATION
Poaching In the 1940s, due to numerous severe outbreaks of sleeping sickness, several villages were evacuated from this area, which became a hunting concession from the 1960s. Although the valley was classified as a national park in 1983, in the mid-1980s, commercial poaching for ivory and rhino horn completely wiped out the park's black rhino population, and threatened to do the same to the elephants. Fortunately, the CITES ban on the world ivory trade did much to stop this; the elephant population in the park is now good, and the Lower Zambezi's game is generally in good shape. That said, as in most national parks, three types of poaching still occur in the Lower Zambezi: commercial ivory, commercial bushmeat and subsistence (mostly snaring). However, ZAWA teams stationed around the park,

with the assistance of Conservation Lower Zambezi, carry out law-enforcement patrols on a daily basis to minimise the impact on wildlife.

Conservation Lower Zambezi Committed to the conservation and sustainable use of the valley's wildlife and natural resources, Conservation Lower Zambezi (CLZ; *www.conservationlowerzambezi.net*) focuses on environmental protection, education and supporting local community development.

Funded principally by the camps in the Lower Zambezi as well as concerned individuals and companies, CLZ provide logistical support – food, fuel and communications – to the ZAWA patrol teams, mounts aerial patrols and facilitates research projects. Schoolchildren from the surrounding communities are also able to learn about their local wildlife through visits to the activity centre. Supporting CLZ helps to protect the wildlife and environment in this area from illegal killing and degradation, both through short-term law enforcement and long-term community involvement.

GETTING THERE There are three means of getting into this area: by road, by air and by boat – or any combination of these. Most visitors stay at one of the private camps as a base, and go for game-viewing drives, walks and trips on the river from there. Arriving by air is certainly the fastest means of transport. Planes land at one of several airstrips in the valley, including Royal Zambezi, Jeki and Kulefu, with the drive to and from the lodges being an activity in itself. A few lodges can arrange for transfers by road and river from Lusaka, though this tends to be very expensive.

More economical, for those with their own vehicle, is to drive to Gwabi River Lodge (page 233) and arrange to be collected from there by boat; again, this is an experience that is an intrinsic part of a trip. Alternatively, the well equipped can drive themselves all the way (see below), but this is neither an easy nor a fast option. A middle ground could be to go with a budget safari operator such as:

Bongwe Safaris m 0978 164038, 0976 012590; e safari@bongwesafaris.com; www. bongwesafaris.com. This Lusaka-based company runs 3-night/4-day budget safaris out of Munyemeshi Lodge (page 244). Meals are prepared by their own staff, & groups are accompanied by an experienced guide to lead game drives, walks, boat trips & canoeing, both in the park & in the GMA. Other than a cash bar in camp, everything is included in the price. There's also an 8-day Kafue/Lower Zambezi combo, with other options on request. *3-day US$810 pp FBA, inc park fees, transfers from Lusaka; 8-day US$1,500 pp inclusive.*

Finally, there are popular canoe safaris (pages 239–40) that run along the river, using simple temporary fly-camps at night.

Visiting independently The adventurous and well equipped can drive in with their own vehicles, either staying at lodges or camping – which means bringing all supplies and camping gear. Note that the only fuel available within the whole area is to be found at Gwabi Lodge (page 233), which also offers minor repairs, including tyres.

The roads into the park need a 4x4 vehicle (ideally two, for safety's sake) but are not difficult driving in the dry season, though the going can be very slow. Get detailed maps of the whole valley before you leave Lusaka, and pack a compass and GPS.

From Chirundu As you enter Chirundu, turn left onto a dirt road signposted to Zambezi Breezers and Gwabi River Lodge, and follow this road for about 8km to the pontoon across the Kafue River (⊕ CHIAWP 15°56.667'S, 28°52.500'E. *Foreign-registered vehicle US$28 one way; Zambian-registered Kw56,000;* ⏲ *06.00–18.00).* The village by the pontoon has a police post and a small, very basic grocery; don't raise your expectations. From here you'll be in the Chiawa GMA, and it's largely a case of sticking close to the river, and following the main track. As far as Chiawa village, this runs alongside fertile fields, where maize, paprika, bananas and beans are the staple crops, and passes numerous small homesteads. About 16km from the pontoon, a sign for Chiawa Cultural Village (⊕ CHIACV 15°50.230'S, 29°07.061'E) marks a fork; for the national park, bear right here, effectively turning into Chiawa village.

The western entrance to the national park, Chongwe gate, lies about 46km from here, or 62km from the pontoon. The route is pretty clear as far as the newly tarred Royal airstrip, which you'll pass on your right. However, about 3km beyond the airstrip you come to a fork (⊕ FKAIR 15°43.046'S, 29°19.308'E); Bear left here, and another 4km or so will bring you to the Chongwe River. From here, the Chongwe gate into the national park (⊕ CHONGG 15°42.093'S, 29°20.045'E) is a further 4km. Once inside the national park itself, the terrain is dominated by broad plains, dotted with baobab trees and inhabited only by plains animals and birds, before eventually dropping down into *albida* forest where shallow lagoons among the trees attract brightly coloured saddle-billed storks.

From the Great East Road For those heading for the eastern side of the park, there's a little-known access road that starts from the Great East Road, some 100km east of Lusaka. It's rough, slow going, and easy to get lost; travelling in convoy is a must and a GPS essential. To find the start of the road, go past Chongwe village, then turn right shortly after the village of Shingela (⊕ TUSHIN 15°14.188'S, 29°10.032'E). From here, follow the road to the Mukanga gate (⊕ MUKANG 15°21.015'S, 29°17.135'E). Shortly after the gate there's another checkpoint marking the entrance to the Chakwenga Mine. The road then drops over the escarpment, a steep descent culminating in a series of sandy riverbeds, and the main game-viewing area on the valley's floor in the Kulefu area, eventually coming out at ⊕ TUCHMN 15°36.577'S, 29°40.167'E, between Jeki airstrip and Old Mondoro. You'll need to allow at least five hours from the Great East Road to Kulefu.

From Lusaka Another equally poor 4x4 track starts from Leopards Hill Road in Lusaka, and gradually deteriorates as it winds its way down the escarpment. It finally emerges at ⊕ EXLEOP 15°55.880'S, 28°57.205'E, opposite cultivated fields and close to Chiawa village.

ACTIVITIES Most of the lodges along the river offer similar activities, concentrating primarily on drives, boat trips, walking safaris, canoeing and fishing, but each has its own individual atmosphere and areas of expertise, and some specialise. Outside the park, some of the lodges also offer village visits, or trips to Chiawa Cultural Village.

Game drives Day and night drives, both in the Chiawa GMA and into the Lower Zambezi National Park (⏲ *Jun–Oct*), are high on the list of priorities for most visitors. They are offered by almost all camps, whether they're located inside or outside the park – though it's worth remembering that the further you are from the national park, the less game you're likely to see; game drives on the west of the GMA can be uneventful.

Walking safaris Walking safaris with a professional guide, and an armed scout, are also widely available, affording the opportunity to get closer to the wildlife on their terms. There are now strict exams, organised by the CLZ (see page 236), for potential guides which match the quality and scope of those in the Luangwa Valley. I would never go walking with an unqualified guide. Most trips are two to four hours, and done as an activity from a lodge or camp.

Birdwatching Birdwatching is usually built into most walks, drives or boating trips if you're interested. With a range of habitats it's a great place for birdwatching at any time, but especially from September to March, when migrants from central Africa can be spotted in the area.

Fishing Fishing on the Zambezi – primarily for tigerfish – is also offered by most outfits, and is at its best when the waters are clear, from around May to June until towards the end of the year. Catch and release is practised by all lodges/camps, both within the GMA and in the national park, where it is obligatory. Fishing is banned between December and February, but many of the lodges are hoping to be allowed to continue to fish on a catch-and-release basis during that period. Those fishing in the national park will need a permit (*US$5 pp/day*).

In recent years a deal has been struck with the local community to prevent over-fishing. In return for financial compensation for the community, it has been agreed that there will be no netting of fish either in the GMA or in the national park.

Canoeing Canoeing on the Zambezi is another firm favourite for the more adventurous. It's a terrific way to relax in the open air and see the river, whilst doing some gentle exercise and game viewing at the same time. Most operators use stable Canadian-style fibreglass canoes which are 5.7m long, and large enough for two people plus their camping equipment and personal belongings. Trips are usually limited to a maximum of five canoes led by a fully qualified canoe guide; while this means that the guide has control over the group, you could still occasionally find yourself closer to a pod of hippos than to your trusty guide.

Broadly there are two different ways to go canoeing. You can canoe as an activity from a lodge or camp, or you can canoe from A to B, sleeping on islands or at points on the bank along the way.

Canoeing guides In the 1990s the question asked about these canoeing trips was always 'Which section should we canoe?' Now the question is more usually 'How qualified is the guide?' Paddling for miles through areas with little game seems to have fallen out of fashion, and now more people are doing less mileage, but aiming to see a lot more game. They want to canoe inside the park, and they want a good guide. (Often this means more canoeing from camps, and fewer paddles from A to B.)

You should understand from the outset that canoeing on this river has a risk attached to it that no guide can ever take away. Even with the very best of guides, it's possible to get into dangerous, even life-threatening, situations with both hippos and crocs. People are killed and injured every year on this river. However, canoeing with, and listening to, a good guide who knows the river will give you the best chance of avoiding dangerous situations, and of escaping those which prove unavoidable.

Day or overnight trips: from a camp or lodge Most of the lodges/camps along the Lower Zambezi will offer options for you to go canoeing for your morning or afternoon activity, taking about three to four hours paddling at a time. Typically, you're driven upstream with the canoes, and you paddle back to the lodge.

This has several advantages. Firstly, there's no hurry, so the guide can build in time to stop and investigate the game *en route*; secondly, if you're at a good lodge then you're probably spending all of your time in a prime game area, within the park; thirdly, you're not committing yourself to more than three or four hours paddling; finally, you've got a comfortable bed lined up for the night back at camp. Occasionally lodges organise full-day or even overnight trips.

Longer trips: from point to point On these trips you put all your kit in the canoe, and paddle downstream for a number of days. Typically, you'll carry tents and food, and camp *en route*.

Physically, you will feel tired at the end of a day, but canoeing downriver is not excessively strenuous (unless you meet a strong headwind), and no previous experience is demanded. To some extent that feeling of exertion often leads to a feeling of achievement at the end of the trip, which increases with the length of the trip and the distance covered.

Canoe safaris were started on the Zimbabwean side in the early 1980s and were led by qualified canoe guides who had to pass National Parks examinations. In the early 1990s, with the emergence of the Lower Zambezi National Parks Wildlife Protection Programme, Zambia also started canoe safaris. As in Zimbabwe, these became enormously popular among more adventurous visitors.

Which section to canoe? Several different canoe safaris run through different sections of the Lower Zambezi River. The first, taking two nights/three days, covers the uppermost section of the river from Kariba to Chirundu, with the Kariba Gorge a highlight early on. The stretch from Chirundu to the mid-Mana Pools region of the Lower Zambezi River features larger numbers of game and birdlife due to the proximity of the national parks on both sides of the river, and takes four nights/three days. The final section, undoubtedly the wildest, runs through the entire length of the two national parks, passing through floodplains and the spectacular Mpata Gorge, and ending at the confluence of the Luangwa River some 163km downstream; for this, allow eight nights/nine days.

Costs include basic camping kit, food (and wine with the evening meal), guide, canoes, paddles etc. Transfers are extra.

Canoeing operators There really isn't the choice of trips, or operators, doing longer canoe trips here that there were in the early 1990s. Several lodges offer canoeing as one of several activities, or even full-day trips, and both Kiambi Lower Zambezi (opposite) and Gwabi Lodge (page 233) organise expeditions lasting from one to four nights. There is also one dedicated specialist:

Zambezi River Adventures aka **River Horse Safaris** m +263 772 235311/ 772 235340/ 773 523848; e zambezi@iwayafrica.com; www. zambezicanoeing.com. From their base close to Chiawa Cultural Village, River Horse operates 2–8-day canoeing safaris on the Lower Zambezi.

These range from the 2-night/3-day Zambezi Short (*US$450 pp*), to the 8-night/9-day Zambezi Explorer (*US$1,198 pp, min 4*); both exc park fees. There's a maximum of 5 18ft 2-man Canadian-style canoes per safari. Trips can also be tailormade. No children under 14 unless by prior arrangement.

Chongwe Falls (⊕ 15°41.173'S, 29°18.581'E) These accessible falls on the Chongwe River, which forms the western boundary of the Lower Zambezi National Park, make a beautiful picnic spot with some good birding. You can clamber up the rocks to see the falls from above, or try your hand at fishing, but don't be beguiled by the still waters; there are large crocs lurking in there so a cooling dip is out of the question.

Cultural tourism Several of the lodges at the western end of the valley offer village trips, some on an informal basis, but others to **Chiawa Cultural Village** (⊕ CHIACV 15°50.230'S, 29°07.061'E; *admission US$10 pp*), which is about 25km east of the pontoon and clearly signposted. Access is either by boat, or by road.

The village was established with funds from the African Wildlife Foundation to showcase the cultural traditions of the local Goba people, and at the same time to raise funds for orphans and other vulnerable people within the community. In this way, people from the villages around the national park get the chance to benefit from the conservation of wildlife and the not-inconsiderable wealth that tourists bring to the area.

Visitors are usually greeted by a group of dancers, an interactive display that can be considerable fun. A guide is on hand to explain the history of the Goba people and to look at many aspects of traditional village life: from cooking and medicinal herbs to clothes, toys and weapons. There are full-size village huts, an interesting museum or interpretive centre, a curio shop, and even a look-out post for elephants (with a great view of the river). Cold drinks are available on site, and a campsite is at the planning stage.

WHERE TO STAY There are several lodges in the valley and a few campsites as well. Almost all are good, although they have quite different styles of operating. For the most part, power is either solar generated or supplied by battery, so needs to be used sparingly. With advance booking and a 4x4, you can drive yourself into any of these, but most people arrange for a transfer by road or charter flight. Establishments to the west of the national park are in the Chiawa GMA. All visitors in the park will be asked to pay a levy of US$2 per person per day towards Conservation Lower Zambezi (see page 236), an organisation committed to the protection of the wildlife and habitat of the national park and the Chiawa GMA. Looking at the various establishments from west to east:

Outside the national park in the Chiawa GMA

🏠 **Kiambi Lower Zambezi** (3 chalets, 8 Meru tents, 2 cottages, camping) m 0977 876003/186106, 0966 655878; e kiambi@ coppernet.zm; www.kiambi.co.za. ⊕ KIAMBI 15°56.170'S, 28°55.520'E. Clearly signposted 12km from the Kafue pontoon, Kiambi is the first lodge that you come to en *route* to the national park; by boat, it's just 5mins from the pontoon. It is set at the confl uence of the Zambezi & Kafue rivers with views across to Kanyemba Island. With relatively easy access & reasonable rates, the camp is popular with w/enders & can get very busy. Power is supplied by mains electricity.

The camp has several accommodation options. The original Meru tents under thatch are erected on polished wooden platforms with a large veranda, some with a river view. Inside are dbl or twin beds (with space for a further 2) & a reed-enclosed shower, toilet & washbasin. More upmarket are en-suite 'luxury' chalets, complete with AC & TV. There are also self-catering cottages sleeping up to 6 in 3 twin bedrooms, or 2 bedrooms & bunks in the lounge, with a bathroom, fully equipped kitchen & a fireplace/braai area overlooking the river. Finally, there's the flat, grassy campsite, where 8 pitches each have their own fireplace & braai, & the ablution block has hot showers privately enclosed by reed & wooden walls. The campsite has its own pool, & an air-conditioned bar with snooker table & DSTV. Snacks are available here, or campers may eat at the lodge by prior arrangement (*dinner US$23*), subject to availability.

High over the river, next to a young baobab, the main camp's lounge/bar has great river views from the terrace. Behind is a cool, thatched dining area surrounded by reed walls, although dinner is normally served around the fire. There's a small pool nearby, & a tiny thatched gym overlooks the river. Kiambi specialises in canoeing, from 3hr trips (*US$37 pp*) to guided overnight expeditions with a crew to set up camp & cook (*US$156 pp/day FB*). Ideally these should be prebooked. Fishing is a prime attraction, too (*US$77/½ day inc 10 litres fuel*) with rod & reels for hire (*US$7/day*), & some tackle for sale. Other activities include cruises in canopied flat-bottomed motorboats, which hold up to 12 people. *Chalet US$181/220, tent US$146/198, all pp sharing/sgl FB; 2 nights inc sunset cruise; 3 nights inc ½-day canoeing. Self-catering cottage US$198–242 (up to 6). Camping US$11 pp; 2-man tent/bedding hire US$8/night).*

🏠 **Kanyemba Lodge** (6 rondavels, 1 house) m 0977 755720; e info@kanyemba.com; www.kanyemba.com. ⊕ KANYEM 15°56.265'S, 28°55.919'E. One of the newer lodges in the valley, just 1km from Kiambi, Kanyemba was opened in 2002 by Zambian-born Italian Riccardo Garbaccio, & refurbished in 2011. From its bougainvillea-adorned entrance to the expanses of green lawns along the river, it's an attractive, well-run place – & foodies will appreciate the Italian-influenced cuisine.

Cool, spacious stone-&-thatch rondavels (1 of them a honeymoon suite with jacuzzi & garden) are tasteful & stylish, with locally made solid wood furniture that includes dbl or twin beds under walk-in mosquito nets; there's also

a walk-in wardrobe area & safe, an en suite shower, & a wooden veranda facing the river. For families, the rondavels can take an extra 2 beds, or there's a larger house with 3 entirely separate en-suite rooms: 2 dbls & 1 with 4 beds. The understated décor runs through the central restaurant/bar, which has an intimate lounge area & library upstairs overlooking the garden & river. To the front, a stone terrace is shaded by a wild mango tree, & chaises longues are set by a small pool near the river. There's a good gift shop, & the lodge is connected to mains electricity.

Activities include game walks on the private Kanyemba Island, where the birding is good & you might encounter wildlife such as elephant, waterbuck, bushbuck & even buffalo. There are also boat trips, canoeing, fishing (tackle included), village walks & sunset cruises. Full-day trips to the national park can be organised (& are included for those staying 3 nights or more); these take a boat to the gate, then driving from there. Unusually for this area, Kanyemba is open almost all year. *US$370/430 pp sharing/sgl Jun–Oct, US$300/350 rest of year, all FBA, exc drinks, park fees.* ⊕ *Closed Feb.*

🏠 **Kanyemba Island Bushcamp** (4 chalets) Contact Kanyemba, above. The largest island on the Zambezi, some 7km long & 2km wide, is privately owned by Kanyemba Lodge, & home to their exclusive bushcamp. It's a rather romantic affair, this, its secluded reed-walled chalets raised high on stilts with canvas flaps opening on to tree-shaded decks over the river & private bathrooms on a platform in the trees. Even the LED 'fairylights' have a slightly romantic quality! More prosaically, there's a radio on hand in case of emergency. Meals – to the same standard as those at the lodge – are served in an open thatched dining area above the river. There's a firepit here, too, as well as a simple bar & a small plunge pool.

With a resident elephant population & good birding, the island is the base for Kanyemba's bush walks; these & all other activities are as at the lodge. *US$470/550 pp sharing/sgl Jun–Oct, US$300/350 rest of year, all FBA, exc drinks, park fees. No children under 12.* ⊕ *Mar–Dec.*

🏠 **Wildtracks** (4 tents, 3 chalets, camping) m 0977 349418; www.wildtracks-zambia.com. ⊕ WILDT 15°56.463'S, 29°00.288'E. Well maintained & very family friendly, the simple Wildtracks is clearly signposted just 3.3km from the road, 18km east of the pontoon. It's geared to the self-catering market, so you need to bring all your own food & drink, but staff are on hand to prepare your food, & there's an attractive new 2-storey boma where an upstairs library is planned. Safari tents & chalets come in various sizes & configurations (2–6 beds). Some are en suite; some share ablutions. At the campsite, where 2 of the 4 pitches are on the river, & firewood & charcoal are supplied, cooking is down to you, so bring everything you need! Wildtracks is popular with school groups, which explains a large swimming pool, child-focused walks, an obstacle course, geocaching & superb climbing on an old baobab tree. Sundowner cruises (*Kw225,000/boat*) & fishing (*Kw450,000/½ day*) round off the options, with rods available for hire. *Tent Kw390,000 sharing (max 5), Kw545,000 dbl en suite; chalet Kw545,000/885,000 4/6 beds. Camping Kw50,000 pp.*

🏠 **Tsika Island Camp** (3 chalets) Contact Chongwe River Camp. ⊕ TSIKA 15°51.205'S, 29°06.583'E. Chongwe's rustic bushcamp is on a small island, 2.5km x 1.5km, about 35km upstream from its parent lodge. Opened in 2010, it's an unspoiled spot, shaded by winterthorn trees & facing east across to Zimbabwe. Rather quirky riverfront chalets have painted ferro walls under thatch, with pole-framed 'windows' & reed blinds. Furnished with a dbl or twin beds under mosi nets, & with solar lighting, each has a pole walkway leading to a toilet, basin & bucket shower. (One chalet can take 2 extra beds.) A simple dining shelter & riverside firepit complete the picture. The island itself offers good birding, with crowned crane nesting here – unusual for the Lower Zambezi. Boat trips & fishing are on offer, as are visits to the cultural village that's almost opposite. Transfers to Chongwe are often by canoe, a pleasant day's drift downstream. *US$800/1,100 pp sharing/sgl Aug–Sep, US$750/1,050 pp sharing/sgl Jul &Oct, US$650 pp Nov, all FBA, inc most drinks, laundry, park fees; exc premium wines/imported spirits. No children under 7.* ⊕ *Jul–mid Nov.*

🅰 **Chiawa Cultural Village** (camping) ⊕ CHIACV 15°50.230'S, 29°07.061'E. The valley's cultural village (page 241) had plans for a simple campsite in 2011. Rates were unconfirmed, but expect to pay around US$15 pp.

🏠 **Kayila Lodge** ⊕ KAYILA 15°47.487'S, 29°11.042'E. In 2011, the long-established Kayila, some 45km from Chirundu & about an hour's drive from the national park, was closed for a complete rebuild. We understand that the new camp will be set further back on the same site, & that it is joining forces with the neighbouring Ntondo. The old Kayila was set in a small group of baobabs on a low rise, with views of the river & surrounding escarpment. Inside the trunk of one of those great trees was a toilet, complete with washbasin, accessed by a small door in its trunk – quite a feature! Let's hope that this, & the tree house set high up in a sausage tree with a bird's-eye view of the river below, will be retained.

🏠 **Mvuu Lodge** (10 tents, camping) ☏ +27 12 660 3820; m +27 79 524 8709; e info@ mvuulodge.com; www.mvuulodge.com. ⊕ MVUU 15°45.913'S, 29°13.122'E. This laidback & flexible lodge is particularly popular with the angling fraternity. It's 18km west of the national park, & visitors either drive themselves here or arrive by boat from Gwabi River Lodge.

The large central area is open on three sides with a stone terrace & a deck over the river. Simply furnished with wooden dining table & chairs, it has a proper bar & a small area with cane chairs. There's a firepit by the river & a small plunge pool on the lawns. Paths through the grass link this to various styles of accommodation. Seven Meru-style tents each have a partially open stone-walled bathroom & a wooden terrace looking across to the river. A further 3 en-suite self-catering tents are in the camping area, with their own braai & fire, & all equipment provided; just bring your own food. Tents are twin or dbl, with 1 for families, & a 2nd family tent in the offing. Lighting is provided by paraffin or battery lamps. Campers share a choice of 4 pitches – 2 on the river – with the local monkey population, with more pitches planned for 2012. Each has its own braai area, firepit, private shower & flush toilet, with an attendant to provide firewood & clean pots & pans. Campers can use the restaurant, but otherwise bring everything with you if you're self catering. Activities include sundowner cruises (*US$35 pp*), fishing (*US$70/120 ½/full day inc tackle*), ½-day canoe trips (*US$80 pp*) & game drives (from US$45 pp). US$400/270 pp sharing FBA/FB; US$170 dbl self catering. Camping US$25 pp. 25% sgl supplement. ⊕ Apr–Nov.

🏠 **Baines' River Camp** (8 chalets) ☎+27 33 3242293; m +27 82 8064074; e reservations@ bainesrivercamp.com; www.bainesrivercamp. com. ⊕ BAINES 15°45.743'S, 29°13.913'E. Rebuilt on the wide riverfront site of the earlier Kiubo Camp, Baines' is just 16km west of the national park, & about 50km from the pontoon, although most guests arrive by plane at the nearby Royal airstrip. With its soft-grey metal roofs, cream-painted walls & glazed windows, it looks solid & cool, every inch the upmarket lodge, with professional yet friendly service to match.

As you step down into the main area, the first impression is of space, oodles of it: in the lounge with its large fireplace, in the rather masculine bar, even in the 'boardroom' that doubles as a library. There's WiFi in the main area, & computer stations with laptops in the lounge. Step outside & you're tantalisingly close to the river – & to a narrow 11m pool, ideal for a proper swim.

Equally close to the river are colonial-style chalets with comfortable furniture on large, private verandas looking across to Mana Pools. Expect AC, glazed windows (backed by netting), carpeted floors, kingsize or twin beds under ceiling fans, & a smart bathroom with separate toilet; each suite boasts a minibar, hairdryer & safe, & 2 feature outdoor showers.

As you would expect, the full range of activities is on offer here. There are also opportunities for the enthusiast to participate in professionally run fly-fishing clinics, birding weeks & workshops for photography or to study elephants – the latter focusing both on their social structure & the threats they face. US$705 pp sharing Jul–mid Nov, US$495 rest of year. FBA, inc most drinks/minibar, laundry, airstrip transfers; exc park fees, premium drinks. 25% sgl suppt in kingsize suite. No children under 14. ⊕ Mar–mid Dec.

🏠 **Munyemeshi Lodge** (22 rooms) ☎0211 231466; m 0977 789786; e agogos@zamnet. zm; www.munyemeshi.co.zm. ⊕ MUNYEM 15°45.437'S, 29°15.309'E. Visitors to this self-catering camp some 10km west of the national park need to bring their own food (for their chef to prepare & serve at the central dining table), their own drink (there's no bar), & their own fishing gear. The lodge itself, though, is

substantial, its stone central building under thatch matched by its chalets. These are all en suite, pleasantly fitted out with twin or dbl beds, & the newer ones share a central kitchen with a separate dining area. Activities comprise game drives (Kw700,000/day) & boat cruises (Kw150,000/hr plus fuel). Kw250,000 pp.

🏠 **Numbayanga** (5 chalets) ⊕ NUMBA 15°44.876'S, 29°16.699'E. This new camp, scheduled for completion in 2012, has all the makings of an upmarket addition to the river. The Cape Dutch style of its cream-painted chalets with green roofs is certainly unusual, & inside they're well appointed – with sliding glass doors, AC, ceiling fans, timber floors, bath, separate toilet & outside shower. Outside, a good-sized infinity pool will have a glass wall over the river,& ornate gazebos add a touch of glamour. However, we have been unable to find out any further information at this stage, & the name given here is, we understand, the name of the investment company.

🏠 **Kasaka River Lodge** (8 tented chalets, family house) www.kasakariverlodge.com; contact via Chongwe River Camp, opposite. ⊕ KASAKA 15°44.242'S, 29°17.982'E. Opened in 2001, but taken into the Chongwe fold in 2010, Kasaka is just 5km west of the national park. It's a family-friendly place, set high above the river, & almost 2 lodges in one. On the 'tame side', en-suite tented chalets on stone-clad platforms sit among neat lawns – which are contentedly chomped by hippo overnight – & facing a small pool. Suspended wooden walkways lead over an ornamental pool past the lounge, bar & dining area to the 'wild side', where more chalets – including a secluded honeymoon suite with an open-air bath – look across the river to Zimbabwe. Let's hope that bathroom upgrades in 2012 won't spoil the best showers in Zambia! For families, there's an entirely separate 2–3-bedroom unit, the 'Hippo Pod', with its own pool, firepit & deck. Cut into the steep hillside is a further lounge area with a deck over the river below.

Alongside day & night game drives & safari walks in the GMA & national park are river cruises, canoeing & fishing trips & cultural visits; the lodge is actively involved with local schools. Those seeking privacy can indulge in bush picnics, private dinners or lunch on Nyamangwe Island, while families are unusually well catered for, with children's menus, games and an entire

'Bush Kids' programme. *US$550/700 pp sharing/ sgl Aug–Sep, US$500/650 Jul & Oct, US$450 Nov, all FBA inc most drinks, laundry, park fees; exc premium wines/imported spirits. No children under 7. Hippo Pod US$2,500 per night Aug–Sep, US$2,200 Jul & Oct, US$2,000 Nov (max 6 people; min 4 adults).* ⊕ *Jul–mid Nov.*

🏠 **Royal Zambezi Lodge** (14 tented chalets) 📞 0211 261265; e royalzambezihq@iwayafrica. com; www.royalzambezilodge.com. ✪ ROYAL 15°43.641'S, 29°18.876'E. Situated just 4km west of the national park, with a full 3km of river frontage, Royal Zambezi was rebuilt in 2007. Many guests fly into Royal airstrip; alternatively you can leave your vehicle at Gwabi River Lodge & transfer by boat; the boat trip takes about 1½hrs.

Imposing gates set the style for the smart reincarnation with shades of the colonial era. Formal lounge & dining areas, each with outsize fireplaces, lead off from a huge lobby. It's unfortunate that the walls appear to be of raw plaster, which jars against the formality of the setting, but service is good & the welcome friendly. Outside, a wide terrace offers more relaxed seating & dining options. A walkway leads to a small pool next to the well-loved Sausage Tree Bar, built around the trunk of a large sausage tree (*Kigelia africana)* but now screened by a wall. Up on a low hill, the Bush Spa offers a variety of beauty treatments.

At the back of the lawned site, a concrete path runs behind a row of en-suite tented chalets under thatch, each rather incongruously separated from the next by rough pole screens. . Inside, though, cream bedlinen on twin or dbl beds & the soft lines of mosquito netting draping the walls add a lightness of touch, & wooden doors open on to a porch looking towards the river. 4 'deluxe' chalets have a private pool & outside bathroom. At the far end, a honeymoon suite, opened in 2011, comes with an outside bathroom & its own pool, guide, boat & vehicle.

Morning & afternoon drives into the park, short walks, fishing, canoeing & 3hr hikes into the mountains are all on the agenda. *US$380/530 Jul–Sep, US$550/700 Oct–Nov, US$650/800 Mar–Jun all classic/deluxe pp sharing FBA inc most drinks, park fees; exc premium drinks, spa. Sgl suppt US$150. Min stay 2 nights.* ⊕ *Apr–Nov.*

🅰 **Chiawa Community Campsite** ✪ CHIAWC 15°43.247'S, 29°19.905'E. On the edge of the national park, this sandy riverside site with some tree shade is primarily used by companies running organised canoeing trips. Aside from simple showers & toilets there are no facilities at all, so visitors need to be entirely self-sufficient. Sadly, though, we understand that the site has been sold for a new lodge. *US$15 pp, per night.*

🏠 **Chongwe River Camp** (8 chalets) 📞 0211 841051/2; e reservations@chongwe.com; www.chongwe.com. ✪ CHONRC 15°42.911'S, 29°20.287'E. Set right on the Chongwe River that marks the boundary between the GMA & the national park, at its confluence with the Zambezi, Chongwe has an enviable location, with a far greater concentration of game here than further west, but without the high charges levied by the park's authorities. Most visitors arrive by private plane at Royal airstrip, or occasionally by boat.

Chongwe today has Meru-style tents set up on platforms along the river, each with dbl or twin beds, a small shaded porch & a semi-open bathroom with ochre-painted ferro walls. To cool off, the honeymoon suite – beautifully situated with views of both the Chongwe & the Zambezi – has its own plunge pool, while others share a pool behind the chalets. Ideal for families or groups of 4 is the smart Albida Suite, enclosed by funky free-form walls. This offers 2 en-suite octagonal tents linked by a canvas-canopied lounge/dining area & its own riverside pool. Guests may dine here in privacy, or in the central sandy dining area, shaded by an old winterthorn (*Faidherbia albida)*, its pods beloved of the local elephant population. There's an informal lounge/bar, too, decked out with cushions on ochre-coloured benches beneath a couple of canvas canopies.

Traditionally popular with fishing groups, the lodge offers all the standard activities, plus the option of walking upstream to return by canoe – or canoeing downstream from its bushcamp on Tsika Island. There's good birding as well, explained in part by the proximity of the Lower Zambezi escarpment. The atmosphere is informal & friendly, with knowledgeable & informative staff & good guiding. *US$700/900 pp sharing/sgl Aug–Sep, US$650/850 pp sharing/sgl Jul & Oct, US$550 pp Nov, all FBA, inc most drinks, laundry, park fees; exc premium wines/imported spirits. Suites US$800/1,100 pp sharing/sgl Aug–Sep, US$750/1,050 pp sharing/sgl Jul & Oct, US$650 pp Nov. No children under 7.* ⊕ *Jul–mid-Nov.*

🏠 **Chongwe River House** e house@
chongweriver.net; www.chongeriverhouse.
com. Contact Chongwe, above, or Robin Pope
Safaris, page 268. ⊕ CHONRH 15°42.488'S,
29°20.259'E. At the end of a massive winterthorn
grove (*Faidherbia albida*), this unique, 4-bedroom
private retreat lies on the banks of the peaceful
Chongwe River, with a spectacular view of the
nearby mountainous escarpment. The entire
house is built of ferro walls & wild wood, so its
structure follows the natural lines of the branches
used. There is not a straight line to be seen! The
main room looks out over the deck & a large pool
to the river & mountains beyond. Furniture in the
living area has been carved from a single huge
fallen winterthorn tree, as if it had come to rest
across the room, while embedded in the ceilings

are pastel-coloured pebbles from the river.
Each of the ground-floor bedrooms is entered
through a tunnel, rather like walking through a
cave; the curved entrance gives privacy without
the need for doors. Their bathrooms have water
pouring out of the stone ceiling instead of the
normal shower rose, & upstairs the showers are
waterfalls. There are wooden 'taps', & the basins
have been carved out of wood & white marble
by the Zambian artist, Eddie Mumba. From the
bedrooms, the sitting room & the deck you will
have game in view, feeding & watering; even the
unusual baths in the upstairs bedrooms afford
a view across the bush, inc the huge elephants
attracted by the house's winterthorn trees.
*US$800 pp Aug–Sep, US$750 pp Jul & Oct, US$650
pp Nov. Min 4 adults.* ⊕ *Jul–mid Nov.*

Within the Lower Zambezi National Park (*Park fees US$25 pp/day; self drivers US$30 pp/day plus US$15 per vehicle/day;* ⊕ *sunrise–sunset Jun–Oct*)

🏠 **Chiawa Camp** (9 tented chalets) ☎ 0211
261588/262683; m 0977 767433; e info@
chiawa.com; www.chiawa.com. ⊕ CHIAWA
15°41.058'S, 29°24.829'E. Small, friendly &
highly efficient, this award-winning camp is set
beneath a grove of mahogany trees, about 8km
(30 mins' drive) inside the national park. Most
guests fly in to Royal airstrip, followed by a short
drive, & a boat ride to the lodge. Private flights
from elsewhere, including the Luangwa, can be
organised.

Being in the park, Chiawa is open only during
the dry season, so is largely built of wood, canvas
& reeds. Though the setting remains rustic, the
camp itself has become considerably more stylish
over the years. Its rooms are well-spaced, insect-
proof, Meru-style tents on raised timber decks
facing the river. With smart, dark-wood furniture,
kingsize or twin beds enveloped in mosquito
nets, a bath, indoor & outdoor showers, & twin
washbasins, they're large, airy, comfortable &
well appointed. And then there's the honeymoon
suite, with its bathtub on the split-level deck,
& seating down below. Every chalet has 12v
lighting & 220v power for charging batteries.

Central to the camp is a comfortable lounge
with a proper bar & a well-designed library area
of books & magazines, while above is a 2nd
seating & viewing area. Meals are taken in a
separate dining shelter, overlooking the river.

From walking safaris & 4x4 trips (inc night
drives), to motorboat & short canoe trips along
the river: activities are exceptionally flexible here.
Few visitors just want to fish, but Chiawa has also
maintained a top reputation for serious fishing
trips for tigerfish (all catch & release). A small,
fenced pool surrounded by decking offers a place
for a cooling dip.

In 2010, out of about 200 game-viewing
days, the camp had 65 separate sightings of
leopard (about half in daylight hrs), & 204 of
lion; unusually, there were also 2 sightings of
aardvark. This is a very good record, but typical
of what a top private camp with good guides can
achieve in Zambia.

On a broader front, as part of its commitment
to the development of conservation education,
Chiawa & its guests fund the education of
140 children in local village schools, & is a top
contributor to the funding of anti-poaching,
environmental education programmes &
conservation in the area. Chiawa is run by a
family team & has carved out a reputation as one
of Zambia's top camps. *US$940/755/565 pp Jul–
Sep/Jun & Oct–Nov/Apr–May, all FBA, inc local
drinks, laundry, exc park fees. No children under 8.*
⊕ *15 Apr–15 Nov.*

🏠 **Sausage Tree** (7 chalets, 1 house)
☎ 0211 845204; m 0977 455448; e info@
sausagetreecamp.com; www.sausagetreecamp.

above **Hippo** *Hippopotamus amphibius*
(SS) page 526

right **Elephant** *Loxodonta africana*
(TH) page 525

below **Herd of buffalo** *Syncerus caffer*
(AZ) page 526

above   Cheetah *Acynonix jubatus* (AZ) page 516

left   Lion cub *Panthera leo* (CM) page 515

below   African wild dog *Lycaon pictus* (CM) page 517

above   **Side-striped jackal** *Canis adustus* (MS/FLPA) page 518

below   **Spotted hyena** *Crocuta crocuta* (PGO/OSF/SpS) page 518

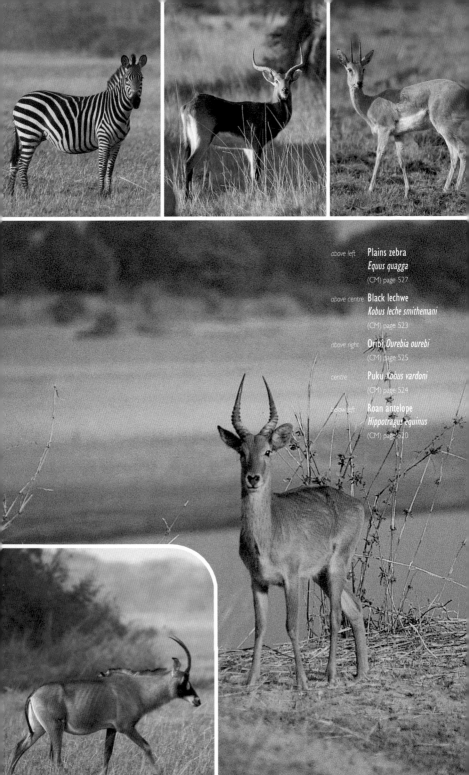

above left   **Plains zebra**
Equus quagga
(CM) page 527

above centre   **Black lechwe**
Kobus leche smithemani
(CM) page 523

above right   **Oribi** *Ourebia ourebi*
(CM) page 525

centre   **Puku** *Kobus vardoni*
(CM) page 524

below left   **Roan antelope**
Hippotragus equinus
(CM) page 520

above left **Greater kudu**
Tragelaphus
strepsiceros
(AZ) page 521

above right **Blue wildebeest**
Connochaetes taurinus
(CM) page 521

centre **Waterbuck**
Kobus ellipsiprymnus
(MB/B/SpS) page 520

below left **Lichtenstein's**
hartebeest
Alcelaphus lichtensteini
(AZ) page 521

below right **Bushbuck**
Tragelaphus scriptus
(CM) page 522

above right **African civet**
Civettictis civetta
(PP/FLPA) page 528

right **Large-spotted genet**
Genetta tigrina
(SS) page 528

below **White-tailed mongoose**
Ichneumia albicauda
(PP/FLPA) page 528

above **Miombo woodland** (C&TS/FLPA) page 30

left **Leopard orchid** *Ansellia africana* (TH)

below left **Protea** (TH)

below right **Blood lily** *Scadoxus multiflorus* (TH)

com. ✆ SAUSTR 15°40.675'S, 29°28.692'E In a beautiful position inside the national park, Sausage Tree is usually accessed by a short flight to either Royal or (closer) Jeki airstrips. A possible alternative is a 2hr boat transfer from Gwabi River Lodge.

Sausage Tree is privately owned & professionally staffed & run, with first-class food & attentive service. Rebuilt in 2008/9, its large, reed-walled chalets retain their signature cream-canvas roofs, but now have ochre-painted fittings & steps down to a matching open-air bathroom cleverly built around indigenous trees; the 2 honeymoon suites have baths, twin basins & their own pools. Similar in style is the private Kigelia House (*min 3 guests*), with a twin & dbl room en suite, a central dining & sitting area, & its own pool, vehicle & guide. Solid teak furniture is used throughout, as are top-class ivory fabrics & linen sheets. Each tent is the responsibility of an individual *muchinda* or butler, & is equipped with an emergency radio. Power is supplied by generator, plus a 24hr inverter.

The cream canvas roofs extend to the riverside living & dining areas (to be enlarged in 2012) & matching umbrellas which shade tables & chairs on the wooden deck. This leads to a small pool, which is shortly to be replaced with a 25m infinity pool. The sausage tree for which the camp was named is now submerged in the shallows; its branches are popular perches for various species of bee-eater. One of the camp's main assets is the proximity of a lovely backwater, the Chifungulu Channel, which runs parallel to the main river for about 14km & makes a great area for a gentle paddle. It's popular with the local hippo population, too, particularly Frank. *Chifungulu* is said to be the local name for *Combretum microphyllum*, the 'flame creeper' with blood-red flowers that grows up winterthorn trees here. Smith's book on the Luangwa's flora, see *Appendix 3*, page 536, observes that some local people used to grind up the roots of this creeper, mix them with dog turds, & then burn the mixture – using the ashes as a cure for lunacy. It's uncertain if anyone at the camp has ever tried this. Expect the full range of day & night drives, canoeing, walking, boating & fishing trips, while in the evening private dinners can be arranged. *US$895 pp mid Jul–mid Oct, US$775 pp Jun–mid Jul & mid Oct–Nov, US$575 Apr–May, all FBA inc drinks, exc park fees; honeymoon US$995/875/675 pp. ⊕ Apr–15 Nov.*

🛏 **Mwambashi River Lodge** (9 tents, 1 chalet) ✆ (UK) +44 (0)7927 534647; e mwambashi@gmail.com. ✆ MWAMRL 15°38.392'S, 29°34.681'E. Mwambashi occupies a well-shaded site in a bend in the river with large *albida* trees, typical of this riverine environment. Most visitors arrive by plane at Jeki airstrip. It is now run exclusively for groups of up to 22 people, who arrive on Sat & stay for 7 nights, & cannot be booked by individual travellers.

Its large, walk-in tents, to be replaced in 2012, are built on wooden platforms with verandas overlooking the river, & canvas shadecloths. Each has a dbl or twin beds with mosquito-netted walls & a large en-suite bathroom at the back; note the funky tiled shower floor! A rather grand honeymoon chalet, open fronted & constructed of wood under thatch, has its own plunge pool. Central to the lodge is a wide thatched structure, with a bar & dining area flanking a substantial lounge; it's light, open & airy, with good river views. With day & night game drives, walking safaris, canoeing, boat trips & fishing, there's plenty to keep a large group occupied. There's even a riverside 'exercise area' to work off excess energy, & a plunge pool to cool off afterwards. *US$42,000–50,000/wk (16 guests) FBA inc park fees, exc alcoholic drinks. Additional guest US$110/day. ⊕ Apr–Oct*

🛏 **Old Mondoro** (4 chalets) www.oldmondoro.com; contact via Chiawa (page 246). ✆ OLDMON 15°37.839'S, 29°41.423'E. This remote bushcamp started life as the old Potato Bush Camp & remains the only bushcamp in the Lower Zambezi National Park – although recent refurbishments have served to reinvent the term 'bushcamp'! Today, it is owned & run by Chiawa Camp, & staffed by an experienced team.

A smart canvas-roofed central area with plenty of cushioned wicker chairs, a dining table & a firepit overlooks the Zambezi, as do the chalets. These are set on temporary concrete platforms with reed walls that are low enough to give views onto the river; canvas sides can be rolled down for greater warmth or privacy. Inside are comfortable dbl or twin beds & teak chairs, plus a basin & curtained toilet; outside there's a proper hot shower & a tempting riverside bath, while on the veranda a daybed complements the usual chairs. It may look rustic, but there's everything you could want, from sockets for charging batteries & running computers to gas geysers for hot water, & good bedside lights. The camp is surrounded by open woodland, with a focus on walking, day & night game drives, game viewing by boat, canoe trips & fishing. We're told that there's an increasing presence of leopard locally – & certainly we were lucky enough to have an excellent sighting on a recent visit. Despite a considerable upgrade, the remote & open location means that this is still very much a bushcamp experience for those seeking an emphasis on guiding & wildlife, though the standard of food & service remains very high. *US$755/1,020 sgl/pp sharing Jul–Sep, US$605 pp Jun & Oct, US$525 pp May, all FBA, inc most drinks, laundry; exc park fees. No children under 12.* ⊕ *May–Oct*

🏠 **Sanctuary Zambezi Kulefu Camp** (7 chalets, max 12 guests) Contact Sanctuary Retreats, page 269. ✛ 15°37.272'S, 29°45.379'E. Deep within the national park, Kulefu is almost cut off from the main track by a small river – & indeed, in 2011 was closed due to flooding. In normal circumstances, most visitors are transferred by boat from the nearby Kulefu airstrip.

Built alongside a channel of the Zambezi, the camp was completely refurbished in 2008. Set up on platforms are large tented chalets with shaded verandas. Inside each are 4-poster twin beds with mosquito nets & ceiling fans, & en-suite shower, bath, toilet & twin washbasins. Teak furniture & white muslin tent linings & tie-back curtains add a touch of luxury. Electric lighting is supplied by a generator.

The spacious lounge is linked to an open dining area on the riverbank, under *Faidherbia albida* & *Acacia robusta* trees, although meals are often served al fresco on one of the nearby islands. A deck leading to a small pool at the water's edge makes an airy place to spend the afternoon, watching game & the river's birdlife.

Activities are flexible, with the camp's location ensuring that game drives & boating are very private. Walking, canoeing & tiger fishing are also options. *US$925/1,205 pp sharing/sgl 15 Jun–Oct, US$680 pp 16 Apr–14 Jun & Nov, all FBA, inc most drinks, laundry, park fees. No children under 12.* ⊕ *16 Apr–15 Nov.*

🏠 **Ana Tree Lodge** ✛ 15°61.013'S, 29°76.990'E. Formerly Mushika Camp, Ana Tree Lodge was demolished in 2011, but plans for its successor have yet to be finalised. Rumours of another small but more upmarket camp are countered by others of a seriously posh lodge with AC & all the trimmings. Assuming that something is built on the site, it lies on the Mushika River a few kilometres east of Zambezi Kulefu & just 4km from an airstrip.

East of the national park
There are normally a few small camps operating east of the national park and the Mpata Gorge. These are usually reached from the village of Luangwa, or Luangwa boma which is some 85km from the Great East Road (see *Chapter 10*, opposite), or can be reached by charter flight from Lusaka. At present, the most reliable is:

🏠 **Redcliff Zambezi Lodge** (7 chalets) ☏ +27 12 653 2664; 🖷 0979 844377/587822; e info@redcliff-lodge.com; www.redcliff-lodge.com. Redcliff Zambezi is tucked away in a GMA between the dramatic scenery of the Mpata Gorge & the village of Luangwa on the Mozambique border. Access is by 30min boat transfer from Luangwa boma.

Accommodation is in en-suite tented chalets, with 2 or 4 beds, the latter layout designed for families. An 'entertainment area' encompasses a TV lounge, dining room & bar, with a pool, campfire & deck overlooking the river. There's limited mobile phone reception & WiFi in case you can't manage without! The lodge is said to be particularly popular for fishing, with a strict catch-&-release policy. Visitors may also take game walks, cultural walks, birding & – at extra cost if specially arranged – boat trips into the national park. *US$275 pp sharing FBA; exc bar.* ⊕ *All year.*

The Luangwa Valley

This lush rift valley, enclosed by steep escarpment walls, is one of the continent's finest areas for wildlife. Four national parks protect parts of the area: South Luangwa, North Luangwa, Luambe and Lukusuzi. Separating these are game management areas (GMAs), which also contain good populations of game. This entire valley is remote but, for the enthusiast, the wildlife is well worth the effort made to get here.

For most visitors, South Luangwa National Park (known locally as just 'the South Park') is by far the most practical park to visit in the valley. This is the largest of the parks, with superb wildlife and many excellent camps. Organising a trip to South Luangwa is not difficult, and its infrastructure is easily the best. However, it is still a very remote park, and so most visitors arrive on trips organised outside Zambia. A few arrive independently and, though this is possible, it does limit their accommodation and activity choices.

The more intrepid may also organise a safari from the South Park into North Luangwa, which is even more remote and exclusive. Its wildlife is now flourishing, thanks to some intensive conservation efforts over the past decade, and the few safaris that do run concentrate on taking small groups for purely walking trips.

Luambe National Park is much smaller than either the South or the North parks, and there's one camp there that makes a perfect stopover if you're heading that way. The birdwatching is good, as with the other parks, though there is less game.

Finally, Lukusuzi National Park is something of an unknown quantity. Few people have even visited this park and there are currently no facilities or camps there.

THE GREAT EAST ROAD

The Great East Road leads from Lusaka to Chipata, the Luangwa's 'gateway', and just over the border from Malawi. It's a long drive: about 555km of tar which is good in places, and pot-holed in others. Alternatively, there are regular buses – though you'll need to take a coach from Lusaka early in the morning to be sure of getting to Chipata by evening. There's relatively little *en route* bar a few fuel stations and some useful places to stop for a meal or to sleep, but beyond Chipata is the little-visited town of Lundazi, notable mainly for its anachronistic castle.

LUANGWA RIVER AREA The impressive suspension bridge over the Luangwa is some 225km east of Lusaka, or 329km west of Chipata. Just 1.9km west of this is a turning to the village of Luangwa (or Luangwa boma), which lies at the confluence of the Luangwa and the Zambezi rivers, close to the border with both Mozambique and Zimbabwe. Near the turning is a small market where there are baskets for sale. The lodge near the start of this road is the obvious place to stay between Lusaka and Chipata (or Malawi).

Where to stay and eat

Bridge Camp (10 chalets, camping) Feira Rd; m 0977 197456/395037, 0979 180475; e bridgecamp@gmail.com; www. bridgecampzambia.com. ✆ 15°00.323'S, 30°12.919'E. This budget camp above the Luangwa River is just 2.8km from the Great East Rd towards Luangwa boma, & clearly signposted. It was rebuilt in 2004 by Will & Lindsay van den Berg, & now offers a range of simple stone chalets, variously furnished with sgl, dbl or twin beds & 3 sleeping 4–5 people. All are thatched with gauze windows, & generator-powered electrics. Some are en suite; others share toilets & showers. There are also 2 separate tree-shaded campsites, with BBQ facilities & their own ablution blocks, & charcoal & wood provided. The bar & restaurant, with an à-la-carte menu, are open to passing visitors, & there's a small pool.

Many guests are in transit, but the camp also organises guided overnight hikes (Kw125,000–250,000 ½/full day) &, in the dry season only, guided canoe trips (*Kw250,000– 500,000 per canoe ½/full day – or Kw150,000 pp for a sundowner trip*). Options include hiking to the confluence of the Lunsemfwa & Luangwa, followed by canoeing back the following morning (*Kw1,000,000 per boat/ day*), & 3–5 nights' trekking in the Lunsemfwa Gorge (*Kw1,000,000 per group/day*). Overnight trips are self catering, & you'll need your own equipment, though the camp will prepare lunch packs & you can hire tents & sleeping bags. *Chalet Kw120,000–165,000 shared facilities, Kw230,000 en suite, both pp sharing; camping Kw45,000 pp.*

NYIMBA Some 98km east of the Luangwa Bridge, huge speed humps announce the presence of this small town, which has both a **fuel** station and a **bank** with an ATM. There's also a small market, a bus station and a **post office**.

Where to stay and eat

Along the road about 2km further east there's a prominent restaurant and bar, **Thula** (⊕ *08.00–22.00 daily*). Serving everything from nshima and chicken to T-bone steak, it's a handy option for a break during a long drive. Right next door, what looked like a new lodge was going up in 2011. From its imposing two-storey thatched central area to a number of A-frame chalets set in landscaped gardens, it looked promising, but to date we have been unable to obtain further details.

PETAUKE Little more than a dot on the map, Petauke nevertheless has a **fuel** station, a **bank**, and a simple **guesthouse**.

KATETE Another fairly nondescript town some 79km west of Chipata, Katete is home to a large mosque, a useful **filling station**, a Finance **Bank**, **post office**, and half-a-dozen grocery **shops**. There's also a Catholic church on the southern side of the road at the western end of town and the St Francis Mission Hospital. If you're interested in volunteering, or in cultural tourism, check out Tiko Lodge (see below).

Where to stay

Aside from a couple of basic guesthouses in town, there is one that is an interesting place in its own right:

Tiko Lodge (17 rooms, 14 dorm beds, 6 tents) Great East Rd; ☏ 0216 252122; m 0977 382875; e tikocc@zamtel.zm; www.tikondane. org. Next to the hospital, about 2km west of Katete, this lodge was set up to raise funds for the Tikondane Community Centre, which brings together a school, skills training & adult education programmes. Guests are welcome to get involved

at several levels, perhaps visiting the hospital, joining a workshop for drumming or dancing, learning the local language or helping out in the centre. A structured programme of voluntary work means that even those with just a few weeks can contribute to the project. Computer skills, fundraising, basic teaching & reading are much valued, but the list is seemingly endless!

In order to help foster local traditions, the lodge works with 3 villages, & organises a number of 'cultural safaris'. One option includes a visit by oxcart to watch some initiation rites, followed by the 'ghost dance' (*departs 16.00,* *returns 24.00, from Kw400,000 (4 people), plus Kw20,000 pp for a meal). Kw60,000/90,000 sgl/dbl en suite; Kw75,000 dbl sharing facilities; dorm bed Kw20,000; camping Kw25,000 pp; 20% discount for volunteers.*

CHIPATA   Chipata (⊕ CHIPAT 13°38.557'S, 32°38.796'E) is a relatively small but busy town that is more than just a gateway to South Luangwa; it is also a border town just 30km from Malawi. Known in colonial days as Fort Jameson, and now the capital of Eastern Province, Chipata stands in a valley, surrounded by quite a fertile area of subsistence farms with low bush-covered hills around. To the east of town is an attractive mosque.

Getting there and away

By air   The easiest way to get to Chipata is by air. The town has a good all-weather asphalt airstrip. Proflight (page 65) has year-round flights linking Chipata with Lusaka on Tuesday, Wednesday and Friday, leaving Lusaka at 07.00, and arriving in Chipata at 08.45.

By bus   There's a regular coach service between Chipata and Lusaka, run by Juldan Motors. These depart daily at 05.30 and 06.30, taking around seven to eight hours to reach Lusaka; tickets cost around Kw130,000 one way. In the other direction, there are buses to Lilongwe in Malawi on Sunday and Wednesday, departing at around 11.00; the fare is Kw70,000 one way. The town's bus station is a little way off the main road, near the main township and market, and is not a place to be hanging around after dark.

Chipata is also the terminus of one of the postbus routes out of Lusaka, with buses departing from Lusaka every Tuesday, Thursday and Saturday at 07.00, arriving in Chipata at 14.00; the fare is K90,000 one way.

Local minibuses ply between Chipata and Mfuwe, leaving only when they're full and costing from Kw60,000 one way; alternatively, there are taxis available.

Where to stay and eat   Most visitors continue to the Mfuwe area, down in the Luangwa Valley, if they can. However, if you arrive late then staying in Chipata is a wise move, and hitchhikers could easily end up here for a night or two due to lack of lifts. There are several good places to lay your head or get a meal, of which Mama Rula's is probably the most geared to travellers rather than the business market.

Protea Hotel Chipata   (40 rooms) Great East Rd; 0216 222905–8; e reservations@ phchipata.co.zm; www.proteahotels.com/chipata. Unexpectedly attractive & with very good service, the Protea is just 2km west of town, 300m from the turn-off to Mfuwe. With all the accoutrements of a good mid-range hotel – twin & dbl rooms with TV, AC, phone, tea station, safe & free WiFi, plus a restaurant & lounge – it's a welcome newcomer to Chipata. Outside, against a backdrop of the Kanjala Hills, the restaurant spills out onto a terrace where there's a good-sized pool in newly planted gardens, with a bar & umbrella shade. **$$$**

Crossroads Lodges   (38 rooms) Umodzi Highway; 0216 222320; m 0975 860266; e chipatacrossroads@crossroadslodges.com; www.crossroadslodges.com. Opened in 2009, Crossroads won't win any prizes for its location, above the main road next to the Total garage, but service is efficient & facilities are good. Twin or dbl rooms have the standard package of corporate extras, including AC & phone, plus a jacuzzi in executive suites. There's a simple dining room, a large, dark bar with seating inside & out, & a small pool at the back. Business, we're told, is 'overwhelming'. **$$–$$$**

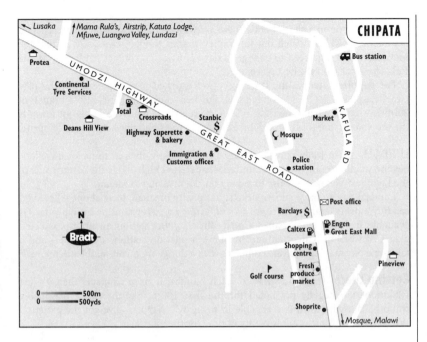

Mosque, Malawi

🏠 **Mama Rula's** (10 rooms, camping)
m 0977 768021/790226; e mamarula@
iwayafrica.com; www.mamarulas.com. Certainly
the best guesthouse in Chipata, Mama Rula's is
well signposted north of town, about 2km off the
main Mfuwe road. It's run by Andrea Breitenbach,
whose passion for plants shows in the colourful,
beautifully maintained gardens. The campsite,
with its own bar & TV, spreads across a large lawn
under a canopy of marvellous red mahogany
(*Khaya anthotheca*) trees & the odd banana or
papaya. The ablutions are clean & well kept, & the
simple twin rooms here – some sharing facilities,
some en suite – are spotless. Dotted around are
more en-suite 'executive' rooms with twin beds.
The large restaurant with a bar & DSTV is open to
both guests & passing visitors, & there's a tree-
shaded pool that's exclusively for guests. Andrea
can arrange trips to the Luangwa & Luambe
national parks & offer advice & information on
Malawi, from crossing the border with a vehicle to
currency exchange. *US$53/65 pp sharing/sgl DBB;
Budget US$15 pp; camping US$7 pp. Special rates
for overland trucks & upgrades available.*

🏠 **Pineview Guesthouse** (35 rooms)
📞 0216 221633; m 0977 232735; e pineview@
coppernet.zm. Clearly signposted opposite
Shoprite, this is one of several guesthouses on a
quiet street. Even the simplest rooms are fine –
with mosquito nets on twin beds, polished floors,
en-suite bath or shower, a TV & fan; a little more
buys a dbl bed & tiled bathroom. There are tables
& a bar in the pleasant garden & secure parking.
$–$$

🏠 **Deans Hill View Lodge** (4 rooms,
6 dorm beds, camping) 📞 0216 221673; m 0977
767221; e deanshillview@yahoo.co.uk; www.
deanshillviewlodge.co.uk. In a clean & tranquil
setting above the town, yet just 500m from the
Total garage, this British-owned lodge has very
simple twin rooms, a 6-bed dormitory & a terraced
camping area, all sharing showers & toilets. A bar
& dining area were nearing completion in 2011,
but for now, veg & non-veg 'plates of food' are
available for Kw30,000. The gardens are attractive,
& there's secure parking – for both individual
vehicles & overlander trucks. *Room/dorm bed
Kw50,000 pp; camping Kw25,000 pp.*

Other practicalities As you arrive by road from Lusaka, the first of several **fuel**
stations is on your right, well placed for those continuing north to Mfuwe. The
heart of the town, however, is a couple of kilometres beyond this, past the police

station and around a sharp bend. There are various **banks**, of which Barclays and Stanbic have ATMs. Watch out for money sharks, though, especially around the fuel stations; if you need to change Malawian kwacha, contact Andrea at Mama Rula's for advice on the best place to go.

For **supplies**, start at the large, very well-stocked new SuperSpar in the new Great East Mall (⊕ *07.30–20.00 daily*). Further southeast there's also a branch of Shoprite, set back from the right side of the road. The main market is out towards the bus station, but for fresh produce check out the small market close to Shoprite.

LUNDAZI About 180km north of Chipata, well off any obvious route for travellers, lies the small, friendly town of Lundazi. It's perched high above the eastern side of the Luangwa Valley, and close to a quiet border crossing to Malawi.

Lundazi has no large supermarkets, but plenty of small, local **shops** where you can buy most essentials. There are a lot of farming areas around, so fresh produce is available. It also has a few **banks**, a **post office**, a police station, an airstrip, assorted places of worship (Christian and Muslim), a mission station, a convent – and a fairy-tale Norman-style castle complete with a dungeon, turrets and battlements.

Getting there The easiest way to reach Lundazi is from Chipata. Then it's just 180km of tar, heavily pot-holed for the first 10km, but thereafter reasonably smooth. Thus the town is accessible in a sturdy 2WD if you've got the patience. Whatever your vehicle, allow plenty of time for the journey.

From the north Reaching Lundazi from Isoka is trickier, requiring a high-clearance 4x4 and even more time and patience. Shortly after the left turning to Isoka on the Great North Road as you head northeast, you come to a turning to the right, signposted to the 'airport bar'. Take this turning, which will lead you through Ntendere and up into the mountains. After about 75km, there's a fork and you turn right, heading almost south to reach Muyombe 50km later. It's a rocky road on the escarpment with many gullies, but the scenery is beautiful. From Muyombe, continue south towards Nyika Plateau and the border with Malawi, dropping down from the mountains as you do so. After around 25km, just before the Malawi border, turn right (southwest) onto a dirt road. This is generally good, though sandy in parts. After shadowing the border for some 70km, there's a fork and Lundazi is signposted to the left, whilst Chama is about 35km away if you take the right turn. Lundazi is now about 110km south of you; making the whole journey a very full day's drive from Isoka.

From the Luangwa Valley Both of the two roads from the Luangwa Valley are impassable during the rains, and even in the dry season require hours of hard 4x4 travel. The better of them leaves the main road on the east side of the valley about 20–25km north of Luambe National Park. It then climbs up the escarpment directly to Lundazi, about 130km away. It's a four–five-hour drive.

The second turns eastwards around the northern boundary of South Luangwa National Park and then cuts up the escarpment through Lukusuzi National Park. It then joins the Chipata–Lundazi road some 60km south of Lundazi (120km north of Chipata).

Where to stay There's only one place of choice (though it's pretty basic). If the castle's full then the town has several other small, basic resthouses, including the **Tigone**, where all the rooms are en suite.

🏠 **Lundazi Castle Hotel** (17 rooms)
\0216 480251. Dick Hobson's excellent *Tales of Zambia* (see *Appendix 3*, page 535) tells of how the district commissioner in the late 1940s, Errol Button, needed to build a resthouse here. Tourism was then taking off & visitors needed to stop between Nyika Plateau & the Luangwa Valley (the same could be said today!). Button designed & had built a small castle in Norman style, with thick walls & narrow slits for archers, overlooking a lake. It has a dungeon, high turrets at each corner & battlements all around. It was christened 'Rumpelstiltskin' after a fairy-tale character favoured by his daughter, & cost a mere £500 at the time. The castle quickly became very popular, & was extended in 1952 to accommodate more visitors.

The castle today is a basic hotel, very cold in winter but with a good atmosphere & often fully booked. All but 4 of the clean but poorly maintained rooms share bathrooms, though running water is not always available – & only the more expensive rooms have hot showers. Simple traditional meals are served, normally a choice of meats with nshima. **$**

SOUTH LUANGWA NATIONAL PARK

(*Park fees US$25 pp/day; self drivers US$30 pp/day plus US$15 per vehicle/day; bed levy US$20/night*) There are many contenders for the title of Africa's best game park. The Serengeti, Amboseli, Ngorongoro Crater, Etosha, Kruger, Moremi and Mana Pools would certainly be high on the list. South Luangwa has a better claim than most. Some of these other areas will match its phenomenally high game densities. Many others – the lesser known of Africa's parks – will have equally few visitors. One or two also allow night drives, which open up a different, nocturnal world to view, allowing leopards to be commonly seen and even watched whilst hunting.

However, few have South Luangwa's high quality of guiding together with its remarkable wildlife spectacles, day and night, in the isolation of a true wilderness. These elements, perhaps, are how the contenders ought to be judged, and on these the South Luangwa Park comes out as one of the highest on the list.

HISTORY
Note on prehistory Some of the earliest evidence of humans in south-central Africa is currently emerging from excavations in and around the South Luangwa National Park. Stone tools dating to at least two million years ago have been found, and all other periods of the Stone Age are represented in the park. There is also evidence emerging of early farmers in the valley, appearing by AD400. As yet there are no sites accessible to the public, but plans have been afoot for some years to build a museum at Mfuwe, on the site of the old cultural centre at Nsendamila, to showcase the valley's rich prehistory.

From the 8th century
With thanks to John Hudson OBE for his help in preparing this text
With the Zambezi established as a trade route by the 8th century, it seems reasonable to assume that small settlements were also appearing on the neighbouring Luangwa River, though it is harder to navigate and was, at that time, probably used mainly to reach the abundant game of the valley, rather than for any trading purposes. Records tell us that Zumbo, on the eastern banks of the Luangwa, was founded in 1546 by the Portuguese – their first settlement in what is now Zambia – and one can only surmise that Luangwa township itself, situated at the strategically important confluence of the Luangwa and Zambezi rivers, must have been founded at around that time too. Both these settlements were subsequently abandoned and resettled, until about 1763 when Zumbo was recorded as having 200 Portuguese families living within its boundaries.

In the 19th century the area was crossed by many European explorers who came to hunt, trade, bring the Gospel or simply to satisfy their curiosity. Around 1810–20, a trading post was opened at Malambo, some 100km north of Mfuwe. This was on the main trade route from Tete to Lake Mweru, which had first been established by Lacerda as early as 1798.

In his last book, *Kakuli*, Norman Carr quotes a Portuguese captain, Antonio Gamitto, as writing of the Luangwa in around 1832:

> Game of all kinds is very abundant at this season of drought; great numbers of wild animals collect here, leaving dry areas in search of water ... we can only say that this district appears to be the richest in animal life of any we have seen.

Later, in December 1866, when Livingstone crossed the Luangwa at Perekani (a place north of Tafika and south of Chibembe), he was just one of many Europeans exploring the continent. He commented:

> I will make this land better known to men that it may become one of their haunts. It is impossible to describe its luxuriance.

In 1904 a Luangwa Game Park was declared on the eastern bank of the river. However, this was not maintained, hunting licences were given out to control allegedly marauding elephants, and the park came to mean little. Then on 27 May 1938 three parks were defined in the valley: the North Luangwa Game Reserve, the Lukusuzi Game Reserve and the South Luangwa Game Reserve – which corresponded roughly to the present park, though without the Chifungwe Plain or the Nsefu Sector.

In the following year, Norman Carr and Bert Schultz were appointed as game rangers and villages within the reserves were moved outside its boundaries. Initially Norman Carr recommended that hunting safaris be started, but over the coming decade he realised that visitors would also come for what are now called 'photographic safaris'.

In 1949 the Senior Chief Nsefu, prompted by Norman Carr, established a private game reserve on the Luangwa's eastern bank, between the Mwasauke and Kauluzi rivers. A safari camp was started here which sent some of its income directly back to the local community. (Norman Carr was ahead of his time!) This soon moved to the site of the present-day Nsefu Camp. The chief's reserve became the Nsefu Sector, which was absorbed into the boundaries of the present park – along with the Chifungwe Plain, north of the Mupamadzi River – when new legislation turned all game reserves into national parks on 15 February 1972.

In the later years of his life, Norman Carr lived at Kapani Safari Lodge, having played a pivotal role in the history of the valley by pioneering commercial walking safaris, upon which South Luangwa has founded its reputation. He remained an important and highly outspoken figure to the end, and devoted much energy in his latter years to development projects designed to help the surrounding local communities to benefit from the park. He was especially involved with local school projects, encouraging the next generation of Zambians to value their wildlife heritage.

His excellent example is increasingly being followed by many of the more forward-thinking safari operators. More and more operators are taking their role in the community seriously, often by sponsoring schools and clinics in the surrounding countryside. Kawaza Village (see pages 292–3) is a highly visible tourism venture run by and for one of the local communities.

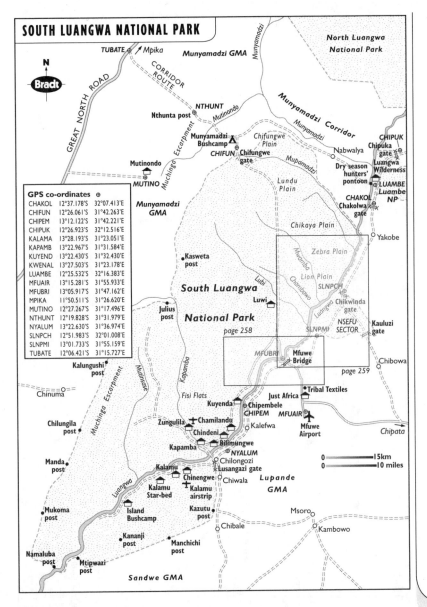

SOUTH LUANGWA NATIONAL PARK

GPS co-ordinates ⊕

CHAKOL	12°37.178'S	32°07.413'E
CHIFUN	12°26.061'S	31°42.263'E
CHIPEM	13°12.122'S	31°42.221'E
CHIPUK	12°26.923'S	32°12.516'E
KALAMA	13°28.193'S	31°23.051'E
KAPAMB	13°22.967'S	31°31.584'E
KUYEND	13°22.430'S	31°32.430'E
KWENAL	13°27.503'S	31°23.178'E
LUAMBE	12°25.532'S	32°16.383'E
MFUAIR	13°15.281'S	31°55.933'E
MFUBRI	13°05.917'S	31°47.162'E
MPIKA	11°50.511'S	31°26.620'E
MUTINO	12°27.267'S	31°17.496'E
NTHUNT	12°19.828'S	31°31.979'E
NYALUM	13°22.630'S	31°36.974'E
SLNPCH	12°51.983'S	32°01.008'E
SLNPMI	13°01.733'S	31°55.159'E
TUBATE	12°06.421'S	31°15.727'E

page 258

page 259

10

GEOGRAPHY The South Park now covers about 9,050km² of the Luangwa Valley's floor, which varies from about 500m to 800m above sea level. The western side of the park is bounded by the Muchinga Escarpment, and from there it generally slopes down to the eastern side of the park, where, except in the extreme south, it is bordered by the wide meanders of the Luangwa River.

Near the banks of the Luangwa the land is fairly flat, and mostly covered with mature woodlands. There are few dense shrubberies here, but many open areas where beautiful tall trees stand perhaps 10–20m apart, shading a mixture of small bushes and grassland. Occasionally there are wide, open grassland plains. The

SOUTH LUANGWA NATIONAL PARK

Mfuwe area

South Luangwa National Park

Bradt

N

0   3km
0   2 miles

Chipela Chansefu

Nsefu Sector

Kawaza Village

Mwongazi

Mfuwe Airport, Chipata

Lupande Bridge

Lupande

Msandile

Lion Plain

Chipela Chandombo

Luangwa

OMANI DRIVE

LUANGWA/WAFWA DRIVE

Luangwa Wafwa

NORMAN CARR DRIVE

04 ROAD

Luangwa River Camp

Monument for Norman Carr

ELEPHANT LOOP

Mushroom Lodge

Mushroom Lagoon

Track & Trail

Thornicroft

Croc Valley

BP

Nsendamila Cultural Village

Marula

Mfuwe Lagoon

Flatdogs

Chinzombo Lagoon

ZAWA office

BAOBAB SHORTCUT

Big Baobab

MOPANI SPUR

05 ROAD

Kakumbi Airstrip

AIRSTRIP SHORTCUT

Mfuwe Lodge

Wamilombe Memorial site

Mfuwe Bridge

RIVERSIDE DRIVE

WAMILOMBE DR

Kapani Safari Lodge

Mushilashi Bridge

MUSHILASHI RIVER DRIVE

Mushilashi

Wildlife Camp

Wakumba

Nkwali/ Safari House/ Robin's House

Nkwali pontoon (for use by lodge vehicles only)

Luangwa

Chief Kakumbi Own Palace

Kafunta River Lodge

Nyamaluma, Petauke

KAPIRI KANFUMU DRIVE

LUPUNGA SPUR

Katete Bridge

Katete

MPUMULO DRIVE

Twin Baobab

KASENGA DRIVE

PRESIDENT'S DRIVE LOOP

Chichele Hill

Puku Ridge

OLD KAUMBA RD

Chichele Presidential Lodge

CHICHELE DRIVE

KASWETA ROAD

RHINO LOOP

RHINO LOOP

Manzi

258

SOUTH LUANGWA NATIONAL PARK
Around the Nsefu Sector

Luambe NP

RIVERR ⊕

Nyakavuma Lagoon

Mwanya (closed)

Kankonko Lagoons

Zebra Plains

Z e b r a   P l a i n

Lumimba GMA

Chikoko Lagoon

Chikoko

⊕ *LUKUZI* Lukusye airstrip

Crocodile Lagoon

Crocodile

Big Lagoon (disused)

Luangwa

Tafika

Chikwinda gate
SLNPCH

Mwamba

Waterbuck Dambo Loop

Mwamba

Elephant Bend Loop

Lion

Kavula Lagoon
Chimbwe Lagoon

L i o n   P l a i n

Fish Eagle Lagoon

Chambowo

Chipela Lagoon

Kaingo

Muwowo Lagoon

Kakonji Pan

Nsefu

Hippo Lagoon

Chichele Salt Pan

Mchenja

Mutanda Plain

Kazikizi Lagoon

NSEFU SECTOR

Lubi

Ebony Grove Loop

Nsolo

Baka-Baka Lagoon

Lunga Lagoon

Kakuli

Tena Tena

⊕ *SLNPMI*
Milyoti gate

N

Bradt

Chisumpa Lagoons

Luangwa Wafwa

| 0 | 8km |
| 0 | 5 miles |

Mfuwe Lodge

Luangwa

Lupande GMA

Luangwa River Camp

MFUWE

MFUBRI Mfuwe Bridge

Chipata

GPS co-ordinates ⊕	
LUARLO	13°04.459'S 31°48.636'E
LUKUZI	12°50.926'S 32°02.060'E
MFUBRI	13°05.917'S 31°47.162'E
MWANYA	12°45.348'S 32°04.555'E
RIVERR	12°41.647'S 32°07.585'E
SLNPCH	12°51.983'S 32°01.008'E
SLNPMI	13°01.733'S 31°55.159'E

IC

The success of safaris in the Luangwa Valley is due in no small measure to one man: Norman Carr. Originally a ranger within the newly formed game reserves in the valley, Carr was quick to spot the potential of tourism as a lucrative source of income for the park. Although originally an advocate of hunting safaris, Carr soon recognised that there was an alternative – and one that didn't involve hunting down and killing the local fauna.

By 1950, Carr had persuaded Senior Chief Nsefu to establish a private reserve on the eastern bank of the Luangwa River. (Interestingly, a reliable local historian maintains that the colonial provincial commissioner was nervous about this. He feared that ultimately the local people would lose both their land and their access to collect salt at the pans in the centre of the Nsefu Sector. His concerns proved valid when, 20 years later, the Nsefu Sector was combined into the national park.) In partnership with the chief, Norman founded Nsefu Camp in 1952. The camp was close to the present-day Nsefu Camp (it's still visible on the Nsefu Luangwa Wafwa), though it was subsequently moved when the river changed its course.

In 1961, Carr set up his own wilderness safaris, based out of another camp, Kapani. This had been established in 1960, when he was warden of the Luangwa Valley, and it was here that he stayed with Big Boy and Little Boy, the two lions that he famously kept as companions. Kapani Camp lay just north of the Nsefu Sector, some 60km upstream of the present-day Kapani Safari Lodge, and close to today's Tafika. In 1961, Carr leased what was later known as Old Lion Camp, close to Kapani Camp but on the opposite (western) bank of the Luangwa River.

In those days the whole operation was basic, with Carr wading across the Luangwa every morning to fetch his clients from Old Lion Camp before taking them on a walking safari. Further camps were tried by the lower Kapamba River in 1963, and the Mwaleshi in the north of the reserve, but none was commercially viable. The venture to Mwaleshi, in North Luangwa, ended with the sad death of one of the guides, Peter Hankin, who was killed by a lioness.

Norman was more successful with his next venture. In 1965, he started walking safaris out of Chibembe Camp, just north of the Chibembe/Luangwa confluence (close to the new Zebra Plains camp, opened in 2011). With this as a hub, he established a circuit of several small pole-and-grass bushcamps, with his clients walking from camp to camp. Nine years later, he built Chibembe Lodge on the east bank; as this was larger and built of permanent materials, it had to be sited outside the park. With this as his main base, he continued to use the old Chibembe Camp as a walking bushcamp. This *modus operandi* of a number of small, temporary walking bushcamps working like satellites for one more-permanent lodge is still used by several of the valley's more traditional operations today.

Norman's clientele in those early days came mainly from the UK, with a few from Southern Rhodesia, South Africa and America. The expense of travelling to and from Zambia ensured that such safaris were a very expensive, elite activity.

Two years after Chibembe Lodge, Mwamba Bushcamp was constructed on the East Mwamba River, close to present-day Crocodile Bushcamp. This was the first exclusive bushcamp, a place where clients could hire the whole six-bed camp and have their own vehicle and guide. Other camps and lodges followed, including Chikoko and Kasansanya (1974). In 1977 Norman founded Chinzombo, which could be reached all year (Chibembe had always been inaccessible during the rains), then later came Kakuli, in 1984, and finally Kapani Safari Lodge in 1986.

NORMAN CARR'S LEGACY Nsefu Camp was the valley's first camp for photographic visitors. From the outset, one of its founding principles was that the indigenous people, the traditional owners of the wildlife, should benefit from the visitors. This mirrors the approach to conservation and development that has been adopted only recently by most of those working in this sector. (In the jargon, it is now called 'community-based natural-resource management'!) Norman Carr was a conservationist far ahead of his time.

Not only did Norman start a number of these camps, he also implemented education projects in the valley, and worked alongside and helped to train many of those who are now the valley's most experienced guides. These include:

- **Phil Berry**, who came to the Luangwa in 1963, and in 1973 joined the Zambian National Tourist Bureau to manage walking safaris, in competition with Norman's safari operations. Three years later they joined forces to start Chibembe. Phil is now the valley's most senior guide, and still leads some walks from his small bushcamp, Kuyenda. He's widely respected not only for his guiding, but also for his meticulous keeping of flora and fauna records, and work with Thornicroft's giraffe.
- **Robin Pope** came into the valley in 1976, working with Phil and Norman at Chibembe and then Nsefu Camp. Tena Tena started around 1983 as one of Nsefu's walking bushcamps, then Robin took it over in 1986 – and branched off to start perhaps the valley's most successful safari operation, Robin Pope Safaris. In 2010 Robin stepped back from the day-to-day running of the safari company and camps, although he still guides some trips, including the mini-expeditions that visit Liuwa Plains.
- **John Coppinger** started as a guide at Nsefu in 1984, whilst Robin was manager. He managed Nsefu for a few years, and then became general manager of Wilderness Trails – which then ran Chibembe, Nsefu, Big Lagoon and a travel agency in Lusaka. Eventually he left there is 1994, to start his own operation, Remote Africa Safaris, based out of Tafika.
- **Isaac Zulu** originally studied as an agriculturalist, but was trained by Norman from 1974. He guided in the valley for many years, including at Chibembe in the late 1980s. Eventually he left the valley in 1989 and worked with Tongabezi in Livingstone, until returning to the valley in 2001 with Chilongozi Safaris (now defunct). Currently he's again guiding with John at Remote Africa Safaris.
- **Abraham Banda** was trained by Norman in 1989, having come straight from the Kapani School (set up by Norman to offer local children the chance of a good education). Now Abraham is one of the leaders of the new generation of Luangwa guides; he manages the safari operation at Norman Carr Safaris, and is manager of their main lodge, Kapani. In addition, he runs a very successful charity to support Yoseffe School, and a number of other community projects.

The way that the Luangwa Valley's safari business has created opportunities for an increasing number of locally born people like Abraham, both in education and tourism, is part and parcel of why Norman Carr started safaris in the Luangwa over 60 years ago. Perhaps his greatest legacy is not the wealth of high-quality walking safaris here, but the impressively strong conservation and development ethics which underpin virtually all of the better, long-standing safari operations in the valley.

largest are Mutanda Plain in Nsefu, Lion Plain just opposite Nsefu, Chikaya Plain north of there, Ntanta around the Mupamadzi's confluence with the Luangwa, the huge Chifungwe Plain in the far north of the park, and the little-known Lundu Plain, south of the Mupamadzi River. These are not Serengeti-type plains with short grass; instead they usually boast tall species of grasses and often bushes. It is their lack of trees that makes them open.

Understandably, the highest density of animals (and hence camps) is around the Luangwa River. However, increasingly camps are being set up elsewhere in the park. The trio of bushcamps run by Norman Carr Safaris is located along the Lubi (or Luwi) River, one of the Luangwa's smaller tributaries, while temporary walking camps run by Robin Pope Safaris are sited beside the Mupamadzi River rather than the Luangwa.

The Luangwa River For the visitor, perhaps the most notable feature of the Luangwa Valley is the pristine river that runs through it. Take a close look at it: very few rivers of this size in Africa (or anywhere else!) have been so unaffected by man. There are no dams on it, no commercial agriculture along its banks, and incredibly little pollution. Hence here you can still see the seasonal fluctuations of water levels and flooding which lead to the dynamic nature of a river in a really natural state. It's not only beautiful but also textbook geography.

Note how the river's twisting curves cut easily through the valley's fertile soil, leaving a sprinkling of crescent-shaped oxbow lakes, or *wafwas*, in their wake. Every year new sandbanks arise as its original banks are cut back and the river's course changes with the floods. Just look at the number of riverside camps and lodges that, over the years, have either moved or gradually been swallowed up by river erosion.

GEOLOGY The Luangwa Valley is a rift valley, similar to the Great Rift Valley of east Africa, though probably older, and it shares its genesis with the adjoining Lower Zambezi Valley. The original sedimentary strata covering the whole area is part of the karoo system, sedimentary rocks laid down from 175 to 300 million years ago.

During this time, faulting occurred and volcanic material was injected into rifts in the existing sediments. One of these faults is the wide valley that the Luangwa now occupies. In geologically recent times, the Luangwa meandered extensively across the wide valley floor, eroding the volcanic rocks and depositing mineral-rich silts. These meanders also left behind them old watercourses and oxbow pools. The most recent of these can still be seen, and they are an important feature of the landscape near the present river.

FLORA AND FAUNA
Vegetation To understand the Luangwa Valley's vegetation, the base of its productive ecosystem, consider the elements that combine to nurture its plants: the water, light, heat and nutrients. Rainfall in the valley is typically 800–1,100mm per annum – which is moderate, but easily sufficient for strong vegetation growth. Occupying a position between 12° and 14° south of the Equator, the valley lacks neither light nor heat. (Visit in October and you may feel that it has too much of both.)

However, the key to its vegetation lies in the nutrients. The Luangwa's soils, being volcanic in origin, are rich in minerals, and the sediments laid down by the river are fine, making excellent soils. Thus with abundant water, light, heat and nutrient-rich soils, the valley's vegetation has thrived: it is both lush and diverse.

Unlike many parks, the 'bush' in the Luangwa is very variable, and as you drive or walk you'll pass through a patchwork of different vegetation zones. See *Flora and Fauna,* in *Chapter 3*, pages 29–33, for more detail, but the more obvious include some beautiful mature forests of 'cathedral mopane'. South of Mfuwe, just outside the national park on the way to the salt pans south of Nkwali, is one area where the mopane are particularly tall.

Along the Luangwa's tributaries, which are just rivers of sand for most of the year, you'll find lush riverine vegetation dominated by giant red mahogany trees (*Khaya anthotheca*, formerly known as *Khaya nyasica*) and *Adina microsephala*. Sometimes you'll also find Natal mahoganies (*Trichilia emetica*), and African ebony trees (*Diospyros mespiliformis*). There are several locations in the park where the latter form dense groves, casting a heavy shade on the sparse undergrowth. Look for such groves where the tributaries meet the Luangwa; there's one beside Mchenja Camp, and another near Kaingo.

Elsewhere are large, open grassland plains. Chief amongst these are probably the plains in the Nsefu Sector. These surround some natural salt springs, which attract crowned cranes in their thousands.

Antelope and other herbivores With its rich vegetation, the Luangwa supports large numbers of a wide variety of animals. Each species has its own niche in the food chain, which avoids direct competition with any other species. Each herbivore has its favourite food plants, and even species that utilise the same food plants will feed on different parts of those plants. This efficient use of the available vegetation – refined over the last few millennia – makes the wildlife far more productive than any domestic stock would be if given the same land. It also leads to the high densities of game that the valley supports.

The game includes huge herds of buffalo, commonly hundreds of animals strong, and seemingly endless family groups of elephants; both are particularly spectacular if encountered whilst you are on foot. Despite Zambia's past poaching problems, South Luangwa's elephants are generally neither scarce nor excessively skittish in the presence of people. Just north of Mfuwe Lodge, you'll find an open plain with few trees, just the skeletal trunks of an old cathedral mopane forest. This has always been attributed to elephant damage from the 1970s, before ivory poaching became a problem, when there were around 56,000 elephants in the park (100,000 in the whole Luangwa Valley) – though very recent research suggests that soil changes and even heart rot disease may have contributed to the trees' demise.

The park's dominant antelope species are puku and impala. Whilst impala are dominant in much of southern Africa, including the Zambezi Valley and throughout Zimbabwe, puku are rare south of the Zambezi. They form small breeding groups which are exceedingly common in their favourite habitat – well-watered riverine areas. Groups are dominated by a territorial male adorned with the characteristic lyre-shaped horns.

Luangwa has a number of 'specialities' including the beautiful Thornicroft's giraffe (*Giraffa camelopardalis thornicroftii*). This rare subspecies differs from the much more common southern giraffe, found in Kafue, south of the Zambezi, and throughout southern Africa, in having a different (and more striking) coloration. Thornicroft's have dark body patches and lighter neck patches; their colour patches don't normally extend below the knees, leaving their lower legs almost white; and their faces are light or white. Fortunately, around the Mfuwe area there is a widespread traditional belief that people who eat giraffe meat will get spots like those of a giraffe. Hence giraffe are rarely hunted by the local people, and are even very common in the GMA to the east of the river, outside the national park.

Cookson's wildebeest (*Connochaetes taurinus cooksoni*), a subspecies of the blue wildebeest found throughout sub-Saharan Africa, are endemic to the valley. They

10

are more common in more northerly areas of the valley, such as the North Luangwa, and Norman Carr's wildlife guide (see *Appendix 3*, page 536) maintains that they also seem to favour the east side of the river, rather than the west. That said, in South Luangwa you've also a fair chance of seeing them in the Nsefu Sector, and on Lion Plain, and particularly around Mwamba Bushcamp area. They differ from the blue wildebeest in having cleaner colours, including slightly reddish bands, and being a little smaller and more compact.

Another special of the Luangwa Valley is Crawshay's zebra (*Equus quagga crawshaii*), a subspecies of the more common plains zebra, which is found in much of the subcontinent. Crawshay's zebra occur east of the Muchinga Escarpment – in the Luangwa Valley and on Nyika Plateau – and lack the brown shadow-stripe that plains zebra usually have between their black stripes.

In contrast to these examples, it is the common waterbuck (*Kobus ellipsiprymnus*) that is found in the valley, rather than its rarer subspecies, the defassa waterbuck (*K. e. crawshayi*), which is found over most of the rest of Zambia. The common waterbuck has the characteristic white 'toilet seat' ring on its rump, whereas the defassa has a white circular patch.

Other antelope in the park include bushbuck, eland and kudu. The delicate oribi occur occasionally in the grassland areas (especially Chifungwe Plain), while grysbok are often encountered on night drives. Reedbuck and Lichtenstein's hartebeest also occur, but not usually near the river, whilst sable are occasionally seen in the hills near the escarpment. Like sable, roan antelope seem to be most frequently seen in the hills – often on the roads south of Chichele, although in the late dry season there are frequent sightings in the Chikoko area, on the fringes of Chifungwe Plain, and in the 'corridor' area between the North and South parks.

A special mention must go to the hippopotami (and crocodiles) found in the rivers, and especially in the Luangwa: their numbers are remarkable. Look over the main bridge crossing the Luangwa at Mfuwe – sometimes there are hundreds of hippo there. Towards the end of the dry season, when the rivers are at their lowest, is the best time to observe such dense congregations of hippo. Then these semi-aquatic mammals are forced into smaller and smaller pools, and you'll appreciate their sheer numbers. These congregations reach their peak in October and November when, for example, you'll find a concentration of 1,000 hippo in just 2km of river, in the Changwa Channel, north of Chibembe. This is probably easiest (and certainly most spectacular) to see by flying over it in a microlight from Tafika.

Predators The main predators in the Luangwa Valley are typical of sub-Saharan Africa: lion, leopard, spotted hyena and wild dog. During the day, the visitor is most likely to see lion (*Panthera leo*), which are the park's most common large predator. Their large prides are relatively easily spotted, at least in the dry season when the grass is low, and to witness one of their hunting trips makes a gripping spectacle.

South Luangwa has made a name for itself amongst the safari community as an excellent park for leopard (*Panthera pardus*). This is largely because leopard hunt nocturnally, and Zambia is one of the few African countries to allow operators to go on spotlit game drives at night. Estimates made whilst filming a BBC documentary about leopards in the park suggest an average leopard density of one animal per 2.5km² – roughly twice the density recorded in South Africa's Kruger National Park. So perhaps the reputation is justified. In my experience, night drives in Luangwa with experienced guides do consistently yield excellent sightings of these cats – at a frequency that is difficult to match elsewhere on the continent. In contrast to this, I'm not aware of any sightings of cheetah for well over 20 years.

Wild dog are also uncommon, though their population seems to oscillate over a period of years. A study of wild dogs in Zambia by Kenneth Buk in 1995 (see *Appendix 3*, page 536) suggested that the Luangwa holds Zambia's second-largest wild dog population, even though this was badly depleted by an outbreak of anthrax in 1987. Since the late 1990s, wild dog have gradually been making more appearances. They're now regularly seen, with a particularly high incidence of sightings south of Mfuwe, near the Nkwali pontoon, from around February to May. Recent research suggests that their numbers are building up (see box, *Carnivores in Zambia's national parks*, page 266).

Birds The Luangwa boasts the rich tropical birdlife that you would expect of such a fertile valley. This includes species that prefer a dry habitat of plains and forests, and those that live close to water. It is difficult to mention more than a few of the Luangwa's 400 species, but several books listed in *Appendix 3* (page 536) cover the region's birds. As the Luangwa is situated between southern and east Africa, keen birdwatchers may want to arrive with two field guides, each describing birds from one region, so that between them they will cover the full range of species encountered in the valley. Better still, bring a good guide to southern Africa's birds, like Newman's guide, and buy Aspinwall and Beel's Zambian guide locally (see *Appendix 3*, which explains the logic of this). Alternatively, get hold of a single guide to the birds of sub-Saharan Africa or the more concise Collins Illustrated Checklist to the *Birds of Southern Africa*.

Species of note include flocks of crowned cranes occurring on the marshes of the Nsefu Sector; the colonies of iridescent carmine bee-eaters that nest in sandy riverbanks in September and October; the African skimmers found along the river; and the giant eagle owls which are sometimes picked out by the spotlight on night drives.

The best time for birds is the summer: the rainy season. The birds' food supply is then at its most abundant, and the summer migrants are around. Just drive into the park during the rains and it becomes immediately apparent that both the vegetation and the birdlife are running riot. Dry plains have sprouted thick, green vegetation mirrored all around in shallow water. Flocks of egrets, herons and storks wade through this, around feeding geese and ducks.

Many species breed here, including storks that often form impressive colonies. There are several sites of tall trees in the Nsefu Sector which, when surrounded by shallow water, regularly become breeding colonies. The most amazing of these has half-a-dozen huge trees filled with nests of yellow-billed storks in their spectacular pink breeding plumage. This is one of the Luangwa's most remarkable sights.

CONSERVATION IN THE LUANGWA
Hunting and poaching South Luangwa has always been Zambia's 'most favoured park'. Over the years it has been given a disproportionately large share of the resources allotted to all of the country's national parks. Many would argue that this has been to the detriment of the other parks, though it did enable it to fight the plague of commercial poaching, which hit the country in the 1980s, with some success. The poachers came for rhino horn – which is sold to make dagger-handles in the Middle East and Chinese medicines for the Far East – and, of course, for ivory.

Sadly the valley's thriving black rhino population was wiped out, as it almost certainly was throughout Zambia; the last confirmed sightings in the Luangwa were in 1987. (One or two sources suggest that a couple of individual animals may be left in the wild, but this is probably just wishful thinking.) However, the good news is that five black rhino re-introduced into a specially protected area within the North Luangwa National Park in 2003 were followed by a further ten in 2006. I was lucky enough to be there to watch as the first animals were each fitted with a radio transceiver, prior to their release. Although two of the rhino have died, further relocations have taken place and several calves have been born, resulting in a population of 29 by 2011. It's a tremendous achievement for conservation in the Luangwa, acknowledging a real *volte-face* in conservation in the valley.

Fortunately, the valley's elephant populations didn't fare as badly as the rhino; they were only reduced. In recent years, thanks in part to the CITES ban on the ivory trade, they have bounced back – and South Luangwa, especially, has very healthy, large herds of relaxed elephants.

Today there is minimal poaching in the park, as demonstrated by the size of the animal populations, and certainly no lack of game. Only in the nervous elephant populations of North Luangwa does one get any echo of the poaching problems of the past.

South Luangwa Conservation Society (e *rachel@slcszambia.org; www. slcszambia.org*) Formed in 2003 in order to support the Zambia Wildlife Authority and Community Resource Boards, the South Luangwa Conservation Society pulled

CARNIVORES IN ZAMBIA'S NATIONAL PARKS

Because large threatened carnivores such as African wild dog, lion and cheetah are naturally wide-ranging and low density they require immense areas to survive, and are therefore very susceptible to human impacts such as habitat loss, disease and persecution. Consequently the presence of these species is synonymous with large relatively intact ecosystems, and Zambia's national parks are a case in point.

With nearly one-third of the country managed for wildlife through national parks and adjacent game management areas (GMAs), Zambia is home to a number of threatened large carnivore species (many of whose populations extend into neighbouring countries such as Malawi). Of these, the African wild dog, or painted dog, once found throughout most of sub-Saharan Africa, is now one of the continent's most endangered carnivores, with Zambia one of only six countries to have a viable population. The immense Kafue National Park is thought to have the country's largest number of wild dogs, followed by the Luangwa Valley.

Intensive conservation work on these dogs was initiated in 1999 in the Lower Zambezi National Park with the formation by Dr Kellie Leigh of African Wild Dog Conservation. This has since broadened into the Zambian Carnivore Programme (ZCP) which, working in collaboration with ZAWA, is focused on conserving Zambia's large carnivores and the ecosystems on which they depend. Fully field-based and operating in eastern Zambia, Kafue, Liuwa Plain and the Bangweulu Wetlands, the ZCP uses an interdisciplinary approach of research, conservation and education to ensure the best chances of survival for Zambia's large carnivores. In addition, because cheetah and wild dog can be individually identified by their coat patterns, any photographs you take of these sightings in Zambia can be invaluable to research and conservation efforts; please submit yours to ZCP direct (e *zambiacarnivores@gmail.com; www.zambiacarnivores.org*).

Chipembele (*0216 246108;* info@chipembele.org; www.chipembele.org; ⊕ CHIPEM 13°12.122's, 31°42.221'E) came about through the determination of Steve and Anna Tolan, who retired from the British police force in 1998 to invest in their dream of educating children in conservation matters. With a passion for African wildlife born of years of travelling and reading, they set about building an education centre, which was finally opened on the eastern bank of the Luangwa River, about 16km southwest of Mfuwe, in 2001. The centre has a large interpretive room complete with displays and exhibits, and visitors are welcome by prior arrangement.

Chipembele's work focuses on teaching through active involvement and fun. Children come for the day from schools all over the area, spending time *en route* spotting game that many of them may never have seen before.

From this central project, Anna has branched out into an extensive conservation outreach programme in the local schools, school improvement projects and a pupil sponsorship scheme, while Steve has taken on anti-poaching work and forestry protection. Rehabilitation of orphaned and injured animals is a further aspect of their work, together with an active involvement in the South Luangwa Conservation Society.

together the work initially undertaken by the honorary rangers and volunteers in the valley. Now with its own premises just outside the national park, it continues to focus on the original aspect of its work, funded by a combination of membership fees and donations. The society directly supports 56 members of staff, most of whom are village scouts with salaries, accommodation, rations, equipment, incentives and ongoing training.

In addition, the society is actively involved in education programmes with the local community. An ongoing anti-snaring programme helps to make both adults and children aware of the impact of poaching and snaring on the wildlife and on the local environment, while a darting programme helps to rescue animals that have been snared by poachers. From another angle, the introduction of chilli fences (see page 330) is helping farmers whose crops are threatened by wildlife.

Conservation and development in Lupande GMA South Luangwa has always been protected from poaching in a way that Zambia's other parks were not. This wasn't always 100% effective, but it was a lot better than elsewhere. Several years ago a project was started in sections of the Lupande GMA, which is immediately adjacent to the national park, to distribute direct cash benefits from the park to the local people.

This has worked very well beside the river (ie: alongside the park), where the animals are plentiful and the hunting income has been very good. Certainly one of the local chiefs has a very nice brick-built palace with satellite television and an impressive new twin-cab Land Cruiser parked in front.

However, further from the park the hunting isn't as good, and the fees have certainly been less. Locals comment that the influx of people into the Mfuwe Bridge area over the last decade has been very noticeable. Even I can see that there are now far more people around that when I first visited in 1995.

Much of the cause of this may be simply the employment prospects generated directly (and indirectly), by the lodges. However, this influx means that the GMA's revenues are being effectively divided among more people. It also puts more strain on the area's agriculture, to increase cultivated land in the area. The danger is that with more people and more cultivation, there will inevitably be a reduction in the GMA's game densities.

This is another Gordian knot for those working on conservation and development in the area to tackle. See *Conservation* in *Chapter 3*, pages 33–5, for a more general discussion of these issues.

LOCAL SAFARI OPERATORS When choosing a camp or local operator, it's important that you pick a good and reliable one. You're in such a remote area that you can't afford to have problems. One safeguard is to seek advice from a good, independent overseas tour operator. For all except the budget camps, you should find that booking your trip through them will be cheaper than booking directly with the camps.

Perhaps also check out Expert Africa's website, www.expertafrica.com (even if you're not arranging a trip with them), as I will be posting updates there for all to see. Many of the smaller one- or two-camp operations are excellent. Meanwhile, here are the contact details and selected snippets of background information on a few of the higher-profile safari operators, in alphabetical order:

Bushcamp Company ✆ 0216 246041; e info@bushcampcompany.com; www. bushcampcompany.com. The Bushcamp Company was formed in 2000 from 2 very old bushcamps (Chamilandu & Kuyenda), both originally owned by Chinzombo, & 2 new ones (Bilimungwe & Chindeni), which were originally owned by Mfuwe Lodge – which is now the hub of their operations. A 5th camp, Kapamba, was added in 2005, & Zungulila in 2008. The company is still run by Andy Hogg, its main founding director, although in 2010 it was bought by a US-based billionaire philanthropist, Paul Allen.

Bushcamp Company has carved out a niche by offering small, remote, high-quality bushcamps. Each camp is different, & although all include walking safaris, all also offer night drives. Guiding standards are high, although be aware that it's usual to just have 1 guide in each camp – & so often all the guests will do the same activity at any one time. Note that it's possible to walk from Chamilandu to Chindeni to Bilimungwe to Kapamba to Zungulila.

Norman Carr Safaris ✆ 0216 246025; e kapani@normancarrsafaris.com; www. normancarrsafaris.com. Norman Carr himself lived at Kapani until his death in 1997, & his family still head up the very capable team who run the company. Operations encompass Kapani Safari Lodge & 4 bushcamps used for walking trips: Nsolo, Luwi, Kakuli & Mchenja. If you want to walk between different bushcamps, going

from one to the next every few days, then the walk down the dry Luwi River is difficult to beat. All are excellent camps & Norman Carr Safaris rightly retains one of the best reputations of any company in the valley. It is currently 1 of only 2 companies to organise regular river safaris in the park (see page 292).

Remote Africa Safaris ✆ 0216 246185; e reservations@remoteafrica.com; www. remoteafrica.com. Founded by John & Carol Coppinger, Remote Africa Safaris is a small but high-quality operator with truly innovative ideas. They run 4 excellent camps: Tafika in South Luangwa, plus the Chikoko Trails walking camps (Chikoko & Crocodile), & Mwaleshi in the North Park; all are regularly refurbished. John used to run Wilderness Trails in the valley, & is regarded as one of the most experienced guides in the region. His guides also include Ernst Jacobs, Isaac Zulu & Stephen Banda, who are experts on the area in their own right.

John is one of the very few people to have canoed the length of the Mwaleshi & Luangwa rivers & was the first to run river safaris in the valley. He also pilots the valley's only microlight aircraft, which is based at Tafika. Remote Africa is unquestionably another of the valley's very best operators.

Robin Pope Safaris ✆ 0216 246090–2; e info@robinpopesafaris.net; www. robinpopesafaris.net, www.robinpopecamps. com. This excellent & highly reliable company was founded by Robin Pope, who was raised in Zambia, trained by Norman Carr, & is another of the top wildlife guides in the valley. His English wife, Jo, was the first woman to qualify as a walking guide in the valley – but it is her efficiency with the marketing & business side of the operation that make her legendary. Together with a very good team they built up what is probably the valley's most complex set of camps & trips, including Tena Tena, Nkwali & Nsefu, river safaris, & a range of different walking safaris (including some true mobiles, the valley's first true bush-camping, & various 'special-interest' safaris in & beyond the valley). In 2010 Robin & Jo handed over the helm of RPS to a Malawi-based Dutch couple, Ton & Margeaux do Rooy – although Robin continues to lead interesting safaris, & Jo's marketing skills are in demand, not least by the Zambia Tourism Board. RPS are unusual in the valley in having no single supplement for most of their camps – although others will often waive this.

Sanctuary Retreats +27 (0)11 438 4650; e southernafrica@sanctuaryretreats.com; www.sanctuaryretreats.com. Sanctuary entered the Zambian market in 2007, taking over several camps from the former Star of Africa. Two of these – Chichele Presidential Lodge & the neighbouring Puku Ridge Camp – are in the South Luangwa, as is the small new Zebra Plains, a seasonal walking camp that opened in 2011. They also have Zambezi Kulefu Camp in the Lower Zambezi, Sussi & Chuma in Livingstone, & (at least in theory) Lechwe Plains Tented Camp in Lochinvar – although there aren't any signs that this will re-open in the near future. Owned by Abercrombie & Kent, Sanctuary also owns a number of small, luxury properties in Botswana & east Africa.

Shenton Safaris (May–Oct only) 0216 246064; e info@kaingo.com; www.kaingo.com. Established by Derek Shenton, Shenton Safaris runs Kaingo Camp & Mwamba, both classic, small camps in a good game area with a strong focus on good guiding & game viewing. Derek was joined a few years ago by Juliet, whose influence has led to a steady rise in standards of service & comfort. Notable are the value they place on using game hides, & – almost unique in the valley – a keenness to organise 3 activities a day, which makes them particularly attractive to photographers. The family also owns Forest Inn, near Mkushi (see page 308).

Wilderness Safaris See page 431.

GETTING THERE

By air Most visitors to the South Luangwa fly in to Mfuwe, which during the main safari season, from June to the end of October, is one of the easiest places in Zambia to reach by air. Currently it is regularly serviced by Proflight (page 397), who schedule up to three flights a day throughout the year. Expect a one-way trip between Lusaka and Mfuwe to cost around US$250 per person; double that for a return. The airline also operates a seasonal service between Mfuwe and the Lower Zambezi.

If you're arriving on an organised trip, then you can relax. A vehicle will be waiting to take you to camp, and there's no need to think ahead.

Mfuwe Airport Mfuwe Airport (⊕ MFUAIR 13°15.281'S, 31°55.933'E) is an international airport, with customs and immigration, but it feels like a small, local one. There's one terminal building, and if you're on one of the smaller flights in and out of the valley, then you're likely to have the pilot coming to find you.

Inside the terminal are toilets, a few small shops and two ATMs, one of which is a Barclays. Just outside you'll find the labelled parking spaces where 4x4s from the lodges wait for their pre-booked incoming passengers. A few yards away is a small café worth investigating:

Sky Trails Café m 0979 337206; ⊕ normally 08.00–17.00, all year. Situated beside the airport, & run by Sky Trails, a charter air company, it's a relaxed place to have a drink as you arrive, or before you leave, or even a tasty bite to eat. The menu includes homemade pizza, toasted sandwiches, meat pies, samosas & various b/fast items. Prices are in kwacha but you can pay in dollars. $

Driving Approaching from Chipata is by far the easiest way to reach the park if you are driving, and once the tarring is complete along this stretch, it will significantly reduce the driving time. Until then, it remains a rather long and tedious drive, but not usually difficult in the dry season provided that your vehicle has a good suspension.

Driving from the north, or Mpika, is a totally different story: it requires a small expedition of at least two well-equipped 4x4 vehicles, driven by experienced bush drivers with a high degree of self-reliance.

From Chipata The turn-off to Mfuwe is clearly signposted just west of Chipata. This takes you along a clearly defined road which in 2011 was largely gravel punctuated with tar, and increasingly rutted as you approach the national park. This road winds down from the high escarpment and into the valley. The views are spectacular, and you will pass many small villages on the way. Keep the windows open and you will feel both the temperature and the humidity rise as you descend.

After around 65km you will pass the Chisengu turn-off (⊕ TUSLNP 13°18.131'S, 32°13.234'E) to the right, where a rough track leads to the Kauluzi and Chikwinda gates. This is part of an old district road which used to connect Chipata and Lundazi, though sections of it further north have not been passable for many years, so it's unlikely to be re-opened.

Continuing straight on, the road leads to Jumbe after about 16km, then there's a short, blissful stretch of tar over Mpata Hill (⊕ HILL2 13°26.728'S, 32°20.489'E). Another 15km brings you to a tarmac T-junction. Turn left for 3–4km to reach Mfuwe Airport (⊕ MFUAIR 13°15.281'S, 31°55.933'E), or right for Mfuwe Bridge (⊕ MFUBRI 13°5.917'S, 31°47.162'E) and the park. From Chipata it's about 95km to Mfuwe Airport, or about 115km to the main bridge into the park, over the Luangwa River.

From Petauke Fully-equipped 4x4 vehicles coming from Lusaka might be tempted to take an earlier turn off the Great East Road, and approach the south side of the park via a turn-off from Petauke. I haven't driven this road; it's very rarely used and is much slower and more difficult than the Chipata road (above), though also more scenic and interesting. It's about 150km to the park's southern gate at Chilongozi, then a further 40km to Mfuwe, during which time you're unlikely to see any other vehicles.

For those who have the back-up and want to try this, here are some old directions and GPS waypoints. Turn off the Great East Road to Petauke (⊕ PETAUK 14°17.730'S, 31°20.253'E) next to the BP filling station (last fuel-up before Mfuwe). It's 4km until you pass the police station, on the right. Then turn left and continue up the hill, taking a left fork after about 200m (⊕ PETS01 14°14.982'S, 31°20.280'E). Head for Ukwimi which is about 50km of ungraded track, following this route:

⊕ PETS02 13°56.842'S, 31°36.867'E	⊕ PETS08 13°37.398'S, 31°34.609'E
⊕ PETS03 13°50.448'S, 31°35.188'E	⊕ PETS09 13°34.183'S, 31°34.183'E
⊕ PETS04 13°48.282'S, 31°34.699'E	⊕ PETS10 13°31.152'S, 31°34.360'E
⊕ PETS05 13°47.971'S, 31°34.555'E	⊕ PETS11 13°25.981'S, 31°33.354'E
⊕ PETS06 13°46.096'S, 31°35.789'E	⊕ PETS12 13°26.011'S, 31°33.593'E
⊕ PETS07 13°38.386'S, 31°34.774'E	⊕ PETS13 13°22.746'S, 31°36.775'E

This brings you to the Chilongozi area and the now-defunct Nyamaluma pontoon (⊕ NYALUM 13°22.630'S, 31°36.974'E). From here you now have to continue roughly northeast, shadowing the east bank of the Luangwa, and you'll eventually emerge into Mfuwe just east of the bridge.

From Mpika via the Corridor Road and '05' Driving south from Mpika, down into the Luangwa Valley between the North and South parks, and then crossing the Mupamadzi into South Luangwa, is possible only in the dry season – but it's probably the trickiest of the ways to get here. See the section on getting to Luambe National Park, entitled *From Mpika via the Corridor Road*, on pages 303–4, for the start of the route. After turning east from the Great North Road (⊕ TUBATE 12°6.421'S, 31°15.727'E) about 40km south of Mpika, you pass Nthunta scout camp (⊕ NTHUNT 12°19.828'S, 31°31.979'E) and then drop over the escarpment and eventually reach the Mutinondo River. About 8.8km after crossing this, there's a left turning which leads to Nabwalya village and the Luangwa River (though the pontoon across the river is no longer operational).

To reach the national park, don't turn left to Nabwalya but continue straight on, then after a further 7.3km you will reach the Chifungwe gate (⊕ CHIFUNG 12°26.061'S, 31°42.263'E), just before the Mupamadzi River. This is the boundary to South Luangwa National Park, reached about 73km from the Great North Road. Crossing the Mupamadzi (which should only be attempted when low) is tricky, but then it's a simple, if long, journey to head due south.

About 3.4km after the Mupamadzi crossing you reach a junction: to the left is a small road to the private Mupamadzi Walking Area; to the right is the '05' road (see also box, page 272) which is very little used but will take you right across the heart of the park, skirting the western side of Zebra Pans. About 55km after the Mupamadzi, you will reach the deep sand of the Luwi River (⊕ 05LUWI 12°56.381'S, 31°45.468'E) near Nsolo Bushcamp, and then some 10km after that you join the network of all-weather roads in the Mfuwe area, just north of the 'Big Baobab' and Mfuwe Lodge (see Mfuwe area map, page 258).

From Luambe See pages 302–3 for details of this route in reverse, and backtrack.

The Luangwa Valley SOUTH LUANGWA NATIONAL PARK

10

By bus/taxi With an increasing population in Mfuwe there are now small minibuses which ply between Chipata and Mfuwe. These cost from Kw60,000 one way (though as a tourist you could expect to pay considerably more) and usually won't leave until full. Small groups of travellers may be able to hire a vehicle for a reasonable rate; make sure you agree on Mfuwe Airport as the drop-off location.

Hitchhiking With plenty of water and stamina, getting to Mfuwe from Chipata is possible. Start hitching early at the turn-off. (There's a basic motel nearby so you can always sleep there if necessary.) Don't accept local lifts going just a few kilometres; there's no point – better to wait for a vehicle going at least to Mfuwe Airport. Some of the camps have trucks doing supply runs to Chipata, there are occasional tourists (though fewer with space to spare) and there is a small amount of local traffic. I took five hours just to get a lift from here one October morning, so expect a long wait.

AROUND THE MFUWE AREA If you are driving (or hitching) to the South Luangwa, then you may be aiming for a dot on the map marked 'Mfuwe'. On the ground, however, this is far from clear. In spirit, the centre of Mfuwe is probably the airport

LESSONS IN BUSH TRAVEL

In early November 2002, two German visitors borrowed a brand-new 4x4 to explore the South Luangwa. The car was a small, low-slung saloon, one of the latest models and very much state-of-the-art. It had on-board computers to control much of the vehicle, from the engine to the suspension.

Coming from Mpika, they entered the Luangwa Valley by the tricky 'corridor' road, successfully reaching the remote Chifungwe game scouts' camp. They planned to take the road known locally as the '05', which passes near the old site of Zebra Pans Bushcamp, before eventually reaching a crossroads near Nsolo Bushcamp, and then the heart of the Mfuwe area. It's a dead straight road (with a bearing of about 5°), mostly through thick bush. It's used very little, and was sure to be very quiet then as all the valley's bushcamps close at the end of October.

All went smoothly until they were crossing the Mupamadzi River, about 3km after the scouts' camp. Halfway across, they got stuck. Then the driver realised that he hadn't locked his hubs (some 4x4 vehicles require one to physically turn a switch on the wheels), so he got out in the river and turned the hubs. Surprisingly, they managed to drive to the other side.

All seemed well and the pair continued south, but 25km further along the road, the car died. Water had got into the wiring; the car's computer had shut down and with it the engine. If the car had broken down in the river, the two men would have been only 3km from the scouts' camp. Now they were 28km away. As is normally wise, they decided to wait with their car for a passing vehicle to summon help. Unfortunately, 24 hours later, not one vehicle had passed by. The '05' is one of many bush roads in Africa which may see only a handful of vehicles per year; just because it's marked on the maps, it is a mistake to assume that it's used frequently!

The men were starting to feel desperate. They had told nobody local what their plans were; nobody was expecting them anywhere. Nobody would raise an alarm. All they had with them was some fruit juice, water, butter and cheese, and the water was running out fast, They decided to walk to find help – southwards towards Mfuwe. After 25km, the elder of the two men, sore and tired, could walk (see page 269), where most of the valley's visitors arrive and depart, and thus frequented by vehicles from the valley's camps.

For the most part, though, the focus of Mfuwe is increasingly the area around the Mfuwe Bridge (⊕ MFUBRI 13°5.917'S, 31°47.162'E) over the Luangwa River. This is 25km northwest of the airport, and is the main entrance to the park's all-weather road network; most visitors entering or leaving the national park pass this way. Here you'll find a very unreliable fuel station with a Zanaco ATM, and some basic shops.

As you approach the bridge, there's a tar road to the left towards Kapani, Nkwali and the lodges and camps on the southern side of Mfuwe. Then, a little further on the right, is the turning to various lodges including Marula Lodge and Track and Trail, and finally there's a turning to the left to Flatdogs.

Along the D104 road between the airport and the bridge you will pass the occasional farm stalls selling vegetables, as well as a school, a church and a clinic – but there is no big town here. There are, though, more small shops, including the well-stocked **Mayana** which sells good cuts of meat as well as milk, eggs, crisps, etc. There's also a small hotel, and the main outlet for Tribal Textiles.

no further. They agreed that he should stop there, whilst the younger, fitter man would continue.

Then their fortunes turned: it rained. The older man, who had been sitting in temperatures of 43°C during the day, took off his clothes and lay on the ground to soak up the water. At 16.00 the next day, he was discovered at the side of the road by a scout patrol. He was naked and approaching delirium; the scouts estimated that he was about three to four hours from death.

Meanwhile, the younger man had continued walking through the night, but lost the main road whilst avoiding a small herd of elephants. Miraculously, in the morning he stumbled across Nsolo Bushcamp. Being November, everything had just closed down for the rains, but a rummage through the bins uncovered tin cans, while the dry river nearby yielded water where the elephants had dug up the bed with their tusks. Boiling the water in the cans on an open fire, the man felt better. The next morning, the scout patrol who had found his friend followed his tracks to Nsolo, and found him there. He was relatively well, although concerned by the two lionesses who had been watching him closely.

Both men were very lucky and now safe – but what of the car? It took nine hours to tow it northwards and back across the river. Then it rained for two days, and the river flooded – making the road impassable. Anyone who knows the area would have told them that November was a crazy time to drive across that river.

Meanwhile, a mechanic flew up to attempt repairs. Plugging his laptop into the car, he restarted its computer and had it working in minutes. Apparently it just needed resetting! Later the men learnt that it would have been possible to shut down the computer entirely.

There are many lessons to draw from this, but the big picture is clear. Unless you're an experienced old Africa hand with a good network of local contacts, unless you take good advice, and drive a vehicle that you know, then driving yourself around the more remote corners of Zambia is asking for trouble. Just because this book indicates GPS positions and bush tracks, it does not mean that these routes are suitable for drivers who aren't experienced in remote African travel.

10

Where to stay near the airport

Just Africa (7 rooms) m 0979 696503;
e lodge@just-africa.com; www.just-africa.com.
⊕ 13°12.123'S, 31°54.949'E. Some 3km from
the airport, Just Africa is owned by an engaging,
entrepreneurial local woman, Misozi Kadewele,
who is also responsible for the 'Snarewear' range
of jewellery made locally from wire snares.
Recommended for those on a tight budget, Just
Africa has 4 chalets & 3 bedrooms, most of which
have an en-suite shower (water heated by wood-
fired boilers) & toilet. These are basic but clean,
the beds have mosi nets & there's electricity for
charging – including an unexpected solar-&-
battery inverter system in the chalets. Game
drives & village visits can be organised. Self-
catering is possible although dinner – typically
nshima & relish (*US$6–10 pp*) & even drinks are
available for residents. **$**

Tribal Textiles (e *marketing@tribaltextiles.co.zm; www.tribaltextiles.co.zm;*
⊕ 13°12.052'S, 31°54.803'E) About 5km from the airport, this well laid-out shop
to the right of the road is marked by large, painted pillars. Started to create local
employment, it sells perhaps Zambia's best hand-painted textiles. Prices are
reasonable (credit cards accepted) and a guide is on hand to explain how the fabrics
are made and to take you round the factory. Don't miss it.

GETTING AROUND

In your own vehicle South Luangwa's network of roads is not as extensive as you
might expect. A few all-weather roads (mostly graded gravel) have been built in the
park around the Mfuwe area – accessible over the main bridge into the park. There's
also an isolated network around the camps owned by the Bushcamp Company, in
the south of the park. These are the only roads that can be relied upon during the
wet season.

Elsewhere, the park has seasonally passable roads that are (optimistically)
marked on some of the maps. Such tracks follow both banks of the Luangwa, north
and south of Mfuwe, and a few penetrate westwards into the park. In the areas near
camps, there are numerous 'loop' roads, which leave these main tracks and return
to them. These are just side roads for game viewing, and trying to be precise about
their position is pointless – they are usually made simply by the passage of a few
vehicles, and will disappear again very swiftly once the vehicles stop.

Note that if you are driving your own vehicle around the park then you are
limited to being in the park from dawn to dusk. You are not allowed to stay in and
drive around after dark; only local safari companies have licences to conduct night
drives. (Note also that the Nkwali pontoon marked on many maps is not for use by
private vehicles.)

Without a vehicle If you do not have a vehicle of your own, then you should
organise your camps or lodges before you arrive. If you haven't done so before you
arrive, then you may be limited to a handful of budget options based in the Mfuwe
area. If your budget is higher, then you might consider stopping at Sky Trails Café
(by the airport) and asking them to radio a few of the more upmarket camps to see
if any have space left. This is unusual, and don't expect bargains (you won't find
any), but it is a real waste to get all the way here and then not make the most of the
park. So if you can, splash out on the best place that you can afford.

There are two other possibilities:

Jackalberry Safaris m 0966 411320; e info@
jackalberry.net; www.jackalberrysafaris.net.
This is a no-frills operation run by Gavin Opie out
of the Wildlife Camp. He offers ad hoc 3-, 4- or
5-day safaris which usually include transfers to
& from Chipata (the pick-up point is Deans Hill

View Lodge). Accommodation is in tents with beds, while washing facilities are shared with other campers. Shorter trips consist of day & night drives in the park, plus a walking safari in the GMA, while the longest features a night at the Wildlife Camp's bushcamp. Gavin is well versed in the area's archaeology, so if you tire of the wildlife ask him to take you on a trip to the nearby saltpans, a key location on the east African slave-trading route. *3-day US$495; 4-day US$645; 5-day US$795.* ⏰ *Apr–Nov (no walking safari in Apr).*

The Personal Touch 📞 0216 246123; 📱 0978 459965; 📧 info@tptouch.com. Owner Ben Koobs rents out 4x4 open Land Rover safari vehicles with 9 seats, geared to game drives within or around the park. An accompanying guide can be arranged on request. Airport/lodge transfers within the South Luangwa NP & trips to Kawaza & other community projects are also possible. *US$125/24 hrs, exc park fees.*

Maps Two different maps of the South Luangwa National Park may be available in Lusaka. One showing South Luangwa and Luambe national parks was compiled for the national tourist board, and is useful in giving the general scheme of the area's roads. Otherwise the information on its reverse side is fairly dated, and so not very valuable.

A second very different map concentrates on just the South Luangwa National Park. This was produced in 1989 using aid donations and shows the landscape and vegetation in considerable scientific detail; it's a scholarly work. Its reverse side details the various land systems in the area: the different combinations of land form, rock, soil and vegetation in the park. This is a fascinating map which has some of the camps marked, but only a few of the existing roads.

In the unlikely event that you need to navigate yourself at all, get both of these and consider also buying more detailed Ordnance Survey-style maps available from the surveyor general's office in Lusaka. Such detailed maps (preferably together with a GPS and good local guide) would be essential for visits to Luambe or Lukusuzi.

🏠 **WHERE TO STAY** I've seen the park several ways over the years – I've hitchhiked here and camped, I've driven myself around, and I've flown in with advanced bookings at lodges and small bushcamps. I think that much of the Luangwa's magic is about being guided by some of Africa's best guides – in a vehicle, or especially on foot. These guys know this area, and its flora and fauna, like the back of their hands.

Upmarket camps and lodges Most of South Luangwa's camps aim at upmarket visitors from overseas. Given the park's remote location, this is not surprising. They incur great difficulties (and costs) in communicating, organising supplies and actually getting their clients into the valley. Then remember that most of them can operate for only for five or six months of the year, after which they pack up, returning to rebuild their camps after every rainy season. Thus, they have some very good reasons to be costly.

The rates at these camps, generally including all meals and activities, and often your bar bill and park fees too, are around US$450–730 per person per day. Most offer a special 'safari rate', typically about 5–10% cheaper than the normal rate, if you stay in camps run by just one operator for seven nights or more. This can be very convenient and is certainly recommended. It will provide a welcome continuity whilst you visit totally different camps. Such combinations include Kapani and its bushcamps; Nkwali, Tena Tena and Nsefu; Tafika and its bushcamps, including Mwaleshi; and Mfuwe Lodge and the camps of the Bushcamp Company.

A few offer discounts in the quieter parts of the season if you are a resident of Zambia, but the best deals are usually available from overseas operators (see

10

pages 44–5) who specialise in Zambia; their volumes of business give them access to significant discounts.

Note that although many of the camps cost around a similar level, their atmospheres and styles differ greatly – so choose carefully. For the sake of completeness, I've included here a few camps whose names are well known, but have now closed.

The valley's camps, in alphabetical order, include:

Big Lagoon Camp Planned in the same mould as Lion Camp (see page 281), but long disused, Big Lagoon Camp is an old safari site on the north side of the Luangwa Valley.

Bilimungwe Bushcamp [map 257]
(4 chalets) Contact Bushcamp Company, page 267; ⊕ BILIMU 13°23.295'S, 31°34.198'E. Some 46km (as the eagle flies) southeast of Mfuwe, Bilimungwe (which means 'chameleon' in the local Kamanga tongue), stands about 100m from the Luangwa, slightly upstream of its confluence with the Kapamba River. Dating back to 1996, it was completely rebuilt in 2011. The central area has been beautifully designed as a thatched roof suspended between the trunks & branches of an old spreading Natal mahogany (*Trichilia emetica*). Comfy chairs, a bar & a dining table occupy the main space, while on a lower deck colourful scatter cushions enliven the bench seating & there's an outdoor dining table with pizza oven. Overlooking a permanent waterhole, it's a fascinating design whose open sides are permeated by a cool breeze.

Very comfortable thatched chalets have walls of cane & reeds topped with mosquito gauze. Concertina doors open on to an extensive deck, above a lagoon that is frequented by elephants. With dbl or large twin beds in the centre, an en-suite shower & twin basins – plus an ingenious stone-enclosed outdoor shower – at one end, & capacious wicker chairs & writing table at the other, the rooms are light, airy – & huge. There's usually just 1 guide in camp, running day & night game drives & walks on a consensus basis. Guests often combine a stay at Bilimungwe with other Bushcamp Company camps, some of them within walking distance. Otherwise, the 3hr transfer from Mfuwe is mainly through miombo woodlands (look out for roan antelope & tsetse flies!). *US$420/560 Nov–Dec, US$590/785 Jun–Oct, all pp sharing/ sgl FBA, inc bar, laundry, airport & inter-camp transfers, exc park fees.* ⊕ *Jun–Dec.*

Chamilandu Bushcamp [map 257]
(3 chalets) Contact Bushcamp Company, page 267. ⊕ CHAMIL 13°19.023'S, 31°38.526'E. About 2hrs' drive southwest of Mfuwe, Chamilandu was set up in 1988 as a bushcamp for walking safaris. Rebuilt in 1999 on a new site, it was refurbished in 2010. Today's Chamilandu is still on the banks of the Luangwa facing the Nchindeni Hills, which look beautiful in the late afternoon sun. Set on high wooden decks, the smart chalets with kingsize or twin ¾ beds under mosquito nets are made of thatch & reeds, entirely open to the front & with open-air showers, dbl washbasins & flush toilets. At night, solar-powered lights augment the light from the moon & stars.

The camp's central area is close to the river, while a short walk brings you to an old hide – now a smart thatched building whose deck overlooks 1 of 7 oxbow lagoons that surround the camp; a great spot for lunch or to watch game. Game drives are offered as an alternative to the usual walks, though note that with only 1 guide on site, the choice is a group decision. Walking between Chamilandu, Chindeni, Bilimungwe & Zungulila – with your luggage taken ahead for you – can usually be arranged as there's only about 10km between each camp. *US$590/785 pp sharing/sgl FBA, inc bar, laundry, airport & inter-camp transfers, exc park fees.* ⊕ *Jun–Oct.*

Chichele Presidential Lodge [map 258]
(10 suites) Contact Sanctuary Retreats, page 269. ⊕ CHICHE 13°10.008'S, 31°42.605'E. About 15km southwest of Mfuwe Lodge, Chichele was built in 1972 as President Kaunda's private lodge in the Luangwa. High up atop President Hill, it's in an area where the Luangwa River starts to come much closer to the escarpment, & it's got a great view! Around it are a variety of environments including miombo woodland & mopane glades, on soil that varies from patches of gravel/sand to patches of black-cotton soil. Later owned by the parastatal 'National Hotels', Chichele fell into disrepair until, with its sister camp, Puku Ridge, it

was completely rebuilt by the now-defunct Star of Africa; in 2007 it moved into the Sanctuary Retreats stable.

Each of its elegant rooms, which include a sgl room (with no sgl suppt) & an interleading family room, boasts a veranda, minibar, AC, hairdryer, tea-/coffee-making facilities, & a mosquito net that's part of the bed's canopy, while en-suite facilities comprise a glass-fronted shower room, bath & twin washbasins. There was an obligation to keep many of Chichele's present buildings for their alleged historical value, so the design has taken these into account, & the place retains a grand, rather colonial feel; it's not difficult to picture a president entertaining his guests here. The communal areas are huge, including a large dining area with candelabra, ceiling fans & even a cappuccino maker, while outside is a relaxing pool & a panoramic view of the surrounding area.

Activities comprise game drives day & night, & guided walks. Small groups or conferences can also be accommodated, in combination with the nearby Puku Ridge. *US$510/665 pp sharing/sgl 15 Jun–Oct, US$400 pp Apr–14 Jun, Nov–Jan, US$320 pp Jan–Mar, all FBA, inc most drinks, laundry, park fees. No children under 9.* ⊕ *All year.*

🏠 **Chikoko Trails** (2 camps) Contact Remote Africa Safaris, page 268. These 2 small bushcamps operate slightly upstream of their parent camp, Tafika, on the opposite bank of the Luangwa. This is around the spot where David Livingstone crossed the Luangwa in 1866, & little seems to have changed since then; it's still a beautiful corner of the valley with excellent game densities.

Being in a wilderness area, there are no roads to these camps & all the luggage & supplies are carried by porters. From Tafika this means a brief drive along the river, followed by a quick crossing by canoe & then a short walk.

At both you'll find a very busy but relaxed air, solar lighting, a simple dining shelter & efficient refrigeration. But to focus on the camps themselves is to miss the point; Remote Africa's guides are amongst the valley's most experienced – so though simple, these are amongst the valley's very best bushcamps. *US$490/730 pp sharing/sgl FBA, inc bar, current park fees, laundry.*

🏠 **CHIKOKO TREE CAMP** [map 259] (3 chalets) Only about 10 mins' walk from the Luangwa, beside the small, seasonal Chikoko Channel, Chikoko's simple, grass-walled chalets

are more like tree houses. Reached by wooden stairs, & raised about 3m off the ground, their bedrooms have low sides & are open to the front, providing a good vantage point for spotting wildlife but with the height giving the nervous an added sense of security. There's a canvas shade above the dbl or twin beds to keep off the sun & any rain, & downstairs is a private flush toilet & shower (hot on request). A 4th, ground-level chalet is available on request. ⊕ *25 May–Oct.*

🏠 **CROCODILE RIVER CAMP** [map 278] (3 chalets) Further from the river, about a 40-min walk, Crocodile is in a great location, beneath a row of ebony trees overlooking a large & usually dry oxbow lagoon. Flashes of vivid colour enliven its dbl or twin rondavels, which are all at ground level, with half walls at the front, & en-suite flush toilet & shower (hot on request), open to the air. ⊕ *Jun–Oct.*

🏠 **Chindeni Bushcamp** [map 257] (4 tents) Contact Bushcamp Company, page 267. ⊕ CHINDE 13°22.056'S, 31°36.426'E. About 7km further upstream than Bilimungwe, Chindeni is also about 3hrs' drive south of Mfuwe. It stands on the banks of a large, semi-permanent lagoon, which stretches away from it on both sides. The main river is about 1km away, & in the near distance rise the Nchindeni Hills, overlooking the park's eastern boundary.

Refurbished in 2010, Chindeni's large, well-spaced tents are tucked into the vegetation beside the lagoon, & raised up on hardwood decks. They're lined with soft-brown canvas, rising to 3 pinnacles, like a trio of miniature big tops. Beneath the centre are twin or dbl beds, flanked by an en-suite shower, loo & twin basins; & open basketwork chairs with cushioned footstools. Outside, twin hammocks on a private shaded veranda invite you to laze away the afternoon. It's all very light: lots of natural wood & neutral fabrics, with just a flash of turquoise. At the heart of the camp, bean bags are lined up on an extensive wooden deck for a front-row view of the lagoon. Ebony & tamarind trees provide shade, while shelter for the separate dining & lounge areas comes from 2 large canvas-topped 'gazebos' held up by heavy poles. Lighting is from paraffin lamps.

It's usual to combine time here with stays at Bilimungwe, or the company's other camps. Here, too, drives, walks & night drives are on the menu

– although be aware that there is sometimes only 1 guide on site, so the choice may be a group decision. *US$590/785 pp sharing/sgl FBA, inc bar, laundry, airport & inter-camp transfers, exc park fees. ⊕ Jun–Oct.*

Chinzombo Although long closed, no mention of the South Luangwa would be complete without mention of Chinzombo, which stood just south of Kapani Safari Lodge. It had a venerable history as one of the valley's first safari camps, but was closed in the early 2000s as the very ground on which it stood was being eroded (about 3–5m of riverbank would disappear per year into the floodwaters). Although there is nothing left on the old site, I wouldn't be surprised to see the name resurrected in a new camp nearby sometime soon!

🏠 **Kafunta River Lodge** [map 258] (10 chalets) ℡ 0216 246046; e kafunta@ luangwa.com; www.luangwa.com. ✪ KAFUNT 13°9.785'S, 31°44.360'E. Kafunta is about 9km from the main road between Mfuwe Airport & the bridge. To get there, turn left before the bridge, signposted to Kafunta, Kapani & other lodges. Then around where the tar ends (just before Kapani) there's a left fork signposted to Kafunta. Believe it or not, this is the main road that runs southwest outside the park & follows the river downstream. There are then 3 clearly signposted left turns: to the Wildlife Camp, to Nkwali Camp, & finally to Kafunta.

On a spacious site beside the river, Kafunta was built from scratch in 1998 by a team including Ron & Anke Cowan, who now own & run the camp. Its central dining/bar area under a huge thatched roof is very impressive – built around a wild mango tree. Dinner is often served by candlelight on an open-air deck to the front, with great views over the floodplains. (There's a small wildlife hide cleverly built into the underneath of this deck.) Beside the bar is a small swimming pool, & a hot tub supplied by naturally hot water from their borehole.

Kafunta's rooms are thatched wooden chalets built on low stilts, about 1m off the ground, which give a slightly alpine feel. Refurbished in 2011, each of the 8 'standard' chalets has 2 ¾ beds under a large, walk-in mosquito net; 2 'luxury suites' have more space, including an upper deck which doubles as a lookout deck, & an extra bedroom for 1–2 children. All chalets have

a shower (hot & cold), twin basins & flush toilet en suite, as well as a minibar, kettle & floor fan – powered by mains electricity. Their windows are gauzed & their verandas have wide views over the river to the plains. They're comfortable, light, well kept & reasonably spacious.

Activities centre around 4x4 game drives (day & night) & walking safaris. Kafunta is 9km from the Mfuwe Bridge, but its drives normally access the park across the Nkwali pontoon, which is only about 1.5km from the lodge. *US$470–520 Jun–Oct, US$360–410 Apr–May, Nov–Jan, all pp sharing FBA, inc laundry, park fees, exc drinks extra except Jun–Oct. Sgl suppt US$80. No children under 6. ⊕ Apr–5 Jan.*

🏠 **ISLAND BUSHCAMP** [map 257] (5 chalets) Contact Kafunta River Lodge (above). About 2hrs' drive south of Kafunta, Island Bushcamp was opened in 2002. It stands on the banks of the Luangwa River, in the far south of the park, where the river no longer forms the border of the national park but rather runs though it. Guests are normally driven from Kafunta. Its chalets are built on raised platforms with open views to the river; all have twin beds, private hot showers & flush toilets. The camp is mainly a base for walking safaris, & limited game drives are possible. *US$470/550 pp sharing/ sgl FBA, inc drinks, park fees. No children under 12. ⊕ End May–Oct.*

🏠 **Kaingo Camp** [map 259] (6 chalets) Contact Shenton Safaris, page 269. ✪ KAINGO 12°55.370'S, 31°55.441'E. Where the seasonal Mwamba River meets the main Luangwa River, this small camp looks over the water towards the Nsefu Sector from beneath an old grove of mahogany & ebony trees. The open-sided sitting room cum dining area is a large thatched *chitenge*, with an amazing bar made from an old leadwood tree trunk. Outside, a deck extends over the river – perfect for game viewing & afternoon tea. Each of the chalets, too, has its own shaded deck over the river, where lunch is served in complete privacy. The chalets themselves, constructed of rendered brick under thatch, have been here for many years, but all now boast an outside bath, & were being redesigned in 2011. Stable-style doors lead in to en-suite rooms where gauzed skylights give a view of the stars as you drift off to sleep. Solid, hand-crafted wood sets the tone – in the headboards backing kingsize or twin beds, in the mirror frames, in the wardrobes. There's also a separate daybed, plus solar lights, & a lockable box.

Close to the camp are 3 hides – the 'elephant' & 'hippo' hides, & the seasonal 'carmine bee-eater' hide – as well as several mobile hides. These are fairly unusual in the Luangwa, & have been widely used by film-crews from both the BBC & *National Geographic*. If you're too active for a late-morning snooze, or are keen on photography, this is the place to keep watch; it's even possible to spend a night in the high elephant hide (*extra US$150/2 people*) – an amazing experience. In fact, photographers are particularly well catered for, with camera dust covers & bean bags provided, & vehicles that allow for each guest to have an outside seat.

Derek Shenton, who owns & runs the operation with his wife Jules, is quiet & unassuming, which has perhaps helped the lodge to attain a solid, established & yet very calm air. It's been open since 1993 & its head guide, Patrick Njobvu, has over 20 years' experience of guiding in this area. As well as the usual walking safaris & day & night drives, there are picnics in the bush & hide trips; many guests take in 3 activities a day. Those staying 7 nights or more with Shenton Safaris can pre-arrange a camping trip with Derek, walking out from Kaingo in the afternoon, camping in the bush overnight & walking into Mwamba Bushcamp the next morning (*extra US$400/2 people*). Note that the Shenton family also run Forest Inn, near Mkushi (see page 308). *US$660 Aug–Sep, US$575 May– Jul & Oct, all pp sharing FBA, inc drinks, current park fees. Sgl suppt US$250.* ⊕ *26 May–Oct.*

🏠 **Kakuli Bushcamp** [map 259] (4 chalets) Contact Norman Carr Safaris, page 268. A camp was first started here in 1984 by Norman Carr, overlooking a wide bend in the Luangwa. *Kakuli* is the local word for an old buffalo bull which has left the main herd, & by association was also Norman Carr's nickname amongst the local people before he died.

Kakuli Bushcamp is linked to Nsolo & Luwi camps, respectively 10km & 20km away, by the seasonal Luwi River, which makes 3-day walks between these 3 sister camps a very interesting option.

Its chalets are rebuilt every year, when their design is often tweaked a little. When last visited,

each had a large thatched roof covering its cream-coloured tent (complete with full mosquito-net lining, kingsize or twin ¾ beds & solar-powered hurricane lamps) & polished deck at the front. Then a door at the back leads to the low reed walls & curved polished surrounds of a large en-suite bathroom, which houses a flush toilet, washbasin & hot shower in an area that feels very open.

The dining-room/bar area is simple & comfortable: a thatched, reed-walled structure with 1 open side, a sprinkling of cushioned chairs & a good bookshelf. A suspended deck overlooks the floodplain, partially open.

The camp seldom takes more than 8 guests, & it concentrates on both walking & driving, though night drives are possible in the area. If 8 guests are in camp, it usually has 3 guides resident; if there are 6 guests, then expect 2 guides. Either way there is some flexibility over activities. A stay here is usually combined with the main Kapani Lodge & some of its sister bushcamps, Luwi, Nsolo & Mchenja. *US$505/685 sgl/pp sharing Jul–14 Oct, US$535 pp May–Jun & 15 Oct–10 Nov, US$450 pp 20 Jan-Mar, all FBA, inc drinks, exc park fees.* ⊕ *20 May–7 Nov, & 20 Jan–Mar for river safaris.*

🏠 **Kalamu Lagoon Camp** [map 257] (8 rooms) Contact Wilderness Safaris, page 431. ✈ KALAMU 13°27.503'S, 31°23.178'E. Overlooking a huge permanent lagoon, Kalamu is the latest of the Wilderness camps in Zambia, accepting its first visitors in Jul 2008. Built on the site of the old Luamfwa Camp, it's in the far south of the park by the Luangwa River, with plains beyond to the treeline. The game here isn't nearly as prolific as further north but the remoteness of this area is a draw. Most visitors fly in to the nearby airstrip, but for experienced drivers with a 4x4 it can (in theory) be approached in the dry season only, using a series of tracks from Petauke.

In addition to twin-bedded en-suite rooms, there are 2 larger family suites, which have a split level where an additional area can be curtained off to create the feeling of 2 rooms. The main lounge & dining area is quite smart but informal: think chunky wooden furniture, big sofas & African art. On the deck outside, there's a firepit & adjacent free-form pool, fronting the river. Activities consist of guided walks & game drives. *US$496/642 pp sharing/sgl FBA, inc local drinks, laundry, taxes, park fees.* ⊕ *May–Nov.*

🔺 **Kalamu Star-bed Camp** [map 259]
(3 timber platforms) Contact Wilderness Safaris, page 431. Sister to Kalamu Lagoon Camp, yet more of a bushcamp, Star-bed Camp is in a similar location. Here, the beds are raised on 3m timber platforms under the stars, with only mosquito net drapes between.Yet each is still very comfortable, with wicker chairs & a hot shower, flush toilet & twin basins en suite. Simplicity follows into the main open-sided area, set on a polished concrete base under light canvas. Guests dine either here or beside the river – where there's a firepit. The camp combines naturally with Kalamu Lagoon Camp & the active may choose to walk the 5km between the 2, & game drives can be taken, too. *US$261/377 pp sharing/sgl FBA, inc local drinks, laundry, taxes, park fees.* ⊕ *Jun–Oct.*

🔺 **Kapamba Bushcamp** [map 257]
(4 chalets) Contact Bushcamp Company, page 267. ⊕ KAPAMB 13°22.967'S, 31°31.584'E. This one of the Bushcamp Company's camps, a 3½hr drive from Mfuwe, is quite different from the rest. Unencumbered by a 4th wall, each of Kapamba's stone-walled chalets (with dbl or twin beds) is open fronted, with sweeping views of a floodplain around the Kapamba River – which is shallow enough to paddle through barefoot or even to sit in during the dry season. Wrought-iron gates span the front of each chalet, offering protection from unwanted visitors & creating a spider-web effect against the African sky. Inside each en-suite bathroom are twin showers above a bath the size of a small plunge pool (a happy accident, resulting from a specification given in centimetres, which the builders assumed was in inches!).

Activities continue the theme, with the camp's guide accompanying guests as they wade through the shallow river on the way to a sundowner or intimate dinner. As at Bushcamp's other camps, walking & day & night game drives are all on the menu. At busy times there are 2 guides in camp, but at others the choice of activity will become a group decision. *US$420/560 Apr–May, Dec–Jan, US$590/785 Jun–Oct, all pp sharing/sgl FBA, inc bar, laundry, airport & inter-camp transfers, exc park fees.* ⊕ *Apr–Jan.*

🔺 **Kapani Safari Lodge** [map 258]
(9 rooms) Contact Norman Carr Safaris, page 268. ⊕ KAPANI 13°7.237'S, 31°46.057'E. Kapani overlooks a beautiful old lagoon within Lupande GMA, just south of the main Luangwa River – thus ensuring that changes in the river's course won't wash away its bank. To get there, turn left just before the Mfuwe Bridge; it's on the right a little over 3km after that junction, & well signposted.

Founded by the late Norman Carr & still part-owned by his son, Adrian, the present camp was built in 1986. Although it has evolved continuously since then, its large brick rooms with their thatched roofs, heavy wooden furniture & cool polished floors still feel reliably solid, spacious & comfortable. Each includes a separate sitting area with large, mosquito-netted windows overlooking a lagoon, its own small drinks fridge, tea/coffee makers & hairdryers. Mains electricity powers efficient (& quiet) ceiling fans, sensibly placed within the walk-in mosquito nets surrounding the beds.

Kapani's focal point is an extensive deck over the lagoon/floodplain, which supports a shaded lounge & bar area, as well as plenty of open-air space where most meals are eaten – Kapani's food is consistently good. A comfortable separate lounge area has a fireplace & a shelf of local-interest books, surrounded by pictures of the area in former times, including some of Norman & his children when young. This makes a cool retreat when temperatures climb, & a warm place for winter evenings. There's also a good curio shop, & a swimming pool.

Activities involve game drives into the park, or occasional walks if requested. The guiding is well up to the valley's high standards; Kapani is notable for having several excellent & long-serving Zambian guides from the local community who were originally trained by Norman Carr. Kapani's community links are especially strong – so activities can include school visits, local theatre productions, pot-making for children & various other community interactions, but do let the lodge know in advance if things like this interest you, as some can take a while to organise.

Kapani also acts as base camp for 4 small, satellite walking camps: Luwi, Nsolo, Kakuli & Mchenja. Together these make a fine combination, with Kapani usually visited for the first few nights (& possibly also the last night), before a combination of the smaller camps. *US$470/650 sgl/pp sharing Jul–14 Oct, US$400 pp*

May–Jun & 15 Oct–10 Nov, US$325 pp 11 Nov–19 May, all FBA, inc drinks, exc park fees. ⊕ All year.

🏠 **Kuyenda** [map 257] (4 rondavels) Contact Bushcamp Company, page 267. ⊕ KUYEND 13°22.430'S, 31°32.430'E. About 75 mins' drive south of Mfuwe, this small, very traditional bushcamp concentrates on walking safaris with the occasional drive. It overlooks the Manzi River, a sand-river tributary of the main Luangwa.

Much of the guiding here is done by Phil Berry – the valley's most experienced guide with a legendary reputation for his knowledge of the area's wildlife. Though Phil no longer leads all the walks, he still spends most of the season at the camp guiding many of the walks & sharing his extensive knowledge of the bush. In the evening, the conversation over dinner can be particularly interesting & convivial, especially when Phil & his partner, Babette, are in camp. The round chalets, made of thatch & reeds, have en-suite toilets & showers open to the sky (hot water is brought on request). Inside are twin queensize beds, or a kingsize dbl, veiled by mosquito netting, & with atmospheric paraffin lanterns. It's understated, nicely finished & very peaceful.

Though walking is the main focus here, drives are also possible – & night drives are always a feature of your time here. Returning to the camp when it's dark is a great pleasure as the whole camp is lit by romantic hurricane lamps which look magical as you approach across a wide sand river. US$590/785 pp sharing/sgl FBA, inc bar, laundry, airport & inter-camp transfers, exc park fees. ⊕ Jun–Oct.

🏠 **Lion Camp** [map 259] (10 chalets) ☎ 0216 246024; e info@lioncamp.com; www.lioncamp. com. ⊕ LIONCA 12°53.089'S, 31°58.032'E. All Africa is here in this large lodge that's a riot of colour, from the cushions of Zambian *chitenje* cloth to beaded Nigerian belts. Situated inside the park around 2½hrs' drive from Mfuwe, it stands on the edge of an oxbow lagoon, or *wafwa*, overlooking an open plain. Having fallen into disuse, it was rebuilt in 2003, & has since been renovated to a standard that wouldn't disgrace a smart hotel.

At the heart of the camp, seating areas under thatch form a horseshoe around a central fireplace. Parallel to the lagoon, a narrow ribbon of deck edges a similarly narrow infinity pool. At the back, the walls lined with black-&-white

wildlife photos, are a large bar & a full-size billiard table; a separate lounge with TV for wildlife DVDs; & a well-stocked curio shop. There's even WiFi in the main area. Dining is flexible – with tables moved from one meal to the next.

High wooden walkways lead to the chalets, themselves on wooden platforms with French windows leading onto decks overlooking the lagoon. They're solid, spacious structures under thatch with wood-clad canvas walls, canvas flaps over gauze windows & stylish interiors: polished wood floors, kingsize dbl or twin beds with walk-in mosquito nets, a fan, en-suite shower & separate toilet, & a day bed for afternoon relaxation. There's 220v inverter power in each chalet, & locks on the doors – a rarity in the Luangwa!

Activities revolve around game drives & walking safaris, & there are photographic safari weeks with Patrick Bentley 3 times a year. It's a professionally run, welcoming lodge, yet despite knowledgeable guiding, a tendency to focus on finding lion on our night drive made it all feel rather rushed. Note that if there are couples in residence, rather than groups, no more than 6 chalets are booked out. US$380/475 Jun–15 Jul & Oct; US$455/565 16 Jul–30 Sep, all pp sharing/ sgl FBA, inc local drinks, exc imported drinks, park fees. 3-night minimum stay. No children under 12. ⊕ May–Oct.

🅰 **Luangwa Bushcamping** See Fly-camping, page 291, for details.

🏠 **Luangwa River Camp** [map 258] (5 chalets) Contact Robin Pope Safaris, page 268. ⊕ LUARLO 13°04.459'S, 31°48.636'E. In a riverside setting 10km northeast of Mfuwe, overlooking the South Park, Luangwa River Camp has been taken over by Robin Pope Safaris & was being refurbished in 2011. The result is a more open river frontage from new & renewed decks, showing off the 2-tier infinity pool to better advantage, but retaining the lodge's former solidity. Panelling of palm stalks features significantly in both the substantial open-plan lounge & dining area & in the spacious, ochre-painted brick chalets under thatch; here it is a backdrop for the en-suite bathroom, complete with sunken bath & separate toilet. Mains electricity enables the use of spotlights, hairdryers, fans & other 'luxuries', making the lodge a good introduction to a safari holiday.

10

Aside from walking safaris & game drives, usually in the national park, there are boat trips when the river is sufficiently high, & cultural trips are easily within range, too, including visits to Chipembele Wildlife Education Centre (page 267), Kawaza Village (pages 292–3), & various other craft & village projects. It's all very flexible – right down to the option of a holistic massage! *US$474 Jul–Oct, US$393 22 May–Jun, US$342 Apr–21 May & Nov, all pp FBA, inc drinks, laundry, airport transfers, exc park & community fees.* ☺ *Apr–Nov.*

🏠 **Luangwa Safari House** [map 258] (4 bedrooms) Contact Robin Pope Safaris, page 268. Built in 2005 near to Nkwali (see below), this large & traditional-looking house has a carefully crafted structure based around the trunks of 25 ancient leadwood trees. From the front entrance, a huge pivoted door opens into the spacious main room, some 12m high, with comfy sofas, large marble dining table & full-height views of the bush through 1 open wall.

There are 4 grand bedrooms, each individually styled & reflecting a different material from copper to glass. Open-tread wooden staircases made from massive reclaimed slabs of wooden banana tree lead to 2 of these rooms; both with balconies supported like drawbridges. All are highly original & styled on a grand scale, with kingsize or twin beds & very large en-suite bathrooms.

Despite that, the focus is on the outdoors. Terraces lead to an infinity pool, & a wooden jetty leads away from the house to an open-sided lounge deck – complete with a large leather sofa, a hanging chair, dining table & chairs for al fresco meals – beneath a group of huge ebony trees in the middle of the often-dry lagoon. Nearby a waterhole attracts families of elephant coming to bathe. During the day, a double-storey wall of the lounge, & a section of each bedroom wall, are opened up completely, turning the outside into a continuation of the living space inside. At night a clever system of insect-proof mesh, wrought-iron grills &, if necessary, waterproof panels slot into place to close up the house & keep it cosy.

The house is usually booked out by one group who – with a private chef, house manager, safari guide & 4x4 – have great flexibility in what they do & when. Although often referred to as a 'family house', Luangwa Safari House really best suits small groups of adults, or at least adults & older children, who will appreciate the openness

of its design & the complete flexibility of its high-quality activities. *US$679 Jul–Oct, US$577 22 May–Jun, US$526 Apr–21 May & Nov, all pp FBA, inc drinks, laundry, airport transfers, exc park & community fees.Min 4 adults; no children under 7.* ☺ *Mid Mar–mid Jan.*

🏠 **Luwi Bushcamp** [map 257] (4 chalets) Contact Norman Carr Safaris, page 268. A further 10km up the Luwi (or Lubi) River from its sister camp, Nsolo, Luwi is at least as rustic. It is set under a group of tall shady trees (*Vitex, Breonadia* & *Khaya anthotheca*), looking out over a small plain. The chalets, which can be twin or dbl, are similarly of reed & thatch, with grass matting covering their polished floors, mosquito nets, storm lanterns, solar lights & a small veranda. All have en-suite facilities, with flush toilets, hot showers & washbasin under the stars.

A very short walk leads to a large, permanent lagoon at a bend in the river (usually frequented by a pod of about 60 hippos). This is purely a camp for walking: either for day walks based here, or for walks linking with Nsolo, Kakuli & Mchenja bushcamps. It's not a camp for game drives – although there's always a vehicle in camp to investigate interesting noises at dusk – & the camp seldom takes more than 7 guests. Time at Luwi is often combined with its sister bushcamps &/or a few nights at Kapani. *US$505/685 sgl/pp sharing Jul–14 Oct, US$435 pp May–Jun & 15–31 Oct, all FBA, inc drinks, exc park fees.* ☺ *20 May–Oct.*

🏠 **Mchenja Camp** [map 259] (5 chalets) Contact Norman Carr Safaris, page 268. Mchenja has been run by Norman Carr Safaris since about 1995. It stands in one of the very best locations of any camp in the valley, beside the Luangwa River at the end of a serenely beautiful grove of African ebony trees (*Diospyros mespiliformis*, which are known as *muchenja* in the local ChiNyanja dialect).

The unusual octagonal chalets all have thatched roofs supported on wooden poles, & each is lined with a cream-coloured canvas. Bedouin-style drapes cover the shade-mesh windows & the double-doors which lead onto a veranda at the front. Inside are a kingsize bed, or twin ¾ beds, plenty of wicker furniture on a polished floor, & a feeling of airy space. Part of the bathroom – with ball-&-claw bath – is inside the tent, next to the bedroom, linked to an open-air reed-enclosed toilet, washbasin & shower with a view.

The airy dining area & small lounge are under thatch, & there is a little slate-grey freshwater plunge-pool set into the deck. Food & activities are reliably good, & the camp usually has at least 2 guides in residence when there are more than 4 guests here, giving a real choice to the activities.

About 30km from Mfuwe, Mchenja stands opposite the Nsefu Sector, between Nsefu Camp & Tena Tena. It makes a good last stop at the end of a walking safari, being an easy 10km walk (3–4hrs) from either Nsolo or Kakuli. *US$605/785 sgl/pp sharing Jul–14 Oct, US$535 pp May–Jun & 15 Oct–7 Nov, all FBA, inc drinks, exc park fees.* ⏰ *20 May–7 Nov.*

🏠 **Mfuwe Lodge** [map 258] (18 chalets) Contact Bushcamp Company, page 267. ✪ MFUWEL 13°4.725'S, 31°47.441'E. Following a significant makeover in 2010, this long-established lodge has emerged stylish & smart. Now the hub of the Bushcamp Company operations, it stands in a prime location overlooking the picturesque Mfuwe Lagoon in the centre of the park's all-weather road network, where the game is prolific & relaxed. The lodge's history dates back many years, having been rebuilt from scratch in the 1990s by the Bizzaro family, owners of the successful Club Makokola in Malawi. It was, & remains, relatively big in the context of the Luangwa's tiny camps.

Each of Mfuwe's painted brick-&-thatch chalets overlooks a lagoon from a broad veranda, complete with wicker hanging chair. Inside are dbl or large twin beds encased in walk-in mosquito nets & cooled by a fan, plus a writing desk, safe, tea/coffee maker, comfy chairs & coffee table. The contemporary bathroom has dual washbasins, a separate toilet, & a shower with a view. Larger family rooms & suites are split level, some with a bath.

It's as well that Mfuwe has a vast lobby, for at the end of the dry season it's the scene of an extraordinary sight: a whole family of elephants coming through to feast on the wild mango trees beyond. For most guests, a large pool, squashy sofas, huge fireplaces & an open-air dining area with pizza oven are the greater draw! The food is good & the bar well stocked. Added bonuses are a proper library with leather chairs, a good curio shop, internet access – & its own lagoon-side spa (page 285). Morning & afternoon/night drives are in Land Rovers with 3 rows of individual seats,

& walks are also possible, though keen walkers would be best to combine a stay here with time at one or more of the bushcamps. *US$295/400 Nov–May; US$445/600 Jun–Oct, all pp sharing/ sgl FBA, exc drinks, park fees. Suite US$30 pp suppt.* ⏰ *All year.*

🏠 **Mushroom Lodge & Presidential House** [map 258] (12 chalets) 📞 0216 246116/7; 📱 0977 758056; ✉ info@mushroomlodge.com; www.mushroomlodge.com. The historic Mushroom Lodge overlooking Mfuwe Lagoon was built in the early 1970s for President Kaunda & his guests, & remained in use until the fall of UNIP in 1991. In the ensuing years, the house fell into disrepair, but it has now been redeveloped as a safari lodge, & was fully refurbished in 2007. To get there from the main park gate, follow the road for about 2km, then turn right as signposted for a further 1.2km.

The substantial en-suite chalets are painted a deep red & shaded under thatch. Each has both a dbl & a sgl bed, its own lounge area with wicker furniture, a minibar, safe, fan, kettle & hairdryer, & a private veranda fronted by the lagoon. Children are particularly welcome, with special meals & games laid on for them, & a babysitting service available. Central to the lodge are a restaurant, lounge & bar area with an extensive veranda & a swimming pool, while nearby is an open-sided *nsaka* where massages are offered. There's extensive WiFi coverage, too. In addition to morning & evening game drives & walks, guests can also take part in tours to Mfuwe & the surrounding villages. *Chalet US$445 pp FB, inc 2 game drives & airport transfers, exc park fees, drinks.* ⏰ *All year.*

🏠 **Mwamba Bushcamp** [map 259] (3 chalets) Contact Shenton Safaris, page 269. ✪ MWAMBA 12°52.973'S, 31°55.940'E. About 6km north of Kaingo, or a morning's walk away, lies Kaingo's satellite bushcamp, Mwamba, at the confluence of the East Mwamba & main Mwamba rivers. The approach to the camp is lovely as the rivers are usually dry & sandy, & the banks open & green. There's an area of mopane forest nearby, as well as ebony groves & grasslands. The camp itself is shaded within a grove of ebonies (*Diospyros mespiliformis*), where there are some particularly beautiful trees. Simple reed-&-thatch chalets have gauze skylights, enabling guests to enjoy the stars from their beds – as they can from the open-air, en-suite bathrooms (with hot bucket shower & flush toilet). There's a comfy dining area by the river, & a well-placed anthill makes a great sundowner spot. The camp has its own hide, too, focused on a waterhole that regularly attracts wildlife. Walking & driving safaris, & hide trips are on offer – & with 2 guides generally in camp, it's very flexible. It's one of South Luangwa's best areas for Cookson's wildebeest, & eland are also sometimes sighted around here. US$585 Aug–Sep, US$535 May–Jul & Oct, all pp sharing FBA, inc drinks, current park fees. Sgl suppt US$250. ⊕ 26 May–Oct.

🏠 **Nkwali** [map 258] (6 rooms, Robin's House, Luangwa Safari House) Contact Robin Pope Safaris, page 268. ⊕ NKWALI 13°6.989'S, 31°44.414'E. Nkwali is the main base for Robin Pope Safaris. It overlooks the Luangwa & the park beyond from the Lupande GMA which encompasses some beautiful tall acacia & ebony woodlands, a favourite haunt for giraffe & elephant. As you turn left just before the main bridge at Mfuwe, Nkwali is well signposted. Take the road for about 5km, then turn left just before the end of the tarmac. Take this for about 2km, then turn right for a further 4km.

Each of Nkwali's comfortable, airy rooms has a thatched roof resting on wicker-work, creamy-white walls, & a dbl or twin beds surrounded by a large walk-in mosquito net. At the back of each chalet the en-suite shower is open to the sky, while the toilet & 2 basins are under cover. All the chalets have views over the river & are on mains power, with a back-up generator.

The camp feels rustic, but very stylishly so, & the high level of attention to detail is clear. Its bar is spectacularly built around an ebony tree, & there's a small waterhole behind the dining room that often attracts game very close to the camp. The food is very good, & you'll usually find exceedingly smooth standards of service.

Note that nearby are 2 private safari houses: the child-friendly 2-bedroom Robin's House (see page 286) & the rather more stylish 4-bedroom Luangwa Safari House (see page 282). Both are close to Nkwali, but both usually run with their own autonomous chefs & guides, so don't impact upon the character of Nkwali at all.

Most activities from Nkwali are drives into the park, which is accessed either by boat across the river, or over the conveniently close Nkwali

pontoon. Walks are led into both the park & in the surrounding GMA; often you'll just cross the river by boat & walk from there. The camp has permission to run walking safaris throughout the year.

It's usual to combine time here with time at Tena Tena &/or Nsefu camps, further north – when Nkwali often works best as the first camp on the itinerary. US$526 Jul–Oct, US$454 22 May–Jun, US$362 Nov–21 May, all pp FBA, inc drinks, laundry, airport transfers, exc park & community fees. ⊕ All year.

🏠 **Nsefu Camp** [map 259] (6 rondavels) Contact Robin Pope Safaris, page 268. ⊕ NSEFU 12°56.236'S, 31°55.289'E. Nsefu is superbly situated on the Luangwa River, in the middle of the Nsefu Sector. It was first opened in 1951 by Norman Carr – making it Zambia's oldest safari camp – & moved to its present location in 1953. Then the camp consisted of raised brick rondavels that were entered via a few steps.

In recent years these deteriorated until, in late 1998, the camp was bought by Robin Pope Safaris, who completely rebuilt & refurbished it. (Robin himself had guided there for many years before starting up his own company, so had always been closely connected with Nsefu.) Now it is once again one of the best camps in the valley.

Nsefu's original row of round rondavels has been retained, but each now has a shady wooden veranda at the front. Inside are twin beds surrounded by a walk-in mosquito net. Soft colours & quality fabrics are used throughout. Large windows look out over the river, stylishly curtained. At the back, each rondavel has had an en-suite shower & toilet added – complete with old-style bath taps (but efficient hot water) – which is partially open to the outside.

The camp has been furnished with taste & elegance, in the style of the 1950s – complete with wind-up gramophone & traditional silver service. The whole effect is impressive &, despite the camp's creature comforts, it has retained an old, solid feel of history.

Nsefu's thatched bar stands beside a huge termite mound, overlooking a small lagoon & a sweeping bend in the river. In a separate dining area, under thatch, the food is very good, & the atmosphere relaxed – although the tables are often laid beside the riverbank, or elsewhere

The Bush-Spa at Mfuwe Lodge (*0216 246123;* m *0979 306826; www.bush-spa.com.* ⊕ *08.00–17.00 daily; from US$45/75 ½/1hr)* must be the most unlikely location for a full-scale spa. Overlooking a lagoon are three treatment rooms – two singles and a double – set within a large, thatched structure which also features a wet deck area and a jacuzzi. Watching elephant while having a massage must be for some the ultimate in game-viewing!

The brainchild of Nathalie Zanoli, the spa was opened in 2007, and offers a chance for local women to work within the tourist industry, which is otherwise largely dominated by men. Nathalie trains them in a range of techniques using indigenous products, such as those extracted from the sausage tree (*Kigelia africana*) or the baobab (*Adansonia digitata*), and taking on board African holistic practices. Massages or wraps, facials or pedicures, hydrotherapy or reflexology. There are numerous options, all priced by the hour rather than according to the treatment.

The spa is open to all comers, and the team also visits lodges owned by Robin Pope Safaris on request.

under the skies. A stay here is often combined with Nkwali, Tena Tena, or one of Robin Pope's walking safaris. *US$617 Jul–Oct, US$515 22 May–Jun, US$434 Jan–Mar, all pp FBA inc bar, laundry, airport transfers, exc park & community fees.* ⊕ *22 May–Oct, & 22 Jan–Mar for river safaris.*

🏠 **Nsolo Bushcamp** [map 259] (4 chalets) Contact Norman Carr Safaris, page 268. Set on a sweeping bend of the seasonal Luwi River, with a permanent waterhole to the front, Nsolo focuses on a central *chitenje* in the shade of mahogany & sausage trees. This is an airy thatched room with a separate open-air seating area & a good library – including the *Nsolo Journals*, written by Craig & Janelle Doria when they managed the camp in the 1990s. Meals are normally taken here, but on special occasions the table is laid in the sand river, lit by the soft glow of hurricane lamps.

The large chalets were designed by Shadrack (Shaddy) Nkhoma, who has managed & guided here for 15 years. Built simply on wooden decks with reed walls & high thatched roofs, each has either twin beds or a dbl under a walk-in mosquito net. En-suite bathrooms are open to the stars with a flush toilet & shower with a view. A dbl door opens onto a tree- or thatch-shaded private deck, with comfortable chairs & a great view over the river. Solar lights are used in the evenings.

The camp was named for the *nsolo* or honeyguide bird (*Indicator indicator*). It lies 9–10km inside the park from the main Luangwa

River, directly west of the Nsefu Sector in a sandy area dominated by mopane trees, with veins of shady riparian forest. Though short game drives during the day & evening are possible, walking is the major attraction. On my first visit to Nsolo in 1995 the ranger accompanying our walks was Rice Time, a sprightly Zambian hunter who strode through the bush with speed & confidence – despite being over 70 years of age. Sadly he died in 2006, but there is a memorial for him in camp, & his stories are still told & re-told. A stay here is usually combined with the main Kapani Lodge & its sister-bushcamps. It is 10km east to Luwi, & about the same to either Kakuli or Mchenja, so a few days spent walking down the sand river between the camps makes a great trip. *US$505/685 sgl/pp sharing Jul–14 Oct, US$435 pp May–Jun & 15–31 Oct, all FBA, inc drinks, exc park fees.* ⊕ *20 May–Oct.*

🏠 **Puku Ridge Tented Camp** [map 258] (7 tents) Contact Sanctuary Retreats, page 269. Barely a kilometre from its sister lodge, Chichele, Puku Ridge opened in 2003, & has since been taken over by Sanctuary Retreats. It stands on the side of a rocky outcrop, overlooking a lovely floodplain on the south side of the park.

Unlike Chichele, the smart Puku Ridge was designed with the safari market in mind, & has a more contemporary, bush feel. Each of its walk-in safari tents has a private veranda, whilst inside are a kingsize or twin beds, surrounded by a walk-in mosquito net with a ceiling fan above the bed. Each private bathroom has twin washbasins & flush toilet, plus indoor & outdoor showers & a bath – demonstrating a relatively high level of luxury by Luangwa standards. Morning tea or coffee are delivered to the tents by your room steward. Activities include walks & day or night game drives. *US$680/885 pp sharing/sgl 15 Jun–Oct, US$450 pp Apr–14 Jun, Nov–Jan, all FBA, inc most drinks, laundry, park fees. No children under 9.* ☉ *Apr–mid Jan.*

⌂ **Robin's House** [map 258] (2 bedrooms) Contact Robin Pope Safaris, page 268. The private, 5-bed Robin's House stands on the riverbank near Nkwali, under a grove of large ebony trees. Inside, the house is very comfortable & very functional, rather than stylish. It has a central sitting room & 2 large bedrooms (a dbl & a trpl), each with its own bathroom. Large windows give great views across the river, & there's a grassy garden complete with small swimming pool. It's all relatively child-friendly, even for small children, & comes complete with a small bookcase full of books. The house has a private guide, hostess & chef, so it's ideal for families &/or those seeking more privacy. Those with older children, & larger groups, might consider Luangwa Safari House (above) as a more appropriate alternative. *US$577 Jul–Oct, US$510 22 May–Jun, US$459 Jan–21 May, Nov–Dec, all pp FBA, inc drinks, laundry, airport transfers, exc park & community fees. Min 3 adults.* ☉ *All year.*

⌂ **Tafika** [map 259] (6 chalets) Contact Remote Africa Safaris, page 268. ⊕ TAFIKA 15°51.250'S, 31°59.811'E. Tafika stands on the bank of the Luangwa, overlooking the national park, & is perhaps the smallest of the valley's main camps. It was founded by John & Carol Coppinger, who managed Chibembe for years until they started Tafika on their own around 1995. John's years of experience in the valley are augmented by the experience of several other top guides working here, including Bryan Jackson, Isaac Zulu, Ernst Jacobs & Stephen Banda; thus Tafika's guiding is amongst the best in the valley.

Four of the reed-&-thatch chalets have 2 dbl beds in each, surrounded by separate walk-in mosquito nets. The family chalet, built around the trunk of a stunning sausage tree (*Kigelia africana*), has 2 rooms, while a new honeymoon chalet was added in 2006, with a kingsize bed,

dbl showers & a private hammock. All have en-suite facilities, including a flush toilet, washbasin, & excellent shower that is open to the skies. Lighting is by solar-powered storm lanterns. The bar/dining area has comfortable chairs & large, circular dining tables, though dinner is a relaxed affair, often eaten together outside. Tafika is not flash or luxurious in any forced sense, though it is very high quality: the food is superb, the atmosphere friendly & unpretentious, & the guiding truly expert.

Game activities include day & night drives, as well as walking safaris. John (who had a commercial pilot's licence at one stage) keeps a microlight nearby, which can take a passenger. If he's in camp, as is usually the case, flights can be arranged for about US$130 per 15mins – let them know in advance if possible. So if you stay here, don't miss seeing the park from an eagle's point of view. Back on land, it's also possible to do a mountain-bike safari – or perhaps to cycle to the school & clinic supported by Tafika. (The camp is, as you'd expect, very closely connected to the local community, which it supports extensively.)

During the dry season, Tafika acts as the hub for Chikoko Trails (page 277), which use 2 walking bushcamps, Chikoko & Crocodile, just over the river in a wilderness area of the park, & also with Mwaleshi Camp's walking safaris in North Luangwa National Park (page 301). *US$565/655/795 pp sharing May–Jun & Nov/Jul & Oct/Aug–Sep, all FBA, inc bar, laundry, current park fees, exc premium wines. Sgl supp't US$240.* ☉ *May–Nov.*

⌂ **Tena Tena** [map 259] (5 tents) Contact Robin Pope Safaris, page 268. Tena Tena overlooks a tributary of the Luangwa River at the southern end of the Nsefu Sector of the park, about 20km northeast of the bridge at Mfuwe. (Its site will move 1km upstream in 2012 since the river ate into its bank, but the fundamentals of the camp will remain the same.) Tena Tena is not only a widely recognised name in safari circles, it's also one of the park's best camps. Its large, comfortable safari tents are under thatch, & fully insect-proof. Each is set on a solid base with twin or dbl beds, & an en-suite shower & toilet at the rear. They are spaced well apart in quite thick vegetation, & 1 side of the tent opens up almost completely to give a full view of a game-productive waterhole only metres away.

Tena has a well-stocked lounge & bar, with low tables, coffee-table books & a small library, & an entirely separate dining shelter overlooking a lagoon. It's lit by a generator in the evening, which is usually switched off as the last person goes to bed. Tena's been built on a lovely sweeping bend in the river, & there's a comfortable seating area set on the bank so that you can relax & watch the river's wildlife just on the edge of camp.

Activities concentrate on morning & afternoon walks, & game drives (including night drives). The guiding, like everything else here, is first-class – it ranks with the best in Africa. A stay here is often combined with Nkwali, Nsefu (camp or bush camping), or one of Robin Pope's walking safaris. *US$617 Jul–Oct, US$515 22 May–Jun, all pp FBA inc bar, laundry, airport transfers, exc park & community fees.* ⊕ *22 May–Oct.*

Zebra Pans Bushcamp Zebra Pans was the location of a small bushcamp deep in the north of the park, 30km from the Luangwa or Mupamadzi rivers, & near the '05' track from Mfuwe to the Chifungwe scout camp on the edge of the Kabvumbu Pans. Run by Robin Pope Safaris, it closed in 1998 because of its high density of tsetse flies (which are thankfully not a problem in most areas of the Luangwa Valley) & inaccessibility. The camp was in a landscape of low undulating miombo woodland, one of very few which were not near a river – so it offered a contrast to the flora & fauna more usually associated with the Luangwa. In the area there are good numbers of uncommon species like hartebeest, roan, reedbuck & eland. As the areas around the Luangwa River become more popular, it's likely that more esoteric bushcamps like this will eventually be re-opened, so watch this space

🏠 **Zebra Plains** [map 259] (4 tents, max 6 guests) Contact Sanctuary Retreats, page 269. ⊕ 12°45.852'S, 32°02.410'E. In the northwest of the park, Zebra Plains is opposite the site where a hunting camp was recorded as long ago as 1932. More recently, this site became the busy Chibembe Lodge, a centre for the long-defunct Wilderness Trails, then was briefly sold to Chilongozi, who went bust in some style. Chibembe had 5 satellite bushcamps, Mumbulu, Kasansanya, Changwa, Nakalyo & Nyakabvumo, all situated in a private walking area within the park to the west of the camp.

The modern Zebra Plains, opened in 2011, is on the site of the old Mumbulu, thus in an area where the walking was, historically, excellent. Set on a beautiful bend of the Luangwa, it feels rather like a traditional mobile camp. From the square tented central area to the large en-suite tented rooms, it sits very comfortably in the bush. Rush matting lines the floors, en-suite bathrooms have bucket showers (but flush loos), & half mokoros do service as bookshelves (with an 'extensive' reference library planned). Mind you, solid wooden campaign furniture, wicker chairs, & mosquito nets enfolding dbl or twin beds & their attendant bedside tables give a sense of solidity, & touches of luxury such as fluffy bathrobes & umbrella-shaded sunloungers add a hint of decadence. Then there's a private *kapaso*, or valet, for each tent. Electricity is solar generated, with an inverter to charge batteries.

Guests at Zebra Plains stay for 3 nights on a fixed-date basis. Game-drive transfers taking around 3hrs are on Mon & Thu from a pre-arranged departure point. There's then a short motorboat crossing to the lodge – or by canoe if the river is low. The next time you'll see a vehicle will be at the end of your stay, for this is entirely a walking camp. It is managed by Garth Hovell, an experienced & knowledgeable guide who leads walks in a predominantly flat, open area dotted with trees & well frequented by wildlife. *US$580/870 pp sharing/sgl FBA inc drinks, laundry, park fees. No children under 15.* ⊕ *Jun–Oct.*

🏠 **Zungulila** [map 257] (4 chalets) Contact Bushcamp Company, page 267. ⊕ ZUNGUL 13°21.117'S, 31°30.928'E. Situated in an untouched part of the park, Zungulila focuses on exploring some of the most untamed sections of bush on foot (though drives are possible). Routes include the Hippo Pools trail along the Kapamba River, or guests can walk to or from its sister camp, Bilimungwe. With its dark wood furniture & kilim-style floor rugs, the camp itself is redolent of the days of the old explorers, though solar lighting augments the paraffin lamps & comfy sunloungers on the deck bring a 21st-century twist. Its large tents, unusually turned sideways with views of the river from the deck or dbl/twin beds, boast many comforts, from partially open-air bathrooms with a separate toilet to a tiny private plunge pool. You can even

10

cool off with a sundowner in the river! Access is usually by 3½hr transfer from Mfuwe Lodge, but there's also an airstrip close by. *US$420/560 May,* *Nov–Jan, US$445/590 Jun–Oct, all pp sharing/ sgl FBA, inc bar, laundry, airport & inter-camp transfers, exc park fees.* ⊕ *May–10 Jan.*

BUDGET AND MID-RANGE CAMPS South Luangwa National Park is not an ideal safari destination for the impecunious backpacker. Hitchhiking into the park from Chipata is difficult (flying is the best way to arrive 'independently'), and there are no touts selling cheap safaris. There are a few budget camps as well as a lot of smaller, more exclusive ones (with all-inclusive rates). The latter don't cater well for unexpected visitors; they're best booked in advance.

If you want to be independent, then come in your own fully equipped 4x4 – as then you can see the park for yourself. That said, although driving yourself around is fun, it's a pale shadow of the experience that you get at one of the better small lodges. Note, too, that self-drive vehicles may not be driven in the national park when it's dark; only registered guides can conduct night drives. Make sure that you bring supplies of food (fresh vegetables and other limited provisions can be bought locally), and the best maps that you can buy in Lusaka.

Most budget travellers who come to the Luangwa arrive in overland trucks. These travel between Malawi and Zimbabwe, stopping here and in Lusaka. They usually stay, together with a few backpackers and independent travellers, at one of Luangwa's less expensive camps, most clustered around the Mfuwe Bridge area.

🏠 **Croc Valley** [map 258] (3 chalets, 12 tents, 10 backpacker beds, camping) 📞 0216 246074; m 0977 175172; e crocvalleycamp@iwayafrica.com; www.crocvalley.com. Upstream of the main Mfuwe Bridge, this leafy & bustling camp has beautifully maintained gardens shaded by Natal mahogany, ebony & sausage trees. To find it, turn right onto a dirt road just before entering the park, in the same direction as Marula Lodge & Track & Trail Rivercamp. When the road splits, follow it to the right; the camp is well signposted. The extensive river frontage, with hippos on the sandbanks & a healthy crocodile population, is dominated by the campsite with 13 pitches, but in 2011 new spacious safari tents were being built along the river with their own dining area & pool. Other accommodation incorporates en-suite chalets on stilts overlooking the bush, 2 family rooms & 3 backpacker rooms (1 dbl, 1 twin, & one 6-bed) sharing an outdoor 'bush' bathroom. There's a 'hippo-friendly' paddling pool (with sloping sides so that bathing hippos can get out), gym, volleyball net, table tennis, a small kitchen for self-caterers & a spacious lounge & bar. If it feels rather crowded in high season, it is still well designed & attractive. Activities comprise walking safaris (*US$50pp*) & 4x4 game drives (*US$35–40pp*). *Stilt chalet/luxury tent US$155/220 FBA low/high season; US$55–45 pp*

room only; dorm bed US$25 pp; camping US$7.50 pp. Park fees extra.

🏠 **Flatdogs Camp** [map 258] (12 tents, 6 rooms, 1 treehouse, 1 family chalet) 📞 0216 246038; e info@flatdogscamp.com; www.flatdogscamp.com. ⊕ FLATDO 13°6.298'S, 31°46.546'E. The local nickname for the crocodile, 'flatdog' was an apt choice when the original campsite was opened in 1992 at the old crocodile camp near the Mfuwe Bridge. In 2000, Flatdogs was moved to its present site on about 100ha of land beside the river, just to the left of the bridge. It's a lovely spot, with plenty of shade from winterthorn, *Faidherbia albida*, & mahogany, *Trichelia emetica*. A lot of game wanders through the area, including a good population of giraffe, attracted by the acacia trees.

Flatdogs today is an extensive & imaginatively designed camp. It includes a 'Dog & Gat' (*sic*) bar; satellite TV & internet café; a swimming pool; a shop for crafts, bush clothes & toiletries; & an à-la-carte restaurant serving meals (including vegetarian food) all day. This is certainly the social hub of the valley – especially during its entertaining Fri-night gatherings. That said, facilities are well spaced out, so you can get as much privacy as you want.

Three thatched, 2-storey units are each split into 2 rooms, although they each easily combine to suit groups & families. Each has a communal kitchenette (self-catering equipment provided) & en-suite bathroom; downstairs is a dbl room with fan & a wraparound veranda, while upstairs is a twin room with a view of the river. A 4th chalet is slightly larger, with 2 sgl beds on a mezzanine floor with viewing deck, 1 room with 3 sgl beds, & 1 with a dbl & sgl, as well as a separate kitchen. All beds have mosquito nets. The Jackalberry treehouse is a rather lovely and innovative addition, with 2 en-suite bedrooms & a completely open sitting room on a tree platform overlooking a small dambo.

There are also 6 'standard' & 6 'luxury' permanently en-suite safari tents. The luxury are larger, and on the riverbank; whilst the smaller standard tents have a bush view. As a radical departure in 2011, Flatdogs decided to close its campsite completely.

Activities include day & night drives in the park (max 6 people per 4x4 vehicle), walking safaris, & all-day drive/walks (*US$50 per activity, exc park fees*). The camp is excellently run & well suited to those on a tighter budget, especially as accommodation & activities can be booked separately. *Chalet US$57–77 pp room only; US$240–300 pp FBA, inc park fees. Standard/luxury tents: US$42–47/US$47–62 pp room only; US$205–255/US$220–285 pp FBA, inc park fees.* ⊕ *Mid-Mar–mid-Jan.*

🏠 **Kawaza Village** [map 258] (6 huts) For details of this cultural village, see pages 292–3.

🏠 **Marula Lodge** [map 258] (13 rooms) 📞 0216 246 073; m 0974 595838; e info@marulalodgezambia.com; www. marulalodgezambia.com. In a classic position just upstream from the main Mfuwe Bridge, Marula is just before Croc Valley & Track & Trail Rivercamp; when the dirt road splits, continue straight to reach Marula Lodge. Despite its beautiful position, this is a very simple camp, used mostly by local groups & businesspeople, as well as those on budget safaris from Malawi, though also receiving some international guests.

Marula's conventional en-suite chalets are dotted over well-kept lawns. All have high ceilings, concrete floors, mosquito nets & a ceiling fan, though the small, louvred windows instil a slight feeling of claustrophobia. Ten have twin beds, the others have 2 twin-bedded rooms sharing a shower & toilet. The camp's focal point

is a large dining/bar area situated under an impressive winterthorn tree. Another 2-storey building has a dormitory for large school groups upstairs & an office below. Mains electricity is backed up by a generator.

Meals are available in the à-la-carte restaurant, or guests can supply & cook their own food (fridges & freezers are available) with the help of one of the camp's chefs. Game drives & walks are offered (*US$40 pp*), & there's a pool near the river. A campsite was under consideration when we visited in 2011. *US$185/205 pp sharing/sgl, inc FB & 2 game activities/day; US$35/50 pp sharing/sgl self catering. Park fees extra.* ⊕ *All year.*

🏠 **Thornicroft** [map 258] (9 chalets) 📞 0216 246247; m 0962 197811; e info@thornicroft-lodge.com; www.thornicroft-lodge.com, www. landlake.net. 1km downstream of the confluence of the Luangwa & the Lupande rivers, Thornicroft aims at both the local market & international visitors – & is more mid-range than budget. Each solid chalet here has stones & wood inset into its walls, large mesh windows & a thin canvas roof (which seems to offer very little heat insulation). Inside is en suite, with comfortable beds & white linen inside a walk-in mosquito net, plus a desk & hanging space. Outside a veranda overlooks the Luangwa, which is eating away at the bank to get closer every year. At the heart of the lodge are a lovely swimming pool & a huge thatched building incorporating the restaurant, bar & lounge area, where tea & coffee is available all day; rather quirkily, there's also a grand piano! As well as morning & afternoon/night game drives, guided walks can be organised in the dry season. *US$205/255 pp sharing/sgl, inc FB, 2 game drives/ day & airport transfers. Park fees extra.* ⊕ *All year.*

🏠 **Track & Trail River Camp** [map 258] (4 chalets, 5 tents, camping) 📞 0216 246020; m 0977 600556; e info@trackandtrailrivercamp. com; www.trackandtrailrivercamp.com. ⊕ 13°09.979'S, 31°79.261'E. This Dutch-owned camp, opened in 2006, is just 5mins' drive from the park entrance. Right next to Croc Valley, it overlooks the river, & is reached along the same track. Thatched, en-suite chalets of a split-level design each have a private veranda, electricity & mosquito nets, & sleep up to 4 people. The spacious en-suite tents, raised up on wooden platforms, are very comfortable with twin or dbl beds & en-suite facilities, & space for an additional bed. Towards the back of the property, the shady campsite offers individual pitches with water, electricity & BBQ facilities. All campers share a central ablution block. Campers can eat in the main camp & the food is reported to be very good. There's an unusual above-ground pool to keep cool, an open-sided gym rondavel & aromatherapy or hot-stone therapy massages in the newly built spa to ensure complete relaxation.

In addition to guided safaris on foot & in an open game vehicle, this is a good place to pick up photography tips from owner-photographer Peter Geraerdts. Village visits are also possible, as are trips further afield. *Chalet US$125/170 pp sharing FB Nov–Jun/Jul–Oct or US$255/325 FBA, inc park fees, airport transfer, laundry; tent US$105/150 FB or US$235/300 FBA. Sgl suppt US$30–95. Camping US$7.50 pp. ⊕ All year.*

🏠 **Wildlife Camp** [map 258] (9 chalets, 5 safari tents, camping, bushcamp) 📞0216 245026/6246026; e info@wildlifezambia.com; www.wildlifecamp-zambia.com. ⊕ WILDLI 13°6.320'S, 31°45.133'E. This popular, buzzing camp, still large by Luangwa standards, has been leased & run from the WECSZ (page 50) by the helpful Herman Miles & Patsy Hahn since 1992. As the lease fee goes towards conservation/development projects, by staying here you are contributing to a good cause. The camp makes a good base if you have your own vehicle, or you can arrange to be collected from Mfuwe Airport (*US$25 pp/min 2*). If you're driving, pass the airport & turn left just before the main Mfuwe Bridge, following the signs to Kapani, Nkwali, the Wildlife Camp & others. Routes differ slightly in the dry season, but in the wet season you pass the entrance to Kapani, then carry on through mopane woodland for about 3km until you see the Wildlife Camp signs; the camp is shortly after that.

Each of the chalets (with 2–4 beds) & twin-bedded safari tents is en suite; all are clean & pleasant, but not luxurious. For those with their own kit, there's a huge campsite set well apart on the river in a large grove of mopane trees. As with any big-game location, don't even think about sleeping outside without a closed tent. In addition to an ablution block, the campsite has thatched shelters, & its own pool & bar. Basic kitchen equipment is available both for the chalets & at the campsite, or with 24hrs notice you can arrange for staff to cook for you (*US$15/day per tent/chalet*). Either way, you'll need to bring your own food; there are a few shops in Mfuwe where you can pick up supplies. Note that there are monkeys in camp, so don't leave food lying around.

The bar/restaurant, with a tiny curio area, is often busy & always relaxed. It overlooks a floodplain & the main Luangwa River beyond, & serves both à-la-carte meals & snacks. There are exceedingly popular day & night game drives (*US$45 pp/min 3*) &, between Jun & Nov, walking safaris (*US$40–50 pp/min 3*) on WECSZ land & in the park; the 4-tent bushcamp (about 2–3km from the main camp) makes a great overnight walking safari option (*US$220 pp all inc*). If you have your own vehicle you can drive yourself into the park during the day, though only licensed guides are allowed to conduct night drives. Village tours are also possible (*US$30 pp*). *Chalet US$60/80 Jul–Oct, US$40/50 Nov–Jun, pp sharing/sgl room only; US$220/250 Jul–Oct, US$150/180 Nov–Jun FBA, inc airport transfers. Safari tent US$40/50 Jul–Oct, US$25/30 Nov–Jun pp sharing/sgl room only; US$180/200 Jul–Oct, US$140/160 Nov–Jun FBA, inc airport transfers. Camping pp US$10 Jul–Oct, US$7.50 Nov–Jun. Park fees & drinks extra. Discount for WECSZ members. ⊕ All year.*

Community campsites around the South Luangwa

🏕 **Munyamadzi Bushcamp** [map 257] (2 rondavels, camping) m 0966 400567, 0978 335467; e info@munyamadzibushcamp.com; www.munyamadzibushcamp.com. ⊕ MUNYAM 12°22.410'S, 31°35.779'E. At the foot of the Muchinga Escarpment, just outside the Chifungwe gate, this community-run site opened in 2010. About 57km from the Great North Rd, it's a useful stop for those heading towards Mfuwe

along the tricky 'Corridor Route' (page 271). There are rondavels & tents for hire, or pitch your own, with hot showers, braai areas, & full board available. Guides (*US$5 pp*) can accompany you on game drives, & to Chibwe Malimba caves & Mutinondo Falls. *Rondavel US$20pp; camping US$10 pp; tent hire US$5. ⊕ 15 May–Nov.*

🏕 **Mwanya Bushcamp** [map 259] ⊕ MWANYA 12°45.348'S; 32°04.555'E. Although closed in 2011, this simple campsite about 100km from Mfuwe may re-open, so keep an eye out. It sits on elevated ground, surrounded by floodplains & the old channel of the Luangwa River, where a lagoon attracts animals almost into camp. Opposite is the island of Chilufya, characterised by smaller lagoons & open plains.

OTHER TYPES OF TRIPS/ACCOMMODATION

Mobile safaris There's a lot of hype about mobile walking safaris. Perhaps images of Livingstone or Stanley striding through deepest Africa with an entourage of trusty porters and guides are to blame. I don't know. But these days, let's be honest, it is somewhat different. The term 'mobile safari' is overused.

It used to mean that you set off with all your kit on the backs of porters and camped where you stopped. Think, for a moment, of the consequences of this. You'll realise that it resulted in either very basic camping stops with few facilities, or more comfortable camps requiring a safari of enormous cost. It also required total freedom to camp where you liked, which is now limited and controlled by ZAWA for very good reasons.

Although the term 'mobile safari' is often abused, there is one operation in South Luangwa National Park that comes close to running a proper mobile operation:

Robin Pope's Mobile Safaris Contact Robin Pope Safaris, page 268. Between mid Jun & Sep, RPS organises about 12 mobile walking safaris along the Mupamadzi River, in the far north of the park. The trip itself lasts 6 days & 5 nights; participants also spend at least 2 nights prior to the trip at Nkwali, & 3 at the end at either Tena Tena or Nsefu – though a few more days either side would be ideal.

The walks are about 10km per day & a truly mobile camp is used, moved by the back-up vehicle to meet you. The camp has comfortable walk-in tents (each with twin beds), shared hot & cold showers, shared long-drop toilets, & a staff of 8 or 9. Typically they'll use 3 different sites for the 5 nights, & the choice depends on the game & the walkers' interests.

These trips are organised on fixed dates each year, & take a max of 6 people. They are always oversubscribed, & sometimes booked up a year or 2 in advance. The real attraction of these trips is, firstly, that they are just walking in a wilderness area. There's no driving, & you are away from everything but the bush. Secondly, you're in a small group that stays together with just 1 guide. You get to know each other & have a lot of time with one of the valley's best guides. They're very relaxing. (As there is no sgl supplement whilst walking, these trips are popular amongst sgl people.) *US$617 Jul–Oct, US$515 Jun, all pp per night at walking camps, plus costs at Nkwali & Tena Tena.* ☺ *Mid Jun–Sep.*

Fly-camping In Africa, the term 'fly-camp' usually means a simple campsite with a campfire and a small, very simple tent – or possibly just a mosquito net. This is obviously a far cry from the luxurious en-suite tents of most modern safari camps – but camping like this out in the bush, with nothing around you apart from the darkness, does have a real appeal for many cosseted travellers. They're ideal for the thrill of no-frills camping in the bush – expect a bucket shower under a tree & a long-drop toilet – but there's certainly no better way to feel close to the wildlife at night.

Lodges have operated fly-camps in some areas of Africa for years – most notably the Selous Game Reserve in southern Tanzania – but they're still new to the Luangwa. The main companies offering them are:

- Robin Pope Safaris (page 268), which terms them 'Bush Camping', and offers them either individually, or as part of a set departure that combines Nkwali, Palmgrove and Luangwa Bushcamping, and Nsefu, each for two nights.

- Norman Carr Safaris (page 268), which offers what it terms 'Luwi River sleepouts' – usually for just one night, for a maximum of four people, and as part of a walk between their bushcamps.
- Shenton Safaris (page 269) have a less well-known option called 'camp-outs' which are normally guided by Derek and which go to the north of Mwamba Bushcamp for one night – again with a maximum of four guests.

RPS uses small, walk-in tents for these nights, whilst Norman Carr and Shentons usually use mosquito nets.

River safaris River safaris are only possible around February to April, depending on the water level in the Luangwa River; then, this is the only way to get around most of the park. See *When to go*, in *Chapter 4*, pages 39–40, for more comment on the wet season – but from that you'll realise that the rain is usually in short, sharp, late-afternoon bursts. The rest of the day is often sunny – for photographers the clarity and quality of the light is extraordinary. So if you've been on safari quite a bit, but only seen the Luangwa (or southern Africa) in the dry season, you should aim to make a trip during the rains. You won't see the density of animals that you'll find in October, but the place comes alive with animals and plants you just don't see in the dry season, and the birdlife is phenomenal.

For ten months of the year most of the river's tributaries are sand rivers, but for just a few months they fill with water. Often they are lined by tall old hardwood trees. In a few areas the trees open out onto wide, shallow floodplains, usually dotted with egrets, waders or geese, while in the middle are several nesting colonies for storks and herons, of which the most well known are those in the Nsefu Sector of the park. These rely on a high water level, and the birds won't nest unless the area is flooded. (This is probably a protection mechanism against nest raiders who would be deterred by the water at the foot of the trees.) The main one of these is a huge colony for yellow-billed storks, which take on a beautiful, delicate pink hue when breeding and collectively make for an amazing sight.

Two operations, Norman Carr Safaris (see page 268) and Robin Pope Safaris (page 268) currently run river trips during the rainy season:

Norman Carr Safaris Their 'Rivers & Rainbows Safari' starts with 4 nights at Kapani followed by a transfer to Kakuli Bushcamp for a further 3 nights. *US$2,650 pp sharing FBA, inc bar, laundry, local transfers & park fees; discount possible for NCS's past visitors.*

Robin Pope Safaris Their 'Emerald Season Safaris' typically spend 7 nights between Luangwa River Camp, Nsefu & Nkwali camps. *US$2,723 pp sharing FBA, inc bar, laundry & local transfers, exc park fees.*

Cultural tourism Though wildlife is often the main draw of the Luangwa Valley, increasing numbers of visitors are enjoying meeting the local people and learning more of their traditional lifestyles. Cultural tourism is gradually taking off. Currently this has two main points of focus:

Kawaza Village (*Contact Robin Pope Safaris, page 268. Day visit US$25 pp inc lunch; overnight min US$50 pp. Robin Pope Safaris charges US$140 pp per night, of which 50% is paid into Kawaza's school fund, & the rest goes to the village*). Jointly developed between Robin Pope Safaris and local villagers, and now part of the wider Project Luangwa, Kawaza is an efficient and viable small business for the village which involves visitors staying either for an afternoon, or (much better) overnight. Here they can spend time with people from this Kunda community and learn more of their daily ways of living, traditions and culture.

It started as an effort to end the villagers' feeling of exclusion. Some of the communities around Mfuwe felt that many overseas visitors arrive and leave without any meaningful form of social contact with them. They also wished to get involved in tourism, to raise funds for their school and to support vulnerable members of their community (orphans and the elderly). The scheme is run by a committee of villagers, with Felix John Kalubu, headmaster of the adjacent school, as secretary. His predecessor, David Mwewa, explained to me that the objectives were 'to provide an authentic Zambian experience and raise money for the community'.

Kawaza is a real village and visitors are encouraged to participate in its normal everyday life – to help the women cook nshima and relish, to visit the local traditional healer, to tend the crops, to try fishing, or to visit the local school, church or clinic. Villagers will tailormake an agenda to suit your interests and time – with an overnight stay (see below) the best option.

The effects of the project on the community are gradually showing. Some of the villagers are learning more English in order to communicate better with visitors. David commented, 'When the visitors first came the villagers could not imagine dancing together with a white person or eating together. But when guests come to the village they join in all the activities … when they see the villagers putting up a roof they join them … The visitors like it that way.' Further, the school is benefiting directly, as a proportion of the income goes straight into its funds. The school's five-year plan now includes erecting more toilets, stocking the library with books and computers, purchasing motorbikes and a school bus to transport both pupils and staff, and providing sports kit for the children.

The village is a 30–45-minute drive from the Mfuwe Bridge, depending on the time of year and the route taken. Transfer costs vary between operators, but expect to pay from US$80 per trip.

🏠 Staying overnight

🏠 (6 huts) A handful of rondavels has been built just for visitors: small, clean huts of traditional design with thatched roofs. These have mattresses on simple wooden bedsteads, with spotlessly clean sheets & mosquito nets. Visitors also have their own separate long-drop toilets & rondavels for bathing (using a large tin bowl & a scoop for the water). The food is grown locally & prepared in the village – including tasty cassava for breakfast, with coffee, tea & milk.

Activities are really just taking part in whatever is going on when you are there, & whatever you are interested in. That might mean going into the bush to the village's plots of arable land, collecting local plants & herbs, preparing the food, or even going to help teach a class at the school. Depending on the time of year, you may be allowed to see some (though not all) of

the initiation ceremonies for the young people. (As you'd expect, men attend only the men's ceremonies & women only the women's.)

Of special interest, usually arranged on request, would be a visit to a traditional healer, or a local clinic, or a meeting with the area's senior chief Nsefu – the paramount chief of the 6 local chiefs. In the evening, the community's elders tell traditional stories or sing songs around the campfire.

If you've never really tried to put yourself in a totally different culture, then spend a night here. It'll make you think about your own culture as much as Kawaza's, & you'll remember it long after you've forgotten the animals.

Guests staying at most camps in the Luangwa can add a night at Kawaza to their itinerary, with rates depending on the individual camp & the cost of transfers (see above).

Nsendamila Cultural Village Very close to the hub of the Mfuwe area, Nsendamila village has been closed for several years, but now offers a small selection

IC

of curios for sale. It is easily found by turning left towards Kapani and Nkwali just before the Mfuwe Bridge, followed shortly by another turning to the left. The village was originally built by the local communities, with funding from various charities and NGOs, its traditional rondavels laid out to demonstrate a local village's way of life. Further plans – for a cultural and heritage centre with drama productions, and for a small museum to house prehistoric artefacts from the Luangwa Valley – have yet to come to fruition. The village is also the site of Uyoba Community School, built and sponsored by the SLCS, at which visitors are welcome.

NORTH LUANGWA NATIONAL PARK

(*Park fees US$20 pp/day; self drive US$25 pp/day & vehicle US$15/day; bed levy US$20 pp per night*) North Luangwa National Park (known usually as 'the North Park') covers about 4,636km² of the Luangwa Valley; it's half the size of the South Luangwa National Park (aka the 'South Park'). It shares the same origin as the South Park, being part of the same rift valley, and its eastern boundary is also the Luangwa River. It has the same geology, soil types and vegetation as South Luangwa, and so its landscapes are very similar.

However, unlike the South Park, which is basically bounded by the steep Muchinga Escarpment to the west, the North Park takes in a lot of this within its protection. About 24% of North Luangwa lies within the escarpment, compared with about 5% of South Luangwa. This means that North Luangwa has a more diverse range of habitats, which is especially interesting for birdwatchers, although there are also mammals found on the hill which aren't normally seen on the valley floor.

From a conservation point of view, it also means that much of the catchment area of North Luangwa's main rivers falls within the boundaries of the park – giving the park authorities more control of its rivers and habitats.

For visitors to the wilderness camps, perhaps the park's most important natural feature is the Mwaleshi River – which is unlike the Luangwa or any of its tributaries in the South Park (except, possibly, stretches of the Mupamadzi). It's a permanent river that flows even in the heat of the dry season, when it's generally very clear and shallow.

THE PARK'S ZONES For the visitor, it's important to understand that North Luangwa is now 'zoned'. Most of the southern side of the park is strictly reserved as a wilderness area. It has very few roads and is currently used only by three small camps, which concentrate on walking safaris. The only way to visit this is to arrange your trip with one of these operators, and stay in one of these tiny camps. If you're not staying at a camp, then you cannot even pass through this area; you'll find clear signs and even booms across the tracks.

However, north of this is a 'zone' that was opened to wider access in 2002. Now it's possible for experienced travellers to bring fully equipped vehicles into the park, and drive through from east to west, or vice versa. Access is strictly restricted to the more northerly zone, which has one main track across it and several side-tracks. This is a new way to see parts of this remote park, whilst getting between Luambe National Park and the Great North Road. It also opens up the possibility of an interesting (if challenging) circular drive around eastern Zambia.

HISTORY
Before the mid 1980s Without the conservation efforts and funds that were devoted to South Luangwa, the country's premier game park, the North Luangwa

National Park has until recently been a 'poor relation'. Poachers hunting rhino and elephant met less resistance there, and local people crossed its boundaries freely in search of food. The impact on the game was inevitable.

North Luangwa remained a wilderness area for many years, officially accessible only to the Game Department, until 1984 when Major John Harvey and his wife Lorna (daughter of Sir Stewart Gore-Browne, of Shiwa Ng'andu) started to run walking safaris here. They were the first safari operators here and their son, Mark Harvey, runs one of the three camps currently in the North Park (*Buffalo Camp*, page 300).

The Owens's ideal In 1986 a couple of American zoologists – Mark and Delia Owens – visited the park in search of an African wilderness in which to base their animal research, and returned in October '87 to base themselves here. They came from a project in Botswana's Central Kalahari Game Reserve, with an uncompromising reputation for defending the wildlife against powerful vested interests. They also had behind them an international best-selling book about their experiences – *The Cry of the Kalahari*. This had brought conservation issues in Botswana to a popular audience, which earned them considerable financial backing for high-profile conservation efforts, including the vital support of the Frankfurt Zoological Society (FZS).

Their presence here was to have a profound impact upon the park. In the early 1980s, elephant poaching was estimated at about 1,000 animals per year. Their second best-seller, the highly readable *Survivor's Song* (called *The Eye of the Elephant* in the US; see *Appendix 3*, page 537), relates their struggles to protect this park from the poachers, and their efforts to find alternatives for the local people so that they would support the anti-poaching work.

Read it before you arrive, but don't be alarmed: the place is much safer now. Also be aware that their book has been written to sell. It's an exciting yarn, but does describe events as if they were a personal campaign. It doesn't mention any real contribution to education, development or anti-poaching from anyone apart from Mark and Delia. Others involved with the park have long maintained that this was not a true picture, and that the Owens's book simply ignored the 'bigger picture' of all the efforts which were going on at the time. Whatever the truth, it's worth reading.

With the dedication of the Owens, and the vital financial assistance that they could attract, poaching has been virtually eliminated. The park's game scouts were paid well and properly housed, and became the most zealous and effective in the country. Local education and development programmes were initiated in villages around the park, aiming to raise awareness of conservation and to provide alternatives for people who relied upon poaching for food.

However, Mark and Delia left Zambia in a hurry in 1996. This followed an alleged incident in which forceful anti-poaching actions went too far. It was precipitated by a documentary screened in the US by the ABC television network, *Deadly Game: The Mark and Delia Owens Story*, in which an alleged poacher appeared to be executed. Mark and Delia have never returned to Zambia.

NORTH LUANGWA CONSERVATION PROJECT Perhaps the real, lasting legacy of Mark and Delia is that they introduced the Frankfurt Zoological Society (FZS) to North Luangwa. The FZS's constant financial support over more than 25 years has done an amazing amount to safeguard this terrific park. Thanks to them, and other important donors, the privately financed North Luangwa Conservation Project continues to support the park and its authorities.

The NLCP's input has concentrated on support for the law enforcement effort, through training and the supply of essential field equipment, rations, vehicles and the building of houses for the field staff. Thus the park's scouts continue to be keen, well trained and well motivated. They also help to conduct regular aerial surveys of large mammals, records of which stretch all the way back to the late 1980s, and to maintain and gradually expand the road network – as well as other aspects of the park's management and conservation.

Various programmes continue to support the communities around the park. These vary from a conservation education programme, with material that is specific to this area, to work on land-use plans – to get the nearby communities to think critically about their future and how they can generate income, whilst safeguarding some of their natural resources for the future.

The rhino Meanwhile, the game goes from strength to strength. In 2003 five black rhino were introduced into a large fenced-off intensive protection zone, at the heart of the park, with a further ten added in 2006, five more in 2008, and another five in 2010. Despite the death of four animals, eight calves have been born in the sanctuary, the latest in July 2011, with the population now totalling 29 in the extended sanctuary area.

These are now probably the only black rhino in the country; their presence is a strong sign of how secure the North Luangwa is, and that the park expects to enjoy the long-term support of the FZS. It's worth noting that while there are 4x4 tracks through the protection zone, no-one is currently allowed to stop within the fenced area. Other animals, however, can get under or over the fencing; it is only the rhino that are kept within the zone.

The future for North Luangwa seems bright – and Zambia's positive experience of having a national park run with the strong support of a donor-funded private organisation has helped it to look to the future in places like Liuwa Plain, where an analogous project is progressing well, and in the Bangweulu Wetlands.

FLORA AND FAUNA In general, the flora and fauna of the North Park are the same as those found in South Luangwa (see pages 262–5). However, the inclusion of the escarpment in the park certainly brings a new dimension to the flora here. An excellent example is the road from Mano down from the escarpment, which is about 12km long. This brings you from the two-storey woodlands of the upper and plateau escarpment, with a lightly closed canopy of semi-evergreen trees 15–20m high, and down through the miombo woodlands on the hills to vegetation more typical of the valley as most people know it.

Often there are bird species here that aren't usually found on the valley floor, and sometimes sable antelope, bushpig or blue monkeys. In the dry season, look also for signs of elephant, which often move into the mountains.

On the valley floor, the ecosystems of the two parks, and the native game species found therein, often seem virtually identical. The North Park has some east African bird species that don't occur further south – like the chestnut-mantled sparrow weaver, the white-winged starling and especially the yellow-throated longclaw – but the differences in species are minor.

However, several differences are apparent. You're more likely to see Cookson's wildebeest (*Connochaetes taurinus cooksoni*), one of the valley's endemic subspecies. The population seems much larger in the north of the valley than in the south. However, you won't find any giraffes here, as they don't seem to occur much north of the Mupamadzi River. (Phil Berry has reliable records of a few sightings here

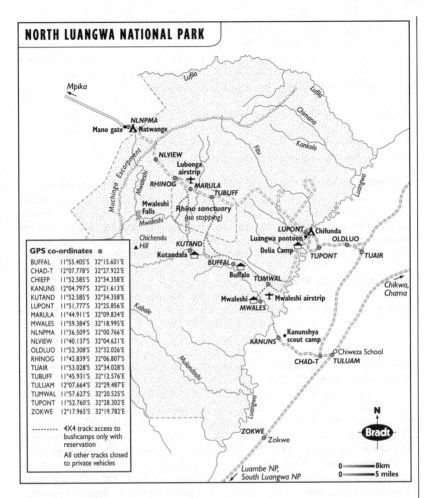

NORTH LUANGWA NATIONAL PARK

GPS co-ordinates ⊕

BUFFAL	11°55.405'S 32°15.601'E
CHAD-T	12°07.778'S 32°27.922'E
CHIEFP	11°52.585'S 32°34.358'E
KANUNS	12°04.797'S 32°21.613'E
KUTAND	11°52.585'S 32°34.358'E
LUPONT	11°51.777'S 32°25.856'E
MARULA	11°44.911'S 32°09.834'E
MWALES	11°59.384'S 32°18.995'E
NLNPMA	11°36.509'S 32°00.766'E
NLVIEW	11°40.137'S 32°04.621'E
OLDLUO	11°52.308'S 32°32.026'E
RHINOG	11°42.839'S 32°06.807'S
TUAIR	11°53.028'S 32°34.028'S
TUBUFF	11°45.931'S 32°12.576'E
TULUAM	12°07.664'S 32°29.487'E
TUMWAL	11°57.627'S 32°20.525'S
TUPONT	11°52.760'S 32°28.302'E
ZOKWE	12°17.965'S 32°19.782'E

-------- 4X4 track: access to bushcamps only with reservation

All other tracks closed to private vehicles

N

0 ——— 8km
0 ——— 5 miles

until about the mid-'80s. John Coppinger comments that in his years operating to the North Park since 1990, he's only ever received a report of one giraffe … and that was probably lost!)

Eland, the largest of the antelope, are more common here, and hartebeest are also seen more often than in the South Park. Given their long lifespan, and slow regeneration after poaching, elephant are skittish in the North Park and still relatively scarce. The population is growing, but it'll take a long time before they are as numerous, or as relaxed, as they are around Mfuwe. Buffalo herds seem to be even larger than those in the South Park, and there are some very strong prides of lion. Hyena are also common; those in the North Park seem to hunt more than those in the South, and have developed a tactic of chasing puku into the Mwaleshi River in order to catch them. Those in the South Park tend perhaps to do a little more scavenging, and less hunting. Then, of course, there are the re-introduced black rhino – see above.

GETTING THERE Prior to 2002, the only way for visitors to see North Luangwa was to come to one of the few camps for walking safaris within the park. That's still the way that most people visit, and certainly the way to get the most out of the park. Typically a three- to five-night stay at one of the walking camps is perfect. Most visitors (and there are only a total of a few hundred in the average year) combine a walking trip here with some time in the South Park, and fly between the two. For the cognoscenti, it's one of Africa's top safari destinations

By air Transfers to and from North Luangwa are normally organised as part of your safari package, on small four- to six-seater light aircraft. A short hop here by light aircraft from Lukuzi or Mfuwe (both in South Luangwa) takes about 20–45 minutes and costs in the region of US$260 per person.

Driving The adventurous and experienced may now drive themselves through the north side of the park. Although the access roads from the Mpika area are graded, and even those within the park are reasonably well maintained, it's a very remote and wild area, so you'll need two fully equipped 4x4 vehicles, the expertise to use them, and a high degree of self-sufficiency. Read *Lessons in bush travel* box, on pages 272–3, before you even consider this! Then directions are as follows:

From Mpika via Mano gate There are now two roads to North Luangwa National Park from the Mpika area, the new route being considerably closer to Mpika. The established route, a turning off the Great North Road (✛ TUNLNP 11°26.378'S, 31°44.307'E), is well signposted just over 60km northeast of Mpika, and 28km south of the turning to Shiwa Ng'andu. There are a few buildings at the junction, a place called Luanya, and the altitude here is 1,556m. This isn't a difficult track, having been recently graded; follow it for about 32km until another sign points left (✛ TUNLN2 11°35.698'S, 31°55.229'E). It's then a further 11km to the Mano gate (✛ NLNPMA 11°36.509'S, 32°00.766'E), by which time you've descended about 390m from the Great North Road.

The new road, opened in 2010, glories in the name of the Kalenga Mashitu Range Road. It starts just over 5km north of Mpika, where you turn east towards the North Luangwa (✛ TU2NLP 11°47.056'S, 31°27.663'E). The only signpost is to Katibunga High School. This, too, is a graded road, initially running parallel to the mountains through woodland, enlivened here and there by the pink and cream blooms of protea flowers. After 38km, you'll go through the village of Katibunga, a prosperous-looking mission station dominated by the Church of Christ the King and now run by Tanzanian monks. A further 21km will bring you to a signpost, where you turn right to the national park. From here the road narrows, and after another 9.4km brings you to the Mano gate.

Mano itself is outside of the park, but this is where you sign in, pay your park fees and find out about the latest park news. The staff are generally very helpful, and usually have reasonably accurate maps charting the route that you are allowed to take across the park. (Unless staying at one of the bushcamps, self drivers are not allowed into the south of the park.) Note that if you're driving to one of the lodges, you must get to the park gate no later than 16.00. If you're camping, the obvious first stop is the Natwange Community Campsite (opposite), not more than 1km further down the road; a second campsite, Chifunda, lies just beyond the pontoon that marks the eastern access point to the park.

From Luambe National Park Approaching North Luangwa from Luambe, you'll be travelling on the east side of the Luangwa River – very much a continuation of the road from South Luangwa to Luambe. (See page 302 for directions.)

Starting at Chipuka gate (⊕ CHIPUK 12°26.923'S, 32°12.516'E), which marks the northern edge of Luambe National Park, you'll be driving north through some very rural country with a scattering of remote villages. About 9km after the scout camp you need to take a very sharp left turn (⊕ TULUA1 12°25.313'S, 32°16.547'E).

Some 17km or so after that turn, you'll reach the very basic Zokwe scout camp (⊕ ZOKWE 12°17.965'S, 32°19.782'E), which is followed by a lovely stretch of fairly undisturbed cathedral mopane woodland. Around 30km after Zokwe, there's a junction in the track (⊕ TULUAM 12°7.664'S, 32°29.487'E) at Chiweza village school. Turn left here, and continue for another 2.9km until there's a right turn onto another track at ⊕ 12°07.778'S, 32°27.922'E.

(Continuing straight on would lead to a crossing of the Luangwa near the old Kanunshya gate, but this entry to the park is exclusive to the operators who work there, and there is no public right of access.)

Hence take a right turn at ⊕ CHAD-T (⊕ 12°07.778'S, 32°27.922'E) and continue north and slightly east for about 28km until you cross an airfield. Just beyond this, turn left (west) at ⊕ TUAIR 11°53.028'S, 32°34.028'E. After another 5km you pass a place called Old Luelo Camp (⊕ OLDLUO 11°52.308'S, 32°32.026'E), and then about 8.5km later, take a right turn (⊕ TUPONT 11°52.760'S, 32°28.302'E). The road ahead is a game track. After almost 7km you'll pass the entrance to Chifunda Bushcamp (⊕ CHIFBC 11°51.645'S, 32°26.066'E), then another 0.4km brings you to a T-junction. Turn right for 200m or so to reach the manual pontoon across the Luangwa (⊕ LUPONT 11°51.777'S, 32°25.856'E; *no charge*) into the North Park. Note that the pontoon takes one vehicle only and is normally operated from 1 June until the end of October, but it's always wise to check in advance. The pontoon is usually monitored by the park's very sharp scouts. In case of vehicle problems they can arrange for help, but a substantial vehicle recovery fee will be payable.

WHERE TO STAY
Northern zone
Outside the park For those who are self-sufficient and driving themselves through the northern zone of the park, there are two simple community camps, one to the west, by the Mano gate, the second close to the Luangwa pontoon in the east of the park. Alternatively, you can camp at Luangwa Wilderness Lodge (see page 304) in Luambe National Park.

⋏ Natwange Community Campsite
(2 chalets, camping) e info@ natwangebushcamp.com, mosesnyirenda@ gmail.com. ⊕ NLNPMA 11°36.509'S, 32°00.766'E. Opened in 2002 with the help of the North Luangwa Conservation Project, Natwange is run by the local Mukungule community, & all the proceeds go into a fund that benefits the community. It's an ideal place to camp on the western boundary of the park. The campsite is set in beautiful thick *mushitu* forest on the banks of the Mwaleshi River, just 1km or so inside the Mano gate. Individual pitches have flush toilets & hot-water showers, tents can be hired (*US$5/ night*), & 2 twin chalets are planned. There are fireplaces for BBQs, & a central shelter, but aside

from water & firewood you'll need all your own supplies.

You can walk along the river from here, arrange a visit to one of the local villages, or perhaps do a little birding or fishing (*guided birding US$5 pp/hr*). Look out for Ross's turaco & the uncommon green twinspot. *US$15 pp.* ☉ *May–mid Dec.*

⋏ Chifunda Community Bushcamp
(3 chalets, camping) ☎ 0216 246127; m 0978 014706; e bushcamp@itswild.org; www.itswild. org. ⊕ CHIFBC 11°51.645'S, 32°26.066'E. This thriving community bushcamp on the Luangwa River, just 0.6km from the Luangwa pontoon, is the only survivor of 3 set up under an initiative sponsored by Community Markets for

Conservation (COMACO), each employing local people – some of them ex-poachers – & with profits shared between local villages.

Surrounded by tall, shady trees, Chifunda is an attractive, well-maintained site overlooking the national park. As well as camping there are simple but spacious thatched chalets, each with large twin beds, solar lighting, open-air toilet & a big shower area. There's a central dining shelter where meals can be provided (*b/fast US$10, lunch/dinner US$15 pp*) or, if you bring your own food, they'll help with preparation. Guided walks (*US$15 pp*) can be organised, as can game drives in your own vehicle (*US$10 pp*), both exc park fees. Village visits (*US$10 pp*) are a further option. *Camping US$12 pp; chalet US$42 pp.* ☉ *12 Jun–Oct.*

Within the park

🏠 **Delia Camp** (4 chalets) ☏ +34 666 828081; e info@deliacamp.com; www. deliacamp.com. We have received very mixed reports about this Spanish-owned camp, which opened in 2006, but was closed for 2011; we understand it will re-open. It is built beside the Luangwa River, to the east of the national park, between the Chifunda gate & the Mwaleshi River. From the turn off to camp (⊕ TUDELC 11°50.956'S, 32°25.573'E), it's a further 10km. As it stands, the camp has open-fronted twin chalets with en-suite facilities, all built of reed & thatch, & raised up on stilts. In similar style, & linked by walkways, the central area has a veranda where meals are taken overlooking the river. Both walking safaris & game drives are offered.

Southern wilderness area

Being very remote, and only accessible for part of the year, the park's southern zone – the walking wilderness area – is a difficult place for a safari company to operate. Hence for many years there have been only two or three camps here, all of which concentrate on walking rather than driving. North Luangwa offers an experience that is even more remote and isolated than the rest of the valley, and you can guarantee that you won't be disturbed by anyone else whilst walking here.

All three of the park's bushcamps stand on the banks of the Mwaleshi, one of the few sources of water for the game, which consequently gravitates to it. It is shallow enough to be easily crossed on foot, allowing you to follow game back and forth across the river. This isn't usually an option beside the main Luangwa, but is easy here. Certainly in the heat of October I relished the cool of paddling across it and even the chance to just sit down in the middle with a drink at sundown. Having such a convenient, cool stream next to camp does make a big difference to both your comfort in the heat and your game viewing.

If you're driving yourself, you will have to leave the park by either the Mano gate or the Chifunda gate. If the latter, do be aware that the road that runs north, parallel to the Luangwa River, is very rarely used, so be prepared for fallen trees, and give yourself plenty of time.

🏠 **Buffalo Camp** (6 chalets) m 0976 970444; e kapishya@shiwasafaris.com; www. shiwasafaris.com. ⊕ BUFFAL 11°55.405'S, 32°15.601'E. Situated close to the Mwaleshi River, surrounded by plains, this small camp is set under some welcome shade. Simple, reed-&-thatch chalets along the river are rebuilt each year, complete with en-suite toilets & hot showers. They're no-frills affairs, but spacious & comfortable, with twin or dbl beds & a low reed wall giving an open view of the river & plains beyond. Relax in a hammock during the heat of the day, or simply cool off in the river; when it's colder, there's a firepit backed by a simple dining shelter.

Buffalo is good value & more offbeat than the other camps in the park; having a laid-back attitude to your time here is a prerequisite to enjoying it! Predominantly a walking camp, it's owned & run by Mark Harvey, who was born & brought up at Shiwa Ng'andu & speaks several local languages; he's a very experienced, knowledgeable & entertaining guide – though note that he isn't always in camp as he also runs Kapishya Hot Springs at Shiwa.

If you're driving yourself through the park, & want to stop for a night or 2, cooking for yourself, it's worth phoning ahead to see if that's an option: Mark will sometimes accept self-catering guests at US$80 (exc park fees/bed levy & activities). Children are welcome (though under 12s cannot walk in the park). *US$300 pp FBA, exc drinks, park fees/bed levy.* ☉ *Mid-Jun–31 Oct.*

⌂ **Kutandala Camp** (4 chalets) e rod@ kutandala.com; www.kutandala.com. ⊕ KUTAND 11°53.325'E, 32°110.237'S. Kutandala Camp was started in 2001 on the south bank of the Mwaleshi River by Rod Tether & his wife, Maelisa (Guz). Rod knows the park exceptionally well, having first guided in the Luangwa Valley in 1989, & he continues to lead all safaris. Guz, a Ballymaloe-trained chef, specialises in conjuring faultless cuisine from minute grass huts with open fires – remarkable stuff! The food & hospitality are excellent, with b/fast & dinner stylishly served al fresco.

Together Rod & Guz spend about 5 months of every year here, in one of the valley's smallest bushcamps. Each of the simple chalets is built of grass & poles, with an en-suite flush toilet & a hot shower open to the stars. Each also has a wide veranda overlooking the Mwaleshi River. Near the bar is an extensive library on natural history & Zambia.

But the main point of Kutandala is to explore the park with Rod on foot. It's strictly a walking camp & most visitors stay here for 4–5 nights. The camp takes 6 people max at any one time – a good number for a walk!

The only easy way to get here is by air; Kutandala is about 50 mins' drive from Mwaleshi airstrip. *US$550/700 pp sharing/sgl FBA, inc drinks, laundry, park fees.* ☉ *7 Jun–7 Nov.*

⌂ **Mwaleshi Camp** (4 chalets) Contact Remote Africa Safaris, page 268. ⊕ MWALES 11°59.384'S, 32°18.995'E. John Coppinger originally set up Mwaleshi Camp for Wilderness Trails in 1989, then retained control of it when he set up his own operation, Remote Africa Safaris. Almost all visitors fly between South & North Luangwa national parks; it's a 35min hop from Lukuzi Airstrip, near Tafika, or 45mins from Mfuwe. A minimum stay of 3 nights is sensible.

Mwaleshi is a delightfully simple yet well-equipped bushcamp whose reed-&-grass chalets are set on the southern bank of a scenic stretch of the Mwaleshi River. Each has a flush toilet & hot shower en suite, under the stars. There's an attractive thatched dining & bar area, also overlooking the river, & a small riverside shelter so you can cool off in the heat of the day. The permanent manager/guide is one of the experienced team from Remote Africa Safaris – so it's a top-class operation & one of my favourite bushcamps in Africa. Walking really is the activity here (very convenient, given the amount you'll be tempted to eat of their excellent food), & the first time you get on a vehicle from camp may well be when you're leaving. That said, the presence of a vehicle enables walks further afield, a day trip to Mwaleshi Falls, or even the occasional night drive. *US$490/730 pp sharing/sgl FBA, inc bar, current park fees, exc premium wines.* ☉ *Mid-Jun–31 Oct.*

LUAMBE NATIONAL PARK

(*Park fees US$15 pp/day; vehicle US$15/day; no fees payable in transit between North & South parks*) This small park, just 254km², is situated between North and South Luangwa national parks and can be reached only between about May and October. The first serious rains turn the area's powdery black-cotton soil into an impassable quagmire – impossible even in the best 4x4. Even in the dry season the roads are not great, as the black-cotton soil sets into a series of hard bumps. The good news, though, is that these – including some self-drive game loops – are re-graded each year.

The park – and the lodge – are administered in conjunction with ZAWA by the German NGO Communities for Conservation Society Cologne (CCSC; *www. conservationsocietycologne.org*), which was formerly Luangwa Wilderness.

FLORA AND FAUNA Luambe is mostly riverine forest, and stretches of mopane woodland; some of this is beautiful, tall cathedral mopane with lots of space between the trees and very little undergrowth. There are also areas of miombo woodland and grasslands – including the open Chipuka Plains that are criss-crossed by streams and lagoons, and regularly visited on game drives.

Although the ecosystem is virtually identical to that of the North and South Luangwa parks, Luambe is a small park in the middle of a large GMA, where controlled hunting is allowed. Thus game densities are lower, though they have recovered significantly under the auspices of the German NGO CCSC, and – as a bonus – the park is less crowded than its larger neighbours. On my last trip through here in June, I saw a sprinkling of small antelope – especially around the lodge and near the river: puku, impala, bushbuck, kudu, and waterbuck are common, and both the shy oribi and the endemic Cookson's wildebeest are occasionally seen. The elephant population is rising, and there are also reports of increased sightings of lion and other cats. With a bird count of around 400 species, it would be well worth investigating further.

GETTING THERE Although there is an airstrip (Waka Waka) just 30 minutes' drive from Luangwa Wilderness Lodge, many of the park's visitors are adventurous 4x4ers passing through, heading to or from the North Park.

If you are not driving, then you'll probably need to charter a six-seater **plane** (pilot plus five passengers) from Mfuwe, which would cost around US$500 for the one-way trip. Alternatively, **road transfers** are regularly done by Luangwa Wilderness Lodge as well as by other lodges in Mfuwe (*around US$650 for 2 people*).

Driving Do read *Lessons in bush travel*, pages 272–3, before you attempt to get to this remote corner by yourself! When you've taken heed of this, the directions are as follows.

From South Luangwa Approaching Luambe or North Luangwa from the South Park, you'll be travelling on the east side of the river. From Mfuwe, head north through the Nsefu Sector, and finally exit the park from Chikwinda gate (◈ SLNPCH 12°51.983'S, 32°1.008'E). It is then about three hours' drive to Luambe, and perhaps seven to the edge of North Luangwa.

On this road, especially near the start, there are a number of small tributaries of the Luangwa to cross. Between about mid-June and the end of October these will usually be fairly easy; outside of that they can be very tricky. About 26km after Chikwinda gate, one of the more notable of these is the Lukusuzi River (◈ RIVERR 12°41.647'S, 32°7.585'E). I know from experience that this is easier to cross going south–north than north–south, as the southern bank stopped me for about five hours on one muddy night in early June. Fortunately, virtually the whole of the nearby village soon appeared – many helped to push and manoeuvre, while some just came for the entertainment. I hope it was better than TV for the villagers, as their unstinting help certainly saved us from a wet and uncomfortable night in the river.

The turning east to the Lukusuzi National Park is (at least in theory) on the south bank of this river, although in practice very, very few people ever venture that way.

About 10km after the river you'll come to the Chakolwa gate (◈ CHAKOL 12°37.178'S, 32°7.413'E), the entry into Luambe National Park. The road through Luambe is primarily thick black-cotton soil so is often hard and bumpy when dry, and impassable when wet.

It's re-graded each year, but was particularly bad when I last travelled this way shortly after the rainy season; leaving second gear was a novelty.

Some 18km later (⊕ TULUA2 12°28.869'S, 32°9.486'E) you'll pass a left turning to Luangwa Wilderness Lodge (page 304), which is almost 3km away. Continuing north, a further 7km will bring you to Chipuka gate (⊕ CHIPUK 12°26.923'S, 32°12.516'E), which marks the northern edge of Luambe National Park.

From North Luangwa See pages 298–9 for the route from Luambe to North Luangwa, and back-track along that.

From Lundazi There's a 4x4 route from Lundazi to Luambe that is passable in the dry season only. It's a scenic drive of 140km or so, but not to be rushed, particularly when going down the escarpment.

From Mpika via the Corridor Road There is in theory a very difficult route into the Luangwa Valley which leaves the Great North Road south of Mpika, and involves the 'Corridor pontoon' across the Luangwa River, but it's a serious undertaking. Even in a good year it's viable only in the dry season – and unless the pontoon is operating, then only in September or October when the river is very low.

The 'Corridor' is the area between the North and South parks, usually used by professional trophy hunters (hunting on a sustainable basis). They have a few simple camps there, they make the roads, and they usually ensure that the pontoon across the Luangwa is working. But if there's no hunting in any given year, then many of the tracks through here will be impassable.

That said, in a normal year you can turn east from the Great North Road about 40km south of Mpika, at ⊕ TUBATE 12°6.421'S, 31°15.727'E – on the track that passes the old Bateleur Farm after 26km. The next landmark is Nthunta Scout Camp (⊕ NTHUNT 12°19.828'S, 31°31.979'E). About 46km from the main road you reach the Nthunta Escarpment, with its breathtaking view over the whole Luangwa Valley.

THE GOUGH MEMORIAL

High on the Nthunta Escarpment, near the Nthunta scout post, stands a small memorial to Mary Gough. Memories of the origins of this are hazy, but it's said that she was a woman who went (against all advice) to camp alone and unprotected for a long time on the Chifungwe Plain in the 1970s. Some remains of her body and clothing were found, from which it was deduced that she had been eaten by lions – and hence she was buried here.

I'm told that a few years later, during the height of Zimbabwe's war for independence, her son from Rhodesia (now Zimbabwe) came here to revisit the memorial. Local sources allege that he was a spy, who fed back information to the Rhodesian armed forces – resulting in the bombing of several bridges along the Great North Road. However, it seems he was never caught or charged with this – so the truth is uncertain.

Perhaps a reader could confirm or refute this rough history, so that I can expand on the facts and stories around this memorial in another edition!

The road is very rough as it descends down the escarpment, but after about 11km (it feels longer) you will reach the Mutinondo River. Cross this, and after 8km there's a turning to the left which takes you to Nabwalya village, in the middle of the Munyamadzi GMA. In the dry season, the hunters usually keep a pontoon across the Luangwa, just south of here (near Nyampala Hunting Camp), which links up with the track between Luambe and the South Park. Unless the river is very low, it's absolutely essential to check that this is operating before you even consider embarking upon this route – since otherwise you cannot get through.

If you were to carry straight on, instead of turning towards Nabwalya, you would be heading directly over the Mupamadzi River into the South Park. For those directions, see the section on getting to South Luangwa, *From Mpika via the Corridor Road and '05'*, on page 271.

🏠 WHERE TO STAY

🏠 **Luangwa Wilderness Lodge** (5 tents, family chalet, camping) 📞 +49 (0)221 971 2079; e reservations@luangwawilderness.com; www.luangwawilderness.com. ✪ LUAMBE 12°25.532'S, 32°16.383'E. Just 3km from the road that links North & South Luangwa, this neat, well-run lodge is an ideal stopover for those driving between the 2 parks. Whilst few overseas visitors will fly over the camps in the South Park to get here, there is a nearby airstrip, & the lodge is increasingly seen as a destination in its own right.

The lodge sits in the cool & dense shade of thick riverine vegetation overlooking a deep section of the Luangwa River where hippos congregate in their hundreds as the water levels drop. Compact but comfortable en-suite tents have good twin beds & a veranda facing the river. A 4-bed family chalet adds another option,

while adjacent is a similarly well-kept campsite with a braai area & good ablutions. The smart central area incorporates a dining table, bar, several comfy chairs & a selection of crafts for sale. Power is derived from solar panels, with battery-powered lights in the tents for night-time. Campers can arrange to eat at the lodge (*b/fast US$15, lunch US$20, dinner US$25–30*) & join game drives (*US$80 pp*).

CCSC staff work with the local community to raise the profile of wildlife conservation & ensure that villagers benefit directly from the presence of tourists, & thus from the presence of wildlife. Part of this programme is linked with schools in the village of Chitungulu, fundraising to improve their facilities, & driving the children into the park to see the wildlife for themselves. For the adults, a series of 'clubs' sets out to teach or foster practical or cultural skills. Tools are supplied to enable men

304

in the carpentry club to produce furniture for both the lodge & other villagers, while men in the craft club hone their skills in basket-weaving & carving to create curios for sale. Seeds donated to the garden club result in fresh vegetables for the lodge; a music club offers entertainment for guests; & a group of women provide meals for visiting tourists, & bake bread to raise money for orphans. Thus by staying at the lodge, every visitor effectively contributes to local conservation work. *US$370/440 pp sharing/sgl FBA, inc laundry, exc alcoholic drinks, park fees; US$190/255 pp sharing/sgl FB. Camping US$12 pp, inc hot shower & firewood, exc park fees.* ⊕ *Jun–Oct.*

LUKUSUZI NATIONAL PARK

This remote park is on the eastern side of the Luangwa Valley, slightly higher in altitude than the other parks in the valley. There are no facilities here at all – just a game scouts' camp near the gate, and an exceedingly poor track leading through the park. Equally, it is uncertain how much wildlife has survived the poaching, though it is thought that the dominant predator here is the spotted hyena, rather than the lion. The vegetation is mostly miombo woodland, dotted with grassland.

GETTING THERE Visiting the park requires a major expedition. There is a track that turns east from the South Luangwa–Luambe track, and then continues through Lukusuzi National Park until it reaches the Great East Road. This track east to the Lukusuzi National Park starts (at least in theory) on the south bank of the Lukusuzi River (⊕ RIVERR 12°41.647'S, 32°7.585'E). See *From South Luangwa*, page 302, for more directions, but don't expect this turning to be very clear or well marked.

This track is bound to be impassable during the rains. The easiest approach to the park would be to take the Great East Road to Chipata, then turn north towards Lundazi. About 110km beyond Chipata there is a track on the left to Lukusuzi. There is a game scouts' camp at the park's entrance, so stop and ask them for advice about the park before you go any further. I haven't driven on either of these routes myself.

LAKE BANGWEULU AREA

Mbala ↑

KASAMA

Chishimba Falls

Luwingu

Isoka

Chinsali

M1

Chambeshi

Chipoma Falls

level crossing

1483m

1528m

1830m

Nsombo

1724m

Shiwa Ng'andu

TUSHIW

T2

TUKAPI

Kapishya Hot Springs

Isangano National Park

TUNLNP

North Luangwa

1841m

Danger Hill

Lake Bangweulu

Mansa

Samfya

Chisonkolo Falls

TU2NLP

MPIKA

Bangweulu Wetlands

185m

Lwitikila

MPIKA

1850m

Chilonga

Munyamadzi Corridor

Luapula

Shoebill Island Camp

Nachikufu Caves

TUBATE

TUNACH

Muwele

Lavushi Manda Nat Pk

TULMGM

Nsobe

TUSBIL

Chiundaponde

LAVUSI

1566m

Mutinondo Wilderness Lodge

Livingstone Memorial

TUMUTI

MUTINO

TULIVI

Lake Waka Waka

TUKASA

Kasanka Nat Pk

1563m

TU2NSA

1559m

NSALUC

Nsalu Cave

TUINSA

1788m

T2

Lake Lusiwasi

TUCHIN

Kanona

KANONA

South Luangwa National Park

0 ____ 50km
0 ____ 30 miles

1528m

1703m

Kundalila Falls

KUNDCA

DEMOCRATIC REPUBLIC OF THE CONGO

SERENJE

SERENJ

Fort Elwes, Changwena Falls

MKUSHI

MKUSHI

T2   Forest Inn

Lusaka

Wonder Gorge

GPS co-ordinates ⊕

KANONA	13°04.204'S	30°38.056'E	TU2NSA	12°44.784'S	30°44.134'E
KUNDCA	13°09.276'S	30°42.104'E	TUBATE	12°06.421'S	31°15.727'E
LAVUSI	12°14.230'S	30°46.856'E	TUCHIN	13°01.146'S	30°27.695'E
MKUSHI	13°38.633'S	29°23.976'E	TUKAPI	11°10.624'S	31°17.454'E
MPIKA	11°50.511'S	31°26.620'E	TUKASA	12°33.250'S	30°23.478'E
MUTINO	12°27.267'S	31°17.496'E	TULIVI	12°29.255'S	30°20.364'E
NSALUC	12°43.202'S	30°40.952'E	TULMGM	12°16.934'S	31°08.037'E
SAMFYA	11°20.437'S	29°33.526'E	TUMUTI	12°22.794'S	31°05.896'E
SERENJ	13°16.159'S	30°14.767'E	TUNACH	12°14.474'S	31°09.041'E
TU1NSA	12°51.351'S	30°46.495'E	TUNLNP	11°26.378'S	31°44.307'E
TU2NLP	11°47.056'S	31°27.663'E	TUSBIL	12°13.451'S	30°35.330'E
			TUSHIW	11°13.334'S	31°49.580'E

Bangweulu Area

The spectacular Bangweulu Wetlands are, after the rains, a fascinating water-wilderness similar in size to Botswana's Okavango Delta. A huge wetland area with its own endemic species of antelope, the black lechwe, it is also a breeding place for one of Africa's strangest and rarest birds: the shoebill.

Nearby Kasanka National Park is a jewel of a reserve, proving beyond doubt that small can be beautiful, while the manor house and estate at Shiwa Ng'andu are a must for anyone seeking an insight into Zambia's colonial history. Meanwhile Mutinondo is a relatively new area, ripe for modern adventurers to explore. Hardcore safari enthusiasts may also want to venture into the stunning and remote North Luangwa National Park (see *Chapter 10*, pages 294–301), which can be accessed by road from these areas. Apart from these main attractions there are numerous fascinating stops – from waterfalls to caves and old colonial monuments – in the area where David Livingstone, literally, left his heart.

If you want to explore Zambia beyond the obvious trio of great game parks (Luangwa, Lower Zambezi and Kafue) then this is perhaps the first area that you should visit. The region is perfect for adventurous self-driving visitors with fully equipped 4x4s, but most of the main highlights here can also be visited on fly-in trips using light aircraft for transport.

THE GREAT NORTH ROAD

Access to much of the region is via the Great North Road out of Lusaka. For the most part this is a good tar road, almost pot-hole-free as far as Serenje, though beyond here watch out for some significant lapses in maintenance.

From the turn-off at Kapiri Mposhi, the road passes Mkushi and Serenje, then on to Mpika further north. None of these towns is a really attractive destination for most visitors, but all can be useful bases for the area's real draws: Kasanka, Bangweulu, Mutinondo and Shiwa Ng'andu.

MKUSHI Some 92km from Kapiri Mposhi, Mkushi (⊕ MKUSHI 13°38.633'S, 29°23.976'E) is 1km north of the Great North Road, across the railway. Far from being just another stop on the TAZARA line, it's a thriving little town, the centre of a prosperous farming area, with a number of large commercial farms in the vicinity keeping cattle and cultivating cash crops. There is a **fuel** station on the main road, and another in town, where there are also plenty of **shops**, a **post office**, three **banks** (and ATMs) and a police post.

Getting there In addition to the TAZARA **trains**, which stop here, several **buses** heading north stop in Mkushi, including the postbus between Lusaka and Kasama.

Where to stay and eat Alongside places in Mkushi itself are a couple of more interesting options within easy reach, while 62km to the west, Forest Inn is particularly geared to the needs of passing travellers.

Loza Guesthouse (10 rooms) 0215 352170; m 0965 353170; e loza@zamtel.zm. ⊕ 13 43.515'S, 29 13.455'E. Some 26km southwest of Mkushi, or 78km from Kapiri Mposhi, is a signpost along a 10km gravel track to this attractive converted farmhouse with a slightly Italianate feel. The most upmarket place in the area, it serves unexpectedly good food, with farm-fresh vegetables, & has a lovely pool – which is open to non-residents. The rooms are simply but personally decorated, each with a dbl or twin beds draped with mosquito netting; most have en-suite bath or shower, & 2 are family rooms. There's also WiFi access. Loza is set on a working farm, which guests are welcome to explore. **$$** *exc b/fast.*

Blu Bubbles Lodge (10 rondavels) Great North Rd; 0215 312236/5; m 0977 412845/977; e blububbles@yahoo.com. Just why a place with bright pink rondavels should be dubbed 'Blu Bubbles' is a mystery. They're clearly visible, though, ranged along a low grassy hill close to the turn-off to Mkushi, & interspersed with animal sculptures. All are en suite, & there's a restaurant/bar serving local dishes. **$$**

ATB Lodge (17 rooms) 0215 325410; m 0955 030051/43. This old house in well-maintained grounds has been in the family since 1973. It's popular with Peace Corps volunteers, who appreciate Agnes's cooking – & the DSTV! – as well as the dark, comfortable lounge with big fireplace. En-suite rooms with mosi nets are clean & pleasant. To find it, head 5km northeast of Mkushi, then follow the signs for a further 5km. **$–$$** *Camping Kw20,000 pp.*

Motel Mariana (8 rooms, 10 chalets) m 0965 760022. On the left as you enter Mkushi, the neat thatched chalets in well-tended lawns have the air of a model village. Twin rooms have TVs & en-suite showers; dbl-bedded chalets also have fridges. There's a simple bar & separate restaurant, where fish, steak or chicken ($) are served every evening. **$** *exc b/fast.*

Forest Inn (11 chalets, camping) Great North Rd; 0215 353003; e forestinn@ iwayafrica.com; www.forestinn-zambia.com. About 62km from Kapiri Mposhi, or 30km west of Mkushi, Forest Inn is to the south of the main road, & is clearly signposted. The 4hr drive from Lusaka makes it a convenient place to stop for lunch or overnight for those heading towards Kasanka, Mutinondo or Shiwa N'gandu.

The inn's thatch-on-brick en-suite chalets, with rustic wooden furniture & electric lights, have recently been refurbished. They are secure, clean & functional rather than opulent, but set in large grounds, with cultivated plants & trees, cut grass, & even an old steam engine. In one area, the campsite has its own well-lit shelter with BBQ facilities, & a good ablution block. The gate is kept closed, but there's a gatekeeper & guard on 24hr duty.

Fresh farm produce is available in the restaurant, which is a good place to stop for b/fast or lunch ($$$). Entertainment in the form of a pool table & darts is in the bar, while the lounge area comes complete with a TV & a real fire for winter evenings. Signposted trails lead along short woodland walks, & birding highlights include Boehm's flycatcher & chestnut mantled sparrow weaver. **$$** *Camping Kw30,000 pp.*

Excursions from Mkushi There are two interesting sites to the north of Mkushi, and one to the south, though you'll need a self-sufficient 4x4 to reach any of them. If heading north, note the proximity of the sites to the border with the DRC (ex Zaire), and check the security situation locally before you go. Make sure that you don't inadvertently drive too far, which would be surprisingly easy to do. Explaining an illegal entry into the DRC might not be fun.

Finally, if you are staying here, you're also within reach of Nsalu Cave and the Kundalila Falls, both covered under *Around Kasanka and Bangweulu* on pages 332–3.

Changwena Falls This is a very pretty waterfall, near to Fort Elwes and Mount Mumpu. It's about two hours north of Mkushi, accessible along a bush track through a forest reserve. These tracks are highly seasonal, so do ask for local directions from Mkushi before you set off. Camping is allowed.

The falls themselves are where a small stream leaves its dambo and cascades through a series of three rock pools. The rocks around are a very attractive copper colour, helping to make this remote spot particularly beautiful. From here you can climb Mumpu and visit Fort Elwes (see below).

Fort Elwes Almost on the border with the DRC, Fort Elwes lies about 40km northeast of Mkushi at an altitude of 1,600m. The tracks to get there are in poor condition and it's not easy to find; ask local directions before you embark upon this trip.

The fort was built around 1896–97 by Europeans who came to seek gold in the area west of the Luangwa Valley. They feared reprisals from the local Ngoni people, if (as planned) the British attacked them near Chipata and the Ngoni were forced west.

It's an impressive place, with superb views of the hills in the surrounding area. Four huge drystone walls, some 2m thick and 3m high, form a rectangular building, which originally had a single entrance under one of them. Today it's disintegrating, but a few remnants of the original wooden structures still survive. The *National Monuments of Zambia* booklet (see *Appendix 3*, page 537) attributes the building to Frank Smitheman.

Lunsemfwa Wonder Gorge This spectacular 300m-deep gorge marks the point where the Mkushi River meets the Lunsemfwa, and both cut into the sedimentary rocks of the Muchinga Escarpment. It is in an extremely remote area, east of Kabwe and about 130km south of Mkushi, further south than what is known as Old Mkushi. Although the road is signposted near the ATB Lodge just northeast of Mkushi, the gorge is more easily accessed from Kabwe; see *Chapter 13*, page 394, for details.

SERENJE Set in a valley in undulating countryside about 3km north of the main Great North Road, Serenje is 110km northeast of the turn-off to Mkushi. An increasing level of agricultural activity in the vicinity is likely to benefit the town, which currently has a Total **fuel** station, a branch of the Finance **Bank**, a Catholic mission, a teacher training college, a **post office**, a police station and a small hospital.

Getting there If you're **driving** yourself, turn off the main road at the BP fuel station (⊕ SERENJ 13°16.159'S, 30°14.767'E). The noisy and busy **bus** station sees several buses a day between Lusaka (*from Kw110,000 one way*) and Kashikishi on Lake Mweru. The Lusaka–Kasama **postbus** also stops at the post office three times a week in both directions. Serenje is also a stop on the **TAZARA** line.

🏠 **Where to stay and eat** Of Serenje's selection of guesthouses, one – the Mapontela – has long shone out above the others; it's also the best restaurant in town. Now, though, there's competition, both from **Villa Mbanandi** (m *0977 836625*) further down the road, and from the Salala, as well as from **MU's** restaurant next door.

🏠 **Salala Executive Lodge** (10 rooms) Ng'answa Rd; m 0964 571190. Close to the junction with the Great North Rd, Salala opened in May 2011 & was still polished & shining when we visited. At the back, rather grand rooms sport DSTV, a fridge, & bath or shower en suite. In the evening, sit down in the pleasant dining room to a plate of meat or chicken with potatoes, pasta, rice or nshima. **$$**

🏠 **Mapontela Village Inn** (8 rooms) m 0977 227522, 0979 587262. Serenje's established favourite is on the right as you enter the town, beyond the police station. It's a small warren of a place, run by a charming Zambian matriarch, Anna Mulenga, & her husband Steve Luker, a retired builder who came to Zambia with the Peace Corps. With its smart green-painted exterior, umbrella-shaded restaurant veranda & spotlessly clean rooms it's a good spot to overnight or for lunch; the menu ranges from sandwiches to omelette & chips to nshima & steak ($–$$). Most of the rooms, each with dbl (or 3) beds, bath or shower, TV, fan & mosquito net, are brick built & lead off a courtyard; the older 2 are slightly smaller (& cheaper) with no fan. **$–$$** *exc b/fast.*

Excursions from Serenje

There are various waterfalls in the area, including the narrow but pretty cascades of **Mulembo Falls** (⊕ MULEMB 13°13.067'S, 30°25.809'E). This is reached by turning off the main road 12km northeast of the Serenje turn-off, towards Kalwa Farm (where the Baptist mission has a guesthouse and campsite). From there drive 4km, then turn left just before the guesthouse, and immediately right. Just over 5km brings you to a rounded, domed rock, and a further 6.2km to the falls themselves. The right track leads to the falls, whilst straight on will take you to the river.

MPIKA

Though no bigger than Mkushi or Serenje, Mpika (⊕ MPIKA 11°50.511'S, 31°26.620'E) is a busy crossroads of a place which has an increasing air of affluence. Here the Great North Road forks: one branch goes to Kasama, Mbala, and Mpulungu on Lake Tanganyika; the other heads directly for the Tanzanian border at Nakonde. It is about a day's travel from Lusaka, Mpulungu or the Tanzanian border, which perhaps explains why one often ends up stopping here overnight.

Getting there

Getting to Mpika is easy, with a choice of public transport if you are not driving.

By bus Daily local bus services link Mpika with Lusaka, Mbala and (to a lesser extent) northeast to Isoka and Nakonde. Buses run by Germins stop next to the BP garage on the main road through town; others, including Juldan Motors, operate from the opposite side of the road. Sometimes, the same buses will pick you up if you wave them down on the side of the road, but not always. The town is also serviced by the thrice-weekly postbus between Lusaka and Kasama: the only bus that doesn't arrive and depart after dark.

Buses to Nakonde leave daily around midnight, with tickets costing Kw80,000–90,000. To Lusaka they depart at around 18.00, 20.00 and midnight, costing Kw110,000–140,000.

By train Mpika is one of the stops between Kapiri Mposhi and Dar es Salaam, in Tanzania, on the TAZARA railway. Tickets on the express train between Mpika and Kapiri Mposhi cost Kw66,000 in first class, Kw46,200 in second and Kw33,700 in third.

The TAZARA station is about 5–6km out of town, a turning off the road towards Kapiri Mposhi that's marked by a new fuel station. Private pick-up trucks operate shuttle runs between there and the central boma in Mpika, fitting as many people onto the vehicles as they can carry. The train rarely arrives on time so be prepared. If you arrive in the early hours of the morning then your options are to get one of these shuttles quickly, or to sleep rough on the station until daybreak and then try to get one. At times like this, the station is crowded but fairly clean and safe.

Mazingo Motel,
Malashi Executive GH,
Shiwa Ng'andu,
Isoka, Nakonde

Shops

GM Trading

Market

PEP

Zanaco

Zambeef

CIMS

Bakery

Police

Bakery

MUSAKANYA KOMBE DRIVE

Melodies
Lodge

KILIMANJARO STREET

Hospital

Finance

Caltex

BP

Bus station

Butcher

ZAWA
office

Post office

Fresh Air Lodge,
St Joseph's Cathedral,
Kasama

Council
offices

Government
Resthouse

0   500m
0   500yds

Tazara station, Zanaco, Tusha Safari Lodge,
Chintu Mukulu Campsite, Kapiri Mposhi

MPIKA

Hitchhiking With clear roads and a reasonable amount of traffic, hitching is a very practical form of transport to and from Mpika. There is probably more traffic going towards Mbala than towards Nakonde, but if you're heading to Lusaka you can hitch around the BP station where both roads join.

If you're going towards Kasama and Mbala, then hitch on the turn-off by the BP station. Alternatively, and especially if it is late in the day, walk a further 2–3km down that tarred turn-off road, until you reach a smart, fenced compound on your right. This is known as the DDSP compound – it houses offices for various aid and semi-governmental groups, and small businesses. You may pick up a lift from one of its workers, who travel widely in the district. You'll certainly see them come and go in a variety of plush 4x4s, and if the worst happens and no lift appears then you can wander across the road and sleep at their simple resthouse.

Where to stay and eat

⌂ **Fresh Air Lodge** (12 rooms) Kasama Rd;
\0214 370095; m 0964 513500, 0967 120100;
e freshairlodge@yahoo.com; www.facebook.com/
freshairlodge. Hidden on the right behind peach-
pink walls topped with razor wire, about 400m
from the main road, Fresh Air Lodge is unmissable.
Its colourful en-suite rooms are enhanced by dbl
beds draped in satin quilts adorned with appliquéd
hearts. You'll always get mosi nets & a fan, while
more exclusive are fridges & DSTV. There's secure
parking at the back. **$**

⌂ **Mazingo Motel** (34 rooms, camping) Great
North Rd; m 0966 803919/804010. ✪ 11°48.570'S,
31°27.091'E. West of the road, almost 3km
northeast of Mpika on the way to Isoka, the
apricot-&-blue chalets of this secure motel lie in
pleasant gardens within a quiet compound. Rooms
with solid wood furniture come in 4 types, all with
en-suite bath or shower, kettle & TV. Campers can
pitch in the parking area, & use the bathroom in
1 of the rooms. Lunch & dinner are from an à-la-
carte menu, & there's WiFi access. **$** *exc b/fast.*

11

311

Melodies Lodge (10 rooms) Great North Rd; m 0977 214223. On the main road through town, Melodies offers simple, clean rooms (5 en suite) – with bright red walls – & secure parking. There's a restaurant ($) & bar, so it could be noisy at w/ends. **$**

Tusha Safari Lodge (4 rooms) Great North Rd; m 0969 291088, 0977 694535. Southwest of Mpika, about 1km north of the turn-off to the TAZARA station, this 2-storey thatched building in extensive grounds looks attractive but promises more than it delivers. En-suite rooms – some dbl, & some for 4 – are adequate, but no more; the traffic is noisy – & 'safari lodge' is a misnomer. **$** *exc b/fast.*

Å Chintu Mukulu Community Campsite (4 chalets, camping) Great North Rd; m 0978 064516; or contact Mutinondo (page 315). ⊕ CHINTU 12°27 42.3'S, 31°04 14.8'E. This community-run site lies close to the road about 83km south of Mpika. It has both simple chalets with bedding, & conventional tent pitches, sharing ablutions. Walks & village visits are on offer, plus farming demonstrations (Nov–Jul), & there's a guide with a limited knowledge of birding. *Chalet Kw70,000 pp; camping Kw35,000 pp.*

✕ CIMS Restaurant Great North Rd. This clean, modern place opposite Melodies Lodge feels more US diner than Zambian restaurant, but the meals combine 'the best chicken & chips in Mpika' traditional with more adventurous offerings such as *ifishimu* – caterpillar. There's a selection of bread, cakes, pies & dairy produce too, making it a good place to put together a packed lunch. $

Other practicalities There are three **fuel** stations right next to each other on the Great North Road, close to the turn-off to Kasama. The most conspicuous of these, BP, has a Barclays **ATM** – and there's another ATM at Zanaco near the turning into the town; there's also a branch of the Finance Bank in town. For **supplies**, GM Trading is worth a glance. A slightly more expensive but very useful supermarket has also opened up on the Great North Road. There's also a busy little market, a couple of bakeries and a good butcher called Zambeef where the meat comes from the Shiwa N'gandu estate.

For **communications**, in addition to a post office, there's an internet café (*Kw2,000/min*) on the main road, close to the junction. Should you be in need of vehicle **repairs**, ask at the turn-off to St Joseph's Catholic Cathedral, 1.5km down the Kasama road.

Excursions from Mpika There are a few interesting caves and waterfalls around Mpika, whilst both Mutinondo and Shiwa Ng'andu (see opposite and pages 316–23) are worthy of large sections of this chapter on their own. To go anywhere away from the main roads you'll really need a self-contained 4x4, even in the dry season.

Nachikufu Caves (⊕ NACAVE 12°13.939'S, 31°08.693'E; *entry US$10/5 adult/child; vehicle US$4; camping US$15 pp inc entry*) The striking setting of this cave complex with their geometric San/Bushman rock paintings may be worth a brief detour, though now that the admission fees have increased, that's debatable unless you're planning to camp.

When excavated in the 1940s Nachikufu Cave was estimated to have been occupied intermittently for about the last 15,000 years. This is no surprise when you consider that all the essentials for survival are here: a regular supply of water from a nearby stream, shelter provided by the cave, firewood in abundance, grass for bedding and a good supply of game and vegetable food sources from the local environment. The cave is also the 'type' site of the Zambian Late Stone Age, which is known to archaeologists as the 'Nachikufan Industry' (25,000–2,000 years ago). A small display of artefacts is kept within the cave entrance and access is only with the official guide who is stationed on site.

Both the rock shelter and the cave look north over a wide plateau, and are formed from a ridge of quartzite rock – perfect for stone tools. There's also a perennial stream about 500m away from the cave. The paintings themselves are fairly simple:

various figures silhouetted in black, including a couple of elephants, a beautifully drawn antelope, and human figures, some of whom are depicted with bows and arrows and one with a spear. It has to be said, however, that they are not brilliant.

The signposted turning (⊕ TUNACH 12°14.474'S, 31°9.041'E) to Nachikufu is about 55km southwest of Mpika. This turning leads you north and west from the main road, over the TAZARA railway, and reaches the cave within about 2km.

Chipoma Falls (*Entry US$10/5 adult/child; vehicle US$4; camping US$15 pp inc entry*) About 20km south of Chinsali, the Lubu River drops 40m over a distance of 500m at this large set of rapids and cascades (⊕ CHIPOM 10°44.998'S, 32°00.284'E). It's a lovely spot for exploring, and there are basic camping facilities here.

To reach the falls from Mpika, head north for Chinsali and Isoka and then turn left about 24km before you reach the turn-off for Chinsali (that's about 57km past the turning to Shiwa Ng'andu). Follow this road for around 6km, taking left turns at all the forks and junctions encountered, until you reach the caretaker's house by the falls. There's an entrance fee of a few dollars.

Chisonkolo Falls (*www.diompika.org; ⊕ 08.00–22.00 daily; entry Kw5,000 pp*) Also known as the Lwitikila Falls, this is a good place for a dip and lunch, or simply to wander. The falls are pretty rather than spectacular, with scope for walking in the surrounding woodland and up to see the views. It lies in a community area, with local people responsible for the site who also sell drinks and snacks. There are even plans for a restaurant, botanic garden and simple accommodation. At present, though, it's quiet except in August when there are various youth camps here. All money raised goes to the school, and visits might be possible on request.

To get to the falls from Mpika, take the road to Chinsali and Isoka for about 20km, until you see a right turn signed to Lwitikila Girls' Secondary School (⊕ TOLWIT 11°43.600'S, 31°28.572'E). Follow this track, which bends round slowly to the left and then goes uphill, until you see some houses on the right. In front of the first house, before the school, a smaller track to the right leads directly to the falls (⊕ LWITIK 11°43.810'S, 31°29.674'E).

Danger Hill A little further north on the Lwitikila River is this tall rock and the falls beneath. There are some lovely views from the top, where in 2011 it looked as though a viewpoint was being built.

AROUND MPIKA

MUTINONDO WILDERNESS AREA Mutinondo Wilderness is a private 100km² reserve, run by Mike and Lari Merrett. It encompasses a pristine area of verdant miombo woodland near the edge of the Luangwa Escarpment, complete with huge granite whalebacks, crystal-clear rivers, stunning waterfalls, pristine woodlands and some small wetland areas. There are great plants and birds, which all make for a lovely ambience.

It's a lovely bit of Africa to explore on foot or on horseback, as well as being terrific value; ideally you should spend at least three nights here. While Mutinondo is quite off the beaten track (if there is a beaten track in this part of Zambia?!), it does have its own airstrip.

History Although this area has been occupied for centuries, as witnessed by the Iron-Age workings about 6km from the lodge, Mutinondo was first really put on the visitors' map in 1994, when Mike and Lari started looking for a place suitable for both conservation and tourism. By 1999 they had finally sorted out all the legalities with the local authorities and chief, and had a direct access road to their lodge site. Throughout the process, they seem to have made every effort to develop the area sensitively, with minimum impact and maximum use of renewable natural resources, such as solar and wind power.

Flora and fauna Some of this area's smaller flora and fauna has been meticulously catalogued – including over 300 different plants and trees, dozens of butterflies and a good range of the varied birdlife.

Flora The main vegetation here is classic miombo woodland, which is in pristine condition with plenty of *Brachystegia* and *Julbernadia* species. This is interspersed with numerous lush, herby dambos, many of which drain into permanent rivers and streams on the reserve. This water, together with the shade of the established woodland, makes the atmosphere relatively moist – which helps to promote such lush plant growth. Beside the rivers, you'll also find thin strips of riverine forest, and occasional patches of moist evergreen forest (*mushitu*). Judging by the thick lichens on the rocks and 'old man's beard' (*Usnea*) hanging from the trees, the air is very clean, and looking into the night sky you'll be hard pressed to spot any light pollution at all.

There is an impressive array of flowering plants, especially during and at the end of the rains. Among these are several species of proteas and a great range of orchids; many of the latter have been carefully relocated around the chalets after they were rescued from the trees felled to build the lodge's access road. During one visit I found a huge cycad in the woodland. At the end of winter, in mid-September, it's a magical place to witness the 'miombo flush', when the fresh new leaves bring a hint of red to the trees. If you're visiting during the rains, keep a look out for specimens of *Termitomyces titanicus*, which is the world's largest edible mushroom. The largest that Mike and Lari have found so far had a diameter of about 85cm but they grow up to a metre in diameter. The local people have known about these for centuries; but it seems that they were first described to science as late as 1980.

Fauna Mutinondo is a good spot for birding and is one of Zambia's 'important bird areas', according to Birdlife International. The bird list available to visitors currently stands at 325 species, and is constantly growing. Obvious 'specials' include Anchieta's barbets, long-toed flufftails, bar-winged weavers, half-collared kingfishers and Ross's turaco.

While Mutinondo is not primarily a game destination, if you spend enough time here you might find a variety of mammals, from duikers and klipspringer to sitatunga – though sightings are infrequent. As the area remains protected, it's likely that larger antelope species like roan and sable, which are already in the area, will become more numerous with time. Of much more interest really are the plants, flowers, trees, mushrooms and smaller wildlife, which also help to make walking here a real pleasure.

Getting there The Mutinondo turn-off on the Great North Road (⊕ TUMUTI 12°22.794'S, 31°5.896'E) is a few hundred metres south of Kalonje railway station on the TAZARA railway. It's about 12km southwest of the turning to Lavushi Manda, and 77km southwest of Mpika, or 364km northeast of Kapiri Mposhi. From the signboard to the lodge is a further 25km along a level track, which is accessible by 2WD year-round.

Mutinondo's airstrip is just over 1km from the lodge (✈ MUTAIR 12°26.998'S, 31°16.954'E), useful for those on a fly-in trip. Its 900m runway is suitable only for single-engine aircraft. Alternatively, with advance notice, it is possible to arrive at Kalonje by train, and arrange for the team at the lodge to collect you.

Where to stay and eat For individual visitors there are three options: the lodge, the nearby campsite and the new self-catering camp, Kankonde. All are open year round, and share the same contact details. Activities available are detailed below. Note that special arrangements can be made for scientific, educational and school groups, which are warmly welcomed.

Mutinondo Wilderness Lodge (4 chalets) m 0978 198198, 0979 862545; e 2mwl@ bushmail.net; www.mutinondozambia.com. ✈ MUTINO 12°27.267'S, 31°17.496'E. The lodge is a lovely spot to stay – though quite idiosyncratic in its way, with both the chalets & the bar & dining areas carefully built around the rocks, each some distance from the other. Every effort has been made to source the building materials locally, & to use local skills & labour in the lodge's construction. The bricks, stone & thatch used were all manufactured, quarried or harvested locally, & all the woodwork, including the furniture, was constructed by a father-&-son carpentry team from the village of Salamo. As you'd expect, most of the staff are from the surrounding villages.

Each of the chalets is large & individually designed: solid, but not luxurious. One has a particularly spectacular balcony, while all have great views over the wilderness. The 'spacious' chalets are effectively suites, ideal for famililes with 2 'rooms' divided by a half wall, 3 beds & glass doors at the front. The 'standard' ones are smaller,–although still very roomy, & are totally open at the front. In each you'll find a wardrobe & some have a fireplace, for when it gets cold. (Given the altitude of about 1,400m, it can get very cold!) 3 of the chalets have an en-suite shower & separate toilet, while the last, arguably the most spectacular, has a separate bathroom with a home-built bath as well as a shower & a 'loo with a view'. Water is heated by individual solar heaters & wood-burning boilers.

Standard Kw450,000/500,000 sgl/dbl; spacious Kw500,000/550,000 sgl/dbl, all FBA; extra bed Kw380,000 pp.

Mutinondo Wilderness Camping (4 pitches). This is a lovely campsite, with raven-proof storage cupboards, good hot showers & clean long-drop toilets. As there are a limited number of pitches you should consider booking in advance if possible. The campsite is adjacent to the lodge; campers are welcome in the bar &, with advance notice, to dine here (*evening meal Kw100,000*). Firewood is available at no extra charge. *Kw60,000 (own tent), Kw340,000 sgl or dbl tent, inc bedding & meals.*

Kankonde Camp (1 chalet, camping) ✈ KANKON 12°24'S, 31°19'E. Some 11km from the main lodge & camp, on a bank of the Mutinondo River, Kankonde offers the independent traveller a further degree of freedom. Its open-air grass chalet has 2 twin beds, & there's ample room for pitching tents. These share a long-drop loo with a view & a bucket shower (with staff to carry hot water). A thatched *nsaka* rounds off the amenities. Firewood is supplied, & water for bathing & drinking is sourced from the Mutinondo & is safe to drink or can be boiled if preferred. Otherwise you'll need to bring your own, along with all bedding, food, crockery, cutlery, etc, though a few basic ingredients are sold in the shop at the lodge. Visitors usually check in at the lodge first to collect a map & other information before heading for Kankonde. *Chalet Kw90,000 pp; camping Kw70,000 pp.*

What to see and do Although Mike and Lari love to guide visitors around when they can, Mutinondo best suits those who feel comfortable exploring. It's a magical place for 'old Africa hands' who want to go off for hours on their own.

It's less ideal for those who are new to the bush, although those with some degree of independence can hire one of the lodge's team to guide them around (*Kw80,000/ day*), and still have a great time. It's not the perfect place if you need your hand held all of the time, or if you're reluctant to abandon your vehicle, as there are relatively few motorable tracks (although there is one dry-season track which extends 25km to the escarpment). For lodge guests, activities are included in the rates; campers and those staying at Kankonde pay extra, as below.

Walking There's a good network of trails, and the country is hilly without being particularly strenuous. The huge granite whalebacks are great for scrambling up, giving you access to superb views of the surrounding country and, in the east, to the Luangwa Escarpment and beyond. It would be very easy to spend three or four days exploring the tracks and whalebacks alone. Trail maps are available at the lodge; I'd also suggest that you take a GPS.

Dedicated and totally self-contained hikers who want something more challenging can arrange longer hikes here, including bush-camping stops. These might encompass the adjacent community-based conservation area, some of the magnificent escarpment waterfalls, or possibly even a long walk down into the Luangwa Valley.

On the water There's a network of very clear rivers and waterfalls, with no crocodiles, hippos or bilharzia. (Though *always* double-check the safety of such a comment locally before you swim, rather than trust any guidebook, even this one!) These have been re-stocked with indigenous fish: red-breasted, three-spot and green-headed bream – so fishing is possible, albeit on a strict catch-and-release policy.

There are two canoes stationed above one of the waterfalls, beside an idyllic section of quiet, tree-lined river. The more adventurous might take advantage of the inflatable tubes, also available, to just float down river. For campers, canoe hire is Kw50,000 per half day.

On horseback Mutinondo has a stable with a number of horses, suitable for all levels of expertise; even complete beginners can arrange to be led by a guide. The horses are surefooted animals, ridden without shoes, and free to roam during the day. It's a very pleasant area for a short walk or a longer hack, with plenty of options. Hard hats are available, adjustable to fit. If you're camping or self catering, riding costs Kw70,000 per hour.

SHIWA NG'ANDU
Background
The early days Shiwa Ng'andu was the inspiration of Stewart Gore-Browne. Born in England in 1883, Gore-Browne first came to Africa in 1902, at the tail end of the Boer War, and later returned in 1911 as a member of the Anglo-Belgian Congo Boundary Commission. On his way back to England, in 1914, one of his carriers guided him north towards Tanzania, passing beside Shiwa Ng'andu, the 'Lake of the Royal Crocodiles'. He intended to settle in Northern Rhodesia, so he negotiated with the local chief to buy the land around the lake – and then, after World War I, he returned to establish himself there. He borrowed money from his beloved Aunt Ethel, and began to build Shiwa.

Gore-Browne was uncomfortable with the colonial attitude towards the African people. He was determined to establish a utopian state, and in his hands Shiwa grew into a vast enterprise with schools and a hospital run with benevolent paternalism. By 1925, Shiwa Ng'andu was employing 1,800 local people.

Gore-Browne passed on skills to them, and together they built neat workers' cottages with tile roofs, as well as bridges and workshops and finally a magnificent manor house, set atop a hill overlooking the lake. Anything that could not be made locally was transported on the heads and backs of porters, along the arduous route from the nearest town, Ndola. At that time it took three weeks to reach Shiwa from Ndola: 70 miles on foot or horseback to the Luapula River, followed by a boat through the Bangweulu Wetlands, and a further ten-day walk from the Chambeshi River to Shiwa.

The heavy English-style furniture was made out of local wood; the large gilt-framed portraits and paintings, silver ornaments, and an entire library of books came from England. Everything came together to create an English country mansion in the heart of Africa – a testament to the determination with which Gore-Browne pursued his vision.

In 1927, when he was 44, Gore-Browne met and married Lorna Goldman, the 'ravishing' 18-year-old daughter of his first love, Lorna Bosworth-Smith. She came to Shiwa, threw herself into her husband's projects, and the estate and its inhabitants prospered. Gore-Browne built a distillery for the essential oils that he hoped to make into a profitable local industry. (Given Shiwa's remote location, the estate's produce had to be easily transportable: a non-perishable, valuable commodity of low bulk.) He had several failures, trying roses, geraniums, eucalyptus, peppermint and lemon grass with no success. Eventually, he succeeded with citrus fruit, which flourished and brought a good income into the estate … until a *tristezia* virus killed off the fruit trees. This hit the estate hard, forcing Gore-Browne to turn to more conventional, less profitable, agriculture.

Regrettably, the stresses of the estate and Gore-Browne's constant travelling took a toll on his marriage; it resulted in his separation from Lorna, who had found it difficult spending such a great deal of time alone at Shiwa with their two daughters, Lorna and Angela. Lady Lorna returned to live in London in 1945. She came back to Shiwa once, in 1958, and then never again. Even in England she would rarely speak of Shiwa; in December 2001 she died, aged 93.

In the meantime, Gore-Browne had become a rare political figure in Northern Rhodesia: an aristocratic Englishman, with excellent connections in London, who commanded respect both in the colonial administration and from the African people. He had been elected to Northern Rhodesia's Legislative Council as early as 1935, and was the first member of it to argue that real concessions were needed to African demands for more autonomy. He was impatient with the rule of the Colonial Office, and resented the loss of huge amounts of revenue through taxation paid to Britain, and 'royalties' paid to the British South Africa Company.

He was knighted by George VI and became mentor to Zambia's first president, Kenneth Kaunda, who, in 1966, appointed him the first ever Grand Officer of the Companion of the Order of Freedom, the highest honour ever bestowed on a white man in Zambia. He died, an octogenarian, in 1967, and today I believe that he remains the only white man in Africa to have been given a full state funeral. He is buried on a hill overlooking the lake at Shiwa – an honour only bestowed on the Bemba chiefs. In the words of Kaunda, 'He was born an Englishman and died a Zambian. Perhaps if Africa had more like him, the transition from colonial rule to independence would have been less traumatic.'

A highly readable and very successful historical account of the life and times of Stewart Gore-Browne and Shiwa Ng'andu, *The Africa House*, was first published in 1999 (see *Appendix 3*, page 535), although note that reservations have been expressed by the family about the historical accuracy of the book.

After Sir Stewart On Sir Stewart's death, the estate at Shiwa passed to his daughter Lorna and her husband, John Harvey, who lived in the house with their four children, Penny, Charlie, Mark and David. However, with the very poor agricultural soils, both the farm estate and the manor house proved difficult to run and maintain. In 1967 the Harveys bought a dairy farm near Lusaka, where both John and Lorna were murdered in 1992. On their deaths, the estate passed to three of Gore-Browne's grandchildren. Initially David took over its management, and by 1995 there were moves to turn the manor house into a museum. Finally, in 2000, Charlie Harvey bought the estate from his siblings and now runs it with his wife, Jo, and their two children, Tom and Emma.

Shiwa reinvented Until 2000, Shiwa typified an old English-style country estate that was gradually slipping back into the African bush. In 2001, Charlie and Jo sold their property and literally 'picked up' their entire farming business just north of Lusaka and translocated it 750km north to Shiwa. Together they brought endless farm equipment, 800 cattle, 600 sheep, 500 assorted wild game animals, eight horses, five cats and five dogs. It was a massive undertaking: for the cattle it was a three-day train ride, followed by a ten-day trek through the bush. With them came two large buses carrying the families – women and children – of the 34 men who had elected to follow the Harveys north.

Soon the house became a hum of activity, with builders and renovators raising much dust and gradually restoring Shiwa's past glory. When I visited Shiwa in 2003, some eight years after I'd first been there, the transformation was startling and impressive. The stranglehold of a slow, tropical decay had been arrested by sheer determination – and the whole feeling of the place had changed. Now it's a thriving family estate, combining a strong sense of history with a vibrant present and a solid future.

Before 2001, Shiwa's only real story – and the only reason to visit – was its history: Gore-Browne and the estate's past glories. Shiwa had been reduced to a curious anachronism in the African bush. By contrast, Shiwa's history is now just that: history. A visit here today will look at the past, but also explore the present: Shiwa's people, its animals and its environment – and how these are developing and changing. At one point during a stay here I saw a young carpenter making one of the internal windows over the courtyard. He was doing a good job, clearly deep in concentration. I asked him if he had also made some of the freshly painted windows on the outside of the house. 'No,' he replied, without pausing, 'my grandfather made those.'

So by all means come to Shiwa to wonder at its past, and the story of Sir Stewart; but expect to leave enthralled by the present – and intrigued by the apparently seamless continuity between the two.

Shiwa today
The manor house As you approach from the main road, the rectangular cottages built for farm workers come into view first, their whitewashed walls and tiled roofs saying more of England than of Africa. Then a red-brick gatehouse appears, its design of Italian influence. An old clock tower rises above its tiled roof, and through its main arch is a long straight avenue, bordered by eucalyptus, leading to the stately manor house.

Climbing up, the avenue leads through typically English gardens – designed on several levels with bougainvillea, frangipani, jacaranda and neatly arranged cypresses. These gardens have been restored with beautiful flowers and well-maintained lawns, though their maintenance represents a continuing battle with bushpigs and the increasing herds of antelope.

Above the front door is a small carving of a black rhino's head, a reminder that Gore-Browne had earned the local nickname of Chipembele, black rhino. At the centre of the manor is the square tiled Tuscan courtyard, surrounded by arches, overlooking windows and a red tiled roof. Climbing one of the cold, stone-slab staircases brings you into an English manor house, lined with old paintings and its wooden floors covered with old rugs.

Much of the old heavy wooden furniture remains here, including the sturdy chests; together with muskets and all manner of memorabilia, such as pictures of old relatives and regiments. Two frames with certificates face each other. One is from King George VI, granting 'our trusty and well-beloved Stewart Gore-Browne, esq' the degree, title, honour and dignity of Knight Bachelor. Opposite, President Kaunda appoints 'my trusted, well-beloved Sir Stewart Gore-Browne' as a Grand Officer of the Companion of the Order of Freedom, second division; it is dated 1966.

The library remains the manor's heart, with three huge walls of books, floor to ceiling, which tell of Gore-Browne's interests – Frouede's *History of England* in at least a dozen volumes, *Policy and Arms* by Colonel Repington and *The Genesis of War* by the Right Honourable H H Asquith. His wife was very keen on poetry: there is a classic collection of works by Byron, Shelley, Coleridge, Eliot and others. Gore-Browne left behind a wealth of diaries and personal papers, and much work is in progress cataloguing and archiving these. Central to the room is a grand fireplace, surmounted by the Latin inscription: *Ille terrarum mihi super omnes anculus ridet* – 'This corner of the earth, above all others, smiles on me'.

It's now possible to stay in the manor house; see *Where to stay*, below, for details.

Shiwa estate The working estate extends to include a farm, a well-stocked game-ranch, a lake, stables and all the support necessary for almost total self-sufficiency – directly employing a permanent staff of around 80, with another 120 or so working on a casual basis. It covers just over 100km² of land, and encompasses the domestic livestock, including about 15,000 laying hens, 1,200 cattle, 40 dairy cows, 700 sheep, 20 pigs and 52 Saanan goats, imported from the USA, whose milk is used to raise orphaned children. Ten years after the move, the game farm has expanded considerably, with over 1,500 head of assorted game, and these are being continuously augmented to improve the bloodlines of the existing herds, and increase the numbers; Shiwa boasts one of the largest breeding herds of pure-bred Boran cattle in Zambia (originally imported from Kenya), its own abattoir on site and a butchery in Mpika. Pasture crops are grown largely to feed the livestock but the workers and their wives are encouraged to cultivate vegetable gardens and blocks of maize for their own consumption and for sale on and to the farm.

Gore-Brown's hospital has been brought back to life, thanks in part to grants from the British and German embassies – whilst smaller grants from diplomatic and private sources have enabled it to complete a very good maternity ward. The two government schools are now thriving once more, supplemented by tuition in IT from visiting international students.

Getting there Shiwa Ng'andu is reasonably well signposted off the main road to Isoka and Nakonde; the turn-off (✪ TUSHIW 11°13.334'S, 31°49.580'E) is about 87km northeast of Mpika. The manor house (✪ SHIWAH 11°11.924'S, 31°44.289'E) is about 13km from this turn-off. The road then continues westwards to Kapishya Hot Springs and onto the Mpika–Kasama road.

Alternatively Shiwa can be reached directly from the Mpika–Kasama road; again turn off about 87km from Mpika (◉ TUKAPI 11°10.624'S, 31°17.454'E). It's then a little over 30km to Kapishya, and about half of that again to the manor house.

🏠 Where to stay There are three very different places to stay on the estate:

🏠 **Shiwa Ng'andu Manor House** (6 rooms) m 0976 070149, 0977 749002; e reservations@ shiwangandu.com; www.shiwangandu.com. ◉ SHIWAH 11°11.924'S, 31°44.289'E. Charlie & Jo Harvey accept paying house guests, & make engaging & energetic hosts. Their guest rooms, hung with paintings from the Shiwa collection, retain many original features, including fireplaces in which fires are lit every night in winter. Traditional hardwood furniture is complemented by new 4-poster bedsteads made on the estate, while en-suite bathrooms add a touch of modernity – but only a touch; some have huge old metal baths rather than modern showers, & an aura of Edwardian style prevails. Meals are very simple farm fare, much of it sourced on the farm, but served with style in the grand setting of a formal dining room. It's very much like staying in an English stately home in Africa – which you'll realise isn't a contradiction in terms when you visit.

Jo & Charlie are very generous with the time that they give to their guests – but there is also a house manager on hand, & a professional guide to take you around the estate. Days are very full, with plenty of activities – you can choose what you'd like to do from a wide range of possibilities (pretty much as below).

Most people come to Zambia on safari, then wonder about adding on Shiwa as an afterthought. That's sad, as I found my last stay here to be among the most interesting & engaging few days that I've spent anywhere in Zambia – a view backed up by the visitors that I've sent here since. If you do come, then allow at least 3 or 4 nights; any fewer would be far too frustrating for you! *US$360 pp, fully inclusive.* ⊕ *All year.*

🏠 **Impandala House** (4-bedroom house) Originally built by Gore-Browne in 1933, to house missionaries translating the Bible from English to Bemba, this quaint & simple farmhouse was renovated by the Harveys & opened to visitors in mid-2009. A 20-min drive from the main house, it, too, retains a sense of colonial times. Its bedrooms – 2 en suite & 2 sharing a

bathroom – are set on 2 levels. The comfortable lounge, dining room & wraparound veranda are furnished simply but appropriately, with some items brought from the main house – though it's not nearly as grand. The house is ideal for families or friends travelling together, & makes a good, low-cost alternative to the main house. It is usually self catering, so come stocked up with food & supplies to last your stay, but catering can be arranged with enough notice. *US$480 per night self catering; US$220 pp FBA, exc horseriding & access to Shiwa House.* ⊕ *All year.*

🏠 **Kapishya Hot Springs** (6 chalets, camping) m 0976 970444; e mark@ shiwasafaris.com; www.shiwasafaris.com. ◉ KAPISH 11°10.263'S, 31°36.057'E. Kapishya is run by Mark Harvey, Sir Stewart's second grandson, a mine of local information & a top local guide. The camp lies on the Manshya River & has been considerably upgraded in recent years, with flourishing gardens where individual plants are carefully labelled & a rustic bar/dining area.

The thatched brick chalets are simple but comfortable, each sleeping 4, & with its own porch & brick floors covered with reed mats. Mosquito-netted windows & en-suite facilities that include large showers are standard. Two of the chalets are dbl-storey, with a particularly good view of the river from the top & their own firepit. Right by the river, the grassy campsite has soft earth that's easy on tent pegs, good hot showers & clean flushing toilets, as well as a dining shelter & BBQ areas. All visitors can order meals, ideally with advance notice (*dinner Kw125,000*), or can cater for themselves (chalet guests can use the camp's kitchen). To spice up the self-catering option, homemade jams & chutneys are for sale.

Kapishya Springs themselves are a great attraction, as is the birding on the property (Ross's turaco is a relatively common visitor) but guests here can also take part in most of the activities on the Shiwa estate; US$20 pp will cover a game drive or a lake trip. Alternatively, there are some lovely waterfalls nearby to explore yourself – see *Excursions from Shiwa,* page 323. Exciting news in 2011 was the discovery of a horde of rock paintings on nearby land – some possibly dating back as far as 60,000 years. Mark plans to guide guests to see these, archaeological work permitting. A series of trails is also being developed, varying from a few hours to a few days with camping along the way.

Kapishya combines well with a visit to Buffalo Camp (see pages 300–1) in North Luangwa National Park, also run by Mark. With lots of advance notice, it's sometimes possible to pre-arrange vehicle transfers between the 2. *US$50/100/140 pp self catering/DBB/FB; camping US$10 pp.* ☺ *All year.*

What to see and do
Shiwa's a great place for a surprising variety of activities, so there's no question of being bored. For those staying at the manor house, these are generally included; for guests at Kapishya they're optional extras. Always bear in mind that numbers of visitors here are fairly small, so where I refer to a 'tour' you should generally visualise half-a-dozen visitors or fewer! Here are just a few of Shiwa's highlights.

Kapishya Hot Springs About 20km from Shiwa Ng'andu, the hot springs in the Manshya River at Kapishya were always a favourite spot of Gore-Browne's and a great place to unwind. Within a shallow part of the cool rocky river, surrounded by *combretum* bushes and gently curving raffia palms (*Raphia farinifera*) is an inviting pool of hot spring water. It makes a great site for bathing. Those not staying overnight on the Shiwa estate can visit for the day for Kw25,000 per person, or US$5.

Boating and rafting There are several activities possible on the water. It's lovely to take a slow boat trip around the edges of the lake, looking out for wildlife, from birds and otters to crocodiles, and it's also possible to do this by traditional mokoro (dugout canoe). During the fishing season, you can bring a rod and reel.

Alternatively, take a full-day trip around the lake, and then from there down the Manshya River. This goes over some small (Grade II) rapids and back to Kapishya Camp – and is a particularly good option for birdwatchers (though do remember to protect any belongings in waterproof containers in case they should be thrown out).

Nature walks and drives Much of Shiwa estate is now a game area, so early morning walks or game drives can be very much a feature of staying here. It's a particularly good place to spot the elusive blue duiker, whilst the more common game includes puku, kudu, defassa waterbuck, Kafue lechwe, Lichtenstein hartebeest, common duiker, oribi, zebra, bushbuck, reedbuck, impala, yellow baboon, vervet monkey, grysbok and wildebeest.

The lechwe and the wildebeest are of a different subspecies than you'll find elsewhere in this part of northern Zambia; they're unlike those in the Luangwa and Bangweulu areas. With patience, sitatunga can usually be spotted from the hide, whilst bushpig, wild cat, civet, genet and clawless otters are around but often less visible. As in many of Zambia's isolated kopjes, there's a resident population of fairly elusive klipspringers.

One of the estate's natural highlights occurs in November, at the start of the rains, when thousands of straw-coloured fruit-bats return to Shiwa to roost. For details of a similar spectacle at Kasanka, see page 327.

Guided walks The Shiwa estate, and the area around it, is a lovely place for scenic walks, with a number of stunning hills and sites of interest. It's as easy to have a good hour's walk alone as it is to stay out for the day with a local guide, perhaps wandering beside the river and getting as far as the Chusa Falls – which are 10km downstream from Kapishya Springs.

Another notable spot is Nachipala Bareback Hill – a large granite whaleback which affords stunning panoramic vistas and a magnificent view of the lake. This is an energetic three-hour walk from the manor house, and on the top a small cairn marks the spot where, on his last journey in 1867, Dr David Livingstone took compass bearings in his final attempt to find the source of the Nile. Kapishya is developing a series of walking trails varying in length, but potentially lasting a number of days. They aim to keep things simple, including fairly basic camping *en route*.

Birdwatching Shiwa has been identified as a priority site for conservation and is listed as one of 31 'important bird areas' in Zambia (see *Appendix 3*, page 536). You can stroll around the estate and game ranch with or without a guide (there aren't usually any lion, buffalo or elephant here, so this is fairly safe), and some of the walks lead through beautiful raffia palm forests.

In total, over 375 species of birds have been seen on the estate. Birding highlights include palm-nut vultures, bat hawks, Ross's turacos, white-cheeked bee-eaters, white-tailed and blue flycatchers, Stanley's bustards, African finfoot, black-rumped buttonquail, long-toed flufftail, greater snipe, grass owls, black-chinned quail finch and a veritable kaleidoscope of different sunbirds. Down by the water, the swamps, rivers and lakes offer a haven for a variety of waterbirds, including pygmy geese; cormorants; yellow-billed, knob-nosed and white-faced teal; giant and lesser egrets; blue, grey, night and goliath herons; Fülleborn's and rosy-breasted longclaws; malachite, half-collared, giant and pied kingfishers; golden-rumped tinkerbird; splendid starlings; black-bellied seed cracker; Bocage's robin; bar-throated apalis; and white-headed saw-wing. Fish eagles and even ospreys may be spotted, as well as transient flocks of pelicans and flamingos.

Horseriding (m 0976 664090; email/website via Shiwa Ng'andu) Horseriding is arranged through Shiwa Horse Safaris, owned and run by Steven and Lucy Rufus who are based at Impandala House, ten minutes from the main house. They arrange rides of varying length for experienced riders only, with good hard hats available. They have beautiful horses, which are exceptionally well trained and respond exceedingly well to instructions. Indeed, some guests commented that the horses here were some of the best they had ever ridden. Day-long excursions can take you all over the estate, though particularly attractive is the hour or so's ride up to the 'View of Angels' – an oft-photographed spot where there is a spectacular view of the lake from the family graves of Sir Stewart Gore-Browne and his daughter and son-in-law, Lorna and John Harvey. Rides must be booked in advance

Around the estate If you've time to spare then take a slow wander around the estate, and perhaps down to the lake, ideally with a guide. You will find an exceedingly positive atmosphere, with the local people very welcoming and friendly, and usually happy to talk about what they are doing.

The farm itself is run on commercial lines, but methods are far from the intensive farming beloved of the West. The environment is a key factor, and nothing is left to waste. This is no place for shiny new gadgets; spending an hour or so watching the sort of machinery usually confined to a museum being coaxed into life can be fascinating in itself. There are numerous community initiatives going on, too, from fish-farming to bee-keeping and bio-gas projects – as well as a variety of projects within the estate's hospital and school.

Tours of the manor house Guided tours of the manor house are by prior arrangement only. If you're staying at the manor house then this is merely a case of asking Jo and Charlie to show you around; it's delightfully informal and totally fascinating.

If you're staying at Kapishya, or just dropping in for the day, the only way to see some of the interior of the house is to book on to a daily 'tour' (*Mon–Sat 09.00–11.00, Sun 10.00–11.00; the fee of US$20 pp goes towards the community fund*). Within the house the tour is limited to the lower floors; the upper floors are strictly for the family and their guests. (Remember that this is a family home first, and a small exclusive guesthouse second, and you'll realise that neither the family, nor their guests, will want a steady stream of visitors looking throughout the house.) Also included are a game drive and a historical guided tour of the estate.

Shiwa's archives Putting Gore-Browne's extensive collection of diaries, letters and papers into an ordered archive has been a long-term project for Jo, and is still not complete. Guests interested in the manor house can have some access to this, on request; it's fascinating to read some of Gore-Browne's old diaries even if you're not an amateur historian. Then there's the enormous library, and Gore-Browne's collection of early records!

Historical tours on the estate Jo is a trained archaeologist, and has been in the forefront of excavating some of the older sites on the estate – already uncovering the kilns that were built to make the bricks and the tiles for the manor house, and the locations of an old summerhouse.

There are a number of other spots of historical interest, including the old hospital, the essential oils distillery, the traction engine and the graveyard – and any can easily be integrated into a historical tour of the estate.

Excursions from Shiwa Shiwa is really a destination in itself, and isn't often used as a base for excursions, although Kapishya makes quite a good base for visiting a few local waterfalls, detailed below. If you ask the team at the springs, they could probably arrange for a guide to go with you to make locating them easier.

Chusa Falls Chusa Falls (✪ CHUSAF 11°09.353'S, 31°33.093'E) are the closest to Kapishya, making a good day trip. On foot, they're a distance of 7km away, or 10km by road. The falls are quite clearly a short series of three steps, each being several metres high.

Senkele Falls These falls (✪ SENKEL 11°06.150'S, 31°21.922'E) are a 15m drop on the Mansha River. The turn-off to them from the Mpika–Kasama Road is at ✪ TUSENK 11°11.712'S, 31°18.903'E, about 3.5km north of the turning to Kapishya and Shiwa. From there the track turns north and continues for 10km. Continue north where the road forks, then after about 2km of high grass, stop at the deserted house; the falls are 100m from here. This might be a lovely place to bush-camp.

Namundela Falls Finally, the stunning double Namundela Falls (✪ 11°06.760'S, 31°27.606'E) are about two hours' drive from Kapishya, followed by a 90-minute walk to the falls along the Mansha River. To get to them, head 28km west from Kapishya, turning north at Chilombo School (✪ CHILOM 11°13.525'S, 31°24.624'E). Follow this track about 13km north and slightly east to the Anderson Farm (✪ ANDERS

11°07.861'S, 31°26.542'E), and then further to the Kapololwe Homestead, marking the start of the walk along the river.

KASANKA NATIONAL PARK

(*Park fees US$10 pp/day; vehicle US$15/day*) This small park is the first privately managed national park in Zambia. It is run by a charity, the Kasanka Trust, and the proceeds from tourism go directly into conservation and development in the park and surrounding communities. It is only 420km² in area, but encompasses a wide variety of vegetation zones from dry evergreen forests to various types of moist forest and permanent papyrus swamps. The park and its camps are so well kept that it is a delightful place to spend a relaxing few days, and keen birdwatchers will find many more pressing reasons to visit.

HISTORY Kasanka was made a national park in 1972, but it was poorly maintained and poaching was rife until the late 1980s. Then an initiative was started by the late David Lloyd, a former district officer, and Gareth Williams, a local commercial farmer. With the approval of the National Parks and Wildlife Department and the local community, they started to put private money into revitalising the park.

In 1990 the National Parks Department signed a management contract with the Kasanka Trust, giving the latter the right to manage the park and develop it for tourism in partnership with the local community. The Trust, which is linked to a registered charity based in the UK and Netherlands (e *info@kasanka.nl*), has trailblazed a model for the successful private management of a Zambian national park. It has been fortunate in gaining financial backing from various donors, but now relies almost entirely on tourism income to fund its activities.

The Kasanka Trust aims to manage the area's natural resources for the benefit of both the wildlife and the local people, and so it closely supports and consults with a locally elected community resource board.

GEOGRAPHY Kasanka is on the southern fringes of the Bangweulu Wetlands, and just 30km from the border with DRC. It is almost completely flat and, lying at an altitude of about 1,200m, it gets a high rainfall during the wet season (about 1,200mm) which results in a lush cover of vegetation.

Although there are several small rivers flowing through the park, the evenness of the land has resulted in an extensive marsh area known as the Kapabi Swamp. There are also eight lakes in the park, though seven of these are really just small, permanently flooded dambos.

FLORA AND FAUNA

Flora The park's natural flora is dominated by miombo woodland, in which brachystegia species figure heavily. The local people use fire as part of their cultivation and hunting/gathering activities, which can spread into areas of the park, so some of this is less tall than it might be – perhaps reaching only 5m rather than its normal 20m. The park operates a programme of limited, controlled burning to reduce the damage caused by hotter fires later in the dry season.

There are also sections of much taller dry evergreen forest, where the tallest trees have an interlocking canopy, and the *mateshi* undergrowth is dense and woody. A good area for this is near the Mulembo River around the Katwa scout post.

Elsewhere you will find evergreen swamp forest, with some superb tall specimens of waterberry (*Syzygium cordatum*) and *mululu*, or red mahogany, trees (*Khaya*

KASANKA NATIONAL PARK

GPS co-ordinates ⊕

TUKASA	12°33.250'S	30°23.478'E
WASALO	12°33.272'S	30°17.740'E
FIBWE	12°35.444'S	30°15.153'E
PONTOO	12°34.362'S	30°14.008'E
LUWOMB	12°30.109'S	30°07.870'E

Livingstone Memorial,
Shoebill Camp

TUKASA
Mulembo checkpoint

Great North Road

Mansa

Conservation
Centre

Mpulukwe Hill

Mlaushi

no entry

Mulembo
airstrip

Chantete
scout post

Wasa Lodge

WASALO
Lake Wasa I

Lake Wasa II

Lake Kalamba
II

Lake Kalamba
I

FIBWE

Fibwe scout post

Musola

Kasanka

PONTOO
Pontoon

Fibwe hide

Kasanka

Kabwe

Boston Bwalya
scout post

Lake
Ndolwa

Kalpabi
Swamps

Nsofu scout post

Mulembo

Bufumu
Forest

Airstrip

LUWOMB
Luwombwa
Fishing Lodge

Chikufwe
Plain

Luwombwa

Bwalyabemba Hill

Serenje

Luwombwa

0   5km
0   3 miles

N

Bradt

nyasica). One of the guides here told me a story of a biologist asking a local Chewa person the name of this tree, and getting the reply '*Khaya*', which means 'I don't know'.

Around the Fibwe scout post is one such area of forest, and the Fibwe hide (see page 331) is perched in a huge *mululu* tree. Similar species also occur in the areas of riparian forest found by Kasanka's small rivers. One notable tree is the wild loquat (*Oxyanthus speciosus*), whose fruit is a major draw for bats.

Interspersed in these forested areas are seasonally flooded grasslands and swamps. The latter include large areas of permanent papyrus beds and *phragmites* reeds, often with very little open water to be seen. The wild date palm (*Phoenix reclinata*) is one of the most common species of tree found here. Keep a lookout, too, for the large tree-proteas that bloom spectacularly around May and June.

Mammals Poaching in the 1970s and '80s drastically reduced the numbers of animals in the park. However, this seems to have had few long-term effects on the species now present. Many of these move into and out of the park quite freely and, as they gradually learn that the park is a safe haven, they are staying longer or becoming resident, and appear to be less shy.

Puku are the most common antelope here, and they are found in a particularly high density along the Kasanka River. Other relatively common residents include bushbuck, reedbuck, Sharp's grysbok and the common duiker. Lichtenstein's hartebeest, sable and roan occur in good numbers, while oribi, zebra and buffalo and defassa waterbuck are more scarce. Elephants move through the park, but a recent count suggested that a population of about 50 were probably resident here.

Of particular interest are the shy sitatunga antelope, which can almost always be seen in the very early morning from the Fibwe hide (see below), near Fibwe scout post. This offers one of the subcontinent's best opportunities for viewing these beautiful creatures in an undisturbed state – far superior to simply getting a fleeting glance of the back of one as it flees from the speedboat in which you are travelling, as with so many sitatunga sightings in places like the Okavango Delta. On occasion, 70 different animals have been spotted in a morning from here. It's excellent. That said, the drive along the Kasanka River between Pontoon and Kabwe campsites is increasingly becoming one of the best parts of the park to see sitatunga.

The smaller carnivores are well represented in Kasanka, with caracal, jackal, civet, genet and Cape clawless otter all regularly recorded. Others, including lion, leopard, serval, spotted hyena, honey badgers and the African wildcat, are more rarely seen.

Mongooses are well represented: the water (or marsh), slender, white-tailed, banded, dwarf and large grey mongoose are all found here.

In the lakes, rivers and swamps, hippo and crocodiles are common. The slender-snouted crocodile, a typical resident of DRC's tropical rainforest rivers, occurs here – though it is far less common than the 'normal' Nile crocodile. Given the park's proximity to the DRC, other species, which are typical of those equatorial rainforests (but rare for southern Africa), can be spotted in Kasanka. For example, the blue monkey is often sighted, occurring together with the area's more common primates: baboons and vervet monkeys.

Probably the most spectacular sight occurs around the start of the rains (in November and December) when an enormous colony of straw-coloured fruit-bats roosts in the *mushitu* forest. Each night they pour out of their resting-place just after sunset, filling the sky as they fly in search of food. The bats have wingspans of up to 1m, making a grand spectacle that is best observed from the area of the Fibwe hide.

Birds Kasanka has lush vegetation with a wide range of habitats including three large rivers, five natural lakes, a papyrus swamp (Kapabi) and real moist evergreen swamp forest. In this small area over 453 bird species had been identified by mid-2011, including many 'specials', and the number continues to rise – so it's a very good place for quiet, undisturbed birdwatching.

The rivers, lakes and wetland areas have excellent populations of ibis, storks, herons, kingfishers and bee-eaters as well as many waterfowl. Water rails, greater and lesser jacanas, white-backed ducks and pygmy geese are common. The larger birds include wattled cranes and saddle-billed storks; around Lake Ndolwa and Wasa there have even been two sightings of the rare shoebill, which breeds in the Bangweulu Wetlands to the north. Reed cormorants and African darters are easily spotted on the more open stretches of water.

Many species common in east or central Africa occur here, on the edges of their ranges (South African bird books just won't be enough!), like the grey apalis, olive sunbird, red and blue sunbird (Anchieta's), green lourie, Boehm's flycatcher,

THE BATS

One of Kasanka's highlights is the magnificent tree-hide, perched high in a red mahogany tree overlooking the Kapabi Swamp. Most come here to spot sitatunga, but if you climb up on a late November afternoon, around the time the rains are beginning, then you'll also witness one of Africa's strangest wildlife spectacles. Between about 18.15 and 18.45, some five million straw-coloured fruit-bats will take to the air above you. These large, fruit-eating bats have wingspans up to about a metre. They start by circling overhead like a vast, slow whirlwind. Gradually, individuals and groups break off and spread out over the forest in search of wild fruits. For an amazing 20–30 minutes the sky is filled, as far as you can see, with squadron upon squadron of bats, heading off into the twilight.

'They come to roost in the evergreen swamp forest, near the Musola River,' Edmund said, gazing down through the canopy. 'It's very unusual vegetation for Zambia – only found near rivers. Tremendously fragile and easily destroyed,' he added. 'During the day the bats occupy just a small area. They hang off the Mushitu trees in such numbers that they pull off the branches, leaving just the woody skeletons to hang on to. This lets light on to the forest floor which, together with the inordinate amount of fertiliser that they drop, promotes very rich undergrowth. Imagine, eight million bats, weighing about 350g each … that's 2,800 tons of animals.' Edmund had clearly done his arithmetic before. 'The equivalent of a thousand elephants, hanging around in perhaps one hectare of forest, suspended from the trees,' he grinned.

Visiting this colony isn't for the faint-hearted, even during the day. Large crocodiles wander under the trees, far from the nearest water, scavenging for dead bats – along with vultures, gymnogenes and a host of other smaller predators. All of which provided further reasons why that high tree-hide was such a wonderful place to be. For the even more adventurous, there are guided walks into the forest at 04.30 or 16.30 to get a closer view of the bats as they return to roost or head out to hunt.

Edited from an article by the author that first appeared in Travel Africa, *and reproduced by kind permission.*

11

Boehm's bee-eater, Sousa's shrike, black-backed barbet, Anchieta's tchagra, and both Schalow's and Ross's turacos (the latter also known as Lady Ross's lourie). Meanwhile, a quiet drift in a canoe down the Luwombwa River should produce sightings of finfoot, giant and half-collared kingfishers, narina trogons and yellow-throated leaflove, to name but a few.

The park was the site for a recent study of hornbill species by a team organised jointly by the universities of Manchester (UK) and Lusaka.

The more common raptors in the area are the bateleur, martial, crowned, Ayre's, African hawk and steppe eagles, plus the snake eagles (black-breasted, western-banded and brown) and the chanting goshawks (pale and dark). Kasanka's fish eagles are often seen and crowned eagles breed here. There arc also several pairs of Pel's fishing owls.

GETTING THERE The entrance to Kasanka, on its eastern border, is marked with a large sign. Coming from Kapiri Mposhi, do refuel in Serenje, as there is no fuel available in the park. Then 36km northeast of Serenje, take the main left turning signposted to Samfya and Mansa. This used to be referred to as the 'Chinese road' because, like TAZARA, a Chinese company built it. After about 55km (the milestones on the left of the road are no longer readable!) turn left, where you will find the the Mulembo scout post and the entrance gate to the park (⊕ TUKASA 12°33.250'S, 30°23.478'E). You may need to register and pay the entrance fee here, but if the post is unmanned then just proceed to Wasa Lodge, bearing left at the fork after 1km or so (turning right here takes you to the new information centre). For those **flying** in, the park has two good 1,200m airstrips for light aircraft – and they're very aviation-friendly.

🏠 **WHERE TO STAY** The Kasanka Trust (*satellite* ✆ +873 762 067957; e *wasa@kasanka.com; www.kasanka.com*) runs all the camps in the park. Although Kasanka can often accommodate 'drop-in' visitors who have their own food, booking in advance is always a good idea. All visitors pay park fees on top of accommodation, except those staying at the conservation centre, which is just outside the park boundary.

🏠 **Wasa Lodge** (8 rondavels) ⊕ WASALO 12°33.272'S, 30°17.740'E. About 20 mins' drive from the main road, in a delightful spot on the shore of Lake Wasa, is the park's main camp. Wherever you are going in the park, you should report here first. There's a variety of accommodation, with dbl, twin & family rooms. All are fairly simple but have en-suite flush toilets & hot bucket showers, & the large, newer ones are quite spacious & comfortable. At night the camp is lit by atmospheric lanterns & small solar-powered lights.

Wasa is well staffed & equipped, & can take both self-catering & fly-in guests. If you're driving in, you can bring your own supplies & the camp's staff will cook them for you. They will also prepare hot water for showers, & are generally around for any reasonable help that you might need. A bar is always available. Alternatively, if you are flying into Kasanka, or don't have your own food, catering can be arranged for you.

Similarly, with your own vehicle you can drive yourself around the park or take a local guide to accompany you. However, if you're flying in then you will need the use of one of the camp's 4x4s & guides, which should be pre-arranged. *Kw280,000 pp self catering, exc park fees; US$370/520 pp sharing/sgl FB, inc activities (best pre-arranged), laundry, & park fees.* ☺ *All year.*

🏠 **Luwombwa Fishing Lodge** (5 chalets) ⊕ LUWOMB 12°30.109'S, 30°7.870'E. This very pleasant & peaceful lodge sits on the bank of the Luwombwa River in the western half of the park. If you're driving yourself, you'll need a high-clearance 4x4 to reach it. Accommodation consists of 3 A-frame thatch-on-brick chalets, 2 with twin beds upstairs plus a sgl & dbl downstairs, & the 3rd on 1 floor only, with a dbl

& sgl bed. All have an en-suite toilet & shower. There are also 2 much simpler chalets with separate facilities. All feel a lot roomier than the older chalets at Wasa, so it's worth coming over to Luwombwa for 1–2 nights if you're staying in the park for any time.

The simple bar & dining area is made of reeds & thatch, & it is dominated by a huge & quite magnificent *mpundu* (or *mobola*) plum (*Parinari curatellifolia*). This has edible fruits, around Oct–Jan, which are variously described as 'sought-after', 'pleasant-tasting' & 'disgusting'.

The camp works on a similar basis to Wasa – you bring your supplies & the camp's staff will look after you, or you make arrangements for meals & drinks with the camp in advance. To reach Luwombwa before dark, make sure that you get to Wasa before 17.00, or it will be too late to continue on here. 5-seater motorboats with guides are available for hire, as are 3-seater canoes. *Kw280,000 pp self catering, exc park fees; US$370/520 pp sharing/sgl FB, inc activities (best pre-arranged), laundry, & park fees.* ⊕ *All year.*

Å **Pontoon Campsite** Set under a beautiful stand of red mahogany (*mululu*) trees (*Khaya nyasica*) near the main Kasanka River crossing (which is currently a pontoon). There are simple bucket showers & long-drop toilets as well as 2 cooking shelters. Staff are on hand to supply firewood, draw water, prepare hot showers, & give basic guidance to visitors. The site can accommodate groups of up to about 15 people. *Kw50,400 pp.*

Å **Kabwe Campsite** Overlooking the Kasanka River plain, this is a smaller site for up to 6 people, with just 1 toilet & 1 shower. It is best booked in advance. *Kw50,400 pp.*

🏠 **Conservation Centre** (4 rooms, dormitory, camping) Accommodation at the conservation centre, 1km from the park gates, is designed primarily for students or long-term researchers. Rooms are set up in pairs, sharing a shower & toilet, & there's a dormitory for larger groups. It's also possible to camp. Some meals can be provided from the on-site kitchen or visitors can cook for themselves. *Room Kw163,000 pp; dormitory Kw94,500 pp; camping Kw50,400 pp. No park fees applicable.*

Fly-camping (*US$370/520 pp sharing/sgl FBA, inc equipment.* ⊕ *May–Dec, though you may have rain Nov–Dec*) Guided walking safaris led by expert, armed game scouts last three to five days and offer a real bush experience. This is the chance to see the many different vegetation types, insects, birds and animals, and to discuss the bush, the project, and anything else at leisure! They usually also include some time canoeing. The fly-camps are simple, but supplies are delivered ahead by vehicle so you don't need to carry a heavy pack. Note that experienced **backpackers** who arrive fully equipped with food and supplies, and who are prepared to carry all their own kit, can often arrange to go for an extended walking trip with an accompanying scout at a much lower cost.

Bat safaris During late November, Robin Pope Safaris (see page 268) organises seven-night safaris which combine their Nkwali property in the South Luangwa (page 284) with a visit to the bat migration at Kasanka, and a day trip to the Bangweulu Wetlands. Costs, including overnight accommodation in Lusaka, are US$4,229/4,852 per person sharing/single.

WHAT TO SEE AND DO During the dry season Kasanka's roads are generally good, and accessible with a high-clearance 2WD. There is a manually operated pontoon (◈ PONTOO 12°34.362'S, 30°14.008'E) for crossing the Kasanka River in the centre of the park, with staff stationed nearby who can assist. (There are plans to build a bridge here eventually.)

Activities organised by the Kasanka Trust include escorted walks, day and night game drives, canoeing, motorboat trips and fishing (bream and tigerfish). I can highly recommend the excellent canoe trips from Luwombwa.

11

Anglers should head for Luwombwa Fishing Lodge (bring your own gear and get a permit in advance from Wasa Lodge), as the best waters for fishing are normally those of the Luwombwa River. The main species found here are vundu catfish and large-mouth, small-mouth and yellow-belly bream. The camp's cooks will prepare your catch for dinner, if you wish, but note that strict rules allow only large fish to be removed for eating. Fishing tackle cannot be hired from the lodges.

With advance notice, there's also the chance to see aspects of some of Kasanka's community-based conservation projects, and meet their participants. One such

CHILLI FENCES

One of the greatest problems facing the successful operation of a national park is managing the conflict between conservation and community. Kasanka is no exception: with a small elephant population in an unfenced park, and a considerable number of arable farms in the vicinity, problems are almost inevitable. Villagers understandably object to elephants trampling their valuable maize and cassava crops, but keeping the animals at bay is rarely straightforward.

In 2000, two researchers in Zimbabwe came up with a simple idea: chilli fences. The aim was to create a barrier that would repel the elephants without resorting to costly and often ineffective barricades or electric fencing. In 1997, Guy Parker and Loki Osborn in Zimbabwe set up the Chilli Pepper Development Project, based on the premise that elephants have a strong aversion to the smell of chillies. Using cheap, easily available materials, they created a fence made of wooden posts linked by sisal rope and hung with strips of mutton cloth that had been doused in used engine oil and chillies. Their results were impressive.

Taking their research as a base, Victoria Paterson, a research student from Glasgow University, spent much of 2007 at Kasanka studying the potential of chilli fences for the villages around the national park. With a focus across five sites, she set up a series of fences, with control experiments to check the efficacy of the combination of materials, and worked with local farmers to explain the methods. Despite considerable resistance, some of the farmers have taken the suggestions on board, with very positive results for their crops. The next stage is to ascertain how long the protective fences will work, assuming that eventually the elephants will overcome their dislike of the chillies. One method of reinforcing the fences is to create a buffer zone between the precious maize crop and the elephant's forest habitat, by growing a secondary crop around it. The European potato, for example, doesn't find favour with elephants, so sowing this between the forest and the maize may be sufficient to persuade the elephant to look elsewhere rather than wading through a field of unappealing fare.

While persuading people to try out new ideas can be an uphill struggle in itself, it's important that putting these ideas into practice should be affordable. With this in mind, villagers have been encouraged to use fibre for rope, and to grow chillies as one of their crops. Here, water is a huge factor, but if the chillies are grown alongside another, profitable crop that requires irrigation, such as rape, then a successful outcome is more likely.

Now, though, the elephants – thwarted of their free meal – have taken to heading for village grain stores, and so the cycle continues.

project was initiated in the Kafinda area in 1997, aiming to raise awareness of the importance of conservation, and to provide alternatives to poaching for the community.

Alternatively driving yourself around is easy, though it's a shame to go by yourself when good guides are available and their community relies on their income. A few places within the park are worth specific mention.

Fibwe hide A magnificent *mululu* or red mahogany tree (*Khaya nyasica*), near to the Fibwe scout post (⊕ FIBWE 12°35.444'S, 30°15.153'E), can be climbed, using a basic ladder, to reach a platform almost 18m above the ground. The views over a section of the Kapabi Swamp are excellent, and if you reach this in the early morning and climb quietly then your chances of seeing sitatunga are excellent.

However, more leisurely risers should take heart: I have seen a number of sitatunga from here as late as midday. In short, this is probably the best place for seeing sitatunga in the wild anywhere in Africa – and so certainly one of the best tree-hides on the continent!

Meanwhile, when you're not searching for sitatunga, it's also a particularly productive birding spot with specials such as Ross's and Schalow's turaco, Boehm's bee-eater, black-backed barbet, Anchieta's chagra, speckled mousebirds and various sunbirds often visible in the nearby forest.

Chinyangale Plain This lies between the Kasanka River crossing and the Fibwe hide. A game-viewing road winds through the open plain with palm clumps and plentiful puku. Another road runs along the western side of the Kasanka, going downstream from the crossing. There are often large herds of puku here, and you'll frequently spot bushbuck and warthog.

Chikufwe Plain The Chikufwe Plain (⊕ CHIFUN 12°33.066'S, 30°09.645'E) is a large open area of seasonally flooded grassland, which is a favourite place to spot sable, hartebeest and reedbuck. There is a good grass airstrip here, and a loop road around the southern side of the plain.

Conservation centre A visitor centre opened in 2007 showcases the park's conservation work and acts as an interpretation centre, with posters, displays, information and videos of the annual bat migration. There is also a limited amount of accommodation designed primarily for students or groups. The centre is 1km from the park gates, but has been built just outside the boundary in the surrounding GMA, so visitors here do not have to pay park fees.

FURTHER INFORMATION Unfortunately, the best source of information on the park, *Kasanka – A Visitor's Guide to the Kasanka National Park*, is now out of print, but you'll find plenty about Kasanka on www.kasanka.com, including information on wildlife, the local habitat and conservation.

AROUND KASANKA AND BANGWEULU

There are several sites of interest in the area around Kasanka and Bangweulu, though you'll need a self-contained 4x4 to reach any of them, and local help for some.

LIVINGSTONE MEMORIAL A plain stone monument, under a simple cross, marks the place where David Livingstone's heart was buried in 1873, in the village of Chitambo. (The village has since moved, but Livingstone's heart – and the monument – remain.) After his death, from dysentery and malaria, his followers removed his heart and internal organs, and buried them under a *mupundu* tree that once stood where the monument is now.

In an amazing tribute, his two closest followers, Sussi and Chuma, then salted and dried his body before disguising it in a tree and carrying it over 1,000 miles to Bagamoyo (on Tanzania's coast). The journey took them about nine months. From there they took the body by ship to London, where Livingstone was finally buried with full honours in Westminster Abbey on 18 April 1874.

Twenty-five years later, in 1899, the Royal Geographical Society in London sent out a small expedition to cut down the *mupundu* tree and bring a section of its trunk, which had been engraved with the names of Livingstone and three of his party, to London, where it remains to this day.

The present Chief Chitambo, Freddy Chisenga, is the great grandson of the chief who received Livingstone. If you are lucky, and willing to pay him for his time and energy, then he will guide you from his home in Cholilo village to the memorial at Chipundu.

Getting there The monument is clearly marked (if sometimes vaguely positioned) on most maps. The easiest route is to turn north off the Great North Road at ✪ TUCHIN 13°1.146'S, 30°27.695'E towards Mansa and Samfya. After some 65km, or 10km beyond the sign for Kasanka National Park, turn right in Cholilo onto a dirt road. There is a signpost and a small market at this turning (✪ TULIVI 12°29.255'S, 30°20.364'E), which is 27km from the memorial.

Follow the main track here for 1km, turning left at Chalilo School (there's a sign to the chief's palace). After 500m, bear right to avoid the chief's palace, or left if you want to visit the chief. Then continue straight on, passing Mupopolo Health Centre, for about a further 25km, till you get to a clinic on the left. Here you should sign the visitors' book and will sometimes be asked to pay a small entry fee. The memorial (✪ LIVMEM 12°17.970'S, 30°17.580'E) is signposted a little way beyond the clinic, to the left, just before Chipundu School. There are toilets on site.

On your return, it's best to avoid forking left along the old road which is marked on many maps, as this takes a very long time to get back to the tarmac road. It is, however, a useful short cut if you're heading towards Lake Waka Waka or the Bangweulu Wetlands.

KUNDALILA (NKUNDALILA) FALLS (✪ KUNDAC 13°09.260'S, 30°42.119'E. *Entry US$10 pp; camping US$25 pp – but rates may vary*) Kundalila, which means 'cooing dove', is one of Zambia's most beautiful waterfalls. Set in an area of scenic meadows and forests on the edge of the Muchinga Escarpment, the clear stream drops 67m into a crystal pool below; it makes a great place for a picnic among the granite boulders. Look out for blue monkeys that are said to inhabit the forests here, and some cheeky white-necked ravens.

At the bottom of the parking area, there is an old bridge across the Kaombe River. The path then splits and the right branch leads you to the top of the gorge – with no safety fences. The left takes you on a longer walk to the bottom, where there's a beautiful pool for swimming, if you can bear the water's chill. Take a close look at a good topographical map and you'll realise that you're in one of Zambia's highest areas, at an altitude of around 1,500m, so it's frequently cool, windy and pleasantly devoid of mosquitoes.

Campers can pitch in the parking area, where there are basic long-drop toilets but no other facilities, although a new shelter was under construction in 2007.

Those with children should be exceedingly careful as there are no fences here, and many of the paths around the falls lead straight to very steep drops at the edge.

Ilse Mwanza reports that the caretaker should also be able to take you to the nearby Kaudina Falls, and possibly also direct you to the Chilindi Chipususha Falls, on the Musumpu River.

Getting there About 65km beyond Serenje, turn southeast off the Great North Road at the small settlement of Kanona (✦ KANONA 13°4.204'S, 30°38.056'E), where a good dirt track is clearly signposted 'National Monument Kundalila Falls, 14km'. (If you were to take another right turn off this track almost immediately, you would reach the local ZAWA offices.)

Soon you'll cross the railway, then 6km further on there's a Kingdom Hall of Jehovah's Witnesses on the left, before finally reaching the falls. Generally you'll sign in with the caretaker, and pay your entry fee, either at the top of the track, or in the parking/camping area at the new shelter.

NSALU CAVE (*Entry US$10*) This huge semicircular cave, cut into Nsalu Hill, stands about 50m above the level of the surrounding plateau, and contains some excellent San/Bushmen rock paintings. Sadly a few years back the caves were vandalised, but since then the graffiti have been fading much faster than the paintings, so once again most of the paintings can still be seen. It may be possible to camp here, in which case you can expect to pay US$10 per person, plus entry fees.

Archaeological investigations have demonstrated occupation for at least 20,000 years, firstly by Middle and Late Stone-Age people, and later by Iron-Age settlers. The oldest paintings are in yellow and include parallel lines, circles and loops. Later drawings were executed in rust-coloured paint, and even later ones in red and white paints used together. The last paints applied appear as grey-white pigments and have been applied rather clumsily. They contain animal fats and are thought to have been the work of Iron-Age settlers within the last 2,000 years.

When you've finished looking at the paintings, the view from the cave's mouth over the surrounding countryside is great – and if you've lots of energy then a scramble to the top gives an even better view.

Getting there The cave is about half an hour's drive from the main road. Head northeast on the Great North Road to the signpost for Nsalu Cave and turn left (✦ TU1NSA 12°51.351'S, 30°46.495'E). This is between Serenje and Mpika, about 30km northeast of Kanona (where you turn to Kundalila Falls) and 15km north of Chitambo Mission Hospital.

Follow this road north for about 14km and then turn left at the rather marvellous sign to 'National Nonument' (✦ TU2NSA 12°44.784'S, 30°44.134'E). After a further 8km this track ends and the cave (✦ NSALUC 12°43.202'S, 30°40.952'E) is visible about halfway up the hill, on which a walking trail is marked. If you continue north past the 'National Nonument' sign, then you're heading to Lake Waka Waka, Chiundaponde and the Bangweulu Wetlands.

LAKE WAKA WAKA If you're looking for some relatively untouched bush and a quiet setting, where you're very unlikely to encounter anyone else, then this lake is a lovely tranquil spot. It's traditionally been good for walking, makes a convenient camping stop on the way to Bangweulu Wetlands, and provides a pleasant lunch spot – though there are no facilities. However, we have heard rumours that the area is being developed, so it would be wise to ask around locally in case access is

11

no longer possible. The views from the surrounding hilltops are panoramic, and I'm reliably informed that the lake is safe to swim in, with no bilharzia, hippos or crocodiles – though I haven't done this myself. There are few settlements around here, and hence a scattering of game is present, including sitatunga and roan antelope, though both are skittish and scarce.

Getting there However you approach, you're really going to need a high-clearance 4x4 once you leave the main tarred roads – and even then you'll find travelling in the rainy season is a challenge.

From the west From the Great North Road, take the road north towards Mansa and Samfya for about 65km, turning right 10km after the sign to Kasanka National Park. (See the directions to the Livingstone Memorial, opposite.) About 1km from the tarmac, keep straight ahead at the Cholilo Basic School, rather than turning left to the Chief's Palace and Livingstone Memorial. Continue past Musangashi School for about 30km, before turning left (⊕ TUWAKA 12°31.524'S, 30°36.366'E) at a sign for Lake Waka Waka. Note that you'll need a high-clearance vehicle for this track at any time of year; it doesn't get much traffic.

From the south There's a wonderful track from the Great North Road to Lake Waka Waka, but the more northerly sections of this are seldom used. Somewhat inexplicably, the whole track was graded in 2004, so with little traffic it is now one of the country's better bush tracks. But don't be lulled into taking half measures; you'll still need a high-clearance vehicle all year round, and a 4x4 during the rainy season.

Start by turning north at the signpost for Nsalu Cave (⊕ TU1NSA 12°51.351'S, 30°46.495'E), 30km northeast of Kanona. After 14km you'll pass the left turning to Nsalu Cave (⊕ TU2NSA 12°44.784'S, 30°44.134'E), but you continue heading north-northwest. This track basically follows a watershed, with the Lukulu to the east, which drains into Bangweulu, and tributaries of the Kasanka to the west, which drain into the park. Thus with no rivers crossing it, it should be passable even during the rains. When I journeyed in late May, this road was particularly beautiful, though I don't think that more than half-a-dozen cars had been through since the previous December. The grass was high, the miombo woodlands apparently untouched, and there were very few villages.

About 22km north of the Nsalu turning, the track bumps over a very rocky hill (⊕ WAKHIL 12°36.573'S, 30°39.333'E), and becomes quite indistinct in places. Carry on, and aim for the junction of this track with the 'main' track from Kasanka to Chiundaponde, at ⊕ TUWAKA 12°31.524'S, 30°36.366'E. This is barely a kilometre from the lake.

CHIUNDAPONDE Chiundaponde is a typical small Zambian village that lies at the heart of the area covered by this chapter. The inhabitants are mainly small-scale farmers from the Bisa tribe. In the fields around the village they grow cassava, finger millet, sorghum, maize and groundnuts as their staple crops. Finger millet and sorghum are also used to make beer for selling; groundnuts are grown as a cash crop. Some also keep goats and chickens, either for subsistence or to sell, and you'll often have to avoid these as they wander across the road in front of your vehicle. Chiundaponde isn't really a destination for most visitors, but you will go through it if you're visiting the Bangweulu Wetlands, and so it's useful to be able to navigate to/from here.

For directions from Chiundaponde to the Bangweulu Wetlands, see page 333.

Getting there and away

From the south or west Follow the directions (see opposite, *From the west* and *From the south*) from the Great North Road to the turning for Lake Waka Waka (⊕ TUWAKA 12°31.524'S, 30°36.366'E). From there, head on the track leading north – which bounces gently though miombo woodlands and, increasingly, small farming settlements. By 17km beyond the lake, you'll pass through a small village with a school where, like anywhere else here, you'll probably be the object of much curiosity and interest – if only from the local children. Although you'll be in third gear and the track is sandy in places, this isn't difficult driving.

After about 23km you'll cross a large dambo (⊕ DAMBO 12°21.947'S, 30°36.321'E), where the track follows a short causeway. A further 9km on and there's another large dambo to cross (⊕ DAMBO2 12°17.384'S, 30°35.407'E), and around 3km later there may be a sign to the new Nakapalayo village (see below) where you can stay. Some 6km after the second dambo, you reach Chiundaponde (⊕ CHSCHL 12°14.724'S, 30°34.741'E), where amongst other buildings you'll find a large school.

From the east Approaching from Mpika, leave the Great North Road about 65km from Mpika, and follow the directions given below to get across Lavushi Manda National Park. In the dry season it takes about three hours to reach Chiundaponde from the turn-off. In the wet season, the Lavushi Manda road is so bad that you should consider an alternative route – perhaps even going all the way to Kasanka, and approaching from the west.

Where to stay Although many people will press on to reach Shoebill Camp, there's one option near Chiundaponde that's worth considering:

Nakapalayo Village (6 local-style chalets, camping) Contact via Kasanka (see page 328). ⊕ NAKAPA 12°16.542'S, 30°34.565'E. This new tourism project, started in early 2004, is about 3–4km south of Chiundaponde, & is signposted from the main track between Chiundaponde & Waka Waka. The village has built extra chalets in the traditional style: neat, rectangular structures made out of traditional mud bricks with smooth, small, arrow-shaped open windows, & twin or dbl beds with mattresses & mosquito nets. They share very clean long-drop toilets, & bathrooms that are simply reed shelters with showers – buckets on a high shelf from which you scoop water over yourself.

Nakapalayo's people have been trained by members of the Kawaza Village community, in South Luangwa, and offer a variety of activities. Most visitors will take a wander around the village with one of the local guides to see, learn & try everyday activities like drawing water, pounding cassava or cultivating the fields. However, there are also opportunities to visit the village headman, or local chief, to learn about the culture & history of the Bisa people; to visit Chiundaponde School, the rural health centre or one of the local churches; to meet the village's traditional healer to learn about the medicinal uses of the area's flora; & to enjoy dancing & storytelling around the fire. If you're staying, then the villagers will also prepare tasty traditional meals for you. This project is still relatively new, but I've had a glowing report from one visitor, who described the people as 'just the most lovely lot in the world'. Nakapalyo is worth supporting if you're passing through the area. *Chalet US60 pp, camping US$30 pp, both inc activities & traditional food. Day visit US$20 pp, inc lunch & activities. Camping only US$7 pp.*

LAVUSHI MANDA NATIONAL PARK (*Park fees US$5 pp/day; vehicle US$15/*day) This park is potentially interesting for its hilly and very pleasant landscape, though sadly it has lost some of its animals to poachers over the last few decades. Lavushi Manda's rocky, undulating land would make parts of it difficult to farm, so, until tourism to Zambia is substantially bigger, there is little incentive for anyone to try to rejuvenate its fortunes by restocking it with game.

The good news is that in April 2011, the Kasanka Trust took over the management of the park. Working as part of a donor-funded development project, they plan to start anti-poaching and roadbuilding immediately. That said, it's likely to take at least a few years before this wilderness area will have the road network and accommodation to accommodate visitors – but watch this space ...

Geography Lavushi Manda is over three times the size of Kasanka, and covers 1,500km² including the Lavushi Hills. It is easily reached from the Great North Road, is almost equidistant from Serenje and Mpika, and the landscape is attractive and undulating. To the north the land slopes away, and the park's streams all drain into the Lulimala, Lukulu or Lumbatwa rivers and thence ultimately into the Bangweulu Basin.

Miombo woodland covers most of the park, with some areas of riparian forest nearer the larger streams and many grassy dambos. Though this is attractive and the scouts report that there are still populations of game left, the area has only one accessible road.

Getting there and around The one east–west road through the park can be dreadful. Driving in the dry season is a challenge with big muddy gullies and areas where the road has just been washed away; when last crossing the park in June, I averaged about 15km/h. In the wet season, I'd expect this to be exceedingly time-consuming at best, and totally impassable at worst.

From the east The turning to Lavushi Manda from the main Mpika–Serenje road (⊕ TULMGM 12°16.934'S, 31°8.037'E) is about 141km northeast of the Chinese road (the turning to Mansa and Kasanka) and about 60km from Mpika. There is currently a large and very old signboard here pointing the way to Lavushi Manda and Bangweulu Swamps – but it looks as if it will disintegrate at any moment.

This road goes across the TAZARA railway line, and 12km later enters the park via a scout post and checkpoint (⊕ MUFUBU 12°16.240'S, 31°2.627'E). After another 20km or so you'll reach a good, solid concrete bridge over the lovely Lukulu River (⊕ LUKULU 12°14.480'S, 30°52.227'E).

From the west There is only one good track which heads east from Chiundaponde, passing the turn-off to Bangweulu. A little over 20km later you'll enter Lavushi Manda at the Lutimwe scout post (⊕ LAVUS1 12°14.230'S, 30°46.856'E) – which is just above a crossing of the Lutimwe River. This is a little over 10km from the good bridge over the Lukulu River (⊕ LUKULU 12°14.480'S, 30°52.227'E) mentioned above.

Where to stay As yet there are no camps or campsites in Lavushi Manda, and doubt over whether camping is even allowed, although the possibility of a small campsite is under consideration. For the present, if you want to camp, contact the Kasanka Trust (e *wasa@kasanka.com*) for the latest information, or drop into the ZAWA office in Mpika and enquire there. If the answer is yes, you'll need all your food, water and equipment.

What to see and do Talk to the team at Kasanka if you're curious about the latest situation here. Driving through the park makes an interesting diversion;

it is a convenient route into the Bangweulu Game Management Area. Although few regard it as a destination in itself, it might make a good area for exploration if you are a very dedicated hiker. If you are planning on venturing off the main road, you'll probably want to arrange for one of the scouts from the gate to accompany you.

THE BANGWEULU WETLANDS

This area is often described, in clichéd terms, as one of Africa's last great wilderness areas. That might be overstating its case a little, but it is certainly a very large and very wild area, which very few people really know and understand.

Though most visitors' image of a wilderness area is an unpopulated, barren tract of land, the Bangweulu Wetlands encompasses numerous small villages. It remains home to some 90,000 local people, who still hunt and fish here, as their ancestors have done for centuries.

PROTECTION OF THE WETLANDS The old way of conserving an area by displacing the people and proclaiming a national park clearly hasn't worked in much of Zambia: witness the minimal game left in many of the lesser-known parks. Thus a more enlightened approach of leaving the people on the land, and encouraging them to develop through sustainable management of their natural resources, is a more modern way to attempt to preserve as much of the wildlife as possible. Despite this approach, the area's population was growing, illegal hunting was rife, and there were fears for the future of the wildlife.

The area was designated a Wetland of International Importance in 1991, and has also been defined as an Important Bird Area. When the WWF became involved in trying to help local communities to manage the area sustainably, the aim was to create a community partnership park (CCP) where illegal fishing would be stopped and the area intensively managed like a national park.

Then, in 2008, African Parks – already successful in turning round the management of Liuwa Plain National Park (see page 487) – was invited by the local chiefs and community representatives to take over responsibility for the park and to protect the region's resources in partnership with the community and ZAWA. The result was the declaration in 2010 of the Chikuni Community Partnership Park, an area of 2,900km² that is augmented by the 3,100km² of the surrounding Bangweulu GMA. Through education, training and law enforcement, it is aimed to restore and protect the environment, while monitoring fishing within the wetlands and implementing a seven-year programme of restocking the larger mammals.

GEOGRAPHY The low-lying basin containing Lake Bangweulu and its wetlands receives one of the highest rainfalls in the country – over 1,400mm per annum. On the northwestern edge of the basin is Lake Bangweulu itself, about 50km long and up to 25km wide. This is probably the largest body of water within Zambia's borders, and an excellent spot for watching the local fishermen but, apart from the lake's remarkable white, sandy beaches, is of little interest to most visitors. It is easily reached at Samfya, a small town on the main road from Serenje to Mansa. See also *Chapter 12*, pages 370–1, for comments on Samfya and the surrounding area.

The more fascinating areas here are the vast wetlands to the southeast of the lake, which cover an area two to three times the size of the lake, and the seasonally flooded grasslands to the south of those wetlands.

The wetlands and grasslands are areas with few roads and lots of wildlife. It's one of the few regions of Zambia where the local communities are beginning to use the wildlife in their GMAs as a really sustainable source of income. There is little development here, just a small, tented lodge and a simple community-run camp for visitors who arrive on their own. The area still has many residents who continue to fish and eke out a living directly from the environment, but gradually the community development schemes are beginning to tap into tourism as a way to fund sustainable development.

FLORA AND FAUNA With access to the wetlands, the birdlife can be amazing and the animals impressive. However, choose the time of year for your visit very carefully: the type of fauna to be seen, and the activities required to see it, will vary hugely with the season.

Animals

The speciality here is the black lechwe, an attractive dark race of the lechwe that is endemic to the Bangweulu area. The only other places where it has been recorded are the swamps beside Lake Mweru, where its status is now exceedingly questionable, and the Nashinga Swamps near Chinsali, where it has been re-introduced. It is much darker than the red lechwe found throughout southern Africa, or the race known as the Kafue lechwe which occur in the Lochinvar area. I think it's by far the most attractive of the three.

The current population in this area is estimated at 100,000 animals, and herds measured in their thousands are common on the dry floodplains around the wetlands. As well as these huge herds of black lechwe you'll find other animals including sitatunga, tsessebe, reedbuck, common duiker and oribi. Zebra are doing very well; about nine were released here at first, translocated from a game farm near Lusaka, and they have now bred up to a healthy herd which is often visible on the plains. Elephant and buffalo are frequently seen; predators are uncommon but hyena and leopard are sometimes observed. Often seen at dusk or dawn, or on a night drive, side-striped jackal are very common. White-tailed mongooses, civets and genets are also frequent nocturnal sightings.

Birds

The Bangweulu area's big attraction is the unusual and rare shoebill (see box, opposite), a massive grey bird sometimes known as the whale-headed stork. The population of shoebills in Bangweulu is reckoned to be as high as 1,000, making this a vital refuge for this very threatened species. They do not migrate, and so are particularly sensitive to disturbance. They breed in the papyrus here, in May and June, and nowhere else in southern Africa – so visitors should be careful not to disturb them when they are sitting on their nests.

Aside from the elusive shoebill, the birdlife in the wetlands is amazing throughout the year, making it well worth the effort required to get here. The commoner birds include the little, cattle, black and great white egrets; black-headed, purple, squacco and grey herons; sacred, glossy and hadeda ibis; knob-billed, yellow-billed, fulvous and white-faced whistling ducks; open-billed storks, pygmy geese, pratincoles and grey-headed gulls. Plovers are well represented, with blacksmith, wattled, three-banded, crowned, Caspian and long-toed varieties – and recently there's also been an influx of spurwing plovers.

Migrants that stop here while the floodwaters are high include flamingos, whilst pelicans and spoonbills are normally resident. Meanwhile Bangweulu is a very important reserve for wattled cranes, which occur in large flocks and are readily seen. (There are greater numbers here than almost anywhere else, with the

The huge, rare and prehistoric-looking shoebill is found only in a few inaccessible spots between southern Sudan and northern Zambia – making it Africa's most sought-after species for birdwatchers.

Shoebills stand up to 1.4m tall, with a strong likeness to the dodo. They have always been named for their ungainly beaks, which resemble a wooden shoe, and older literature refers to them as whale-headed storks, whilst Arab traders knew them as *abu markub,* which means 'father of the shoe'. Their scientific name, *Balaeniceps rex,* means 'king whalehead'.

Shoebills can look rather sinister when viewed head-on, with their massive beaks and a frowning glare, but in profile they appear charmingly dolphin-like with a mouth that apparently smiles, and huge eyelashes. Despite this beguiling look, their mandibles are razor sharp; their upper bill ends in a curved hook that's used to pierce and hold their slippery prey. Their plumage is bluish slate-grey, with a slightly darker head which sports a small tuft of feathers that can be raised to form a crest. Their legs are long and dark, and their toes lack any webbing.

Shoebills inhabit a precise ecological niche: they specialise in feeding on large fish that live in poorly oxygenated waters of swamps and wetlands – particularly lungfish. They are usually seen standing motionless beside slow, deep-water channels, particularly in areas where fish concentrate – like the narrow channels where spreading waters spill out onto seasonally flooded areas. They remain still for hours, waiting for fish to surface for air, when they ambush with a swift and powerful strike. They will prey on species other than lungfish, and are also said to take amphibians, water-snakes, monitor lizards, terrapins, rats, young waterfowl and, some sources report, even young crocodiles.

Although they prefer to hunt in fairly open areas, where it's easy for them to take off if disturbed, they nest in large, flat nests found in denser vegetation – often papyrus. Between one and three eggs are laid, though only one chick usually survives. It takes about four and a half months for this silvery-grey chick to fledge and become independent, then a further three or four years until it first breeds.

Taxonomists have long debated if the shoebill is a member of the stork, the heron or the pelican family, as various characteristics suggest one or another. However, DNA studies now conclude that shoebills are closely related to pelicans, but in a family of their own.

Given their restricted and remote habit, shoebills are incredibly difficult to study and consequently relatively little is known about them. Estimates of the total world population seem to be around the 5,000–10,000 mark. We know that their main stronghold is in the Sudd, in southern Sudan, and that they are also found in Murchison Falls National Park in Uganda, the Moyowosi-Kigosi Swamp in western Tanzania, Manovo-Gounda-Saint Floris National Park in the Central African Republic, and, allegedly, in Akagera National Park in Rwanda (though nobody on the ground in Rwanda seems to know about them!).

We also know that they are, sadly, occasionally sold for meat by local people and for profit by foreign collectors – as shoebills are one of the most expensive birds in the trade. So if you are fortunate enough to see them, try to keep your distance and minimise any disturbance.

Bangweulu Area   **THE BANGWEULU WETLANDS**

11

possible exception of the Kafue Flats.) The wetlands' shallow waters are ideal for smaller waders, like sandpipers, godwits and avocets. Other smaller birds worthy of particular note include the swamp flycatcher, lesser jacana, white-cheeked bee-eater (aka blue-breasted in east African literature) and Fülleborn's and rosy-breasted longclaws (which is the local name for the birds known as pink-throated further south). There are plenty of raptors around, with fish eagles, marsh harriers and bateleur eagles particularly common. On the flat grass plains around the wetlands, Denham's bustards are frequently seen striding around.

WHEN TO GO There are many reasons to come to Bangweulu – only one of which is the birding. So choose your season carefully.

January and February are the heart of the rainy season, when the waters are rising. It's the worst time of year for the small, biting lechwe flies and other insects, so insect repellent is vital. Arriving with a head-net, covering your face and neck below your hat, would not be going too far.

This is a great time for birding, as many of the residents will be in breeding plumage, and there will be lots of migrants around – although shoebills usually arrive only at the end of February. The lechwe are in the swamps at this time, whilst other mammals have retreated to the woodlands on the margins of the water.

Water levels peak in **March**, though the rains draw to a close only around April. From **May** the water levels start slowly to recede and travelling begins to get easier by the end of the month. This is the best time to go for shoebills, which are often seen within sight of Shoebill Camp, along with countless other wading and water-loving species. Like many of these birds, visitors to Bangweulu will often spend a lot of time wading if they're keen to see shoebills at close range!

Towards the end of this period and into **June and July**, the waters pull back from the flat, seasonally flooded plains around the wetlands, exposing large areas of fertile, open grasslands – like the Chimbwi Plain. These attract huge herds of black lechwe along with tsessebe and other herbivores from the woodland margins. It's a great time for game drives, with night drives often yielding genets, side-striped jackals, civets and various mongooses. In the wetlands, the water has receded further and the shoebills have moved closer to the lake – so seeing them involves longer mokoro (dugout canoe) journeys from Shoebill Camp. That said, in early June I managed half-a-dozen sightings in one long day – and even later in July you are still almost guaranteed to see a shoebill if you apply enough effort. Though days are warm, the nights are very cold – with temperatures dropping to almost freezing.

In **August and September** the floodplains and outer reaches of the wetlands become even drier; Shoebill Camp is no longer an island, and most wildlife viewing is done on foot or by 4x4. The shoebills have retreated into the permanent swamps, and it takes a bit of determination (and a mini-expedition) to get close to them, though in recent years it has been very possible to see them at this time of year. The Lukulu River is the focus of much wildlife, whilst concentrations of storks and other birds form 'fishing parties' in the remnants of drying pools where fish and snails are stranded.

By **October** the land is parched and dusty everywhere except deep in the heart of the wetlands, far from Shoebill Camp. In **November and December** the first rains bring some relief, as well as a flush of new grass on the plains, which attracts massive herds of black lechwe back from the wetlands, and tsessebe in more moderate numbers from the woodlands.

GETTING THERE Getting to Bangweulu isn't always easy. You'll need to do one of the following:

- Organise a special 'mobile' trip here with an experienced safari company. (I know of none that regularly runs trips here – although the Kasanka team will sometimes organise 4x4 transfers to/from Bangweulu.)
- Fly into here, and then continue by flying out. This is how most people visit; although not cheap it is the easiest way to organise, and the most relaxing way to visit.
- Drive in here with your own fully equipped 4x4. This isn't easy or quick, but it can be fun if you've an adventurous streak and can be self-sufficient.

Organised trips There's only one company working on the ground in this area at present: the Kasanka Trust (see page 328 for contact details, and www.kasanka.com for an informative website). They run Kasanka National Park and Shoebill Camp. You can book a trip with them directly or, more usually, arrange it through the tour operator (see pages 44–5) who is organising the rest of your trip in Zambia for about the same price as booking direct.

Fly-in trips These must be pre-arranged. You can fly in to Shoebill Camp, as there is an airstrip (called Chimbwe) at Chikuni, just 3km from Shoebill. You'll be transferred to the camp from there, and your activities will be arranged for you. There is currently no 'schedule' for these flight transfers, and so they are relatively costly for one person because you need to hire the whole plane. Consequently, the price becomes more economic for two or three passengers. Flying in will give you a view of the wetlands and surrounding plains that you can't get from the ground – it's fascinating!

In early May, Robin Pope Safaris (see page 268) operate a six-night 'Shoebill Safari' that combines a trip to Shoebill Camp with their Nkwali lodge in the South Luangwa (*US$4,067/4,767 pp sharing/single FBA, inc transfers from Lusaka*).

Driving yourself From around November to early May, driving yourself on any of these routes can be very challenging – not to say wet, muddy and very slow. If you don't know what you're doing, you're likely to get stranded. By contrast, in the dry season it is fine, although note that there are very few vehicles on some of these tracks, and you always need a fully equipped 4x4 – with your own food and supplies.

From Chiundaponde to Chikuni If you're approaching from Waka Waka, then to reach Bangweulu just continue straight through Chiundaponde, heading roughly north. After leaving the village, you'll find the track bends slowly round to the right before crossing a small bridge. Barely 500m after this bridge is a left turn (✛ TUSBIL 12°13.451'S, 30°35.330'E) onto a track which is small and easy to miss; this leads northwest to Bangweulu. This turning is about 4km east of Chiundaponde, and a fraction under two hours' drive from Waka Waka.

Barely 100m north of the turning is a scout post – and it's always worth checking with the scouts here for the latest news and directions. (There's a fairly reliable radio here that's in close touch with Chikuni and, in case of problems, could even reach Kasanka.) Follow the track northwest, and after about 19km you'll pass Mwelushi Middle Basic School. In another 20km you'll reach Muwele village (✛ TUMUWE 11°59.226'S, 30°22.850'E) where the track splits; the left fork leads in a more westerly direction towards Chikuni. At times this track resembles more of a footpath than a road, but don't give up!

About 6km after the village, the road forks (✛ TUNSOB 11°59.098'S, 30°19.720'E), with the left turn going to Nsobe Camp. If you continue straight on, without turning to Nsobe, you will soon emerge from low scrub into a plain of open grass, stretching for as far as you can see. (Look around you – that dark reddish colour on the horizon may just be thousands of black lechwe!) Here you'll see the start of a long causeway leading to Chikuni; this is in poor condition, and generally not used. In recent years it has been better, in the dry season, to follow the vehicle tracks which run parallel to the causeway. In the wet season you really need experienced, up-to-date local advice – which, when levels are low, will generally be to splash through the water on existing tracks. During periods when water levels are very high, Chikuni has been inaccessible by vehicle.

However you are proceeding across the plains, about 8km after the turning to Nsobe, you reach the small scout post of Chikuni (⊕ CHIKUN 11°58.097'S, 30°15.279'E). Chikuni literally stands out as it's on top of a small rise in the plains, marked very clearly by a tall eucalyptus tree. This is one of the few trees within sight on the plains; there is another at Kaleha, about 8km east along the Lukulu River.

If you're going to Shoebill Camp then you need to have pre-arranged your stay, and Chikuni is often the rendezvous point where you leave your vehicle, and continue by mokoro; in any case, you should stop, check with the scouts, and sign the register. The scouts here have a radio to contact Shoebill Camp (as well as the ZAWA scout post on the road from Chiundaponde). Somewhere beyond Chikuni, depending on water levels, the wetlands begin.

From Chikuni to Shoebill You should pre-book your time at Shoebill Camp, so take advice from the Kasanka team about how to get from Chikuni to Shoebill at the time of year when you are going. If the water's high (typically January to June) then you may need to leave your vehicle at Chikuni and reach the camp by mokoro (*Kw75,000 pp*).

Later in the year you should be able to drive, in which case you sign in with the scouts at Chikuni and then pass straight through. Follow the direction of the airstrip for part of its length, and then hit out at 30° to your right, where you should find the tracks of other vehicles to the Shoebill Island causeway. If in doubt, try scanning the flat horizon for Shoebill's distinctive rectangular water tower amongst a patch of small trees.

Facing the camp, you will need to bear slightly to the left in order to join the beginning of the causeway (or later on, depending on the water levels). However, the route varies a lot with the particular season, and so it's vital that you get directions from the team at Kasanka, or the scouts at Chikuni, before you try to drive here.

🏠 **WHERE TO STAY** There are two main camps in the Bangweulu area: Shoebill and Nsobe. If you're on an organised trip, or flying in, then you'll be staying at Shoebill. Nsobe was historically a hunting camp on the edge of the swamps, but now that that area has been afforded higher protection it has been taken over by African Parks. Although closed at the time of writing, it is expected to re-open as a photographic camp.

If you're driving yourself in a self-contained 4x4 with all your supplies (there is no other sensible way!) then you could possibly stop at Nakapalayo village on the way to Bangweulu (the campsite at Muwele village is no longer recommended except in an emergency). However, note that Shoebill Camp is further into the wetlands than the other camps – so most trips end up there at some stage!

🏠 **Shoebill Island Camp** (5 Meru-style tents, 2 chalets, camping) Contact via Kasanka (page 328). ⊕ SHUBIL 11°57.099'S, 30°14.300'E. Shoebill Camp stands on a small, permanent island, just 2.5km northwest of Chikuni as the stork flies. During the rains & for a few

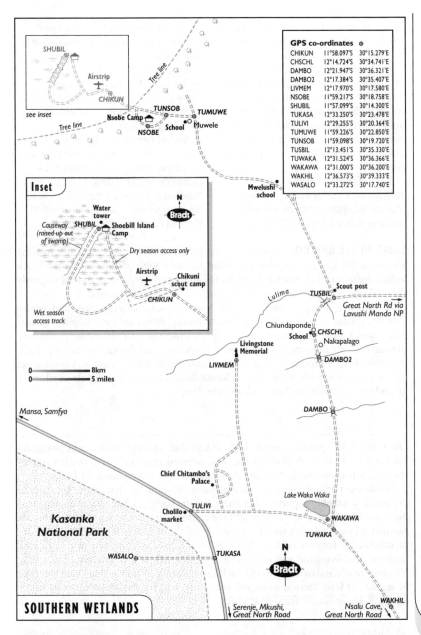

Inset

SHUBIL

Water tower

Causeway (raised up out of swamp)

SHUBIL

Shoebill Island Camp

Dry season access only

Airstrip

Chikuni scout camp

CHIKUN

Wet season access track

0 ——— 8km
0 ——— 5 miles

Mansa, Samfya

Kasanka National Park

WASALO

TUKASA

SHUBIL

Airstrip

CHIKUN

see inset

Tree line

TUNSOB

Nsobe Camp

NSOBE

School

TUMUWE

Muwele

Mwelushi school

Lulima

TUSBIL

Scout post

Great North Rd via Lavushi Manda NP

Chiundaponde

School

CHSCHL

Nakapalago

DAMBO2

Livingstone Memorial

LIVMEM

DAMBO

Chief Chitambo's Palace

Cholilo market

TULIVI

Lake Waka Waka

WAKAWA

TUWAKA

WAKHIL

WASALO

TUKASA

Serenje, Mkushi, Great North Road

Nsalu Cave, Great North Road

SOUTHERN WETLANDS

GPS co-ordinates ⊕		
CHIKUN	11°58.097'S	30°15.279'E
CHSCHL	12°14.724'S	30°34.741'E
DAMBO	12°21.947'S	30°36.321'E
DAMBO2	12°17.384'S	30°35.407'E
LIVMEM	12°17.970'S	30°17.580'E
NSOBE	11°59.217'S	30°18.758'E
SHUBIL	11°57.099'S	30°14.300'E
TUKASA	12°33.250'S	30°23.478'E
TULIVI	12°29.255'S	30°20.364'E
TUMUWE	11°59.226'S	30°22.850'E
TUNSOB	11°59.098'S	30°19.720'E
TUSBIL	12°13.451'S	30°35.330'E
TUWAKA	12°31.524'S	30°36.366'E
WAKAWA	12°31.000'S	30°36.200'E
WAKHIL	12°36.573'S	30°39.333'E
WASALO	12°33.272'S	30°17.740'E

months afterwards, this is within the wetlands, surrounded by channels & lagoons. Later in the year, it's left high & dry & accessible by 4x4 from Chikuni (see opposite).

Facilities are simple in this old-style safari camp. The original walk-in Meru-style tents each have a private bucket shower (hot water supplied

on request) & a flush toilet outside at the back. Added to these are 2 rather larger reed-&-thatch chalets, also with private flush toilets. During the drier months when the campsite isn't flooded, it is possible to camp.

The camp's other buildings, including a bar/ dining area & a breakfast room-cum-lookout point, also have thatched roofs on grass walls. During your stay, do make the effort to climb the water tower for camp's best view over the swamps.

Activities depend on the time of year; if there isn't enough water to travel through the swamps by canoe, the usual form of water transport, then the guides will take you walking over the floating reed bed in search of shoebills & other wildlife. Alternatively, drives will take you to the drier areas of the plains & into the surrounding woodlands.

Shoebill Camp isn't luxurious by modern safari standards, but it is comfortable and remains by far the best option in this area, where the environment, flora & fauna are fascinating, &

the activities can be excellent. This is a great destination for the adventurous who are keen on their wildlife, but it really needs to be booked in advance. *Kw280,000 pp self catering; US$370/520 pp sharing/sgl FB, inc activities (best pre-arranged), laundry, park fees. Camping Kw50,400 pp. Boating & guides extra.* ⏰ *All year when accessible – usually Mar–Jan.*

⚑ Nsobe Camp On the edge of the plains, Nsobe is a pretty basic campsite with just rooms for washing, a dining area & a kitchen, but its location on the edge of the plains is a big plus. In time there may be reed-&-thatch chalets here, too, but at present it's purely for those with all their own camping kit. *US$15 pp.*

WHAT TO SEE AND DO Driving, walking (often wading!), boating and canoeing are the activities here, all of which must be done with guides. While the black lechwe are spectacular, the birdlife is Bangweulu's main attraction, and the ungainly shoebill (see box, page 339) is a particular favourite among visitors.

As you might expect from an area which is seasonally flooded, and whose name translates as 'where the water meets the sky', Bangweulu is a largely trackless wilderness. It is easy to get lost if you simply head into it by yourself, and indiscriminate driving does much damage to both the soil structure and the ground-nesting birds. It is strongly recommended on safety and conservation grounds that 4x4 owners use one of the camps as a base for their explorations; and take local advice about where to go and how to minimise their environmental impact.

ISANGANO NATIONAL PARK

(*Park fees US$5 pp/day; vehicle US$15/day*) East of Lake Bangweulu, Isangano National Park covers 840km² of flat, well-watered grassland. The western side of the park forms part of the Bangweulu Wetlands, which are seasonally flooded.

While the park's ecosystem was originally the same as that of the Bangweulu GMAs, it is reliably reported that the game in Isangano has totally disappeared because of settlement, agriculture and the consequent subsistence hunting. There is no internal road network within the park at all, though there is quite a high density of subsistence farmers settled within its boundaries. With this in mind, it's very doubtful that Isangano will ever become a national park in anything but name. Visitors are advised to look toward the Bangweulu area if they want to visit this type of region. At least there is some infrastructure, and the local communities in the area will derive benefit from your visit.

12

Northern Zambia

To explore northern Zambia properly, and to visit the national parks here, requires some determination, or at least advance planning. All of the area's three main national parks have suffered from neglect over the years. However one, Sumbu, is hanging on with a couple of small lodges that could lead to a promising future. This large reserve is bounded by GMAs and Lake Tanganyika, one of the largest lakes in east Africa's Great Rift Valley, with a rich aquatic life found nowhere else. As well as more traditional safari pursuits, it offers snorkelling, diving and fishing, and it's a pleasant place to relax.

The north's other two parks, Mweru Wantipa and Lusenga Plain, may take more to get them back on the map, as neither has organised facilities for visitors, or good roads. Years of poaching have reduced the populations of game animals within them, and what animals are left remain shy and understandably wary of humankind. Outside of the national parks, this part of northern Zambia is a fascinating area, and there are numerous sights and waterfalls at which to stop and wonder.

Finally, a word about Nyika, a high plateau that straddles the Malawi border and provides the Luangwa with many of its tributaries. There are national parks on both sides of the border. Nyika Plateau National Park, on the Zambian side, is unlike anywhere else in the country: high mountains clothed in rolling heathlands and often draped with mist. It's a great walking destination, a cool respite after the heat of the Luangwa Valley and home to numerous endemic species. However, it's easiest to access from the east, from Malawi, and so it's often forgotten when talking of Zambian national parks.

GETTING ORGANISED Most tour operators based in Zambia specialise in wildlife safaris, but one specialises in northern Zambia (as well as further afield):

Thorn Tree Safaris \ 0214 221615; m 0966 436267; e thorntreesafaris@yahoo.com; www. thorntreesafaris.com. Run by Claire Powell, daughter of the owners of Thorn Tree Guesthouse, the mobile-safari operation of the same name covers the whole country but specialises in the north. All trips are tailor made, & can combine such diverse activities as diving & dhow safaris on Lake Tanganyika, small-group cycle tours through Zambia, Malawi & Tanzania, & tigerfishing on the Chambeshi River, with more conventional wildlife safaris. Thorn Tree also works closely with the charity Tanganyika Children.

THE GREAT NORTH ROAD TO MPULUNGU

The Great North Road stretches from Lusaka through Kapiri Mposhi to Mpika. Here it divides, with one fork going through Kasama and on to Mbala and Mpulungu – about 1,150km. This is the region's main artery, tarred all the way

and – having been resurfaced in 2009/10 – now largely free of the pot-holes that have dogged it for years.

KASAMA Kasama is centrally located, about 860km from Lusaka. Visitors to northern Zambia will invariably end up spending some time here, even if only to refuel and buy a few soft drinks. It is a busy little town, the regional capital, with lots going on. As it acts as a supply centre for much of the north of the country, there are some well-stocked stores, and a relatively large amount of traffic coming into, and leaving, town.

Getting there

By air Having been without an air service since 2005, Kasama now has a regular connection with Lusaka, via Ndola. Flights operated by Proflight (page 65) leave Lusaka on Monday and Thursday at 07.00, arriving at 10.00, and return at 14.00, all via Ndola. For charter flights, the regional specialist is Sky Trails (page 65).

By train The TAZARA station is about 7km south of town, on the right as you enter from Mpika. This is your last chance to disembark at a major town before the railroad turns east, away from Lake Tanganyika, towards the border at Tunduma. The express train from Kapiri Mposhi to Dar es Salaam passes through Kasama early on Wednesday at 03.09 and the slower train on Saturday at about 02.49, returning at 22.07 on Tuesday and 00.11 on Sunday respectively. A one-way express ticket to Dar costs about Kw93,000 in third class, rising to Kw160,000 in first class. For details, see pages 395–6.

By bus Kasama is an important regional hub for buses between Lusaka and the north, linking the town with Mbala and Mpulungu on Lake Tanganyika. Confusingly, each bus company has its own terminus, though the most reliable – Germin and Juldan Motors – are both based on Golf Road.

Regular buses run from both Lusaka and the Copperbelt to Kasama and on to Mpulungu. Departure and arrival times are the same in each direction: leaving

GPS REFERENCES FOR NORTHERN ZAMBIA

CHAMON	10°54.634'S, 31°05.344'E	MPULUN	08°45.907'S, 31°06.368'E
CHIMBR	09°33.082'S, 29°26.937'E	MUMBUL	10°55.801'S, 28°44.178'E
CHISHI	10°06.465'S, 30°55.100'E	MUSON	10°42.856'S, 28°48.858'E
FALLST	09°32.239'S, 29°27.874'E	MUTUNG	08°33.839'S, 30°12.405'E
KABWEL	09°31.432'S, 29°21.267'E	MWANSA	09°49.250'S, 28°45.350'E
KALAMB	08°35.831'S, 31°14.397'E	MWERUP	08°53.572'S, 29°28.878'E
KAPUTA	08°28.503'S, 29°39.990'E	NSAMA	08°53.448'S, 29°56.896'E
KASAMA	10°12.440'S, 31°11.290'E	NTUMBA	09°51.167'S, 28°56.652'E
KAWAMB	09°47.605'S, 29°04.675'E	SAMFYA	11°20.437'S, 29°33.526'E
KUNDAB	09°13.058'S, 29°18.258'E	SAMTJN	11°21.126'S, 29°29.453'E
MAMBIL	10°33.791'S, 28°48.858'E	SUMBU	08°31.221'S, 30°28.629'E
MANSA	11°12.076'S, 28°53.451'E	TOKAPU	09°07.531'S, 29°12.996'E
MBALA	08°50.694'S, 31°22.325'E	TOMWAN	09°49.317'S, 28°45.474'E
MBERES	09°44.078'S, 28°47.350'E	TOSHCT	09°27.486'S, 31°13.136'E
MPOROK	09°21.831'S, 30°07.432'E	TOSHC2	09°40.270'S, 30°41.628'E

Travellers on the TAZARA train will cross into Tanzania at Tunduma, some 245km northeast of Kasama. This is also a major crossing point for vehicles, with all the attendant queues and hassle that you might expect.

A Tanzanian visa, currently US$50, can be purchased at the border, but you'll need to pay in US dollars cash. There's a foreign exchange service at the bank near the immigration office.

To cross the border with a vehicle, you will require a temporary import permit (TIP) in place of a carnet, supplied on presentation of copies of both your passport, the vehicle's registration document and the exit document from Zambia. A month's road tax costs a further US$25, also payable in US dollars cash, and you'll also need to purchase third party insurance.

Lusaka, the Copperbelt or Mpulungu at midday, to arrive at their final destination at 04.00 the following morning. Fares are Kw150,000 each way.

There is also a postbus to Kasama from Lusaka, arriving in the town every Monday, Wednesday and Friday at 17.00.

For those heading west to Luwingu, the bus station is on the Luwingu Road towards the airport.

Going east is usually fairly straightforward, The road to Nakonde is pretty good, though it's worth checking the state of the roads at the end of the rainy season. If any of the pontoons are out of action, there's usually a sign on the way out of town saying so. An alternative option is to take the TAZARA train to Nakonde, at the border, then continue south by bus.

Hitchhiking Kasama is a good place for hitching. If you want to go north, to Mbala or Mpulungu, walk out beyond the roundabout with the crocodile statue, near the market, and start hitching there.

If you're heading south towards Mpika then you need to walk out past the TAZARA station, or perhaps a little further, hitching as you walk. There are some memorable speed humps on this road, which should slow down even the most ardent of speed-kings to a crawl.

Heading west or east is more difficult, as there is much less traffic. However, a traveller going in either direction is something of a rarity, so novelty value will encourage potential lifts. That said, most drivers will not have a clue where you're heading for.

Where to stay and eat There's no shortage of places to stay in Kasama, which boasts over 30 guesthouses. Of these, a few stand out, with Thorn Tree and Kasembo particularly recommended. Note that here more than ever price is no guide to quality.

In town
Kasama Lodge (11 rooms) Zambia Rd; 0214 221039; e enquiries@zambiahostels.com; www.zambiahostels.com. Opposite Thorn Tree Guesthouse, & professionally run by the Hostels Board of Management, this small hotel has an airy location overlooking the escarpment. En-suite rooms are clean & modern, each with TV, kettle, mosi net & fan, & some with a sofa & fridge too. There's a bar & restaurant serving all meals ($$), & at the back is a pleasant courtyard. $$–$$$

⌂ **Dauson Lodge** (7 rooms) Luwingu Rd; ☏ 0214 221440; m 0977 760900/896278. Just off the Luwingu Rd to the airport, & a 5-min walk from the crossroads, this is a quiet, pleasant lodge. Its en-suite rooms, each with a dbl bed, fan, mosi net, TV & fridge, are spotlessly clean, & for TV addicts there's a large lounge with a big screen. Meals, such as chicken or beef stew, are available to residents. **$–$$**

⌂ **Thorn Tree Guesthouse** (7 rooms) Zambia Rd; ☏ 0214 221615; e kansato@iconnect.zm. Hazel & Ewart Powell came to this area of Zambia to teach in 1969 & stayed on to combine teaching with running a guesthouse. Consequently they've a fund of knowledge on the local area & its people, & can help you get the best out of the region.

Thorn Tree lies about 1km southwest of town, on the edge of an escarpment with a great view; it's a 2-min drive or 10-min walk. Coming from Lusaka, turn left at the main crossroads & continue for about 300m. Pass a park on your right, the government offices on the left, & a police station on the right, then take the right-hand fork & carry on for a further 650m; the

guesthouse is on the left. Alternatively, you can arrange for Ewart to collect you from the airport, station or buses.

Aside from a dbl room in the main house, rooms are in a purpose-built block overlooking the garden. All have mosquito nets, fans & TV, & all share a lounge, bar & dining area. Good, family-style meals are served, with most of the ingredients – from oranges & limes to eggs, coffee & tea, & even the jams & peanut butter – produced on the farm. It's a very homely place, suitable for children, where you can easily feel part of the family.

Thorn Tree has a small plunge pool in the grounds, & if you want to play tennis or golf, or swim, or if you need transport to a local attraction such as Chishimba Falls or Mwela Rock Paintings, they can help. For trips farther afield, Claire Powell runs a personal safari company, Thorn Tree Safaris (see page 345) with a particular focus on the Northern Province. **$–$$**

⌂ **JB Hotel** (30 rooms) Golf Rd; ☏ 0214 221452; m 0977 844149. With its central location opposite the town's fuel stations, JB is a pleasant hotel set in unexpectedly attractive

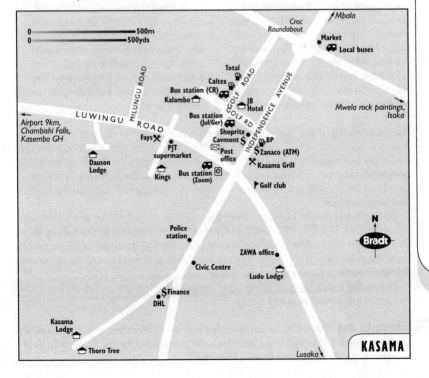

KASAMA

12

gardens, with a restaurant, an outside bar & shaded gazebos. Inside, the rooms, 19 of them en suite, lead off rather institutional corridors but all are clean & cool, with tiled floors, TVs, mosi nets & fridges. **$**

🏠 **King's Guesthouse** (14 rooms) 2 Mulilansolo Cres; ☏ 0214 221028; 📱 0977 513255. Tucked away behind gates off Luwingu Rd, King's seems to be larger inside than would appear possible. Rooms & chalets are dotted around the mature gardens, some with a veranda & chairs, & all en suite. Thatched sunshades

shelter groups of tables & chairs among the trees, interspersed with life-size models of kudu, hippo & other animals. Inside there's a central lounge with a seriously ornate TV, & a dining area. **$**

🏠 **Ludo Lodge** (9 rooms) Mpika Rd; 📱 0977 794804/486741. On the right of the road to Lusaka, just past the golf club & next to the ZAWA offices, Ludo Lodge is well managed & very clean. En-suite rooms are nicely appointed with pine furniture & tiled floors, as well as a TV, fan & fridge. All meals are served in the restaurant. **$**

Out of town

🏠 **Kasembo Guesthouse** (14 rooms) Luwingu Rd; ☏ 0214 230065; 📱 0977 748453; e bshone@zamnet.zm. ⊕ KASEMB 10°13.714'S, 31°07.506'E. Some 8km west of Kasama, Kasembo Guesthouse is on the farm of the same name. To get there, take Luwingu Rd east for about 750m beyond the airport, then turn left down a farm road (⊕ TOKASE 10°13.239'S, 31°07.665'E), signposted to Kasembo Farms, & follow the signs for about 1km to the guesthouse.

Kasembo Farms was founded 50 years ago & is now owned & run by the Missionaries of Marianhill. It stretches for about 400ha, & keeps around 175 Friesian cows (40 are milked), 150 pigs, 150 sheep, 2,000 hens for egg laying, & a few thousand chickens for the pot. The priests say that they leave things as natural as possible. 'Our vegetable garden has never seen a grain of fertiliser in its existence,' commented one. With

most of the basic ingredients grown on the farm, it's no surprise that meals are a highlight here.

Accommodation for visitors (of any creed) consists of large rooms grouped in pairs around a grassy central area, shaded by indigenous trees, & near a good pool. Each pair of rooms shares a toilet & separate shower, while each room has locally made pine furniture with a dbl or twin beds, mosquito nets, a fan, fridge & TV. Just one has its own bathroom & separate lounge. It's a cool, tranquil spot, completely without hassle.

The missionaries make a point of ensuring that the service is attentive & discussions with them can give you an interesting insight into the area. Several types of local beer & a few spirits are on offer during meals. If you arrive in town & want to stay then ask at the Kasembo Farms shop, behind PEP Stores & near the Caltex fuel station. **$** *exc b/fast.*

Bushcamping If you just want a quiet place in the bush to camp 'rough' around Kasama, then one very experienced old Zambian hand recommended the old (defunct) Kalungwishi State Ranch to me, about two hours' drive from town. He comments that it's a fantastic place to explore and is enormous with very few local people about and lots of nice habitat for birds, including good miombo woodlands and large dambos.

To get there take the Luwingu Road, then turn north before you reach Luwingu (about 20km). Drive past Chitoshi and aim for the headwaters of the Kalungwishi River. (You'll need a good map of the area!) Pass the trig-point tower (from which there is a good view, if you climb it) and take a left into the old ranch. There are two entrance roads to Kalungwishi, and at least one still has a sign.

The reality is that you can camp safely pretty well anywhere in this region – just be sure to ask if you are near a village.

✗ **Where to eat** For a bite to eat there are lots of small cafés, including **Fays** on Luwingu Road. For something a bit more substantial, head for the **Kasama Grill** on Independence Avenue, close to the crossroads.

If you are driving towards Mbala, you won't go hungry on the road, since 107km north of Kasama you come to a collection of **roadside stalls** near Senga Hill (⊕ SENGA 09°21.968'S, 31°14.496'E). These sell all manner of fast food, including chicken and chips, fritters, and delicious potato samosas that almost justify a stop in their own right.

Other practicalities Shoprite has come to Kasama, and with it a vast array of foodstuffs and commodities are now obtainable that were very difficult to find previously.

Should you need information on the national parks, there's a **ZAWA office** in town, next to Ludo Lodge on the Lusaka road.

Excursions around Kasama

Mwela rock paintings (*Entry US$15/7 adult/child; vehicle US$5/day; camping US$15 pp, inc entry*) There are over 700 cave paintings outside Kasama, most of them to the east of the town, making this one of the richest areas for rock art anywhere in Africa. While a few of the images are representational, the tradition here is of enigmatic geometric designs that defy easy interpretation. The art is generally considered to be the work of the Twa people, around 2,000 years old, but has variously been dated to late Stone-Age peoples.

The paintings are spread over a wide area across six recognised sites: Sumina, Mulundu and Changa are to the south of the road; Mwela and Muankole to the north; while Luimbo lies in the opposite direction, just beyond the airport on the left. To reach the main sites, take the road towards Isoka, east of Kasama, for about 6km until you see a sign indicating that this is a national monument. Sign in at the kiosk with the caretaker, and he will lead you around the paintings (and would appreciate a tip at the end).

While it's possible to spend hours here, for most casual visitors just a few paintings will suffice to give an idea of the style and scale of the work. Highlights include the Lion at Sumina, and a series of three paintings on the Mwela site (⊕ MWELA 10°12.250'S, 31°13.958'E). An excellent book on the paintings, *Zambia's Ancient Rock Art: The Paintings of Kasama*, is available in Lusaka; for details, see *Appendix 3*, page 537.

Chishimba Falls (*Entry US$15/7 adult/child; vehicle US$5/day; camping US$15 pp, inc entry*) The Luombe River at Chishimba is harnessed partially to run an unobtrusive hydro-electric station, but the water that is left makes for a super series of waterfalls: one artificial and the other two natural. The first, Mutumuna, has a drop of about 20m where it descends onto a rocky riverbed, and it's probably the prettiest of the three. In the centre, protected by a weir, is Kevala, more of a series of rapids than falls, with a large pool created by the weir. The third, Chishimba itself, is a short walk downstream. Here, water spouts over steep cliffs into a deep, rocky canyon that is, according to legend, inhabited by spirits. If you walk right down to the bottom you can stand behind the curtain of water with the rock face at your back and the water in front of you.

Close to the central weir are a sheltered picnic place and a campsite with flush toilets, and a visitor information centre. Walkways have been constructed between the falls, with thatched viewing shelters at strategic points, but note that at Chishimba Falls in particular there is a sheer drop that is not fenced, so it is important to take extra care. The helpful caretaker is usually happy to act as a guide.

To get to Chishimba (✪ CHISHI 10°06.465'S, 30°55.100'E), head west out of Kasama on the tarred Luwingu Road towards the airport. Continue along here for 25km, to the end of the tar, then turn right onto the wide gravel road to Mporokoso. Follow this for about 11km to a clear signpost to the falls (✪ TOCHIS 10°06.176'S, 30°55.694'E), where you turn left, then right again after about 200m, and continue for a further 500m to a parking area.

Chilambwe Falls (*Entry US$5; camping US$10 pp*) About 72km from Kasama on the Mporokoso road, these attractive falls are worth a day trip – though there are no designated facilities for campers. Visitors can also hike to the top of the falls and follow the river through open fields.

Chambeshi Monument (*Entry US$10/5 adult/child; vehicle US$5/day; camping US$15 pp, inc entry*) At the north end of the bridge over the Chambeshi River, about 85km south of Kasama, is a monument beside the road (✪ CHAMON 10°54.634'S, 31°05.344'E). It marks the place where General von Lettow-Vorbeck, Commander of the German forces in East Africa during World War I, surrendered to Hector Croad, the British District Commissioner, on 14 November 1918.

Von Lettow-Vorbeck and his forces had marched south from German East Africa (now Tanzania). They didn't realise that the war in Europe had been over for three days until told by Croad. Upon hearing the news from the British the Germans agreed to march back to Abercorn (now called Mbala) and there hand over their prisoners to the British. It seems as if it was all very civilised.

Part of the monument is a breech-loading field gun, made in 1890, which was the type that the German forces used during World War I.

Tigerfishing on the Chambeshi River One of Zambia's more remote fishing rivers, the Chambeshi offers tiger fishing in almost guaranteed isolation. Trips of two nights or longer are run between September and April by Thorn Tree Safaris (page 345), using large canvas safari tents complete with hot bucket showers, and with three-course dinners served under the stars.

MBALA The small town of Mbala lies just off the road from Kasama to Mpulungu. From here, the road to Mpulungu descends into the merciless heat of the rift valley – so enjoy the relative cool whilst you can.

Known as Abercorn when the country was under British rule, Mbala was where the German General von Lettow-Vorbeck handed over his prisoners to the British at the end of World War 1 (see above). Today, it is a quiet backwater notable for the Moto Moto Museum, which is one of the country's best museums. It is also the access point by road for Kalambo Falls (see page 354).

Mbala has a couple of **fuel stations**, two **banks**, a **post office** and even a small prison (the old prison building is now a historic monument). You can buy most things in the **shops**, including a decent selection of fresh fruit and vegetables from Tafisa Trading, opposite the bus station.

Getting there and away Regular long-distance buses ply the route between Lusaka and Mpulungu, stopping at the bus station on Mbala's main street. Typically, southbound buses leave Mbala in the early hours of each morning. The one-way fare to Lusaka is around Kw175,000.

There are also buses to Kitwe run by both Germins and Zoom, between them covering every day except Monday, and leaving Mbala shortly after midnight.

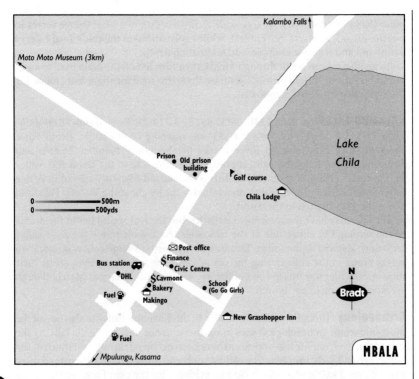

Kalambo Falls ↑

Moto Moto Museum (3km)

Lake
Chila

Prison ● Old prison
building

▶ Golf course

Chila Lodge ⌂

0 ————— 500m
0 ————— 500yds

⊠ Post office
$ Finance
Bus station 🚐 ● Civic Centre
● DHL
$ Cavmont
Fuel ⛽ $ ● Bakery   School
● Makingo   ● (Go Go Girls)

N

⌂ New Grasshopper Inn

⬥ Fuel

⟋ Mpulungu, Kasama

Bradt

MBALA

⌂ **Where to stay** Just outside town, Lake Chila Lodge is a welcome newcomer to Mbala. In town itself, the New Grasshopper Inn is the only place worthy of recommendation. The Makungu Guesthouse, formerly the Abercorn Arms, has seen better days – and I have had a report that it is not safe. The Christy Inn, 2km outside town, has sunk into a state of disrepair.

⌂ **Lake Chila Lodge** (5 rondavels)
m 0977 795241/824499, 0968 503431;
e lakechilalodge@yahoo.com. ⊕ 08°50.389'S,
31°23.085'E. Just 1km northeast of town & right on the perennial Lake Chila, this new lodge in pleasant gardens is currently Mbala's best accommodation. Individual en-suite rondavels are spacious with dbl beds & a fridge. There's a bar & a restaurant whose menu ranges from nshima to pasta & other Western-style dishes. **$**

⌂ **New Grasshopper Inn** (22 rooms)
Makanta Rd; m 0977 504580. In a relatively peaceful location, but within walking distance of the centre, the New Grasshopper's rooms are pretty basic, but it's a friendly & reasonably secure place to stop for the night. Substantial meals such as chicken with nshima or potatoes are served in the simple restaurant, but the cavernous bar next door could become rowdy at w/ends. **$** *exc b/fast.*

What to see and do

Moto Moto Museum (⊕ MOTOMO 08°49.265'S, 31°21.416'E. ⊕ 09.00–16.45 *daily exc Christmas & New Year; entry US$3 pp*) Opened in 1974, Moto Moto is perhaps the best place in the country for Bemba history and artefacts. At its heart is an extensive and well-presented collection of tools, craft instruments, and exhibits connected to traditional ceremonies and witchcraft, originally assembled by Father Corbeil, a missionary stationed at the nearby Kayambi Mission. The museum takes its name from Corbeil's nickname, Bwana Moto: he was renowned for calling for

12

moto (KiSwahili for 'fire'). A large-scale reconstruction of a local village serves to put the various artefacts into context, while explanations of the traditional roles of a husband and wife, for example, add fascinating depth.

To get there, head north through Mbala, then turn left off the main road towards Kalambo Falls by the old prison. Continue along this road for about 3km, following the signposts; it's clearly signposted.

KALAMBO FALLS (⊕ KALAMB 08°35.831'S, 31°14.397'E; ⊙ 06.00–18.00 daily; entry US$15/7 adult/child, vehicle US$5/day, camping US$15 pp inc entry) For a short distance the Kalambo River marks the boundary between Zambia and Tanzania. At the Kalambo Falls, it plunges over the side of the Great Rift Valley in one vertical drop of about 221m. This is the second-highest waterfall in Africa (after South Africa's Tugela Falls), about double the height of the Victoria Falls, and about the 12th-highest in the world.

The falls may have the impressive statistics, but the real appeal lies in the drama of the setting. On either side of the falls, sheer rock walls frame the river valley far below: Zambia to the south, Tanzania to the north. A large colony of marabou storks breed in the cliffs during the dry season. The falls themselves are at their most spectacular towards the end of the wet season, in February or March, though are worth visiting in any month.

Archaeology Though few visitors realise it, the Kalambo Falls are also one of the most important archaeological sites in southern Africa. Just above the falls, by the side of the river, is a site that appears to have been occupied throughout much of the Stone Age and early Iron Age. The earliest tools and other remains discovered there may be over 300,000 years old, including evidence for the use of fire.

It seems that the earlier sites of occupation were regularly flooded by the river. Each time this occurred, a fine layer of sand was deposited, thus preserving each layer of remains, tools and artefacts in a neat chronological sequence. Much later, the river cut into these original layers of sand and revealed the full sequence of human occupation to modern archaeologists.

For years Kalambo provided the earliest evidence of fire in sub-Saharan Africa – charred logs, ash and charcoal have been discovered amongst the lowest levels of remains. This was a tremendously important step for Stone-Age humans as it enabled them to keep warm and cook food, as well as to use fire to scare off aggressive animals. Burning areas of grass may even have helped man to hunt. However, more recent excavations of older sites in Africa have discovered evidence of the use of fire before the time when we believe that the site at Kalambo was occupied.

The site is also noted for evidence of much later settlement, from the early Iron Age. Archaeologists even speak of a 'Kalambo tradition' of pottery, for which they can find evidence in various sites in northern Zambia. It seems that the early Iron-Age farmers may have gradually displaced indigenous hunter-gatherers from about the 4th century AD: no further Stone-Age remains are found after that date. However, oral history from northern Zambia, along with the extensive rock art around Kasama, speaks of a recent survival of hunter-gatherers alongside farming peoples.

Getting there
By boat-taxi The mouth of the Kalambo River is around 17km from Mpulungu, so adventurous backpackers can take a boat upstream to near the base of the falls, then return the following day. From the lake it is a fairly strenuous but enjoyable

2½-hour walk to the top of the falls, where camping is allowed. You will need to bring all your own food and equipment.

There's a regular boat service along this route (see pages 360–1), on Monday, Wednesday and Friday, taking two hours in each direction. Boats leave the village of Chipwa very early in the morning, returning from Mpulungu the same day at around midday; as a *mzungu* (white person), you can expect to pay around Kw15,000. Since the times are very approximate, you could end up walking into the falls after dark, so it may be better to negotiate a private trip with one of the fishermen in Mpulungu.

A better option by far is to bring all your provisions and stay at one of the lodges nearer the falls – Mishembe Bay or (if either is open) Kalambo or Isanga Bay. Then you can make a day trip to the falls, perhaps even walking there.

Alternatively, small boats that ply between Mpulungu and Kasanga, in Tanzania, can drop you off one day, and pick you up the next.

Driving The falls are about 38km from Mbala, along a good track that has been recently graded. In the dry season it's perfectly possible to get through with a 2WD vehicle. Head north out of Mbala on the tar road towards Zombe and the Tanzanian border. Just past the golf club and lake to the right, the tar comes to an end. Beyond the bridge, take the left fork and continue to a clear signpost (✪ TOKALA 08°45.543'S, 31°06.884'E); turn left here – it's about 6km from Mbala. The road goes through villages and woodland, passing the currently impassable track to Isanga Bay Lodge (✪ TOIBL 08°41.634'S, 31°17.969'E) to the left. After 29km, you'll come to a fork (✪ 08°36.619'S, 31°14.133'E); bear right and follow the road as it descends steeply to the entrance to the falls.

Because of Kalambo's border position, policing it has been difficult in the past, and vehicles left unattended have been likely targets for theft. While this is still a potential hazard, there is a caretaker on site in daylight hours, so the threat is now considerably less.

⚠ Where to stay You can camp here, with stunning views to the west across the rift valley. There's a caretaker on site all day, but aside from a small shelter, facilities are limited to a couple of long-drop toilets.

LAKE TANGANYIKA AND ENVIRONS

LAKE TANGANYIKA Lake Tanganyika is one of a series of geologically old lakes that have filled areas of the main East African Rift Valley. Look at a map of Africa and you will see many of these in a 'string' down the continent: lakes Malawi, Tanganyika, Kivu, Edward and Albert are some of the larger ones. Zambia just has a small tip of Tanganyika within its borders, but it is of importance to the country. Access to Lake Tanganyika grants Zambia a real port with transport links to a whole side of Tanzania and (during peaceable times) direct access to Burundi. It also makes this one corner of Zambia totally different from the rest of the country, with a mix of peoples and a 'tropical central Africa' feel.

There are some well-established lakeside lodges, those to the east within striking distance of Kalambo Falls, and two in the vicinity of the little-known but viable Sumbu National Park.

Geography Lake Tanganyika is the deepest of the Rift Valley lakes of central/east Africa, with a maximum depth of about 1,470m, and is the second-deepest lake in

12

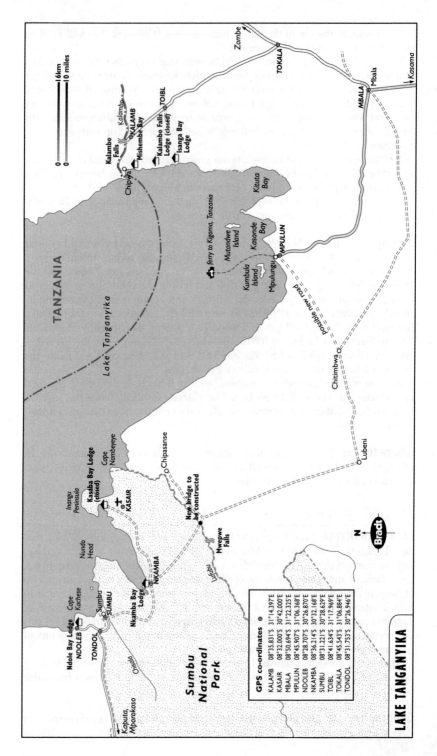

LAKE TANGANYIKA

GPS co-ordinates ⊕		
KALAMB	08°35.831'S	31°14.397'E
KASAIR	08°32.000'S	30°42.000'E
MBALA	08°50.694'S	31°22.325'E
MPULUN	08°45.907'S	31°06.368'E
NDOLEB	08°28.707'S	30°26.870'E
NKAMBA	08°36.214'S	30°32.168'E
SUMBU	08°31.221'S	30°28.629'E
TOIBL	08°41.634'S	31°17.969'E
TOKALA	08°45.543'S	31°06.884'E
TONDOL	08°31.753'S	30°26.946'E

the world. It has an area of around 34,000km² and is estimated to be about 10–15 million years old. The surface layers of water are a tropical 24–28°C and support virtually all of the known life in the lake.

Well below these, where it is too deep for the sun's light to reach, are separate, colder waters. Below about 200m, these are deprived of oxygen and hardly mix with the upper layers. They are currently the subject of much scientific study.

The lake has a variety of habitats around its 3,000km or so of shoreline, ranging from flat sands to marshy areas and boulder-strewn shores.

Flora and fauna

Flora The geology of the rocks around the lake has led to the water being unusually hard (between 7° and 11° dH), alkaline (average 8.4 pH) and rich in minerals for a freshwater lake. It is not an ideal environment for normal aquatic plants, so these are generally found near the entry of rivers into the lake but not elsewhere. Various species of algae have adapted to fill this ecological niche, and extensive 'lawns' of grass-like algae cover many of the lake's submerged rocks.

Animals The water's excellent clarity, the lack of cover and the rocky shores do not encourage either hippo or crocodiles, though both are more common around the relatively undisturbed shores of Sumbu National Park. They are also seen regularly near the mouths of rivers, and their presence must always be considered before you swim. The lake is a reliable source of water for game, which often comes to drink during the dry season.

Birds The birdlife on the shoreline is generally good, and the species found here also tend to represent many more of the typical east African birds than can be found elsewhere in Zambia. The area's more unusual residents include purple-throated cuckoo-shrikes, white-headed saw-wings, stout cisticolas, and Oustalet's white-bellied sunbird.

CICHLIDS

Cichlids are generally easy to keep in home aquaria, being small, colourful, and fairly undemanding. Several operations have sprung up around the lake in recent years to catch specimens for the pet trade, and fly them out to Europe and America. Indeed, one of the lake's lodges used to make most of its living from this, with tourism really just a sideline.

One of the characteristics of cichlids is the ability of individual species to adapt their colour at a very local level. Thus, one of the most popular cichlids for aquaria are the *Trophus sp*, which can be found in over 30 different colour morphs in different areas of the lake.

The largest of the cichlids found in Lake Tanganyika, indeed the largest in the world, is the nkupi (or emperor cichlid, to avoid confusion with the very different Zambezi fish, nkupi), *Boulengerochromis microlepis*, which grows up to 4kg in weight – in marked contrast to the tiny *Lamprologus multifaciatus*, which reaches a maximum length of just 1cm.

For a fascinating insight into the cichlids to be found in the lake, get hold of a copy of *Tanganyika Cichlids in their Natural Habitat* (see *Appendix 3*, page 536).

12

Fish Lake Tanganyika and the other lakes in the rift valley continue to fascinate both zoologists and aquarists as they have evolved their own endemic species of fish. So far, well over 450 have been identified in Tanganyika, of which over 252 species are in the Zambian part of the lake (and of those, 82 have been identified as endemic in a report by the Ramsar Convention, under which much of Lake Tanganyika and the surrounding area is protected). Most of the lake's fish species are from the *Cichlidae* family – or cichlids (pronounced sick-lids; see box, page 357), as they are known. Many of these are small, colourful fish that live close to the surface and the shoreline. Here they inhabit crevices in the rocks and other natural cavities, avoiding the attention of larger, predatory fish that patrol the deeper, more open, waters.

The lake is the most southerly home of both the goliath tigerfish and an endemic species of perch from the *Lates* family, the silver or Tanganyika perch, *Lates angustrifrons*. Three smaller species of perch are to be found in these waters, too, including the smallest, the buka, which along with kapenta is the target of commercial fishermen. There are also freshwater jellyfish which, interestingly, don't sting, and – very occasionally – a freshwater coelacanth is sighted.

Reptiles Two reptiles are endemic to the lake: the fish-eating Tanganyika water-snake, *Lycodonomorphus bicolor*, and the venomous Tanganyika water cobra, *Boulengerina annulata*.

What to see and do in and around the lake
Most of the lodges around the lake can organise a range of watersports and fishing, though it's as well to be aware that if these involve a boat trip, costs will reflect the high cost of fuel. For additional activities around Sumbu, see pages 368–9.

Swimming, snorkelling and diving Tanganyika is a marvellous lake in which to go snorkelling, or even scuba diving, as the numerous fish are beautifully coloured and there is seldom any need to dive deeply. Visibility depends on the state of the water, but can be as high as 10–20m in places. Halfway between Sumbu and Mpulungu is a series of cliffs and drop-offs that are of particular interest to divers, while other popular diving spots include the area around Katete.

If you plan on any watersports, you must consider the **safety** issues. Both crocodiles and hippos are common in parts of the lake, but can be very localised. There is also the venomous if non-aggressive Tanganyika water cobra, which grows up to 2m. While it usually avoids swimmers as terrestrial snakes avoid walkers, you should still watch out for it. There is some doubt about the existence of bilharzia in the lake but you should be aware of the possibility (and see pages 96–7 for general guidelines). If you are considering taking a swim, ask advice from the locals about the precise place that you have in mind. They may not be infallible, but will give you a good idea of where is likely to be safe, and where is not.

Fishing Lake Tanganyika (and especially the Sumbu area) has a first-class reputation in freshwater angling circles, because of the variety of fish that can be caught on rod and line. It is not unusual for visitors to catch a dozen different species in a single visit. The greatest appeal comes from the nkupi, the goliath tigerfish and the Nile perch, the last of which can reach an impressive 80kg in weight.

The best time for fishing is between November and March. Each March sees the annual fishing competition held at Sumbu off the point near Nkamba Bay Lodge. Fly-fishing is becoming increasingly popular, particularly for nkupi and the perch species. Some of the tropical cichlids will also rise to a smaller fly.

There is considerable concern about the sustainability of commercial fishing on the lake, with the spotlight falling on both over-fishing and the impact of global warming on the breeding habits of the fish. Although fishing with nets is illegal within national park waters, the ban is regularly flouted by local fishermen. Nevertheless, commercial fishing is of significant importance, primarily for two species: the buka and the much smaller kapenta.

MPULUNGU Sitting in the heat of the rift valley, about 38km from Mbala, Mpulungu is Zambia's largest port. It's a busy place and visited by many travellers, most of whom are Africans but with the odd backpacker thrown in too. The atmosphere is very international, a mix of various southern, central and east African influences all stirred together by the ferries which circle the lake from port to port.

There is a strong local fishing community and a small but thriving business community, complete with a small contingent of white Africans, expats and even aid workers. So though Mpulungu might seem like the end of the earth when you get off a bus in the pitch-black evening, it isn't.

Getting there and away
By bus Mpulungu is at the most northerly end of the main bus route from Lusaka, via Kabwe, Kapiri Mposhi, Mkushi, Serenje, Mpika and Kasama, and Mbala. Buses from Mbala tend to arrive around 07.00, and those heading south leave in the small hours. The fare to Lusaka is around Kw180,000. There are several operators on the route, of which the best is considered to be Juldan Motors. The 'terminus' is on the main road, beside the market – you cannot fail to go through it.

There are also buses to Kitwe every day except Monday, departing around midnight.

Driving Mpulungu is the final town on the Great North Road out of Lusaka. Long pitted with huge pot-holes, the descent from Mbala is now smooth tar and affords some great views of the lake. If you're transferring to one of the Sumbu lodges, a taxi from Kasama airport to Mpulungu can be arranged for up to ten passengers, albeit at a hefty US$500 for the return trip.

Hitchhiking Hitching here from Mbala in the afternoon is very easy, with lots of lifts. However, getting out in the morning is virtually impossible. Everybody who has a little space in their vehicle goes to the bus terminus near the market and fills up with paying passengers, so few are interested in a stray hitchhiker walking away from the bus station. So, if you want to get out of Mpulungu, go with the crowd and hang around the main market area, quizzing any likely buses or vehicles. Because of the steep, twisting road out of the valley, heavy or under-powered vehicles can be painfully slow, so get a lighter, more powerful lift if you can.

By ferry Only one of the large international Tanganyika passenger ferries on Lake Tanganyika, the MV *Liemba*, is still operational. In theory it calls at Mpulungu every other Friday morning at around 07.00 and leaves the same afternoon at around 13.00 – though actual times very much depend on the cargo. For precise dates, bookings and other information, contact either Thorn Tree Safaris (page 345) or Nkupi Lodge (page 361).

From Mpulungu the ferry sails over the Tanzanian border to Kasanga, then to Kigoma in the north of Tanzania, with countless places in between. The journey

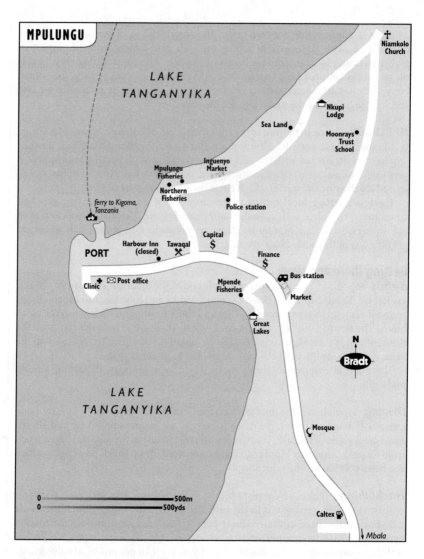

Niamkolo
Church

LAKE
TANGANYIKA

Nkupi
Lodge

Sea Land

Moonrays
Trust
School

Inguenyo
Market

Mpulungu
Fisheries

Northern
Fisheries

ferry to Kigoma,
Tanzania

Police station

Capital
$

PORT

Harbour Inn
(closed)

Tawaqal

Finance
$

Bus station

Clinic

Post office

Mpende
Fisheries

Market

Great
Lakes

N

Bradt

LAKE
TANGANYIKA

Mosque

0   500m
0   500yds

Caltex

↓ Mbala

takes up to two days, technically arriving in Kigoma on Sunday at around 13.00, and departing on Wednesday at about 16.00.

Ferry tickets fall into three classes. In first-class cabins (*US$65 pp*), there is a double bunk with a basin, while second-class cabins (*US$56 pp*) sleep four. Third-class passengers pay US$41 each, but take pot luck of seating around the ship. There are also en-suite VIP and family cabins (*US$260/4 people*). Bikes may be taken on the ferry, but not cars. Tickets must be bought on the ship, but both the above can assist with bookings. Food and water are available on board.

By boat-taxi If you need a short trip out to one of the **lodges** on the lake then hire a boat-taxi from the beach-side market, next to Andreas Fisheries. You will need to make sure that the driver knows the lodge that you want, and exactly where it is, and you may want to bargain over the rate a little. Alternatively, if time is on your side, you can use one of the regular boat-taxis that go up the lakeside to the Kalambo River (a 2½-hour walk from Kalambo Falls) on Monday, Wednesday and Friday, stopping at several villages and taking around two hours in each direction. Boats leave the falls area very early in the morning, returning from Mpulungu the same day some time after midday; one-way tickets should be Kw4,000, but a *mzungu* can expect to pay nearer Kw15,000.

Visitors to **Sumbu** (see pages 362–9) usually depart from Mpende Fisheries (previously Samaki Fishing) by prior arrangement with one of the lodges. To get there turn left down the gravel road opposite the bus station, which is about 1km after the Caltex garage. Boats usually arrive from Sumbu on Monday, Wednesday and Friday morning, returning in the afternoon. All passengers must first report to the immigration authorities at the port to notify them of their destination.

No matter where you are heading, it's essential that you have a crystal-clear deal over the price for the trip, including you and all your baggage, before you set off from Mpulungu – as disagreements on arrival (or worse still, on the lake) are bad news for you and the person running the boat.

Getting organised To organise accommodation, or anything else in the area, your best bet is to speak to Claire Powell at Thorn Tree Safaris (see page 345). The company maintains a dhow on the lake at Mpulungu, and can organise transfers for up to 15 people, as well as accommodation and trips around the area.

Where to stay If you are backpacking through, or have arrived late in the day, staying in Mpulungu itself for a night or two is probably your best option. Effectively this gives you the choice of the established backpackers' favourite, Nkupi Lodge, or the smaller Great Lakes. If both are full, you could try **Chamuluzi Guesthouse** opposite the market, or the **district resthouse**, but these wouldn't be top of my list.

In town For those wishing to stay longer the choice is widened by a number of lakeside lodges, though these tend to come and go. Almost all are accessible only by boat.

Nkupi Lodge (9 rooms, camping) 0214 455166; m 0977 456742, 0955 455166, 0966 69397; e nkupilodge@hotmail.com. This relaxed backpackers' retreat has become something of a legend with overlanders, largely because of its laid-back owner, Denish, & a total lack of competition. To find it, follow the tar road past the main bus/market area almost to the port, then turn right & follow the coast road; Nkupi Lodge is on the right. While there are more direct roads leading from the market, it's a confusing area, & this is the clearest route. It's about 15–25 mins from town, or Kw15,000 by taxi.

Now managed by the very helpful & knowledgeable Charity, the lodge has several large thatched rondavels with stone floors, mesh windows, mosi nets & a fan – on mains electricity. The campsite, & all except 1 room (a simple but spacious en-suite dbl), share clean hot showers & toilets. Beer is available, as is scrupulously boiled water. Self-catering is an option, or African & Indian meals can be ordered a couple of hours in advance (*Kw15,000–45,000*); particularly popular is *nkupi*.

Charity can organise all sorts of activities, from visits to Kalambo Falls to paddle-boat trips to one of the islands, to include a picnic & swimming. Just ask her! *Chalet Kw75,000/125,000 sgl/dbl sharing facilities, Kw175,000 dbl en suite; camping Kw25,000 pp (own tent); Kw50,000 pp in room without bedding.*

Great Lakes (5 chalets) m 0966 436566, 0977 173874; e patrickkatema@yahoo.com, mwansapauline@yahoo.com. Centrally located opposite the mosque, Great Lakes has thatched en-suite chalets, & its own restaurant. **$**

Lakeside lodges

⌂ **Isanga Bay Lodge** (6 chalets, camping) m 0966 646991, 0977 393868; e isangabay@ gmail.com; www.isangabay.com. North of Mpulungu, about halfway to the Tanzanian border & within hiking distance of Kalambo Falls, Isanga Bay Lodge is usually reached by a ½–1hr boat transfer from Mpulungu (*US$105 per boat, 10–12 people*); there is safe parking in the town. In theory you could drive in from the Kalambo Falls road north of Mbala, but the poor 26km track can't be recommended, even in a 4x4.

3 thatched wooden chalets stand on stilts on a beautiful white sandy beach, surrounded by coconut palms & indigenous vegetation. Each has a dbl bed & 2 sgls, all draped with mosquito nets, plus an en-suite shower & toilet, & a veranda facing the lake. Overlooking the rocks are a further 3 stone chalets, similarly equipped. There's also a campsite with hot showers, braai stands & firewood available, & campers can arrange to eat at the lodge. Very good meals are served in a central thatched *insaka*, where there's also a bar. Day visitors are welcome, with activities that include good snorkelling among the rocks, hikes to Kalambo Falls, kayaking, fishing, bird walks & even waterskiing or tubing. *Chalet US$130 pp FB; camping US$15 pp.*

⌂ **Kalambo Falls Lodge** (7 chalets) Zambia's first upmarket lodge on the lake, 16km from Mpulungu, was closed & reported to be up for sale in 2011. It originally started as a base for catching aquarium fish for export, then curious aquarists arrived for trips, staying in thatch-on-stone chalets, each en suite & with a private veranda.

⌂ **Mishembe Bay – Luke's Beach** (3 chalets, camping) Contact via Thorn Tree Safaris, page 345. Mishembe is real Robinson Crusoe stuff – just a pure white sandy beach sheltered in its own bay – the last on the Zambian side of the shore. It is accessed in 30mins by private boat (US$150 return, up to 8 people), or by water-taxi from Mpulungu taking 1–3hrs (Mon, Wed & Fri). Hidden among the trees on wooden platforms overlooking the lake are simple open-sided chalets under thatch, built entirely of local materials & with roll-down canvas walls for protection against the rain. Inside are walk-in mosquito nets around twin or dbl beds, & an en-suite shower & flush toilet. Meals are served under a large fig tree. Under the palm trees, amongst the baboons, monkeys & birds, there's space for campers, who should bring all their own food & equipment. It's a magical place, totally isolated & very good value.

There is very good snorkelling right in the bay, with visibility up to 10m, depending on the wind. The bay is also ideally situated for walks up to Kalambo Falls, about 2½hrs each way. On a more personal level, Mishembe has strong links through Thorn Tree Safaris with the local community, supporting & building schools in nearby Chipwa & Miyamba villages, taking visitors to attend church services, & inviting local choirs to sing at the lodge. *US$150 pp FB; camping US$25 pp.* ⊕ *All year.*

What to see Just a few kilometres east of Mpulungu, beside the lake, you may see a tall, rectangular turret rising above the shoreline as you head to Kalambo Falls or one of the lodges in a water-taxi. This isn't a fort, but the remains of one of Zambia's oldest churches, **Niamkolo Church**. It was originally built by the London Missionary Society around 1893–96, but abandoned in 1902 because of health problems suffered by the missionaries. The original buildings were burned, but in 1962 the walls were restored to their former height and cemented into place. Now they're all there is to see. At 80cm thick in places, they may last for another century yet.

SUMBU NATIONAL PARK

Park fees US$10 pp/day; vehicle US$15/day; fishing US$5 pp/day) Sumbu National Park covers about 2,020km², and borders on Lake Tanganyika. It also covers a small part of the lake, which means that those boating in these waters are subject to park entry fees, as well as those on land. To the north- and southwest, the park is adjoined by the 360,000ha Kaputa GMA, while between this and the park to

SUMBU NATIONAL PARK

Kaputa

Chishera Swamp

Lake Tanganyika

Lake Mweru Wantipa

Bulaya

Chikasa

MUTUNG **MUTUNG**

Kampala

NDOLEB
Ndole Bay Lodge
TONDOL

Cape Kachese
C Kabwe
Ngosye

Cape Inangu

Nundo Head

SUMBU
Sumbu

Cape Nambeyeye

Kasaba Bay
(closed) **KASAIR**

Mutundu gate

Cisala

Nkamba Bay
NKAMBA

Mbola

Nsama, Mporokoso

Tondwa Swamp

Lufubu

Lukwesa *Yendwe Valley*
Ngozya viewpoint

Tondwa GMA

Chansamosaka Escarpment

Mwenze

Kambole Mission

Masakwa Flats

Chambeshi

Kaniki

Lufubu

GPS co-ordinates ⊕

KASAIR	08°32.000'S 30°42.000'E
MUTUNG	08°33.839'S 30°12.405'E
NDOLEB	08°28.707'S 30°26.870'E
NKAMBA	08°36.214'S 30°32.168'E
SUMBU	08°31.221'S 30°28.629'E
TONDOL	08°31.753'S 30°26.946'E

Malula

N

Bradt

Lubeni

0 ———— 8km
0 ———— 5 miles

the west is the smaller Tondwa GMA, which is leased out to a small professional hunting operator. These two act as a very effective buffer for the park, keeping the local subsistence hunters/poachers out and giving the game numbers a chance to increase. Combined with the presence of two (and potentially three) lodges in this area, this has made Sumbu's future look very promising indeed.

On another promising note, Sumbu is one of several parks in Zambia that have been designated as being 'viable game parks' under a study funded by the EU. Plans are afoot to change the way the parks are run, and EU money is set to help the less developed parks to become self-sustaining. Eventually, each of Zambia's parks should have greater autonomy, which will allow them to use their own funds for community development schemes as well as anti-poaching operations. This is vital if the wildlife of parks like Sumbu is to recover and tourism is to become a worthwhile source of revenue.

FLORA AND FAUNA Sumbu protects populations of elephant, and a range of antelope including blue and yellow-backed duiker, roan, sable, bushbuck, waterbuck, sitatunga, the occasional zebra and a large number of puku; there are also reports of eland in the hills. Buffalo herds range up to about 400 individuals, and move around between Sumbu and the neighbouring GMA. The park's main natural predators are lion and leopard, though numbers are uncertain. Although poachers continue to kill occasionally, the animal populations are increasing.

A study in the 1990s concluded that there were still wild dogs in the park and its surrounding GMAs, though there has been no follow-up, and their continued long-term survival was in doubt. I don't know of reports of wild dog since then.

Although Sumbu cannot yet boast huge herds of the larger antelope, elephant or buffalo, there is sufficient game to make a trip to the park worthwhile. Its vegetation and environment are, on the whole, in pristine condition and offer a real Zambian wilderness experience.

The birding is good, with 295 species recorded in the park and the adjacent Tondwa GMA. A number of east African species occur here that you won't find in the rest of southern Africa. Look out especially for the bare-faced go-away bird, common on the open floodplain areas; also a waxbill known as the red-cheeked cordon bleu, occasional ospreys, palmnut vultures and red-faced crombecs. Pel's fishing owl and bat hawks also occur, though not more commonly than elsewhere.

In the lake itself, there are plenty of hippos and a very healthy population of crocodile – including both Nile crocodile (*Crocodylus niloticus*) and its smaller, endangered cousin, the slender-snouted crocodile (*Crocodylus cataphractus* or *Mecistops cataphractus*). Some are sufficiently large to dissuade you from even thinking of dipping your toe in the water. For details of fish and other reptiles in the lake, see pages 357–8.

GETTING THERE Access has long been the main problem for visitors to the Lake Tanganyika area, and getting to Sumbu is an added challenge. It's difficult, or time-consuming, or very expensive.

By air The 1,500m airstrip at Kasaba Bay (⊕ KASAIR 08°32.00'S, 30°42.00'E) was being upgraded to international standards in 2011, and should be operational by the end of the year. In time the new airport is expected to have customs and immigration facilities.

Limited amounts of AV-Gas are usually available from the lodges, by prior arrangement.

Normally both Ndole Bay and Nkamba Bay lodges will collect passengers from the airstrip by boat, taking about 30 minutes to Nkamba Bay, or 40 minutes to Ndole Bay, but Nkamba Bay also has its own airstrip.

There are scheduled flights on Monday and Thursday between Lusaka and Kasama via Ndola, arriving in Kasama at 10.00 so that it's possible to get to Sumbu the same day. From Kasama, it is possible to charter a flight to Sumbu, though at around US$2,400, this is not a cheap option.

By boat Though they're at least 75km across the lake, the lodges in Sumbu most commonly arrange to transfer their guests by boat from Mpulungu, where both use the harbour facilities of Mpende Fishing (page 361). Each has different speeds and sizes of boat available, at different costs, but expect to pay around US$350 per boat each way. A 'banana boat' (a long, thin chug-chug motorboat with space for up to six people) will take about four hours to reach Sumbu, whereas a traditional wooden dhow, although larger, can take up to six hours. Ndole Bay operates a large, high-speed catamaran that covers the distance in two hours, taking 2–10 passengers at US$750 return, with the option (by arrangement) of snorkelling/diving *en route* at Cape Chaitika.

Transport boats Crowded transport boats ply up and down the lake with frequent stops, so if you don't have a transfer organised, these might be an option – though be prepared for a long wait (sometimes days). Expect to pay from about Kw70,000 for the trip, which takes between ten and 18 hours, depending on the number of stops. Alternatively, you could negotiate to hire the whole boat for around US$150 plus about 75 litres of fuel, but make it quite clear that you wish to go direct to your destination, or you could still find yourself stopping everywhere. Either way, ask around at Mpende Fisheries in Mpulungu, or by the water taxis at the main market, or – in Sumbu town – on the beach. Remember that the lake can be rough (and thus you could get wet), and that you'll need to take all food and water for the journey with you.

By road Sumbu National Park can be approached relatively easily in a 4x4 via Kaputa or Mporokoso, though neither is a fast option. There is also a 4x4 track from Mbala as far as the Lufubu River, which defines the park's eastern boundary, with a new bridge under construction to link it through to Sumbu.

From Mporokoso For the majority of drivers, the most direct approach to the park is from Mporokoso (✪ MPOROK 09°21.831'S, 30°07.432'E; see pages 379–80), a network of dirt roads that was upgraded in 2007 and is largely in good condition. Initially, the road heads more or less north through the village of Munyele and on towards **Nsama** (✪ NSAMA 08°53.448'S, 29°56.896'E), close to the eastern shores of Lake Mweru Wantipa, where there are a few shops, a secondary school and a Catholic church. Keen birdwatchers should note that just north of Nsama there's a patch of miombo woodland where the relatively uncommon white-winged starling is easily spotted. Beyond the town, there are numerous small villages lining the road, but nowhere of note. Despite mention of Bulaya on most maps, don't expect a town here: it's nothing more than a dot on the map.

About 135km from Mporokoso, and 39km before Sumbu, you'll reach the Mutundu gate (✪ MUTUNG 08°33.839'S, 30°12.405'E), a game checkpoint that marks the beginning of the national park. This is also where the road from Kaputa (the area's administrative centre) joins the road from Mporokoso to Sumbu.

From here the road runs along the northwestern edge of the park towards Sumbu town (see page 369), with sweeping views over the bay as it descends from the plateau. Some 31km after the Mutondo gate, there's a left turn to Ndole Bay Lodge (✪ TONDOL 08°31.753'S, 30°26.946'E). To reach the national park gate, continue along the increasingly poor main road for a further 8km or so to the turn-off to Sumbu town. This also marks the entrance to the national park, at Sumbu gate, and is where you'll have to pay park fees. The road then continues to Nkamba Bay Lodge and Kasaba Bay, within the national park.

From Nchelenge via Kaputa For the first stretch of this route, see *The road to Mweru Wantipa and Kaputa*, pages 369–76.

Beyond Kaputa, the road widens, passing through numerous villages as it crosses the narrow strip between Lake Mweru Wantipa and the DRC border. The lake itself remains out of sight, although fishing nets laid out to dry indicate its proximity to the road. As the road descends, the land around becomes increasingly marshy, with papyrus beds and reeds, and pools dotted with purple water lilies. It's a haven for waterbirds, with reed cormorants, pied and malachite kingfishers, and African jacanas all easy to spot. Eventually, some 83km from Kaputa, you'll emerge onto the Mporokoso–Sumbu road (see above) at the Mutundu gate (✪ MUTUNG 08°33.839'S, 30°12.405'E), marked on some maps as Kampela, where you turn left for Sumbu.

Note that the dirt road from Mununga to Nsama (✪ NSAMA 08°53.448'S, 29°56.896'E) along the southern side of Lake Mweru Wantipa is very bad and becoming impassable.

Cross-country from Mbala For many years the poor track between Mbala and Sumbu has ended abruptly at the Lufubu River, the park's southeastern boundary, with no bridge across. In 2011, however, the combined forces of a looming election and external finance resulted in work on grading the road, and rebuilding the bridge over the river. By summer 2011, the first 30km out of Mbala were complete, with a passable track from there almost to the river. Work on the section down the escarpment, and the bridge itself, was expected to start at the same time, with completion anticipated by September, in time for the elections – though it is important to check this information locally before setting out. From the Lufubu River west to Sumbu a new road covers the remaining 50km.

The reinstatement of this link between the two sides of Lake Tanganyika will offer an attractive option in the dry season for experienced drivers with a strong sense of adventure.

According to Gerard Zytkow at Ndole Bay, 'the countryside is wonderful and the drop from the escarpment into the Yendwe Valley is breathtakingly beautiful.' Nevertheless, a 4x4 with spare wheels and a winch are likely to remain essential, and flooding during and after the rains will almost certainly render the road largely fictional. Be aware, too, that the road is allegedly used regularly by poachers.

At present, the start of the track is about 5km west of the Mbala T-junction on the road towards Mpulungu. However, once work is complete, the turn-off is expected to be just 100m or so from the T-junction, with a second access road from just outside Mpulungu.

GETTING AROUND THE PARK The network of roads in the park may have been extended in the last few years but these are largely only game tracks, devised by the lodges for their own use. For practical purposes, the only passable roads in the park are between Sumbu Town and Nkamba Bay, then on to Kasaba Bay, or east to the Lufubu River. While these are open all year, you'll still need a 4x4 at any time.

Boat trips in national-park waters can be organised through one of the lodges (see below).

WHERE TO STAY Despite the difficulty of access, Sumbu's future for tourism is looking bright. Two lakeshore lodges, Nkamba Bay and Ndole Bay, are currently operational – the first inside the national park; the second, more casual, just outside the park's northwestern boundary. A third, Kasaba Bay Lodge on the Inangu Peninsula, has been closed for several years, but following privatisation it is anticipated that three new lodges catering to different budgets will be set up on the peninsula within the next couple of years. Historians will note that it was at the original lodge that Mozambique's president Samora Machel met regional leaders before catching his fatal flight in 1986 from the lodge's airstrip.

All three lodges have a chequered history. Originally, both those in the park were run by the government, but by the early 1990s both were in terminal decline: expensive yet poorly maintained. Eventually they were put up for tender in late 1995 and snapped up by private operators, although later fortunes have been mixed. Ndole Bay Lodge was originally privately owned, but was taken by the government in 1989, only to be closed in the early 1990s when its trade disappeared. Now it has reverted to its previous owners and is once again thriving.

Ndole Bay Lodge (15 chalets, camping) +88 2165 207 7085; m 0966 780196; e info@ ndolebaylodge.com; www.ndolebaylodge.com.

NDOLEB 08°28.707'S, 30°26.870'E. Owned by Gerard & Barbara Zytkow, & run by their son, Craig, & his partner, Elise, Ndole Bay Lodge stands beside Lake Tanganyika in Cameron Bay, just northwest of the national park boundary, & offers the opportunity to swim, snorkel or fish from its private white-sand beach (which is considered to be perfectly safe).

Visitors usually arrive by boat, sometimes following a taxi transfer from Kasama airport. Drivers should take the well-signposted left turning as they approach Sumbu, about 5km before the town (⊕ TONDOL 08°31.753'S, 30°26.946'E). The lodge is 7km down a partly rocky track, for which you'll need a high-clearance vehicle at all times.

It's a lovely wild spot &, despite creature comforts such as the recent addition of mains electricity, still feels at one with the African bush. Both the chalets & the main central building are set back from the beach, well spaced among mature gardens on a gentle slope. The main area links the dining room with the bar & a library under a grand thatched roof, all surrounded by a low stone wall. It's a practical design – cool & airy. Under a thatched shelter, hammocks swing in the breeze, just the place to relax after a dip in the small pool, while over the water is a large, shaded wooden deck with more hammocks, sunbeds & steps into the lake. On a practical note, there's a shop for essential toiletries, local crafts & fishing lures, & WiFi throughout the site.

The chalets are built of stone with thatched roofs, & most are en suite. They're large & comfortable, without being luxurious, some with space for extra beds. 2 more upmarket chalets & a dbl suite open onto the beach, each with a private deck & outdoor shower, & a self-catering house is scheduled for completion in 2011. Set to one side on the beach, beneath beautiful winterthorn trees, *Faidherbia albida,* is a campsite, equipped with running water, BBQ stands, & a new ablution block with hot-water showers & flush toilets. Campers can book into the lodge for meals, & can use its facilities, provided they do not disturb other guests.

There's plenty to do, but don't come expecting to be organised; this is a laidback spot that is very much in tune with its location. You can hire various types of boat (*US$7–25/hr, or US$30–180/day plus fuel*), as well as snorkelling equipment & basic fishing tackle. As a qualified PADI instructor, Craig has established a PADI IRA resort at the lodge, the first on the lake, offering courses from 1-day try dives (*US$100 pp*) through to Rescue Diver. Other activities include game drives, nature walks, birding trips, lake cruises & waterskiing. Further afield, it's possible to visit some local hot springs, a traditional village (the lodge funds various community projects in Ndole village) & perhaps a village healer, or to organise a night trip to watch the operation of a kapenta fishing rig. A custom-built dhow, designed both for cruising & diving, allows extended trips such as a 5-night lake safari to Sumbu NP and Kalambo Falls, or 4 nights in the park, to include the Lufubu River Valley. There's also a 1-night trip at a fly-camp near Nundo Head, including walks to the balancing boulders & Kampasa Rainforest, or the option of multi-day hikes up the Lufubu River. *En suite US$121/136; shared US$99/110, both sgl/pp sharing FB, inc snorkelling, kayaking & floating sunbeds from the lodge, guided walks, village visits, sunset paddle, laundry. Self-catering US$65/50 sgl/pp sharing. Camping US$10 pp. ⊙ All year.*

🏠 **Nkamba Bay Lodge** (9 rooms) ℮ info@nkambabaylodge.com; www.nkambabaylodge.com, or contact via Voyagers, page 150. ⊕ NKAMBA 08°36.214'S, 30°32.168'E. Nkamba Bay re-opened for business in 2006, firmly positioning itself upmarket. The lodge is located on a low rise above the lake shore some 20km from the Sumbu Park gate; there's a signpost indicating the turn-off. You'll need a 4x4 for this road, but most guests (& all in the rainy season) are transferred by boat from Mpulungu (2–4hrs). The airstrip at Kasaba Bay is currently closed for expansion & redevelopment, but for those wishing to travel by air, Nkamba Bay has its own airstrip.

Accommodation consists of 4 spacious rooms built in a block around a couple of old fig trees overlooking the lake, & a further 5 chalets set further back with partial lake views. All have been stylishly renovated to be modern but comfortable, combining crisp white linen softened by fabrics & paintwork in more earthy tones. Each room has a kingsize bed hung with walk-in mosquito nets on a minimalist concrete plinth, smart en-suite shower, & a wooden veranda that – in the lake-view rooms – is partially enclosed, a useful extra during the rains. Note that some rooms are quite high up, so are not suitable for children.

At the lodge's heart is a large, airy *insaka* sheltering a bar/dining area, hung with huge wooden masks & outsize baskets. To one side, squashy sofas & low *mukwa* tables are fronted by a small (but deep) pool – parents beware – & the lake beyond. The nearby conference room has become a cosy place to relax, with tea & coffee on tap, & a small library. There is also a small gift shop. Power, until recently supplied by generator, was expected to be linked to the mains during 2011.

Activities comprise game walks from the lodge or into the rainforest, game drives, beach dinners, boat trips, sundowner cruises, canoeing & fishing, for which tackle is available to hire. This is no place to swim, though – as attested by a quick glance at the crocodiles basking in the waters off the beach. It is possible to arrange a trip to local landmarks such as the waterfalls on the Lufubu River or a nearby beach, as well as to Chieftainess Chomba's village. *US$420 pp FB, inc drinks (exc bottled wine & imported beers), airstrip transfers, & land-based activities. Boat US$150/ day plus US$3 per litre of fuel. Park fees extra, payable to ZAWA. ⊙ All year.*

WHAT TO SEE AND DO Each of the lodges can organise a range of activities both on and off the water, but there are one or two local highlights that are worth singling out, detailed below. See also *Swimming, diving and snorkelling* and *Fishing* (page 358). Further afield, it's possible to organise excursions to Mpulungu (pages 359–62) or Kalambo Falls (pages 354–5).

Balancing rocks One spot well worth an excursion is the balancing rocks (one large rock balancing on three small ones) that stand on the Nundo Head Peninsula – a favourite trail destination shrouded in local mystery. Each year around early June, a pre-fishing ceremony in honour of the spirit, Nundo, is held here to mark the beginning of the five-month period in which local fishermen can fish within a small area of national-park waters. Visitors can arrange to witness the ceremony through Ndole Bay Lodge.

Game viewing and birding As the lodges extend their influence and the number of animals increases, game viewing is increasingly drawing visitors up here. Apart from the ubiquitous puku, most antelope species are still re-establishing their populations; so although you won't see huge herds, you should see some good game here. The lodges have all worked to increase the road network for game drives, and the animals themselves are becoming much more relaxed as a result. Fortunately, with a large area and only a few lodges the roads are very quiet and other vehicles are a pleasant rarity. The birdwatching here has always been excellent: look out for Pel's fishing owl, palmnut vultures and numerous east African migrants.

Guided walks About 5km from Nkamba Bay Lodge and within the national park is the small Kampasa Rainforest, a favourite spot for guided walks. Trips usually involve a boat transfer, then a three- to four-hour walk from the beach, and are accompanied by an armed ZAWA scout.

The rainforest itself covers only about 300m² and is centred on an underground stream that bubbles up out of the ground most of the year. Mature woodland species such as sausage trees, *Kigelia africana*, and Natal mahogany, *Trichilia emetica*, grow alongside plants that include the flame creeper, *Gloriosa superba*. Before entering the forest, the trail leads past a dense reed bed where sitatunga are often seen. The area surrounding the reed beds is also rich in puku and is a well-used route for elephant, while the forest itself is regularly traversed by a pod of hippos on their way to the plains behind it. The park's lion frequent the area, too, and can often be heard from Nkamba Bay Lodge. Among the birds that are likely to be encountered are Pel's fishing owl, African broadbill, Angolan pitta and Narina trogon; crowned cranes are often seen on the plain, and during the rainy season the reed beds are the haunt of the black coucal.

A second walk option leads to the Muzinga Falls on a small stream to the east of Sumbu town, about an hour's walk from the lake.

SUMBU TOWN On the edge of Sumbu National Park, about 8km east of the Ndole Bay turn off, Sumbu town has grown considerably over the last few years and now has an estimated 20,000 residents, largely employed by the national parks, police, immigration or council – or in commercial fishing. As a result, there's talk of upgrading the status of the town, and there are even rumours of eventually tarring the road through to Kaputa. For now, though, a major improvement was the arrival of mains electricity in 2011.

While the town isn't nearly as cosmopolitan as Mpulungu (!) it can be fairly lively. In the town square, a short walk from the harbour, small shops and bars surround the water pump, alongside a popular pool table. It's possible to buy most things, including fresh fruit and milk, if you ask around, and simple meals such as nshima and chicken are to be had for around Kw10,000–15,000. If you're after a bed for the night, there are a couple of simple **guesthouses** charging around Kw20,000 a night: one in the market and a second at the harbour.

An open-air **market** for vegetables, dried fish and second-hand clothing spills from the square down to the harbour. There is also a government-run clinic, with a medical officer (but seldom any drugs), and a ZAWA post. **Fuel** – both petrol and diesel – is sometimes available in drums; just ask around in the square.

The Zambian military maintains a presence by the harbour, but now that the beached Congolese naval vessel has been returned to the DRC, their interest is largely in checking the ID of passengers off the transport boats from Mpulungu.

THE ROAD TO MWERU WANTIPA AND KAPUTA

The western side of this region, skirting the shores of Lake Bangweulu to Samfya then continuing up the Luapula River north to Lake Mweru, is known to only a handful of visitors, but offers plenty of rewards. The river is a draw in itself, as are the waterfalls that characterise much of this area, while the journey is enlivened by countless small villages, their square, brick houses topped with a mop of loose thatch and often decorated in striking geometric patterns.

If you're coming northeastward on the Great North Road from Kapiri Mposhi, it's wise to refuel at Serenje (see map, page 306). Then, after a further 36km, take the main left turning signposted to Samfya and Mansa (and Kasanka National Park). This is the artery that runs over some 580km of very good tar to Nchelenge, in the far northwest corner of the country.

The section of road up to the T-junction just west of Samfya used to be referred to as the 'Chinese road' because it was built, like the TAZARA railway, by the Chinese. After about 55km on this road you'll pass the entrance to Kasanka National Park (see pages 324–31), then 10km later the right turn to the Livingstone Memorial (see pages 331–2) and Bangweulu. Continuing north, the road crosses the impressive 3km-long Luapula Bridge, on the border with the DRC. During and after the rainy season, from around December to July, the river overflows onto the surrounding plain, which is dotted with miniature islands topped with palm trees. In the flooded fields, water lilies flower and water birds brighten the landscape. Permanent villages are augmented by temporary fishing camps, their inhabitants making the most of the months of plenty, and along the roadside fishermen tout their catch of bream or kasepa for sale.

Beyond the Luapula Bridge, watch out for the occasional pot-hole, although generally the road remains very good. About 350km from the Great North Road turn-off, or 115km from the Luapula Bridge, you'll reach a T-junction (⊕ SAMTJN 11°21.126'S, 29°29.453'E). Turn right here and a further 9km will bring you to the small town of Samfya.

SAMFYA With its location beside the powder-fine, white-sand beaches of Lake Bangweulu, Samfya seems to have the potential for a top resort. However, on closer inspection it's less tempting than it looks: accommodation could do with a serious shake up, strong winds blowing off the lake can be decidedly disruptive, and for the most part the lake is full of crocodiles, so this is really more of a stopover than a destination in its own right. (While people do bathe in the clear waters by the hotels, local advice is mixed; think carefully before wading in.)

On a more practical note, the town has a rather unpromising-looking **fuel** station, as well as a Finance **Bank**, a **post office**, a small **market** and a range of basic **shops**.

Getting there Several **buses** a day run between Lusaka and Kashikishi via Kabwe, Kapiri Mposhi, Serenje, Samfya, Mansa and Nchelenge. Those heading north stop at the market in Samfya at around 08.00, but southbound buses must be boarded at the T-junction 9km west of town, at a similar time.

Regular **postboats** used to ply Lake Bangweulu, collecting and delivering mail to the island communities on the lake. Like the postbuses, these would happily take paying passengers, but in recent years the service has been contracted out to private concerns, and information is patchy. Even in Samfya itself it is difficult to ascertain any form of timetable, but the boat used to depart every Thursday at 10.00, calling at Mbabala Island, Chisi Island and Muchinshi amongst others. To get to the port, turn left at the crossroads as you enter the town and follow this dirt road, with shops on either side, for about 300m to the end.

Where to stay and eat Samfya's accommodation options seem to come and go, but the addition of a new lakeside lodge broadens the choice for visitors. In town, several basic (and cheaper) options include the reasonable and clean restaurant, **Watch Me Grow**, with two central locations.

Bangweulu Bay Lodge (6 chalets) 0211 266927; m 0977 780080; e info@ amazingzambia.com; www.bangweulubaylodge. com. Just 200m from the beach, this new lodge opened in 2010, with 2 new chalets added a year later. Each of the thatched, en-suite chalets has a wooden deck overlooking the lake, & is furnished with twin or dbl beds (or a family room with a dbl & a sgl), & a fridge. Activities are primarily water based: fishing, sailing & sunrise cruises, but there are also beach BBQs & dancing displays. Swimming in the lake (considered by the lodge to be hippo & croc free) may be a further option. It's also possible to organise a visit to the Bangweulu Wetlands (US$65 pp) or to Mambilima Falls (US$180/5 people). Many of the staff here come from the nearby Chipepa village, where the lodge is planning to build a school. US$150–180 pp sharing FB, inc laundry & 2 activities/day.

Samfya Beach Hotel (9 rooms) m 0977 371136. With its prime location on the lake shore, & a huge beachfront lapa for shade, this established hotel at the entrance to the town should be a little goldmine, but lack of maintenance & high prices tell their own story. En-suite rooms are large but basic, albeit with plenty of hot water, & in the so-called bar & restaurant a knock on the kitchen door reaps little reward. $ exc b/fast.

Luni Guesthouse m 0978 048179, 0979 291456/345593. One of several basic offerings, this one near the bus terminus. $

LUBWE It would be well worth exploring the road north of Samfya towards Lubwe, on the western side of the lake. Lubwe itself is home to a Catholic mission hospital built in 1926 and now run by the Sisters of Mercy. Active fundraising since 2000 has resulted in significant improvements both at the hospital and in attendant projects to improve the lives of the local people; for details, see www.lubwezambiafund.org.

MANSA About 72km from the T-junction, or 81km from Samfya, Mansa is the capital of Luapula Province. It's a thriving provincial town, with tree-lined roads and an appealing air of prosperity.

Getting there and away Mansa's links to the rest of the region are enhanced by its position close to the Luapula River and the DRC border. A tarred road leads southwest to the border town of Chembe, where there's a pontoon over the river, then a road link across the DRC to Mufulira in the Copperbelt. There is currently talk of replacing the pontoon with a bridge.

By air The re-introduction by Proflight (page 65) of a twice-weekly service between Lusaka and Mansa via Ndola has improved regional connections considerably. Flights depart from Lusaka on Tuesday and Friday at 11.15, returning at 13.45.

By bus Long-distance buses are operated by Zamsaf, Sierra, Juldan Motors and Germin. Most leave from Mulenshi Road in the centre of town, though each operator has its own departure and arrival point; the most obvious is that used by Zamsaf next to the Civic Hotel. Regular buses connect Mansa with Lusaka and Kashikishi on Lake Mweru, as well as to Kawambwa. Buses to Lusaka leave in the

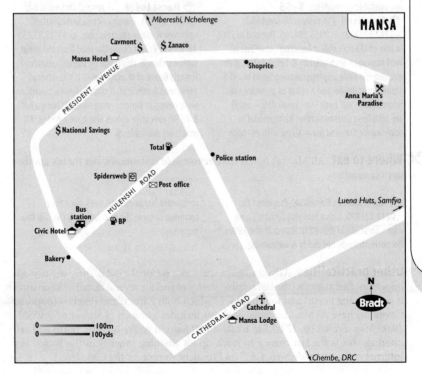

morning, Zamsaf at 07.00, Juldan Motors and Germins at 08.30, taking about nine hours to complete the journey. Northbound buses load at 04.00 (buy a ticket the day before) and 16.00. Fares to Lusaka are around Kw150,000 one way; to Samfya Kw110,000 and to Kawambwa Kw180,000.

Where to stay

Mansa Hotel (30 rooms) President Av; 0212 821607. Central & well established, the Mansa is immediately next to Cavmont Bank & down the road from Shoprite. Its brick-built rooms, arranged round a series of courtyards, are simply furnished but very clean & pleasant; each has an en-suite toilet & bath, as well as TV, fridge, ceiling fan & mosi nets. The hotel also has a couple of well-stocked bars, & a restaurant serving b/fast, lunch & dinner ($$). It's a cut above the average of Zambia's town hotels, professionally run with helpful staff; even the president stays here! **$$**

Chukwuma Guesthouse (12 rooms) 0212 821560; m 0977 240457. This pleasant guesthouse is just north of town; to find it, head north from Shoprite, go over the bridge, then turn right. Simple en-suite rooms built in a low block are fronted by a formal grassed area. Meals are available to residents. **$–$$**

Civic Hotel (16 rooms) Mulenshi Rd; 0212 821930; m 0955 304765. Opened in 2006 in one of Mansa's oldest buildings, the Civic is well managed with friendly & helpful staff. If the exterior is a little unprepossessing, solid wood & stone floors inside give a sense of permanence. Rooms (with 'sgl' beds – ie: small dbls – only) are off a long corridor, rather institutional in appearance but well maintained with en-suite

showers, tea/coffee-making facilities, fans, mosquito nets & TV. The 1st-floor restaurant & bar, overlooking the road from a long veranda, serves à-la-carte meals all day. Unlikely extra facilities include a hairdresser, barber, 2 shops & an internet café. **$**

Luena Huts Lodge (18 rooms) Samfya Rd; m 0966 807555, 0978 003880. ⊕ 11°12.279'S, 28°54.700'E. To the east of town on the north side of the road, individual rondavels sit in a row behind a secure gate, each with a neat garden plant-lined path – including tomatoes. A TV, fan, nets, fridge & dbl bed are standard; some share facilities, while others are en suite. Away from these, a 2-storey bar attracts a cool breeze & is very popular at w/ends (closing time Mon–Thu 22.00, Fri–Sun 24.00), so the place could be noisy. Between the 2 there's a simple restaurant, serving meals all day, every day. **$** exc b/fast.

Mansa Lodge (17 rooms) Cathedral Rd; 0212 821301; e enquiries@zambiahostels. com; www.zambiahostels.com. ⊕ 11°12.132'S, 28°53.357'E. Just down the road from the main Catholic church, this is run by the nationwide Hostels Board of Management. It's functional, very clean & efficient, if slightly soulless, with en-suite rooms in various categories. All have a bath & DSTV; executive rooms also have a fridge. All meals are available. **$**

Where to eat
All Mansa's hotels have reasonable restaurants, but there's another option nearby:

Anna Maria's Paradise President Av; 0211 821890. Italy's loss was Zambia's gain when Anna Maria moved to Mansa in the 1990s. Recently, though, her shady & welcoming

restaurant has been sold. Let's hope they continue to serve the best bream & chips in the region.

Other practicalities
As you might expect in a regional capital, there are two all-important **fuel** stations (the last reliable source of fuel for several hundred kilometres if you're going north) and four **banks**, of which both Zanaco and Barclays (opposite Cavmont) have ATMs. The range of **shops** includes a branch of Shoprite (⊕ 08.00–19.00 Mon–Fri, 08.00–17.00 Sat, 09.00–13.00 Sun); if you're heading north and self catering, this is the last chance to stock up on anything other than the basics. For **internet** cafés, try Spiderweb, C&C on President Avenue, or the Civic Hotel.

NORTH OF MANSA Some 9km north of Mansa the road splits. The left turn leads to Mwense, Mbereshi and Nchelenge, while the road straight ahead is for Kawambwa. Both appear beautifully tarred, but don't be fooled; after the first 25km or so the Kawambwa road deteriorates rapidly into a bad dirt road, which is well worth avoiding, while the road to Nchelenge is pretty good tar for most of the way. Thus, if you're heading towards Kawambwa, take the road towards Nchelenge via Mwense, then turn right at Mbereshi for Kawambwa. It's both easier and quicker.

The Nchelenge road follows the verdant valley of the Luapula River as it flows north into Lake Mweru, forming the border with the DRC and widening all the way to the lake. A succession of villages lines the road, which crosses several rivers, all flowing west towards the Luapula from Zambia's higher ground in the east. It's an easy but interesting drive, particularly after the rainy season when the flooded plains attract temporary fishing camps, as further south. The route is further enhanced by views across the river to the DRC and the lure of several attractive waterfalls (see below), many of which offer a good spot for a picnic or to camp.

There are two fuel stations along this stretch, one at Mwense, 111km north of Mansa, the second 18km further north in the village of Chiluba, but neither is reliable, so do fill up in Mansa.

The Luapula waterfalls Along this route are numerous lovely waterfalls, many virtually unmarked, including the following:

Mumbuluma Falls (⊕ MUMBUL 10°55.801'S, 28°44.178'E; *US$10/5 adult/child; vehicle US$5/day; camping US$15pp inc entry*) About 32km north of Mansa (167km from Mbereshi) there's a signposted turning to the left (⊕ TOMUMB 10°55.536'S, 28°47.945'E), where there's a gate. After about 8.4km of rather bad track you'll reach the falls The water goes over a two-stage drop, about 30m across. There are attractive rapids in between and a deep pool at the bottom – but no facilities at all, though there is a village nearby and camping is possible, with a good spot about 100m east of the falls.

Musonda Falls (⊕ TOMUSO 10°42.2952'S, 28°48.784'E) About 60km north of Mansa (141km south of Mbereshi) you cross the Mwense Bridge over the Luongo River. There is a reasonable set of scattered cascades (⊕ MUSON 10°42.856'S, 28°48.858'E) near here, but you first need to get permission to view them from the nearby hydro-electric power station; stop at the bridge and ask ZESCO security. This can be time-consuming, and there's not much to be seen as the river disappears into the power station.

Mambilima Falls (*US$10/5 adult/child; vehicle US$5/day; camping US$15pp inc entry*) About 90km north of Mansa (111km from Mbereshi) there's a set of lovely rapids on the Luapula River. These used to be called the Johnstone Falls and are scattered over a 5km stretch of the river. Turn off the main road about 5km south of Mambilima village, at a sign to the Christian Brethren Church Conference Centre (⊕ TUMAMB 10°32.260'S, 28°40.037'E). From here, follow the track for about 3km to the centre, where you can gaze over at the DRC or walk along the river for close-ups of some of the larger rapids. It's a very pleasant spot for lunch.

MWANSABOMBWE The village of Mwansabombwe (⊕ MWANSA 09°49.25'S, 28°45.35'E), just to the east of the main road (⊕ TOMWAN 09°49.317'S, 28°45.474'E) and 13km south of Mbereshi, is the focus of the colourful Mutomboko Ceremony – the Dance of Victory – that takes place every year on the last Saturday of July (see box, above), starting at 08.00. Visitors are welcome to watch, but photographers will need a pass costing Kw120,000 for the day. A statue at the entrance to the village commemorates the event.

If you're heading east to Kawambwa, don't be tempted to take a 'short cut' before Mbereshi by turning off the road at Mwansabombwe; this may look promising at first, but quickly disappears into a series of tracks that aren't the easiest to follow; stick to the main road unless you've time to explore!

MBERESHI The importance of Mbereshi (✪ MBERES 09°44.078'S, 28°47.350'E) to the visitor is threefold. It has a **fuel** station, though the supply at Kawambwa is rather more reliable. It is also the junction where you turn off for Kawambwa, Lumangwe Falls and Mporokoso. And finally, just after you turn onto this road, there's a **church** to the left on the hill that is one of Zambia's earliest. It was built in the early 1900s by the London Missionary Society, which was responsible for several other buildings in the vicinity, the rest of which are now in varying states of disrepair.

There are some serious speed humps at each end of the village; if you're driving yourself, be warned.

NCHELENGE This small town near the shores of Lake Mweru is the base for an occasional ferry service out to the two populated islands in the lake: Kilwa and Isokwe. In addition to a **post office** and small **market**, there is **fuel** available, albeit not necessarily reliable.

Getting there and away Buses heading north from Lusaka via Samfya and Mansa stop in Nchelenge, continuing on to Kashikishi which marks the end of the tar road.

Where to stay There are two places to stay in town:

Lake Mweru Water Transport Guest House 0212 972064. Rooms at this waterfront guesthouse are clean with en-suite facilities, & meals are available. This is also the place to organise boat trips out to Isokwe &

Kilwa, though you'll need your own tackle if you want to fish. **$**

Nchelenge Resthouse (19 rooms) This rather less attractive alternative is nearby. It's run by the council & is at least cheap. **$**

What to see and do The area by Lake Mweru will seem just like a continuous series of lakeside fishing villages. The fishing is (apparently) excellent, but there's also an abundance of crocodiles.

Birdwatchers might like to take a detour, using the track to the shore next to Chabilikila Primary School, which is just south of Nchelenge. This will lead you to some areas of papyrus near the mouth of the Luapula – a promising spot for finding swamp-dwelling species.

BEYOND KASHIKISHI TO MWERU WANTIPA NATIONAL PARK Some 3km beyond Nchelenge, at Kashikishi, the tar road comes to an end and the road deteriorates dramatically, so if you're aiming to get to Kaputa, allow plenty of time. Continue north along the edge of Lake Mweru for a scenic 30km or so, towards the village of Mununga then follow the road as it veers away from the lake until you reach the Kalungwishi River.

At the village of Mununga, turn right, then after around 30km go left (TOKAPU 09°07.531'S, 29°12.996'E) towards Kaputa. There are often market traders at the junction, so it's a good place to pick up whatever produce is in season. The stretch of road from this junction through Mweru Wantipa National Park to Kaputa is stony but reasonably level; it was re-graded in 2007 and is far better than many would have you believe, though you'll still need to drive with care. After 44km you'll come to a barrier, which marks the entrance to the national park (MWERUP 08°53.572'S, 29°28.878'E). From here, continue straight through the national park and across the top of Lake Mweru Wantipa to Kaputa (see opposite).

Mweru Wantipa National Park (*Park fees US$5 pp/day; vehicle US$15/day*) This is another large tract (3,134km²) of Zambia that was once a thriving national park, renowned for large elephant and crocodile populations. Now poaching has much reduced these, though reports suggest that some big game still lives here, and claims are made that sitatunga can be found among the dense papyrus beds on the lake shore. Sadly, though, to the casual observer the park appears to be singularly devoid of life; even the birds seem to have deserted the place.

That said, the whole area, including the lake, was designated a Ramsar site in 2007, at the same time as three other wetland areas in Zambia. Ramsar reports that the diversity of habitats along the lake, featuring riverine forest, wetlands and miombo woodland, attracts numerous waterbirds, including the wattled crane, black stork and Goliath's heron.

The road to Kaputa goes straight through the park, on the western side of Lake Mweru Wantipa, a sedimentary and highly seasonal lake which itself forms part of the national park. Along this road, you'll come to a ZAWA scout post (MWSCOP

08°47.807'S, 29°30.519'E). If you anticipate camping here, or even exploring away from the road, then ask if one of the scouts can accompany you.

KAPUTA Despite being the district capital, Kaputa (⊕ KAPUTA 08°28.503'S, 29°39.990'E) is a rather unattractive place, its main street strewn with rubbish, and with the dejected air of a border town. There's a branch of the National Savings and Credit Bank in town, an internet café, a few shops and a **market** where you can pick up basic foodstuffs. The presence of a few simple guesthouses (all **$**), including **JMC Roadside Guesthouse** by the barrier as well as **Chelewa Chalets** and **Twalifwaya Twalanaka**, is unlikely to deter most visitors from pressing on towards Lake Tanganyika (see pages 355–62).

FROM MBERESHI TO KASAMA

THE ROAD TO MPOROKOSO Turning east at Mbereshi, towards Mporokoso, you turn off the tar and onto a reasonable gravel road. Note that the pontoon across the Kalungwishi River at Chimpembe, about 86km from Mporokoso, has now been replaced by a solidly constructed bridge.

Places of interest along and around this road include:

Ntumbachushi Falls (⊕ NTUMBA 09°51.167'S, 28°56.652'E; *US$15/7 adult/ child; vehicle US$5/day; camping US$15 pp inc entry*) These falls are very clearly signposted about 23km east of Mbereshi and 18km west of Kawambwa, and 20km from the valley turn-off (⊕ 09°50.666'S, 28°56.450'E). They are just 1.2km south of the road along a good track, and surrounded by some beautiful thick *mishitu* forest.

The main falls drop about 40m into a dark pool, with a second cataract alongside. Don't swim in the main pool, as there are strong currents and undertows that can pull you under the falls themselves. However, both the pool at the foot of the second cataract and the gentle rapids above the first falls offer perfect places for a cooling dip or a proper swim. Clear footpaths lead from the car park in both directions.

Despite the derelict bungalows at the back of the car park, this is an idyllic spot to camp. Facilities, currently limited to a single long-drop toilet, were being upgraded in 2011. You can pitch either by the car park or – more secluded but away from the toilet – above the falls. It is also an ideal base from which to visit other waterfalls in the area.

In the rainy season, there is a further set of falls, the **Witch Doctor's Falls** a short walk away, so called because there used to be *ng'anga* shrines at its base, one containing millet, the other a model canoe carved from bone. If you'd like to visit, ask the helpful caretaker to guide you there, and remember to offer him a tip.

Kawambwa Rather smaller than most maps of Zambia might suggest, Kawambwa is a pleasant backwater 18.6km from Ntumbachushi Falls, with little to detain the visitor. It is, though, widely known for the large Kawambwa Tea Estate, east of the town, which was privatised in 1996. Production has slowed considerably in the last few years, giving added poignancy to a road sign proclaiming that Kawambwa will be 'poverty free by 2030'.

There's a reasonably reliable fuel station at the junction with the Mbereshi road, and a small market in town, as well as a range of shops and a branch of the Zanaco Bank.

A regular bus service operates every day except Monday between Lusaka and Kawambwa via Mansa, stopping next to the fuel station.

If you're driving straight through the town from Mbereshi, you'll come to a T-junction; to stay on track, turn left here (right takes you into Kawambwa), then almost immediately right (at ⊕ KAWAMB 038 09°47.605'S, 29°04.675'E). After a further 24km you'll come to the end of the tar, just by the tea estate.

Where to stay There are a few guesthouses in Kawambwa, including:

🏠 **Lusenga Lodge** On the left as you enter town, this relatively new place linked to the Lusenga Trust offers spotless en-suite rooms decked out in sunny paintwork. Each has dbl beds with DSTV, tea station & direct-dial phone. **$$**

🏠 **St Mary's Guesthouse** (12 rooms)
m 0979 648746. This simple but central establishment is linked to the Catholic church. Rooms have mosquito nets over the beds, & share bathroom facilities. **$**

Lusenga Plain National Park (*Park fees US$5 pp/day; vehicle US$15/day*)

Lusenga Plain was originally designated as a park to protect a large open plain, fringed by swamp and dry evergreen forest and surrounded by ridges of hills. On its northeastern side it is bordered by the Kalungwishi River, which passes over three beautiful waterfalls: Lumangwe, Kabwelume and Kundabwika.

Sadly, without enough support, Lusenga is now a park in name only. Poaching has reduced the game considerably and, with no internal roads in the park, there are few reasons to visit.

Perhaps the formation of the Lusenga Trust and a community resource board will eventually serve to turn round its fortunes and revitalise its once-abundant wildlife.

Getting there The park is usually approached from the Kawambwa–Mporokoso road, and you should be very well equipped for any attempt to reach it. Some visitors have had success in reaching the park by getting a game scout as a guide from the ZAWA in Kawambwa. Otherwise the park is hard to enter.

Falls on and around the Kalungwishi River

The Kalungwishi River forms the boundary between the Luapula and Northern regions of Zambia, and also the eastern boundary of Lusenga Plain National Park. Along the river are three major waterfalls in relatively close succession: Lumangwe, Kabwelume and Kundabwika. While Lumangwe is the most straightforward to reach, and well worth the visit, the greater draw is Kabwelume, 5km further on and a must for anyone in the vicinity. Getting to Kundabwika is altogether more demanding.

In addition to the falls themselves, there are miles of pleasant walking upstream, so consider staying overnight to give time to explore the other falls further downstream.

Pressure for electricity in Zambia is likely to impact on the river, with plans for a hydro-electric power station between Lumangwe and Kandabwika falls.

Where to stay There are **campsites** with flush toilets at Lumangwe, Kabwelume and Kundabwika Falls, but we have been unable to contact the owners of the self-catering Cascade Cottage nearby. However, in case the situation should change, it is signposted from the Kawambwa–Mporokoso road about 300m from the Chimpempe bridge, then a further 2km down the track.

Lumangwe Falls (*US$15/7 adult/child; vehicle US$5/day; camping US$15 pp inc entry*) To reach these, turn left off the Kawambwa–Mporokoso road about 2km east of the Chimpempe bridge (⊕ CHIMBR 09°33.082'S, 29°26.937'E), which crosses the Kalungwishi River some 65km from Kawambwa and 86km from Mporokoso. There's a clear signpost to Lumangwe and Kabwelume Falls on the north side of the road, on the outside of a bend (⊕ FALLST 09°32.239'S, 29°27.874'E). The track is narrow, level and fairly straight, continuing for about 10km to a fork (⊕ LUMAFK 09°32.466'S, 29°23.296"E), where there's a new information centre. Bear left here; the falls are just 300m away, manned by a caretaker.

Lumangwe is a solid white-and-green wall of water, 100m across and 30m high. It's perhaps the most spectacular of the waterfalls in this region and bears comparison to Victoria Falls. The noise is deafening and the air is filled with fine mist. There are two viewing points, one overlooking the main falls from the front, and a second – much drier! – from the top of the falls where you can see how a large island splits the river's flow. The energetic might want to climb to the bottom of the falls in order to reach the end of the rainbow that's seen on most days. There are no pots of gold here though, and the climb comes with a warning: instead of steps, you'll be making your way down (and then up) a rope using the cliff side for balance.

You can camp at the falls in safety; an ablution block with flush toilets has been built close to the falls, with a campsite behind. The former guesthouse is to become a curio shop.

Kabwelume Falls (⊕ KABWEL 09°31.432'S, 29°21.267'E; *US$15/7 adult/child; vehicle US$5/day; camping US$15 pp inc entry*) These falls are 5km downstream from Lumangwe, which makes a pleasant walk for two or three hours through the forest. Ask for precise directions at Lumangwe. Alternatively you can drive yourself, provided that you have a good 4x4: the track is very poor in parts and it's slow going. Simply return to the fork close to Lumangwe Falls, then turn left and continue for 5km or so to a small parking area. There's also a new campsite with ablution block.

Unlike that around many of the area's waterfalls, the vegetation at Kabwelume has been left to grow wild, enhancing the approach to the fall – provided that you come prepared (this is no place for flip-flops!). The increasingly overgrown path takes you across the river on stepping stones (probably inaccessible in the rainy season), then through thick vegetation dotted with bright flowers and alive with butterflies, and finally down a steep, slippery slope. You'll emerge after 300m or so to a most magnificent waterfall – a curving curtain of water 20m high and 75m across. Below is a deep pool, which itself flows over a second fall of 20m. On the left are two cataracts falling the whole 40m; on the right water pours down the cliff face. Look about you and this makes 180° of water – with the cataract, the main waterfall and the waterspout. It's a truly beautiful sight, worth savouring.

Kundabwika Falls (⊕ KUNDAB 9°13.058'S, 29°18.258'E; *US$10/5 adult/child; vehicle US$5/day; camping US$15 pp inc entry*) These are the last major falls on the Kalungwishi before it flows into Lake Mweru. Despite that, they are accessed from a different road, which may be impassable after rain; ask for advice locally, perhaps from Joseph at Ntumbachushi.

There are two routes to the falls, both requiring a 4x4. The normal route is from the Kawambwa–Mporokoso road. About 21km east of the Chimpempe Bridge (⊕ KUNDTO 09°27.945'S, 29°36.447'E), or 63km west of Mporokoso, turn northwest onto a narrow, very poor track; it's just west of a road barrier and signposted to Chikwanda Basic School; some maps mark this as a place called Mukunsa. Continue along this track, which is deeply rutted and pot-holed, for about 50km. It passes through villages for about 30km, then descends into less populous woodlands. It's very slow going so allow around two hours to the turn-off. The turning towards the falls (⊕ TOKUND 09°11.397'S, 29°19.890'E), is into woodland, and almost invisible when the grass is high, so ask one of the villagers to point it out. From here, there's a straightforward 5km track that leads to the river.

Approaching from the opposite direction, drive 65km north of Nchelenge to the village of Mununga, on the banks of Lake Mweru. From there it's 35km to the falls on a reasonable dirt road, turning south at ⊕ TOKUND, as above.

The woodland track brings you out by a series of gentle rapids, known as the upper falls. An expanse of open grassland offers plenty of room to camp, with no villages nearby, and just the occasional fisherman for company. To reach the main falls, a further 1km downstream, involves clambering over boulders along the riverbank.

Kundabwika itself is a geometrical waterfall, a 25m-wide rectangular block of green-and-white water. It's not possible to get very close to the falls, but there are good long-distance views from the top of the rock outcrop.

As you approach the falls, about 3km from the road and to the left of the woodland track, there's a rocky outcrop where rock paintings can clearly be seen. You can explore yourself or, if you have time, ask if one of the villagers can take you to see them. A new if basic campsite at the site, with flush toilets, is a bonus after the long drive in.

Mumbuluma Falls II These falls (⊕ MUMBII 09°13.024'S, 29°20.681'E) lie 3km from the Kundabwika Falls turn-off, between Nyausa and Lumpa villages. Just before Nyausa School and past Kakoma Stream there's a 1km winding path to the falls. To be honest, it's little more than a rapid (they're also known as Mwesa Rapids) but it's quite scenic, with views of the Lusenga Plain National Park.

Yangumwila Falls There is said to be another set of falls, Yangumwila, on the Itabu River. From Lumangwe Falls, head towards Mporokoso. The falls lie a three-hour walk away from Chiwala Primary School. Ask around for details.

MPOROKOSO Mporokoso (⊕ MPOROK 09°21.831'S, 30°07.402'E) is a useful small town in the heart of northern Zambia. It lies at a T-junction on the Kawambwa–Kasama road, and is also the main access point for Sumbu National Park (see pages 364–6 for directions to the park). The centre is to the west of the T-junction, along a wide, tree-lined avenue. Here you'll find a branch of the National Savings and Credit Bank, a police station, post office, shops and a small market – in short, a normal Zambian town.

The town's recent history is very much tied up with that of refugees from the war in the DRC. In early 1999, a number of refugees and loyalist Congolese troops fled across the border to Zambia, crossing around Kaputa and Sumbu. They were looked after by the UNHCR, the Red Cross, Oxfam and other agencies at Mwange Camp, about 60km outside Mporokoso, on the way to Kawambwa. Many of the aid agencies retain a presence here, and there's also a fairly large government hospital (with doctors but generally poor medicines and equipment), serving a large area of the country.

Getting there and away Most people coming to Mporokoso will be on the main Kawambwa–Kasama road – although it's in pretty poor shape from Kawambwa - and only a little better from Kasama.

If you're approaching from Mpulungu or Mbala, there is a road that avoids Kasama, although it's over 70km long, and rough going (you'll need a 4x4) even in the dry season – so it's hardly a 'short cut'. To find it, head towards Kasama from Mbala. About 74km from Mbala you'll see a turning to the right (⊕ TOSHCT 09°27.486'S, 31°13.136'E). This joins up with the Kasama–Mporokoso road at ⊕ TOSHC2 09°40.270'S, 30°41.628'E, about 8km northwest of Kapatu Mission (81km southeast of Mporokoso).

For those heading to Luwingu, there's also a way to avoid Kasama. To find it, follow the road southeast to Kasama for around 55km to a right turning. Take this road, continuing southwest until it joins the Kasama–Luwingu road. It's not in superb condition, but is just passable in a normal car during the dry season, though you would certainly need a 4x4 when it's wet.

🏠 **Where to stay** If you wish to break your journey here, there are a few very simple guesthouses, including:

🏠 **Riverside Hotel** (20 rooms) Reader Mieke Symoens recommends this secluded & secure hotel on the north of the Kawambwa–Mporokoso road, at the entrance to the town. Campers may be allowed to pitch a tent in the garden, but will need to pay for a room for the use of a bathroom. Drinks & local meals ($) are available. **$**

Waterfall excursions from Mporokoso

Kapuma Falls These small but delightful falls (⊕ KAPUM 09°23.235'S, 30°05.675'E), cascading over scattered wall-like rocks, make a pleasant half-day trip from town and are a great picnic spot. Around 7km southwest of Mporokoso, past the district hospital, turn left just before the Agricultural Training Centre, from where it's around 2km to the falls. The road ends on a private farm, so if somebody is home do ask permission to see the falls.

Pule Falls Also known as Chipulwe Falls, these (⊕ PULEF 09°30.573'S, 30°17.001'E) lie just off the road to the (other) Luangwa River. Take the dirt road southeast of Mporokoso for 24km, turning off east after the Luangwa bridge onto a motorable path for 1km. There's a 500m footpath through cassava fields and banana plantations to these scenic, but not very deep, falls (about 15m drop). They're worth the two-hour trip from Mporokoso.

Mumbuluma Falls III These falls (⊕ MUMIII 09°33.211'S, 29°44.736'E) are surprisingly impressive; surprising, as neither they nor the river that spawns them, the other Luangwa, are well known. Sadly, although they offer good places for camping, with no villages nearby, access has been blocked in recent years. Should the situation change, you reach them by heading 33km west out of Mporokoso to Angelo village (⊕ ANGELO 9°26.771'S, 29°49.511'E). Turn south here for 14km, then west for 4km, where there's a footpath to the falls across the clearing.

Lupupa Falls These (⊕ LUPUPA 9°16.441'S, 29°46.910'E) make for a pleasant outing when combined with Mumbuluma Falls III, possibly by having lunch at the former and camping at the latter. To reach them, head west out of Mporokoso on the 28km fair dirt road to Njalamimba. From here, head on 10km to Chandalala, then take the 3km motorable footpath before finally crossing the bridge on foot. The main attractions are the views from the falls down the gorge along the Mukubwe, over the hills and into the pool itself.

MPOROKOSO TO KASAMA Perhaps surprisingly for what might appear to be a fairly important artery, the 196km road between Mporokoso and Kasama is for the most part very poorly maintained, so it's not a journey to rush; you should allow around four hours, without stops. There are few villages along this stretch, either, so little to alleviate the monotony of consecutive pot-holes and deep ruts.

After 106km you'll come to the Kapatu Mission (⊕ KAPATU 09°43.148'S, 30°43.845'E) on the left of the road, where there are also a few shops. A further 54km brings you to the turn-off to Chishimba Falls (see pages 351–2), shortly after crossing the picturesque Luombe River. The falls are close to the road and it's well worth stopping here for an hour or two. From the falls, it's just 11km to the tar road, then at last a smooth final 25km to the centre of Kasama (see pages 347–51).

NYIKA PLATEAU NATIONAL PARK

(*Park fees Malawian side US$5 pp/day; vehicle US$2/day*) Nyika Plateau is a marvellous area for hiking, and has some unusual wildlife. It lies mostly in Malawi, with just a slim Zambian national park hugging the border, and is best approached from the Malawian side. For this reason, below is a description of the plateau as a whole, and how to see it, including directions within Malawi.

GEOGRAPHY Zambia's tiny Nyika Plateau National Park, just 80km², adjoins Malawi's largest: Nyika National Park, which was established in 1965 and extended to 3,134km² in 1978. At the heart of both parks lies the gently undulating Nyika Plateau, which averages over 2,000m in altitude.

In addition to the main plateau, the Malawian national park also protects part of the eastern slopes of the Nyika range, where grassland and forest are replaced by thick miombo woodland.

FLORA AND FAUNA
Flora Nyika is notable for its wonderful montane scenery, and as being an ideal hiking destination. The lower slopes harbour miombo woodland, which is replaced by more open grassland at the higher altitudes. Of particular interest to botanists are the roughly 200 orchid species recorded in the park, which generally flower in January and February; of these 11 species are endemic to Nyika.

Mammals Nyika protects a rich diversity of mammals – almost 100 species have been recorded – including an endemic race of plains zebra, *Equus quagga crawshaii*, and a very high density of leopard.

Game viewing is good all year round, and the open nature of the plateau ensures excellent visibility. In the area around Chelinda Lodge, visitors are practically guaranteed to see roan antelope, scrub hare, zebra, reedbuck, bushbuck and eland. Your chances of seeing leopard around Chelinda are good.

The lower slopes of miombo woodland support good populations of buffalo and elephant, though these animals only rarely move up to the grassland of the plateau. Lion and cheetah are also infrequent visitors to the plateau.

Birds With well over 400 species recorded, Nyika supports a great diversity of birdlife. However, many of the species included on the checklist are found only in the miombo woodland of the lower slopes, which are best accessed from the Malawian side of the park, near the main entrance gate at Thazima, and are thus unlikely to be seen by visitors who stick to the plateau.

The grassland around Chelinda Camp is inhabited by several tantalising birds. Foremost are the wattled crane, Denham's bustard and the exquisite scarlet-tufted

12

Chisenga, Nkonde

Karonga

2017m
Mpanda
Bleak House

N. Rukuni

Kawozya

Nthalire

Chipome

Jalawe

Chisenga, Isoka

Mahowe 1881m

Domwe

Nganda 2606m

Bemba

Kongera 2187m
Kaperekezi

Chisanga Falls

Lake Kaulime

Chelinda Lodge/ Camp

ZAMBIA

site of Zambian Resthouse (closed)

Chelinda Campsite

Chosi

Chelinda

Muyombe

Chire

Sangule Kopje

Nyika Plateau National Park

Chelinda Falls

2148m
Mwanda

MALAWI

Juniper forest

Fingira Rock

Thazima

Chama

Rumphi

N

Nkhonjera

Bradt

0 — 8km
0 — 5 miles

Katumbi

Rumphi, Mzuzu

malachite sunbird (distinguished from the commoner malachite sunbird by its much longer tail). As rewarding as the grassland for general birding are the forests, particularly the large Chowo Forest near the Zambian resthouse, where localised species such as Sharpe's akalat, bar-tailed trogon, olive-flanked robin, white-breasted alethe and a variety of other robins and bulbuls may be seen.

Four birds found at Nyika (yellow mountain warbler, churring cisticola, crackling cloud cisticola and mountain marsh widow) have been recorded nowhere else in Malawi, while the Nyika races of red-winged francolin, rufous-naped lark, greater double-collared sunbird and Baglafecht weaver are all endemic to the plateau.

There are also three butterfly species endemic to the plateau, and one species each of chameleon, frog and toad which are found nowhere else.

The rivers and dams on the Nyika Plateau are stocked with rainbow trout, and are thus popular with anglers.

GETTING THERE AND AWAY

By air By far the easiest way to Nyika is by air. Charter flights between Mzuzu and Chelinda (*US$200 pp one way, min 2*) should resume soon, but in the meantime it is possible to get a charter flight from Lilongwe. If you've picked a clear day with few clouds, the views from the aircraft are stunning, and you can clearly see the foothills, the patches of natural forest, the plantations in Linnaean symmetry and the open expanses of rolling heathland.

Driving Chelinda Camp lies roughly 115km from Rumphi in Malawi, and is reached along recently re-graded roads which shouldn't present any problem in the dry season but which may be challenging after heavy rain; a high-clearance 4x4 is recommended at any time. Although the route is not signposted, from Rumphi you take the S85 (the only road out of town) westwards for 45km, then keep right where the main road bends left to Katumbi. Thazima entrance gate is 8km along this road. About 40km past the entrance gate, a signposted turn-off to the right leads to Chelinda, a further 20km away. The best place to stock up on food before you reach Nyika is Mzuzu, and the last place where you can be sure of fuel is Rumphi.

In the dry season, the journey between Lilongwe and Nyika is a comfortable eight–nine-hour drive; during the rains, it can be done in a day but it's a very long slog; allow ten hours. You may want to overnight in Mzuzu *en route* or perhaps at one of the northern lakeshore areas near Chintheche. To check current road conditions, contact Wilderness Safaris (m *+265 (0)888 822398, 24hrs*). They also offer road transfers from Mzuzu, priced accoding to the number of guests.

By bus/hitchhiking There is no through public transport to Chelinda, although in the dry season, there is a twice-weekly bus between Rumphi and Chitipa which will drop you at the last turn-off, from where you'll either have to walk the last 20km to Chelinda (it's reasonably flat!) or else hope to hitch a lift. In the rainy season, there is no bus but you can easily get a *matola* from Rumphi along the S85 (ask for a vehicle heading to Katumbi), then walk the 8km from where you will be dropped to the entrance gate. Provided you have a tent, it is permitted to camp at the entrance gate, though facilities are basic.

If you want to hitch all the way, you'd be wiser trying to get a lift from Rumphi through to Chelinda, to be sure of not getting stuck halfway. The best days to hitch are Fridays and Saturdays, which is when Malawian residents tend to head to the park (but also when accommodation is most likely to be fully booked – not a problem, of course, if you have a tent).

Organised safaris and hikes Reasonably priced safaris to Nyika can be organised from Nkhata Bay, starting at around US$120 per person per day. More adventurously, the Rumphi-based Matunkha Eco-Tours offer a two-day hike up to Chelinda from Rumphi.

At the other end of the spectrum, Robin Pope Safaris (see page 268) run ten-night trips each October that combine the Nyika Plateau with their Nsefu Camp in the South Luangwa and Pumulani on Lake Malawi (*US$7,242 pp FBA, inc drinks, laundry & internal flights*).

WHERE TO STAY The only viable places to stay in the area are at Chelinda Lodge or Chelinda Camp, formerly leased to the Nyika Safari Company, but taken over in 2009 by Wilderness Safaris (+265 (0)1 771393/771153; e reservations@wilderness. mw; www.wilderness-safaris.com). Both places were refurbished prior to re-opening in July 2010.

Chelinda Lodge (8 cabins) Built from timber & stone collected from the plateau, this upmarket lodge lies on the edge of pine forest with stunning views across the montane grasslands. Its 2-storey cabins have a viewing area upstairs above an open-plan lounge & twin bedroom where a central fireplace comes into its own in winter – roaring log fires are exactly what you need. The cabins are en suite with a private veranda, too, & there's a slightly larger version for families. Central to the lodge are a dining area & lounge that open onto a deck, & are linked to the rooms by wooden walkways. Activities from both here & the camp include 4x4 game drives day & night, mountain biking, walking & trout fishing. *US$420–540/640–880 sgl/dbl FBA, inc park fees.*

Chelinda Camp (6 rooms, 4 chalets, camping) Overlooking a beautiful small dam, & encircled by extensive pine plantations, Chelinda Camp is a little lower down than the lodge. Recently renovated dbl rooms, each with a toilet & bath or shower en suite, are simple & solid. These share a dining area, lounge & bar with its own fireplace. Alongside are individual chalets, each with 2 dbl bedrooms, bathroom,

lounge, dining area with fireplace & a small, fully equipped kitchen.

Guests can self cater in the chalets & do their own morning & day drives, or can opt for a fully catered stay with all meals & activities provided. For self caterers, a resident chef does all your cooking for you, but since you must bring it all with you, this is only an option if you are driving here: the nearest shop is 4hrs away in Rumphi, & even that is very limited. However, self caterers can also take occasional meals in the restaurant. *Rooms US$235–260 pp FBA; self catering US$120/ night (max 4).*

Chelinda Campsite About 2km from the main camp, the campsite is in a lovely spot in the forest with sweeping views over undulating grassland. There are no permanent tents here, so you'll need your own tent, but there is a large, clean ablution block with hot showers. Campers should keep food well out of reach of the resident hyenas – which have even been known to gnaw on car tyres! You can eat in the main camp provided that you book in advance (b/fast US$15, lunch, US$20, dinner US$25). *Camping US$10 pp.*

WHAT TO SEE AND DO Nyika National Park has many very scenic spots and archaeological sites, and several different hiking and driving options along an extensive network of roads and trails. Mountain bikes can be hired at Chelinda Camp (*US$15/day*). While visitors are free to walk where they please by day (and to explore the park by road if they have private transport), all guided activities and night drives must be organised through Wilderness Safaris Malawi (above).

The following synopsis of major attractions serves as a taster only.

Walks around Chelinda Plenty of roads radiate from Chelinda Camp, and it would be quite possible to spend four or five days in the area without repeating a walk. The marshy area immediately downstream of Chelinda Dam (which lies right in front of the camp) is a good place to see bushbuck and a variety of birds, and the dam itself attracts nocturnal predators such as hyena and leopard. A good short walk for visitors with limited time is to the **two dams** near Chelinda. The road here follows a dambo (a seasonal or perennial marsh) and the area offers good game viewing, as well as frequent sightings of wattled crane. The round trip covers 8km and takes two hours.

Another good short walk (about an hour) is from behind Chalet Four to the Kasaramba turn-off and then left along Forest Drive through the pine plantation back to Chalet Four. At dusk, there is a fair chance of seeing leopards along this walk, and daytime sightings are not uncommon.

A longer walk takes you to **Lake Kaulime**, which lies 8km west of Chelinda. This is the only natural lake on the plateau and is traditionally said to be the home of a serpent which acts as the guardian to Nyika's animals. More certain attractions than legendary serpents are migratory waterfowl (in summer) and large mammals, particularly roan antelope and zebra, coming to drink. It is also a very attractive spot, circled by indigenous trees.

Night drives Spotlit night drives out of Chelinda offer the best opportunity to see nocturnal predators. Leopard and serval are often seen on the fringes of Chelinda Forest, while spotted hyena and side-striped jackal are common in grassy areas. When we last visited, we were lucky enough to see a pair of honey badgers crossing the road – a first for both of us. Especially in winter, the plateau gets really cold at night, and you should take all your warm clothing with you in the vehicle.

Horseriding A stable of around 25–30 horses used to be kept at Chelinda, with animals suitable for both novice and experienced riders. At the time of writing, Wilderness Safaris were considering re-introducing these for 2012, but this should be checked in advance.

Fishing The rivers and dams on the Nyika Plateau have long been popular with anglers for their rainbow trout, but stocks are currently seriously depleted. At present, fly fishing is available in some places by arrangement with Wilderness Safaris.

Walks and drives further afield Many of the more interesting points in Nyika are too far from Chelinda to be reached on a day walk, though they are accessible to visitors with vehicles.

Jalawe Rock About 1km on foot from a car park 34km north of Chelinda. The views here are spectacular, stretching over a close range of mountains to Lake Malawi's mountainous Tanzanian shore. With binoculars, it is often possible to see buffaloes and elephants in the miombo woodland of the Mpanda Ridge below. A variety of raptors, as well as klipspringer, are frequently seen around the rock, and the surrounding vegetation includes many proteas.

Nganda Peak At 2,605m, this is the highest peak on the plateau. It lies about 30km northeast of Chelinda, and can be reached by following the Jalawe Rock road for about 25km then turning left on to a 4km-long motorable track. It's a 1.5km walk from the end of the track to the peak.

Kasaramba Viewpoint This viewpoint lies 43km southeast of Chelinda. You can drive to within 1.5km of the viewpoint and then walk the final stretch. When it isn't covered in mist, the views to the lake are excellent, and you can also see remnants of the terraced slopes built by the early Livingstonia missionaries. The most extensive rainforest in Nyika lies on the slopes below Kasaramba, and visitors frequently see the localised crowned eagle and mountain buzzard in flight. From Kasaramba, a 3km road leads to the top of the pretty 30m-high Nchenachena Falls.

Further along the road to Kasaramba, also 43km from Chelinda, is a large juniper forest, the most southerly stand of *Juniperus procera* in Africa. A short trail offers the opportunity of sighting forest animals such as leopard, elephant shrew, red duiker, bushpig and a variety of forest birds. The forest can also be explored from the firebreaks that surround it.

Zovo Chipola Forest   Near the old Zambian resthouse, Zovo Chipola is of special interest to birdwatchers, and also harbours several mammal species, the most commonly seen of which are bushbuck, blue monkey and elephant shrew. An unmarked trail runs through the forest, which is best visited with a local guide, at least if you hope to pick up the calls of such elusive forest birds as the bar-tailed trogon.

Chowo Forest   Larger than Zovo Chipola Forest and nearer to the old Zambian Resthouse in the Zambian part of the park, this used to be popular with people staying at the resthouse, but it is now somewhat off the beaten track.

Fingira Rock   A large granite dome lying 22km south of Chelinda. On the eastern side of the rock, a cave 11m deep and 18m long was used as a shelter by humans around 3,000 years ago – excavations in 1965 unearthed a complete human skeleton and a large number of stone tools. Several schematic rock paintings can be seen on the walls of the cave. A motorable track runs to the base of the rock, 500m from the cave. The miombo woodland around Thazima entrance gate is rich in birds and noted for unusual species.

Wilderness trails   Six wilderness trails have been designated within Nyika National Park, ranging from one to five nights in duration. There are two options for visitors. Those wishing to do a more basic hike must supply their own camping equipment and food, and are required to make an advance booking through Wilderness Safaris Malawi (page 384), who will organise a national parks scout, and porters if required. Alternatively, Wilderness Safaris offers fully serviced and catered trails with large tents and expert guides; costs depend on the size of group.

The cost for most of the basic hikes is US$30 per person for the first night and an additional US$20 per night thereafter for the first two people. Additional people are charged US$5 per person per night. The Livingstone Trail commands a one-off additional payment of US$50, on top of this. There is a small extra charge for porters. Of particular interest are:

Livingstonia Trail *(US$80 for 1 or 2 people; US$10 pp for each additional person)* The most popular of Nyika's wilderness trails leads from Chelinda all the way to Livingstonia on the Rift Valley escarpment east of the national park. This three-day, two-night guided hike is recommended only in the dry season. Hiking the route in reverse is not permitted, as a guide and park fees cannot be organised at Livingstonia, though this may become possible in future.

Jalawe and Chipome River Trail   Of particular interest for wildlife viewing is this four-night trail, which passes through the miombo woodland in the northern part of the park. It offers the opportunity to see elephant, buffalo, greater kudu and a variety of other mammals that are generally absent from the plateau.

FURTHER INFORMATION   If you can, get hold of a copy of Sigrid Anna Johnson's out-of-print but excellent guide to the plateau, *A Visitor's Guide to Nyika National*

Park, Malawi (see *Appendix 3*, page 537). There is a copy in the library at Chelinda. A small booklet containing a detailed map of the Chelinda area is sold at the park reception for a nominal charge.

Another useful resource is the website of the **Nyika Vwaza Trust** (*www.nyika-vwaza-trust.org*), a UK-based organisation dedicated to preserving the wildlife and habitats of Nyika and Vwaza.

The above description of Nyika Plateau has been edited from an original section in the excellent *Malawi: The Bradt Travel Guide* by Philip Briggs. If you plan an extended visit to Malawi, then get hold of a copy of this before you travel – it's the standard reference on travel in Malawi.

THE COPPERBELT

DEMOCRATIC REPUBLIC
OF THE CONGO

13

The Copperbelt

The Copperbelt is Zambia's industrial base, a prosperous area around Ndola, Kitwe and Chingola dotted with mines: the area's production of copper and cobalt is of global importance. The population density here is high, and the environmental impact of so many people can clearly be seen. Despite this, the centres of the Copperbelt's cities are pleasant and not the sprawling industrial wastes that might be expected.

For the normal visitor, these areas have very few attractions and so this chapter is deliberately concise. For simplicity's sake, this text also covers three of the main towns around the Copperbelt – Kabwe and Kapiri Mposhi to the south, and Solwezi to the west – even though these are outside the confines of the Copperbelt Province.

The region tends to attract a higher level of rainfall than Lusaka, so bear this in mind if you are planning to travel in the rainy season. Note, too, that land in the Copperbelt is at a higher altitude than that further south – Ndola, for example, is 1,296m above sea level, and Solwezi higher still. As a result, it's generally cooler here than in the capital, so do remember to bring warmer clothes, especially for the evenings.

THE HISTORY OF THE COPPER

Zambia's rich copper deposits have been exploited since around the 6th or 7th century AD. There is evidence that the early Iron-Age inhabitants of Zambia mined, smelted and even traded copper with their neighbours – bracelets and bangles have been found at several sites.

However, large-scale exploitation of these reserves waited until the 20th century. Around the turn of the century, the old sites where native Africans had mined copper for centuries, like Bwana Mkubwa southeast of Ndola, were being examined by European and American prospectors. The demand for metals was stimulated from 1914 to 1918 by World War I, and small mines opened up to satisfy this need. They worked well, but these small-scale productions were only viable whilst the price of the raw materials remained high. Copper, zinc, lead and vanadium were among the most important of the minerals being mined.

Given Zambia's location, and the high costs of transporting any produce out of this land-locked country, it made economic sense to process the mineral ores there, and then export the pure metal ingots. However, this would require considerable investment and large-scale operations.

After the war, demand for copper continued to increase, fuelled by the expansion in the worldwide electrical and automotive industries. Large-scale mining became a more feasible option. In 1922 the British South Africa Company, who claimed to have bought all of the country's mining concessions in various tribal agreements, started to allocate large prospecting areas for foreign companies. Exploration skills

The Copperbelt   THE HISTORY OF THE COPPER

13

389

from overseas flowed into the country, locating several large deposits of copper – well beneath the levels of the existing mining operations.

By the early 1930s, four large new mines were coming on stream: Nkana, Nchanga, Roan Antelope and Mufulira. These were to change Northern Rhodesia's economy permanently. Despite a collapse of the prices for copper in 1931, the value of the country's exports increased by 400% between 1930 and 1933 – leaving copper accounting for 90% of the country's exports by value. Thus began the mining industry which in 2010 accounted for about 11% of Zambia's GDP and 85% of Zambia's export earnings.

Over the last decade, the price of copper has fluctuated, first sending the Copperbelt's newly privatised industry into the doldrums, then elevating interest in the 'green rock' to goldrush levels. As a result, the industry has expanded beyond the traditional confines of the Copperbelt, with both Kansanshi Mine at Solwezi and the huge Lumwana Mine another 65km to the west now up and running.

LUSAKA TO KAPIRI MPOSHI

The Great North Road out of Lusaka, the T2, rapidly slips off the city's dirty industrial belt for open bush and mile after mile of farmland, planted with everything from soya beans to maize and coffee. It's a good, tarred road, increasingly undulating beyond Kabwe, with the only problem likely to come from slow-moving haulage trucks transporting goods to or from the region's mines.

At intervals along the roadside, local produce is offered for sale. Look out for **honey** in large plastic containers to the north of Kabwe, and various small **markets** that you'll pass *en route*.

WHERE TO STAY If you're heading in this direction, but looking for somewhere to stay reasonably close to Lusaka, there are several options before the town of Kabwe. The best of these are listed below, from south to north. Chrismar Hotels are planning to construct a new lodge in this area, too.

Protea Hotel Safari Lodge (40 rooms) Great North Rd; 0211 212843–6; e chisamba@zamnet.zm; www.proteahotels. com. Set in a private game reserve 45km north of Lusaka. For details, see page 139.

Fringilla Farm Lodge (46 rooms, 5 chalets, 2 flats, 2 houses, camping) Great North Rd, Chisamba; 0211 213885/214364; e fringillalodge@gmail.com; www.fringillalodge. com. Situated about 51km north of Lusaka towards Kabwe (look out for the sign on the east side of the road), Fringilla is part of a large, working farm that has expanded to include a butchery, a dairy, a clinic & even a post office; the bank that was on site is now 500m up the road on the opposite side.

Gone is the erstwhile small B&B, its place taken by a rather ramshackle selection of accommodation that capitalises primarily on the conference trade. The reception & conference room occupy the old farm building, but the restaurant & bar have moved to a spacious new building centre stage ($$; ⏰ 06.30–21.30 *daily*). Dining here, or outside, concentrates on farm produce: sausages, steaks & chops, with a braai at w/ends. That, plus an extensive children's playground, farm walks, & the option of horseriding (no hard hats provided), make it a good venue for day trips. Behind the restaurant are a range of simple but well-kept rooms, all en suite (some with just a low partition) & with ceiling fans, fridge, kettle, nets & the obligatory TV. Well back again is a small shady campsite & basic ablution block, shared by 12, 2-bed chalets. With friendly & helpful staff, the atmosphere is pleasant & relaxed. $$–$$$ b/fast extra. Camping Kw25,000 pp.

Chaplin's Barbet (7 rooms) 0211 213762; m 096 848267; e arulussa@zamnet. zm. This simple camp on an organic farm, named for Zambia's only truly endemic bird, was opened for the eclipse in 2002, but isn't really geared to walk-in visitors. It's situated 73km north of Lusaka, about 1km west of the Great North Rd along a track that's level but deceptively slippery in the wet season. With their earthy red tones, the square brick chalets under thatch are unpretentious but pleasant enough, each having a stone floor, twin beds with mosquito nets, & en-suite shower. Meals can be provided in the small boma by prior arrangement. Visitors are welcome to look round the farm, which produces (& sells) essential oils for aromatherapy. **$$**

🏠 **Ibis Gardens** (39 rooms) Great North Rd; 📞 0211 213764; m 0966 954080; e ibis@zamnet. zm; www.ibiszambia.com. East of the Great North Rd, some 74km from Lusaka, Ibis is set in 18ha grounds down a level 1km drive. With its painted chalets neatly arranged across flat, well-kept lawns dotted with banana & guava

GEOLOGY OF THE COPPERBELT   *Steven Lewis*

The Central African Copperbelt spans the border of northwestern Zambia and southern DRC and represents one of the largest copper provinces in the world. Known deposits falling within the Zambian Copperbelt contain approximately 88 million tonnes of copper.

Archaeological evidence for copper mining in Zambia dates as far back as the 4th century when malachite was mined and smelted into cross-shaped ingots known as *nsanshi*, which were used for trading. Large-scale copper production, however, didn't start until around the turn of the last century when early European explorers were shown the out-cropping copper deposits near present-day Ndola, Kitwe and Solwezi. As a result, commercial mines were opened shortly after the Cape-to-Cairo railway line reached Ndola from the south, and mining has continued to the present day.

However, the full story of the Zambian Copperbelt began around 877 million years ago, when the oldest rocks of the so-called Katangan Supergroup were deposited in a series of basins that now form the heart of the Copperbelt. The earliest rocks of this group are made up of conglomerates and sandstones that were deposited by rivers and deltas in a series of narrow troughs during the early stages of the evolution of the basins. As the basins developed and deepened, the character of the rocks changed in response to the changing depositional conditions, resulting in dolomite-dominated rocks that were deposited on platforms under fairly shallow water. In response to further basin deepening a later group of rocks, comprising a transition from dolomite, through a mixed series of dolomites and siltstones to a dominant siltstone were deposited, indicating an accumulation of material in a deep-water environment. At this point, a major change in the geological environment occurred, indicated by the presence of a thick unit of debris flows known as the 'Grand Conglomerate', with overlying siltstones. The Grand Conglomerate is a remarkable unit that can be traced for hundreds of kilometres and probably reflects the breaking up of the Rodinian Supercontinent around 740 million years ago.

The origin of the copper deposits contained in these rocks has long been debated by geologists studying the Copperbelt. Early theories leaned towards a 'syngenetic' origin, suggesting that the copper was deposited at the same time as the rocks in which it occurs. More recent research favours a longer, multi-stage 'diagenetic' origin, in which the copper was introduced into the rocks via major fault systems over a very long period of perhaps 300 million years or more, long after the rocks were deposited.

trees, the place has a rather suburban feel. The impression persists inside the dbl or twin rooms, with their white walls & simple but modern furnishings. Yet if it's quite corporate, it's also very clean & pleasant. AC/heater, safe, fridge & tea-/coffee-making facilities come as standard, as does a huge en-suite shower. Larger houses have 2 or 3 bedrooms, a lounge & a kitchenette.

During the week this is very much a business venue, with internet café, restaurant & bar, but at w/ends it morphs into family mode, with pizzas & braais on offer, & sports facilities that include tennis, volleyball, basketball, a gym & a large, free-form pool complete with its own island. A further 33 rooms should be completed by 2012. **$$**

KABWE This small town (✪ KABWE 14°26.655'S, 28°26.717'E) is situated little more than 60km south of Kapiri Mposhi and about 142km north of Lusaka. It was built on the old colonial model of a central business area with a perpendicular road-grid, surrounded by pretty, spacious suburbs and with 'satellite' townships containing lots of high-density housing for poorer people. These divisions have melted a little, but the centre still has wide streets – albeit now lined with a variety of fuel stations, banks and fast-food outlets alongside the shops.

History Kabwe, when under colonial rule, was known as Broken Hill. In 1921 an almost complete human skull was unearthed here during mining operations, at a depth of about 20m. Together with a few other human bones nearby, it's estimated to be over 200,000 years old, making these the oldest human remains known from southern central Africa. Originally classified as *Homo rhodesiensis* by scientists, the remains are now generally attributed to *Homo heidelbergensis*, a large-brained species that was the common ancestor to *Homo sapiens* in Africa and the Neanderthals in Europe. However, to most people this human is best known as 'Broken Hill Man'.

In more recent times, the town's economy has been closely linked with mining, most recently for zinc and lead (with very high-quality silver as a by-product). Although the mine, which was only about 2km south of the centre, was closed in 1994, a lucrative deal to process the tailings was signed in 2011. The town is also widely known for the large Mulungushi Textiles factory, from where cotton from all over the country is brought together then exported to China.

Getting there and away Regular long-distance **buses** connect Kabwe with both the Copperbelt and northern Zambia each day, as do **postbuses** on both the Lusaka–Ndola and Lusaka–Kasama routes. The Lusaka bus terminal is on Freedom Way, close to Tuskers Hotel; other buses use the area near the Kobil fuel station on Independence Avenue.

🏠 **Where to stay** Most visitors to Kabwe are in transit, and accommodation is limited to one decent hotel in the centre of town, plus several simple guesthouses – of which Travel Executive Lodge is not untypical.

🏠 **Tuskers Hotel** (35 rooms) Buntungwa St; ☏ 0215 222077; m 0966/0977 712909; e tuskers@zamnet.zm; www.tuskerszambia.com. On the southern side of town, on the corner of Freedom Way, Kabwe's main hotel survives predominantly on the trade in local conferences. But the staff are helpful, & it's better than it looks at first glance. En-suite dbl & twin rooms are clean

& a decent size, with all that you'd expect from a small-town hotel, including AC, safe & fridge. The hotel has a bar & a cavernous restaurant, but nicer is to have a drink on the terrace near a good-sized pool in a pleasant garden. **$$**

🏠 **Kabwe Lodge** (14 rooms) Marshall Av; ☏ 0215 224297; e enquiries@zambiahostels.com; www.zambiahostels.com. As at other government-run hostels, the en-suite rooms here are simple but reasonably modern, & there's a restaurant & bar – all set in pleasant gardens. **$$**

⌂ **Travel Executive Lodge** (8 rooms) 33A Independence Av; ☏ 0215 222885. Central, simple & perfectly adequate, the Travel Executive offers en-suite dbl rooms (& 1 family). There's a small garden with a bar, & meals such as nshima & chicken on offer for dinner. **$**

✗ **Where to eat** Don't expect anything fancy in the food stakes, though **Tuskers** does a reasonable line in barbecued steaks and fish, and the pizzas there are said to be good. There are fast-food outlets near the fuel stations on Independence Avenue, though, so if you're passing through and in need of a quick break, it's a perfectly reasonable place to stop for a bite to eat.

Out of town, the offerings are more promising. To the north, about 13km along the tar road, **Tony's Stop** is a useful snack bar with a pleasant garden where you can sit with a drink and a fritter. To the south, altogether in another league, is:

✗ **Fig Tree Café** Great North Rd; m 0977 872966, 0968 652413; ⊕ 06.00–18.00 Mon–Sat. This excellent pit-stop between Lusaka & the Copperbelt is west of the road, some 10km south of Kabwe. Stop for what have been described as Zambia's best burgers, plus a healthy wraps, tarts & excellent homemade cakes. You can eat indoors or out, or just drop in for a takeaway. **$–$$**

Other practicalities The main **shop** in town is the big Shoprite supermarket, just off Freedom Way, but there are other, smaller, shops – including a bakery – or you could try the large market, to the south of town near the railway line. Both Barclays & Zanaco have **ATMs** in town, including one near Shoprite. For motorists, there are a number of **fuel** stations on Independence Avenue, and should you be in need of spares, try Autoworld (☏ 0215 221574), just west of the Kobil fuel station.

Excursions from Kabwe

Mulungushi Dam (*Admission Kw20,000 pp*) Some 60km southeast of town is the Mulungushi Dam – a 27km-long manmade lake that was formed in 1925 when the Lunsemfya River was dammed to provide hydro-electricity for the mine in Kabwe. The Mulungushi Boat Club has a a swimming pool over the lake, but at present, no boats. All the same, nature and bird walks can be arranged, and there's plenty of scope for exploring both by 4x4 and on foot – perhaps with a picnic. With care, it's possible to clamber down to the spillway, and on to the dam wall. With sufficient notice, you may be able to get permission from the Lunsemfwa Hydro Power Company (*0215 224957*) to view the powerhouse.

Getting there Entering Kabwe from the south, turn right just before you cross the railway. Follow this road parallel to the railway, cross a railway sidetrack, then swing left and cross a bigger railway crossing. On the other side are two roads; take the dirt track on the right – it may be signposted 'Mulungushi Boat Club 55km'.

Where to stay and eat

Mulungushi Boat Club (6 chalets, 2 rooms, camping) m 0978 123366; e danzambia@gmail.com. In addition to en-suite chalets, there is a campsite, & a couple of twin rooms in the Bell Tower, with ablutions available at the clubhouse. The club has a restaurant & bar with views from the balcony across the lake. *Chalet Kw250,000; room Kw 200,000, both inc admission & b/fast; camping Kw30,000 per tent, plus admission fee.*

Lunsemfwa Wonder Gorge East of the dam, and about 80km from Kabwe as the pied crow flies (or 130km from Mkushi), is the spectacular and steep gorge marking where the Mkushi River meets the Lunsemfwa, as both cut 300m into the sedimentary rocks of the Muchinga Escarpment. This is a very rural, remote area so you'll need a reliable and sturdy 4x4, good maps of the area, and someone to come and look for you if you get stuck.

The best vantage point is Bell Point. It was apparently named after a Miss Grace Bell, a friend of the first European to see the gorge, who visited in 1913. The easiest approach is from the south. Bell Point is designated as a national monument but there are places you can camp. You can either scramble down to the bottom to keep exploring the gorge, or get to a vantage point and sit and enjoy. The latter is recommended.

Getting there Follow the directions for Mulungushi Dam, above. From here, continue across the Mulungushi, following the power lines northeast to Kampumba and on to Lunsemfwa. Crossing the bridge over the Lunsemfwa, take the RD204 to Old Mkushi.

The turn for Bell Point, a track on the right that seems to head back the way you came, lies around 20km from Lunsemfwa. Bell Point itself (14°38.500'S, 29°08.600'E) is 35km away from this turning. After 1km there's a fork: take the right track. Ignore all turn-offs for 21km then, following an area of farmland, take a left onto a less used track. The last village on the route lies at 22km, after which the scenery grows ever more beautiful despite the presence of a car wreck at 32km (a casualty, so it is said, of the Rhodesian war).

KAPIRI MPOSHI Kapiri Mposhi's main claim to fame is that it stands at one end of the TAZARA railway. There is a constant flow of people, buses and trucks through town which makes it lively, if slightly aggressive, but not safe. Kapiri is a town which visitors often pass through, but where they seldom linger. Expect people around at all times of the day and night, and be on your guard against opportunist thieves. This particulary applies if you're using the ATM at the new Barclays Bank.

Only one **fuel** station remains in the town itself. Presumably the others were put out of business by the 24-hour Continental Oil station that sits at the junction where the Great North Road splits from the road to the Copperbelt. Despite its advertised amenities there are just toilets and an almost empty shop here, but as elsewhere in Kapiri, you'll come across people selling cheap pirate DVDs, CDs and cassette tapes, which are put together in Tanzania and brought in over the border.

To the east of town you'll notice a small, rather incongruous-looking hill that gives the town its name: *kapiri* means 'mountain'. The town is the home of the glassworks KGP, which uses stone mined from the hill, and as you head north towards the Copperbelt you'll see traders selling glasses and mugs alongside the road.

Getting there and away Kapiri Mposhi is a linear town, but with its location just south of the junction where the Great North Road splits from the road to Ndola, it is effectively a major crossroads for those travelling northwards from Lusaka, with excellent links to the rest of the country. Drivers should watch out for the large speed humps at both ends of the town on the main road.

By bus Kapiri Mposhi is easily reached by minibus, long-distance coach or postbus, as it stands on the main routes between Lusaka and both northern Zambia and the Copperbelt. There are very frequent arrivals and departures, especially to/from Lusaka and the Copperbelt; a ticket between here and Lusaka costs from around Kw55,000. The bus terminus is in the centre of town, on the left if you're travelling north, behind a variety of market stalls. The town is on the postbus route between Lusaka and Ndola.

By TAZARA train If you continue along the road going north, it will soon cross a railway line. Turn right just before this and follow the road for about 1km to reach the bustling and quite imposing TAZARA terminus.

If you did not buy one at the TAZARA office in Lusaka (page 125), this is the place to buy your ticket through to Dar es Salaam, 1,860km from Kapiri, or to stations *en route* within Zambia as far as Kasama and the border at Nakonde. The station becomes exceedingly busy around train departure times, and foreigners will encounter considerable hassle. To avoid this, arrive well before the train is due to depart and take great care of your belongings. If you need to buy a ticket, then allow at least an extra hour.

TAZARA TRAIN PRICES (IN KWACHA) FROM KAPIRI MPOSHI

Fares below are for the express service, one way. Fares on the slow trains are about 20% cheaper.

To	1st class (sleeper)	2nd class (sleeper)	3rd class
Mkushi	18,900	14,500	11,900
Mpika	66,000	46,200	33,700
Kasama	79,200	66,000	52,800
Border (Nakonde/Tunduma)	105,600	79,200	66,000
Dar es Salaam	237,600	198,000	145,200

13

TAZARA services have long held a generally good reputation for time-keeping, though that's starting to look a little tarnished. Just two trains a week run on the route in each direction: the express on Tuesday, and a slower train stopping at all stations on Friday. Both trains return the following day. Express trains leave Kapiri Mposhi at 16.00 on Tuesday, and arrive in Dar es Salaam at 12.35 on Thursday. The return leaves Dar at 15.50, also on a Tuesday, arriving back in Kapiri Mposhi on Thursday at 09.26. These trains stop at the major stations *en route*, including the Zambian towns of Mkushi, Serenje, Mpika, Kasama and Nakonde.

The slower, all-stations service departs from Kapiri Mposhi on Friday at 14.00, arriving in Dar es Salaam on Tuesday at 15.00; it returns on a Friday, leaving Dar at 13.00 and reaching Kapiri Mposhi on Sunday at 16.00.

Tickets are available in first, second and third classes. Both first- and second-class compartments are sleepers (although there are second-class seaters, too), accommodating four and six passengers respectively; in third class, it's seating only. Good food is available on the trains, as is bottled water, and in first class you can expect to be provided with bedding, towels and soap too.

Remember to check in advance with the Tanzanian High Commission (page 148) if you'll need a visa to enter Tanzania. Travellers to Zambia can usually get their visa on the train, but again, do check your status first. (For details of visas, see pages 52–3.)

Hitchhiking Hitching to or from Kapiri Mposhi is fairly easy. Your best bet is to walk out of town for a kilometre or so until you find space. Alternatively ask around the truckers in town for a lift. If you are going north, then get a short lift or a taxi to take you the 2km or so to the Continental Oil fuel station, where the road to Ndola splits from the Great North Road to Mpika and beyond. This is an excellent hitching spot. (But do remember that hitching in Zambia is not a free ride; you will be expected to contribute to the cost of the journey.)

🏠 **Where to stay and eat** There are a few run-down hotels, including **Chanika Lodge** on the main road and – possibly better – **Peniel Executive Lodge** to the south of town. These and others like them are basic and noisy, often with rooms rented by the hour as well as by the night. Kapiri Mposhi is not a place to stay unless you have to.

Seasonal produce is available in the **market**, so expect bananas and oranges in the middle of the year, and perhaps tomatoes, peanuts and sweet potatoes at the end of the rainy season. There's a bakery opposite, and lots of takeaways.

NDOLA

About 325km north of Lusaka, Ndola is the provincial capital of the Copperbelt, but slightly smaller than its neighbour, Kitwe. It is a pleasant city with broad, leafy streets and little to indicate its industrial base. With the recent boost in the price of copper, the town has witnessed a parallel resurgence in prosperity, with several new guesthouses and restaurants in evidence.

Aside from mining, Ndola benefits from an unusually pure water supply, which explains why it is home to the large Mosi brewery.

GETTING THERE AND AROUND
By air Ndola's airport is on the southern side of the centre of town, clearly signposted off to the right as you enter town from the south. It is well served by

regional specialist Proflight, with several flights per day to Lusaka. There are also direct flights to Johannesburg with Zambezi Airlines and SAAirlink, and to Nairobi with Kenya Airways.

The open-air café at the airport is one of the more pleasant places to while away time awaiting a flight. Inside, you'll find all you'd expect from a small-town airport: a bank, bureau de change and ATM (though this may not be the most reliable of machines), a curio shop, car-rental office, internet access, and offices for all the local airlines.

✈ **Kenya Airways** ☎ 0212 620709/620725; www.kenya-airways.com. Daily flights to Nairobi.
✈ **Proflight** ☎ 0212 611796; m 0977 207957; e ndolaterminal@proflight/zambia.com; www.flyzambia.com. Daily scheduled flights between Lusaka & Ndola, & on weekdays to Solwezi.
✈ **SAAirlink** ☎ 0212 612206; www.saairlink.co.za. One flight a day to Johannesburg.

✈ **Zambezi Airlines** ☎ 0212 613151/611066; m 0978 778771; www.flyzambezi.com. Daily flights to Johannesburg. Also has offices in Solwezi, ☎ 0218 821620, & Kitwe, ☎ 0212 220108/228006; m 0978 778774.
✈ **Zambia Flying Doctor** ☎ 0216 11417/8; m 0977 290656; e zfdradio@zamnet.zm. This small outfit operates charter flights across northern Zambia.

By bus Ndola's main bus terminus is at the southern end of Chimwemwe Road, less than 1km south of the Savoy Hotel – though coaches to Lusaka start from around the Broadway Cinema or Buteko Avenue. There are very frequent links to the other towns of the Copperbelt (*Ndola to Kitwe Kw16,000 by minibus*), and also Lusaka (*from Kw65,000*). To reach northern Zambia (accessed via the road through Mkushi and Serenje), take a southbound (probably to Lusaka) bus and change at Kapiri Mposhi.

A **postbus** service operates between Lusaka and Ndola several times a day except Sunday, stopping in Kabwe and Kapiri Mposhi. The journey takes 3½ hours with a one-way fare of Kw50,000. The postbus also operates between Ndola and the Northern Province three times a week (*Tue, Thu & Sat; Kw100,000 one way*), and between Ndola and Livingstone on Monday, Wednesday and Friday, leaving Ndola at 05.30, and costing Kw140,000 one way.

By train Although trains run twice a week between Kitwe and Livingstone via Ndola, stopping at all stations, they are far too slow to be of use to many travellers.

Car hire
🚗 **Avis Airport** [398 D7] ☎ 0212 620741; m 0977 800756; www.avisworld.com
🚗 **Voyagers/Europcar** [398 C3] Arusha St; ☎ 0212 620990/620314; airport ☎ 0212 617062/

620604; m 0966 860648, 0977 860648; e carrental@voyagerszambia.com; www.voyagerszambia.com

Hitchhiking Ndola is quite a big town, meaning that good hitch spots are a long walk from the centre – so consider getting a taxi for a few kilometres.

If you want to get to northern Zambia, via Mansa, then resist the temptation to 'cut the corner' by crossing into and out of the DRC – it's far too dangerous.

🏠 **WHERE TO STAY** There is a small choice of hotels in Ndola, and a growing number of guesthouses, but all aim at visiting businesspeople and prices are correspondingly high. For most visitors, the better guesthouses are generally a more appealing option than the town's hotels. That said, a new Protea Hotel is scheduled to open in Ndola in 2013.

13

NDOLA

A
B
C
D

1   MACHA   MWATIANVWA   BOUNDARY   Castle Lodge   CHIPULUKUSU   1
Northrise Shopping Precinct

KWACHA   TANZANIA AVENUE   NORTHRISE   Ndola Hill   LOWENTHAL   VITANDA

2   Technical College   FITENTE   Brewery   PRESIDENT   2
Kansenshi Shopping Precinct
Mary Begg Clinic
CHINTU
MULOBEZI

ROAD   KABINGA   Kaps Villa   Chez Ntemba   Railway station   Palace
KANSENSHI   LEWANIKA   DR DAMIE   SHINDE   ARUSHA STREET   Voyagers
3   KABELENGA   Setanga Lodge, Kumbali Lodge, Kitwe, Luanshya   KOPA ROAD   Indigo   BP   Bus station (north)   Caltex   Power station   3
LUANGWA   Starscape   Vanilla Bread   BROADWAY   Savoy   Autoworld   Deja Vu
Michelangelo   Anglican Cathedral   Copperbelt
Catholic Cathedral   CHINWEMWE   Barclays   MOFFAT   Ndola Boating Club
Central Hospital   NKANDABWE   BLANTYRE   Total   Zambia   Stanbic
High Court   CHINWEMWE   Danny's   MAINA SOKO   DEPOT
4   HILL CREST   Swimming pool   Lowenthal Theatre   BUTEKO   Stanbic   DAG HAMMARSKJOELD   4
KANONGESHA   Civic Centre   Police   Starscape   CHISOKONE
Fire station   INDEPENDENCE WAY   Shoprite   CHINWEMWE
Squash Club   KAUNDA   Stanbic   Plaza Cinema   Bus terminal (south)
Rugby Club   BP   MATELO
NKANA ROAD   Hilltop Hospital   PRESIDENT AVENUE   Slave Tree
5   KANINI   MAKOLI   Caltex   Kafubu   ITAWA   5
N
Bradt   Ndola Golf Club

6   Kafubu   Chabanga Lodge   Total   CHIKOLA CRES   6
RIVER   Bei Tempi   Millennium Lodge
KABUSHI   MASALA   KABWE ROAD   AIRPORT ROAD   DAG HAMMARSKJOELD DRIVE
Musa Kasonka Stadium
7   0   500m   Caltex   Airport   7
0   500yds
Jacaranda Mall, Mukuba Hotel, Showgrounds, Kabwe, Lusaka

A
B
C
D

Hotels

🏠 **Mukuba Hotel** [398 D7] (54 rooms) ☎0212 651000–3; e mukhotel@microlink. zm, mukhotel@zamtel.zm; www.mukubahotel. com. The Mukuba is located about 6km south of town, adjacent to the Showgrounds. If you want the amenities of a hotel, & can live with the 10-min drive from the centre of town, this is far more attractive & better value than the Savoy. To get there, head towards Kabwe, then turn right into the industrial area onto Arkwright Rd, then Crompton Rd. A good-size floor rug softens the corporate effect in each room, where you'll find AC, tea/coffee maker, phone, DSTV & a fridge. The hotel is built around a central courtyard where peacocks strut around the fishponds, while beyond roams a small resident herd of impala. There's a bar & restaurant, & an internet room. **$$$**

🏠 **Savoy Hotel** [398 C3] (146 rooms) 12 Buteko Av; ☎0212 611097–9/611101–3; e info@savoyhotel.co.zm; www.savoyhotel. co.zm. Despite priding itself on its casino & 'suspended swimming pool situated on the mezzanine floor' (open to non-residents Kw30,000), the Savoy's image is decidedly tarnished nowadays. It stands just off Maina Soko Rd, near the eastern end of Broadway, with a secure car park. Its rooms, if relatively small & functional, are reasonably comfortable, with AC, DSTV, free WiFi, & both bath & shower en suite. Lunch & dinner are served in the restaurant. **$$$**

🏠 **Palace Hotel** [398 C3] (52 rooms) Cnr Vitanda St & Kabelenga Av; ☎0212 621840; e palacehotel@gmail.com. Under the same management as the Edinburgh Hotel in Kitwe, & at the heart of Ndola's business district, the Palace is quite an old hotel, having opened in the mid-1940s. Over the years it has had several different names, including the Coppersmith Arms, Naaznina, Travellers' Lodge &, more recently, the Royal Hotel. Its en-suite rooms are old-fashioned but adequate, each with satellite TV, direct-dial phone, minibar/fridge & tea/coffee machine. Downstairs there's a restaurant, a bar & secure parking. **$–$$$**

Guesthouses

🏠 **Michelangelo** [398 A3] (11 rooms) 126 Broadway; ☎0212 620325; m 0966 780036; e michelangelo@m-lodge.com; www.michelangelocafe.com. The Italianate Michelangelo, with its columns, cool tiles & courtyard pool, is currently Ndola's best guesthouse. The theme continues in the rooms arranged round the pool, where warm terracotta colours are offset by limed furniture & good, soft lighting. Each is dominated by a large bed with all-round mosquito net, but there's still room for a desk with internet point, TV & hairdryer, & an en-suite bath & shower. The restaurant is warm & inviting, & the bar is popular in the evenings as well. Credit cards accepted over US$15. **$$$–$$$$**

🏠 **Castle Lodge** [398 C1] (8 rooms) 19 Sheila Dare Rd, Northrise; ☎0212 641175; m 0955 784727; e information@castlodgendola.com; http://castlelodgendola.com. Reports suggest that this imposing guesthouse is quite a find: quiet, set in lawned gardens with a pool & secure parking, plus a good restaurant ($$) & WiFi. **$$$**

🏠 **Chabanga Lodge** [398 C6] (18 rooms) Nakatindi Rd; ☎0212 622353; m 0955 888195; e chabangalodge@zamtel.zm. Down a narrow road close to the airport, Chabanga Lodge is well placed for travellers, though the yappy dogs may be off-putting to some. The warm apricot wash of the walls & toning fabrics give a modern feel to the large, light rooms, offset by wrought-iron furniture & tiled floors. Each has a dbl bed & is equipped with AC, mosquito nets, DSTV, kettle, phone & fridge. In the public rooms, ornate formality contrasts with a decidedly simple dining area, where very good evening meals are available on request ($$$). **$$–$$$**

🏠 **Indigo Lodge** [398 B3] (5 rooms) 1 Kopa Rd; ☎0212 610043; e info@indigolodge. co.za; www.indigolodge.co.za. Light, modern & quite homely in style, this new lodge boasts a restaurant, bar, pool & patio. Rooms have fans & the standard accoutrements: DSTV, minibar, tea/ coffee station, plus mosquito nets, with all but 1 en suite. **$$–$$$**

🏠 **Millennium Lodge** [398 D6] (7 rooms) 3 Chikola Cres; ☎0212 610940/1; e info@millenniumparklodge.com; http:// millenniumparklodge.com. With a swimming pool & jacuzzi surrounded by manicured green lawns, this is an attractive option. Modern, en-suite rooms have AC, DSTV, fridge & WiFi access. A full English b/fast is served in the restaurant, where other meals are available on request, & there's also a bar. $$–$$$

🏠 **Kaps Villa** [398 A3] (6 rooms) 2 Mulobwezi; 📞0212 615765; m 0977 117747; e vkaps@yahoo.com. Mutale Kapoka brings a lively but professional approach to the management of her father's new guesthouse. All rooms are en suite with TV, with larger ones having a kitchenette (& a higher price & only a cont b/fast). The small covered dining area has a TV & bar. It's an affordable & pleasant alternative to Ndola's more upmarket offerings. $$

🏠 **Kumbali Lodge** [398 A4] (7 rooms) 3416 Chibwe Cres, Kansenshi; m 0964 012453. En-suite rooms at this new guesthouse with a pretty garden & pool all have AC, tea & coffee facilities, DSTV & a fridge, & meals are available, too. $$

🏠 **Setanga Lodge** [398 A4] (14 rooms) 578H Freedom Way; 📞0212 680002; e setanga@ zamtel.zm. The attractive Setanga is a cut above most of Ndola's guesthouses, with a large lounge for guests' use & a pool dominating the garden. Bedrooms, some en suite & others sharing facilities, have well-chosen fabrics with pine & wrought-iron furniture; each has a dbl bed, TV & fan. That said, the lodge was relocating in 2011, with no date for its re-opening available. $$

Around Ndola

🏠 **Nsobe Game Camp** (5 tents, 9 chalets, camping) 📞0212 671008/671097; e reservations@nsobe.com.zm; www. nsobegamecamp.com. Some 9km from the Great North Rd, the turn-off for Nsobe Game Camp is about 50km south of Ndola, or 65km north of Kapiri Mposhi; the track is accessible by 2WD all year. The camp is set on a 1,500ha game farm in predominantly miombo woodland, with 3 dams (manmade lakes), 15 species of antelope, including black lechwe, sable, eland & the rare sitatunga, & over 320 species of birds. The atmosphere is one of upmarket camping – & indeed there is a campsite at one end of the site, right on the lake with braais & hot-water showers, but no power. En-suite safari tents on raised wooden platforms have no frills, but everything you need, including a wooden veranda overlooking the lake; similar chalets sleep 2–5 guests. The nearby TV lounge & separate restaurant are especially popular at w/ends, when Nsobe is a favourite with local visitors. About 5–10 mins' walk away are 2 self-catering chalets, sleeping 6 or 8 people respectively. Food – much of it farm produce, from fresh orange juice & fish to venison & pork (& their own sausages) – is good & plentiful, & there's a shop selling their produce too.

This is a working farm, with around 1,000 pigs, bream-stocked fishponds, & a citrus orchard. Aside from farm visits, activities include fishing, bush walks, visits to their reptile park, & game drives in your own vehicle or theirs (this is no place for serious guiding, but there's a useful bird checklist & an identification sheet for the antelope). Day visitors can use braai sites, picnic tables & benches set near the water's edge. On the water itself, there's canoeing (lifejackets provided) or even swimming – the dams are said to be croc free. Or just chill in the grounds, or take advantage of the jacuzzi or sauna. *Tent/chalet Kw375,000/300,000 sgl/pp sharing DBB; self-catering chalet Kw1,000,000–1,250,000 6–8 people; camping Kw35,000 pp. Day entry Kw25,000. Game drive Kw50,000 pp (min 3); self game drive Kw50,000; canoe Kw10,000/hr. No credit cards.*

🏠 **Mukuyu Camp** (5 chalets) Contact via Nsobe, above. Some 10 mins' drive from Nsobe Game Camp, Mukuyu is a private, secluded camp that sleeps up to 10. With its thatched central dining/seating area & solar lighting, it is more upmarket than Nsobe, relaxing & comfortable without being luxurious. Everything was made on the premises, using locally sourced elephant grass for the walls & thatch, wood from the farm, & handmade clay bricks, while simple baskets adorn the walls. Square, thatched rooms have a small veranda overlooking a waterhole, & at the back is an open-air shower in a semi-open bathroom (1 has a sunken stone bath, too). With its own staff & kitchen, the camp is entirely self-contained, a perfect hideaway in the bush. In case the setting palls, there's a tiny plunge pool & night drives are on offer.

For something more romantic, try the private Miombo Woodland View. Perched on a rocky hill are an open-air dbl bedroom under thatch, a separate bathroom beneath the stars, & a dining area. *Kw500,000/750,000 pp FB/FBA; min 4, 1 group only. Miombo View Kw600,000 pp DBB.*

🏠 **Lowden Lodge** (13 rooms, camping) ✆ 0212 515001; m 0966 701150/ 781105/904291/907154; e lowden@iwayafrica. com; www.lowdenlodge.com. Almost equidistant between Ndola & Kitwe, & about 1km off the main road in the direction of Luanshya, this small guesthouse with dbl, twin & sgl rooms is attractively set in well-kept gardens. Those in search of exercise will welcome the large pool, exercise room & jogging track, while others may find the sauna, bar & TV lounge more to their taste. Dinner, with home-grown produce, is available to guests, & there's free internet access. **$$$**

🏠 **Kafue Lodge** (8 rooms) Book via Voyagers, page 402. ✪ 13°22.127'S, 27°58.166'E. Some 2hrs' drive, or 92km, from Ndola, Kafue Lodge is popular with Copperbelt residents for a w/end break. Although it is just 32km from Mpongwe, a huge farming area northwest of Kapiri Mposhi, it is most easily accessed from the north. To get there, head towards Kitwe, then turn off to Luanshya after about 20km; continue through Luanshya & Mpongwe then, after a further 7km,

turn right onto a dirt road & follow this for some 20km, bearing left after 1km; once you get to the airfield, turn left, continuing for a final 5km.

The lodge is on a 20km^2 game farm on the banks of the Kafue River, stocked with 10 species of antelope, including sable & kudu, & with excellent birding opportunities: Bob Stjernstedt, the Zambian birding expert, advises that it's a particularly good place to see Pel's fishing owl.

Relatively simple rooms have been built in pairs, 2 to a chalet. Each is en suite, with wrought-iron furnishings, twin beds, sliding windows, & rugs laid on the cement floor. Outside, to one side of the shared veranda, is a sink, crockery, cutlery & a tiny fridge (you'd need a coolbox & ice if you're self catering), while on the other is a BBQ area. If self catering doesn't appeal, there's a bar & restaurant (*lunch Kw65,000–95,000 pp*), with produce from the lodge's organic vegetable garden on the menu.

Walks & game-viewing tracks meander through tall miombo woodland & dambos, characteristic of this part of Zambia. It's also a popular spot for fishing, or for a cruise along the river, while close by is Lake Kashiba. **$$$** *exc b/fast.*

✗ **WHERE TO EAT** There are plenty of takeaways and fast-food joints around town, including the ubiquitous **Hungry Lion** near the police station on Blantyre Road [398 B4], and several outlets anticipated to open in **Jacaranda Mall** [398 B7]. For more substantial meals, either at lunch or in the evening, the choices are no longer limited to the main hotels, although the **Mukuba's** restaurant is perfectly adequate. At midday, the **boat club** overlooking the river [398 D4] is a dark but cool place for lunch (there's a gym and sauna here, too).

✗ **Danny's** [398 C4] President Av; ✆ 0212 621828; ⊕ 12.00–14.30, 19.00–22.30 daily. With its predominantly Indian menu (but with more than a hint of other cuisines thrown in), Danny's is one of the best places to eat in town. **$$$**

✗ **Deja Vu** [398 D3] President Av N; m 0977 752589; ⊕ 12.00–14.30, 18.30–22.00 daily. A super Indian/Chinese restaurant nr Broadway roundabout. The curries & masalas come highly recommended. **$$$**

✗ **Michelangelo** [398 A3] 126 Broadway; ✆ 0212 620325; ⊕ 08.00–14.00 & 19.00–22.30 Mon–Sat; Sun residents-only dinner. As you might expect, the menu at Michelangelo is dominated by Italian fare, boasting freshly made ricotta cheese, & listing a big range of pizzas & pastas. At lunchtimes, the emphasis is on salads, stuffed pitta bread & omelettes. **$$$**

✗ **Starscape** [398 C4] Buteko Av; ✆ 0212 612248; ⊕ Tue–Sun. Another Indian offering, shortly moving to Broadway [398 A3]. **$$**

🖵 **Bei Tempi** [398 D6] Dag Hammarskjoeld; ⊕ 08.00–22.00 Tue–Sun. An unlikely find next to the Total garage, close to the airport, this is the place to seek out if you're craving a decent coffee or tea, or smoothies & shakes. The menu consists of mezze, pancakes, stuffed pittas, quiches & salads, though at around Kw30,000 a throw, it's on the pricey side. **$$**

🖵 **Vanilla Bread** [398 B3] Broadway; ✆ 0212 620476; ⊕ till18.00 Tue–Sun. This top-class café makes a popular lunch venue, serving excellent coffees & teas as well as light meals.

These include pizza, wraps, burgers, focaccia & panini. $

NIGHTLIFE Most of Ndola's residents spend the evening at one of the town's restaurants or clubs, with the bar at the **boat club** a favourite. **Chabanga** [398 C6] and **Michelangelo** (see above) are pleasant after-dinner haunts. What the town's nightlife lacks in sophistication, it makes up for in sheer numbers. In addition to **Circles** and the **Garage**, there are no fewer than five **East Wing** clubs – labelled simply East Wing 1, East Wing 2, etc – and not to be recommended. For more hard-core drinking, places such as **Chez Ntemba** [398 C3] are popular with locals.

SHOPPING Ndola isn't somewhere that you'd seek out for a shopping spree, but with the advent of the new **Jacaranda Mall** on the southern outskirts of town ([398 B7] *Kabwe Rd*), things are looking up. To find it, take the first turning right after the Masala roundabout on your way south. Here you'll find a large branch of the Pick 'n' Pay chain (considered to be the best grocery shop in the Copperbelt), and an outlet for Bobbili Gems, with various fast-food outlets in the offing. Elsewhere, there's an established branch of Shoprite on Chisokone Avenue [398 C4].

At the Renaissance Wellness Centre in the same building as Vanilla Bread ([398 B3] *Broadway*), owner Shelagh Brown showcases cosmetics, jewellery, local textiles and various holistic products, as well as practising body alignment therapy.

For those planning a trip further afield, Ndola has its own Lands Office opposite the Lowenthal Theatre ([398 B4] *Independence Way;* ✆ *0212 620276*) where Ordnance Survey type **maps** similar to those at Mulungushi House in Lusaka are on sale.

OTHER PRACTICALITIES

Banks There are ATMs at Barclays, FNB and Standard Chartered banks, all on Buteko Avenue [398 C4].

Communications Internet cafés are located both next to and opposite the Savoy Hotel on Buteko Avenue [398 C3], and opposite the Bank of Zambia on Broadway. Expect to pay around Kw200 a minute, with a minimum charge of Kw2,000.

Health The best clinic in Ndola is considered to be the Mary Begg Clinic ([398 A2] *Chintu Rd;* ✆ *0212 614333*). There's also Ndola's Hilltop Hospital ([398 B5] *Independence Av;* ✆ *0212 611051/2;* m *0977 757272*), or you could try the Miramar Medical Centre (*54/55 Ndibu Dr, Kansenji;* ✆ *0212 680077*). The town has several pharmacies, including Chemopharm on Chisokone Avenue, opposite Shoprite [398 C4].

Travel agents If you're in town and need help with local arrangements then contact:

Voyagers [398 C3] Arusha St; ✆ 0212 621333–6; e headoffice@voyagerszambia.com; www. voyagerszambia.com. Ndola is the heartland of the generally highly regarded Voyagers, who have their head office in town. It's worth noting that they can collect travellers from the Kasumbalesa/Mokambo border post.

WHAT TO SEE AND DO Most activities in the town centre around the local sports clubs: cricket, rugby, golf ([398 A5] with an 18-hole course) and sailing. There's also a swimming pool on Nkandabwe Avenue [398 B4] with a separate garden bar.

For the first-time visitor a walk to the top of the low, grassy **hill** [398 C2], in a residential area just north of the centre, gives a good sense of location, with an excellent view across to the DRC – and the cement factories. In town itself, the oft-overlooked **Copperbelt Museum** ([398 C4] *Buteko Av, entry Kw5,000*) hosts small exhibitions on the geology and cultural history of the Copperbelt, with a rather unusual look at toys in the form of intricate wire models of mining machinery and the like, made by local children. Downstairs is a shop selling a range of baskets and other curios. There are long-term plans for the museum to move to new premises on Independence Avenue, between the High Court and the Civic Centre, and to change its name to the Museum of Science and Technology. For now, though, the museum is of only passing interest.

Not far from the museum, the old **Slave Tree** on Makoli Avenue is of historical importance, though behind its locked gates it seems rather neglected, and taking photographs may not be welcome. The tree is a very old pod mahogany (*Afzelia quanzensis*, known locally as a *mupapa*), on which two species of figs are parasitic. In 1880 the Swahili slave-traders frequented this area and built a stockade, using the shade of the tree as a meeting place. It was also a place where slaves were bought and sold between the various traders. The slave trade was abolished in Zambia in the early 1900s, as the British established a colonial administration. Ndola was founded in 1904 and now just a representation of the tree features on its coat of arms, while a plaque at the foot of the tree reads:

This plate has been placed on this mupapa tree to commemorate the passing of the days when, under its shade, the last of the Swahili traders, who warred upon and enslaved the people of the surrounding country, used to celebrate their victories and share out their spoils.

DAG HAMMARSKJOELD

The death of UN Secretary-General Dag Hammarskjoeld in a plane crash on 17 September 1961 shocked the world, not least because the circumstances of the crash were steeped in controversy. Sixteen people died when the DC6 travelling *en route* from Congo to Ndola crashed into a tree on farmland just outside the town. Whether the crash was a result of pilot error, or whether the plane was shot down by mercenaries fighting on the side of the Congolese against the United Nations, has never been ascertained, although no evidence was ever found of foul play, or indeed of any mechanical failure. Attempts to find out the cause of the crash were hampered by looters who were at the scene before the arrival of the rescue services.

Mr Hammarskjoeld was eiected to the post of secretary-general in 1953, and takes the credit for introducing the idea of establishing a United Nations' peace-keeping force. At the time of his death, he had been taking part in talks in Leopoldville (now Kinshasa) to try to resolve the conflict, which by 1961 had been dragging on for a number of years. The talks ended in deadlock, and the delegates were travelling to neutral territory under cover of darkness, although stories of decoy planes and other spy-story antics are much exaggerated.

The memorial's curator, M K Nasilele, has written a (somewhat controversial) account of the incident in *Crashed Hopes Revived*, published privately in 2006 and available at the Copperbelt Museum. To give the memorial a more lasting significance, Mr Nasilele was also involved in the establishment in 2002 of the nearby Dag Hammarskjoeld Memorial School.

13

A second slave tree, Chichele Mofu Tree, lies in the centre of the dual carriageway to Kitwe, about 11km from Ndola – having fallen down in the last couple of years.

A couple of kilometres closer to Ndola, and signposted to the north of the road, the **Dag Hammarskjoeld Memorial** (*entry US$7*) commemorates the United Nations Secretary-General who was killed here in 1961 (see box page 403). Designated a national monument, and a World Heritage Site, it lies along a 5km track through farmland, lined in part with tall pine trees from the secretary-general's native Sweden. In addition to a stone cairn on the site, there is a memorial garden and a visitors' centre displaying information about Mr Hammarskjoeld and his role in the UN, and documenting the circumstances leading up to the crash. Outside, pine trees at the memorial are laid out in the shape of a plane. It's a shame that the entrance fee is now so high.

EXCURSIONS FROM NDOLA Relatively near Ndola are two lodges which are destinations in their own right, and are often visited on long weekends from Lusaka or the Copperbelt: Nsobe Game Camp (page 400) and Kafue Lodge (page 401).

Sunken lakes The landscape around Ndola and Kitwe features a series of water-filled limestone sinkholes which manifest themselves as lakes. Of these, two are particularly popular – and each tends to be known as simply 'the sunken lake'. The first, **Lake Chilengwa**, is about 16km southeast of Ndola, where fishing and boating make for a popular day trip.

Considerably further afield is the better-known **Lake Kashiba** (*entry Kw5,000 pp*), also known as the 'sacred lake', a reflection of its status in traditional beliefs. Go for a picnic, to swim or simply just to explore. It's located 70km south of Ndola, to the southwest of Mpongwe, and near Kafue Lodge (page 401).

KITWE

Situated a few kilometres southwest of the large Nkana Mine, Kitwe is 59km from Ndola, the two towns linked by a very good dual carriageway. The extensive pine forests lining the north side of the road extend as far as the border with the DRC, and were planted by President Kaunda as part of a timber export initiative. Kitwe is Zambia's second-largest town and relies for its prosperity on copper mining, whose presence is all too visible in the extensive slag heaps on the edge of town.

Like most of the Copperbelt towns, Kitwe was in the doldrums for several years with a steady decline in amenities, activities and general infrastructure. However, in the last few years it has seen a resurgence in prosperity following privatisation of the mines and a rapid rise in the value of copper on the world market. Today, it's a thriving town with plenty of amenities.

GETTING THERE AND AWAY
By bus Getting to or from Kitwe is easiest by bus. Kitwe's main bus terminus is in Martindale (shown on some maps as the 'second class trading area'), next to the main town centre. Here you'll find many departures for Ndola (*from Kw15,000*), plus daily connections to Chingola (*Kw8,500*), Solwezi, and Lusaka (*Kw70,000*). There are also regular buses to the Luapula area and northern provinces, although buses on these long-distance routes will hang around until they fill, even if this takes a day or two.

By air The town's Southdowns Airport is about 25km to the west on the Kalulushi and then Kalengwa roads, but Proflight's link between Kitwe and Lusaka is no longer operating. The region's main airport is at Ndola.

By train Kitwe is the end of the line for trains from Livingstone that pass through Ndola and Lusaka. The service is painfully slow, running just twice a week and taking a full 48 hours to complete the journey. Take the bus!

Hitchhiking Like Ndola, Kitwe is a large town, so good hitch spots are a long walk from the centre. It is best to get a taxi for a few kilometres.

WHERE TO STAY

In Kitwe When the first edition of this book was written, there was little choice of accommodation in Kitwe, and that which existed was poor value. However, that's all changed as small guesthouses such as the Mukwa seem to have sprung up everywhere, leaving the large old hotels like the Edinburgh with little choice but to reform radically or go out of business. That said, increased pressure on rooms in the town has seen many of the guesthouses expand, not always for the best.

Most of the following accept Visa and MasterCard credit cards.

Edinburgh Hotel [406 B4] (76 rooms) Obote Av; 0212 222444; e reservations@ edinburgh.co.zm; www.edinburgh.co.zm. Kitwe's main hotel is in traditional mould, rather dark & very old-fashioned, despite a recent change of ownership. Situated just west of the business district, it's centrally located close to the main railway & bus stations. Within the hotel, on its ground floor, are some useful service agencies – like a travel agent, & an internet café. Just behind the hotel is the Edinburgh Arcade, which has a variety of small shops.

The Edinburgh has a range of rooms at different prices. There are various suites, luxury & deluxe rooms, & a whole floor of somewhat dilapidated 'standard' rooms – all of which have en-suite facilities, AC, kettles, fridges, phones, satellite TVs & WiFi. The Highlander Restaurant – complete with dance floor – is the focus for meals, & there are several bars, a casino, a swimming pool & secure parking. **$$$–$$$$**

Africaza Guesthouse [406 C1] (8 rooms) 11 Mushitu Cl, Parklands; 0212 221097; e dcole@ iconet.zm. Africaza is centred on one of the town's best restaurants, Arabian Nights (see page 407), but its rooms – albeit varied in style – are no afterthought. The best of them, in the main house, are large & stylish, if slightly busy, with mod cons that include AC, phone & fridge, balanced by cane furniture, African-themed pictures & elephant-print fabrics. Those built in a separate

block are slightly less cohesive in style, but have more modern shower rooms to compensate – & a slightly higher price tag. **$$$**

Jasmin [406 B2] (34 rooms) Jasmin Cl, off Poinsettia Dr, Parklands; 0212 215124; m 0966 192925; e jasmin@microlink.zm; http:// copperbeltlodging.com/jasmin. Considerable expansion at Jasmin has resulted in lots of nooks & crannies, & some of the rooms spilling over across the road. If the communal areas feel a bit random in design, the en-suite rooms are all compact, modern & clean, with DSTV, phones & AC or fans. Accommodation ranges from sgl brick rondavels to 4-bed family units & 3 twin rooms within the main house. Outside is a swimming pool, overlooked by the restaurant & bar. Parking is outside the gate, under the supervision of a nightwatchman. **$$$**

Mukwa Guest House [406 C3] (13 rooms) 26–28 Mpezeni Av; 0212 224266/77; e mukwa@zamsat.net; www.mukwalodge. co.zm. The old colonial-style building at Mukwa is surrounded by attractive gardens with a swimming pool. Each of the spacious rooms has satellite TV, direct-dial phone, good WIFI, fridge, complimentary fruit basket & a tea/coffee station. The lounge, with its Africa-centric décor, is notable for the absence of a TV, so makes a pleasant spot to read a book, but the greatest attraction is the smart Indian/continental restaurant (see page 407). **$$$**

KITWE

A — Southern Cross, Chingola, Solwezi
KWACHA ROAD
INDEPENDENCE AVENUE
Schools D
FREEDOM AVENUE
Schools
KUOMBOKA DRIVE
Total
Parklands shopping centre
Caltex
Fire station
Central Hospital
Arabian Nights
Africaza
Town House
CHIBULUMA ROAD
POINSETTIA DRIVE
Jasmin
NATIONALIST WAY
FREEDOM AVENUE
Bradt
N
CHIPIMPI
Out of the Blue
Il Panino
Parklands
CHIWALA AVENUE
NYERERE ROAD
ZOMBA ROAD
Caltex
Autoworld
FREEDOM AVENUE
FREEDOM AVENUE
CHIBOTE AVENUE
Kobil
Pamo
PAMO
Sherbourne AVENUE
PRESIDENT AVENUE
Dawat
MPEZENI
Mukwa
Old mine tailings
After 10
INDEPENDENCE AVENUE
Bus station (long distance)
Market
Voyagers
Zanaco
Exodus
Stanbic
Library
CHISOKONE AVENUE
MUKATA AVENUE
Post office
CITY SQ.
Police
OBOTE AV
ZAMBIA WAY
Barclays
Civic Centre
BP
Edinburgh
Shoprite
Buses (local)
Std Chtd
Market
OXFORD ROAD
KANTANTA
Railway station
Bus station (long distance)
Total
level crossing
KARIBA
open pit
NINTH
CENTRAL
0   300m
0   300yds
CENTRAL AVENUE
ELEVENTH
Cricket Club
CLUB
Showgrounds, ↓ Ndola
KITWE

☖ **Sherbourne Guest House** [406 C3]
(23 rooms, annexe) 20 Pamo Av; ☎ 0212 222168;
m 0955 782778; e bookings@sherbourne.co.zm;
www.sherbourne.co.zm. Following significant
extension the Sherbourne is now quite cramped,
though it still has a 4-room annexe at 14 Mpezeni
Av. Rooms each have twin or dbl beds, as well
as satellite TV, minibar/fridge, internet access

& phone. A swimming pool & playground are
set in established gardens with tables on the
lawn. A separate restaurant (⊕ 12.00–14.00,
18.00–21.00 daily), including a Sun buffet & hog
roast, is open to all comers. **$$$**
☖ **Town House Lodge** [406 D1] (8
rooms) 65A Mabvuto Ct, Freedom Av; ☎ 0212
221855; e townhouse@coppernet.zm; www.

copperbeltlodging.com/townhouse. If the corridors at this friendly & relaxed place feel rather old-fashioned, its rooms are modern & nicely appointed, with flashes of bright blue or touches of brown to enliven an otherwise neutral décor; the honeymoon suite, though, goes heavy on the leopard print. Each room has en-suite shower or bath, as well as AC, DSTV, minibar/fridge, safe, & kettle for tea & coffee. Guests can relax on a sunny veranda or in the TV lounge, & there's a small dining room, too. **$$$**

⌂ **Pamo Lodge** [406 C3] (10 rooms) 2 Pamo Av; ☏ 0212 222769; e pamo@zamnet.zm. One of the town's less expensive offerings, Pamo Lodge makes a feature of mix 'n' match furniture & décor that's heavy on the florals & frills. Rooms are clean, if dark, with en-suite shower or bath, & fan, fridge, DSTV & kettle. **$$**

Around Kitwe

⌂ **Shamabinga Retreat** (9 rooms) 174 Wolfram Av, Itimpi; m 0977 486354/852782; e brucosa@yahoo.com. Shamabinga lies 15km from Kitwe on the Chingola road, in an area which in colonial days was developed as a sort of market garden to feed the towns of the Copperbelt. To get there, follow the main road for about 12km, then take a right turn towards Itimpi. Turn left at the roundabout, then right at the T-junction; Wolfram Av is the 1st turning on the left. Owned & run by the delightful Constance Shiaka, it's a large old colonial house fronted by an attractive, English-style courtyard garden & lawns in a 2ha plot. En-suite dbl rooms are configured in 4 separate buildings. Of these, 4 share a lounge, dining room & kitchenette, & 2 suites have these to themselves. All are comfortably furnished & feature local Zambian curios & crafts. Meals are served on an outdoor veranda area. **$$** *inc laundry.*

✗ **WHERE TO EAT** Like Ndola, Kitwe has plenty of takeaways, with reliably hygienic standards – if not haute cuisine. The most notable include the **Hungry Lion** ([406 B4] opposite the main post office in the centre of town) for hamburgers and pies, and **After 10** ([406 C4] in Martindale – the 'second-class trading area') for snacks, sandwiches, pizzas, curries, Chinese and even Arabian dishes. The latter, predictably given its name, stays open late.

For a good evening meal you need to look more carefully. Try the following (and note that in addition to the restaurants listed here, both the **Jasmin** and **Sherbourne** guesthouses and the **Edinburgh Hotel** will accept non-residents for meals).

✗ **Arabian Nights** [406 C1] 11 Mushitu Cl, Parklands; ☏ 0212 221097; ⏰ daily. Sister restaurant to the one in Lusaka's Arcades, Arabian Nights specialises in Indian & Pakistani cuisine with a sprinkling of other dishes & a few special vegetarian options. It's a classy place, sited both indoors & on a covered veranda, next to a series of fish pools with a fountain. It's dark & atmospheric, & has an excellent reputation – this is a place where you could justify dressing up. & the on-site guesthouse means you can stay over, too. **$$$$**

✗ **Out of the Blue** [406 C2] Old Greek Club Premises, Bridge Walk; m 0976 526480; ⏰ 10.00–late. Despite the location behind the Greek church, there's no link with Greece here – except perhaps the late-night music (live at w/ ends) & drinking. A standard, albeit expensive, menu is served in an open, café-style setting, with a pool table at the back & a large bar. **$$$$**

✗ **Dawat** [406 C3] Independence Av; ☏ 0212 228281; ⏰ 09.00–22.00 Tue–Sun. Another good Indian restaurant, also serving steaks & fish. **$$$$**

✗ **Mukwa Restaurant** [406 C3] 26–28 Mpezeni Av (off President Av); ☏ 0212 224266; ⏰ 11.00–15.00, 18.00–21.30. Part of the guesthouse of the same name, Mukwa is an elegantly stylish restaurant serving a good variety of Indian food, as well as more usual continental fare. **$$$–$$$$$**

✗ **Mona Lisa** [406 D1] Parklands; ☏ 0212 229677; ⏰ 10.00–22.00. Although once the place for pizzas, as well as pasta, steaks & grills, we hear that standards here have slipped. It's a popular watering hole, too, with a DJ or live music some evenings. **$$$–$$$$**

Il Panino [406 A2] 3044 Lilongwe Rd; 0212 212329; ⊙ 08.00–16.00 Mon–Fri. An unexpected find in the industrial area of Kitwe, this is a cool, modern place for b/fast or light meals, including pancakes & salads. There's a delicatessen on site, too, so you can top up on supplies at the same time. $$

NIGHTLIFE As you might expect, many of the local restaurants are popular watering holes in the evenings, with **Mona Lisa** offering live music on Friday, and a DJ on Wednesday, Friday and Saturday. There are several nightclubs in town – though do take local advice as the current 'in' places change regularly. The most popular are probably **Circles** ([406 D1] *Parklands*) and **Club Zero** (*Kwacha East township; turn right at traffic lights for Buchi on Independence Av, & it's about 3km down the road*), but you could also try **Exodus** [406 C4] or **Hangover**. All have pool tables, dance floors and disco music, tending to stick to rhumba and rhythm and blues. Expect to pay around Kw25,000 admission.

As in other cities, these clubs are frequented almost exclusively by black Zambians, and they generally open until very late. Normally they have a very lively and friendly atmosphere, so overseas visitors should have no problems. If/when trouble develops, the owners of the clubs are generally quite good at sorting it out. You should, of course, take the standard precautions that apply in any such busy places to avoid the attention of thieves and pickpockets – by dressing down and not carrying valuables.

SHOPPING While there's everything you need in Kitwe, the town doesn't as yet have anything in the form of a modern shopping centre, though there are rumours of a large new complex to be built soon. For now, Shoprite [406 B4] has a branch just off Zambia Way, near the Edinburgh Hotel, and there's a new convenience store called SuperSave at Parklands [406 D1]. More interesting perhaps is the main **market** [406 B5], which runs alongside the railway, close to the Edinburgh Hotel. Adjacent to this, near the long-distance bus station, and right at the end of Obote Avenue past the Edinburgh Hotel, is the large Chisokone Curio Market [406 D5]. Alternatively, you could take a look at Medusa Crafts [406 D1] in Parklands. For books, it may be worth checking out Kickstart Bookshop, also in Parklands ([406 D1] 0212 222594).

Out of town along the Kitwe–Chingola road, a shopping mall and hotel were scheduled to be incorporated within the new Copperbelt City, but in 2011 building had stopped and there is a questionmark over its completion.

OTHER PRACTICALITIES
Car spares and repairs Toyota have a franchise at the Caltex garage ([406 A1] *Chingola Rd;* 0212 217571/2217335), and Ford spares can be obtained from the Vehicle Centre. Spares for Mercedes, Mitsubishi and Chrysler vehicles can be obtained from Southern Cross Motors ([406 A1] *2503 Independence Av;* 0212 210035). More generally, a range of car spares is also available from either Autoworld ([406 B3] *off Freedom Way;* 0212 221960) or Daniel's Motor Spares (0212 223927).

Communications There are various **internet cafés** around town, including one on the ground floor of the Edinburgh Hotel [406 B4] and another, Sundiland, on City Square. One of the best is Botech (*Ontario Shopping Centre, Freetown Rd;* ⊙ 08.00–20.00) with decent computers, and costing Kw150 a minute. The main **post office** [406 C4] is just off Zambia Way, opposite Shoprite and Barclays Bank.

Health If you fall ill in or near Kitwe, contact the **Wusakili Mine Hospital** (0212 224144). To find it, take a left at the first set of traffic lights as you enter Kitwe from Ndola, and go past the mine. There are several pharmacies in the town.

For situations that are more serious, and may require immediate evacuation, contact **Speciality Emergency Services** (*SES; Lilongwe Rd;* 0212 211182; m *0977 770306–7;* e *seskitwe@zamnet.zm*), and see page 89 for details.

Money and banking Most of the large banks have branches in the centre of town, around the junction of Oxford Road and Zambia Way. There are also plenty of bureaux de change, including one by the Edinburgh Hotel [406 B4].

Travel agents and car hire
Voyagers [406 C4] Enoschomba Rd;
0212 225056/229102–3; e kitwe@
voyagerszambia.com; www.voyagerszambia.com

WHAT TO SEE AND DO In itself, Kitwe has few intrinsic attractions; as in Ndola, activities tend to centre around the local sports clubs. That said, the town is sufficiently close to Ndola for the two to share local attractions (see pages 402–4). Nearer Kitwe itself, there are a number of places of interest, including the **crocodile ponds** at Chililabombwe – the last town to the north before the border with the DRC. It is also possible to visit a women's **weaving project** at Chililabombwe (m *0977 863626*), part of a church group. Understated cotton throws and table mats in natural colours are available at competitive prices; you can expect to pay around US$35 for a cream throw.

Chembe Bird Sanctuary (*Entry Kw5,000 pp*) This woodland reserve, owned by the WECSZ (page 50) and about half-an-hour's drive to the west of Kitwe, is just off the road between Kalulushi and Kasempa. Centred on a small lake, it's a haven for birders, with over 300 of Zambia's listed birds recorded here; *chembe* is the local name for the African fish eagle, a regular visitor. Line fishing is permitted on the lake, where spotted-neck otters may be seen, but this is no place to swim: crocodiles are plentiful. Rather safer is the 7km Chinkamba Drive around the lake, offering a two-hour walk or short drive: it's navigable by 2WD in the dry season. There's a picnic and camping site, with charcoal available from the warden.

In the same direction is **Mindolo Dam**, home of Kitwe Boat Club (where you can get drinks and snacks) and a good spot for picnics, boating and quadbikes.

CHINGOLA

Chingola lies at the western end of the Copperbelt, about 50km west of Kitwe on a good road with just the occasional pot-hole. Beyond here you either head west towards Solwezi and Mwinilunga, or proceed north towards Lubumbashi in the DRC. The town is dominated by the huge KCM open-pit mines – the largest in Zambia – that have gouged the landscape on the eastern side of the town. Signs of renewed prosperity are everywhere, with investment attracted from all over the world.

GETTING THERE AND AROUND Work started in 2011 on a dual carriageway between Kitwe and Chingola, improving further the link between the two towns. Chingola itself is well served by buses to and from other towns in the Copperbelt and as far as both Solwezi and Lusaka. For details see under *Kitwe*, pages 404–5.

If you're driving yourself, note that several of the town's side streets are blocked at one end, making the concept of 'driving round the block' somewhat challenging! Note, too, that development of the KCM mine to the north of town has resulted in changes in the road layout from that shown on many maps. Finally, be aware that the road between Kitwe and Chingola is considered to be extremely dangerous in terms of potential accidents.

WHERE TO STAY While a few visitors choose to stay overnight at the **Chimfunshi Wildlife Orphanage** (pages 412–15), most opt to base themselves in Chingola, either at the new Protea or at one of the guesthouses, and visit the orphanage as a day trip.

In town

Protea Hotel Chingola [411 D4] (40 rooms) Kabundi Rd; 0212 312810; e proteachingola@zamtel.zm; reservations@ proteahotels.com; www.proteahotel.com/ chingola. Opened in 2002, the Protea came like a breath of fresh air to Chingola. It's an L-shaped building, all blues & terracottas, set in an open position just outside town, fronted by trees & a large parking area. From its cool blue reception area it is modern, light & very well kept, with plenty of solid wood furnishings. Rooms have en-suite bath & separate shower, AC, armchair, kettle, TV, desk & WiFi. They are set out in 2 wings either side of an apex formed by a pool & terrace, & backed by a smart but comfortable restaurant (06.00–22.00). Here, à-la-carte menus offer everything from light meals to pastas to grills. Alongside the conference rooms are a business centre with internet (office hours only), & a steel-&-chrome bar with upstairs lounge that can be heaving at w/ends. **$$$–$$$$**

Mokorro Grill & Lodge [411 B4] (3 chalets) Kabundi Rd; 0212 310079; m 0966 521230/742238; e mokorro@iconnect.zm; www. chingolagrill.com. New thatched chalets at this central restaurant are en suite with DSTV. **$$$**

Mukwa Lodge [411 D3] (10 rooms) 73 Mkushi Rd; 0212 310042; e mukwachingola@zamsat.net; www. mukwalodge.co.zm. Sister establishment to Mukwa in Kitwe, this new lodge has airy rooms in a courtyard arrangement. There are 8 elegantly furnished 'colonial-style' dbls, 1 twin & a family room, all with fridge, AC & DSTV. Continental meals are served in the residents-only restaurant. **$$$**

Rosewood Guesthouse [411 C5] (14 rooms) 5 Freedom Av; 0212 313114;

m 0966 239770/786131; e rosewood@zamnet. zm, info@rosewood.co.zm. The traditionally homely Rosewood has been completely rebuilt on a new site, left of the roundabout as you enter Chingola. Each en-suite room now boasts a flat-screen TV, fridge, tea/coffee station, wall fan, WiFi & safe. Both b/fast & home-cooked dinner are served in the new dining room, & packed lunches can be prepared on request. **$$$**

The Willows Guesthouse [411 C5] (7 rooms) 57 President Av; m 0966 906544/ 992002, 0955 746099; e info@willows.co.zm. Just off the main roundabout, this is another Zambian-owned guesthouse, rather institutional in design, with little embellishment. That said, twin rooms, off a long corridor are clean, with en-suite shower & toilet, as well as AC, fan, TV, kettle & safe. There's a well-appointed sitting/ dining room, WiFi access, & an attractive garden where a braai area is formed between paths of railway sleepers that reflect the owner's work on the railways. **$$$**

Hibiscus Guesthouse [411 C5] (9 rooms) 33 Katutwa Rd; 0212 313635; m 0966 781045; e hibiscusguesthouse@gmail.com. Located just south of the roundabout, Hibiscus is set in attractive gardens with a small pool. All rooms are now en suite with DSTV & a fridge. Guests have a lounge, kitchen & dining room for their own use, with packed lunch & substantial dinners available on request. **$$**

Mica's Guesthouse [411 C2] (12 rooms) 59 5th St; 0212 313653; m 0977 188782. Close to the hospital, Mica's has clean dbl & family rooms, each with TV, fan, mosi net, & en-suite bath or shower & toilet. There's a bar in the entrance, & meals can be provided on request. **$$**

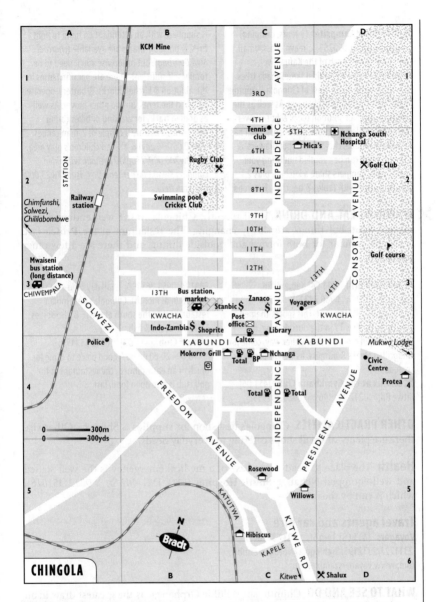

CHINGOLA

⌂ **Nchanga Hotel** [411 C4] (31 rooms)
Kabundi Rd; m 0955 829115. The old-fashioned
Nchanga in the centre of town may have been

renovated, but don't hold your breath. On the
plus side, it's relatively cheap & has a decent beer
garden. **$**

Out of town
⌂ **Nabona River Lodge** (8 rooms)
Chililabombwe Rd; m 0966 992900, 0969
302424; e nabonadn@yahoo.com. Set on a
farm on the banks of the Kafue River, Nabona
is about 15mins' drive from both Chingola &

Chililabombwe. All rooms are en suite, with an
additional 10 rooms under construction. Guests
have the use of a bar with games area, a dining
room, & a lounge with TV & internet access, plus
a braai area in the garden. **$$**

Ӿ Riverbend Campsite (3 tents, camping) m 0966 997410/990251; e reevo.chas@gmail. com. On a 4km stretch of the Kafue River, Riverbend is situated amidst large, shady trees on a farm some 35km west of Chingola – approx 10km from the chimp orphanage. As well as the campsite, with an ablution block & hot showers, there are simple en-suite walk-in tents. Each has twin beds, a table, chairs & chest of drawers, & a firepit; linen can be supplied but bring your own towels. Campers share a kitchen, plus 2 thatched *lapas* with tables & benches. Firewood is supplied, with an attendant on hand to light fires, & portable braais are available (*charcoal Kw4,000/bag*), but otherwise you'll need to be totally self sufficient. There are paraffin lamps in the ablution & kitchen blocks, & battery-operated lamps in the tents, but no other power. As well as graded tracks for walking or bikes (bring your own), there are a couple of 2-man canoes (*Kw30,000/½ day*) & a small children's play area. *Tent Kw200,000/250,000 without/with linen. Camping Kw40,000 per tent. Day visitor Kw25,000 (children free).*

Ӿ WHERE TO EAT AND DRINK Until recently, Chingola wasn't well endowed with places to eat, but things are slowly changing. The restaurant at the **Protea** (see above) is popular for both formal and poolside dining, and there are a few other options.

Ӿ Mokorro Grill [411 C4] Kabundi Rd; ☎ 0212 310079; m 0966 742238/521230; ⊕ 10.00–21.00 Mon–Sat. This sports-themed diner offers sports TV in the outside *lapa*, or more peaceful dining inside. Either way, come for chargrilled steaks & burgers, as well as pizzas & seafood. $$$$
Ӿ Shalux at the Gymkhana Club [411 D6] Kitwe Rd; ☎ 0212 311346; m 0966 781955/ 908124, 0955 263090; ⊕ all day Mon–Sat, 1st & last Sun of month). Chingola's best Indian restaurant is to the south of town, & also serves Chinese, steaks & fish. $$$$
Ӿ Golf Club [411 D2] ☎ 0212 311179; ⊕ 10.00–20.00 daily. A good place to come for lunch or an early dinner , the restaurant at the golf club is also open for b/fast. $$

OTHER PRACTICALITIES Chingola's best shop for **supplies** is Shoprite. Otherwise there are plenty of small shops catering to everyday needs.

Health The place to head for in case of a medical emergency is the well-staffed and well-equipped **Nchanga South Hospital** ([411 D2] *4th St;* ☎ *0212 351018*), which is run by the mine.

Travel agents and car hire
Voyagers [411 C3] 14th St; ☎ 0212 311642/ 2311722/2312195; e chingola@voyagerszambia. com; www.voyagerszambia.com

WHAT TO SEE AND DO Chimfunshi Wildlife Orphanage is the greatest draw in an area whose attractions are otherwise linked to the town's sports clubs. There is also **Hippo Pool**, a designated national monument and a favoured picnic spot, a few kilometres outside the town.

Chimfunshi Wildlife Orphanage (*PO Box 11190 Chingola;* ☎ *0212 311293;* m *0966 208405;* e *chimfunshiwildlife@iwayafrica.com; www.chimfunshi.org.za; admission Kw50,000 pp*) Probably the most popular excursion from Chingola is to Chimfunshi Wildlife Orphanage. This refuge for some of Africa's great apes is very much a working wildlife sanctuary. Although tourists are welcome to watch the chimps being fed and at play, it is not specifically geared to visitors. It's well off the main Zambian tourist trail and, aside from a number of dedicated supporters, is virtually unknown outside the country.

Chimfunshi started off as a normal 4,000ha cattle farm beside the banks of the Kafue River, close to the border with the DRC (formerly Zaire). It was run by Sheila Siddle and her late husband, David. Over the years, the Siddles established a reputation for rescuing wild animals in need. Then, in October 1983, Sheila's son-in-law brought her an orphaned chimpanzee, named Pal, who had been confiscated from Zairean poachers. Pal was sick and malnourished, and had been physically abused, yet against the odds Sheila eventually nursed him back to health.

It had been known for some time that Zambia was a conduit for the illegal export of chimps from Zaire, but as the authorities had nowhere practicable to release any confiscated animals, they had not been over-zealous in trying to stop the trade. Gradually they confiscated more chimps; and, by mid-1988, the Siddles had 19 chimps at Chimfunshi. At first, all were kept in cages, but taken out for regular forest walks. Then, as sending rehabilitated chimps back to Zaire wasn't a safe option, the Siddles decided to build a large enclosure at Chimfunshi. With minimal backing, they built a 4m-high wall around 2.8ha of their own forest land, and gradually introduced a group of chimps into the area. Unexpectedly, these chimps eventually melded into a coherent family-type group, which was clearly a great success. By this time orphaned chimps were being sent here from many corners of the globe, so in 1991 a second, 5.6ha enclosure surrounded by a solar-powered electric fence was constructed to accommodate another group of chimps.

A few years later, the Siddles acquired an adjacent 5,400ha farm, and made over the land to the Chimfunshi Wildlife Orphanage Trust, ensuring that the chimps would have a permanent home – something that is particularly important for animals whose lifespan in captivity mirrors that of humans. The northern boundary of the farm is the Kafue River, which butts onto 1,000ha of dense forest, with large grassy areas of river floodplain and several small tributaries of the Kafue River. There is also a particularly beautiful patch of tropical forest, which follows a narrow gorge. Generous donations enabled the construction of two large 500ha enclosures with

INDIGENOUS CHIMPS?

Chimpanzees are not generally thought to be indigenous to Zambia. Currently the southernmost population of wild chimps is thought to live in a remote (and relatively little-documented) corner of the Rukwa Region of Tanzania – around the Loasi River Forest Reserve on the eastern shore of Lake Tanganyika.

Chimpanzee distribution in the wild is limited by suitable habitat, and especially by the distribution of suitable vegetation and the wild fruit on which they live. Although there are remaining populations in woodland areas, most occur in moister, thicker forests – where the availability of wild fruits is higher. The relatively open, dry miombo woodlands in northern Zambia wouldn't be a typical habitat, although in some areas chimps do inhabit more arid woodland areas.

Sheila Siddle maintains that chimps could have once lived in Zambia. She cites oral evidence, reported from older local people in Mbala, just south of Lake Tanganyika, who refer to a species of animal which is now extinct in the area as *socamuntu*, meaning 'like a man' in the Bemba language.

plenty of mature *musambya* (*Chrysophyllum magalismontanum*) trees, followed by two smaller enclosures of 200ha each. Each of these has a concrete 'feeding centre' – essentially a building with a door onto the open enclosure, and bars for windows, and the larger two have a rooftop observation area.

In 2000, Sheila and David were jointly awarded the MBE for their work with the chimps, and travelled to London where their medals were presented at Buckingham Palace by the Queen.

Chimfunshi today Today there are 120 chimps on the property. Over the years, several chimps have been born on the farm, but several of the animals are now fitted with contraceptive implants. The larger enclosures housed 47 and 23 chimps respectively, while a further 15 were in the first of the 200ha areas, and the fourth enclosure was waiting for a new family to move in. A herd of impala grazes the land between the two large enclosures.

The chimps spend almost all of their time outside, coming inside only at feeding times, which means that they are close enough to be inspected by the keepers for any health problems.

Each of the 'family' groups is made up of animals that have been gradually introduced to each other until they become a cohesive unit, and only then can they be allowed into one of the large enclosures together. Those whose social groups are as yet incomplete live in a variety of pens and large cages near the house, with space at the back where they are free to roam for part of the day, when the keepers are around. Inevitably, there are a few chimps for whom socialising is a step too far, or who have escaped once too often, and these problem animals remain caged for safety's sake. It's not pretty, but the animals are well cared for, and the cages are almost certainly better than where the animals were before coming here; active fundraising is taking place to help improve their lot.

In addition to the chimps, Chimfunshi also rehabilitates various other orphaned animals. At any one time, you're likely to find a menagerie of furry, feathered and warm-blooded beings here, all either being nursed back to health, or being kept on after recovering. A typical story is that of Billy, the hippo, who joined the family in 1992. At ten days old, she was discovered on the bank of the Kafue, next to the body of her dead mother. She was adopted by Sheila, who kept her in the house when small. Now, at well over 1,500kg, she's fully grown, yet she still comes to the house each morning for her bottles of milk and wanders around the campsite and the farm with nonchalant disregard for her bulk – and anything that gets in the way of it. (Do remember, though, that she's still a wild animal, and treat her with respect.)

The orphanage is supported by a trust. If you would like to help, contact the Friends of Chimfunshi (e *adoption@mweb.co.za*). And to find out more, get hold of a copy of Sheila's book, *In My Family Tree* (see *Appendix 3*, page 537).

Getting there It takes about an hour and a quarter to drive to Chimfunshi from Chingola. Take the tar road towards Solwezi for about 42km until you come to a sign pointing right (✪ TUCHIM 12°28.476'S, 27°29.150'E) to the orphanage. If you're coming from Solwezi, it's around 118km to this signpost. From the turn-off it's a further 18km along a reasonably good farm track to the orphanage (✪ CHIMFU 12°21.460'S, 27°33.242'E), taking about 40 minutes to drive in the dry season. There are no buses to the orphanage itself, but plenty of transport plies the route between Solwezi and Chingola, so it would be easy to be dropped at the turning, although hitching (or walking) along the access road could take some time.

Where to stay Chimfunshi was not designed with the tourist in mind, so forget all ideas of upmarket lodge-style accommodation. Those wishing to stay at the sanctuary have the choice of simple, dormitory-style rooms or a riverside campsite. Either way, you'll need to come with all your own food; meals are not provided. Do note, too, that communications out in the bush can be very poor, so if you're planning to stay, you need to allow plenty of time to set up your visit.

Education centre This modern centre is about 12km from the main farmhouse & incorporates accommodation for 20–30 people. It is used mainly for school classes, youth groups & undergraduate students from overseas, but when it is empty, private visitors are welcome to use the facilities. The buildings are simple modern prefabs, with small dormitory-style rooms, some with 7 beds, others with 2; bedding & towels are provided. All are clean, & are set around an open courtyard, with a large braai area, communal kitchens, & separate buildings with hot showers & long-drop toilets. Water is supplied from the site's own borehole. A cheerful classroom features posters showing the chimp 'family' groups, complete with individual portraits, while outside, each of the trees is labelled with both its Bemba & scientific names. *Kw100,000 pp.*

Campsite Set on a gently sloping bank of grass leading down to the river, the campsite is close to the house owned by Sheila's daughter, Sylvia. Campers share old but hot showers & long-drop toilets, & it's usually possible to borrow a few pots & pans if you need them. Those without their own tent can make use of the (very basic) caravan that's parked at the educational centre. *Camping Kw50,000 pp; Kw100,000 deposit for caravan.*

What to see and do Some visitors prefer to spend a few days here, taking advantage of the freedom to explore the farm's extensive walks and excellent birding (over 350 species have been recorded), and affording the time to watch the chimps at leisure. Most, though, come for just a half day, or perhaps bring a picnic and spend the day here.

The chimps are divided between the two main enclosures, and a variety of large cages and smaller enclosures near the farmhouse. These, the educational centre and the campsite are a considerable distance apart, making some form of vehicle very useful; you can walk between places, but it takes a while! Visitors can drive themselves, or you can arrange to be collected from the educational centre or campsite to go to the farmhouse, where the bush walks and feeding of the baby chimps takes place.

The chimps follow a straightforward routine, which makes it relatively easy to plan a day out. Feeding times are at 07.00, when the babies are fed their milk in bottles, and balls of nshima are shared out among the older animals. Visitors are welcome to visit for the 11.30 feed of fruit and vegetables, and more milk for the whole group, or at 13.30 for the day's final offering of milk. (Milk provides the chimps with their protein requirement, substituting for the meat which would form a small part of their diet in the wild.) Outside of feeding time, when one of the keepers will explain something of the chimps' behaviour and routine, there are two options. Individual visitors are welcome to explore the enclosures themselves, observing the animals at tree level from the roof of the feeding centres, which makes for some excellent photographic opportunities.

Those staying overnight may have the opportunity to take part in a two-hour morning bush walk with some of the younger chimps (*US$100 pp; min age 19*), in the company of one of the keepers. If the idea of a baby chimp jumping into your arms or riding piggyback across the bush to a natural playground appeals, then don't think twice. Just remember that this is no place for smart clothes, and remove any jewellery or other items before the chimps do it for you.

There has been a history of copper mining from the Kansanshi Hills north of Solwezi for hundreds of years, but commercial mining started only in the 20th century. Riding on the success of the Kansanshi Mine, Solwezi has evolved in just a few decades from a small village to a busy little town – and is still growing. While it's not an attraction in itself, it is useful for supplies if you're coming from Lusaka and heading west, or driving into Kafue from the north.

GETTING THERE AND AWAY The main tarred road leading from Chingola runs right through Solwezi (⊕ SOLWEZ 12°10.931'S, 26°23.960'E). It's a distance of 180km, and is in reasonable condition, but there are sufficient pot-holes to catch out the unwary – not to mention the goats, pigs and cyclists all along the road. To the east, the tar road towards Kasempa has been improved in recent years and is now in good condition.

By air Solwezi's airstrip is west of the town. Proflight operates flights between here and Ndola every weekday, and to and from Lusaka twice a week. With so much industrial development in the area it's no surprise that there are plans to upgrade the airstrip to take international flights.

By bus Regular buses link Solwezi with Chingola, Kitwe and Lusaka, with departures from Solwezi usually in the early morning and early afternoon. Expect to pay around Kw25,000–35,000 to Chingola one way; Kw45,000 to Kitwe, and Kw80,000 to Lusaka. The bus station straddles the main road, next to and opposite the market, at the western end of town.

WHERE TO STAY Like so many of Zambia's northern towns, Solwezi has benefited from the resurgence in the mining industry. Now, in addition to several larger, old-style motels, and an ever-increasing variety of small guesthouses, there are one or two entirely different places to stay, from the upmarket Royal Solwezi to the simple but well-run Floriana. Of the rest, most are reasonable – and reasonably accessible from the main tar road through town.

Kansanshi Hotel (30 rooms, 4 villas)
\0218 821221; m 0965 611611; e info. kansanshihotel@gmail.com. In a forested location about 2km from the main road, this new hotel is some 10mins both from town & from the Kansanshi Mine. Its thatched buildings incorporate rooms of various standards, all en suite with internet access & DSTV; there are self-catering villas too. Guests can dine à la carte in the restaurant, or eat in the pizzeria & sports bar near the pool. **$$$–$$$$**

Royal Solwezi (48 rooms) 147 Old Chingola Rd; \0211 821620; m 0966 271422; e reservations@solwezi.com; www.solwezi.com. Opened in 2007, the Royal Solwezi is set on a low hill on the eastern edge of town, about 0.5km from the main road. Good views to the east make this a prime spot, & there's enough space to make it the envy of many a hotelier. Rooms are huge – sgls have a dbl bed; dbls have 2 of them – with ultra-modern bathroom fittings, a TV & safe as standard. Bright splashes of colour & trendy photos documenting the hotel's phases of construction enliven tinted cement floors & bed plinths, & solid *mukwa*-wood desks. The rooms are built in 2-storey blocks, 2 each side of the cavernous central area. Patio doors from each lead onto a balcony or straight out to wide lawns stretching across the pool & a sports bar with plasma TV screens – sufficiently far away for noise not to be an issue. Towards the bottom of the plot, 10 2-bedroom villas cater to long-stay visitors.

The veranda is an attractive & relaxed place for a drink, contrasting with the formality of the

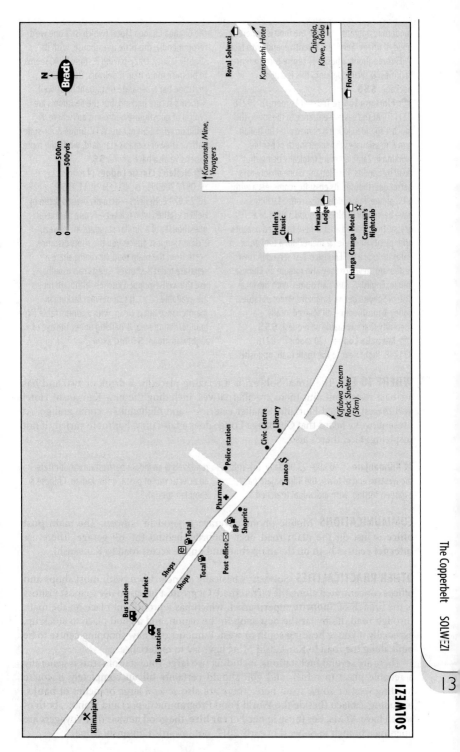

modern restaurant – where the food is generally good, if pricey. Service is attentive, and with fast WiFi throughout, a business centre & conference facilities, & secure parking, this is a good package. **$$$**

🏠 **Floriana Lodge Trust** (41 rooms) ☏0218 821130. At the eastern entrance to the town, this much-expanded lodge is named after an Italian nun & missionary who spent much of her life working in Zambia before tragically being shot dead by bandits. The Floriana is one of Solwezi's better guesthouses. Its en-suite rooms, each with a TV, phone, fan, fridge & tea/coffee facilities, have been built in blocks around 3 sides of a grassy, tree-shaded area, where thatched gazebos offer plenty of shade (& shelter) for a cool drink. Rates include a full English b/fast served in their restaurant, in which they also conjure up Chinese, Indian, English & Zambian dishes, with the local dish of Solwezi beans, *kingovwa* sweet potatoes, honey & mushroom – all sourced locally – a speciality that's available on request. **$$$**

🏠 **Mwaaka Lodge** (20 rooms) ☏0218 821248. Right next to the main road, opposite

the Changa Changa Motel (which isn't one we'd recommend!), this little guesthouse, with its slightly jaunty, crazy-paving & stone look, seems to promise more than it delivers. Outside, a thatched bar & separate restaurant bode well, & there's secure parking, but the bedrooms are typical of guesthouse bedrooms anywhere, & could do with a bit of care. A TV, fridge & en-suite bath or shower come as standard, while the more expensive also have a sofa. **$$**.

🏠 **Hellen's Classic Lodge** (4 rooms)
📱 0977 706995; ✪ HELLEN 12°11.165'S, 26°25.074'E. Hellen's – actually owned & run by Hellen's father, who is a vet – is one of several guesthouses of a similar standard in Solwezi; a clear signpost directs you the short distance north from the main road. Its rooms share a separate toilet & shower. Guests can usually use the well-equipped kitchen, although meals are available ($$). It's somewhat lacking in maintenance but is clean, with a comfortable TV lounge/dining area, & parking under the eye of a nightwatchman. **$** *b/fast extra*

✖ **WHERE TO EAT** The Royal Solwezi is a relaxing place for a drink or two and has a smart restaurant, but there are alternatives, including the new Kansanshi Hotel and the established Floriana. Smaller eateries – and nightclubs – come and go. At present, we've heard that Chabanga Lodge does a fair curry. For more varied (if not inspiring) fare, there's also:

✖ **Kilimanjaro** ⏰ 06.00–22.00 daily. Towards the western end of town, the Kilimanjaro has a garden setting, with individual thatched

rondavels & an indoor bar/restaurant. It offers an eclectic mix of pasta, grills, Indian, Chinese & Zambian specials. **$$**

COMMUNICATIONS Mobile phone coverage is good in Solwezi. The main **post office** is just off the main road near Shoprite, behind the BP garage. There are **internet** centres both on the main road and on the access road to Kansanshi.

OTHER PRACTICALITIES Solwezi is basically a linear town, with most shops and offices concentrated along the tarred road. Of greatest practical use to most visitors is the branch of **Shoprite** supermarket, which has a prominent place on the main through road. It's by far the best shop in the region, and a good place to stock up, especially if you're heading south or west. Rumours of a new shopping centre to be built along the road to Kansanshi Mine have yet to materialise.

There are several **fuel** stations, including two large Total stations; this is generally a reliable place to refuel, and you should certainly fill up completely if you're heading west or south from here. There are also several large branches of **banks**, including Zanaco (beside the World Food Programme depot) and Stanbic, both of which have ATMs. For those in need of **car hire**, the good news is that Voyagers are opening a branch in Solwezi in early 2012, out towards Kansanshi Mine.

In an emergency, there's a 24-hour Medical Centre (0218 821225). For other medical issues, the best place to go is Hilltop Hospital (m 0977 567892), just off the main road through town.

WHAT TO SEE AND DO Solwezi may not be a tourist mecca but there are still one or two places that offer an interesting diversion if you're passing through. For those visiting Kansanshi Mine, there is also an unexpected bonus. Since the approach road to the mine is largely privately owned, it is surrounded by security fences, which in turn keep out poachers. As a result, you can expect to see herds of impala along here, which comes as something of a surprise in an area not noted for its wildlife.

Kifubwa Stream Rock Shelter *(Entrance US$15 pp; ⏰ 09.00–18.00 daily)* Quite
close to the centre of Solwezi, where the Kifubwa Stream runs through a narrow gorge, there's a series of enigmatic engravings under an overhanging rock, dating to the late Stone Age. Although these had been known to local people for many years, they were first brought to wider attention in 1928. Subsequent archaeological surveys uncovered evidence of both quartz tools and charcoal fires, giving a clear indication of the site's provenance. Unfortunately, the engravings themselves have suffered at the hands of vandals.

To get there, turn off the main road to the south, towards the Teachers' College; it's signposted 'National Monument'. After about 3km, you'll come to the college; continue for a further 3km or so to a boom across the road. Stop here to pay the entrance fee, then you can either walk or drive the last couple of hundred metres down towards the river. Here, well-marked trails lead to the engravings, and interpretive signboards explain how they were discovered. It's an attractive picnic spot, but don't try swimming; there are some serious undercurrents.

Mutanda Falls *(Entrance US$10 pp)* About 36km from town is the Mutanda
River, where there's a series of attractive rapids, the Mutanda Falls. To get here, follow the tar road west out of town, go past the airport, and continue almost to the river. Just before this, take a left turning off the road and follow this track for about 1km.

🏠 Where to stay
🏠 **Mutanda Falls Leisure Resort** Dotted around the area are some basic chalets & there's a bar area with superb views of the rapids. Food here seems to be very hit & miss: some talk of chicken, steak, fish & nshima at reasonable rates; others describe it as awful.

The Copperbelt SOLWEZI

KAFUE RIVER BASIN

14

The Kafue River Basin

Southwest of the Copperbelt, the Kafue River Basin covers a large swathe of central Zambia stretching almost from the DRC to the west of Lusaka. It encompasses large areas of very sparsely populated bush as well as the Kafue, Blue Lagoon and Lochinvar national parks.

Much of this region of Zambia is difficult to visit, consisting of endless seasonal bush tracks which link occasional farming settlements. At its heart lies the huge Kafue National Park, which has some superb game-viewing areas within its boundaries. The best of these, the Busanga Plains, is not the most accessible, but at times it ranks with the subcontinent's most impressive game areas.

East of the park, there are seasonal floodplains that sustain game and attract a rich variety of birdlife – like the Lukanga Swamps and the Kafue Flats. Part of the latter is in theory protected by two small national parks – Blue Lagoon and Lochinvar – but most such areas remain outside the parks. The Kafue River Basin is a wild area, with some excellent game and endless possibilities for exploring, but very little development.

TOWNS AROUND KAFUE NATIONAL PARK

Southern Kafue is relatively near to Livingstone, and usually accessed from Kalomo or one of the other towns on the Livingstone–Lusaka road (see *Chapter 9*, pages 213–18). Northern Kafue has three towns around it which aren't usually destinations in their own right, but may be useful jumping-off points for the northern side of the park: Kasempa in the north, Mumbwa to the east, and Kaoma in the west.

KASEMPA The small town of Kasempa is set in the midst of rolling, hilly country. Although there are many villages in the surrounding bush, the overall population density doesn't feel very high as much of the area seems to be miombo woodland. The only **fuel** station is closed, but black-market fuel is available here – for a price. Better is to head southeast for 5km to the Mukinge Hospital (see box, page 422), which offers both petrol and diesel for sale to the public.

Getting there and away Three roads run into Kasempa, meeting at a T-junction. To the north is an excellent, tarred road from Solwezi. That meets two reasonably good gravel roads: one just north of town (✪ TUKAOM 13°27.388'S, 25°49.771'E), heading southwest to Kaoma; the other heading southeast towards Mumbwa, with a turn-off to the Kafue National Park's Kabanga gate. For detailed directions on this route, see *Driving from Kasempa to Mumbwa*, below.

There's a direct **bus** between Kasempa and Lusaka, via Solwezi. Buses stop in the square.

From Solwezi The good tar road southwest from Solwezi passes the airport then continues in a more southerly direction towards Kasempa, passing close to the Mutanda Falls. After some 140km, at ⊕ TUKALU 13°3.302'S, 25°59.199'E, the M11 from Kalulushi joins this road from the west, then a few kilometres further on there's another junction (⊕ TUKASE 13°6.226'S, 25°52.252'E). The road straight on, heading west, is the good M8 to Kabompo, with tarring nearing completion in 2011. For Kasempa, turn left and follow the tarred D181 for 43km to the small town (⊕ KASEMP 13°27.404'S, 25°49.779'E).

🏠 **Where to stay** There are a few basic guesthouses in town, including the very rundown (but very cheap) **TTG** close to where the buses stop, but the best of the bunch is a little way out of the centre:

🏠 **Maka Guesthouse** (9 rooms) 📱 0977 435332. ⊕ MAKAG 13°27.382'S, 25°49.645'E. 3km north of town on the road towards Kaoma, this simple, friendly guesthouse offers clean rooms with fans, 3 en suite & the rest sharing a bathroom. There's a living room with TV, & in the evening you can get nshima & chicken ($), but no b/fast is served. **$**

Other practicalities Most of the town's shops and other facilities form a square just off the main road. There's a branch of the National Savings and Credit Bank here, but to **change money** you'll have to wait for the mobile Zanaco Bank on a Tuesday or Friday. Other amenities include a **post office**, a Catholic church and a few very basic **shops** – including the virtually empty Poshrite supermarket.

MUKINGE HOSPITAL

Mukinge Mission (*www.webmissions.org/mukinge*) started around 1925 when the Rev C S Foster came to this area as an evangelical missionary. His son, Bob, was born here, studied medicine in Toronto, and then returned in 1950 to found a mission hospital – even supervising its construction.

Today, Mukinge Hospital serves a huge area that can result in patients travelling on foot or by bike for up to five days. With about 200 beds, it cares for around 140 in-patients a day (including three or four births on average) as well as 160–180 outpatients. The seven in-patient wards include one for malnutrition and another for isolation. There are also two operating theatres, a new eye clinic, a laboratory, a range of X-ray equipment, a physiotherapy department, a training school for nurses and a pharmacy with basic drug supplies. In short, it's the best hospital for a very long way.

Mukinge is still supported by the Evangelical Church in Zambia, as well as by the government, but funds for day-to-day expenses such as food and equipment are tight. To this end, the hospital has its own **fuel station**, with both diesel and petrol sold from large drums. Prices are on a par with black-market outlets, around Kw8,500 per litre in 2011, but there are no issues about the quality here, and you have the added feel-good factor of knowing that you have contributed to a worthy cause.

To get to the hospital (⊕ MUKING 13°28.894's, 25°51.409'E), head south of Kasempa for about 4km, then turn right (⊕ TUMUKI 13°28.264'S, 25°51.902'E), following the signs for a further 1km. There are buses between here and Kasempa.

Driving from Kasempa to Mumbwa This once-difficult road has been graded in recent years, and is now an easily navigable and pleasant drive, skirting round the eastern edge of the national park. Along the way, the road is lined with a few small rural settlements and a lot of open areas. After 4km, you'll pass the turning to Mukinge Mission, then a further 75km brings you to a right-hand fork signposted to the Kabanga gate (⊕ TUKABA 13°57.930'S, 26°11.858'E), on the northern border of Kafue National Park. The gate itself (⊕ KABANG 14°5.808'S, 26°7.036'E) is some 19km along a bumpy, sandy track. For Mumbwa, however, continue straight along the graded road, passing through lush green woodland and the occasional village, and keeping right where there's a fork in the road after 11km (⊕ KAFORK 13°57.905'S, 26°17.459'E). A total of almost 28km will bring you to the Lunga pontoon (⊕ FERRYL 13°58.984'S, 26°20.784'E; ⊕ *06.00–18.00 daily; Kw56,000 per vehicle*).

About 3km before the pontoon is a turning to Lunga River Lodge (⊕ TULUNG 13°58.626'S, 26°20.076'E). This is the start of a very bumpy, black-cotton soil track that shadows the east bank of the Lunga River for around 25km to what is currently a hunting lodge, on the boundary of the park. A continuation then heads northwest to the Kabanga gate (⊕ KABANG 14°5.808'S, 26°7.036'E). Most drivers, however, cross the Lunga River, then continue for another 70km along a good, but winding road to the Lubungu River (⊕ LUBUNG 14°33.750'S, 26°27.250'E); watch out for fallen trees and other debris *en route*. Note that the pontoon here (⊕ *06.00–18.00 daily; Kw56,000 per vehicle*) is smaller than its counterpart over the Lunga, so not capable of taking large vehicles.

From the Lubungu River, it's another 75km or so to Mumbwa, a straightforward if rather uninteresting journey taking around two hours. While this section of the road isn't quite up to the standard of that to the north, it's still a largely good, if narrow, gravel road – a far cry from the nightmare track of old.

For directions in reverse on this section, see *Driving north from Mumbwa*, page 424.

Note that the southern parts of this route, from around the Lunga pontoon, are within a GMA, so you are not free to camp – or indeed to do anything other than simply pass through.

MUMBWA Mumbwa's proximity to Lusaka gives it a palpable urban buzz, entirely different from the rural feel of small towns further west. The presence of a large mosque with a dominant minaret only serves to enhance this feel.

The town is 4km north of the main tar road between Lusaka and Mongu, and is the last place for anyone heading into the Kafue National Park to change money or stock up on fuel. That said, you'd be wise not to bank on either of these amenities.

Getting there
By bus Between the town's two roundabouts, in the bustling market area, is the local bus station, where buses between Mongu and Lusaka stop in both directions. It's a relatively busy route, with arrivals and departures at all times of day, though the highest frequency is the middle of the day, when buses that left from Lusaka or Mongu in the morning pass through the town. One-way fares to Lusaka are around Kw4,290 on a small minibus, or Kw7,000 on a larger one.

Driving from Lusaka About three hours' drive from Lusaka (148km), on the Great West Road towards Mongu, a large modern factory looms next to the road, and orderly warehouses stand behind well-watered lawns. This is perhaps the country's biggest cotton ginnery. A few kilometres further west is a turning off the

14

road to the north, which leads – after about 4km of pot-holed tar – to the thriving town of Mumbwa.

⌂ **Where to stay** There are a couple of overnight choices in Mumbwa, of which the best is the Hacienda.

⌂ **Hacienda Hotel** (7 rooms, 6 chalets) ☎ 0211 800287/8. ✪ HACIEN 14°59.041'S, 27°03.720'E. This old hotel in a quiet location has been recently revamped, with good service & pleasant staff. To find it, turn left off the main road at the 2nd roundabout heading north, then it's on the left. Rooms are en suite with spotless tiled floors, dbl or twin beds & mosi nets, AC, fridges & DSTV. The clean, tiled foyer leads to a separate bar with TV, & a restaurant ($), serving decent meals of beef stew or chicken curry &

rice for Kw15–25,000, or Zambian dishes such as pumpkin leaves & groundnuts at Kw10,000. There's a good pool in the pretty gardens, too. **$$**.

⌂ **Mumbwa Motel** (22 rooms) ✪ MUMBMO 14°59.710'S, 27°03.622'E. Mumbwa's other option, on the right as you drive into town, is cheaper, tatty & less welcoming. Small rondavels are en suite, & for amenities it boasts a cocktail bar, restaurant & public phone. **$** *exc b/fast*.

Other practicalities Mumbwa has a fairly reliable Total **fuel** station (✪ TOTALM 14°59.451'S, 27°03.642'E) on the main roundabout into town. It's the only one for miles around, but it would be wise to phone ahead (☎ *0211 800094/218/307*) to check that fuel is available. In addition to the town's **market**, located between the two roundabouts, there are endless small local **shops**, including the good Gilson's bakery close to the fuel station. Opposite the market is a branch of Barclays Bank (⊕ *08.30–14.30 Mon–Fri*) with a useful **ATM**. Again, it's not entirely reliable, so don't run your cash too low.

Driving north from Mumbwa

To the Lubungu pontoon From the tarred Great West Road, there is now a generally good gravel road along the eastern side of the park to the Lubungu pontoon via the Kabulushi gate, and on to Kasempa. A high-clearance vehicle remains advisable, however, and if you're heading for Hippo Lodge or McBrides' Camp (see pages 439–40), then a 4x4 is essential in the rainy season. Note that it is no longer possible to drive due north into the park from the Nalusanga scout post.

To access this eastern road from the Great West Road, turn north into Mumbwa, then left at the first roundabout by the Total garage (✪ TOTALM 14°59.457'S, 27°03.617'E), Continue through a market and after about 1.1km, at the top of the next rise, take a right turn onto the Kasempa road, a reasonable gravel road that goes to Lubungu pontoon. The 66km stretch from here to the Kabulushi gate (✪ KABULU 14°40.727'S, 26°39.338'E) passes through wooded areas and some farmland. The surface is showing signs of wear, but as you continue north, so it improves. No fees are payable at the gate by those just driving through; if you're staying at Hippo Lodge or McBrides' Camp, park fees should be paid at the lodges themselves.

After a further 20km, or nearly 86km from Mumbwa, the road passes through an area with huge rounded boulders. A fork (✪ TUHIPP 14°37.866'S, 26°29.659'E) to the left, clearly signposted from the south (but not from the north) leads to Hippo Lodge and McBrides' Camp – and also the old Hippo Mine (see page 439). For the Lubungu pontoon (✪ LUBUNG 14°33.750'S, 26°27.250'E; ⊕ *06.00–18.00 daily; Kw56,000 per vehicle or US$20 if foreign registered; 12 ton limit*) continue on the main road for a further 10km – and note that this pontoon is smaller than its Lunga counterpart.

If you're driving to Lunga (which very few people do) you could alternatively take the longer route through the park which, although significantly slower than this one, is likely to offer some good game sightings.

From the Lubungu pontoon to the Lunga pontoon See *4x4 routes within and around northern Kafue*, page 434, for directions along this route.

KAOMA Kaoma is a small district town about 3km north of the Great West Road between Kafue and Mongu, and about 76km west of Kafue National Park. Though not close to Kafue, it's on the edge of the Western Province, so is very much a gateway to the area. Whichever way you're travelling, it's wise to fill your fuel tank (and spare fuel drums) here.

If you have space in your vehicle, you'll find no shortage of people wanting to share the journey. Given the shortage of transport, and the insight that hitchhikers can give to visitors, don't appear rude to the locals by refusing a lift.

Getting there and away

By bus All the buses stop at the bus station behind the Total filling station in the centre of town. Buses to/from Lusaka take about 5½ hours; those to/from Mongu about two hours.

Driving

From Kaoma to Lukulu If you're heading west to Lukulu, take the tar road towards Mongu for about 25km, then there's a gravel road on the right, signposted as 195km to Lukulu. After 16km on this road it forks: keep to the right. Later there's a sign heralding a turn to the right, to the M8, which leads to the Watopa pontoon (⊕ FERRY4 14°2.338'S, 23°37.744'E).

Lining this road are small villages, each consisting of thatched huts built in varying sizes. Oxcarts are also a frequent sight, straight out of a biblical scene.

From Kaoma to Kasempa From the Great West Road at Kaoma, there's a reasonable gravel road that heads north and then northeast to Kasempa.

Where to stay and eat There's a choice of small local guesthouses in Kaoma, of which the best is at the Kaoma Cheshire Orphanage. Others include **Luena View Guesthouse**, on the north edge of town, **Mak's Guestvilla**, opposite the bus station, and the recently opened **Chief's Boma Guesthouse** on the Great West Road. All have fairly clean rooms and may be able to arrange simple meals. Mak's also has a bar.

Kaoma Cheshire Orphanage Guesthouse (6 rooms, 6 rondavels) m 0977 221782. With a beautiful view of the Luena valley, the guesthouse has decent, clean rooms in 2 semi-detached houses (1 with a living room & DSTV, the other with a dining room) or in individual rondavels. There are mosquito nets in each room. Guests share communal hot showers & a kitchen where you can prepare your own food. Alternatively, simple meals can be provided with sufficient notice. By staying here you support the orphanage in raising funds for Zambia's ever-increasing number of AIDS orphans. *Kw100,000 pp; b/fast Kw20,000.*

Tom Kok reports on three places for a drink and a chat along the main street: **Maseka** (which has an outside terrace, where you can meet plenty of local people), **Liye Liye** and **Luvu**. C&C near the Zamtel mast serves good nshima, chips or rice,

14

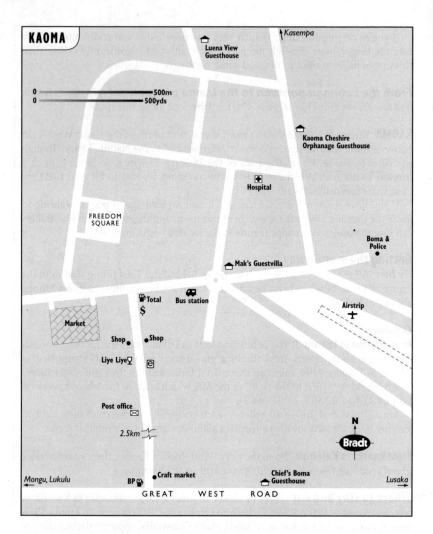

KAOMA

↑ Kasempa

Luena View
Guesthouse

Kaoma Cheshire
Orphanage Guesthouse

⊞ Hospital

FREEDOM
SQUARE

Boma &
Police

Mak's Guestvilla

Total
$

Bus station

Airstrip

Market

Shop •   • Shop

Liye Liye

ℯ

Post office
✉

2.5km

N

Bradt

Mongu, Lukulu

BP

• Craft market

Chief's Boma
Guesthouse

Lusaka

GREAT   WEST   ROAD

0 ────── 500m
0 ────── 500yds

with beef, chicken or occasionally fish and a drink ($), and is a pleasant place to spend an evening. More and more bars have satellite television.

Other practicalities Kaoma has a **post office**, a Finance **Bank**, numerous **shops** (of which the best stocked is Cheap & Best along the main road) and local eateries, and two vital **fuel** stations: vital to anyone travelling west, that is. The most reliable of these is the BP station on the main road, but as always, don't run your supplies too low. If you're looking for **crafts**, take a look at the small craft market opposite the BP station. Established with funding from the WWF, it offers baskets, woodcarvings and other crafts at affordable prices.

What to see and do Local artist Kozhi Kawina has painted several murals that are well worth a visit. You can find them on the walls of the district hospital, the doctor's residence and the Cheshire orphanage. If you contact him direct (m *0979 314215*) Kawina can also take you to see his work at his studio in the nearby village of Chilombo, a nice walk of some 3km. In addition to his painting, the artist leads a cultural drum and dance troupe that has established quite a reputation in Zambia.

KAFUE NATIONAL PARK

(Park fees US$20 pp/day; vehicle US$15/day or Kw15,300 if Zambian registered. Fees payable at Hook Bridge, Dumdumwenze, Kabanga & Musa gates, & at some lodges. ⊕ *06.00–18.00)* Kafue is a huge national park, two-and-a-half times the size of South Luangwa. Sadly, in the 1980s and early '90s, few resources were devoted to its upkeep and anti-poaching efforts were left to a couple of dedicated souls from the few safari lodges that remained in the park.

Now the situation is better. A steady trickle of visitors into the park helps add weight (and finance) to the ongoing effort to build the park back up to its former glory. Even the park's elephants are visibly recovering (both in number and in terms of losing some of their shyness), although it will be a while before they return to their former strength. It is very heartening to see that the rest of the game is thriving, and occurring in a volume and variety that bodes well for the future.

The camps here are not generally as plush or well-oiled as the corresponding camps in the Luangwa, but in Kafue's best areas the game can be very good. In particular, game viewing on and around the Busanga Plains can be stunning, so don't visit the park without at least a side trip into this remarkable area.

In a move to develop tourist facilities in the park and its surrounding GMAs, and thus improve the income of the local people, discussions are in hand with the US-based Millennium Challenge Corporation (MCC). If the project goes ahead, it is anticipated that funding of around US$100 million will be allocated over a five-year period towards constructing all-weather roads along the park's north–south axis, upgrading the airstrips, protecting the park and improving management systems.

GEOGRAPHY Established in 1924, the Kafue National Park covers some 22,400km² (about the size of Wales, or Massachusetts) of very varied terrain and is one of the world's largest national parks. Naturally, its geography varies considerably. Throughout the park, the permanent Kafue River follows a well-defined course, and widens in a few places where barriers of harder rocks near the surface force it into shallow, rocky rapids – Kafwala and the area beside KaingU Safari Lodge being the obvious examples. Bordering the eastern side of southern Kafue is Lake Itezhi-Tezhi – a large, manmade lake that was created in 1977. The primary function of its dam is to regulate the water levels experienced by the Kafue Gorge Hydro-electric Dam, further downstream, although it also generates some electricity.

The map clearly shows that the tarred Great West Road between Lusaka and Mongu bisects the park. This road provides the easiest route into the park, and also a convenient split that allows me to refer to 'northern' and 'southern' Kafue as simply meaning the areas to the north and the south of the road. These have slightly different habitats and species, and also very different access routes. As far as casual visitors are concerned, they could almost be two separate parks.

Surrounding the whole are no fewer than eight game management areas (GMAs), which provide a valuable buffer zone for the park's wildlife.

FLORA AND FAUNA
Flora Most of Kafue is an undulating mosaic of miombo woodlands and dambos, within which you'll find smaller patches of munga woodland, and bands of riparian forest and thickets along the larger rivers.

14

In the extreme northwest of the park are the permanently wet **Busanga Swamps**, surrounded by adjacent floodplains and now a designated Ramsar site. These are dotted with raised 'tree islands', notable for some mammoth specimens of sycamore figs (*Ficus sycomorus*) amongst other vegetation. The floodplains are ringed by a 'termitaria zone' of grasslands.

Northern Kafue receives slightly more rain than the south, resulting in richer, taller vegetation. In many areas such woodland is dominated by the large-leafed munondo tree (*Julbernardia paniculata*), though you'll also find 'Prince of Wales feathers' (*Brachystegia boehmii*) and the odd mobola plum (*Parinari curatellifolia*).

Southern Kafue is dominated by areas of Kalahari sand, and also has a slightly lower rainfall than the north. Large stretches of Kalahari woodland are the norm here, typified by silver-leaf terminalia (*Terminalia sericea*), poison-pod albizia (*Albizia versicolor*), and *Combretum* species. Within this there are a few patches of mature teak forest – the Ngoma Forest being one of the most spectacular examples – whilst further south, on patches of alluvial clay, are some beautiful groves of cathedral mopane (*Colophospermum mopane*).

In the far south of the park, the **Nanzhila Plains** are a fascinating area. Wide expanses of grassland are dotted with islands of vegetation and large termitaria – often with baobabs (*Adansonia digitata*) or ebony trees (*Diospyros mespiliformis*) growing out of them.

Fauna Covering such a large area, with a variety of habitats, Kafue is rich in wildlife and many of its species seem to exhibit strong local variations in their distribution. This is a reflection of the wide variety of habitats in such a large park.

Antelope Kafue has a superb range of antelope, but you will have to travel throughout the park if you wish to see them all.

The **Busanga Swamps**, in the far north of the park, are permanently flooded and home to the secretive sitatunga, which is uniquely adapted to swamp life. These powerful swimmers will bound off with a series of leaps and plunges when disturbed, aided by their enlarged hooves which have evolved for walking around on floating papyrus islands. They will then stand motionless until the danger passes, or even submerge themselves leaving just their nostrils above the water for breathing.

The **Busanga Plains**, a little further south, is a much larger area that is seasonally inundated. This only starts to dry out around June (it's totally impassable by vehicle until then), when it's possible to visit and see large herds of red lechwe and puku, with smaller groups of zebra and blue wildebeest. Oribi are found throughout the park, but are particularly common here, and you also have a good chance of seeing roan and the beautiful sable antelope.

Across the rest of the northern half of the park, there's a good range of mixed bush environments, and here kudu, bushbuck, eland, reedbuck, common duiker, grysbok and defassa waterbuck (a subspecies without the distinctive white ring on the rump) are all frequently seen. Even within this there are local differences; the Kafwala area, for example, is notable for good numbers of Lichtenstein's hartebeest and sable. Numerically, puku dominate most of the northern side of the park, though they gradually cede to impala as you move further south.

On the south side of Kafue, the game has been more patchy. Generally it thrives in areas around lodges, which provide some sanctuary from poaching, but away from these it can be scarce. However, the success of anti-poaching measures and the presence of three lodges in the GMA on the eastern side of the river are certainly having an impact, and the game is improving as a result. The area around Puku Pan and KaingU Safari Lodge is particularly rich in impala and bushbuck, and the game is fairly relaxed.

The area from Itezhi-Tezhi south to Ngoma has Kafue's densest elephant population, with some groups also frequenting the Chunga area. In just a day around the Ngoma area and Riverside Drive, where the game was relaxed and fairly prolific, we found not only a number of elephant herds, but also a large herd of over a hundred buffalo, plenty of impala and puku, family groups of Lichtenstein's hartebeest and waterbuck, and numerous bushbuck, warthog and baboons.

South of Ngoma, the picture is improving too. When I first visited in the early 2000s, the game was sparse indeed, and skittish. It was interesting that the only really good sightings that we had of large animals were around the Chilenje Pools loop and what is now Nanzhila Plains Safari Camp – so once again the animals were congregating in areas associated with visitors. Now we're getting credible reports that numbers are increasing, with species ranging from blue wildebeest and eland to roan and sable antelope, as well as waterbuck, kudu and impala.

Large predators   Lion are relatively widespread all over the park, but the larger males are increasingly uncommon, with inevitable consequences for numbers as a whole. On the Busanga Plains, prides – including the so-called Busanga pride, notable for climbing trees – stalk through nervous herds of puku and lechwe nightly, using the natural drainage ditches for cover with deadly efficiency.

Leopard remain very common throughout the main forested areas of park, though they are seldom seen on the open plains. They are most easily observed on night drives, and continue with their activities completely unperturbed by the presence of a spotlight trained upon them. In particular, Lufupa has a reputation for great leopard sightings, although this may have been as a result of a few particularly good guides.

KAFUE LION PROJECT

What happens to the lions of the Busanga Plains in the wet season? This is part of the focus of a research project (www.kafuelionproject.org) started in July 2010 by PhD student Neil Midlane, in conjunction with Panthera, ZAWA, Wilderness Safaris and the Wilderness Trust.

Most experts agree that there has been a dramatic decrease in the lion population in recent years, and that there are fewer than 30,000 lions left across the whole of Africa. Although, as Africa's largest national park, the Kafue is potentially a stronghold for the species, very little is known about its lion population. For that reason, Neil, from the University of Cape Town, is centring his three-year study of lion behaviour on the northern Kafue. His initial aim is to ascertain the number of lions within the park and – more importantly – whether that population is stable, increasing or decreasing. Armed with that knowledge, the next stage is to establish the cause of any decline that might have occurred, and what can be done to reverse it. As a first step, by the end of 2010 members of four lion prides had been collared, with more to follow, in order that their movements can be tracked.

At the same time, Neil is working with staff from ZAWA to assist in building up their monitoring and research capabilities. Once he has completed his fieldwork, this will help to ensure the long-term sustainability of the project.

14

Spotted hyena are seen regularly, though not often, throughout the park. They appear to occur in smaller numbers than either lions or leopards. Cheetah are not common anywhere, but they're most frequently seen in the north of the park, and around the Nanzhila/Konkamoya area to the south. It's certainly the best place in Zambia to look for cheetah.

Although wild dog remain uncommon in any locale, occasional sightings occur all over the park (though fewer around the road on the east side), which is one of their strongholds in Zambia. The park's huge size suits their wide-ranging nomadic habits and I have had a number of reports of them being seen on the north side of the park in the last few years. Areas around the Busanga Plains seem a particular favourite.

Other large animals Elephants occur throughout Kafue, though overall their numbers are still recovering from intensive poaching during the 1970s, and their density varies hugely within the park. Just south of Lake Itezhi-Tezhi, around Chunga and, especially, Ngoma, there are large herds and a thriving population – though they're not always relaxed, so drivers there need to be very wary of getting too close to them. South of Ngoma, the situation was much gloomier, although anti-poaching measures have resulted in a resurgence in the elephant population.

On the north side of the park elephant densities are lower than around Ngoma, but they have improved a lot. When I first visited Lufupa in 1995, a few elephants spotted a kilometre from the lodge were a reason for excitement, causing us to leave dinner and jump into a vehicle. Now family groups are commonly seen in the Lufupa and Lunga areas, and are a lot less skittish than they used to be. Visiting in 2010, we saw some very relaxed elephants on the Busanga Plains.

Buffalo, common in the 1970s and '80s, are rarely seen nowadays, though herds do frequent the Busanga Plains. Sadly, black rhino are thought to be extinct throughout the park, after sustained poaching decades ago.

The Kafue River and its larger tributaries like the Lunga are fascinating tropical rivers – full of life and infested with hippo and crocodile, which occur in numbers to rival the teeming waters of the Luangwa. Vervet monkeys and yellow (*not* chacma) baboons are common almost everywhere, and you'll usually find porcupines, mongooses, civets and a wide variety of small mammals on night drives. One other curious but interesting fact: there seem to be more pangolins than aardvarks in North Kafue, which is a very unusual situation indeed!

Birds The birding in Kafue is very good. There have been about 495 species recorded here, suggesting that the park has probably the richest birdlife of any Zambian park. This reflects Kafue's wide range of habitats, because in addition to extensive miombo woodlands (quite a Zambian speciality!), Kafue has plenty of rivers, extensive wetlands and – in the north – seasonal floodplains.

The wetlands and floodplains have the full range of herons (including the black heron), storks and ibises, plus crowned and wattled cranes, Denham's (or Stanley's) and kori bustards, secretary birds, and geese (spur-winged and Egyptian) by the thousand.

In the long, verdant stretches of riverine vegetation you're likely to spot Ross's turaco, Narina trogons, MacClounie's (black-backed) barbet, olive woodpecker, brown-headed apalis and the yellow-throated leaflove. Pel's fishing owl is also found here, with birding expert Bob Stjernstedt noting that there are pairs around Ntemwa, and African finfoot frequent the shady fringes of the slower rivers, swimming under the overhanging trees with part of their body submerged.

Kafue's extensive miombo woodlands have endemics such as pale-billed hornbill, miombo pied barbet, grey tit, miombo rock thrush, Sousa's shrike, chestnut-mantled sparrow-weaver, spotted creeper, and three species of eremomela. In the south, on the Nanzhila Plains, the black-cheeked lovebird – near-endemic to southern Zambia – is relatively common.

HUNTING AND POACHING During the 1980s and early '90s there were few efforts or government resources devoted to protecting Kafue, and poaching was rife. This ensured the extermination of black rhino, and a sharp reduction in elephant numbers at the hands of organised commercial poachers. Fortunately the park is massive, surrounded by GMAs, and not easily accessible. So although the smaller game was hunted for meat, this was not generally on a large enough scale to threaten their populations. Nor did it adversely affect the environment.

Organised commercial poaching is now relatively rare, and the remaining incidence of smaller-scale poaching by locals (for food) is being tackled by a number of initiatives. The ZAWA team protecting the park has become much more active in recent years, having received a lot of training and more resources.

Some of these initiatives concentrate on increasing the physical policing of the park, the most obvious being anti-poaching patrols, which have been partially funded by some of the lodges. Others try to tackle the underlying reason for this poaching, and attempt to offer practical alternatives for the local people of the surrounding areas that are more attractive than shooting the game. For example, one such project allows local people in neighbouring areas to come into the park to collect natural honey. Both types of initiatives work with the help and support of some of the more enlightened local safari operators.

GETTING THERE AND AROUND To get to Kafue, and to get around once there, you have three choices. First, you can fly in and stay at one of the better camps or lodges – and the team from the camp will walk, drive and boat you around their area of the park. Second, you can drive yourself into and around the park in a 4x4. Or third, you can arrange for a company from outside to drive you in, and around the park.

By air or scheduled transfer This is certainly the most relaxing way to get to the park, especially if your time is relatively limited, or you like the idea of a holiday here rather than an expedition. There are various airstrips dotted around the park and some are in good repair. There are no scheduled flights into the park, but several charter companies in Lusaka will fly you in or out on request and Wilderness Safaris usually transport their guests by air.

Wilderness Safaris www.wilderness-safaris. com. Although well established in Namibia & South Africa, Wilderness's operation in Zambia is more recent. In addition to their camps in the Kafue National Park, they have 2 camps in the South Luangwa. Wilderness deals only with agents, so reservations for their lodges should be made through a tour operator (pages 44–5).

By road If you want to drive within the park, then think of it as an expedition. You will need two good 4x4 vehicles, plenty of water and – if you're planning to camp – all your provisions, as places to re-supply are few and far between. If you have problems, you must be able to solve them yourself, as you can expect little help. Although there are many camps listed in the sections below, only a handful would be able to offer aid in an emergency.

However, if you come well equipped then the park is wonderful. Several operators – especially in the east and south of the park – also have excellent campsites. If you do come, then you can be assured of seeing very few other vehicles during your stay in this stunning area.

Arrive with the best maps of the place you can find, and use them in conjunction with those in this book. Do bring a GPS; you will need one. Note that the speed limit within the body of the park is 40km/h – though in reality you'd often be hard pressed to come even close to that.

For those just bisecting the northern and southern areas along the tarred Lusaka–Mongu road, there's no need for a 4x4. However, aside from the obvious danger of colliding with an animal in this area, there are several speed bumps and these – together with the odd pot-hole – mean that sticking to the 80km/h limit is essential.

Budget safari operators The Lusaka-based Bongwe Safaris runs four-day/three-night trips (*US$690 pp/max 7*) into the private and well-stocked Mushingashi Conservancy, bordering the park's secluded northeast, where you can expect to see no other vehicles. Groups are based in rustic chalets at Delai Camp (page 441) within the Mushingashi Conservancy. For more details, see page 237.

Mobile operators in Kafue A couple of safari operators run mobile trips into the Kafue. Some work well, though without a long-term presence in the park, they clearly don't know the ground as well as the established camps. Further, if they encounter serious difficulties, they seldom have the logistical support to solve their own problems. (There are tales of one inexperienced company that recently came up into the Busanga Plains too early, and ended up with its vehicle stuck in mud for two days.)

Perhaps more importantly, most of the established camps work hard to maintain the park's roads and minimise poaching. Few, if any, of the mobile operators contribute to this vital work.

As Kafue starts to receive a few more visitors, the Busanga Plains (especially) is becoming better known and the focus for more attention from small mobile operators. However, if you want to get the very best from it, and effectively contribute to the work to preserve the area, then I recommend that you support the area's permanent operators.

NORTHERN KAFUE The northern section of the park is a slightly undulating plateau, veined by rivers – the Lufupa, the Lunga, the Ntemwa, the Mukombo, the Mukunashi, and the Lubuji – which are all tributaries of the main Kafue, whose basin extends to the border with DRC.

The main Kafue River is already mature by the time it reaches the park, though it has over 400km further to flow before discharging into the Zambezi. Thus within the park its permanent waters are wide, deep and slow-flowing, to the obvious pleasure of large numbers of hippo and crocodile. Tall, shady hardwoods overhang its gently curving banks, and the occasional islands in the stream are favourite feeding places for elephant and buffalo. In short, it is a typically beautiful, large African river.

Occasionally it changes, as at Kafwala. Here, there is a stretch of gentle rapids for about 7km. The river is up to about 1,000m wide and dotted with numerous islands, all supporting dense riverine vegetation – making a particularly good spot for birdwatching.

GPS co-ordinates ⊕	
AIRHIP	14°40.191'S 26°23.417'E
BRIDGI	14°24.687'S 26°09.180'E
BUSANG	14°12.199'S 25°50.115'E
BUSAPC	14°10.488'S 25°49.223'E
FERRYL	13°58.984'S 26°20.784'E
HIPPO	14°40.610'S 26°22.526'E
HOOKBR	14°56.477'S 25°54.384'E
KABANG	14°05.808'S 26°07.036'E
KABULU	14°40.731'S 26°39.330'E
KAFRC	14°29.841'S 26°31.206'E
KAFTUR	14°46.126'S 26°04.393'E
KAPING	14°12.351'S 25°48.577'E
LUBUNG	14°33.750'S 26°27.250'E
LUFUPA	14°37.080'S 26°11.626'E
LUNGAC	14°11.665'S 26°21.483'E
LUPEMB	14°13.317'S 26°28.833'E
MCBRID	14°41.537'S 26°73.107'E
MOSHI	14°24.348'S 26°09.474'E
MUSANZ	14°23.237'S 26°02.026'E
NALUSA	14°58.258'S 26°42.718'E
POLEBR	14°06.149'S 26°10.229'E
SHUMBA	14°13.091'S 25°52.233'E
TREETO	14°24.141'S 26°02.524'E
TUKARC	14°30.920'S 26°29.202'E
TUCHGA	14°56.832'S 25°51.222'E
TUHIP	14°37.890'S 26°29.658'E
TULEOP	14°32.700'S 26°28.050'E
TULUNG	13°58.625'S 26°20.076'E
TUMUSH	14°40.853'S 26°40.430'E
TUTZTZ	14°58.268'S 26°27.168'E

NORTHERN KAFUE

Most of the park's northern section, between the rivers, is a mosaic of miombo and mopane woodlands, with occasional open grassy pans known as dambos. The edges of the main rivers are lined with tall hardwood trees. Raintrees (*Lonchocarpus capassa*), knobthorns (*Acacia nigrescens*), jackalberries (*Diospyros mespiliformis*), leadwoods (*Combretum imberbe*), and especially sausage trees (*Kigelia africana*) are all very common.

The Kafue's tributaries are smaller, but the larger of these are still wide and permanent. The Lufupa is probably the most important. It enters the park from the Kasonso-Busanga GMA in the north, and immediately feeds into a permanent wetland in the far north of the park: the Busanga Swamps. In the wet season these waters flood out over a much larger area, across the whole Busanga Plains, before finally draining back into the river, which then continues its journey on the south side of the plains.

The swamp and seasonal floodplain together cover about 750km², and are a superb area for game. The seasonal floodwaters on the plains are shallow, but enough to sustain a healthy growth of grasses throughout the year on the mineral-rich black-cotton soil. These open plains are dotted with numerous small 'islands' of wild date palms (*Phoenix reclinata*), and wild fig trees (various *Ficus* species).

The area is perfect for huge herds of water-loving lechwe and puku, which are joined by large numbers of zebra, wildebeest and other plains grazers as the waters recede at the end of the wet season. However, the Busanga Plains are very remote, and normally impossible to reach by vehicle until about July. Until recently, few people (even in the safari business) had heard about them, let alone visited them, but now this remarkable area is firmly on the map.

4x4 routes within and around northern Kafue You really need a high-clearance 4x4 for any of the routes within the park. Despite that, you'll have problems on all of them during the rains, and anything close to the Busanga Plains is impassable between about November and July.

From the north via the Kabanga gate The Kabanga gate (✪ KABANG 14°5.808'S, 26°7.036'E) is the park's most northerly entrance point, affording access for those coming from Kasempa and the Copperbelt. For directions to the gate, see *Driving from Kasempa to Mumbwa*, page 423.

From the gate, the clear, largely sandy track that proceeds southwards into the park is considerably better than the approach road to the gate from Kasempa. The track keeps east of the Ntemwa River, passing the site of the old Moshi Camp (✪ MOSHI 14°24.348'S, 26°09.474'E), until – after almost 39km, or roughly three-quarters of an hour's drive – it reaches a couple of bridges at the confluence of the Ntemwa and Lufupa rivers (✪ BRIDG1 14°24.687'S, 26°09.180'E).

From here, the road continue south towards Lufupa, Kafwala and the Hook Bridge.

To the Busanga Plains Just south of the second of these bridges there used to be a turning west towards Treetops and the Busanga Plains, but despite the signpost this is now completely impassable. If you're heading for Busanga, continue south for a further 2.5km, where there's a sharp turn to the right (✪ TUBUSA 14°25.806'S, 26°08.967'E). Note, however, that the signpost (to Treetops) is visible only if you're coming from the south. From this junction, it's a further 50km northwest to Shumba on the Busanga Plains. During the dry season, it's a relatively good track, despite the inevitable bumps, pot-holes and sand patches.

From the south: Lusaka–Mongu road The last fuel stations you'll find before you reach the park are at Mumbwa (coming from Lusaka) or Kaoma (if you're coming from Mongu). Either way, if you are driving north into the park from here, to Lufupa or the Busanga Plains, simply turn north off the main road at the Hook Bridge gate beside the Kafue's west bank, just west of the Hook Bridge itself (⊕ HOOKBR 14°56.477'S, 25°54.384'E). From here the track (⊕ KAFTUR 14°46.126'S, 26°4.393'E) heads northeast through the heart of the park for about 44km, where a right turn leads east to Kafwala Camp. Continuing roughly northeast for about a further 26km will lead you to Lufupa (⊕ LUFUPA 14°37.080'S, 26°11.626'E). In the dry season it's basically a good track, fine for a 2WD with high clearance, though designed more for game viewing than speed. In the wet it is impassable due to the toffee-like consistency of the black-cotton soil.

This track is the main vehicular artery through northern Kafue, and continues north over the Lufupa and Ntemwa rivers to the Kabanga gate (⊕ KABANG 14°5.808'S, 26°7.036'E). About 82km from the Hook Bridge, you'll pass a clear turning to the left (⊕ TUBUSA 14°25.806'S, 26°08.967'E) signposted to Treetops and leading to the Busanga Plains. For details of this route, see *To the Busanga Plains*, above.

From the M9 Lusaka–Mongu road to the Lubungu pontoon See *Driving north from Mumbwa*, pages 424–5, for more details of this route around the northeast side of the park.

North from the Lubungu pontoon to the Lunga pontoon Once dubbed the 'road of death' by one very experienced old hand, this 75km stretch of road has been transformed into a good, graded road that makes for pleasant, relatively straightforward driving. That said, it remains quite narrow, and fallen trees can be a hazard, while pot-holes could well materialise in the rainy season.

Starting at the Lubungu pontoon (⊕ LUBUNG 14°33.750'S, 26°27.250'E), it's about 2.5km north to the right turning (⊕ TULEOP 14°32.700'S, 26°28.050'E) to Leopard Lodge. About 6.5km beyond that is another turning (⊕ KAFRC 14°29.367'S, 26°28.583'E) on the right which leads to the erstwhile Chamafumba Camp, now re-opened as Kafue River Camp. Both of these are on the north bank of the river, upstream from the pontoon.

From this second turning, it's some 70km to the Lunga pontoon (⊕ FERRYL 13°58.984'S, 26°20.784'E; ⊕ 06.00–18.00 daily; Kw56,000 per vehicle), north of which the road continues as far as Kasempa (see *Driving from Kasempa to Mumbwa*, page 423, for details).

As you cross on the pontoon, you might wish to reflect that the journey that took you just a couple of hours would all too recently have taken at least eight, and required at least two very sturdy vehicles.

🏠 **Where to stay** Though the range of camps listed here appears to be long, most non-Zambian visitors are probably best to choose a combination of one of the camps in the centre of the park, with a second on or near the Busanga Plains – and perhaps Hippo Camp or McBrides' to the east. While many of these camps have been here for years, several have been completely rebuilt and some are brand new. Each offers a different experience, yet all are closely involved with the park and its conservation.

Camping is easily arranged at McBrides' (page 440) and Mayukuyuku (page 448), and there are also a couple of well-placed sites just outside the park, to the east: Kafue River Camp and Leopard Lodge. Alternatively, Kafwala Camp is relatively inexpensive

– for WECSZ members. There are no campsites on the Busanga Plains, and you are not allowed to just camp anywhere. This rule is both wise and effectively enforced.

Busanga Plains With the exception of Mukambi's Busanga Plains Camp, Wilderness Safaris currently has a monopoly here, transferring their guests from Busanga airstrip by helicopter. Camps in this area are featured largely heading from east to west.

⌂ Musanza Tented Camp [map 433] (6 rooms) Wilderness Safaris, page 431. ✪ MUSANZ 14°23.237'S, 26°02.026'E. Musanza under Wilderness ownership has been moved south to the site of the former Ntemwa Camp, a lovely leafy spot right on the Lufupa River, beloved of kingfishers, paradise flycatchers & the resident hippos. Formerly only for groups, it opened to independent visitors in 2011.

Green canvas tents with coir matting & twin beds set the scene, with a canvas basin & mirror outside, & an en-suite handbasin, bucket shower & separate flushing toilet. In the 2 newer tents, the shower & toilet are outside, enclosed by thatching grass. Sand paths lead to a tented awning shading a large circular table, a small seating area & a bar/coffee station. Beyond lies the river, where directors' chairs are set beneath a huge ebony tree entwined with a strangler fig. A hammock hangs tantalisingly by the river, adding a touch of colour, & for the ultimate relaxation there's a queensize bed suspended nearby. In the heat of the day, brunch is served on a cool platform up a bank, while at night, lantern-lit dinners can be served in the bush. With a range of activities, including game drives, safari walks across the river, & river cruises, this is an attractive camp that manages to retain a sense of wilderness. *US$380/520 pp sharing/sgl FBA, inc local drinks, park fees.* ⊕ *Jun–Oct.*

⌂ Shumba Camp [map 433] (6 chalets) Wilderness Safaris, page 431. ✪ SHUMBA 14°13.091'S, 25°52.233'E. Rebuilt from scratch in 2007, Shumba is set in the middle of the plains on an 'island' of large fig trees, some 15–20 mins' drive south of the base of the permanent swamps. With wooden decks & walkways raised some 2m off the ground, the camp is relatively safe for older children – & the height makes for some interesting wildlife possibilities, too: in 2007, a lion kill right under the buildings made riveting viewing.

Both its wide, rectangular chalets & the main area face the plains, their tented walls with gauze panels topped with a mop of thatch, & with large glazed doors to offer protection from the wind that whistles across the plains. Inside the chalets (1 suitable for families), all is space & light, the wooden floors offset by white linen & neutral décor. As well as twin 4-poster beds enveloped in white mosquito netting, there's a sofa or armchairs, a writing desk, & ample storage space with a safe – not to mention a sherry decanter & glasses. The bathroom area, with twin basins, shower & separate toilet, leads through to an outdoor shower. Solar panels heat the water & there's 24hr electricity. Running the length of each chalet is a split-level wooden deck with a table & chairs, & cushioned seating.

Central to the living area is an open bar fronted by bar stools, around which several 'rooms' are kitted out with comfy seating & a long dining table. There's also a small shop stocking safari clothes & a few curios. An extensive split-level deck incorporates an outdoor eating area with a fire, a small infinity pool & a very relaxing chair-swing. Meals can be taken as a group or at individual tables – & the food is very good.

Activities revolve around day & night game drives, guided walks, & boat trips (May–Sep, water permitting). Guests can also take scenic flights in a balloon or by helicopter, both based at Kapinga. *US$649/809 pp sharing/sgl FBA, inc local drinks, park fees. No children under 8.* ⊕ *Jun–Nov.*

⌂ Kapinga Camp [map 433] (4 chalets) Wilderness Safaris, page 431. ✪ KAPING 14°12.351'S, 25°48.577'E. Just a short drive from Busanga Bushcamp, Kapinga is of a similar standard to Shumba, but smaller & softer in design, more at one with the environment yet unexpectedly elegant. Its large tented rooms are on dark wooden decks facing the plains: 2 to the east & 2 to the west. Neutral in décor, with splashes of red, they are deceptively luxurious, with 4-poster dbl or twin beds draped with mosi nets, comfortable chairs, a ceiling fan & electric lights. A camp bed can be added for a child.

Curtained to one side are twin basins, a separate loo (with a hand-carved seat!), & inside & outside showers, while on the deck, reached through double doors with gauze screens, there's built-in cushioned seating. Sand paths link the rooms to the central area here, so it's not a place for the nervous or those with young children.

The heart of the camp, in a grove of trees that include a huge sycamore fig, is a stylish open-sided area under a canvas roof. It's dotted with armchairs, coffee tables, magazines & even a crystal decanter on a silver platter, & faces the plains across a small circular pool. More comfy seating surrounds the adjacent firepit, ideal for cool mornings & evenings, & below is a tree-shaded deck set with sunloungers. Dinner is a movable feast, with the location of the table regularly changed.

In addition to game drives (families with children 6–12 must have a private vehicle), there are flat-bottomed boat trips when there's enough water (Aug/Sep). The helicopter, which is based at Kapinga, also offers scenic flights down the Lufupa River (*US$900 per ½hr, max 4 people*). More in keeping with the environment are hot-air ballon rides over the plains (*US$400 pp, Aug–Oct; min 2*), taking off 1hr before sunrise & culminating in a champagne b/fast. *US$649/809 pp sharing/sgl, FBA, inc local drinks, laundry, park fees. No children under 6.* ☺ *mid Jul–Oct.*

🏠 **Busanga Bushcamp** [map 433] (4 tents) Wilderness Safaris, page 431. ☺ BUSANG 14°12.199'S, 25°50.115'E. This deceptively simple camp is on a small fig-tree island in the middle of the plains, a short distance from Shumba & Kapinga. Accommodation is in walk-in tents on polished concrete floors, each with comfortable twin beds & solar-powered bedside lights wrapped by mosquito nets, & a shaded deck with a couple of directors' chairs. Curtains separate the bedroom from an en-suite hot shower & flush

toilet, plus a dressing area. It's well equipped, but not luxurious.

Sand paths lead to a tree-shaded boma, with views over the plains. In the seating area, there's a small library, with a self-serve bar, & tea & coffee available all day. Meals are often prepared over an open fire & served al fresco. This is a close-to-nature experience, with a wooden viewing deck up in an old sausage tree, & day & sundowner drives in search of the area's super game. Balloon flights can be arranged. *US$543/689 pp sharing/sgl FBA, inc local drinks, laundry, park fees.* ☺ *Jun–Nov.*

🏠 **Busanga Plains Camp** [map 433] (4 tents) Contact via Mukambi, page 448. ☺ BUSAPC 14°10.488'S, 25°49.223'E. This intimate tented camp is also known as Mukambi Plains Camp, & not to be confused with Busanga Bushcamp. It lies on the eastern side of the Lufupa River, in a peaceful location that's a 5–6hr drive through the park from its sister lodge. A wooden walkway leads across a plain of floating grass to the camp, hidden among wild date palms on a photogenic tree island. It's a relaxed, welcoming place, a shady oasis with its main living area set beneath an extensive mobola tree (*Parinari curatellifolia*) overlooking the plains. Here, red lechwe are in their element, regularly seen from the open deck – & from the spacious open-air bathrooms alongside each of the comfortable tented rooms. Bucket showers & lighting from paraffin lamps & candles lend a back-to-nature feel – offset by flush toilets & excellent food!

With no more than 8 guests at a time, activities can be flexible – with both game drives & walks around Kapinga Island an option. *US$625 pp sharing FBA inc drinks, park fees & game–drive transfer to Mukambi (max 8 people). Fully inclusive 5–7-night packages with Mukambi US$500 pp/ night, inc Lusaka transfers.* ☺ *Late Jul–early Nov.*

Centre of the park and northeast As on the Busanga Plains, almost all the accommodation in this area is operated by Wilderness Safaris. Access is simplest from the Hook Bridge gate: simply turn north from the Great West Road to the west of the bridge, then follow the road north. Camps are listed here from south to north, with road distances given from the gate.

🏠 **Mayukuyuku Bush Camp** For details of this camp, which lies in the northern Kafue but within easy reach of the main Lusaka–Mongu road, see page 448.

🏠 **Kafwala Camp** [map 433] (2 chalets, 2 rondavels) \ 0211 251630; m 0977 771347; e kafwala@zamtel.zm, ashworth@zamnet.zm, wescz@zamnet.zm; www.conservationzambia.com.

14

org. This camp is built on the bank of the Kafue River in a stunning location, about 700m below the start of the Kafwala Rapids. To get there, follow the road through the park northeast for about 44km, then take the right turn to Kafwala.

The camp can be booked only in its entirety, and is restricted to WECSZ members (page 50), who must book in advance. If you're thinking of staying here then join the society in Lusaka: it does a lot of good & needs more support. Accommodation comprises 2 simple 3-bed chalets that are linked by a walkway with 2 more beds, & 2 rondavels, 1 with a dbl bed, & 1 twin. Toilets, shower & bathroom are communal, as are the lounge, dining & BBQ area. Deep freezes, fridges, lamps, crockery, cutlery & bedding are provided – but you must bring all your own food & drink, as well as a decent torch. The camp's staff will cook for you, so don't forget to bring flour & yeast if you'd like fresh bread. If you bring light fishing tackle then the cook will fillet & prepare your catch for dinner. The staff will also service the rooms, do the washing, & help with anything else that is reasonable. (You should tip them at the end of your stay.) *US$300 up to 12 people.* ⊕ *All year.*

⌂ **Lufupa Bush Camp** [map 433]
(4 rondavels) Wilderness Safaris, page 431. ⊕ LUFUBC 14°48.090'S, 26°11.177'E. Formerly Kafwala Rapids Camp, the newest Wilderness camp was rebuilt in 2010 in a stunning location very near to Kafwala Camp – but about 1½hrs' drive from the other Lufupa camps. Lots of wild date palms line the banks of the river, lending a lush, tropical air to the place. However, the wildlife in this area isn't as prolific as around Lufupa Tented & River camps, but it is a particularly good area for sightings of Lichtenstein's hartebeest & sable.

Each of the rooms is a neat en-suite rondavel, not large but perfectly comfortable & well appointed. There are 2 main areas under thatch where you can relax & where meals are served, as well as a firepit closer to the river.

Note that the hippos & crocs in this area have not read the textbooks, & seem to be living happily in & around the fast-running water of the rapids – so don't be tempted to take a cooling dip, however inviting the gently bubbling water looks. *US$380/520 pp sharing/sgl FBA, inc local drinks, park fees.* ⊕ *May–Nov.*

⌂ **Lufupa River Camp** [map 433] (7 tents) Wilderness Safaris, page 431. ⊕ LUFUPA 14°37.080'S, 26°11.626'E. Overlooking the confluence of the Lufupa & Kafue rivers, this camp is the centre of activity in the northern Kafue. Access by road takes about 5–7hrs from Lusaka, including a break for a packed lunch. If you're driving yourself, follow the road past Kafwala, & continue north for a further 26km to Lufupa. In 2011 the camp was reserved for groups on set tours with the American operator OAT (page 45), but this might change in 2012.

Accommodation is in spacious safari tents that face the Kafue River, each with en-suite shower, toilet & washbasin; 2 of these are family tents; the rest are twins.

Buffet-style meals are served in the central dining area &, while there is little choice, the food is good (& any dietary restrictions well catered for). There's a comfortable bar, & you can always help yourself to tea & coffee. The atmosphere is friendly, casual & very unpretentious. The camp prides itself on a no-frills approach, so you won't be waited on hand & foot, but there's always someone to help when you need it.

Under normal circumstances the lodge runs several activities at once. Most are by 4x4 & boat (an afternoon boat trip on either the Lufupa or the Kafue is excellent), though walks can be organised on request. *US$380/520 pp sharing/ sgl FBA, inc local drinks, park fees. Camping US$10 pp exc meals & activities which can be booked separately.* ⊕ *All year.*

⌂ **Lufupa Tented Camp** [map 433] (8 tents) Wilderness Safaris, page 431. ⊕ LUFUTC 14°36.832'S, 26°11.285'E. Located right next door to Lufupa River Camp, this is similar in design, with identical rooms, but a slightly more exclusive air. However, despite being in a good area for wildlife, it was like Lufupa River Camp reserved for groups on set tours in 2011.

⌂ **Lunga River Lodge** [map 433] ⊕ LUNGAC 14°11.398'S, 26°21.286'E. Located on the bank of the Lunga River, overlooking Kafue from its northern boundary, Lunga River Lodge was once a top-class photographic camp. At present, however, its guests come to hunt, which is outside the remit of this book. I have, though, listed it here in case the situation should change.

top   **Nile crocodile** *Crocodylus niloticus* (CM) page 517

above left   **Nile monitor lizard** *Varanus niloticus* (PGO/OSF/SpS)

above right   **Flap-necked chameleon** *Chamaeleo dilepis* (TH)

below   **Pan-hinged terrapin** *Pelusios subniger* (SS)

top left	**African fish eagle** *Haliaeetus vocifer* (SS)
top right	**Little bee-eater** *Merops pusillus* (AZ)
above left	**Giant kingfisher** *Megaceryle maxima* (CM)
above right	**Carmine bee-eater** *Merops nubicoides* (MA)
left	**Yellow-billed stork** *Mycteria ibis* (CM)
below	**Pelicans** *Pelecanus onocrotalus* (CM)

above left   Wattled crane *Bugeranus carunculatus* (AZ)
above right   Shoebill *Balaeniceps rex* (S/FLPA) page 340
right   Three-banded courser *Rhinoptilus cinctus* (AZ)
below left   African darter *Anhinga rufa* (AZ)
below right   Giant eagle owl *Bubo lacteus* (AZ)

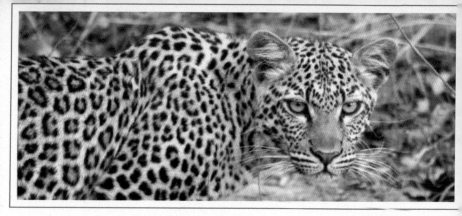

HOME of the LEOPARD

Kafue has many special places to explore,
and one very special place to stay.
Come and enjoy our famous hospitality,
beautiful setting, expert guiding and
fabulous game viewing, especially leopards.

MAYUKUYUKU

Kafue National Park, Zambia
www.kafuecamps.com
info@kafuecamps.com

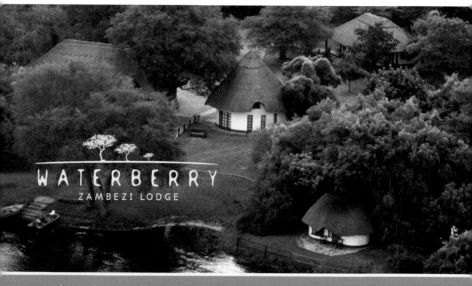

WATERBERRY
ZAMBEZI LODGE

Close to Victoria Falls, but far away from everywhere.

Stay at Livingstone's loveliest, friendliest lodge
where you can be as active or as relaxed as you choose.

reservations@waterberrylodge.com   www.waterberrylodge.com
PO Box 61294 , Livingstone, Zambia   Tel/Fax +260-21 3 327455

The perfect start & end to any safari

The gateway to Zambia, we're Lusaka's most relaxing lodge.
Just 20 minutes from the airport, it has a true safari feel.

PIONEER LODGE & CAMP
LUSAKA, ZAMBIA

Tel : +260 966 731 420
Email : info@pioneercampzambia.com
Web : www.pioneercampzambia.com

*Owner Chris Cooke's guiding is matched only by the beauty
of our location; our new luxury tented accommodation;
and the diversity of our
plentiful game....*

Konkamoya
follow the wind

Lake Itezhi–Tezhi,
Kafue National Park
www.konkamoya.com

Zambezi
Safari & Travel Company

We're a well-established, seasoned and proudly independent family-owned safari company; a small and mature team of confident, "can do" individuals.

Tel: +44 (0)1548 830059
email: info@zambezi.com
Africa House, Poundwell St, Modbury, PL21 0QJ, UK

www.zambezi.com

ZAMBIA

Tailor-made safaris to Luangwa, Lower Zambezi, Kafue, Victoria Falls & beyond

SAFARI CONSULTANTS

Individually tailored and small group safaris to East and Southern Africa

+44 (0) 1787 888 590   info@safariconsultantuk.com
www.safari-consultants.co.uk
Africa House, 2 Cornard Mills, Great Cornard, Suffolk, UK

The Lubungu pontoon area Of the lodges and camps in this area, two – Hippo Lodge and McBrides' – are south of the pontoon, near the old Hippo Mine, and most of the others just to the north, outside the park boundary.

Getting to Hippo and McBrides' From the main road between Mumbwa and Kasempa, about 10km south of the Lubungu pontoon, take the fork to the west (⊕ TUHIPP 14°37.866'S, 26°29.659'E). Although this is clearly signposted from the south, it's easy to miss if you're coming from the north. For Hippo Lodge, follow this road, passing through a gate (⊕ MINEGT 14°39.169'S, 26°25.025'E) after 5km, and later turning left at the whitewashed buildings of the old Hippo Mine (⊕ HIPMIN 14°39.169.S, 26°25.025'E; see box below). Continue for a further 4km to the airstrip (⊕ AIRHIP 14°40.191'S, 26°23.417'E). From here, it's barely 2km to Hippo Lodge (⊕ HIPPO 14°40.610'S, 26°22.526'E) – or 3km to McBrides'.

For the more direct route to McBrides', take the same fork off the main road, but after 4.5km turn left (⊕ TUMCBR 14°39.158'S, 26°27.871'E), as signposted. Follow the yellow arrows both here and after a further 5.2km (⊕ T2MCBR 14°41.512'S, 26°26.775'E), then continue for another 7km or so until you reach the camp (⊕ MCBRID 14°41.537'S, 26°23.107'E).

🏠 **Hippo Lodge** [map 433] (4 chalets, 2 tents) ☎ 021 1295398; m 097 7788910; e hippolodge@zamnet.zm, igor@zamnet.zm; www.hippolodge.com. ⊕ HIPPO 14°40.610'S, 26°22.526'E. On the site of the old Lubungu Camp, but renovated in 2002, Hippo Lodge is now run by one of its owners, the capable Bruce Whitfield – who ran Lufupa Lodge for many years in the late 1990s. For access, see above.

Quirky stone-&-thatch chalets all have fine river views, large unconventional baths & en-suite showers & toilets, yet each is different. 2 dbls have an A-frame design; 1 – slightly more conventional – has both dbl & twin rooms. The largest, Stony House, comes with a dbl room, a twin loft room, & a spacious kitchen/living area with 2 sgl beds. Simpler are twin-bedded safari tents under thatch, each with a small veranda &,

at the back, a large stone-walled bathroom that's partially open to the sky. The main lounge/dining area overlooks the river, with a separate bar to one side. Alongside, sunloungers are set around an attractive stone pool. There is no electricity, but battery-powered lights are provided, & batteries can be charged.

Just 1km from camp is a marvellous natural hot spring, within which a rough stone wall has been constructed to section off a sand-bottomed 'jacuzzi' from the area favoured by Shim, the resident hippo. This is just 1 of several possible guided walks, either close to camp or across the river, whilst the energetic can arrange a rendezvous with 1 of the lodge's boats. Whilst the game isn't quite as prolific or varied as further west, what's around is becoming increasingly relaxed, with elephant regularly seen in & around

HIPPO MINE

Zambia's first commercial copper mine was discovered in 1903 by Jacob Elliott – though how he got here, in an area infested with tsetse flies and therefore inaccessible on horseback, remains a mystery. Elliott died only a couple of years later, killed by a hippo, it is said – hence the name of the mine. His grave at the site is marked by a marble gravestone.

Operations at the mine itself commenced in 1911, and it remained active until 1971. Today, the rusting machinery that remains has its own appeal, though there is little left apart from this. The entrance to the mine is marked by a cluster of white buildings and a large log on the track leading to Hippo Lodge (⊕ HIPMIN 14°39.169.S, 26°25.025'E), which can arrange visits to the mine.

camp, & the shy sitatunga occasionally spotted. Boat trips are a major feature, with fishing & birdwatching favourite activities, perhaps combined with an island b/fast or lunch. Bruce is a good guide who knows northern Kafue well, and he & his team conduct day & night drives. And for self drivers, there's a 40km network of game-viewing loops that has been graded. If you want to continue to Lufupa, some 40km downstream, after staying here, a boat transfer can be arranged, as can trips to the Busanga Plains. *US$420 pp FBA, inc most drinks, park fees; Stony House US$360 (6 people, house only).* ⊕ *Mar–Nov (airstrip* ⊕ *May–late Nov).*

🏠 **McBrides' Camp** [map 433] (9 chalets, camping) e mcbrides.camp@uuplus.com; www. mcbridescamp.com. ✪ MCBRID 14°41.537'S, 26°23.107'E. Informality sets the tone at this very personal camp (to get here, see above), where animals wander through & the birdlife is quite a feature, too. In the style of a small 'walking' bushcamp like those in the Luangwa Valley, it was started in 2002 by Chris & Charlotte McBride, knowledgeable & engaging hosts who lead all activities themselves. Both have spent most of their lives in the bush. Indeed, Chris's MSc thesis was on lions, & he went on to write 3 books on the subject, including *The White Lions of Timbavati*.

Dotted around the grassy site are some rather quirky reed-&-thatch chalets, comfortable but with none of the 'design' element that is common to many safari lodges. Six have a dbl & a sgl bed, while the others are smaller, with just a dbl or twin beds. All have mosi nets over the beds, skins or rugs on the floor, a solid wooden chest of drawers, & chairs & a table on a small veranda. Attached to each is a large bathroom, with hot shower, basin, & flush toilet, partially sheltered under a strip of thatch. Lighting is a mix of candlelight, paraffin lanterns & solar power, & batteries can be charged. There's also a simple campsite, with toilets, basins & hot showers in 2 open-air ablution blocks, but no marked pitches. Campers are welcome to eat at the main camp (*dinner US$20 pp*), & to take part in activities (*from US$15–40 pp, depending on activity*).

Set back from the Kafue River *is an open-fronted lounge & dining room,* a homely, slightly cluttered place with throws & cushions on the old squashy sofas, plenty of books & artefacts, & a lovely view of hippos wallowing in the river.

Moored close by are the camp's boats, the *Finfoot* (a 2-storey aluminium craft used for river cruises), the *River Lion*, used for drifts, & a banana boat for fishing. Otherwise activities major around walking safaris, although game drives are available on request. Alternatively it's possible to make a trip to their fly-camp, 14km downstream. *US$330–400 pp sharing FBA, exc transfers & alcohol; sgl suppt US$60–80. Camping US$20 pp & park fees.* ⊕ *Apr–Dec.*

🏠 **Kafue River Camp** [map 433] (4 tents, camping) m 0977 933000; e kafueriver@ iwayafrica.com; www.kafueriver.com. ✪ KAFRC 14°29.841'S, 26°31.206'E. Popular with w/enders from Lusaka, this relaxed camp is in the GMA on the northeastern border of the park, on a secluded stretch of the river & a great spot for fishing. It was opened in 2009 by Beatrice & Chriss Wienand, on the site of the old Chamafumba Camp, just upstream from the Lubungu pontoon. The entrance is clearly signposted (✪ TUKARC 14°30.920'S, 26°29.202'E) from the main road, then it's a further 4.5km (along either track) to the camp; you'll usually need a high-clearance vehicle.

Large, tented chalets under thatch have all the essentials – but absolutely no frills: comfortable twin beds, functional wooden furniture, & a brick-built toilet & shower at the back with piping hot water. There are plans for 2 more chalets – a twin & a family – plus, eventually, a fly-camp on the Lunga River. For now, a little way upstream, a campsite with braai areas & 2 solid ablution blocks was nearing completion for 2011.

Most guests are self catering, & use the kitchen where there's a cook to help with preparation. Nearby is an open *citenge*, or living area, with a wooden deck extending over the river & great views in both directions. On the river, choose from trips in an aluminium fishing boat or 1 of 3 RIBs (*US$25 pp*), or a full day fishing (*US$120/max 3*). On land, there are game drives & guided walks (*US$50/45 pp, inc park fees*), while just behind the camp, a substantial hide overlooks a well-frequented waterhole. *US$50/100 self catering/FB pp sharing; camping US$20 pp.* ⊕ *Easter–Nov.*

🏠 **Leopard Lodge** [map 433] (5 chalets, camping) \ +27 82 416 5894; e info@leopard-lodge.com; www.leopard-lodge.com. ✪ LEOPLO

14°32.823'S, 26°28.960'E. Close to Kafue River Camp, & reached by turning off the main track at ⊕ TULEOP 14°32.700'S, 26°28.050'E, Leopard Lodge also lies on the river, but here it is more open. Large, modern en-suite chalets look promising with their thatched roofs & cream paintwork, & downstream there's an attractive campsite with private reed-screened facilities & open river views, but when we visited over a bank holiday both the chalets & the restaurant were closed & the campsite looked empty. Despite what appears to be significant investment – including a large airy lapa with a firepit & a deck over the river, & the introduction of solar power in 2011 – it all felt rather sterile. Fishing, boat cruises, & game drives can be arranged, as can visits to some hot springs about 4km from the lodge. *US$365–450 pp sharing FBA, inc local drinks, park fees. Camping US$25 pp;* ◷ *All year, but must be pre-booked.*

🏠 **Mushingashi Conservancy** [map 433] (2 houses, 3 camps; camping) m 0977 846978; e darrellwatt@yahoo.com; www.mushingashi.

net. ⊕ TUMUSH 14°40.853'S, 26°40.430'E. About 65km from Mumbwa, the unfenced 405km² Mushingashi Conservancy runs for 18km along the Kafue River & shares a 37km boundary with the national park. Primarily used by anglers, it also boasts some good wildlife, including elephant, sable, eland & roan, predators such as lion & cheetah, & over 400 bird species. There are self-drive game loops, & guided walks can be arranged.

From the road, it's 30km to the main Kabalushi Camp, with well-marked turnings to this & other simple, self-catering camps in the conservancy (bring *all* your own supplies). All are located on the river & with en-suite facilities. **Delai** & **Khosikoto** camps each have 6 rustic thatched chalets & a campsite; then there's **Kalonga Waloba** (14 chalets), & **Kabalushi** (8-bed & 2-bed houses). Most guests bring their own boats, but there are fully equipped boats for hire too (*US$100 per day & fuel*). Nearby are the Piamanzi (or Mutoyi) hot springs, bubbling out of black-cotton soil – so not suitable for swimming. *US$50 pp; camping US$25 pp.*

SOUTHERN KAFUE

Stretching about 190km southwards from the main road, the southern part of the park is long and thin, although it is only about 85km wide at its broadest point. On its eastern boundary are the Kafue River and the Itezhi-Tezhi Dam: 300km² of water. Itezhi-Tezhi differs from many dams as, apparently, it is not made of continuous concrete but instead is filled with earth, in order to render it less vulnerable to tremors and minor earthquakes.

The vegetation and geography of the southern side are similar to the north – see *Geography and Flora and fauna*, page 427 – although there's more Kalahari sand in the south, and it's notable for a few really beautiful teak forests.

4x4 routes within and around southern Kafue

Mukambi, Chunga and Mayukuyuku are very near the main road, and are clearly signposted around the main bridge over the Kafue in the centre of the park. At present, to reach the heart of the southern section of the park you must either take one of the routes through the GMA, or approach from the south from Monze, Choma or Kalomo on the Lusaka–Livingstone road. Note, however, that there is talk of reinstating the spinal road down the western side of the Kafue River. For now, all routes require a 4x4 throughout the year, and in the wet season, only the D769 from the north is practical.

From the M9 Lusaka–Mongu road to Lake Itezhi-Tezhi

Despite a fiction perpetrated by distant cartographers, the 'road' south from Chunga to Lake Itezhi-Tezhi, following the western bank of the Kafue, has been impassable for many years. The good news, though, is that this track – said to be a lovely road, with many bridges across no fewer than 11 rivers – is expected to re-open within the next few years. Until that happens, access into the park from the Lusaka–Mongu road into the southern section of the park is restricted to the eastern side

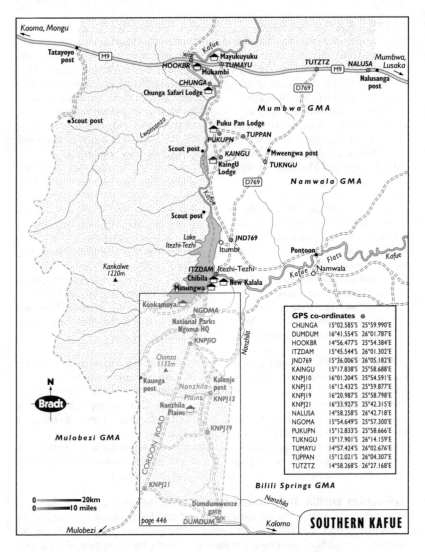

Southern Kafue map

Kaoma, Mongu

Tatayoyo post

M9

Kafue

Mayukuyuku

HOOKBR *TUMAYU*

Mukambi

CHUNGA

Chunga Safari Lodge

•Scout post

Lwansonza

Mumbwa G M A

TUTZTZ   NALUSA   Mumbwa, Lusaka

M9

Nalusanga post

D769

Puku Pan Lodge

PUKUPN   *TUPPAN*

Scout post

KAINGU   •Mweengwa post

KaingU Lodge   *TUKNGU*

D769

Namwala G M A

Kafue

Scout post

Lake Itezhi-Tezhi

JND769

Itumbi

ITZDAM Itezhi-Tezhi   Pontoon   *Flats*   Kafue

Chibila   New Kalala   *Kafue* Namwala

Musungwa

Kankalwe 1220m

Konkamoya

NGOMA

National Parks Ngoma HQ

KNPJI0

Chonza 1132m

Kaunga post   Kalenje post

Nanzhila Plains   *KNPJI3*

Nanzhila Plains

KNPJI9

Mulobezi G M A

N

Bradt

Nanzhila

GPS co-ordinates ⊕		
CHUNGA	15°02.585'S	25°59.990'E
DUMDUM	16°41.554'S	26°01.787'E
HOOKBR	14°56.477'S	25°54.384'E
ITZDAM	15°45.544'S	26°01.302'E
JND769	15°36.006'S	26°05.182'E
KAINGU	15°17.838'S	25°58.688'E
KNPJI0	16°01.204'S	25°54.591'E
KNPJI3	16°12.432'S	25°59.877'E
KNPJI9	16°20.987'S	25°58.798'E
KNPJ21	16°33.927'S	25°42.315'E
NALUSA	14°58.258'S	26°42.718'E
NGOMA	15°54.649'S	25°57.300'E
PUKUPN	15°12.833'S	25°58.666'E
TUKNGU	15°17.901'S	26°14.159'E
TUMAYU	14°57.424'S	26°02.676'E
TUPPAN	15°12.021'S	26°04.307'E
TUTZTZ	14°58.268'S	26°27.168'E

CORDON ROAD

KNPJ21

Bilili Springs G M A

Nanzhila

0 — 20km
0 — 10 miles

page 446   Dumdumwenze gate   DUMDUM   Kalomo

Mulobezi   **SOUTHERN KAFUE**

of the Kafue River and Lake Itezhi-Tezhi, through the Mumbwa and Namwala GMAs. On the plus side, there are safari camps in both of these, and the game is increasingly good.

Of the two viable routes, one follows the all-season D769 through the GMA, while a second – the 'river route' – is dry season only, being impassable in the rains. (There is also a third route between the two, known as the 'hunters' road', which is used by local people, but is not a right of way.)

The D769 to Itezhi-Tezhi Heading west from Lusaka, the road bypasses Mumbwa after some 150km then about a further 37km brings you to the Nalusanga scout post (⊕ NALUSA 14°58.258'S, 26°42.718'E), at the entrance to the Kafue National Park. After a further 28km, there's a turning left (⊕ TUTZTZ 14°58.268'S, 26°27.168'E) into the south of the park, along the D769. If you're approaching from the west, that's a fraction more than 51km from the main Hook Bridge over the Kafue River. It is clearly signposted to Itezhi-Tezhi and – in the rainy season – is the only viable road south.

This road has been appalling for years, earning it the title of the country's worst 'tar' road: 120km of pot-holes taking five to six hours in a good, sturdy 4x4, even in the dry season. Then what was left of the tar was removed, but the road remained dreadful. It took a presidential visit for the surface to be graded, but by mid 2011 it was at last a viable option. That said, this is likely to deteriorate with the rains, so do take that into consideration. And be aware, too, that whole sections are popular with tsetse flies, making air conditioning a valuable accessory for your vehicle.

About 45km after the turning, you will pass the Mweengwa scout checkpoint (⊕ MWEENG 15°16.539'S, 26°14.950'E), where you must stop to sign in. About 2km south of that, there's a turning clearly marked for KaingU Safari Lodge and Puku Pan (⊕ TUKNGU 15°17.901'S, 26°14.159'E).

About 39km from the scout post you'll stop at a veterinary control post; then a further 22km and you reach **Itezhi-Tezhi village** (⊕ ITEZHI 15°44.252'S, 26°2.202'E). This is about 106km from the main Lusaka–Mongu road. Continue for about 2km, bearing left and uphill until you reach a ZESCO checkpoint. At this point, a right turning on to a tar road takes you into the village (see page 444) where you can organise fuel and take in some commanding views of the lake. To continue straight to the southern section of the park then drive on below the dam wall (⊕ ITZDAM 15°45.544'S, 26°1.302'E). You'll pass three lodges, which are well signposted on the right-hand side of the road, then it's just a couple of kilometres further to the Musa gate (⊕ MUSAGA 15°47.802'S, 25°59.938'E). This is where you pay your park fees into the southern section of Kafue National Park. Interestingly, the gate itself is located outside the park boundary, which you'll cross (albeit without any sign) just before Lake View Drive.

The river route to Itezhi-Tezhi Between June and November, there's an altogether more scenic, albeit longer alternative to the D769, following a series of tracks along the Kafue River and passing close to both Puku Pan and KaingU safari lodges. The route crosses the Mumbwa GMA, and is absolutely legal, but note that this is also a hunting concession – so safari-goers may not always be welcome. That said, when we asked directions of a hunter, we were treated with absolute courtesy and shown the right turning without any fuss.

To find the river route, leave the M9 Lusaka–Mongu road opposite the turning to Mayukuyuku (⊕ TUMAYU 14°57.424'S, 26°02.676'E), signposted to Kafumbakwale (a very underused community campsite). Follow this narrow but good gravel track more or less southwest for about 5km, keeping an eye out for a track to your left into the bush (⊕ RR1 14°59.603'S, 26°01.020'E). There's no signpost, and it's not terribly clear, but if you overshoot it you'll soon get to the river so just retrace your steps. The correct, sandy track winds southeast through the bush for about 4km until, at ⊕ RR2 14°59.584'S, 26°01.031'E, you come to a confusing medley of tracks in a rough clearing. It's easy to become disorientated here, but continue broadly south, bearing slightly left in the clearing, then right into a steep gully at ⊕ RR3 15°00.604'S, 26°02.666'E, and emerging into a thick patch of sand. From here, the track continues roughly south, through bush and across open plains, crossing several river beds, and sometimes with glimpses of the river to your right. Precise route directions are of little help, but the following GPS co-ordinates mark some of the riverbeds and other landmarks *en route* to KaingU Safari Lodge:

RR4	15°01.884'S, 26°02.283'E	Riverbed; graveyard termitaria both sides; river on right
RR5	15°03.934'S, 26°01.525'E	Riverbed
RR6	15°05.394'S, 25°59.764'E	Riverbed
RR7	15°05.997'S, 25°59.302'E	Ignore track to left
RR8	15°06.788'S, 25°58.971'E	Ignore track to right along river
RR9	15°07.905'S, 25°58.488'E	Hunting camp to right on river
RR10	15°10.734'S, 25°58.973'E	Take right fork
RR11	15°12.199'S, 25°58.748'E	Keep right at fork
TUPPN2	15°12.389'S, 25°58.708'E	T-junction with good gravel track. Turn right for Puku Pan and to continue south
TUKAI2	15°13.877'S, 25°59.484'E	Take right fork to KaingU and south
POLEBR	15°17.306'S, 25°59.130'E	Cross the pole bridge and turn immediately left (continue straight on for KaingU Safari Lodge)

Continuing south from the pole bridge (and the turning to KaingU), you'll cross several more riverbeds and – after around 21km – you will pass the palace of Chief Kaingu to your left, followed 7km later by Bushinga village. From the pole bridge to the junction with the D769 (✪ JND769 15°36.006'S, 26°05.182'E) is around 43km. From here, you turn right towards Itezhi-Tezhi village. Useful GPS co-ordinates along this stretch include:

RR12	15°21.495'S, 25°59.695'E	Dip, and pool to left
RR13	15°22.469'S, 25°59.866'E	Double river crossing
RR14	15°25.006'S, 26°00.286'E	Take left fork
RR15	15°25.760'S, 26°00.064'E	Deep river crossing
RR16	15°29.762'S, 26°00.436'E	Stone bridge
RR16	15°34.815'S, 26°03.240'E	Bear left at fork

Itezhi-Tezhi village For those heading into the park, the village is an invaluable source of both fuel and supplies. Instead of following the main road south, turn right and you'll pass a police station immediately on your left, followed by a **post office** and a branch of the Zanaco **Bank**. Pass the school and you'll get to the ZESCO offices (◷ *08.00–12.30 & 14.00–16.30*), where you can arrange for **fuel** supplies. By this time, you'll be high up and overlooking the lake. (The fuel itself is dispensed back on the main road, on the way towards the dam wall.)

From the south
Kalomo to Dumdumwenze gate The small town of Kalomo (page 214) is about 126km from Livingstone on the way to Lusaka, and marks the turning towards the southern section of the Kafue. There's a **fuel** station here (✪ KAFUEL 17°01.661'S, 26°29.271'E), where you should fill up before setting out for the park. Just north of this, a clear sign points west to the Dumdumwenze gate. Almost immediately the road becomes a dirt track, passing through a busy **market** (a good place for supplies) to a T-junction. Turn right here and follow the road as it curves left (ignoring right-hand turn-off).

Continue over a railway bridge, followed shortly afterwards by a river bridge (✪ KALBRI 17°0.915'S, 26°29.468'E), then take the next left fork. Continue following the main track, ignoring any turnings and keeping left at forks. After a few kilometres you should be travelling northwest, passing through the occasional village. About 40km from the main road, you will start leaving the villages behind to climb through some hills. Eventually, after about 74km, the road drops down gradually to Dumdumwenze gate (⊕ DUMDUM 16°41.554'S, 26°1.787'E), where the game scouts will sign you into the park. (Note that Dumdumwezi is the local spelling and pronunciation.)

The road has been recently graded, and the route is clear, but watch out for some particularly vicious speed bumps which materialise before and after both villages and river bridges, often with no warning signposts. Watch out, too, for goats, cattle and hens along the road.

North from Dumdumwenze Always ask the scouts at the gate for advice – if only to determine how wet the roads are, and so if it's safe to go on the much

more interesting Nanzhila River route. Whichever route you take, drive north into the park for 2.3km to the first junction (⊕ KNPJ20 16°40.332'S, 26°1.722'E).

Between about December and July, there's little choice: you will have to take the **Cordon route**, which skirts around the southwest side of the park through woodlands. This gets to Ngoma without crossing any substantial rivers, and so while it does have the odd sticky dambo, an experienced driver with a 4x4 should be able to get through even in the rains. Note, however, that high sand can pile up in the centre of the road, so a high-clearance 4x4 is as essential for this route as for any other within the park.

For this route you go into the park, heading north for about 2.3km, then take a left turn at your first junction (⊕ KNPJ20 16°40.332'S, 26°1.722'E). From here you proceed about 40km, through fairly thick forest, heading slightly north of west, until you reach a junction (⊕ KAFU01 16°33.927'S, 25°42.314'E), which indicates the southwestern tip of the park. There you turn right, to head north and slightly east on a basically straight road that passes through the heart of the southern end of the park. This ultimately meets other roads near Ngoma at junction ⊕ KNPJ10 16°1.204'S, 25°54.591'E.

During the dry season, consider taking the **Nanzhila River route**, which is much more interesting. This shadows the river north, crossing it several times and skirting around the eastern edge of the Nanzhila Plains. From ⊕ KNPJ20 16°40.332'S, 26°1.722'E, continue straight ahead. The vegetation along this route can be exceedingly thick even in June, so it's best to wait until at least July to drive along here.

From that first junction it's about 19km until you cross to the east bank of the Nanzhila River at ⊕ NANRV2 16°30.905'S, 26°0.164'E. Although the river isn't very deep, its banks are steep and can be slippery, so if there's any danger of you getting stuck, make sure that you have a back-up plan. Continue north, and after about 19km, there's a concrete marker sign at ⊕ KNPJ19 16°20.987'S,

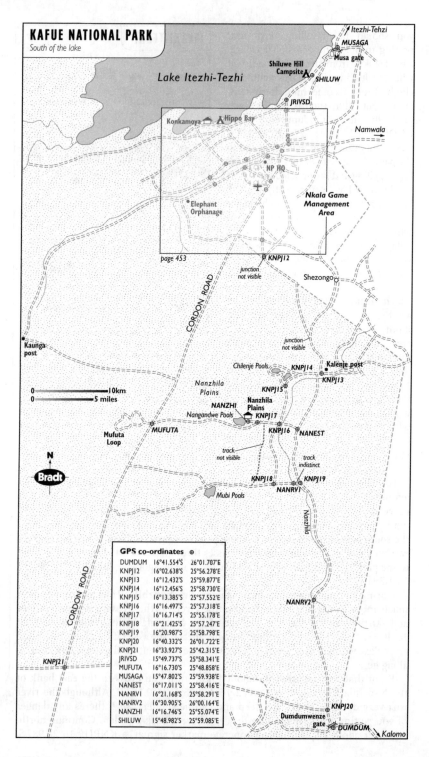

KAFUE NATIONAL PARK
South of the lake

Itezhi-Tehzi

MUSAGA
Musa gate

Lake Itezhi-Tezhi

Shiluwe Hill
Campsite
SHILUW

JRIVSD

Konkamoya   Hippo Bay

Namwala

NP HQ

Nkala Game
Management
Area

Elephant
Orphanage

page 453

KNPJI2

junction
not visible

Shezongo

CORDON ROAD

junction
not visible

Kaunga
post

Chilenje Pools   KNPJI4   Kalenje post

KNPJI3

Nanzhila
Plains

KNPJI5

0   10km
0   5 miles

NANZHI   Nanzhila
Plains

Nangandwe Pools   KNPJI7

Mufuta
Loop

MUFUTA   KNPJI6   NANEST

N
Bradt

track
not visible

track
indistinct

KNPJI8   KNPJI9

NANRVI

Mubi Pools

Nanzhila

GPS co-ordinates	⊕	
DUMDUM	16°41.554'S	26°01.707'E
KNPJI2	16°02.638'S	25°56.278'E
KNPJI3	16°12.432'S	25°59.877'E
KNPJI4	16°12.456'S	25°58.730'E
KNPJI5	16°13.385'S	25°57.552'E
KNPJI6	16°16.497'S	25°57.318'E
KNPJI7	16°16.714'S	25°55.178'E
KNPJI8	16°21.425'S	25°57.247'E
KNPJI9	16°20.987'S	25°58.798'E
KNPJ20	16°40.332'S	26°01.722'E
KNPJ21	16°33.927'S	25°42.315'E
JRIVSD	15°49.737'S	25°58.341'E
MUFUTA	16°16.730'S	25°48.858'E
MUSAGA	15°47.802'S	25°59.938'E
NANEST	16°17.011'S	25°58.416'E
NANRVI	16°21.168'S	25°58.291'E
NANRV2	16°30.905'S	26°00.164'E
NANZHI	16°16.746'S	25°55.074'E
SHILUW	15°48.982'S	25°59.085'E

NANRV2

CORDON ROAD

KNPJ21

KNPJ20

Dumdumwenze
gate   DUMDUM

Kalomo

25°58.798'E, and you may spot a very faint track heading west, to your left. Although this track has virtually disappeared, don't let that put you off. Turn left as if it were there (it should be!), across the vegetation if necessary. In about 800m you'll reach a river crossing (✥ NANRV2 16°30.905'S, 26°0.164'E). Continue over this and for a further 2km on a better track until you meet a road junction (✥ KNPJ18 16°21.425'S, 25°57.247'E). Turn right to take a really lovely road north. It passes the Nanzhila Plains, and bends east at the Chilenje Pools, and then leads to Kalenje scout post. If you didn't go west at KNPJ19, then continuing straight would also bring you to Kalenje.

From Kalenje there's a variety of game drive roads which will lead you slightly west of north to Ngoma. Note that as you head towards the airstrip, there are some particularly deep patches of sand, so take extra care in that area.

From Monze on the Lusaka–Livingstone road From Monze take a turning on the north side of town towards Chongo, heading northwest towards Lochinvar National Park. You may need to ask local directions to get on the right track, but it passes through waypoint ✥ TULOCH 16°15.465'S, 27°28.632'E. After 7–8km you will pass Chongo – keep left there as the track divides after the village. About 8km after Chongo the road forks (✥ T2LOCH 16°10.054'S, 27°23.610'E): right leads to Lochinvar National Park; left leads to Namwala and thence the Ngoma area of Kafue.

About 35km later, on a dusty (or, if wet, muddy) and rather pot-holed track, you will reach Chitongo, and a T-junction. Here you find an implausibly good tarred road! (If you turned left onto this, you would find that the tar turned into poor gravel about 60km before Choma.) For the Kafue turn right at Chitongo, and follow this heading slightly west of north, then due west. About 50km after Chitongo you will reach the larger village of Namwala, on the southern edge of the Kafue's floodplain (where, incidentally, there's a pontoon over the Kafue). From Namwala, the track leads about 60km southwest, into the park. This is bumpy and pot-holed gravel, but is passable during the rains. It enters the park past the site of the old Nkala Mission, joining the road network at ✥ TUNAMW 15°53.894'S, 25°57.854'E, about 2km north of Ngoma.

🏠 **Where to stay** If you're just passing through the park on the main Lusaka–Mongu road, consider stopping for a night or two in the area around Mukambi – but if you have more time, it's well worth penetrating deeper into the park. The southern Itezhi-Tezhi area, and around Ngoma, has the most spectacular game in this part of the park, whilst KaingU Safari Lodge is built beside a unique and very lovely part of the river.

If you're driving and taking camping kit, there is plenty of choice, even though both the national parks' campsites in the southern Kafue have closed. You can probably afford to turn up at the lodges along the Lusaka road and those around Lake Itezhi-Tezhi, and even at Hippo Bay, but would be advised to book the smaller, more remote campsites at KaingU and Nanzhila Plains Safari Camp. For those on a fly-in trip, on a flexible budget, the options in this area include KaingU, Nanzhila Plains Safari Camp and Konkamoya.

For ease of reference, I've split the southern Kafue's camps into three distinct areas: 'Near the M9 Lusaka–Mongu road', 'Further south in the GMA' and 'Around Itezhi-Tezhi Dam and south'.

Near the M9 Lusaka–Mongu road There are several places to stay very near the M9 road, but for most people those listed here are likely to be the best bet. All are on the river, and either in or opposite the national park – with Mayukuyuku just inside the northern Kafue.

🏠 **Mayukuyuku Bush Camp** [map 442] (4 tents, camping) e kafuecamps@btinternet. com, info@kafuecamps.com; www.kafuecamps. com. ⊕ MAYUKU 14°54.975'S, 26°03.925'E. Small, personal & welcoming, Mayukuyuku was set up in 2006 by Patrick Moyo & Pippa Turner, who worked together at Lufupa for years. It's a simple place, more camp than lodge, & capably run by an entirely Zambian team. It lies 5.7km north of the main Lusaka–Mongu road, from where it is clearly signposted (⊕ TUMAYU 14°57.424'S, 26°02.676'E), some 107km west of Mumbwa.

Walk-in tents under shaggy thatch are set on a sandy, tree-shaded site by the river, opposite a small island & within the national park. Each has dbl or twin beds, floor mats, solar lighting, an open-air reed-enclosed shower & separate flush toilet – & a shady porch with its own hammock. A little way upstream is a separate campsite with 4 pitches (*tent hire US$15–25*); backpackers can be collected at Hook Bridge (*US$30 per vehicle*). Closer to the camp are a simple lounge/ bar/dining shelter – with meals available to allcomers with advance notice – & a reception area with small shop.

Both guests & day visitors can take boat cruises or fishing trips on the river, as well as guided walks & game drives (*all US$35 pp*). Alternatively, you can hire a guide to accompany you in your own vehicle (*from US$25/2hrs*). *US$250/350 pp FBA inc park fees; US$250 FB; no sgl suppt. Camping US$15 pp. Transfers extra.* ⊕ *All year.*

🏠 **Mukambi Safari Lodge** [map 442] (9 chalets, 1 villa) 📞 0211 840953; m 0976 914493; e info@mukambi.com; www.mukambi. com. ⊕ MUKAMB 14°58.656'S, 25°59.599'E. In the capable hands of Linda & Jacques van Heerden, Mukambi is a well-built, comfortable lodge in the GMA, with consistently high standards. It is signposted from the main Lusaka–Mongu tar road (⊕ TUMUKA 14°57.584'S, 25°59.721'E), about 9km east of the Hook Bridge over the Kafue. The camp is 2km from the main road – easily accessed in a normal 2WD.

Thatched, cream-painted chalets (4 twin, 4 dbl, 1 family, & a family villa) are solidly built with beautifully carved wooden doors. There's

no AC or fan, but the circular shape, tree shade & netted windows help to keep them cool, & each has a small veranda with chairs. Inside are 4-poster beds under mosquito nets, the neutral décor enlivened by ethnic wall hangings & wood carvings. Stone-tiled showers in the bathrooms are solar-heated, with a geyser in the villa.

Significant refurbishment in 2011 has brought a more open, relaxed feel to the wooden central area, which overlooks the Kafue River to the national park. Food is good, served buffet style in the substantial restaurant, while lower down is a relaxed seating area over the river. There's a swimming pool with a deck, & a cosy lounge/ bar with a fire for the winter months. Day visitors are welcome & can join in activities subject to availability.

A range of boating and 4x4 game-viewing trips is available, with no more than 8 guests in each safari vehicle. Overall game densities in the Chunga area (where they usually drive) have improved considerably since the camp was opened in 1997 & anti-poaching measures put in place. In addition to some lovely herds of elephant & buffalo, there are now regular sightings of lion, leopard, cheetah & wild dog. Guests may also visit the local primary school, which is supported by the lodge. *US$200–260/ 320–375 pp sharing, chalet/villa, FB. Walking, boating & game drives US$40 pp, exc park fees.* ⊕ *All year.*

🏕 **Mukambi Bushcamp** [map 442] (7 pitches) Contact via Mukambi, above. A short wander upstream from the main lodge is Mukambi's campsite, with individual thatched shelters & a couple of pre-erected tents with bedding & towels for those without their own kit. There are areas for braais, & campers share a spotless ablution block, & a purpose-built camp kitchen with sinks, power, tables & chairs. Camp staff are on hand to help with fires & food preparation. Campers are welcome to eat at the lodge & join in with activities if there's space, & with advance notice. *US$15 pp. Pre-erected tent US$55.* ⊕ *All year.*

🏠 **Chunga Safari Lodge** [map 442] (5 rondavels, camping) m 097 9427589, 097 7148987; e bobmalambo@yahoo.com, nexim@

zamnet.zm. ⊕ CHUNGA 15°2.585'S, 25°59.990'E. This old-style camp has an attractive riverside setting in the national park, with bushbuck wandering nonchalantly through. To find it, turn south off the main road, immediately west of the main Kafue Hook Bridge (⊕ HOOKBR 14°56.477'S, 25°54.384'E). A gravel road heads south for about 14km until a crossroads: left leads to the College of Wildlife Management, but continue straight on for a further 4km to the National Parks' Chunga HQ & the neighbouring lodge. You are now about 8.5km due south of Mukambi Safari Lodge, but on the opposite side of the river.

Chunga's ochre-washed thatch-on-brick rondavels were refurbished in 2010, to include en-suite showers & toilets, & it's also possible to camp here. The camp is largely self catering, with a thatched kitchen/dining area & small bar, but meals can be provided on request (*Kw50,000 pp*).

Walking safaris, game drives & boat cruises (US$25 pp) can be organised, but facilities are very limited. That, & its relatively high prices, means that few people feel it's worth the effort. *Rondavel US$75 pp; camping US$20 pp. Park fees extra.* ☼ *All year.*

Further south in the Namwala GMA There are two more southerly lodges beside the river in the GMA, too far from the Mongu–Lusaka road to be mere stopovers. Both have campsites, and both are best booked in advance. There has long been game in this area, effectively protected from poaching by the presence of the lodges. That said, although the game is building up, it isn't as good as in the park's best corners – but the river here is stunning!

⌂ **KaingU Safari Lodge** [map 442] (4 tented chalets, 1 family chalet) ℮ lodgemanager@kaingu-lodge.com, reservations@kaingu-lodge.com; www.kaingu-lodge.com. ⊕ KAINGU 15°17.838'S, 25°58.688'E. KaingU stands in an idyllic setting on the east bank of the Kafue; as the bee-eater flies it's about 40km from the M9, or 10km south of Puku Pan. To get here from the D769 (see page 442) turn west at the signpost to KaingU ⊕ TUKNGU 15°17.901'S, 26°14.159'E. This bush track twists & winds through dense miombo woodland for about 23.5km until you fork left at ⊕ TUPPAN 15°12.021'S, 26°4.307'E. From there it's just under 18km to the lodge, during which you cross a small pole bridge (⊕ POLEBR 15°17.306'S, 25°59.130'E). An alternative approach in the dry season is via the river route (page 443).

Broadly traditional in design, & finished with a high degree of care, the lodge was fully refurbished in 2011. Each of its large, green Meru-style tents is raised on polished wooden decking under thatch, with a big veranda facing the river. Large, high-quality beds stand on hand-woven rugs, & it's possible to open up the whole of the front of the tent to be 1 big mesh window. At the back, an attractive stone bathroom has an indoor & outdoor shower (or bath), & individual touches like a towel rail of knurled wood. There's hot water aplenty & small 12v solar-powered

lights. A new chalet with a private garden should be completed in 2011, ideal as a honeymoon suite or for private dinners.

The lodge is run by Tom Heinecken, & his wife Viviane. Tom's passion for the wildlife & the natural environment is manifest in the emphasis on walking – including in the park – & river trips, though day & night game drives & fishing excursions are offered too. A short walk from the river, overlooking a waterhole, the 'puku hide' allows guests to spend as long as they like watching game or birds. Meander down the Kafue in an inflatable boat; take off on an overnight camping trip; or, when the water is low, relax in the pools above the rapids. Alternatively, you can visit a gemstone mine, hot springs, or an old iron smelter that has been coaxed back to life (with proceeds contributing towards the upkeep of a new school). With such a small lodge, & a high degree of enthusiasm, there's plenty of flexibility.

The river beside the lodge is as lovely as any stretch of African river that I know: it's worth coming here just to spend a few days afloat. KaingU stands beside an area where the river broadens to accommodate a scattering of small islands, each consisting of vegetated sandy banks & huge granite rocks interspersed with rapids. Imagine someone throwing half of Zimbabwe's Matobo Hills into a wide, shallow river & you'll

14

get the picture. So to potter round here in a boat, or even just to go fishing, is a real journey of discovery. With endless side channels & islands to explore, there's something different around every corner, plenty of vegetation everywhere – & birds all around. It's a real gem of an area. *US$265–375 pp FBA, inc park fees & local drinks.* ☺ *All year.*

⚠ KaingU Campsite [map 442] (2 private campsites, 1 shared site) Contact KaingU Safari Lodge, above. KaingU has 2 private riverside pitches, each with its own spotless & very well-designed reed-walled ablutions (flush toilet, hot shower & washbasin), a cooking grid, a fireplace, a tap & a table for washing up. These private sites can each take up to 8 people & 2 vehicles. Set apart from these is another, larger site, which can take up to 16 people (4 vehicles max) sharing ablutions. All the sites are pleasant & grassy, under trees, & firewood is provided. However, you must bring all your food as meals are available at the lodge only if you've arranged them well in advance. *US$22 pp.* ☺ *Apr–Dec.*

🏠 Puku Pan Safari Lodge [map 442] (10 chalets, camping) ☎0211 266927; m 0977 780080; e pukupan@zamnet.zm; www.pukupansafarilodge.com. ⊕ PUKUPN 15°12.833'S, 25°58.666'E. Puku Pan has a lovely

situation on a 200m stretch of the Kafue River, overlooking the park from the GMA & as the fish eagle flies about 10km north of KaingU. Though it's possible to fly in, most people drive. By road, follow the directions for KaingU (above) to ⊕ TUPPAN 15°12.021'S, 26°4.307'E. Fork right here, & it's just under 14km to the lodge, passing the airstrip (⊕ AIRPUK 15°12.202'S, 26°1.989'E).

One of the Kafue's first camps, it remains simple. Each of its cottages, built of mud-finished blocks & wood under thatch, has a veranda overlooking the river, plus flush toilet & bath or shower with hot water; there is solar power. There's also a large if basic campsite with shared ablutions, including hot showers, & a couple of simple tented chalets. At the back of the site, a thatched open-sided lounge area overlooks a waterhole where puku – & the occasional elephant or lion – come to drink. Guests & day visitors can take part in boat trips & day or night game drives (*US$20 pp*), or fishing & game walks (*US$15 pp*). Activities are currently in the GMA, but there are plans for drives & walks in the park, too, when park fees will be payable. *US$195–225 pp FB; activities extra. Self catering US$80–128 pp. Tented chalet US$46–60 pp. Camping US$20–30 pp.* ☺ *All year.*

Canoe trails

Mawimbi Trails Camp ☎+ 263 486 1286; m +263 772 261831, 774 186336; e nathalie@mawimbi-adventure.com; www.mawimbi-adventure.com. This new fly-camp, established in 2011 in partnership with KaingU Safari Lodge, is the base for a canoe trail along a 90km stretch of the Kafue River. Starting at Mukambi, participants paddle in inflatable canoes as far as Itezhi-Tezhi Dam.

Accommodation, inside the national park, is in simple twin-bedded tents with bedside table & hurricane lamps, set up by staff who go ahead by motorboat. Dinner is served under the stars or – if necessary – in a gazebo. It's a flexible system, with a basic 3-day package that can be extended to incorporate walking in the national park. *US$290–400 pp/night FB, depending on numbers.*

Around Itezhi-Tezhi Dam and south Grouped in the GMA to the southeast of Lake Itezhi-Tezhi, and just south of the dam wall, are three fairly old-style camps catering more to Zambian tastes than to overseas visitors. They're relatively inexpensive – and some would regard them as good value. There's also the option of a small new lodge in Itezhi-Tezhi village.

In the national park itself, and right on the lake, the new Konkamoya offers superb guiding in a relatively simple context, while further south, Nanzhila Plains Safari Camp has made this remote area of the park accessible once again to adventurous visitors. Although both national parks' campsites have been closed, most of the lodges offer camping, and there's also the simple Shiluwe Hill site near the Musa gate.

🏠 **Lakeside Lodge** [map 445] (7 rooms) Itezhi-Tezhi village. ⊕ LAKESD 15°44.768'S, 26°00.604'E. About 1.5km beyond the ZESCO offices, & geared largely to the corporate market, this new lodge was nearing completion in 2011. Built on a steep slope leading down to the lake, it has 2 rooms in a single block, each with a dbl & sgl bed, & 5 more spacious thatched rondavels with kingsize beds. All are en suite with AC, fridge & TV, & all have lake views. A restaurant & bar will complete the package. **$$$**

🏠 **New Kalala Safari Lodge** [map 442] (13 chalets, camping) ☎ 0213 263179/265375; e info@newkalala.com; www.newkalala.com. ⊕ NEWKAL 15°46.583'S, 26°00.538'E. Well signposted south of the dam wall, New Kalala overlooks the lake from a stunning perch on a granite kopje where you'll see the odd rock dassie scurrying about. Recent refurbishment has brought a new lease of life to the large chalets that are dotted around well-tended gardens above the lake. Although they remain rather stark, all have en-suite bathrooms, fridge & AC. It is also possible to camp on the lake shore. Overlooking the lake, the restaurant/bar serves lunch (*Kw60,000*) & dinner (*Kw80,000*). Guests can take part in game drives (*Kw170,000 pp & park fees*); boat cruises (*Kw150,000 pp, or boat hire from Kw550,000/½ day, plus fuel*); & a hot springs tour (*Kw60,000 pp*), & there's a nice pool here, too. *Chalet Kw500,000/800,000/900,000 dbl B&B/HB/FB. Camping Kw70,000 pp.*

🏕 **Chibila Camp** [map 442] (3 chalets, camping) ☎ 097 7794036; e 890121@zm.celtelplus.com, wecsz@zamnet.zm; www.conservationzambia.org. ⊕ CHIBIL 15°46.638'S, 26°00.407'E. Almost next door to New Kalala, Chibila (or Chibala – formerly the David Shepherd Camp) stands between large granite boulders on the shores of the lake. It was built for members of the Wildlife Conservation Society of Zambia (the present WECSZ, page 50), & remains available to members only. Each chalet has 4 beds, en-suite shower & toilet, & a private veranda. It's a self-catering camp, but staff are on hand to help cook & there's a fully equipped kitchen & BBQ area. *Kw120,000 pp; camping Kw50,000 per group.*

🏠 **Musungwa Safari Lodge** [map 442] (40 chalets, camping) ☎ 0211 273493; e zamker@zamnet.zm. ⊕ MUSUNG 15°46.987'S, 26°00.329'E. On the shore of Lake Itezhi-Tezhi,

Musungwa is about 5km south of the dam wall, & just 2km north of the Musa gate. Though it's seen better days, it remains the largest lodge in the area, & is a popular base for local gatherings & fishing competitions. Twin & 4-bed en-suite chalets have tiny private verandas overlooking the lake. Housed in 3 large rondavels are the reception, bar & restaurant, open to day visitors, plus a small curio shop. Just below is a swimming pool commanding a stunning view of the lake, & surrounded by pleasant gardens, complete with grass, bamboo, bougainvillea & the odd palm. There are tennis & squash courts, too. Activities include boat cruises, game drives &, of course, fishing. **$$$**

🏕 **Shiluwe Hill Campsite** [map 446] ⊕ SHILUW 15°48.982'S, 25°59.085'E. Facilities at this basic lakeside campsite, 3km southwest of the Musa gate, comprise just a toilet & shower. A couple of chalets were under construction in 2010. *US$10 pp.*

🏠 **Konkamoya** [map 453] (6 chalets) ☎ 0211 213362; e info@konkamoya.com; www.cookesafricansafaris.com, www.konkamoya.com. ⊕ KONKAM 15°52.040'S, 25°52.976'E. In a prime position on the lake shore, Konkamoya opened in 2007. Many visitors fly in to Ngoma, a ½hr game drive to the south. If you're driving yourself, follow the main track from the Musa gate, turning right after 5km on to Lake View Drive. From here, keep to the lake shore until after 18km you come to a crossroads (⊕ TUKONK 15°53.061'S, 25°52.671'E) signed to Howard Cooke Safaris. Turn right & the lodge is within 2.5km.

Konkamoya sits on a wide grassy plain, fronted by drowned trees & a small island rising from the lake. Wide steps leading up to an airy lounge/bar & a crescent of infinity pool give a rather grand feel, dashed somewhat by rustic balustrades of painted concrete that add a faintly Mexican touch. That's fortunate, for the lodge is by no means grand. On the contrary, it feels rather homely, & many of the staff come from owner/manager Chris Cooke's family farm, which explains the slightly paternalistic atmosphere.

That this is the 1st lodge to open right on the lake, within the national park, is somewhat surprising – for game levels are improving (Chris claims to have seen a noticeable increase in game in the area since he arrived), the views are excellent, & the options of both land- & water-

The Kafue River Basin   KAFUE NATIONAL PARK   14

based activities afford plenty of variety. It can get windy, though, which explains the location of Konkamoya's rustic but well-appointed chalets – in a sheltered corner with no view of the lake. However, in 2011, 3 new lakeside chalets on stilts under thatch, with a wooden decking – & solar power – will come on line, too.

But to concentrate on the buildings is to miss the point. Chris is an interesting & knowledgeable guide, leading game drives, walks, boat trips & fishing with equal enthusiasm, & capable of enlivening anything from a lioness stalking her prey to an apparently inanimate termite mound. Konkamoya may not have all the bells & whistles, but this standard of guiding speaks for itself. *US$370 pp FBA.*

Å Hippo Bay Campsite [map 453] (2 pitches) Contact via Konkamoya, above. Well away from the lodge, Konkamoya's no-frills campsite is set back from the lake. There's a good solid ablution block with hot water, plus a supply of firewood & – a real bonus – drinking water, but otherwise campers need to be entirely self sufficient. They can, though, join in lodge activities for US$25 pp, ideally with advance notice. *US$25 pp.*

⌂ Nanzhila Plains Safari Camp [map 446] (6 chalets, camping) \ +267 2413740; e info@nanzhila.com; www.nanzhila.com. ◈ NANZHI 16°16.746'S, 25°55.074'E. In the remote south of the park, this comfortable camp is surrounded by woodland & plains. To the front, the large, grass-fringed Nangandwe Pool attracts good herds of game, including roan & sable antelope, defassa waterbuck, Lichtenstein's hartebeest & eland – which in turn draw predators such as wild dog & cheetah. Birdlife is good year round; look out in camp for paradise flycatchers & red-headed weaver birds, while the near-endemic black-cheeked lovebird is regularly spotted on game drives.

Most visitors arrive by air at Ngoma, followed by a 2hr game drive, but a new airstrip under construction in 2011 will be just a short walk from camp. To drive in you'll need a 4x4, & plenty of time. From the Musa gate, continue 22km to the park HQ at Ngoma, then follow the Cordon Rd, turning left after the airstrip for a further

35km to the Kalenji scout post, then right for a further 15km to camp. From the Dumdumwenze gate, follow the track for 3km to a fork; if it's dry, continue straight ahead to the east of the river, but when wet you *must* turn left & head north for 65km on the Cordon Rd, before turning right to the camp.

Facing the pool is an open-fronted thatched boma, raised up beneath a mature ebony tree (*Diospyros mespiliformisi*). With a lounge, dining area & extensive wooden deck, this is the focal point of the camp, its largely wicker furniture offset by comfy cushions & a selection of books. In the evenings, guests congregate by the firepit, before adjourning to a communal table for dinner.

To one side of the pool are 3 solidly built thatched chalets, each with an en-suite shower, toilet & twin washbasins, & a combination of netted windows & doors to allow a through breeze. Although not particularly spacious, they're furnished with care, to include dbl or twin hardwood beds & matching bedside tables under wraparound mosi nets, & good storage space. Opposite, 3 twin Meru-style tents under shadecloths offer a simpler alternative, with partially open en-suite facilities at the back, & the bonus of a small veranda overlooking the pool. Donkey boilers heat the water, & paraffin lamps add a slightly romantic touch, with a solar-powered generator useful for charging camera batteries etc – usually when guests are out of camp.

The campsite, upgraded in 2011 with flush toilets & proper showers, lies away from the chalets. By arrangement, campers can sometimes join in meals or activities at the lodge, but otherwise need to be entirely self sufficient, except for firewood.

Flexibility is the key here, with a series of loops for day & night drives, plus guided walks, & trips to Lake Itezhi-Tezhi or – by arrangement – to Shezongo village, the Elephant Orphanage or Ngoma Forest. In the winter months, Jul–Sep, bush b/fasts can also be organised. *US$350 pp sharing FBA, inc local drinks, park fees. Camping US$15 pp & park fees.* ⊕ *May–Nov.*

Places to visit in Southern Kafue Southern Kafue suits exploration in your own 4x4 well, so to concentrate on a few places to visit is really to miss the point. However, a few notable highlights are:

GPS co-ordinates ⊕	
AIRNGO	15°57.867'S 25°56.422'E
ELEPHO	15°58.044'S 28°51.632'E
KNPJ01	15°53.436'S 25°58.195'E
KNPJ02	15°54.142'S 25°57.623'E
KNPJ03	15°54.105'S 25°57.549'E
KNPJ04	15°55.290'S 25°54.238'E
KNPJ05	15°56.596'S 25°53.280'E
KNPJ06	15°57.043'S 25°53.033'E
KNPJ07	15°55.583'S 25°54.910'E
KNPJ08	15°57.076'S 25°56.872'E
KNPJ09	15°58.663'S 25°55.984'E
KNPJ10	16°01.204'S 25°54.591'E
KNPJ11	16°01.456'S 25°56.228'E
JNAMI1	15°51.410'S 25°58.228'E
JNAMI2	15°53.050'S 25°58.204'E
NGOMA	15°54.649'S 25°57.300'E
TUNAMW	15°53.894'S 25°57.854'E

Lake View Drive This area is home to some of the best game in the south, enticed in the dry season by lush grassy plains next to the lake. Protection of the game is afforded both by the presence of a new lodge, Konkamoya, and the proximity of the national park's Ngoma headquarters (⊕ NGOMA 15°54.649'S, 25°57.300'E), about 20km from the Itezhi-Tezhi Dam wall. At Ngoma itself, there are various offices and houses for the park's staff, and you can drop in, but it's not in great condition, and isn't really set up for visitors. About 5km south of here is an all-weather airstrip (⊕ AIRNGO 15°57.867'S, 25°56.422'E).

Ngoma Forest In the Ngoma area of the park's southern section, between two junctions (⊕ KNPJ07 15°55.583'S, 25°54.910'E and ⊕ KNPJ08 15°57.076'S, 25°56.872'E), is a fairly clearly signposted track that is seldom driven. This is a shame, as it weaves its way through the beautiful and intriguing Ngoma Forest which, when devoid of leaves at the end of the dry season, is decidedly eerie. It is made up of a dense stand of mature trees which are largely Zambezi teak (*Baikiaea plurijuga*); see box, page 455.

Elephant Orphanage (e *elephantorphanageproject@gmail.com; entry US$10/5 adult/child;* ☉ *guided tour 11.00 daily;* ⊕ ELEPHO 15°58.044'S, 25°51.632'E) The relatively new Elephant Orphanage (see box, page 454) is located just a few kilometres from the ZAWA headquarters at Ngoma, an area that has an established population of around a thousand wild elephants. It offers visitors the opportunity to watch and take photographs through viewing holes in a fence as the young herd returns to their 'boma' for lunch and a bathe. This isn't a place to get up close and personal with the elephants. Indeed, human contact is kept to

ELEPHANT ORPHANAGE PROJECT

Established in 2001 with the aim to 'rescue, rehabilitate and release' elephants orphaned as a result of human actions, such as poaching, the Elephant Orphanage Project is based on a similar model in Kenya run by Daphne Sheldrick. Under the auspices of the Zambian NGO Game Rangers International, and with the support of the David Shepherd Foundation (*www.davidshepherd.org/project/000002/elephant*), it is one aspect of three elephant-focused projects, which also include park protection and training, plus – crucially – education and awareness. In the long term, it is hoped to extend the remit to include both research and community development.

By the mid 2011, the unit comprised seven elephants, from the youngest, 11-month-olds Musa and Rufunsa, to the oldest, six-year-old Chidoba. They, like the others, were traumatised on arrival, having lost not just their mothers but also their social bonds within the herd, but with time and care they adapt to both their new companions and the strange environment. The little ones in particular receive protection from Chamilandu, who at just five years old is the only female currently here. Their keepers – ten of them working on a 24-hour rota – form part of a wider 'family' network, bottle-feeding the babies every three hours until they are weaned at around two–three years.

The elephants are up early, heading out into the bush at 06.00 with two keepers and a ZAWA scout, and returning only at lunchtime. The afternoon routine is similar, leaving at around 14.30 and returning at 18.00, which allows time for regular monitoring, ranging from measuring the orphans to checking the colour of their tongues as a guide to appetite. At night, for safety's sake, most of the youngsters are stabled, but as they grow new perimeter fences are being constructed to maintain their security.

Already, the youngsters are interacting with the wild population, although it is not until they reach maturity – and full independence – that they have a hope of being accepted into the herd. With an average maturation of around 15 years for males, and from nine to 15 for the females, this is a long-haul project, with each elephant expected to stay at the orphanage for at least ten years.

For those interested in helping, there's a programme (*US$1,500 pp FB*) through which volunteers spend a month working in pairs in the areas of community development and education – but emphatically not with the elephants. The project runs during the dry season only, between July and November.

an absolute minimum, in order to give the animals the best chance of survival when they are eventually returned to the wild. But if you'd like an opportunity to find out a little about the social systems of elephants, and the complexities of raising orphaned elephants with a view to releasing them back into the wild, then it's an interesting place to spend an hour or so. Note that it's important to arrive promptly at 11.00, so that you have time for a briefing and to don the regulation green coat before the elephants return from the bush.

Chilenje Pools Further south, several pools lie at the heart of two large, neighbouring grassy dambos which are a major attraction for game during the drier months. In theory there's a track going round this area; in practice you may have to make your own across a bumpy expanse of solidified mud.

Mufuta Loop West of Nanzhila Plains Safari Camp, this is another interesting game-drive loop that takes in more undulating terrain, fringed by woodland and dotted with pools that attract numerous waterbirds. Keep an eye out in particular for the magnificent sable antelope.

Nanzhila Plains If you're travelling through the south of the park, then two tracks run east–west. Take these towards the start of the dry season, and you'll often find yourself in plains with grass several metres tall, which is lovely but doesn't

---

THE DEMISE OF THE TEAK FORESTS

In the past, stands of teak forest probably covered fairly large areas of the Kalahari, and certainly of southwestern Zambia. They are comprised largely of Zambezi teak (*Baikiaea plurijuga*), previously called Rhodesian teak – a tree that occurs only in undisturbed areas of Kalahari sand in northern Botswana, northern Namibia, southern Angola and western Zambia. Now, however, this tree is severely threatened, its demise typical of that of several other hardwood species that were once common here, like *mukwa* (*Pterocarpus angolensis*), and rosewood (*Guibourtia coleosperma*).

Zambezi teak trees reach up to 20m in height, with a dense, spreading crown of leaves, and smooth, grey-brown bark. The trees flower from December to March, bearing lovely pinky-mauve flowers. Seedpods follow, from June to September, cracking open explosively to catapult their seeds a distance to the ground.

The tree's wood is dense and hard, but also very even-grained and strong. Although it has never had many traditional uses, as it was too hard to cut, it was a sought-after timber that was (and sadly is) commercially very valuable. It's been widely used for bridge-building and railway sleepers, and Coates Palgrave (see *Appendix 3*, page 536) reports that 'when the London corn exchange was rebuilt in 1952 a special grooved floor was designed to take the grain thrown down by the merchants, and *B. plurijuga* was selected for the parquet blocks because of its ability to withstand abrasion without splintering'.

Baikiaea plurijuga has been commercially logged in Zambia since around the start of the 20th century. Zambian timber production probably peaked in the 1930s, but by the 1960s huge tracts of teak forest had been lost. Now, although the export of *Baikiaea* logs is banned, export licences are still being issued for *Baikiaea* timber, predicated on (difficult-to-enforce) promises to leave a minimum number of the trees, and then not log the same area for 20 years.

Meanwhile, experts suggest that a 300-year cycle would be needed to allow the forests to regenerate. They note that fire is often used as a tool by loggers, to open up the dense under-storey of vegetation (known as *mutemwa*) in *B. plurijuga* forests, and that the debris left behind after logging will often lead to fires. *B. plurijuga* is particularly sensitive because its thin bark renders it very susceptible to fire; once burnt, these forests degrade forever and don't recover.

In recent years the poverty in the area, combined with major commercial pressures, has led to many of Zambia's remaining 'forest reserves' being degazetted, which then opens them up for commercial logging. So, sadly, a beautiful teak forest like Ngoma is an increasingly rare sight.

14

make for good game viewing. It's also surprisingly easy to get lost here! (Beware of inflammable seeds in your radiator – see *Driving through high grass*, on page 105.) Later in the year, when the grass dies back, visibility is excellent.

Within this area you'll also find woodland sections, tree-islands and even the odd lone baobab tree (*Adansonia digitata*). There are several pools here, too, which attract relatively large herds of game and some wonderful birdlife.

South of Nanzhila, however, the lack of wildlife tells a sorrier tale, with just the odd reedbuck putting in an appearance among the tree squirrels and hornbills; poaching in this area of the Kafue is a serious problem.

FURTHER INFORMATION The Kafue Trust has sponsored publication of *The Kafue National Park, Zambia – A Visitor's Handbook*, by Peter Moss, with photographs by Ian Murphy. For details, see *Appendix 3*, page 538.

LOCHINVAR AND BLUE LAGOON NATIONAL PARKS

Further down the Kafue's course, east of Ngoma, are two small national parks that encompass opposite sides of the Kafue River's floodplain. Their geography and ecosystems are very similar, but despite continuing efforts to rejuvenate both parks, their infrastructure has all but collapsed and wildlife has suffered heavily from poaching in the last few years.

Historically, both Blue Lagoon and Lochinvar have had populations of people living and farming around their borders, and often inside the park. Most are poor cattle herders, and probably aren't averse to supplementing their diets with (technically illegal) subsistence hunting. Their ancestors probably hunted here before these areas were either taken over as farms, or declared national parks; hence it could easily be argued that these lands belong more to these people than they do to ZAWA. Clearly any long-term solution needs to include these people – which is not an easy task.

Neither park receives many visitors, and those who do visit should arrive with their own supplies; there is currently no lodge accommodation or camping facilities here.

GEOGRAPHY Both parks are very flat, and the sections nearer the river are seasonally flooded. The resulting watery grassland reflects the sky like a mirror, for as far as you can see. It is quite a sight, and a remarkable environment for both animals and waterfowl.

In both parks you'll find a variety of quite clearly defined environments, as you move away from the waterways to the dry, permanent woodlands. Immediately beside the water, you'll find very large areas of open grassland which are seasonally flooded – a classic **floodplain** environment. On the drier side of this, where the grassland does not receive a regular annual flooding, termitaria can exist – with high solid mounds (often looking like chimneys) to keep their occupants safe from drowning in the occasional exceptional flood. This is a very distinct area in the grasslands, known as the **termitaria zone**.

Further away still, where there's absolutely no risk of flooding, you'll find a variety of trees in the woodlands which extend across the south of Lochinvar and the north of Blue Lagoon.

FLORA AND FAUNA

Flora The landscapes in both parks change with proximity to the river, especially above the 'high flood' line. Within parts of the termitaria zone you'll find some low bushes like the paperbark acacias (*Acacia sieberana*), zebrawoods (*Dalbergia* melanoxylon), fever trees (*Acacia xanthophloea*) and rough-leaved raisin bushes (*Grewia flavescens*). Drier patches here, such as the area around the tented camp, often have pretty acacia glades with large and shady white thorns (*Acacia polyocantha*) and smaller blue thorns (*Acacia erubescens*).

As the plains gradually merge into woodland, you'll find some of the typical species from *munga* woodlands (see *The Natural Environment*, page 30) including sickle-leafed albezias (*Albezi harveyi*), pepper-leafed commiphoras (*Commiphora mossambicensis*) and the distinctive woolly caper-bushes (*Caparis tormentosa*).

Slightly higher and further from the water, the tree-belt becomes more established and varied, containing different bands of mixed woodlands. The belts of mopane woodland are particularly distinctive, dominated by *Colophospermum mopane*, but also including leadwoods (*Combretum imberbe*), raintrees (*Lonchocarpus capassa*), and even the occasional knobthorn (*Acacia negrescens*).

Finally, well away from the water, you find stands of classic miombo woodland becoming the dominant environment – for example, as you travel south out of Lochinvar. (As an aside, it was interesting to see some notable specimens of Natal mahogany, *Trichilia emetica*, in this particular woodland.)

Fauna The very different bands of vegetation in these parks give rise to a wide variety of birds and animals – although this also means that some of the species found here are restricted to fairly small areas of the parks and so you need to move around if you're to have a chance of seeing a good range of them.

Animals Traditionally, the parks have been home to huge herds of Kafue lechwe – a little-known subspecies of the red lechwe, endemic to the Kafue's floodplain. Historically the Kafue lechwe used to occur here in enormous numbers. In the 1930s, population estimates suggested about 250,000 Kafue lechwe lived across the whole Kafue Flats area. By the 1950s an aerial survey put the population at about 95,000 lechwe. By 1988 this was revised down to 65,000, and in 1999 estimated the population as down to about 45,000. Since then, poaching has continued almost unabated; we have to move swiftly to conserve them, and their habitat.

Alongside the Kafue lechwe, many other species occur here – although all have reduced in numbers drastically over the last few decades. Typical of this area are buffalo, eland, roan, plains zebra, Lichtenstein's hartebeest, blue wildebeest, puku, reedbuck and the delightful, diminutive oribi antelope; whilst in the thickets on the edge of the plains you'll find kudu, baboon and vervet monkeys. That said, last reports were that reedbuck had disappeared from Blue Lagoon, and that bushbuck numbers were in single digits.

Birds The best season for birds on the Kafue's floodplain is probably around April/May, when the waters are at their highest levels. Then the resulting lagoons attract a great variety of migrant birds – giving a staggering spectacle of waterfowl. Often you'll find large numbers of just a couple of species in one area. This may be dominated by fulvous ducks, pratincoles, sandgrouse, or waders like sandpipers, avocets, ruff, Kittlitz's plovers, little stints and black-winged stilts. In the last ten years, Lochinvar has become a major wintering ground for black-tailed godwits, 3,000 or more of them. Lapwings – or plovers – are usually plentiful, including long-toed, crowned, white-crowned and the ubiquitous blacksmith.

Pelicans are always around, both white and pink backed, and sometimes so are small numbers of flamingos. Cranes, both wattled and crowned, are there, usually in flocks of a hundred or more, plus spoonbills and a variety of storks and ibises

14

(notably sacred and glossy). In both parks the best areas for watching waterbirds are unpredictable. They depend on the water levels, which in turn depend on the flood regime of the Itezhi-Tezhi Dam upstream.

However, during the early rains, the grasslands are always full of harlequin quails, Luapula cisticolas, Ethiopian snipe, yellow-crowned bishops and a sprinkling of streaky-breasted flufftails. Later in the season when the plains are dry, secretary birds pace around in pairs, whilst in the air are plenty of raptors – bateleur, martial and African hawk eagles, plus brown and black-breasted snake eagles. Amongst the thousands of lechwe there are always recent deaths, so there are four species of vulture present, plus large numbers of marabou storks.

LOCHINVAR NATIONAL PARK (*Park fees US$10 pp/day; vehicle US$15/day*) Lochinvar's northern boundary is the Kafue River. The land on which the park stands was originally obtained from the local Chief Hamusende in around 1908 by a Mr Horne, a man known locally as 'the Major'. Horne was a Scottish cattle farmer from Botswana who registered the land on behalf of the British South Africa Company, and built the old Lochinvar Lodge as his farmhouse.

Previously little of this land had been used for farming because of the game here, including lion and leopard. To convert the land into a cattle ranch, Horne set about exterminating these. In a ruthless programme of annihilation, populations of sable, roan, eland, warthog and wildebeest were wiped out, as well as lion – the last of which is thought to have been killed in 1947.

However, in 1966 Lochinvar Ranch (as it was then called) was bought by the Zambian government with the help of a grant from the WWF, and converted into a GMA; but the extra protection afforded to the wildlife by this designation was not enough to prevent its numbers from diminishing further, and so in 1972 Lochinvar was upgraded to a national park.

Subsequently the park has been designated as a 'wetland of international importance', and at one point a WWF team was working with the local people to help manage the park on a sustainable basis.

There are a lot of settlements around Lochinvar, and local people still come into the park – as they have done for centuries. Many were unhappy with Lochinvar Ranch – and have always felt that this is their land. They come to gather wild foods and fish, and even to drive their cattle from one side to the other; so although major conservation efforts are being made in Lochinvar, building up the diversity and number of game species here is not an easy task.

Getting there Lochinvar is easiest to approach from Monze, on the Livingstone–Lusaka road – about 287km from Livingstone and 186km from Lusaka. The road that heads northwest from Monze, signposted for Namwala, is just north of the grain silos on the Lusaka side of town. From town head for the point ✪ TULOCH 16°15.465'S, 27°28.632'E.

It passes Chongo village and forks (✪ T2LOCH 16°10.054'S, 27°23.610'E) about 8km afterwards. Ask local advice to find this junction if necessary. Take the right fork, or you will end up in Kafue. Follow this road for about 10km and then turn left at another sign (✪ TULV14 16°3.718'S, 27°22'E). It is then about 14km to the park gate. This last section of the track twists and turns, but all the tracks that split off eventually rejoin each other and lead to the park. There are also a few more signs so, if you become unsure, ask a local person and they'll show you the way. The gate to Lochinvar (✪ LOGATE 16°0.737'S, 27°15.569'E) is about 48km from Monze.

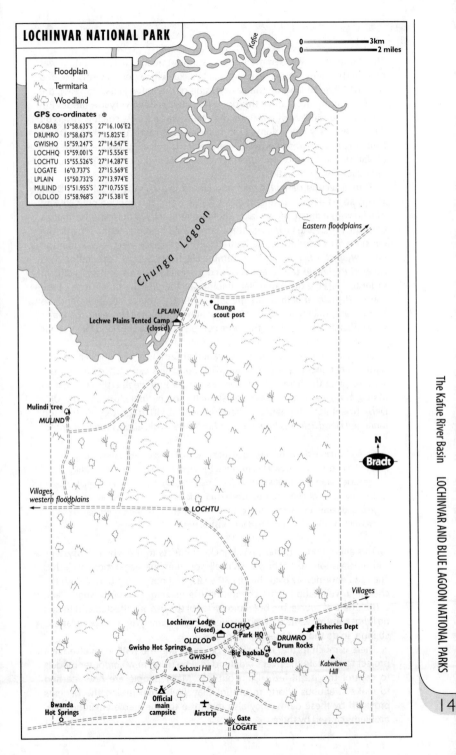

LOCHINVAR NATIONAL PARK

Floodplain
Termitaria
Woodland

GPS co-ordinates ⊕

BAOBAB	15°58.635'S	27°16.106'E2
DRUMRO	15°58.637'S	7°15.825'E
GWISHO	15°59.247'S	27°14.547'E
LOCHHQ	15°59.001'S	27°15.556'E
LOCHTU	15°55.526'S	27°14.287'E
LOGATE	16°0.737'S	27°15.569'E
LPLAIN	15°50.732'S	27°13.974'E
MULIND	15°51.955'S	27°10.755'E
OLDLOD	15°58.968'S	27°15.381'E

Kafue

0 ————— 3km
0 ————— 2 miles

Chunga Lagoon

Eastern floodplains

LPLAIN ⊕
Lechwe Plains Tented Camp
(closed)

● Chunga
scout post

Mulindi tree
MULIND ⊕

N

Bradt

Villages,
western floodplains

⊕ LOCHTU

Villages

Lochinvar Lodge
(closed)   LOCHHQ
OLDLOD ⊕   ⊕ Park HQ   ⚑ Fisheries Dept
Gwisho Hot Springs ⊕   DRUMRO
GWISHO   Big baobab ⊕ Drum Rocks
Big baobab⊕ *BAOBAB*
▲ Sebanzi Hill   *Kabwibwe*
Hill

Bwanda
Hot Springs ○   Ⓐ
Official
main
campsite   ✈
Airstrip   Gate
⊕ LOGATE

The Kafue River was dammed in two stages. Initially, in 1971, a dam was built in the Kafue Gorge, just south of Lusaka, which permanently flooded 800–1,100km^2 of land on the eastern side of the Kafue Flats. However, the gradient of the river above this point had always been very low (about 8m drop in over 200km of river), so the result was a huge, shallow reservoir with a relatively low volume (785 million cubic metres). The Kafue Dam's primary purpose was to provide hydro-electric power: it supplies up to 75% of Zambia's electricity. To guarantee this it needed a reservoir which was effectively larger than this.

Thus a second dam was built and closed in 1977: the Itezhi-Tezhi Dam. This is about 450km upstream of the Kafue Dam, and flooded only 300km^2 of land with a much deeper lake – holding about 4,925 million cubic metres of water. Hence the flow from Itezhi-Tezhi could be regulated to provide the constant flow needed by the Kafue Dam to generate electricity. When the dams were constructed, ZESCO (Zambia Electricity Supply Corporation) was obliged to ensure that there was a continuous flow out of Itezhi-Tezhi, in order to preserve the Kafue Flats habitat, and service the other users of the water. (The largest of these are the sugar industry around Mazabuka, and the municipality of Lusaka, which extracts water for the city.) However, this was a very difficult task – made all the more complex because the flood takes about six weeks to get from Itezhi-Tezhi to the Kafue Dam.

Before the dams, the river's flow varied enormously with the season: the Kafue Flats flooded every year and the floodplains experienced a long dry season. Since the dams, ZESCO has released a four-week artificial 'flood' in March, but clearly it has failed to simulate the natural situation. The UK's Department for International Development (DFID) reported in 2001 on *Managed Flood Releases from the Itezhi-Tezhi Reservoir*, and within that noted:

> Since the dams, the flooding pattern has changed considerably. There has been a reduction in the seasonal fluctuations. The annual minimum flood area has increased from about 300km^2 to approximately 1,500km^2. In places permanent lagoons have formed where ephemeral aquatic habits had existed before.
> In broad terms, the western half of the Flats is drier, whilst the eastern half is wetter than they were prior to dam construction.

This altered flood pattern has knock-on effects to the whole ecosystem. Old-time visitors to Lochinvar will tell you that the vegetation there has changed enormously over the last 30 years, and not for the better. With the change in vegetation come changes in the grazing – for both wildlife and cattle. Then, of course, the breeding cycles of the fish are affected and there's no longer any movement of fish upriver past the dams. When fish populations change, so do those of many bird species.

There is much further research to be done, and the WWF is involved in a project to simulate the river's old flood regime using new computer models to control the Itezhi-Tezhi Dam outflow. Many people are now starting to make strenuous efforts to ensure that whilst maximising the benefits provided by these dams, they also minimise the inevitable environmental problems caused by them.

Maps An excellent (albeit very out of date) 1:50,000 visitors' map to Lochinvar was published by the surveyor general in 1986, and is still available at their main office in Lusaka. It indicates the vegetation types and also gives photographs and short descriptions of some of the park's interesting features and wildlife. Most of the 'camps' depicted are now disused, and some of the roads now seem as if they were figments of a cartographer's imagination.

Where to stay

The original red-brick Lochinvar Lodge, built in the colonial style of 1912, was used as a farmhouse until 1966, when it was sold to the government. As the state of the park gradually deteriorated, the lodge was put up for tender to private safari operators in 1996. Eventually, Star of Africa agreed to take it as part of a 'package' of old government properties around the country. Renovating it would have been a huge job, so instead they built a tented camp (✪ LPLAIN 15°50.732'S, 27°13.974'E) which, for a while, was the only camp or lodge in the park. In 2007, the camp was taken over by Sanctuary Lodges & Camps, but since then it has remained closed.

Camping Until Lechwe Plains Tented Camp is re-opened, your only option is to camp, for which you will need all your own supplies. There have been several sites here, but it's best to ask the scouts at the gate for the latest news. To reach what was the official campsite, drive about 2km past the gate into the park, and take the second left turning. Continue for about 5km. This site in theory has water, a long-drop toilet and a simple cold shower, with firewood and a barbecue provided. It is close to the hot springs at Bwanda, near the old Lupanda Wildlife Camp. If you wish to pick up a scout from the gate to guide you, then it's advisable to arrange this in advance.

What to see and do

With the rapid depletion of the game, the birds are the main attraction at Lochinvar. The best birding is generally close to the water, on the floodplain. For this it's probably best to walk north and east from Mulindi Tree or north of Chunga towards Hippo Corner. It's vital to avoid driving anywhere that's even vaguely damp on the floodplain as your vehicle will just slip through the crust and into the black-cotton soil – which will probably spoil and extend your stay in equal measure. A few sites to note include:

Lochinvar Lodge (✪ OLDLOD 15°58.968'S, 27°15.381'E) This is the site of the old farmhouse built by Horne, and later the old government-run lodge. There are plans to renovate this dilapidated, crumbling old building. It does have superb views over the park, and with a lot of work, and money, a lodge here would be an attractive option. However, until enough people come to Lochinvar to make even the tented camp economically viable, it's likely to remain an evocative old ruin.

Gwisho Hot Springs (✪ GWISHO 15°59.247'S, 27°14.547'E) Gwisho Hot Springs are near the southern edge of the park. To get here drive from the main gate to the old lodge, and then turn sharp left immediately in front of the old lodge's gates. From the campsite, drive north out of the camp and turn right towards Sebanzi Hill, following the edge of the plain. After about 2.5km turn left at a stone cairn and palms. The springs are signposted, and just a few kilometres further on, about 2km west of the old lodge.

The springs were formed by a geological fault which stretches along the southern end of the park, on the edge of the Kafue Flats Basin. Associated with this is a deposit of gypsum, the mineral used to make plaster of paris, which was mined at

Gwisho from 1973 to 1978. You can follow the white rocks which mark this fault from Bwanda Hot Springs past the old campsite and Sebanzi Hill through Gwisho Hot Springs to the lodge, and past Drum Rocks.

The water which wells up into these springs has been heated far below the surface, and thus is independent of the rainfall or local surface water conditions. It varies from about 60°C to 94°C, and contains a high concentration of sodium, chlorine, calcium and sulphates.

The thick vegetation around the springs is surrounded by a picturesque stand of real fan palms (*Hyphaene petersiana*), whose small fruits, when opened, are seen to have a hard kernel known as 'vegetable ivory'. In the thick, wet vegetation here keep a lookout for birding 'specials' including black coucal and Fülleborn's longclaw. Also look out for the stand of knarled old trees on the rocks at the top of the small rise beside the springs. These may look a little like deformed baobabs, but they are in fact African star-chestnut trees (*Sterculia africana*).

In the early 1960s, when the remains of late Stone-Age settlements were excavated here, it was described as one of the best-preserved and oldest sites in southern Africa. Among the findings were Arab-style trading beads, suggesting that the local inhabitants had traded the salt collected here far and wide, possibly as far as east Africa. Some artefacts discovered here are on display at Livingstone Museum.

Talk to the local people and they will tell you that the Gwisho area was the location of several fierce battles between the Tonga/Ila people and the Batwa, with hundreds of men being killed at a time – hence the existence of several mass burial sites nearby.

Bwanda Hot Springs Bwanda Hot Springs lie in the southwest of the park, surrounded by a large area of reed beds. They're quite close to Limpanda scout camp, and so are often used for bathing and washing by the local people – and even sometimes as a place to water their cattle.

Sebanzi Hill This national monument marks the position of an Iron-Age village on the top of the hill, which was excavated during the 1960s. Archaeologists say it has been inhabited for most of the last millennium. Originally known as Ko-Banza, the village continued to exist right up to the first half of the 20th century when the villagers were evicted, presumably by the ranch owners. Looking out from this site you have an excellent view over the park and the springs, and hence realise why it was a strategically important site in times of turmoil.

The giant baobab on Sebanzi is said to be 2,500 years old, and is often used by nesting white-backed vultures. There are also said to be some caves in the side of the hill, though these are now hidden behind deep, impenetrable thicket. The hill is still probably home to some threatened southern African species, including pangolin and aardvark, as well as hyenas, jackals, bush pig, bushbuck and small wildcats. Notable birds often seen here include the African broadbill.

Drum Rocks Close to the lodge, in the south of the park, is an outcrop of rocks (⊕ DRUMRO 15°58.635'S, 27°16.106'E) that echo when tapped, producing a curious, resonant, almost metallic sound. These are the Drum Rocks, or Ibbwe Lyoombwa in the local language. Ask the scouts to direct you to these: they are fascinating. (Similar rocks, on the farm called Immenhof, in Namibia, were originally discovered by San/ Bushmen and are now known locally as the 'singing rocks'.)

Considered sacred by the locals, these rocks are actually just the remnants of much larger boulders that were dynamited by the ranch's owners, curious to know the secret of their sound. They play an important part in the local religious calendar. As part of an elaborate rite of passage, it is traditional for a young man to come with his cattle to the rocks, chant '*Ibbwe Lyoombwa*' and then perform a dance and various rituals designed to prove his manliness. At the end, he should leave with his cattle without turning back, for fear of seeing his dead ancestors, and then stay away from his village until the beginning of the rains. If he has proved himself sufficiently, he will then be considered an adult and will be able to take a bride on his return. Even today, visitors are supposed to chant '*Ibbwe Lyoombwa*' to prevent bad luck befalling them.

Nearby is a large baobab ($\oplus$ BAOBAB 15°58.637'S, 27°15.825'E) with a completely hollow trunk that can be entered from a crack in the side (which is the size of a small doorway). According to Chief Hamusende, the hollow was formed by an old man who, given a magic club, decided to try it out by bashing it against a nearby baobab; a broken tree and the formation of the hollow were the result of his experiment. It was actually used as a shelter by the district commissioner during the 1800s, and local legend has it that anybody who refuses to believe in the customs and beliefs of the villagers will enter into the hollow and never return, the tree sealing up and closing behind them.

Chunga This group of large winterthorn trees (*Acacia albida*), is roughly where the main track meets the lagoon. It's the site of the old wildlife camp, and a good spot to camp provided you don't mind being disturbed by the odd vehicle.

Mwanachingwala Conservation Area

Although east of the national park boundary, Mwanachingwala lies in a similar environment to Lochinvar National Park, but is normally accessed from Mazabuka. For details, see page 218.

BLUE LAGOON NATIONAL PARK

(*US$10 pp/day; vehicle US$15/day*) Blue Lagoon is on the north side of the Kafue River. It was originally owned by a farming couple turned conservationists, the Critchleys, but more recently, especially during KK's reign, the Ministry of Defence restricted access to the military, plus a few privileged politicians and generals who used the old farmhouse intermittently as a hunting retreat – with predictable impact on the local wildlife.

Since then, the team from Mukambi Safari Lodge in Kafue have been working with the WWF to try and resuscitate the park. Given that the environment is still in reasonable shape, and the natural flooding regime of the river can be re-established, it is hoped that there is every chance of success in the long term. However, the park's Nakeenda Lodge has been closed since 2007, so the future remains uncertain. Reports suggest that many of the park's trails are very overgrown and that, while the birding is excellent, and antelope are to be seen near the lagoons, other wildlife is little in evidence.

Getting there Blue Lagoon is reasonably well signposted, and there are several ways to reach it. Note, however, that it's not possible to reach it from the south, unless you're arriving by boat during the floods!

From Lusaka The easiest route from Lusaka is to take the Great West Road towards Mumbwa, then turn left after about 22km, opposite the filling station. This all-weather gravel road leads to the national park's scout camp at Naleeza. If you're heading for Nakeenda Lodge (currently closed) then follow the sign left.

From the west From the west, pass through Kafue's Nalusanga scout post and about 81km from here, beyond Mumbwa, look for a Total garage near Nangoma.

BLUE LAGOON NATIONAL PARK

Fill up here, then continue towards Lusaka for a few hundred metres, before taking the first right turn after the filling station, following the power lines. In less than a kilometre, turn right at the crossroads and keep following those power lines! (This junction is on a local bus route, so if you ask directions you will probably end up with a guide and their luggage; a fair deal all round!) Continuing for 9km brings you to Myooye village, where you should take the left fork that passes the clinic on the right-hand side.

Follow this track for 31km to a T-junction, ignoring smaller side tracks. (If the group of huts on the left, halfway along this road, has a flag flying, it means that the Tonga chief who lives here is in residence.) Turn right at the T-junction, and continue for 22km, ignoring a right-hand turn, passing through the first gate and finally reaching the scout post. Sign in here, pay the park and camping fees, and check the current camping rules with the scouts.

Where to stay The only place to stay in the park, the old-style self-catering Nakeenda Lodge, has been closed for some years. Located behind the Critchleys' simple farmhouse and right next to the old causeway, its thatched, en-suite chalets had lovely views over the flats.

With luck it will be just be a matter of time before this is re-opened, but in the meantime it may be worth asking one of the scouts at the gate if you can camp at one of the old national park sites.

What to see and do The park is dominated by the Kafue Flats, which are flooded in the rainy season. This is certainly the best time for birdwatching here, and the park is generally at its best. In the dry season the view is not as stunning but still worth a visit.

The Critchleys built a causeway that extends for about 5km over the marshy flats, enabling a vehicle to drive out onto the flats for a wonderful view of the stunning birdlife; there's even a turning circle at the end. Along the causeway are several memorial stones, one reading:

> Erica Critchley 1910–1976
> To the memory of the
> one who loved Zambia
> so much she cared for
> human and natural resources.
> Let what she stood for
> not be forgotten by Zambians
> especially by its youth.
>
> Kenneth Kaunda
> President of Zambia
> March 30 1976

In the dry season, when the end of the causeway doesn't usually reach the water, a ranger from the scout post will take you on walks around the flats. Aside from the wildlife, do visit the old farmhouse that used to be owned by the Critchleys. It's fascinating.

14

DEMOCRATIC REPUBLIC OF THE CONGO

1527m ▲

Ikelenge ● Nchila Wildlife Reserve
NCHILA ● Source of Zambezi

1457m ▲

MWINIL ● MWINILUNGA

ANGOLA

1414m ▲

West Lunga

Ntambu

Solwezi

1194m ▲

West Lunga NP

Kabompo

Kasempa, Solwezi

M8

1371m ▲

JIVUND
Jivundu ● Mufumbwe
TUJIVU

1219m ▲

Kasempa

Chavuma

TUCHIN

Chinyingi Mission
CHINYI

ZAMBEZ ● Zambezi

KABOMP ● TUMWIN

1094m ▲

MUMBEJ

KABOMPO

Dongwe

1178m ▲

Watopa pontoon

WATOPA

1073m ▲

Lungwebungu

SANCTA

Lukulu pontoon ● Lukulu

Liuwa Plain National Park

Barotse Tiger Camp
○ Mbanga

Libonda pontoon

Luena

Kaoma

M9

Lusaka

HARKAL
Kalabo

Barotseland floodplain

LIMULU
Limulunga

LEALUI
MONGU
Lealui ● MONGU

Kafue National Park

FERRY3

Sandaula

Luanginga

Southern Lueti

Lui

0 — 80km
0 — 50 miles

Luampa

Kataba

Luanja

SENANG ● SENANGA
Pontoon

Kalongola
Sitoti

FERRY2
Pontoon

Shangombo

Kwando

TUSHAN

Mbeta Island

Njoko

NPSIOM
Sioma

Ngonye Falls NP
Maziba Bay
Kavumbu

Mulobezi

1109m ▲

Sioma River Camp

KABULA
Kalabolelwa

Kabula

MUTEMW
Mutemwa

Ngambwe Rapids

Nina Lodge
Sakazima

Zambelozi

Shackletons

ANGOLA

Sioma Ngwezi National Park

Katima Zambia

SESHEK ● SESHEKE

M10

Katima Mulilo

Livingstone
Kazungula

○ Imusho

Pontoon ●

WESTERN ZAMBIA

NAMIBIA

15

Western Zambia

This remote area of western Zambia is difficult to visit but can reward intrepid travellers with some of the country's most interesting experiences. The Barotse floodplains, near Mongu, offer a glimpse of rural Zambian life that is still largely untouched by the 21st century, while Liuwa Plain National Park has excellent game and few visitors. It may be the venue for one of Africa's last great wildlife migrations, or 'gatherings', which has remained largely unknown because of the difficulty of getting into the area. Other parks, Sioma Ngwezi and West Lunga, do not have the same reputation for wildlife, but Sioma Ngwezi at least is still a very wild place to explore with a well-prepared group of 4x4 vehicles.

Common to almost the whole area are the related problems of supplies and transport. Much of the region stands on deep Kalahari sand where vehicles need a high-clearance 4x4 capability. If you are going off the main roads, then a small expedition is needed consisting of several vehicles, in case one runs into problems. During the rainy season, many of the roads are impassable, and even the pontoons (ferries) across the rivers will often stop working. Being stranded is a very real possibility. Thus the area's paucity of visitors is largely explained by the sheer difficulty of getting around.

The Christian missions have a very well-established network here. On the whole, these do remarkable work for the communities in the area, being involved with schools, hospitals, churches, development projects and many other aspects of local life. The courteous traveller can learn a lot about the region from these missions, and they are also good places to find English-speaking guides to accompany you on your travels – who will prove invaluable for just a few dollars per day.

I've divided this chapter into three sections: southwestern Zambia, Barotseland and northwestern Zambia. These don't slavishly follow provincial divisions; rather they reflect the differences between the areas as I understand them and are a convenient way to organise the text. I have also written the first part of the chapter, through southwestern Zambia, as a tour, starting from the border towns of Kazungula and Sesheke, and continuing north up the Zambezi to Mongu.

SOUTHWESTERN ZAMBIA

Compared with the rest of Zambia, the southwest of the country has been largely neglected, with few roads (which are generally poor) and no major towns. This does mean that its sights, like the marvellous Ngonye Falls, are very quiet. However, with the arrival of the long-awaited tar road running parallel to the Upper Zambezi and investment in Sioma Ngwezi National Park this region is set to see an increase in visitors.

The big draw of the Upper Zambezi, and the *raison d'être* of the camps along the river, has always been fishing – for bream and tigerfish. While an increasing numbers of visitors are coming for other attractions, such as Ngonye Falls and the excellent birdlife, it is fishing that retains the greatest appeal.

HIGHLIGHTS

Fishing on the Upper Zambezi The Zambezi River here is generally wide, although in parts of its course between Sesheke and Senanga it becomes shallow, broken by forested islands and rocky outcrops, and you'll also find waterfalls and rapids. So there are conditions suitable for challenging fly-fishing and spinning.

Tigerfish are the most sought-after challenge, whilst various bream species, particularly the predatory yellow-belly and the thin-face breams, make good sport fishing in the faster sections. In the slower sections, fishermen find the more sedentary three-spot, red-breast and greenhead bream.

Birdlife For a more gentle interaction with some of the wildlife, this area offers some excellent, undisturbed birdwatching – with various species frequenting different areas of the river and the surrounding vegetation. A few of the river's 'specials' include rock pratincoles, seen darting about the rocks of many sections of rapids; African finfoots, which lurk at the water's edge in areas of thick, overhanging vegetation; African skimmers, which nest on some of the river's exposed sandbanks; and Pel's fishing owls resting in some of the old riverine trees. You'll also have the chance to spot Schalow's and Lady Ross's turacos, yellow-spotted nicator, narina trogon and wood owls (the Mutemwa Lodge area is particularly good for these).

WEST TO SESHEKE There's an excellent tarred road, the M10, running parallel to the Zambezi from Livingstone to Sesheke. After 63km, a turning left leads after nearly 3km to the small border town of Kazungula. Continuing past this turning brings you to Sesheke, where there's a bridge over the Zambezi, and a border post with Namibia.

Kazungula This small town marks the location of a **ferry** over the Zambezi into Botswana (⊕ *06.00–18.00*). This can take just one truck and two or three cars at a time, so can get very busy. As well as a fee of around US$25 per vehicle, depending on size, there are all sorts of other paperwork (and payment) required – insurance, immigration, car import permit, carbon and road tax, police levy – so it's often worth enlisting the help of one of the many 'agents' who are likely to hassle you. And be prepared with plenty of cash.

On the main M10 road, just before the turn-off, the Kazungula Reststop offers snacks and more substantial dishes to passing travellers. Then, just before the ferry itself, there are a few **shops**, a small **market** (⊕ *early–18.00 daily*) and the simple Zipazi **restaurant**. This is also where local buses stop.

Getting there and away A twice-daily bus service run by Mazhandu Family Bus links Livingstone with Sesheke. If you're heading for Botswana, then hop on one of these and get off at Kazungula; you can expect to pay around Kw30,000 from Livingstone, or Kw40,000 from Sesheke. The ferry to Botswana is a good place to hitchhike. After that, to get into Kasane or to head for Nata, you should walk the short distance to the disease control post, which makes a perfect hitchhiking spot as vehicles have to stop here anyway.

Where to stay Kazungula itself has nowhere of note to stay, but there are a couple of fishing lodges to the west that welcome visitors:

🏠 **Sekoma Island Lodge** (9 tents) m +27 83 708 3787; e info@sekoma.co.za, sekoma. island@gmail.com; www.sekoma.co.za. ⊕ SEKOMA 17°44.900'S, 25°10.533'E. Set on an island of the Zambezi near the Mambova Rapids, Sekoma is well placed for the angler in search of tigerfish or Zambezi catfish (all catch & release), while outside the fishing season it attracts keen birders, with walks & boat trips available. The lodge is accessible only by boat from Mambova village; to drive to the jetty, turn off the main road about 5km west of Kazungula & follow this for about 5.5km. Safari-style twin tents (& 1 for families) are right on the river, each with a small porch, & a tiled bathroom at the back, & – during the fishing season (May–Sep) – each allocated a speedboat & guide. There's a riverside deck, too, & a large, cool dining room. *R1,980 pp (SA rand) FBA, exc bar, fishing tackle & transfers.* ⊕ *mid May–mid Jan.*

🏠 **Shackletons Lodge** (6 chalets, 5 tents) m 0977 934149; e info@shackletons.co.za; www.shackletons.co.za. ⊕ SOKACA 17°29.793'S, 24°46.519'E. Around 170km from Livingstone, or 55km east of Sesheke, Shackletons lies 3.5km down an easily navigable sandy track (turn-off ⊕ TUSOKA 17°28.010'S, 24°46.948'E), overlooking an island beside the Zambezi. Beyond are wide floodplains, typical of the seasonally flooded eastern end of Namibia's Caprivi Strip.

En-suite twin chalets with netted windows are solidly built under thatch & overlook the river from their wooden verandas. Further back, simple walk-in tents share an ablution block. At the heart of the lodge, the split-level main building incorporates a lounge, dining area & riverside bar, with a fire & small pool nearby & a deck over the river shaded by an ebony tree. It's a relaxed, unpretentious place, with the emphasis firmly on fishing, but there are river cruises & plenty of birding opportunities, too. *Chalet US$320 pp sharing FB, inc fishing (20 litres fuel), exc drinks & transfers; tent US$75 pp DBB.* ⊕ *Apr–Dec, depending on floods.*

Sesheke Sesheke sits on the eastern side of the Zambezi River, linked by a 900m bridge to a smaller town on the other side, known locally as Katima Zambia. The bridge, financed largely by Germany, was opened in 2004 by the presidents of Zambia and Namibia. It lies about 5km inside Zambian territory, and was only the fifth bridge to span the width of the Zambezi – the others being the road bridges at Chirundu, Tete and Livingstone, and the footbridge at Chinyingi Mission. (A sixth bridge, just south of Ngonye Falls, has now reached the drawing board, and a seventh – at Kazungula – is also in the pipeline.)

Sesheke itself (⊕ 17°28.599'S, 24°17.208'E), has a few **stores**, a small branch of the Finance **Bank**, a simple hospital, a police station (listen for their early-morning marching songs if you're staying overnight!), a **post office** and a few small **guesthouses**. There's also a **fuel** station here – although fuel is considerably cheaper across the border in Namibia's Katima Mulilo. Supplies are more plentiful there, too, so Sesheke can be very quiet.

The smaller Katima Zambia, right next to the border with Namibia, has just a police post, a small market and a few local stores.

Getting there and away Sesheke is easily reached from either Livingstone or Katima Mulilo, in Namibia, on excellent tarred roads. There's a twice-daily bus service from Livingstone, costing Kw55,000 one way, with onward connections to Lusaka (*Kw95,000*) and Kitwe (*Kw150,000*).

If you're driving from Livingstone to Sesheke, read *Driving west* in *Chapter 8*, page 161. Access to or from the north, until recently, was challenging, but with tarring of the road expected to be finished in 2012, this is set to improve dramatically.

Western Zambia SOUTHWESTERN ZAMBIA

15

469

Where to stay Sesheke's limited accommodation options are both unsophisticated and correspondingly inexpensive, with the best being Brenda's Baobab. If you're driving yourself, you'll find several lodges along the river, both to the east of town (page 469) and on the way north to Ngonye Falls (see below).

Brenda's Baobab (4 chalets, camping) Mulambwe St; m 0979 011917; ⊕ SESHES 17°28.833'S, 24°17.571'E. Popular with backpackers, this unexpected gem is just over 1km east of the town centre, opposite the hospital, & accessed down a drive between the civic centre & St Kizito Roman Catholic Church. It's owned by Brenda & her husband, a Dutch GP, who travel regularly to Europe, & their en-suite chalets under high thatch are certainly the best rooms in town – with a fridge, TV & fan. Down by the river are grassy lawns dotted with shady picnic tables & a campsite. Nearby are clean

toilets & showers, & an expanse of wooden decking around a large central baobab. They'll serve food, drinks, & an eclectic range of beers drawn from Namibia, Zambia & South Africa. **$$** *Camping Kw30,000 pp.*

Sisheke Lodge (9 rooms) ☎ 0211 481086. On the left as you drive into Sesheke from Kazungula, & just before the fuel station, this friendly place has simple but clean en-suite rooms. There's a lounge, porch area & dining room, with a self-catering kitchen a useful add-on; if you bring your own food, they'll even cook it for you. **$**

DRIVING NORTH FROM SESHEKE TO NGONYE FALLS The road north from Sesheke follows the western bank of the river for 190km, as far as Sitoti. Even by Zambian standards it's exceptionally poor. In late 2010, what remained of the gravel was fissured with pot-holes, some filled with patches of deep sand, and a high-clearance 4x4 was essential.

By the time you read this, however, the long-overdue tar road along this section should finally have come to fruition. Originally expected to open in 2008, it has been beset with delays, but by spring 2011 the new surface was complete as far as Nina Lodge, and 2012 should see the whole section tarred. In time, it is anticipated that a new bridge will be built over the Zambezi just south of Ngonye Falls, taking the road over to the eastern bank at that point, then continuing north to meet the tar road at Senanga. In reality, though, construction of the bridge is unlikely for at least another three years.

Aside from the perennial appeal of the fishing, and other river-based excursions, the main reasons for visiting this area of southwest Zambia are the Ngonye Falls (often referred to as the Sioma Falls; see pages 475–6) and the Sioma Ngwezi National Park, which lies to the west of the river, and is expected to be encompassed within the new KAZA park (see page 473). With travel further north often being very slow, this is also a good area to break the journey for a few days on your way north or south.

Where to stay Along the Upper Zambezi, between Sesheke and Ngonye Falls, you'll pass signposts to several places to stay – primarily fishing camps. The following are listed in the order in which they are encountered when driving north from Sesheke. Note that about 17km north of Sesheke bridge you'll come to a fork in the road (⊕ RDFORK 17°21.956'S, 24°09.064'E); keep to the left – unless you're heading for the sawmill!

Sakazima Island Lodge (7 bungalows, camping) ☎ +264 662573; m +264 811 2466; e tutwa@mweb.com.na; sakazima@tiscali.co.za; www.sakazima.co.za. ⊕ TUSAKA 17°17.868'S,

24°08.230'E. Some 2hrs' drive from Livingstone, down a 2.5km track about 26km north of Sesheke, this small, peaceful fishing camp was under new management in 2010. It is built on a group of 5 islands in the Zambezi, with its own campsite on the mainland. The original owners were careful not to remove any of the island's trees when building the lodge, & there's still a lush, tropical feel about the place – lots of wild date palms (*Phoenix reclinata*), African mangosteens (*Garcinia livingstonei*), ebonies (*Diospyros mespiliformis*), knobthorns (*Acacia nigrescens*) & the occasional pod mahogany (*Afzelia quanzensis*). Whole groups can book the lodge on a self-catering basis.

Each of the reed-&-brick bungalows has a wooden deck above the river, & an en-suite shower, washbasin & separate toilet at the back, with water heated by individual gas boilers. The main dining area & bar are entirely of wood, with a small river-water plunge pool on the deck in front, plus a firepit & a couple of shaded hammocks. The lodge offers great fly-fishing opportunities on the rapids & the birding is good, too. Mokoro trips, short nature drives in the nearby bush, guided birding walks & day trips to Ngonye Falls & Livingstone can be booked in advance. *R1,100 pp sharing FB inc sunset cruise. Self catering R550 pp. Camping R100 pp (all rates in South African rand).* ⊕ *All year.*

🏠 **Nina Lodge & Fishing Camp** (6 rooms, 2 houses, camping) m 0979 571407; e ninafishing@gmail.com; www.ninafishing. com. ⊕ TUNINA 17°12.340'S, 24°05.387'E. Some 43.5km from Sesheke, or 11km north of Lusu Mission, Nina's overlooks the Lusu Rapids within the proposed KAZA park. Owned & run by Nicky & Dalene Rossouw, it's a rather ramshackle self-catering camp, with a range of accommodation & a bar, plus a simple new restaurant. Flooding in 2010 caused significant damage to the 2-bedroom house & self-contained fishing camp – with its own kitchen & 4 bedrooms – but these & the campsite were being rebuilt when we visited. (You can still camp on their private island, or use this for a picnic or dinner.) Over the rapids are 2 stone-built rooms with gauzed windows, homemade furniture & contemporary bedding, & sharing a kitchen. A 3-bedroom family house with 2 bathrooms & a deck was in hand for 2011. Most guests come for the fishing (tackle can be hired), but there's good birding, too; other activities include bush walks & mokoro excursions with members of the local community. *US$50 pp.*

🏠 **Mutemwa Lodge** (6 tents) ⚲ (Namibia) +264 608 043581; m 0976 555186; e reservations@royalbarotsesafaris.com; www. mutemwa.co.za. ⊕ MUTEMW 17°6.449'S, 24°2.508'E. About 55km north of Sesheke, Mutemwa has been owned & run by Gavin Johnson, the former Springbok rugby player, & his wife, Penny, since 1996, & is home to their 3 daughters. From the neatly signposted turn-off (⊕ TUMUTE 17°7.056'S, 24°1.861'E), it is just 2km to the lodge. Although the best lodge in the area, it retains a simplicity that – coupled with a family atmosphere – is particularly appealing.

Meru-style twin tents are spread out along the river, shaded by the remaining tall trees in the riverine forest – mostly pale-bark waterberries, as well as pod mahogany, jackalberries & sausage trees – & backed by an expanse of cropped grass. Each tent has a basin, flush toilet & (gas-heated) shower behind a reed screen, & a small deck overlooking a channel of the Zambezi. A large central thatched roof shelters a bar, lounge & dining area, & there's a small pool nearby. The food is good, wholesome fare, with b/fast & lunch served on the lower deck overlooking the river, & dinner at individual tables arranged around a fire. Lighting comes from paraffin lamps; the camp has no electricity save for a generator that is handy for charging batteries.

Guests, from independent self drivers to larger, fly-in groups (the lodge has its own landing strip), come primarily for the fishing; the camp has 7 good motorboats & several guides, including Gavin himself. More broadly, birding trips & sundowner cruises are also on the menu, as are canoeing excursions, perhaps followed by a champagne b/fast on an island in the river, & guided walks on a 1km-long island opposite the lodge. An added option is to combine a trip here with its sister lodge, Maziba Bay, 70km upstream near Ngonye Falls. For keen anglers, Mutemwa also runs annual fishing camps near Lukulu (page 499). *US$300 pp sharing FBA, exc drinks & lost or broken fishing tackle, Charter plane from Livingstone US$400 pp/10 people.* ⊕ *Closed during heavy rains (Jan–Feb).*

🏠 **Kabula Tiger Lodge** (7 chalets, camping) ⚲ +27 82 550 8642, +27 82 672 5168; e info@ kabulalodge.com; www.kabulalodge.com. ⊕ KABULA 17°02.404'S, 24°00.892'E. This self-catering lodge is primarily geared to families coming in search of fishing & birding, though with high open decks it's not ideal for younger children. It is clearly signposted at ⊕ TUKBTL 17°03.363'S, 23°59.706'E, about 10km north of Mutemwa; it also has its own airstrip.

Simple, thatched dbl or 4-bed reed chalets are en suite & most have decks overlooking the river. Lights that operate off your vehicle battery are provided, but there is no other power. 2 communal kitchens are equipped with gas fridges, a cooker & basic utensils. For campers, there's a tree-shaded campsite with 6 pitches & ablution facilities in individual rondavels rather than a block. Each pitch has a tap & its own washing-up area, with wood-fired boilers for hot water, & there's a thatched *lapa* with tables & benches beneath a venerable pod mahogany.

In addition to guided fishing trips (*R170/hr 3 people*), there are opportunities for walking & birding (*R50 pp*) on Kabula Island, just upstream of the lodge, where over 200 species of birds have been recorded. *Chalet R545/845 twin/4 bed; camping R105pp (South African rand)* ⊕ *All year.*

🏠 **Kavumbu Camp** (3 chalets, camping) 📞 +1 858 342 9220/350 9445; e kavumbu.camp@att.net; www.kavumburivercamp.com. Kavumbu stands in riverine forest beside the Zambezi, within the proposed KAZA Park. The turn-off (⊕ TUKAVU 16°56.461'S, 23°53.004'E) is about 27km north of Mutemwa, or 87km north of Sesheke, with a further 3km track to the camp. Alternatively, it's possible to fly in from Livingstone.

In late 2010 Kavumbu was undergoing considerable refurbishment, with a view to the '4-star family market'. Large, 2-bedroom chalets overlook the river, each with a bathroom at the back & self-catering facilities with a deck at the front. There's also a sandy, tree-shaded campsite with a reed ablution block. Central to the camp, a lounge & restaurant are to be built over the river. Mains electricity should be on line once the tarred road is complete.

Prime attractions are fly-fishing & birdwatching, with a low deck being constructed for birders (& a 2nd, lower down, creating a bar), but it's quite possible simply to explore the river. There are also mokoro trips, & 2-day canoe safaris with a night on an island in the river. *US$220–420 pp sharing FB, inc drinks, boat hire & river guide; sgl suppt US$80. Camping US$10 pp.* ⊕ *All year.*

🏠 **Sioma River Camp** (10 tents, 2 chalets, camping) m 0977 771098; e siomacamp@gmail.com; www.siomacamp.com. ⊕ SIOMRC 16°42.525'S 023°38.571'E. At his desk in the Danish embassy in Lusaka, Hans Aaskov dreamed of establishing a lodge – & this is it. Just 11km south of Ngonye Falls, or 115km north of Sesheke, Sioma River Camp occupies a hilly site that overlooks a narrow but deep stretch of the Zambezi, where in the dry season sculpted sandbanks are exposed on both sides. It's a simple, no-frills place, ideal for self-drive visitors & within easy reach of the falls.

As well as simple dome tents, there are walk-in tents with open-air bathrooms set on elevated wooden decks, some under thatch. In 2010, a couple of thatched chalets were under construction in 2010. The narrow main building, with half walls to allow a through breeze, incorporates a restaurant/bar with a lounge area overlooking the river (*meals US$5–25*). On the hill above sits a stone-built library with comfy chairs, a cosy fire – & a selection of single malt whiskies. Well away from the camp, in the woods above the river, the campsite overlooks a broad sandbank. A simple ablution block is set higher up still, secure from any flooding after the rains.

A highlight here is a boat trip upstream to Ngonye Falls (*US$30 pp/min 3*). Other activities include fishing (*from US$30 pp*), trips to the Lumbe River where it's possible to swim (*US$20 pp/min 3*), & to a village (*US$25 vehicle plus US$10 pp*). *Chalet US$75/110 pp B&B/FB; dome tent US$40 pp. Camping US$10 pp.*

🏠 **Maziba Bay** (camping) Contact via Mutemwa Lodge, above. ⊕ MAZIBA 16°40.594'S, 23°37.647'E. About 120km north of Sesheke bridge, & less than 10km south of Ngonye Falls, Maziba Bay – under the same ownership as Mutemwa Lodge – has a superb location on the western bank of the Zambezi. A spectacular beach of fine white sand would (but for the local crocodile population) put it on a par with the best of the Indian Ocean islands, & it is close enough to the falls to offer ½-day trips (*US$30 pp & park fees*), as well as fishing trips (*US$50/hr up to 4 people; bring your own tackle*). Sadly, though, flooding during 2009 & 2010 caused considerable damage, & it now operates primarily as a campsite, with no food or drinks available. *US$10 pp.* ⊕ *Closed during heavy rains (Jan–Feb).*

SIOMA NGWEZI NATIONAL PARK (*Park fees US$5 pp/day, vehicle US$15/day*) Of all Zambia's remote and seldom-visited parks, Sioma Ngwezi would probably be one of the easiest to regenerate. It is really very close to the Victoria Falls/Livingstone area, which has a huge reservoir of visitors keen to do short safari trips. Tourism to Namibia's Caprivi Strip is rapidly taking off, and with the main road between Sesheke and Senanga now being tarred, access to the vicinity of the park is very good.

Against this background, the park has been incorporated into plans for a new 'peace park' (*www.peaceparks.org*), the Kavango-Zambezi Transfrontier Conservation Area. Known locally as KAZA, it will cover around 287,132km², connecting Sioma Ngwezi and the surrounding GMAs with protected areas in neighbouring Botswana, Zimbabwe, Angola and northern Namibia – and notably including the Okavango Delta and Victoria Falls. As with all the peace parks, the primary aim is to create a corridor to allow migratory animals to move freely between the various reserves, unencumbered by manmade boundaries. In particular, this would be a step towards ending the absurd situation where Chobe has too many elephants ... yet this corner of Zambia, just over the border, has too few!

Although Sioma Ngwezi's tourist infrastructure is still very rudimentary, rough tracks are being cut so that self-drive visitors can explore the park, provided that they take a game scout to show the way. There are as yet no signposts or maps, but construction of a new parks office was expected to start in 2011.

Geography Positioned in the far southwestern corner of Zambia, Sioma Ngwezi National Park covers 5,000km², making it the third largest of Zambia's national parks. It shares a long border with Angola, along the Kwando River, and a short border with Namibia in the south. This corner is less than 50km from northern Botswana, and its vegetation and landscape owe much to the Kalahari sand that lies beneath it.

Most of the park is flat, dry and quite densely wooded – covered with a mosaic of miombo and acacia woodland, with the occasional area of teak forest. There are a few open dambos and sometimes these surround the occasional pool in the bush – but surface water is rare here during the dry season.

Geographical problems Bordering both Angola and Namibia's Caprivi Strip, Sioma Ngwezi was always going to be a difficult park to keep secure and well managed. Following years of civil war, Angola has only recently started on the long road back to peace, let alone prosperity. Namibia's Caprivi Strip, too, has had its security problems in recent years. Sioma Ngwezi itself was a stronghold of Namibia's SWAPO fighters in the early years – and later of the Angolan rebels.

While cross-border poaching is rarely as prevalent as many in Africa will claim (people from 'over there' always make easy scapegoats for crimes), it certainly is a problem in this area.

Looking at the park's geography, you'll realise that most of the animals must either survive entirely without surface water, or need to drink from one of the two rivers nearby: the Kwando on the western border, or the Zambezi which is east, outside of the park. Study a detailed map and you'll realise that what settlements there are in this area are strung out on the banks of these same rivers. So after around July, by which time the park's few dambos have dried out, much of the game needs to run a daily (or more likely, nightly) gauntlet of the riverside villages to drink.

A further problem is how much the logging, which has decimated the oldest hardwood trees in most of Zambia's western provinces, has encroached illegally into this park.

15

Flora and fauna Sioma Ngwezi is the only Zambian park, outside the Luangwa Valley and the Mosi-oa-Tunya National Park, where giraffe have historically been found. It is claimed that rather than being the same subspecies as those in Luangwa (Thornicroft's giraffe), these are an 'Angolan' subspecies, which is different again from the normal 'southern' variety found throughout the subcontinent. Native antelope species include roan, sable, eland, tsessebe, blue wildebeest, zebra, reedbuck, kudu, steenbok, oribi and possibly lechwe on the Kwando River. The major predators are lion, leopard and spotted hyena, and there have been occasional sightings of wild dog, although these are quite possibly packs visiting from the strong population in northern Botswana. Small numbers of elephant, too, frequent the park, especially in the dry season.

Current game populations Sioma Ngwezi's game populations have taken a battering in recent years. Poaching (aka subsistence hunting) is common, and made much easier by the trek to water that much of the game makes – thus bringing it into close contact with the settlements beside the two main rivers. The predators have also suffered, as they're attracted to the easy meat of grazing cattle from nearby local villages, which then bring them into direct conflict with the local people.

Thus, although small populations of most of the main game species still occur here, it is both scarce and skittish, and the casual visitor is likely to see virtually no game at all. That said, indications are that the wildlife is recovering slowly and that species like sable, roan, tsessebe, eland and reticulated giraffe are increasingly being spotted.

When to go The best time to visit Sioma Ngwezi is probably just after the end of the rains, between May and November, when the dambos inside the park still have a little water and are attracting game. Alternatively, spend time beside the Kwando later in the year, when it's the only water source around.

Getting there and getting organised There is a track leading to the eastern corner of the park and around the boundary from the Sesheke–Ngonye Falls road, about 16km south of Mutemwa Lodge – although I couldn't find this when I last passed this way. A second, 51km further north at Silumbu (⊕ TUSNNP 16°54.674'S, 23°51.117'E), close to Sioma, is clearly signposted. This heads southwest around the perimeter of the park to the Kwando River. Here it joins up with a track that runs parallel to the river from Shangombo in the northwest almost to the park's southern boundary. However, the track across the park that links these two access points has been inaccessible for many years. On the plus side, a new border post with Namibia along the Kwando River is expected to open soon, making it considerably easier to travel between the Zambezi and Kwando rivers.

Driving is difficult and requires the backing of a couple of 4x4s. The Kalahari sand can be slow going, and is also very heavy on fuel – so remember that this is available only at Sesheke or Katima Mulilo in the south, or Senanga and Mongu to the north.

Permits for the park are available from the national park office at Ngonye Falls (⊕ NGOFNP 16°39.820'S, 23°34.264'E). If you intend to explore this area independently, then get a scout from the office to guide you, and perhaps show you to a good spot for camping. There are, as yet, no designated campsites within the park. Alternatively, you can take a two-night guided trip to the park with Mutemwa Lodge (page 471), and day or overnight trips can be organised by Hans Aaskov at Sioma River Camp (page 472).

Security note Note that there is some question over the precise location of the border, as pre-1970s it used to be the eastern edge of the Kwando floodplain. Then Zambia 'moved' it to the middle of the river. Wherever it is, you don't want to stray over it accidentally.

🏠 **Where to stay** Aside from two-night camping trips organised by Mutemwa Lodge, there is a simple camp near the park boundary:

⛺ **Sioma Bush Camp** (4 tents) m 0977 771098; e siomacamp@gmail.com; www. siomacamp.com. ⊕ SIOMBC 16°45.074'S, 23°25.246'E. Some 35km from its parent Sioma River Camp, the Bush Camp is in the GMA, near the border of the national park & next to a couple of waterholes. Campers can take their own kit, but there are also simple 3x3m dome tents under thatch.

In addition, there's a basic bush kitchen with a thatched dining shelter overlooking 1 of the waterholes, & a couple of viewing platforms. Full board 2-night packages (*US$300 pp*) & bush walks/drives can be arranged (*US$15/30 pp plus park fees*), with transfers from Sioma River Camp at US$60 return (min 2 people). *Dome tent US$50 pp sharing; own tent US$10 pp.*

NGONYE FALLS NATIONAL PARK (*Entry US$5 pp; vehicle US$5;* ⊕ *06.00–18.00*) The most recent of Zambia's national parks, and very much the smallest, was proclaimed in December 2009. Conceived in partnership with the local community, it lies about 127km north of Sesheke and covers just 200ha on each side of the river, although it is envisaged that it will eventually encompass a total of 1,760ha. The park is centred on the spectacular Ngonye Falls (often referred to as the Sioma Falls), with fencing of the surrounding land in hand during 2011 in order to start restocking it with game.

Livingstone passed this way, having come north through what is now Botswana. He noted:

30th November, 1853 – At Gonye Falls. No rain has fallen here, so it is excessively hot. The trees have put on their gayest dress, and many flowers adorn the landscape, yet the heat makes all the leaves droop at mid-day and look languid for want of rain. If the country increases as much in beauty in front, as it has done within the last four degrees of latitude, it will indeed be a lovely land.

For many miles below, the river is confined in a narrow space of not more than one hundred yards wide. The water goes boiling along, and gives the idea of great masses of it rolling over and over, so that even the most expert swimmer would find it difficult to keep on the surface. Here it is that the river when in flood rises fifty or sixty feet in perpendicular height. The islands above the falls are covered with foliage as beautiful as can be seen anywhere. Viewed from the mass of rock which overhangs the fall, the scenery was the loveliest I had seen.

This was about two years before Livingstone journeyed further down the Zambezi and saw the Victoria Falls for the first time.

Flora and fauna Once the fences are in place, plans to stock the park will be kickstarted with the introduction of both zebra and several species of antelope – impala, kudu, bushbuck and sitatunga – as well as warthog and bushpig. As the park boundaries are widened, so the number of species will be increased.

Back on the river, one of the wildlife highlights is the presence of cape clawless otters, which cavort in the fast-running waters and rest on the sandbanks.

Getting there and away The park entrance (⊕ NGOFNP 16°39.820'S, 23°34.264'E), is about 127km north of Sesheke, or 57km southeast of the Sitoti pontoon, and is clearly signposted to the east of the road. Here you can pay your entry fees, leave your vehicle safely, and find a guide to take you down to the falls themselves.

Where to stay There are plans to open a lodge near the falls, but for the moment the only accommodation on site is for well-equipped campers. Also worth consideration are Maziba Bay and Sioma River Camp (page 472), both just south of the falls.

⋏ Campsite The basic campsite here is close to the river, a short walk from a beautiful sandy beach (strictly no swimming!) & the falls themselves. Its 2 large pitches each have a firepit at the front, with a bucket shower & separate composting toilet; it's all very environmentally friendly. A semi-sheltered camp kitchen offers a food-preparation area, useful if the heavens open at the critical time. Firewood is available, but you need to bring all other food & supplies. *US$5 pp.*

What to see and do Although nothing like as high as Victoria Falls, the Ngonye Falls are still impressive, and if the former didn't exist then they would certainly draw visitors. The geology of the area is the same as that of Victoria Falls, and these falls were formed by a similar process, with erosion taking advantage of cracks in the area's basalt rock.

Ngonye's main falls form a rather spectacular semicircle of water, with lots of smaller streams and falls around the edges. Some of these create little pools, ideal for bathing, though be careful to remain at this point as the main river has too many crocodiles to be safe. They are at their most beautiful during the dry season, from July to December, when the drop is at its greatest. Earlier in the year, the Zambezi floods, so the drop between the falls and the next stage of the river can all but disappear.

Seeing the falls from the western bank is easy – it's a 15-minute walk from the park gate, just beyond the campsite. However, most of the main falls cannot be seen from the bank, and you certainly won't appreciate them fully. To get a really good view, you must cross onto an island in the river in front of the falls. At low water, the park scouts can organise a mokoro to take you across (*US$5 pp, inc guide*), although when the river is in flood, this becomes too dangerous.

The alternative is to contact one of the nearby lodges. Both Sioma River Camp and Maziba Bay have motorboats that they use for trips to the falls, so it's worth asking at either of these. The white-water rafting trips that used to be run here are no longer operating.

For notes on birdwatching in this area, see page 468.

DRIVING NORTH FROM NGONYE TO SENANGA
From Ngonye to Sitoti From the park's office at Ngonye Falls it's about 61km northwest to the Sitoti pontoon, or Kalongola. Don't expect any respite from the road further south, though. This is equally poor, although the presence of Chinese trucks and villages for the roadworkers in early 2011 suggests that the tar may not be too far away.

On the way you'll pass through the village of Sioma, where the presence of a tyre repair place could well prove welcome. (This is where you turn off for Sioma Ngwezi National Park, too.) A little later you come to Nangweshi (⊕ NANGWE 16°23.787'S, 23°19.465'E), where you can stock up on drinks and snacks. Of a handful of guesthouses here, the **Nangweshi Inn**, on the left, boasts guestrooms and a restaurant – albeit very basic.

About 45km north of Ngonye, and 16km south of the ferry, there's a substantial road junction (TUSHAN 16°21.424'S, 23°16.668'E) with a sign pointing west to **Cuando Lodge** (which proudly advertises that it has 'showers and lights'), and the Shangombo Mission (140km) on the Kwando (or Cuando) River. This turning is beside a small settlement known as Matebele, where there's a bridge over a tributary to the Zambezi.

Just north of this, the road forks (TUSITO 16°21.085'S, 23°16.498'E). The right fork drops down onto the lower-lying grasslands of the Zambezi's floodplains – and thence to the Sitoti pontoon. The left fork probably leads to what, in theory, is a very difficult and sandy track along the western side of the Zambezi floodplain to Kalabo; see *Driving from Kalabo to Sitoti*, page 486, for details.

Sitoti pontoon The pontoon across the Zambezi (FERRY2 16°14.716'S, 23°14.251'E; 06.00–18.00; Kw40,000 per vehicle), at Kalongola, is a little over 20km south of Senanga, and 9km north of Sitoti village. It's a good, large pontoon which can take several vehicles at a time, setting off when it's full; there's no set schedule. In the wet season, when the crossing is longer, the fare is considerably higher.

Stallholders close to the pontoon sell drinks and seasonal produce such as tomatoes; there's also the simple God Knows Restaurant – which doesn't instil too much confidence.

When (if!) the new bridge across the Zambezi near Ngonye Falls is finally built, the pontoon will almost certainly close. For now, though, it provides a vital link for travellers heading north or south through the Western Province.

SENANGA Coming from the south, Senanga is the first 'proper' town since Sesheke, and you're now back on tarmac. Bliss! On the eastern bank of the Zambezi, it's a pleasant place, linear in layout with trees lining the main road and a tall radio mast near the centre. Here you'll find a vital BP **fuel** station (which usually even has fuel), a **hospital** (almost opposite the BP garage), a **post office**, a **market** and a handful of **shops** and small bottle stores – but you still can't shake off the feeling that it's out on a limb.

Getting there and away The 104km stretch of road from Senanga to Mongu is good tarmac all the way, having been resurfaced in 2008.

From the south, see *From Ngonye to Sitoti*, above. From the Sitoti pontoon to Senanga it's a further 20km, for which you need to allow around 40 minutes until the new tarred road is complete. If you're heading south, you have to cross to the west bank on the Sitoti pontoon – at least until the advent of the promised bridge; there is no navigable road on the east side of the Zambezi beyond here.

There are buses as far as Senanga from Mongu, but as yet none heading further south.

🏠 **Where to stay and eat** Although there are several basic guesthouses, of which the Greenrite is not untypical, a much better bet is Senanga Safaris Lodge. You can eat there, too, or perhaps at the very basic **Mombochima** restaurant on the opposite side of the road.

🏠 **Senanga Safaris Lodge** (26 rooms, camping) 0217 230156. SENANG 16°6.153'S, 23°17.963'E. Rooms at this simple hotel are spaced around a grassy bank dotted with mature trees & sloping down to the Zambezi. Spacious, en-suite rondavels offer the best value (*Kw150,000 dbl*), with fridge, TV, AC & cont b/fast tempting even diehard campers to think twice! It's easy to while away an hour or 2 in the evening watching the mokoro 'rush hour' from the riverside bar, with views across to the floodplains. Meals are served in the dining room – but be prepared for a very long wait: in our

case, nearly an hour for b/fast of a cup of tea & 2 slices of bread. **$–$$$** *Camping Kw50,000 pp.*
🏠 **Greenrite** (4 rooms) m 0977 429535, 0979 524415. This small guesthouse on the main road, next to the turning for Senanga Safaris, would make a reasonable 2nd choice of place to stay. Some rooms share facilities; others are en suite. **$**

BAROTSELAND

The heartland of the former British protectorate of Barotseland, now the Western Province, covers the floodplains which surround some of the upper reaches of the Zambezi. It is the homeland of the Lozi king, the Litunga, and his people – a group who have retained much of their cultural heritage despite the ravages of the past century. They were granted more autonomy by the colonial authorities than most of the ethnic groups in Zambia's other regions, and perhaps this has helped them to preserve more of their culture. The Litunga has winter and summer palaces nearby, and a hunting lodge in Liuwa Plain. (Chapter 47 of John Reader's excellent *Africa: A Biography of the Continent* covers some of the history of this area in fascinating detail. See *Appendix 3*, page 535, for details.)

For the traveller this means that some aspects of life here have altered relatively little since pre-colonial times. Most of the local people still follow lifestyles of subsistence farming, hunting and gathering, and when rains are good they must still move to higher ground to escape the floodwaters. Be aware, though, that political feelings occasionally run high over the level of autonomy that is permitted by the government.

BAROTSE FLOODPLAINS The area bordering the Zambezi River as it runs west of Mongu represents the second-largest wetland in Zambia, and was designated as a Ramsar site in 2007. After the rains, the Barotse or Zambezi floodplains are transformed with small islands of vegetation dotted through the expanse of water. Ramsar (*www.ramsar.org*) notes that 'there is sparse riparian vegetation, small stands of *Acacia albida* in the floodplains, *Syzygium guineens* along the main river channel and patches of *Diplorhynchus* scrub and *Borassus* forest in the northern areas. Semi-evergreen woodlands found on the Kalahari sands have economically important species like *Baikiaea plurijuga* and *Pterocarpus angolensis*'.

MONGU Perched high on a ridge overlooking the eastern edge of the Barotse Plains, Mongu is the provincial centre for western Zambia – and the only large town this side of Livingstone or Lusaka. Very few tourists reach here, so there are few people who aren't Zambian, and almost all of those work with or for the fairly permanent contingent of NGO personnel. The areas around Mongu are amongst Zambia's poorest and many are isolated by seasonal floods, so there is often need for relief workers here.

The town is easily reached from Lusaka and Senanga, and is the best place in the region to get **fuel** or **supplies**. Otherwise there is little to attract visitors, apart perhaps from the good **baskets** to be found here. However, make the most of the amenities and relative comforts here – as there are precious little of these to the north or west.

Mongu has long had a bad reputation for theft, but perhaps police vigilance over the years has paid off, since there was little hint of this on our last visit in 2010.

Geography Mongu is about 25km from the dry-season course of the Zambezi, or immediately adjacent to the water when the river is in full flood. The town is spread out on a ridge above the plains, with no real centre but several quite different busy areas. Small villages and cattle dot the dusty plains during the dry season, but when wet it is all transformed into a haze of green grass on a mirror of water that reflects the sky. Then, when the water is fairly high, the views west over the floodplain are spectacular: myriad channels snaking through apparently endless flat plains.

Orientation The tarred M9 from Lusaka meets the tar road heading south to Senanga at a central roundabout (⊕ MONGU 15°16.159'S, 23°08.007'E). North of this is a vibrant, packed old town area with shops, a heaving market, a bus station and an army barracks; if you pass these, then ultimately you'll find a tar road north to Limulunga. West of the roundabout lies a small hill, upon which you'll find most of the government buildings. Beyond, on the other side of this hill, you drop down to the harbour, and to the road across the floodplain which leads to the Zambezi, Kalabo and Liuwa Plain.

Getting there and away Good tar roads link Mongu to Lusaka (638km) and Senanga (103km), but vehicular access to both the north and west is seriously challenging.

By air In 2011, Proflight were planning to introduce scheduled flights between Lusaka and Mongu Airport (⊕ AIRMON 15°15.227'S, 23°9.376'E). Chartering a plane, although possible (Livingstone or northern Kafue are closest), would be very expensive.

By bus Several buses link Lusaka to Mongu every day – expect a minibus to cost around Kw75,000 and a coach about Kw100,000. The bus station is beside the old market, while long-distance coaches stop behind the Catholic church on the main road.

Hitchhiking Hitching to Mongu along the Great West Road is possible for the determined. Hitching to get around the surrounding countryside is very slow and difficult – but it is how most of the local population travel.

Driving west to Sandaula on the Zambezi Much of the promised new tar road between Mongu and Kalabo, which was to head west along a causeway across the floodplains, has been abandoned (see box, page 481). What is left comprises sections of slowly crumbling causeway, with yawning gaps that require you to drop down onto parallel tracks on the floodplain. It'd be wise to ask around in Mongu about the road's current state before you leave, but expect it to be largely impassable when the plains are flooded, between about December and July. Even in the dry season, the sand can be very deep and troublesome – so a high-clearance 4x4 remains essential.

To get to this road, head west over the hill from the main Mongu roundabout, pass the post office, then turn left down towards the harbour (⊕ HARMON 15°16.293'S, 23°07.180'E). There you'll clearly see a road to the right dropping down onto the Barotse floodplain. Remember to fill up with fuel in Mongu before you leave; there are no fuel stations west of here.

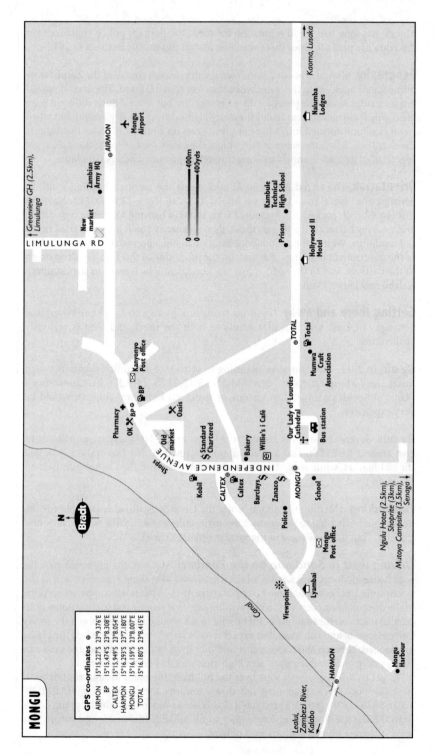

MONGU

GPS co-ordinates ⊕

AIRMON	15°15.227'S	23°9.376'E
BP	15°15.474'S	23°8.308'E
CALTEX	15°5.949'S	23°8.054'E
HARMON	15°16.293'S	23°7.180'E
MONGU	15°16.159'S	23°8.007'E
TOTAL	15°16.180'S	23°8.415'E

N

Bradt

↑ *Greenview GH (2.5km),*
Limulunga

LIMULUNGA RD

New market

Zambian Army HQ

⊕ *AIRMON* ✈

Mongu Airport

↑ *Kaoma, Lusaka*

☐ Nalumba Lodges

400m
400yds

0
0

Pharmacy ✚

OK ✗ BP ⊕
⊠

⊕ BP

Kanyonyo Post office

✗ Oasis

Kambule Technical ● High School

● Prison

Hollywood II ☐ Motel

⊕ TOTAL
☐ Total

Mumwa Craft Association

Slops

Old market

$ Standard Chartered

INDEPENDENCE AVENUE

● Bakery

✚ Our Lady of Lourdes Cathedral

☐ Willie's i Café

☐ Bus station

Kobil ●

CALTEX ⊕
● Caltex

Barclays $

Zanaco $

MONGU ⊕

● School

Police ●

⊠ Mongu Post office

✳ Viewpoint

☐ Lyambai

↓ *Ngulu Hotel (2.5km),*
Shoprite (3km),
Mutoya Campsite (3.5km),
Senaga →

Canal

⊕ *HARMON*

↑ *Lealui,*
Zambezi River,
Kalabo

● Mongu Harbour

NYAMINYAMI AND THE MONGU–KALABO ROAD

Contracts signed in March 2002 started the construction of a 74km tar road from Mongu, via Kalabo, to the Angolan border which, it was envisaged, would completely open up wet-season access to impoverished areas west of the Zambezi and into Angola.

The project planned to connect Mongu and Kalabo, and ultimately Lusaka, with Angola – spanning not only the Zambezi River, but also the width of the Zambezi floodplain. This entailed 35km of raised causeway above low-lying plains that are seasonally inundated when the river breaks its banks. Initially it was scheduled for completion in 2004, but exceptional flooding washed away part of the structure, prompting a major reassessment of the design. By then, funds for the project were starting to run seriously short, and a hydrologists' report suggested that the section of causeway east of the Zambezi River (from the Zambezi to the canal at Mongu) wasn't strong enough to support a road.

Despite these problems, the 22km section of tar road running from the western edge of the floodplain to Kalabo was eventually opened, but the rest of the project has been abandoned. Perhaps the road's builders have finally realised what their predecessors at Kariba Dam already knew – that Nyaminyami, the old river god of the Zambezi Valley's Tonga people, is very hard to tame.

The road heads roughly northwest, so it's difficult to get lost. There are plenty of people to ask, too, all heading roughly between Mongu and the ferry at Sandaula. About 14km from Mongu's harbour, you'll reach the village of Lealui (⊕ LEALUI 15°13.446'S, 23°1.077'E; see page 484). This would have been a ten-minute drive if the tar had been finished, but is more likely be an hour's slalom. Lealui itself is the location of the isolated summer palace of the Litunga, the Lozi king, and a centre for the Lozi administration. Visitors are advised to show courtesy and respect, even if it doesn't appear to be different from any other small African village.

A little over 10km northwest of Lealui, after another half-hour's tortuous driving, you'll reach the ferry across the Zambezi, at Sandaula (⊕ FERRY3 15°12.291'S, 22°55.297'E). See *Kalabo*, pages 485–6, for details of the route continuing to the west.

Driving north to Lukulu There's a good tarred road for 15km north of Mongu, basically as far as the Litunga's winter palace at Limulunga. Then there's nothing more than vanishing local tracks across the Barotse floodplains between there and Lukulu. These are passable in the dry season – see *Lukulu*, pages 495–6 for directions – but otherwise consider driving to Lukulu on all-weather (albeit relatively poor) roads via Kaoma.

Getting around The Mongu police appear to be vigilant, and there are often roadblocks around town where they will check your vehicle and its papers. If you're driving, make sure that you're wearing your seatbelt and moving slowly. The taxi rank and bus station are located between the market and the BP garage.

Driving Apart from the main tar roads to Lusaka and Senanga, most of the area's roads are little more than vehicle tracks, and they degenerate into patches of deep sand quite frequently. A 4x4 is essential here, even in the dry season, and the worst

15

of these tracks will require almost constant low-range driving through long sections of Kalahari sand.

During the wet season, from around December to July, the whole area north of Ngonye Falls is subject to flooding. Then the Barotse floodplain becomes a large, shallow lake. Much of the population moves to higher ground to live, and boats are the only option for getting around. Don't even think about trying to drive anywhere off the tarred roads then.

By boat For much of the year, boat transport is the best way to see the immediate area around Mongu, and it is the only way if the flood is high. The best way to find a suitable boat is to ask at the harbour office in Mongu.

For a few dollars you can hire a mokoro to take you out on the waterways, and – except at the end of the dry season – perhaps down towards Lealui and the main channel. Spend a few hours like this, on the water, and you will appreciate how most of the locals transport themselves around. You will see everything from people to household goods, supplies, live animals and even the occasional bicycle loaded onto boats and paddled or poled (punted) from place to place.

For rather more, there are two larger ferries with outboard motors that will take 20 or so people on longer journeys; once the floods start, there's typically at least one of these per day between Mongu and Kalabo.

There is also a privately run postboat on the Zambezi that carries passengers, the mail and cargo, including the occasional vehicle – but note that ferrying a vehicle is likely to be a very expensive option.

Where to stay There's a choice of accommodation in Mongu, much of it of fairly poor quality. Both of the relatively large, old-style hotels are in dire need of refurbishment, leaving a gap filled by a rash of small, private guesthouses. These cater mainly to top local businesspeople, foreign aid workers and expats, so standards of accommodation and security among the best are reasonable, if nothing special. Note that price is seldom a useful guide to quality here – and as new places spring up they will often be better than the older establishments. Try to book accommodation in advance, too, as the better places are often full – especially around the time of the Kuomboka ceremony (page 21). That said, many won't take reservations unless you pay at the time of booking.

In the past, Mongu has had a bad reputation for theft, so it's wise to take maximum precautions against losing your belongings, even in the hotels. If you can't make it into town, but need to stay in the area, then it's better to ask at a village than to camp alone.

Nalumba Lodges (13 rooms) 0217 221199; e nalumbalodges@iconnect.zm. NALUMB 15°15.939'S, 23°09.118'E. Number 2 of 3 Nalumba Lodges in Mongu, this one is on the site of the old Crossroads Lodge, on the south side of Kaoma–Lusaka road, about 2km from the main roundabout. It has fairly small but very clean & functional rooms – all with en-suite shower & flush toilet, TV, fridge, kettle, mosi nets & AC. There's a small dining room, & a pleasant bar in the courtyard with seating in individual round gazebos. Parking is very secure behind an electric gate. $–$$

Country Lodge (13 rooms) Independence Av. Close to Barclays Bank in the centre of town, this well-placed lodge is recommended by Sister Pat from Lukulu's Catholic mission. En-suite rooms have TV & fridge, & the food, she tells us, is both good & plentiful. $

Green View Guesthouse (23 rooms, camping) Limulunga Rd; 0217 221029; m 0955 769599, 0979 522132; e mongu@ limagarden.com; www.limagarden.com/ guesthouse_mongu_zambezi.html. GREENV 15°13.960'S, 23°8.721'E. One of the better options near Mongu, this small, quiet guesthouse is a 15min drive from the Litunga's winter palace. To reach it head north on the tarred Limulunga Rd for about 2.5km, where there's a sign to the left, behind the New Apostolic Church. Being attached to a church seems to lend a very happy, relaxed air – & it's far enough from town for security to be less of an issue. Significant enlargement in 2011 will result in 16 new twin or dbl chalets, each en suite & with AC. The older twin rondavels, with a fridge, kettle, TV, fan & mosi nets, are also en suite. Camping is a further option, but facilities for campers are limited. B/fast (*Kw5,500–22,000*) & dinner (*Kw27,500*) are available on request. **$** *Camping Kw20,000 pp.*

⌂ Hollywood II Motel (20 rooms) ☎ 0217 722230; m 0976 653037. On the main road almost opposite the prison & with secure parking, this new motel should be fairly safe unless there's a break out. Clean, tiled rooms in a single block are simple & quite small, but all have AC, fridge, TV, mosi nets & en-suite shower room. There are bars both upstairs & downstairs, & a separate restaurant (Kw25,000 pp). **$**

⌂ Lyambai Hotel (17 rooms) ☎ 0217 221138; e comacs@coppernet.zm. Mongu's oldest hotel, fairly near the harbour, has en-suite rooms laid out in 2 long rows across a courtyard. It's desperately in need of renovation, but the views from its cool courtyard make up for a lot. There's also a restaurant & bar, & secure parking. **$**

⌂ Ngulu Hotel (18 rooms) ☎ 0217 221414/221258; e nguluhot@zambia.co.zm. This old-style hotel, used primarily for local conferences, is almost 2.5km south of the roundabout, on the left as you head towards Senanga & just before the turning to Shoprite; the guarded car park has a good view of the floodplains. We're assured by the helpful manager that there are plans for change, with tour packages including village stays on the agenda, but for now, it's in need of a hefty makeover. Dbl & twin rooms are all en suite with toilets & baths; there are mosi nets, fans & TVs, & some rooms have AC. The restaurant is open for lunch & dinner. **$**

⋏ Mutoya Campsite m 0977 449699; e paul@zam.co.za; www.zam.co.za. ⊕ MUTOYA 15°18.337'S, 23°08.900'E. About 3.5km south of the roundabout, there's a clearly signposted turning (⊕ TUMUTO 15°17.778'S, 23°08.870'E) to the west to this pleasant, well-kept campsite with a strong Christian foundation. You'll need a 4x4 for the steep, sandy access road, but once at the bottom it opens out into a series of grassy, level pitches, with fresh water from a borehole, electric hook-ups, & – higher up – clean ablution blocks. If you don't have your own tent, you might be able to use 1 of the pre-erected dome tents on site. The site shares its grounds with a school for orphaned children, for whom it doubles as a place to explore. *Kw40,000 pp.*

⋏ Where to eat Some of the hotels have restaurants and others serve meals on request, or you could put together a picnic from Shoprite. For something a little different try the **OK restaurant**, or the reliable:

⋏ Oasis Restaurant ☎ 0217 221931; ⊕ 07.00–23.00 daily. On the road behind the old market, this large restaurant has tables both inside & out. Dishes such as T-bone steaks, fish & burgers are served with chips & salad, with daily specials, too. The Oasis doesn't have an alcohol licence – but ask nicely & they'll send someone out to buy drinks for you. **$**

Other practicalities There are three main **fuel** stations: Caltex just 400m north of the roundabout; BP another kilometre further on, past the old market; and Total just 700m east of the roundabout.

For banks, there's an ATM at Zanaco beside the roundabout, and another at the adjacent Barclays; both are reasonably reliable. On the other side of the road, further up, is a Standard Chartered Bank. The main **post office** (⊕ POMONG 15°16.256'S, 23°07.566'E) is to the west, high on the hill above the harbour; it is also an agent for Western Union. The town also has an **internet** café, Willie's i Café, opposite Barclays Bank.

15

Shopping Mongu is the obvious place in the Western Province to buy **supplies** and get organised. The best place to head for is the large and well-stocked Shoprite (✪ SHOPRT 15°17.186'S, 23°09.047'E; ⏱ *08.00–18.00 Mon–Fri, 08.00–17.00 Sat, 09.00–13.00 Sun & public holidays*), by far the biggest and best store in town. It is reached by heading about 3km south of town towards Senanga, then turning left (signposted to Lusaka along the M9) for around 0.8km.

The huge old **market** in town is a good place to buy locally produced fresh fruit and vegetables (and, I'm told, bread also).

For **crafts**, take the main road to Lusaka from the roundabout, and on the south side, just before the Total (✪ TOTAL 15°16.180'S, 23°08.415'E), you will find the Mumwa Craft Association (✆ *0217 221263*; e *mundiakk@yahoo.com*; ⏱ *08.00–17.00 Mon–Sat, or by appointment*). This non-profit-making society was established in 1994 to improve the economic, social and cultural well-being of the local communities by representing a network of several hundred local producers throughout the Western Province. They concentrate on good basket weaving, as well as woodcarvings, pottery and metalwork. Items on sale vary according to the season but may include the large and very beautiful linen baskets that are woven using skills developed over the centuries by the Lozi people in making their fishing traps. You won't find better baskets supporting a more worthy cause, or at lower prices. During and after the rains, when many of the craftsmen gather here during the day, you can also watch them at work.

What to see and do Aside from wandering around the old market or visiting the craft association (above), there are no specific sights in Mongu. You may, though, like to visit the lively and very traditional **harbour** (✪ HARMON 15°16.293'S, 23°07.180'E). The two main attractions, however – the Litunga's summer and winter palaces – are both excursions from town.

The greatest of Zambia's cultural festivals, the **Kuomboka** (see *Chapter 2*, page 21), is the tradition of moving the Litunga, the Lozi king, plus his court and his people, away from the floodwaters and onto higher ground. If the rains have been good and the floodwaters are rising, this spectacular ceremony takes place around February or March, often on a Thursday, just before full moon. It involves a flotilla of boats for most of the day, plus an impromptu orchestra of local musicians and much celebration. Don't miss it if you are travelling in western Zambia at the time.

The Litunga's summer palace at Lealui About 13km west of Mongu, amidst the floodplains, the Litunga's summer palace (✪ LEALUI 15°13.637'S, 23°01.107'E) is set in a large grove of trees that is easily seen from the escarpment on which Mongu stands. If the road is flooded, you can hire a mokoro to bring you out from Mongu.

Don't expect a Western-style palace; this appears to be a normal small African village with thatched huts. However, it is not only the king's summer residence, but also the main Lozi administration centre. Visitors are warmly welcomed, though are strongly advised to show the utmost courtesy and respect to their hosts. Indeed, until very recently it was normal to introduce yourself to the Kuta (the traditional court) as a courtesy, especially if you planned to continue on to Liuwa. See *Driving west to Sandaula on the Zambezi* on page 479 for directions of how to get here from Mongu.

The Litunga's winter palace and the Nayuma Museum and Heritage Centre (⏱ *08.00–17.00 Mon–Fri; entry Kw2,000*) North of Mongu, next to the Litunga's main winter palace, this museum houses some interesting exhibits on the history and culture of the Lozi people, with a strong focus on conserving and promoting the region's heritage. Its director, Manyando Mukela, is also *Ngambela* (prime minister) to the Litunga. A small craft shop sells some really beautiful basketwork from the area, at very reasonable prices.

To get here, take the tarred Limulunga Road north from Mongu's new market for around 15km, then turn left down a tarred side road opposite the water tower at the centre of Limulunga. Follow this round and after a kilometre or so you reach a barrier, with the museum on the left, and the Lozi palace on the right. This royal complex is all fairly grand and impressive, complete with keen security guards from about March to June, when the Litunga is in residence.

KALABO This small, rambling town by the Luanginga River is the gateway to Liuwa Plain National Park. The name is derived from the Lozi word *silambo*, meaning 'paddling stick'.

Coming from Mongu, you'll arrive at a T-junction where you turn right into a wide main street lined by grand old buildings with verandas, most in various states of decay. It's usually very quiet, though clearly the shopkeepers have active imaginations with the 'Just Imagine' and 'Hard Work Makes Dreams Come True' restaurants.

Continue down this main road to reach the **harbour**, where there is a small pontoon (⊕ HARKAL 14°59.248'S, 22°41.001'E; *Kw40,000 return*) over the Luanginga.

Getting there and away With the proposed tar road from Mongu now abandoned, Kalabo is not easy to reach, and is inaccessible from the east between about December and June. In fact, anywhere west of the Zambezi remains expedition territory at any time. 'Roads' here are usually just tracks in the Kalahari sand, which need days of low-range driving. They require not only a 4x4 (preferably several, in case of emergency), but also large quantities of fuel. This can be replenished only in Mongu, so long-range fuel tanks and lots of jerrycans are vital. See *Driving in sand*, pages 104–5, for more advice – and note especially the points on higher fuel consumption and misleading milometer readings.

Water is also a problem, as it tends to seep through the Kalahari sand rather than forming pans on the surface. Hence no potable water can be relied upon, even in Kalabo, so if you're heading west, take some good containers and fill up in Mongu.

During the wet season, Kalabo remains cut off by road from the east of the country. Then you have three options: to wait for the Zambezi ferry to start up again after the floods; to use the expensive postboat from Mongu, which takes one vehicle at a time – enquire locally to find out if it can be arranged; or to tackle the sandy track from Sitoti on the west side of the Zambezi (see below).

Kalabo has its own airstrip (⊕ KALAIR 14°59.501'S, 22°38.484'E), so it is at least possible – albeit very expensive – to charter a plane into the area.

Driving from Mongu via Sandaula See the directions for *Driving west to Sandaula on the Zambezi* on page 479, for the route from Mongu to the pontoon across the Zambezi.

The Sandaula pontoon (⊕ FERRY3 15°12.291'S, 22°55.297'E; ⊕ *06.00–18.00*; *Kw40,000 per vehicle*) is large enough for three vehicles – although it will often leave with just one or two. During the dry season, when the Zambezi is confined within its banks, the crossing is only a hundred metres or so, and the ferry is about 27km from Mongu. Once the area is flooded, the pontoon ceases to operate.

From the pontoon, Kalabo is about a 46km drive in the dry season. For the first 11km or so, you'll be negotiating a series of deep, sandy tracks which diverge confusingly as they cross the floodplains. Follow these in a westerly direction for about 11km, a journey of about half an hour, before joining the new tar road – the only part of the ambitious Mongu–Kalabo road that was completed – for the final 34.7km northwest to Kalabo (⊕ KALABO 14°59.820'S, 22°39.602'E). At the T-junction, turn right; it's then just 2.9km to the harbour, and the pontoon across the river to Liuwa Plain National Park.

Driving from Mongu via the Libonda pontoon In theory it should be possible in the dry season to cross the Zambezi higher up the river, at the Libonda pontoon – and then to head westwards, and slightly south, on small paths and tracks across the floodplains. However, we have reports that the pontoon is no longer operational, presumably put out of business by the now abandoned plans for the new road.

If you do try this way, then you should certainly take a local guide (hitchhiker) to help you navigate – and you will see plenty of these throughout the area. You will pass men, women and children carrying everything from luggage to mattresses and supplies on their heads. Given the area's lack of transport, if you have room in your vehicle then you should offer lifts whenever possible.

Driving to Liuwa See *Getting there*, under *Liuwa Plain National Park*, page 491, for details.

Driving from Kalabo to Sitoti There is a track on the western side of the Zambezi between Kalabo and Sitoti, but it is thick sand with no fuel (or much else) on the way. You'd probably be wise to take local hitchhikers as guides. The route heads south and slightly west (average bearing of about 157°) from Kalabo to the Sitoti pontoon (see page 477); aim for ⊕ TUSHAN 16°21.424'S, 23°16.668'E.

This is 164km as the heron flies, and a lot more on the ground. I haven't driven this route, but am reliably informed that it's about 12 hours of driving. If you were forced to do this, it would take much more time and fuel than going via Mongu and Senanga. So if you cross from Mongu west of the Zambezi during the wet season, bear in mind that this could be your only way out.

Other practicalities There is **no fuel** available in Kalabo – and although you can get the basics in the market or in local shops, you'd be well advised to buy all your **supplies** in Mongu before you arrive. There are, though, often people selling fish along the roadside, and there are a few general stores close to the harbour. There's also a basic **café** there – ideal if you have to wait for someone to fetch the pontoon for you! And if you've longer to spare, the **market** is well worth a visit in its own right.

Kalabo has a mission with a large **hospital** (⊕ HOSPKA 14°59.111'S, 22°40.654'E), and a basic government **resthouse**.

The **immigration** office is behind some of the shops near the harbour, on the left of the Luanginga pontoon.

Liuwa Plain National Park Tourism Centre Of vital importance to most visitors is the tourism centre for Liuwa Plain National Park, which is conveniently located on the left just before the harbour, next to the park's headquarters. This is where you get permits for Liuwa Plain National Park, book your campsites, and get directions for the park. It's also the place where you can organise a guide to accompany you, if required.

LIUWA PLAIN NATIONAL PARK (m 0977 158733, 0977 758603; *reservations* e *liuwatourism@african-parks.org*, *information* e *liuwainfo@african-parks.org*;

www.african-parks.org. Park fees US$40 pp per day; camping US$10 pp/day. Guide fee US$13/day. ☻ Self-drive 06.00–18.00 Jun–Dec) Liuwa Plain is as wild and remote as virtually any park in Africa; at the right time of year, its game is also as good as most of the best. The cliché 'best-kept secret' is applied with nauseating frequency to many places in Africa by copywriters who can't think of anything original; this is perhaps one of the few places that would deserve it.

Liuwa Plain has long been a very special place. It was declared a 'game reserve' as early as the 19th century by the king of Barotseland, and subsequently administered by the Litunga, or Lozi king. Traditionally, the park was the Litunga's private hunting ground, and the people whose villages were located around the land were charged with looking after the animals for him. Then in 1972 it became a national park, and its management was taken over by central government. Although the local people retained utilisation rights of the park, grazing their animals, fishing in the rivers and pools, and harvesting plants for use in traditional crafts, their cultural connection with the land was broken, and poaching became rife. It was not until 2003, when the park was taken over by African Parks and the link with the Litunga reinstated, that the villagers regained stewardship. Now, in addition to their utilisation rights, they run campsites for visitors, and once more have an interest in the preservation of the wildlife.

The word *liuwa* means 'plain' in the local Lozi language. Legend relates how one Litunga planted his walking stick here on the plain, where it grew into a large *mutata* tree. The tree in question can still be seen from the track which leads from Minde to Luula: after leaving the first tree belt, look in the distance on your left side when you are halfway to the next tree belt.

Liuwa Plain is certainly the most fascinating park in the region, but getting here almost always requires an expedition. For this reason, visitor numbers are tiny: in 2010 fewer than 500 visitors entered the park. Yet even these figures dwarf those in some of the previous years: only 50 tourists visited in the whole of 2000. While these figures are gradually increasing, the number of vehicles admitted at any one time is limited to 40 in order to preserve the park's fragile ecosystem.

Geography
Although a network of sand game-viewing tracks has been established in the 3,662km² park, it remains largely untouched. Most of it is a vast honey-coloured grass plain, stretching about 70km long and 30km wide. Within this there's just the occasional open pan, cluster of raffia palms, or small tree-island interrupting the flatness. In places you can look 360° around you and see nothing but a flat expanse. The environment is unlike any other park in Zambia – the most similar places are probably Katavi, in western Tanzania, and, possibly, the much smaller Kazuma Pan in Zimbabwe.

Large areas of this plain are totally flooded from around December to April, with the waters rising in the northwest and spreading southeastwards. It's this flooding which drives the wildebeest migration, or 'gathering', as the herds move in search of new, fresh grazing.

In the centre, and especially the southern side, of this enormous grassy plain, you'll find a scattering of open pans, many of which hold their water well into the dry season. These are well worth investigating. Although in the dry season some will appear almost lifeless, others will have great concentrations of birds or antelope.

FLORA AND FAUNA
Flora Liuwa Plain's main plant life, on first glance, appears to be vast areas of grasslands, within which species like *Vossia cuspidate* and *Echinocloa stagnina* are

amongst the most important for the herds of grazing herbivores. On tree-islands, and around the edges of the plain, you'll find the small false mopane, or copalwood (*Guibourtia coleosperma*); the silver cluster-leaf (*Terminalia sericea*), which is so typical of the Kalahari; stands of Zambezi teak (*Baikiaea plurijuga*) and weeping wattle (*Peltophorum africanum*), while around the pans are occasional stands of palms including the odd tall *Hyphaene*.

Mammals and reptiles As is common in vast open areas, many of Liuwa's larger mammals tend to group together into great herds when on the plain – and these are much of the park's attraction. The 1991 wildlife census estimated populations at 30,000 blue wildebeest, 8,000 tsessebe, 1,000 zebra and 10,000 other large mammals which would have included herds of buffalo, red lechwe, eland, Lichtenstein's hartebeest and roan antelope as well as assorted pairs of reedbuck and the delightful, diminutive oribi which are so common here.

Later surveys suggested that game numbers had declined by around a third, with buffalo, eland, Lichtenstein's hartebeest and roan antelope possibly wiped out

AFRICAN PARKS

African Parks (*www.african-parks.org*) was founded by a group of businesspeople and conservationists who recognised that African governments had limited resources to pay for conservation or the social development which is needed to accompany it. Their first major venture required about US$15 million to buy the land for, and completely redevelop, Marakele National Park, in South Africa's Waterberg Mountain – in an amazingly short time.

Backed by finance and expertise from a multi-millionaire Dutch businessman, Paul Fentener van Vlissingen, that first project was a huge success. Van Vlissingen's family own the multi-national SHV – one of the Netherlands' largest companies. (It controls numerous companies worldwide, including the Makro chain of wholesale stores.)

African Parks, now fully based in South Africa, is concerned with the long-term sustainability of some of Africa's national parks by forming agreements with governments to manage and finance national parks. They aim to work with the inclusion of local communities, to safeguard the flora and fauna and to relieve local poverty. Ultimately, they aim to make their parks into sustainable, self-financing business units. However, they are willing to provide substantial funds to 'kick start' failing parks and areas – and also act as a channel for grants received for this from other donors.

The initial lease agreement for Liuwa Plain National Park was finally signed in Lusaka on 31 May 2004. The event was attended by the Litunga, the Ngambela, other representatives from the Barotse Royal Establishment, the minister of tourism, ZAWA representatives and the ambassadors of the USA and Netherlands. This agreement extends to 2024, with a possibility of renewal for a further 20 years if all partners agree.

Initially, African Parks committed US$2 million to Liuwa Plain over a five-year period, but a total of US$9 million has been invested since 2004. Signs that poaching was coming under control (for example, wildebeest meat is no longer available in the local markets) have been swift to follow.

Now, at last, the picture for the park's wildlife is beginning to look more positive.

completely. However, with more active protection, numbers are building up again; the 2011 count revealed 42,700 wildebeest, around 4,400 zebra and increasing populations of all herbivore species. Both roan antelope and wild dogs have returned to the park, and the population of red lechwe is recovering well. Eland and buffalo have been re-introduced, and the scouts say that sitatunga are still found in some of the rivers on the edge of the park.

The largest herds currently seen in the park are the blue wildebeest which mass here in their thousands during the rains. Amongst them, you'll find zebra and tsessebe. Though widely regarded as a 'migration', some suggest that it may in fact just be a gathering on the plain of all the game that has previously been in the surrounding bush, rather than an actual migration from, say, Angola. Regardless, if you can catch it at the right time, it's a stunning sight: flat, open plain with animals as far as the eye can see.

That said, I think it's quite wrong to concentrate on the sights in November and, in effect, dismiss the rest of the year. I last visited for a few days in the month of September which yielded plenty of wildebeest on the plain, including one herd of over a thousand; several smaller herds of zebra, tsessebe and red lechwe, one of the last numbering over 120 individuals; and some of the most spectacular birding that I'd ever seen in southern Africa.

Predators have also been well represented in Liuwa, with lion, leopard, cheetah, wild dog and hyena all occurring here. Although by 2007 there was just one remaining lioness, popularly known as Lady Liuwa, two male lions were brought in to join her in 2009; at the time of writing, there was still no sign of cubs and plans are being finalised to introduce two or three young lionesses. Wild dogs are recovering in the park, with two different packs now breeding successfully here.

Leopard occur within the national park, though the surrounding forest is a better habitat for them than the plain itself. Hyenas are fairly commonly seen, and are cheeky enough to come to the edge of your firelight's glow.

With sharp eyes you're also likely to spot smaller curious omnivores like side-striped jackal, troops of banded mongooses, and possibly porcupines. I've had reports of some particularly large snakes living here – though (thankfully) been unable to verify these.

Birds Liuwa boasts a total of about 334 bird species which, even when I visited during a dry month like September, were amazing: spectacular groups of crowned cranes often numbered several hundred birds; wattled cranes, so endangered in many places, thrive here with numerous pairs and smaller groups of up to 30 individuals; while one particular flock of pelicans included several hundred birds. I saw all of these in just a few days in early September – and so when it rains, the park's birding must be quite unbelievable.

Then, when the pans fill up, open-billed, yellow-billed, marabou and saddle-billed storks arrive, with spoonbills, grey herons, egrets, three-banded and lots of blacksmith's plovers, pygmy and spur-winged geese, and many other waterbirds. Slaty egrets are seen in groups, a rare occurrence elsewhere.

Bob Stjernstedt, a Zambian birding expert, comments that Liuwa is relatively rarely visited, and so many more birds are sure to be added to this list. Secretary birds and Denham's and white-bellied bustards are common; and the park is famous for thousands of the migrant black-winged pratincoles, a finely-marked swift-like bird which is rare further east. Other 'specials' here include the pink-billed and clapper larks, rosy-breasted longclaw, swamp boubou, long-tailed widow, sharp-tailed starling and white-cheeked bee-eater. The plain is also a great area for raptors

LIUWA PLAIN NATIONAL PARK

0 ━━━━━━━━ 16km
0 ━━━━━━━━ 10 miles

Luambimba

peak dry season only

Lukulu

MUTVAA
Mutvaa ○

SIKALE ⊕ ▲ Sikale

Mataba B Local Forest

KALAB
Mukalabumbu
Tower ●

MIYAND
● Miyanda
Pool

Mataba A Local Forest

N

Brad t

Kuuli Local Forest

WILDB1 ⊕ ▲ Katoyana

○ Liuwa
School

Matamanene Camp 🏠 ⊕ **MATAMA**

Lone palm 🌴⊕ **IPALM**
⊕ **PELICA**

WATER2 ⊕
WATER1 ⊕

**West Zambezi
Game Management Area**

LYANGU ⊕ ▲ ⊕ **LIUWA4**
Lyangu

KWALE
▲ Kwale
LIUWA3 ⊕

LIFORK ⊕
LIUWAP ⊕

**ZAMBEZI

FLOODPLAIN**

*Sikundu
Local Forest*

LIUWA2 ⊕ Kayala
▲ **KAYALA**
Kalabo ● ⊕ **HARKAL**
Pontoon

Mongu ▼

	GPS co-ordinates ⊕				
🌿 Forest	IPALM	14°40.876'S	22°35.388'E	LIUWAP	14°53.234'S	22°39.102'E
Wetlands	HARKAL	14°59.248'S	22°41.001'E	LYANGU	14°48.822'S	22°32.735'E
Settled area	KALAB	14°24.335'S	22°37.554'E	MATAMA	14°39.237'S	22°38.218'E
	KATOYA	14°36.700'S	22°42.126'E	MIYAND	14°25.167'S	22°39.109'E
National park	KAYALA	14°58.360'S	22°41.129'E	MUTVAA	16°16.106'S	22°33.616'E
	KWALE	14°49.111'S	22°41.015'E	PELICA	14°41.439'S	22°36.786'E
	LIFORK	14°52.366'S	22°38.803'E	SIKALE	14°17.560'S	22°33.150'E
	LIUWA2	14°57.718'S	22°40.119'E	WATER1	14°45.334'S	22°37.395'E
	LIUWA3	14°50.594'S	22°37.971'E	WATER2	14°44.848'S	22°37.279'E
	LIUWA4	14°47.287'S	22°37.484'E	WILDB1	14°36.645'S	22°38.851'E

from the greater kestrel to bateleur and martial eagles, fish eagles and palmnut vultures. Pel's fishing owl is found along the rivers, the Luanginga to the south and the Luambimba to the north.

When to go With the exception of guided fly-in trips, the park is open to independent visitors only between mid July and December. For many people, Liuwa is at its best during November, when the gathering of wildebeest on the plains reaches its peak. That said, the park is worth visiting whenever you can get there – there's always some amazing wildlife to be seen!

Before you visit it's important to understand the weather and the game movements in the park.

From **January to about May**, a large area of the plain is covered in shallow water, and all the pans in the south of the park are full. Although the park is closed to visitors until mid April, these conditions are perfect for the large herds of herbivores which gather there, and the large numbers of birds which also arrive. However, **around June/July** the plains dry up, the waters recede northwards, and gradually the herds move that way also. They desert the waterholes of the southern side of the plain, and move back northwest, eventually melting back into the woodlands which surround the park. Plenty of resident wildlife remains, relying on a scattering of pans which retain their water for most of the year.

From **August to October** the herds start drifting southwards again. At first, in September, you'll find just a few herds, typically just a few hundred wildebeest, venturing south onto the northern areas of the plain – but gradually as the rains approach these increase in number and move further south into the park.

In **November and December** the first rains are falling, and the plains are teeming with game, including young animals, for this is also the calving period. November is classically the best time to visit the park – a balance between catching the best of the game, and ensuring that you can get out rather than getting stuck.

Getting there and away Until recently, driving yourself was the only means of exploring Liuwa Plain, but a couple of interesting options are now available. If you'd like to explore independently, you can hire a vehicle with driver from African Parks (*US$150/day plus fuel*). They will also arrange transfers from Kalabo airport (*US$45 pp return*) or Mongu (*US$290 pp return by car dry season; US$425–520 pp by boat wet season*).

Alternatively, Robin Pope Safaris (see page 494) operate weekly fly-in trips both during May and June, when the park's birdlife is at its best, and from November to December.

Self driving For independent drivers (4x4 only), access to the park is technically from July to 15 December only; either side of this and you would stand a strong chance of getting completely stuck in deep mud. In July, however, it's important to check the state of the Zambezi River well in advance, as if this is too high, then it cannot be crossed. In some years it is late July before the crossing is possible. A GPS is essential – and indeed may soon be mandatory.

From Kalabo First head to the tourism centre on the 'harbour' (⊕ HARKAL 14°59.248'S, 22°41.001'E) to get your permits, then take the pontoon across the Luanginga River (*Kw40,000 per vehicle one way*)

From the pontoon, there are multiple tracks heading to and around the park; it's very confusing. You should head for route markers ⊕ LIUWA1 14°59.044'S,

22°40.900'E, which you'll pass after barely 500m, and then ✪ LIUWA2 14°57.718'S, 22°40.119'E, which is a further 3km away. From here, take the right track. Beneath you is deep Kalahari sand, and the driving is a very steady, slow plod in low-range third or fourth gear, with an average speed of about 15km/h. There are a few small villages, but little game along the early part of the drive, although here and there lilac-breasted rollers brighten up the tops of trees along the roadside with dazzling flashes of blue as they fly.

There's no 'official' park entrance, though there used to be a signboard at ✪ LIUWAP 14°53.234'S, 22°39.102'E. One way into the park is to head about 13km north and slightly west of the pontoon. Shortly afterwards there is a small fork in the track at ✪ LIFORK 14°52.366'S, 22°38.803'E, from which both branches continue into the park. The right-hand track continues all the way to Matamanene Camp – and given the higher level of traffic that is likely to travel this way, this might be the best one to follow. However, on my last visit I took the left branch, which continues towards waypoint ✪ LIUWA3 14°50.594'S, 22°37.971'E.

As you get further into the park the trees start to spread out, grouping themselves into small, slightly raised islands, surrounded by a sea of knee-to-thigh-deep golden grass. Carry on for a further 10km or so after ✪ LIUWAP (above) to ✪ LIUWA4 14°47.287'S, 22°37.484'E, by which time you're basically out of the trees, and onto the southern edge of the plain. Here, the track into the park starts to become much less distinct – and ultimately vanishes. (If you're coming back out of the park, then head for this point to pick up the track out.)

Whichever fork you take, you should expect two or three hours of rough, sandy driving after you leave the pontoon before you are well into the park. The good news is that although getting into the park is a slow slog through deep sand, most of the tracks within the park are generally much firmer, easier and more pleasant to drive. Do keep to these tracks – and enjoy!

North and east to Lukulu While almost all visitors to Liuwa enter and leave via Kalabo, it is nevertheless possible in the peak of the dry season to drive out of the north of the park, crossing the Luambimba River before turning east towards Lukulu. Note that it can't be done in reverse, since both entry permits and campsite bookings for the national park can be organised only at Kalabo.

If you're considering this route, you'll need at least one self-contained 4x4 vehicle (and preferably two), and the services of a local guide (ask at Sikale campsite) in order to negotiate the Luambimba River, since it's a tortuous route that changes according to the level of the river and the time of year. A GPS is also essential.

From Sikale (✪ SIKALE 14°17.933'S, 22°33.226'E), head due north to Mutvaa village (✪ MUTVAA 14°16.106'S, 22°33.616'E). Just after the village, turn right at ✪ MUTVA2 14°15.884'S, 22°33.437'E onto a narrow track through the trees, emerging after 0.5km back on to the plain. Shortly after this, at ✪ MUTVA3 14°15.761'S, 22°33.655'E, take the left fork towards the woodland, following a sandy track with the trees on your right. At ✪ LUAMBI 14°15.524'S, 22°33.842'E, descend through the trees to fiddle your way through deep sand across a series of channels that make up the Luambimba River. At ✪ LUAMB2 14°15.380'S, 22°34.068'E, emerge from the wood and cross to two wooden stakes; go left, keeping the stakes on your right, into more woods. At ✪ LUAMB3 14°15.027'S, 22°34.322'E, there's a junction; turn right here, still in the woodland, on to a good track – well used by oxcarts – with the plain on your right. About 10km from Sikale (40 minutes' drive), or 4.6km from the river, you'll come to the village of Silange (✪ SILANG 14°15.201'S, 22°35.951'E). Bear left into the woodland once more, then follow this track eastwards for close on 77km to the Zambezi River, opposite Lukulu (⊕ LUKZAM 14°22.410'S, 23°13.933'E). For details of crossing the river, see page 497. Approaching the river, the woodlands thin out, the number of villages increases, and isolated fan palms dot the plains. Significant landmarks along the way include:

⊕ TOLUK1 14°14.166'S, 22°43.125'E	Village on right. Bear left just after village, keeping in woodland.
⊕ TOLUK2 14°14.896'S, 22°46.927'E	Take right fork.
⊕ TOLUK3 14°15.130'S, 22°47.949'E	Continue straight on at crossroads in small village, across a riverbed, then into woodland.
⊕ TOLUK4 14°16.912'S, 23°00.060'E	Track diverts around a pool then returns on other side across the plain, keeping village on right.
⊕ TOLUK5 14°19.045'S, 23°03.899'E	Take left fork.

Getting around The only means to explore the park, unless you're on an organised safari (see *Where to stay*, below), is by private 4x4. (For local vehicle hire, see *Getting there and away*, page 491) Game-drive loops have been designated for independent visitors, who are provided with a simple map of the park at the tourism centre in Kalabo. Staff here can advise on getting around the park, too. A 30km/h speed limit is largely self policing; you'd rarely be in a position to drive faster than this anyway.

There's no real need to take a scout as a guide – provided that you're fully equipped with a reliable GPS and have a back-up plan in case of an emergency (see *Safety precautions*, below). However, if you do take a guide (*US$10 per day, inc food*), then you may learn quite a bit from him or her, as well as helping the park with a valuable extra source of employment. The scout also carries a radio that can be used to communicate with the park headquarters in case of emergency.

Safety precautions A GPS system is essential for anyone planning to visit the park as landmarks are few and the tall grass can obscure views. Early in the season it's essential to have netting on your vehicle to stop grass seeds which will clog up your radiator and may combust (see *Driving through high grass*, on page 105). It's also wise in a park that's this remote to travel in convoy, with a reliable satphone in case of emergency.

Should an emergency arise, African Parks may be able to help, either by supplying fuel (*Kw1,500/litre surcharge*), or with the rescue of a vehicle (*US$90 exc fuel*). Do note, however, that availability of fuel cannot be relied on; this is absolutely a last resort.

⌂ Where to stay Several campsites have been established as a joint venture between the community and African Parks, thus making the park accessible if you are in a position to drive yourself in a small expedition. Remember, though, that – aside from water and firewood – you must be totally self-sufficient.

Over the years, attempts to set up permanent camps in Liuwa, however, have all failed; it's just too remote. While mobile safaris initially met a similar fate, these are now operated again by Robin Pope Safaris, who base their seasonal trips out of Matamenene Camp.

With the advent of flights between Lusaka and Mongu in 2011, access to this area will be improved, so plans are being drawn up for new camps in 2012–13.

🏠 **Matamanene Bush Camp** (4 tents)
Contact via African Parks (page 486) or
Robin Pope Safaris (page 268). ⊕ MATAMA
14°39.272'S, 22°38.188'E. Visible for its radio
mast from some distance across the plains,
Matamanene is a fully equipped self-catering
camp (*max 10 guests*). At certain times of the year,
it is used exclusively by Robin Pope Safaris, who
run set departures during May & Jun, & later in Nov
& Dec. At the edge of woodland overlooking the
plain are en-suite Meru tents under a canvas fly
sheet, each with twin beds & hotwater showers. A
large central tent shelters a comfortably furnished
lounge & dining area.

The camp is adjacent to the base camp of
the Liuwa Carnivore Project, a joint research
effort by African Parks & the Zambian Carnivore
Programme that focuses on wild dog, cheetah,
lion & hyena within the park & its significance
to transfrontier conservation efforts with
Angola. The project is run by Zambian ecologist
Jassiel M'soka, who is extremely helpful in
providing information on the whereabouts &
dynamics of these animals. *Self catering US$60
pp exc park fees. Robin Pope US$3,568/4,180
pp sharing 4/5 nights FBA, inc transfers from/
to Lusaka.*

Campsites (*US$10 pp*) There are four community campsites around the park,
three of them within a 15km radius of Matamenene Camp, along the wildebeest
migration route, and the fourth in the north of the park. A fifth site, Kayala, is
located 2km from Kalabo, south of the park entrance. Note that the camping fee
goes to the Liuwa Community Development Fund, administered by African parks
and the area chiefs. Some of this goes towards running the camp; the rest is used for
community projects such as schools and teachers' housing.

No more than five vehicles can be accommodated on each site at any one time.

With the exception of Sikale, where facilities are more basic, each of the sites has
two (cold) showers, two flush toilets, a washbasin and water from a well. You're not
allowed to collect firewood in the park, but it's supplied at no extra charge by the
attendant at each campsite; better still, bring your own fuel.

It is sometimes possible to arrange with the campsite attendant to be shown a
range of local crafts, or for traditional dances to take place at the campsites or to
be invited to a nearby village. Similarly, for those interested in fishing, traditional
techniques can be demonstrated or even taught, while other options may include
boat trips or guided walks, the latter with an armed scout.

Ă Kayala ⊕ KAYALA 14°58.360'S, 22°41.129'E.
Opened in 2010, Kayala is just 2km north of
Kalabo, so ideally placed for those arriving later
in the day.
Ă Kwale ⊕ KWALE 14°49.111'S, 22°41.015'E.
Situated in the southeast of the park, 19km (1hr)
from Kalabo, Kwale is a shady site bordering open
grassland. The wildlife is at its best from the end
of Oct.
Ă Lyangu ⊕ LYANGU 14°46.822'S,
22°32.735'E. 26.4km (1½hrs) from Kalabo, in
the southwest of the park, this is a woodland site
with plenty of indigenous flora. It is within easy
distance of the Lone Palm & several self-drive loops
affording excellent birding & game viewing.

Ă Katoyana ⊕ KATOYA 14°36.700'S,
22°42.126'E. With a central location about
42km (2½hrs) from Kalabo, Katoyana occupies
a peaceful wooded site on the edge of the plain,
not far from Liuwa School.
Ă Sikale ⊕ SIKALE 14°17.560'S, 22°33.150'E.
The most isolated of the park's campsites, 78km
(3½hrs) from Kalabo, Sikale is in a wooded glade
overlooking the plain at the northern edge
of the park, close to the route taken by local
fishermen as they return with their evening
catch. Immaculately maintained, it has a long-
drop toilet & 2 washing enclosures, with water
drawn from a waterhole & heated by the camp
attendant.

Places to visit Liuwa is all about exploring on your own – provided that you stick
to the existing roads. (This is important; the vegetation is extremely fragile and

easily damaged. Note, too, that drivers found off road could well incur a fine.) That said, there are a few spots worth noting:

- ❁ WATER1 14°45.334'S, 22°37.395'E This great waterhole seemed to be a magnet for cranes, with a huge flock of crowned cranes always around it, augmented by parties of wattled cranes.
- ❁ WATER2 14°44.848'S, 22°37.279'E Another lovely spot which was generally quieter, though did seem to be visited daily by a herd of red lechwe.
- ❁ 1PALM 14°40.876'S, 22°35.388'E This is the spot known as 'Lone Palm', for obvious reasons. There's also a huge waterhole here where the general birding was excellent.
- ❁ MIYAND 14°25.167'S, 22°39.109'E Miyanda Pool, one of the park's larger pools, close to the Mukalabumbu Tower. Even when devoid of water in mid October, a thousand or so wildebeest formed a cordon around the lake, interspersed with up to a hundred zebra, numerous waders, and a fair few scavengers – vultures and marabou storks – anticipating their dinner.

LUKULU The riverside town of Lukulu is the main town in the district, with a collection of government and local council offices in the boma, or central area. Supplies of **fuel**, from a drum rather than a pump, are both expensive and not terribly reliable, although at least the quality is considered to be acceptable. As always in outlying areas, you'd be wise not to run your tank too low.

The town, with its primary school, two high schools and a district hospital (now with very limited facilities), was founded as a Catholic mission, and remains typical of rural Zambia; visitors – especially those with fair skins – are something of a novelty. It has a public water pumping and distribution system, which means running (drinkable) water most of the time, but despite the presence of a ZESCO plant (Zambia's electricity supply company), supplies of electricity are erratic. Lukulu is also notable for having a **post office**, but no vehicle, so post to or from Lukulu is often transported by one of the Catholic nuns who work at the mission!

Getting there and away There are good all-weather roads linking Lukulu (❁ SANCTA 14°22.749'S, 23°14.236'E) with Kaoma, which is just off the Lusaka–Mongu road, Kabompo and Zambezi. Despite the proximity of Mongu, the route between the two towns is nothing but a series of inter-village footpaths across the Barotse floodplain; it is usually faster to travel via Kaoma. There are no reliable roads on the west side of the Zambezi, though crossing the river and finding a route through to Liuwa Plain is possible in the height of the dry season (see page 492).

From Mongu across the Barotse floodplain By far the quickest and best route to Lukulu starts near the Kaoma turn-off, on the Lusaka–Mongu road. However, if it is well into the dry season, then there is another possibility described here: heading cross country across the floodplains.

Leaving Mongu past the new market, the tar ends after the shops at Limulunga (❁ LIMULU 15°7.769'S, 23°8.635'E) and shortly the track forks. Head down the hill, towards the small river. Fording the first shallow channel of this, take a hard right onto a motorable track and follow this. There are lots of people down here, and if you can pick up a hitchhiker to guide you, then do so. You'll probably give lifts to several before the day is out!

As you head north the tracks split and fork, getting smaller all the time, until about midway to Lukulu. Then there appear to be no good tracks. However, gradually, as you continue, they get clearer again as you approach Lukulu. Think about it and you'll realise that they are all made by the local people, travelling from village to village, and (crucially) to their nearest town – so they radiate out from the towns. This is the typical pattern made by the smallest thoroughfares in most rural areas.

There's little point my trying to describe the precise route here, as every vehicle will end up on a slightly different track – which is half the fun! Instead I'll list a few waypoints, south to north, so that those travelling with a GPS can keep track that they're heading roughly in the right general direction:

⊕ NANGIL 14°52.659'S, 23°4.478'E Nangili School where an engaging headteacher presides over about 350 children, from grades one to nine.
⊕ AIRNGU 14°36.687'S, 23°6.977'E Ngulwana Airstrip, which is occasionally used by fishermen coming on private trips up to this corner of the Zambezi.
⊕ KAWYA 14°28.827'S, 23°13.999'E Near the school at Kawaya. If coming south towards Mongu, this point marks where you deviate from the track to Mbanga, turning right down a steep bank. Coming north, you join a better track here.
⊕ TUMONG 14°24.515'S, 23°15.588'E Where the bush track from Mongu/Mbanga meets the reasonable Kaoma–Lukulu road.
⊕ SANCTA 14°22.749'S, 23°14.236'E The Sancta Maria Mission at Lukulu.

The countryside is lovely, with open fields and plenty of patches of various interesting palm trees. You'll pass through a variety of tiny villages and settlements – mostly subsistence farming of rice and maize. On very rural routes like this it's important that you give lifts to other travellers; they're often poor people for whom there probably isn't any other form of transport. Conveniently, they'll often be able to direct you to the nearest town, too, making the second half of your journey much easier than the first. It's about 99km as the stork flies between Mongu and Lukulu, and going over the floodplains will take you about five to six hours.

From Kaoma to Lukulu The bumpy gravel road between Kaoma and Lukulu offers year-round access to the town. When the Barotse Plains are flooded, it is also the only access route for vehicles from Mongu, which must head east to Kaoma along the tar road, then northwest to Lukulu; the alternative is to go by boat.

Buses ply between Kaoma and Lukulu a couple of times a week, costing around Kw70,000 one way. VSO worker Karun Thanjavur described the road as 'an axle breaker … the buses creak and groan from abuse'. She advises travellers coming this way on public transport to travel with a good stock of food and water (at least for two days), and a sleeping bag (with mosquito net/coils) etc – just in case the bus breaks down.

From Lukulu to Kasempa Heading north-northwest you pass the school and then the old market before leaving town. This is a reasonable gravel road for which a high-clearance 4x4 would be wise in the rains – but otherwise it is a main artery by local standards on which you can reach 50–60km/h. Traffic is light, primarily oxcarts, as the road undulates past a mix of bush and settlements, with plenty of mango trees and cassava crops being grown.

It's about 63km to the Watopa pontoon (⊕ WATOPA 14°02.338'S, 23°37.744'E), where there are a few small shops. If you were to follow the road southeast from the ferry you'd get back to meet the road to Kaoma. For Kasempa, however, take the pontoon across the Kabompo River (*Kw56,000 per vehicle*) and follow the similarly good gravel road for almost 22km, heading slightly east of north until you come to a T-junction with the east–west M8. This is Mumbeji (⊕ MUMBEJ 13°51.653'S, 23°40.327'E), notable only for a range of small stalls and grocery shops with names such as 'God's Chance' and the 'Work like a Slave'.

From here the good all-weather M8 gravel road (50–60km/h when dry!) goes west to the town of Zambezi (⊕ ZAMBEZ 13°32.262'S, 23°06.158'E), and east about 67km to Kabompo (⊕ KABOMP 13°35.610'S, 24°12.125'E). Although there has clearly been some logging here, much of this road goes through thick woodland with very few settlements.

Without your own vehicle, the only means of public transport around these areas are private local 4x4s, assorted lorries and vans. The charge varies (depending whether you wish to ride in the cab or in the open back, braving the elements) but you can get from Lukulu to Watopa or Kabompo, for example, for about US$6/Kw30,000. Some drivers will inevitably charge more if you are fair-skinned, as you are perceived to be a wealthy *makuwa* (white person). On average, this is probably a fair assumption – so pay and smile, and don't complain!

From the west There is a pontoon crossing at Lukulu, but it's by no means regular, and there are no real roads on the other side – just a series of paths that link the small villages there.

Crossing here and then driving south to Liuwa and/or Kalabo is possible in the height of the dry season (see page 492), but a GPS and a local guide are essential. Kalabo is much easier to reach by crossing the river further south.

If you do want to use the pontoon at Lukulu, you'll need both plenty of time and, quite possibly, some local help, since even if the pontoon is on your side of the river (it's usually on the Lukulu side), the chances of it being manned are slim. The fare is a matter of local negotiation with pontoon operator Mr Kayombo (m 0979 146388). We were charged a hefty Kw140,000: Kw70,000 each way – since the pontoon was on the 'wrong' side of the river and had to cross to fetch us. There's room for only one car on the pontoon and as the riverbanks are steep and sandy on both sides, you'll need to reverse onto it in order to be in a position to drive off in forward gear.

🏠 **Where to stay** Basic accommodation comes in the form of a **government guesthouse** (**$** *exc b/fast*), reached by turning southwest off the main road near the post office, then following it round to the right,. There's also the **Mary Inn** (**$**) in the new market, a slightly better option than its namesake in the old market.

There are no campsites, but if you ask permission you may be able to **camp** in front of the Sancta Maria Mission. The mission itself has rooms, although these are usually occupied by local people working in the town. Either way, the sound of children singing at the local school is likely to be balanced by that of late-night revelry from across the river! If you'd prefer to camp out of town, there are many lovely spots along the river, especially just across from Lukulu on the far bank, where a well-equipped traveller can camp in peace in the dry season. Ask whoever owns the nearest homestead for permission.

For details of fishing camps in the area, see opposite.

✗ Where to eat There are several basic restaurants, mostly in the old and new markets. All usually offer rather meagre fare of nshima and some form of relish ($). With a few hours' notice, **Fernando's Butchery**, in the old market, may be able to serve slightly more elaborate meals.

If you're self catering, it's wise to arrive with a good stock of food and drink. The shops in the old and new markets have only the most basic essentials, and the chances of finding even canned food are not great. Both soft drinks and beer depend on a truck supplying them from Lusaka; news of its arrival spreads like wildfire through the town.

The local people live by subsistence farming and fishing, eating just what they cultivate or catch, so not much fresh produce reaches the market either. That said, you'll probably find one or two varieties of seasonal fruits and vegetables, plus dried fish, eggs and roller meal for nshima. Try Fernando's Butchery in the old market for meat. Bread supplies are erratic, but scones are sometimes available as an alternative. As to the wares at the Ziba Zako Endless Love Shop, who knows?

What to see and do Lukulu doesn't have many obvious attractions, though the nearby Zambezi River and floodplains are very scenic, with excellent views from the Sancta Maria Mission (see box below). As in many of the area's smaller places, privacy can be a problem as an outsider is regarded as a source of free entertainment by some of the local community. Karun, a VSO volunteer living here, commented, 'If the visitor is willing to offer to the local people the same right to watch that s/he has assumed, then we have a happy relationship; if not, we have an unhappy visitor

---

SANCTA MARIA MISSION

The peaceful Sancta Maria Catholic Mission (⊕ SANCTA 14°22.749'S, 23°14.236'E) at Lukulu was founded in the 1930s by Father Phelem O'Shea, later Bishop of Livingstone. Painted a dark pink, it has a stunning setting high on one bank of the Zambezi, overlooking palm-fringed woodlands opposite, and is a beautiful place from which to watch the sunset.

Over the years, several different Catholic missionaries have worked here, including the Sisters of the Holy Cross, who established the girls' school. The sisters tell of one day, in the 1950s, when the bell in the tower started ringing wildly. On investigation the bell ringer proved to be a spotted hyena – probably from Liuwa – which had seized the rawhide rope in its jaws, and was trying to pull it off and eat it.

The building itself now functions as a community guesthouse, but the mission continues its community and social work, particularly in the areas of schools, welfare and health.

There is a Sunday service in Lozi that offers a fascinating blend of Catholicism and Lozi culture – with lots of singing and dancing.

but content locals. Except for an occasional visit by a group of Makishi dancers, there are no other festivals that take place in Lukulu.'

Fishing camps around Lukulu In the early 1990s several fishing camps started up between Mongu and Lukulu, focusing on the superb tigerfishing in the area. However, it proved a difficult and expensive place to run a camp and several failed. Today, the only camp operating is Barotse Tiger Camp.

During July and August, there are fully catered five-night fishing camps on the Lungwebungu River, northwest of Lukulu on the western side of the Zambezi River, run by Mutemwa Lodge (page 471).

🏠 **Barotse Tiger Camp** (6 tents) 📞 0213 327489; m 0977 707829/586353; e anglezam@ microlink.zm; www.zambezifishing.com. Some 20km south of Lukulu, this classy fishing lodge under the ownership of the Livingstone-based Angle Zambia is on a stretch of river where numerous fishing world records have been attained over the years. Guests fly in to Lukulu airport & transferred to the camp by vehicle & boat. There is no vehicular access to the camp itself.

This is a traditional tented camp, spread out along the river. Tents have dbl or twin beds under mosi nets, & en-suite facilities with flush toilets & outdoor showers. At the heart of the camp are 2 large mess tents: 1 with a bar & lounge, comfortably kitted out with sofas & armchairs; the other the dining area. As for the fishing, with waters teeming with fish & 18ft aluminium boats with GPS fish-finding technology, anglers will be in their element. *US$450/585 pp sharing/sgl FB, inc laundry, fishing, exc drinks & fuel.* ⏲ *Apr–Oct.*

NORTHWESTERN ZAMBIA

West of the Copperbelt, squeezed between Angola and DRC, this area is distant from most of Zambia. This is reflected in its flora and fauna which, in parts, are much more like those of the wet tropical forests which occur to the north than those of the drier areas of the Kalahari to the south.

Despite being out on a limb, the roads here generally work well, with a tar road from the Copperbelt to Mwinilunga and another being constructed over the top of the good gravel road known as the M8, which links Solwezi with Zambezi via Mufumbwe and Kabompo.

MUFUMBWE Once little more than a dot on the map, the linear town of Mufumbwe (✤ MUFUMB 13°08.212'S, 25°00.251'E), 108km west of the turn-off to Kasempa and 121km east of Kabompo, is growing rapidly. For those driving through on the M8, it's notable for a reasonably reliable if very expensive **fuel** station (diesel only at the time of research) and a **tyre-repair** place. These, as well as a **bakery** and a small **market**, are invaluable if you're planning a detour into West Lunga National Park.

WEST LUNGA NATIONAL PARK (*Park fees US$10 pp/day; vehicle US$15/day or Kw15,300 if Zambian registered;* ⏲ *Jun–Oct*) Some 150km northwest of Kafue, as the pied crow flies, West Lunga is another of Zambia's parks which is both very wild and little visited. It was originally gazetted as a game reserve in the late 1940s, mainly to preserve its population of yellow-backed duiker. Then elephants were also abundant, along with a multitude of antelope species including Angolan (giant) sable and Lichtenstein's hartebeest. There was big game here – including buffalo, lion and leopard – but probably never in the volumes found in the Luangwa or Kafue. However, in the last few decades it's been used very little, except for hunting and fishing by the local communities. As a result, the game has been seriously depleted, and vegetation overgrown.

Despite signs during the last decade that, possibly, with a lot of dedication and hard work, it might be coming back to life, there is as yet little evidence of this on the ground. One positive move has been the formation of the West Lunga Trust, to try to conserve some of this pristine corner of Zambia. The surrounding population density here is relatively low, and almost entirely adjacent to the main roads. Thus, with the help and drive of the local chiefs, they've been able to mobilise many of the local communities to help patrol and monitor the environment. Community Resource Boards (CRBs) have been introduced with a view to controlling the natural resources in each of the surrounding areas, and derive a financial benefit from any operations there. It is to be hoped that the willingness of the park's staff, which is considerable, and their tough approach to poaching, will in time translate into improvements in both the infrastructure and environment within the park itself.

Geography, flora and fauna West Lunga National Park covers 1,684km²
of forests, dambos, open grasslands and papyrus swamps. It is bounded by the Kabompo River to the east and south (adjacent to which are most of the park's swamps) and by the West Lunga River to the west. The environment is still pristine miombo, interspersed with large grassland plains, flooded dambos and some particularly attractive *Cryptosepalum* forests. It's very beautiful and wild, but the grass and vegetation are thick and difficult even to walk through. The rivers that flow through the park are great for canoeing and boating – with some sections of rapids, and some where you canoe beside rock walls.

Buk's 1993–94 survey (see *Appendix 3*, page 536) reported two sightings of wild dog in West Lunga, although noted that poaching remained heavy and the species was probably declining here. Rob Munro reports that he saw buffalo, impala, puku and warthog in the park on a trip in mid 1999.

Ten years later, Dorian Tilbury (a first-class guide with a long history in Zambia's more remote areas) confirmed sightings of puku, hippo, crocodile, vervet monkey, yellow baboon and numerous excellent sightings of samango monkey, plus spoor of bushbuck, bush pig, cane rat, thick-tailed bushbaby, civet and genet. There are certainly still puku, vervet monkey, hippo and crocodile here, and the scouts at Jivundu claim recent sightings of elephant, defassa waterbuck, hartebeest, sable and blue duiker. In the north of the park there is talk of buffalo, bushbuck, reedbuck, civet and bushpig, too. It's also quite likely that there will be a few sitatunga around, plus common and yellow-backed duiker. There are probably no lion or leopard remaining, though both certainly used to occur here.

Of course with an untouched environment, the birding remains excellent – and even a short visit along the rivers should yield sightings of half-collared kingfishers, African finfoots and large numbers of black saw-wing swallows amongst many more common species. Zambia's turacos do well here, with Schalow's and Ross's more common than the grey lourie or go-away bird.

Getting there West Lunga is still exceptionally wild – so you will require an independent streak both to get here, and to get around.

The park's main entrance, near the village of Jivundu (⊕ JIVUND 13°06.139'S, 24°41.522'E), is accessed from the main M8 road, 64km east of Kabompo, and 41km west of Mufumbwe. There's no signpost here, so it's easy to miss the turning (⊕ TUJIVU 13°12.151'S, 24°40.907'E). This leads on to a sandy track, which runs through woodland for 11.5km to the ZAWA scout post on the south bank of the

CRYPTOSEPALUM FORESTS AND THE WHITE-CHESTED TINKERBIRD

Almost exclusive to Zambia, *Cryptosepalum* forests are distinctive dry evergreen forests which occur in the area of the Kabompo River. They are regarded by botanists as forming the largest area of tropical evergreen forest in Africa outside the equatorial zone.

Dominating these forests is the *mukwe* tree (*Cryptosepalum pseudotaxus*), which grows on relatively infertile Kalahari sand where there is no permanent surface water. This lack of water means that these areas remain relatively uninhabited. Other trees often found here include the much-exploited rosewood (*Guibourtia coleosperma*). Further south, the character of these forests gradually changes and they become dominated by Zambezi teak trees (*Baikiaea plurijuga*; see *The demise of the teak forests*, page 455). Hence logging is a serious threat to them.

The under-storey in *Cryptosepalum* forests is usually dense and tangled, including *Liana* and *Combretum* species which form impenetrable thickets. Epiphytic lichens are common, and the forest floor is mainly covered in mosses. It's very difficult to walk through unless a path has already been cleared.

The avifauna is usually particularly rich, with a mixture of bird species which frequent moist evergreen forests, woodlands and riverine forests. Amongst specials found in these forests are gorgeous bush shrikes, crested guineafowls, purple-throated cuckoo-shrikes, Margaret's batises and square-tailed drongos. However, the area is famous amongst ornithologists for the controversy surrounding its one and only endemic species: the white-chested tinkerbird. Just one of these birds has ever been found, and that was the 'type specimen' netted in 1964. Numerous subsequent attempts to find more have failed.

Some feel that they have simply been defeated by the dense foliage, and that a population of these birds exists deep within the thickets. Others argue that the one specimen found was probably an aberrant individual of the similar golden-rumped tinkerbird, which also occurs in these forests. Whatever the truth, it makes these forests a magnet for birdwatchers, all keen to catch a glimpse of the world's second white-chested tinkerbird!

Kabompo River. Here you pay your entrance and campsite fees, and can arrange for a scout to accompany you across the river into the park.

The easiest ways to get to West Lunga are either from the Copperbelt or from Kafue National Park's eastern boundary, via Kasempa. Approaching from Lukulu is straightforward, but from Mongu is very time-consuming – whether via Kaoma or across the plains, when a good 4x4 is essential even in the dry season.

From the Copperbelt Take the tar road through Kitwe and Chingola to Solwezi (⊕ SOLWEZ 12°10.931'S, 26°23.960'E), from where it turns south until crossing the Mutanda River at Mwelemu (⊕ MWELEM 12°23.661'S, 26°14.276'E). On the other side of the river, there's a good tar road on the right, which heads west to Mwinilunga. For West Lunga, continue on the road south, towards Kabompo and Kasempa. After almost 90km it is joined from the east by a road from Kitwe (which would have made a shorter, but more time-consuming, approach), via the village of Ingwe.

About 16km later there is a road left to Kasempa, and one straight on to Kabompo (⊕ KABOMP 13°35.610'S, 24°12.125'E). Take the road going straight. By 2010, this section of the M8 had been tarred as far as Kabompo and is a super road – though

A personal view of canoeing the West Lunga, from Dorian Tilbury

> Twisting and turning, your feelings are burning,
> You're breaking the girl … she loves no one else…

The song rolls around my head like the incessant chant of some rhythmic revolution; and it's not from listening to the Red Hot Chili Peppers either. We've been on the road around Zambia for some time and don't have the track in our collection but we spent the night with a Peace Corps volunteer in a village outside Kasempa and he played us a tune one night … strummed his guitar around the dancing firelight and sang the Chili Peppers song. It stuck.

This mission is an odd one. There are two girls involved, one whom I would love to break, the other I would most definitely not. The latter is my wife, newly wed and the single most important person in my life; the former is the West Lunga River down which we are canoeing for the next six days … twisting and turning … my fears are returning … I'm breaking the girl …

There is no road for resupply or extraction, no radio communication, no boat, no village, no Burger King drive-through if it all gets too much. Once we launch our canoe we are committed to the river, to the exit point six days and more than 70km away. But we are well prepared and once we're in and drifting with the oscillating current, we're twisting and turning … our senses enduring … we're breaking the girl …

The water is crystal clear, cutting its snaking path through this emphatic and wild terrain. The banks are high, sometimes even carved from black rock, sheer and straight, almost overbearing in grace and stature. Freaky euphorbias and silver figs emerge from the granite, their roots entwined through crags and crevices, creeping and drifting down secret passages until somewhere their food source is found. When there are no rocks, the banks bulge and swell with matted trees all clambering for a front-row seat, a room with a view, a perch on the edge of this marvellous show. Everything, it seems, was caught suspended in time making a rush for this river.

We cannot see through the trees. We creep down this mystic rhythm with just the noise of our paddles gliding the surface and a multitude of birds flashing blues and yellows, scarlets and purples, every colour of every rainbow on temporary display. Schalow's lourie, half-collared kingfisher, African finfoot and black saw-wing swallows provide the entertainment and make up the pixels within this big picture charade. And all the while, pyjama-clad samango monkeys dance through the trees, turn and look, then sheepishly disappear.

We don't know what awaits us with this girl … we hit rapids and rock pools, hippos and croc dives. We catch glimpses of memories … just a flash then they're gone … evidence of poachers in the shadows of a distant past, long since departed along with the game. There are times when it is almost silent and eerie, the forgotten relic of a time gone by, a time of animal crowding. One day perhaps the forests will again echo and cry with the howl of territory calls, the crack of feeding branches, the whistles of alarm. But for now, the silent majesty flows her irrefutable path down a million years of creation. She carries her life blood and snakes her course, relinquishing the secrets of her past, oblivious to the prospect of her future … twisting and turning … her feelings are burning … we're breaking the girl …

you still need to watch out for pedestrians and animals. After 140km you'll come to the turning off the M8, above.

From Kafue Follow the directions in *Chapter 14*, page 423, to approach Kasempa from Mumbwa via the Lubungu and Lunga pontoons, stopping at Mukinge Hospital for fuel, then head north from Kasempa onto the road from Mwelemu to Kabompo. Alternatively, take the tar road to Kitwe and Solwezi, and then cut southwest; this is likely to be easier and probably faster.

⌂ Where to stay

⚠ Fishing Camp ⊕ WLNPFC 13°06.480'S, 24°40.552'E. The park's campsite, confusingly named the 'fishing camp', is located outside the park on the southern bank of the Kabompo River, just 2.2km from the park gate, & 3km from the confluence of the Kabompo & West Lunga rivers.

Simple but well maintained, it's a large, fenced site, sandy underfoot but with plenty of tree shade, & direct access to a picturesque bend in the river for boats. Facilities comprise a wooden shower enclosure with a donkey boiler for hot water, & a separate toilet. *US$5 pp.*

What to see and do A new vehicle pontoon across the river was installed in 2010, and ZAWA's stated aim is to clear the road through the park from Jivundu to Ntambu in the north during 2011, making it within reach of the Solwezi–Mwinilunga road. By late 2010, however, even the first few kilometres were sufficiently overgrown to make access all but impossible. Until the track through the park has been properly cut, then, it's best to leave your vehicle at Jivundu, under the watchful eyes of the scouts, and take a scout/guide from there to walk with you into the park, returning to camp in the evening.

If you'd like to go out on the river, boat trips (*US$20 pp plus Kw30,000 & fuel for the boat, plus park fees*) can be arranged, provided that fuel is available. Thus these are best booked in advance. Similarly, fishing – with your own kit (*US$30 pp/day*) – is another option. Boats can be launched from the campsite, where it's possible to negotiate a mokoro trip on the river with one of the local fishermen.

Although the rivers here are in stunning condition, with some class III rapids, the canoeing trips that used to be organised by Mwinilunga Ventures between June and October are no longer operating. Perhaps it's only a matter of time before another operator with an adventurous streak will be persuaded to start these again.

KABOMPO This small town beside the surging Kabompo River, in the sparsely populated northwest, is at the centre of Zambia's remaining teak forests – and 121km from Mufumbwe. There is a long-established Catholic mission here, as well as a **market**, a hospital, a **post office**, a branch of the Finance **Bank**, several small **shops** and a handful of guesthouses. **Fuel**, supplied from drums, is not guaranteed, although diesel is more reliable than petrol; ask around near the restaurant opposite the water tower for a dealer.

Getting there and away Navigating to and from Kabompo (⊕ KABOMP 13°35.610'S, 24°12.125'E) is very easy, as it's on the main M8 road. By early 2011, the ongoing but slow programme of tarring had included the town centre, and was continuing to both east and west.

From Mwinilunga The turning northwards to Mwinilunga (⊕ TUMWIN 13°26.082'S, 24°19.978'E) is 25km east of Kabompo, and although it's signposted, is easily missed. After about 4.5km this road splits; the road to Mwinilunga takes the right fork over the tributary, and then bends back to the left, heading roughly north-northwest with the Manyinga River on its left. See the section on getting to Mwinilunga, page 509, for more about this road.

Just 2km east of the turning is the busy roadside town of **Manyinga** (⊕ MANYIN 13°25.095'S, 24°19.901'E), spread out between two bridges – over the Kabompo River on the east side, and the scenic Manyinga River to the west.

By bus Buses to and from Zambezi (*Kw40,000 one way*) stop every day except Sunday outside the Big Tree Restaurant on the main road, almost opposite the water tower. There are also three buses a week between Chavuma and Solwezi (*Kw85,000 one way*), and on to Kitwe (*Kw150,000*), all stopping in Kabompo.

Where to stay and eat A clutch of simple guesthouses (**$**) is signposted off the main road towards the river. Among these are two that boast river views: the **Kabompo Riverview** (m *0967 921799*) and the **Zambezi Source** (⊕ KABOGH 13°36.283'S, 24°12.793'E). To get there, turn off the main road at ⊕ TUGSTH 13°35.618'S, 24°12.156'E, continue over a rather incongruous but neatly planted roundabout, and you will find them on the left-hand side.

If you need to pick up some food, you might try the **Slow by Slow Restaurant** or the **Struggling Grocery**, close to the water tower – where there's also a bakery.

ZAMBEZI Like many regional centres in Zambia, Zambezi is referred to locally as 'the boma'. It's a small town with a few very basic **shops**, a **post office**, a Catholic mission and a small local **market**. Most of its amenity buildings, including the police station and government offices, are situated just off the main road, behind the 'new' **fuel** station (⊕ ZAMBEZ 13°32.262'S, 23°06.158'E), which when we visited was showing no signs of opening. In fact, if you're driving into this area,

---

THE WORLD'S PUREST HONEY

Driving around the Kabompo area, you'll often see what look like hollow logs, suspended high in the trees. These are beehives, and beekeeping has long been a tradition in these forests, with fathers handing down to their sons not only the skills, but also traditional hives of grass, bark and hollow tree trunks.

Now this traditional process has developed into a thriving industry with global reach. This started as a Zambian government initiative, initially supported by funding from the German Technical Development Agency, to improve the marketing of the local honey that was produced here, and thus increase the income of the rural population. Then there were only a few hundred local producers, but in 1979 North Western Bee Products was established.

Now this company is owned by the producers and it buys honey and beeswax from about 3,000 traditional bark hive beekeepers in Zambia. It supplies almost half the African honey exported to the EU, at prices typically 50% above the average price paid for other imported honey, and this was the first honey to be certified organic by the Soil Association.

It exports most of its wax and honey to Tropical Forest Products, in the UK (*www.tropicalforest.com*), which then markets and distributes it as a premium product to shops such as Fortnum & Mason, Sainsbury's, the Body Shop and others.

See their website for more about this model of sustainable development.

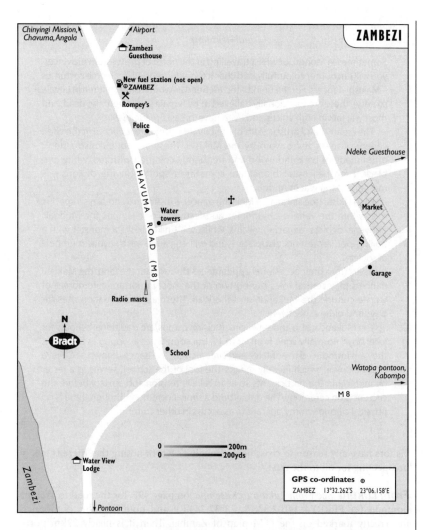

Chinyingi Mission,
Chavuma, Angola

Airport

Zambezi
Guesthouse

New fuel station (not open)
⊕ ZAMBEZ

Rompey's

Police

Ndeke Guesthouse

CHAVUMA ROAD (M8)

Water
towers

✝

Market

$

Garage

Radio masts

N

Bradt

School

Watopa pontoon,
Kabompo

M 8

0 ——————— 200m
0 ——————— 200yds

Zambezi

Water View
Lodge

GPS co-ordinates ⊕
ZAMBEZ   13°32.262'S   23°06.158'E

Pontoon

do so with very large reserves of fuel. The town's old fuel station closed some time ago, leaving drivers dependent on black-market fuel. Supplies of this are erratic, but diesel is more reliable than petrol, albeit at a very expensive Kw8,500 per litre. Do be aware that watered-down petrol from illicit sources – known as 'bush fuel' – is sometimes sold to unsuspecting travellers, so ask locally for a reliable source.

Getting there and away The road west from Kabompo, the M8, is a remarkably good gravel road (gradually being tarred), that continues north to the Angolan border at Chavuma. Along the road are relatively few villages and lots of thick teak forests. In the dry season the smoke from occasional bush fires will be seen drifting in the sky, above areas of scorched and blackened ground. It's a measure of the improvements in the road infrastructure that the journey to Lusaka that used to take five days can now be completed, via Lukulu and Kaoma, in around ten hours.

There's a pontoon across the river just below Water View Lodge (*Kw45,000 per vehicle*), although most people pay just Kw500 to be ferried over by mokoro. Few

Sometimes in Mongu, or whilst travelling in the north of the western provinces, you will encounter colourfully clad characters adorned with fearsome costumes – Makishi dancers. For the uninitiated (defined as women and children in Luvale society), these are traditionally believed to be female spirits from the dead, and most will talk in high voices and even have 'breasts' made of wire.

The creative and artistic skills of the Luvale people are reflected in the wide variety of mask styles worn by the Makishi. These are huge constructions, often made of bark and wood and frequently coloured with red, white and black. Even helicopter blades are sometimes spotted in the designs – a memory of the war in Angola.

Each Likishi (the singular of Makishi) dancer is distinctive and plays a specific role within the various ceremonies and festivals. For example, the Mungali, or hyena, depicts menacing villains, whilst the Chikishikishi, a monster with a boiling pot, represents discipline – and will consume mischievous members of society.

Apart from their occasional appearances throughout the land, the Makishi dancers play central roles during two of the most important ceremonies of Luvale culture: the Mukanda and the Wali. These are the initiation rites for boys and girls respectively.

The Mukanda, also known as circumcision camps, are traditional 'schools' for local boys, normally aged from 12 to 17, but sometimes as young as five. Here, they are introduced to adult life and circumcised. The dancer known as Chileya cha Mukanda, which literally means 'the fool of the school', serves as a jester by mimicking the participants so as to relieve tension and anxiety before the circumcision ceremony. The girls attend a similar ceremony, though there is no physical clitoridectomy operation, as occurs in other cultures.

visitors have any reason to cross here, though it's worth noting that there is talk of prospecting for oil to the west.

From Lukulu See *From Lukulu to Kasempa*, on page 497, for the road to Watopa pontoon (⊕ FERRY4 14°02.338'S, 23°37.744'E), and note that this pontoon is incorrectly marked on the ITM map of Zambia. Then it is nearly 22km north to Mumbeji (⊕ MUMBEJ 13°51.653'S, 23°40.327'E), where you turn left on to the good M8 for a further 75km west and northwest to Zambezi (⊕ ZAMBEZ 13°32.262'S, 23°06.158'E).

Where to stay and eat Perhaps unexpectedly, Zambezi has a handful of guesthouses, including **Ndeke Guesthouse**, and those below - both of which have restaurants. Alternatively, try the simple **Rompey's Restaurant**, next to the 'new' fuel station.

Water View Lodge (14 rooms) m 0979 379449. Perched high above the Zambezi, & clearly signposted from the main road, this pleasant guesthouse has 3 types of room. An inventive pricing structure means that the best, at Kw100,000, are also the best value – rather grand, with en-suite shower, TV, fridge, fan & b/fast included. Meals of nshima with chicken or fish are served in a thatched restaurant overlooking the river, where there's also an open rondavel, ideal for sunset drinks. **$** *B/fast Kw10,000 pp.*

🏠 **Zambezi Guest House** (5 rooms, camping) off Chavuma Rd; 📞 0218 371124; 📱 0978 642882; e zambezi@limagarden.com; www. limagarden.com. Renovations are expected to add another 20 rooms to this guesthouse, which currently has en-suite brick-&-thatch chalets with TV, fridge & dbl beds. **$**

What to see and do

Traditional dancing About 17km north of town are the palaces of the Lunda and the Luvale senior chiefs, on the east and west sides of the road respectively – as you might predict from the rough distribution of languages mapped out in *Chapter 2*, page 21. The Luvale chief's palace is the venue for the Likumbi Lya Mize (see page 25), as well as for traditional dancing which is held here several times a week.

CHINYINGI SUSPENSION BRIDGE

with thanks to Richard Miller, Cheshire, Connecticut, USA

The Chinyingi Mission was founded in 1953 to minister to villagers on both sides of the Zambezi, bringing them education and healthcare. However, at this point the river is over 210m wide, very deep, and subject to annual flooding, yet the only means of crossing it in the early days of the mission was by dugout canoe.

When he first arrived at the mission, Brother Crispin was responsible for transport, maintenance and cooking, and in order to help bring heavy supplies as well as people over the river he introduced a pontoon ferry. However, in 1971 four people were drowned while bringing a woman to hospital in a dug-out canoe, and he vowed to prevent any further accident by building a bridge over the river. While his was an unlikely background for the engineering feat he had undertaken, Brother Crispin didn't lack faith. From a picture of a suspension bridge in Nepal that he had seen in *National Geographic*, he set to work, identifying people who could help him in the design of the bridge, sourcing the materials, and securing funds to pay for the project. He pulled together a team of just five young labourers, then spent all his free time working alongside them; for safety reasons, no work was undertaken unless he was present.

The project was not without significant setbacks. At just 6m high, the original towers at each end of the bridge proved to be too low for the cables to span the river at the right height, and had to be rebuilt twice to reach the necessary 18m. The suspension cables, when first hung, swung wildly, until Brother Crispin was advised to install guy wires to hold them in place. And every element of the supplies had to be trucked up to 800km across unforgiving terrain in all weathers. Little wonder that it took over five years for the bridge to be completed.

The result, though, has stood the test of time. Since its opening in 1977, the 300m bridge has continued to provide a lifeline to people on the opposite side of the river to the mission, and a supply line for the mission itself. While Brother Crispin has now returned to his native Italy, as many as 500 people a day continue to cross the 1m-wide metal walkway (the original wood was replaced by Brother Crispin before he left), that he and his team suspended some 13m above the waters. They come on foot, on bicycles, and even on mopeds, up to 60 at a time, taking for granted the work of a Capuchin monk who built their bridge on faith.

15

Chinyingi Mission About 23km north of Zambezi, just after the Makondu River, is a sandy track heading west (⊕ TUCHIN 13°20.450'S, 23°03.674'E). It's signposted to Chinyingi Mission, which is a further 8km along this track, for which a high-clearance 4x4 is essential.

The mission (⊕ CHINYI 13°21.146'S, 23°00.834'E), which stands on the western bank of the Zambezi, was founded in 1953 by a group of Capuchin brothers. It is perhaps most famous for the Chinyingi suspension bridge – one of only four bridges to span the width of the Zambezi at the time of its construction (see box, page 507), though a fifth, at Sesheke, has since been built – and two more, at Ngonye Falls and Kazungula, are likely to follow. If you walk across the bridge to the mission (you can park by the bridge), you get a real feel for its 300m span, and some beautiful views along the river, too.

Although the mission is not currently inhabited, the school and a rural health centre are still operational, as is the mission church, and visitors are welcome to look around. It's a tranquil spot, lit up by frangipani and flame trees. The church itself is simple but light and spacious, drums at the ready for the next service, and notable for its cross of scaffolding bars.

CHAVUMA Some 80km north of Zambezi, or 6km south of the Angolan border, Chavuma lies at the point where the Zambezi re-enters Zambia. The land around here is arid, and the soil mostly grey in colour, which makes villages in this area look dull compared with those further south. Proximity to the border means that the town has attracted a number of illegal Angolan diamond sellers.

The Brethren Missionaries, who live in a large compound up on the hill by the town, have their own camping spot by the river, which they may allow you to use, or they may be able to direct you to other suitable places to stay.

Fuel supplies are very intermittent, so it's important not to rely on filling up here.

Getting there The M8 here from Solwezi via Kabompo and Zambezi is a decent gravel road. If you're approaching from the south via Lukulu then it's best to cross the Kabompo River at the Watopa pontoon (⊕ FERRY4 14°02.338'S, 23°37.744'E), then join this road from there (see *From Lukulu to Kasempa*, page 497).

What to see and do
Chavuma Falls This is not nearly as spectacular as the Zambezi's drops at Ngonye and Victoria Falls, but makes a good picnic site for an afternoon. The falls are found by taking the footpath near the pontoon.

No-man's-land Every morning there is a small market in no-man's-land, between the territories of Zambia and Angola. Both Zambians and Angolans come to barter for goods, under the watchful eyes of the armed border guards. It is a fascinating occurrence. As a foreigner, make sure you have very clear permission from the border guards before you even consider joining in, and don't take any photographs without permission.

MWINILUNGA Mwinilunga is a large, thriving outpost of a town, raised up in the remote northwest corner of Zambia. The town isn't on the national grid, and there's no fuel station (you might be able to get fuel from drums, but don't rely on it). On the plus side, there are shops with basic supplies and a sizeable local **market**, plus several **banks**, a large **post office** and a small Franciscan mission.

Getting there and away By far the easiest way to get to Mwinilunga is via the Copperbelt, Chingola and Solwezi. To reach it, travel through Chingola and then take the turn to Solwezi. This is tarmac, but in a variable state of repair.

About 28km after Solwezi there's a junction at Mwelemu (⊕ MWELEM 12°23.661'S, 26°14.276'E). Mwinilunga is signposted to the right, and from there it's about 288km of largely reasonable tarmac away. Eventually you'll descend a hill, cross the West Lunga River, and drive into town. Beyond the tar, a good gravel road leads north into the DRC via Ikelenge. Alternatively, head for Angola via Kalene Hill, and the border at Jimbe Bridge just over 100km away.

From Kabompo See Kabompo's section on *Getting there and away* (pages 503–4) to locate the turn-off for Mwinilunga from the M8 (⊕ TUMWIN 13°26.082'S, 24°19.978'E). Then after 4.5km, take the right fork, and bend around left. It's a beautiful drive along a good but narrow road on which you can average about 30–40km/h in the dry season. On either side are occasional subsistence farming communities, and large areas of forest. It does cross one or two large dambos, which could be very sticky during the rainy season. Note that this route goes relatively close to Angola, and you'd be well advised to check the security situation locally before coming this way. Equally, don't be tempted to divert off to the west of the road unless you know exactly where you're going.

After about 49km you'll pass the village of Lunsongwe (⊕ LUNSON 13°02.068'S, 24°13.385'E) – spelled 'Lusongwa' on some maps – where there's a school and a small grocery shop. Around 54km later, you pass the very spread-out village of Kanyilambi, notable mainly for its church and beautiful silvery fields of rice – and then you're almost halfway to Mwinilunga.

Continuing north, the forests and other vegetation start to get thicker whilst the atmosphere becomes perceptibly warmer and more humid – despite the slight but steady rise in altitude. In places the forest is thick enough for the canopy of trees over the track to interlock – and for some of the birding 'specials' found in Mwinilunga to occur here too.

Eventually you reach a T-junction (⊕ TUKABO 11°45.158'S, 24°26.114'E) with the main Mwinilunga–Solwezi tar road, and the centre of town is a few kilometres west. In the dry season it takes about five hours to cover the 219km from Kabompo.

Where to stay Mwinilunga has an assortment of largely unremarkable places to sleep and/or eat, all fairly inexpensive, but the following are among the better choices. Many visitors will proceed straight to Hillwood Farm and Nchila Reserve, and campers might do better alternative to head for the campsite at the source of the Zambezi (see pages 513–14).

Kwakuwahi Lodge (3 rooms) In an attractive setting on the banks of the Lunga River, this relatively new lodge is owned by a Christian husband-&-wife team, Roma & Catherine Nyukambumba. Its neat chalets are backed by manicured lawns dotted with trees & shrubs. Inside, clean en-suite rooms come with queen or dbl beds, AC, DSTV, radio & fridge – & (very welcome) hot water. There's a modern lounge & the food is reasonable. **$$**

Elidos On the main street through town, Elidos is popular with backpackers & volunteers, either for a bite to eat or as an overnight stop. **$**

HILLWOOD FARM AND NCHILA WILDLIFE RESERVE Hillwood Farm is an improbable place. It's an oasis of peace and order in a corner of Zambia which the world's media might expect, given its position between Angola and the DRC, to be under permanent siege. What's more, within its bounds, Hillwood has a very special reserve, Nchila, which has flora and fauna that are unique to Zambia: it contains a slice of equatorial forest that's been preserved and nurtured. The family who own this farm, the Fishers, have been working in close partnership with the local communities here for generations.

In recent years the family has placed an increasing emphasis on hunting, and – since hunting and photographic guests don't mix – there are very few weeks of the year that are available for other guests. That said, they still welcome campers, ornithologists and photographers whenever they can.

So while it's exceedingly 'out of the way' by anyone's standards, and there are restrictions on the times when non-hunting guests can stay, Hillwood remains a totally fascinating place that's delightful to visit and contains some amazing wildlife. If you're anywhere near here, do contact them to see if you can stay.

Getting there and away To reach here from Mwinilunga, continue through town on the main road, past the turn-off to the airport. After about 7km, the road changes from tar to well-maintained gravel road. Over its course it then crosses a series of rivers, and you'll drive over four bridges. (Whilst you don't need a 4x4 for this in the dry season, there are several steep sections that could become tricky in the wet season.) In sequence, the rivers include Luakela, the Chitunta and the Kaseki.

About 47km from Mwinilunga there's a right turn that is clearly marked (⊕ TUZAMB 11°23.321'S, 24°16.632'E). After about 4.6km, this leads to the source of the Zambezi (see pages 513–14 for details). Then about 3km after that turning, you cross the final river, the Sakeji. About 9km after this there is a clear signpost to the right (⊕ TUHILL 11°17.040'S, 24°16.663'E) proclaiming that Hillwood Farm and Nchila Wildlife Reserve are about 7km away. This final road felt a little like a local footpath through a village to us, but eventually you do reach Hillwood Farm (⊕ HILLWO 11°14.989'S, 24°18.852'E) – an oasis of order.

Note that on the way from Mwinilunga to Hillwood you pass (although may not notice) the Luakela Forest Reserve and later Chitunta Plain, both of which have some of the birds which attract ornithologists to this corner of the country. Luakela Forest Reserve is noted for lots of bar-winged weavers, whilst Chitunta Plain is very important for many species, including the Angola lark, Grimwood's longclaw, the dambo (black-tailed) cisticola, the black and rufous swallows and short-tailed pipits. Venture several kilometres up the stream there, and you've a good chance of seeing another very uncommon bird, Bocage's weaver.

Hillwood is about 68km from Mwinilunga and, if you don't stop for any birdwatching, will take a bit less than two hours to drive. Alternatively, Nchila can be reached by a short (though not very cheap) charter flight from Lusaka or (marginally less costly) from Lunga River Lodge in northern Kafue.

What to see and do Although most people will stay on the reserve (see below), there is lots to see around the farm. Most people will also detour to the source of the Zambezi, and keen ornithologists will frequently head into the surrounding area in search of the 'specials' found in this corner of Zambia.

Hillwood Farm Zambian farms don't come much more remote or well established than Hillwood. Relatively speaking, it's had a lot of time to build up a very self-sufficient yet interdependent community of people.

Of interest here is the farm itself, which these days relies on beef and dairy cows, cereal and, increasingly, tourism to generate income. The orphanage and the school are also fascinating; the boarding school is used by some of Zambia's more affluent residents, so it's not at all impoverished by local standards.

If you have the opportunity to chat with Pete, Lynn or Pete's father, Paul – do so. You'll get an intriguing insight into the area's past and present. They have always worked closely with the surrounding communities – Pete meets with the local village headmen once a month to inform, involve and share out the maintenance and development work on the reserve fairly between the villages. Roads, bridges, fences

THE FISHER FAMILY

Pete Fisher is Zambian – part of the fourth generation of Fishers in Zambia. Lynn, his wife, is Californian, but has always lived in Zambia. They live in the oldest house on Hillwood Farm with their two sons, Sonny and Christopher. Pete's father, Paul Fisher, and his sister Melanie, and her family, also live and work at Hillwood.

The history of the Fisher family is an interesting one, and inextricably linked with the development of the local area. The story begins in the late 19th century. Inspired by David Livingstone's and Fred Arnott's aspirations to end the slave trade in Africa by establishing Christianity and legitimate commerce in its place, Walter Fisher was a willing recruit to the missionary quest. In 1889, freshly qualified as a doctor and with a gold medal for surgery at Guy's Hospital, Walter Fisher left the UK with a party of seven other men and women, bound for the Angolan coast. Suffering from various hardships on arrival, the party moved out of Portuguese territory to Kalene Hill in Northern Rhodesia. Indeed, the ruins of the houses and store rooms they built in the Angolan style, with bricks made of baked anthill, can still be found there.

Kalene Hill eventually became the home of a mission hospital and an orphanage after Walter's wife, Anna Fisher, rescued a newborn baby. She found the child after it had been lying on its mother's grave for two days – where it had been placed as it was believed to have caused her death (the mother had died in childbirth). The orphanage is now on Hillwood Farm, in the care of Paul and Eunie Fisher, and its emphasis is on keeping a traditional African way of life so that the children can return to their village at about six years old. Until then, they are taught, fed and clothed to give them a good start. As has always been the case here, each baby comes with a female family member to assist with its care. There are currently 30 orphans; visitors are warmly welcomed. Esther Townsend and Helen Finney, two English orphanage mothers, currently manage the day-to-day needs of the orphanage.

In addition to the orphanage, Anna Fisher was also responsible for establishing the Nyamuweji village for old ladies, where they cultivated the land and were protected by the Fishers from customary witch-hunts. Such women, too old to work hard, often came for refuge. There remain six to eight women at Kalene, and they are more or less self-supporting.

Sakeji School started in 1925, next to Hillwood. It has a very wide catchment area for its size, made possible by road links and the well-maintained Sakeji airstrip. The school teaches Grades 1 to 7 (Junior) and is funded and staffed by mainly Canadian and American missionary workers from an organisation called 'Christian Churches in Many Lands' (CCML). In 1962 the Bible was translated into Lunda by Singleton Fisher. A new version by Paul Fisher and Joan Hoyt is under way for the Zambian Bible House.

and shelters are all built and maintained with local labour and materials wherever possible. This 'Nchila Committee' also helps a great deal to prevent poaching, kept to a minimum thanks to the excellent rapport within the community as a whole. This is built on many years of talking together, mutual trust and help.

Nchila Wildlife Reserve (*www.nchilawildlifereserve.com;* ⏴ *15 May–15 Nov; entrance US$10 pp*). Nchila Wildlife Reserve is a 40km² area of virgin bush within the boundaries of Hillwood Farm. It's a great area for game drives and walks, always accompanied by a guide from Nchila (hence the need to book in advance). See below for more on the flora and fauna, but note that even if you're not a keen 'twitcher', the rolling country is very pleasant walking, with patches of evergreen forests adding a welcome touch of shade.

The prime time to visit is August to end-October for the birding.

Flora and fauna Nchila attracts a steady stream of ornithologists, herpetologists, zoologists and other keen observers of the natural world. Most come for the reserve's pockets of pristine wet, evergreen forest (rainforest). These are typical of large areas of its neighbouring countries – so you'll find species here which you can't see anywhere else, unless you're prepared to brave the instability of either Angola or the DRC.

Note that you'll find some exceedingly comprehensive details of Nchila's flora and fauna on the reserve's website so here I'll just mention a few of the more obvious highlights.

Flora This beautiful, rolling and hilly area has large areas of moist open plains dotted with termitaria. These are veined by miombo woodland and, in the lower areas, patches of wet, evergreen (mishutu) forest which surround many permanent streams.

Animals The larger wildlife here includes possibly Zambia's largest herd of sable antelope (some of which appear to have some genes in common with Angolan giant sables, given their appearance), and very good numbers of roan and eland that are generally very relaxed and approachable. In addition, there are plains zebra, defassa waterbuck, impala, Lichtenstein's hartebeest, Kafue lechwe, puku and kudu. Oribi are very common on the plains, warthog are sometimes seen grubbing around, and there's a herd of blue wildebeest.

Sitatunga frequent the denser, wetter patches of forest – and, like the bushbuck which are found here, sometimes venture out along the edge of the open plains; it's here that I had one of the clearest sightings of these shy antelope that I've ever experienced. The Nchila team say that there are two different subspecies of sitatunga here: 'normal' sitatunga such as are found to the south in Zambia and the rest of southern Africa, and an 'Angolan' subspecies.

In the forest patches you'll find vervet and blue monkeys, as well as common and blue duiker. (With some luck and much skill, the guides can sometimes call the curious blue duiker in to approach you!)

Birdlife The birdlife here is a real draw; it's a very special place. The forests contain 30 species not found anywhere outside of the DRC, Angola and this area – most of which do not even occur around Mwinilunga (only 70km south of Nchila). However, for some of this area's 'specials' you may have to go a further 50km north to the very tip of Zambia – around the source of the Salujinga and the Jimbe. The borders with Angola and the DRC are very sensitive – so take local advice before you venture that far.

The source of the Zambezi and the Sakeji River, which runs through Hillwood, is a microcosm of the DRC forests. Many of the birds which occupy ecological niches south of here are replaced by different, but closely related, species. The area's 'specials' often need work to spot, and a fair amount of searching with one of Nchila's guides who knows where to look. They include afep and bronze-naped pigeons; black-collared bulbuls; grey-winged robins; rufous ant thrushes; Fülleborne's and rosy-breasted longclaws; honeyguide greenbuls; shining blue, white-bellied and blue-breasted kingfishers; olive long-tailed cuckoos; orange-tufted, green-throated and Bates' sunbirds; buff-throated apalises; Laura's and bamboo warblers; white-cheeked bee-eaters; red-bellied paradise flycatchers; and splendid glossy starlings.

Where to stay Both the bushcamp and the campsite are on the reserve, and reservations for both are essential, since hunters are never mixed with other guests. In addition, they may not otherwise have the space, staff or supplies to accommodate you. Your two options are:

Nchila Camp (3 chalets) e nchila@ nchilawildlifereserve.com, nchilawildlife@ iwayafrica.com; www.nchilawildlifereserve. com. ⊕ NCHILA 11°14.945'S, 24°19.642'E. Nchila's small bushcamp overlooks a large plain & dambo from the edge of riverine forest & miombo woodland. Recently upgraded, it can take a maximum of 6 people (8 if squeezed!) in well-furnished chalets with solid wooden furniture, stylish fabrics & imaginative touches. One stunning chalet, which wouldn't be out of place in the most stylish of lodges, has a kingsize bed & a big en-suite bathroom, incorporating a large, slightly sunken bath beside the window, & a good shower. A good 2nd chalet has 2 twin rooms which share a flush toilet, shower & a bath with another shower over it. Both are spacious, built of stone with thatched roofs, & with water heated by wood-fired boilers. A smaller chalet (comfortable for 1 person, or 'cosy' for 2) has its own en-suite shower & toilet.

At the camp's heart is a thatched dining & lounge area, the two separated by a large log fire. With a lovely view over the dambo, it makes a pleasant place to sit & watch the wildlife. The food is good but simple: very fresh wholesome farm fare. A 90-min game drive costs about US$30 pp. *US$300 pp FBA, inc entry fee.* ⊕ *15 May–15 Nov.*

Nchila Campsite Nchila's campsite, in a lovely shady spot next to the Sakeji River, has a new ablution block with showers & flush toilets. There's also a dining area & a kitchen with a small wood stove & hot water. Lighting is courtesy of a connection to your car battery. Firewood is provided & a staff member is available to draw & heat water for showers. You'll need to come with all your own camping kit & most of your food, although limited amounts of fresh produce may sometimes be available from the farm. It's best to agree this in advance with Nchila. *US$25 pp plus entry fee US$10 pp.* ⊕ *15 May–15 Nov.*

Excursions from Hillwood and Nchila

The **Zambezi rapids** near to Hillwood are a very popular day trip – as a lovely spot to play in the water and float down on inflatable inner tubes. This is a particularly good place for birdwatchers to search for the rare Forbes plover, which hunts for insects on the bare rocks.

Further north, around the **source of the Jimbe River**, is the best place to look for the compact weaver and white-spotted flufftails; a recent sighting of the shrike flycatcher was a new discovery for Zambia.

Source of the Zambezi About 12km south of the entrance road to Nchila is a turn-off (⊕ TUZAMB 11°23.321'S, 24°16.632'E) to the official spot at Kalene Hill where the mighty Zambezi begins its 2,700km journey to the Indian Ocean. Protected both as a national monument and a World Heritage Site, the site itself is unexceptional, but the surrounding dense forest canopy, part of a 36.8ha reserve, is impressive.

A copper plaque, unveiled in 1964 to celebrate Zambia's independence, marks the site, at an altitude of about 1,500m. There's a good thatched shelter here, ideal for picnics, and it takes about half an hour to walk to the source. Note that the short access road is, in part, the boundary between Zambia and the DRC.

Appendix 1

WILDLIFE GUIDE

This wildlife guide is designed in a manner that should allow you to name most large mammals that you see in Zambia. Less common species are featured under the heading *Similar species* beneath the animal to which they are most closely allied, or bear the strongest resemblance.

CATS AND DOGS

Lion *Panthera leo* Shoulder height 100–120cm. Weight 150–220kg.

Africa's largest predator, the lion is the animal that everybody hopes to see on safari. It is a sociable creature, living in prides of five to ten animals and defending a territory of 20–200km². Lions often hunt at night, and their favoured prey is large or medium antelope such as wildebeest and impala. Most of the hunting is done by females, but dominant males normally feed first after a kill. Rivalry between males is intense and takeover battles are frequently fought to the death, so two or more males often form a coalition. Young males are forced out of their home pride at three years of age, and cubs are usually killed after a successful takeover.

When not feeding or fighting, lions are remarkably indolent – they spend up to 23 hours of any given day at rest – so the anticipation of a lion sighting is often more exciting than the real thing. Lions naturally occur in any habitat, except desert or rainforest. They once ranged across much of the Old World, but these days they are all but restricted to the larger conservation areas in sub-Saharan Africa (one residual population exists in India).

Lions occur throughout Zambia, and are very common in the larger parks with better game densities – Luangwa (North and South), Kafue and Lower Zambezi. Spend a week in any of these with a good guide and you'd be unlucky not to see at least some lion! They occur in smaller numbers in the more marginal parks and GMAs, and more sparsely in areas with more human population.

Leopard *Panthera pardus* Shoulder height 70cm. Weight 60–80kg.

The powerful leopard is the most solitary and secretive of Africa's big cats. It hunts at night, using stealth and power, often getting to within 5m of its intended prey before pouncing. If there are hyenas and lions around then leopards habitually move their kills up into trees to safeguard them. The leopard can be distinguished from the cheetah by its rosette-like spots, lack of black 'tearmarks' and more compact, low-slung, powerful build.

The leopard is the most common of Africa's large felines. Zambia's bush is perfect for leopard, which are common throughout the country, as they favour habitats with plenty of cover, like riverine woodlands. Despite this, a good sighting in the wild during the day is unusual.

Leopard

515

In fact there are many records of individuals living for years, undetected, in close proximity to humans. Sightings at night are a different story and, because Zambia's national parks allow night drives, it's probably Africa's best country for seeking leopard.

South Luangwa National Park was recently chosen by the BBC for the filming of their remarkable documentary, *Night of the Leopard*. Leopard sightings often become the main goal of night drives there. Your chances of spotting them are equally good in the Lower Zambezi, whilst consistently first-class sightings are also reported from Lufupa Lodge in Kafue. Remarkably they usually seem unperturbed by the presence of a vehicle and spotlight, and will often continue whatever they are doing regardless of an audience. Watching a leopard stalk is captivating viewing.

Cheetah *Acynonix jubatus* Shoulder height 70–80cm. Weight 50–60kg.

This remarkable spotted cat has a greyhound-like build, and is capable of running at over 70km/h in bursts, making it the world's fastest land animal. Despite superficial similarities, you can easily tell a cheetah from a leopard by the former's simple spots, disproportionately small head, streamlined build, diagnostic black Cheetah 'tearmarks', and preference for relatively open habitats. It is often seen pacing the plains restlessly, either on its own or in a small family group consisting of a mother and her offspring. Diurnal hunters, cheetah favour the cooler hours of the day to hunt smaller antelope, like steenbok and duiker, and small mammals like scrub hares.

Zambia has a small but growing population of cheetah, centred on Kafue National Park. They're very rare in the Luangwa, and have recently been re-introduced into the Lower Zambezi (though with mixed success).

Similar species The **serval** (*Felis serval*) is smaller than a cheetah (shoulder height 55cm) but has a similar build and black-on-gold spots giving way to streaking near the head. Seldom seen, it is widespread and quite common in moist grassland, reed beds and riverine habitats throughout Africa, including Zambia. It does particularly well in some of the swampier areas. Servals prey on mice, rats and small mammals, but will sometimes take the young of small antelope.

Caracal *Felis caracal* Shoulder height 40cm. Weight 15–20kg.

The caracal resembles the European lynx with its uniform tan coat and tufted ears. It is a solitary and mainly nocturnal hunter, feeding on birds, small antelope and young livestock. Found throughout the subcontinent, it easily adapts to a variety of environments and even occurs in some of Zambia's populated areas. Despite this, being nocturnal it is rarely seen. Caracals normally stalk their prey as closely as possible, before springing with surprise.

Caracal

Similar species The smaller **African wild cat** (*Felis sylvestris*) is found from the Mediterranean to the Cape of Good Hope, and is similar in appearance to the domestic tabby cat and a little larger. It has an unspotted torso, a ringed tail and a reddish-brown tinge to the back of its ears. Wild cats are generally solitary and nocturnal, often utilising burrows or termite mounds as daytime shelters. They prey upon reptiles, amphibians and birds as well as small mammals.

African wild dog *Lycaon pictus* Shoulder height 70cm. Weight 25kg.

Also known as the **painted hunting dog**, the wild dog is distinguished from other African dogs by its large size and mottled black, brown and cream coat. Highly sociable, living in packs of up to 20 animals, wild dogs are ferocious hunters that literally tear apart their prey on the run. They are now threatened with extinction, the most endangered of Africa's great predators. This is the result of relentless persecution by farmers, who often view the dogs as dangerous vermin, and their susceptibility to diseases spread by domestic dogs. Wild dogs are now extinct in many areas where they were formerly abundant, like the Serengeti, and they are common nowhere. The global population of fewer than 3,000 is concentrated in southern Tanzania, Zambia, Zimbabwe, Botswana, South Africa and Namibia.

African wild dog

Wild dogs prefer open savanna with only sparse tree cover, if any, and packs have enormous territories, typically covering 400km² or more. They travel huge distances in search of prey and so few parks are large enough to contain them. In Zambia wild dogs have their strongest base in Kafue, closely followed by the Luangwa, though even in these parks they are regarded as an uncommon sight. They are sometimes seen in Liuwa, Lower Zambezi and Sumbu areas. Elsewhere their existence is less certain.

NILE CROCODILE   *Mike Unwin*

Nile crocodile (*Crocodylus niloticus*) Length over 5m. Weight over 1,000kg.
Few visitors to Zambia's mighty rivers will want to miss the opportunity to see this antediluvian creature. With its powerful serrated tail, horny plated skin and up to 100 peg-like teeth crammed into a long, sinister smile, the Nile crocodile is the stuff of nightmares and action movies. Contrary to the more lurid myths, crocodiles generally avoid people (understandably, given the slaughter they have suffered). Yet while they will not usually launch themselves into boats or come galloping after you on land, humans are still potential prey for a big one, and tragedies do occasionally occur. When in crocodile country, it is sensible to keep your distance from the water's edge.

Crocodiles can live up to 100, but reach sexual maturity at 12–15 years. They inhabit lakes, rivers and swamps. Whereas youngsters are boldly marked in black and green, adults are generally a muddy grey-brown colour – usually lighter in rivers than in lagoons. Theirs is an amphibious life: basking on land, jaws agape to lose heat, or cruising the waters, raised eyes and nostrils allowing them to see and breathe undetected. As well as eating fish such as bream and barbel, adult crocs will ambush mammals up to the size of buffalo, grabbing them with an explosive sideways lunge from the water, before dragging them under to drown. Large numbers of crocodiles gather to scavenge big carcasses, churning up the water as they thrash and spin to dislodge chunks of flesh. They will even leave the water to steal a nearby lion kill.

Similar species The endangered **slender-snouted crocodile** (*Crocodylus cataphractus* or *Mecistops cataphractus*) occurs in Zambia only in two places. In Lake Tanganyika, it is largely confined to the quieter sections of the lake around Sumbu National Park. Historically it is also said to occur in the upper streams of the Congo basin around Kasanka, although there have been no reliable sightings reported for many years.

Side-striped jackal *Canis adustus* Shoulder height 35–40cm. Weight 8–12kg.
Despite its prevalence in other areas of Africa, the side-striped jackal is common nowhere in Zambia, although it occurs throughout the country. It is greyish in colour and has an indistinct pale horizontal stripe on each flank and often a white-tipped tail. These jackals are most often seen singly or in pairs at dusk or dawn. They are opportunistic feeders, taking rats, mice, birds, insects, wild fruits and even termites. The side-striped jackal is Zambia's only species of jackal.

Spotted hyena *Crocuta crocuta* Shoulder height 85cm. Weight 70kg.
Hyenas are characterised by their bulky build, sloping back, rough brownish coat, powerful jaws and dog-like expression. Contrary to popular myth, spotted hyenas are not exclusively scavengers; they are also adept hunters, which hunt in groups and kill animals as large as wildebeests. Nor are they hermaphroditic, an ancient belief that stems from the false scrotum and penis covering the female hyena's vagina. Sociable animals, hyenas live in loosely structured clans of about ten animals, led by females who are stronger and larger than males, based in a communal den.

Spotted hyena

Hyenas utilise their kills far better than most predators, digesting the bones, skin and even teeth of antelope. This results in the distinctive white colour of their faeces – which is an easily identified sign of them living in an area.

The spotted hyena is the largest hyena, identified by its light brown, blotchily spotted coat. It is found throughout Zambia, though is increasingly restricted to the national parks and GMAs. Although mainly nocturnal, spotted hyenas can often be seen around dusk and dawn in the Luangwa, Kafue and Lower Zambezi. Their distinctive, whooping calls are a spine-chilling sound of the African night. Note that neither of the spotted hyena's close relatives, the brown hyena and aardwolf, are thought to occur in Zambia.

PRIMATES
Baboon *Papio cynocephalus* Shoulder height 50–75cm. Weight 25–45kg.
This powerful terrestrial primate, distinguished from any other monkey by its much larger size, inverted U-shaped tail and distinctive dog-like head, is fascinating to watch from a behavioural perspective. It lives in large troops that boast a complex, rigid social structure characterised by a matriarchal lineage and plenty of inter-troop movement by males seeking social dominance. Omnivorous and at home in almost any habitat, the baboon is the most widespread primate in Africa, frequently seen in most game reserves. With their highly organised defence system, the only predators that seriously affect baboons are leopard, which will try to pick them off at night, whilst they are roosting in trees.

Common baboon

There are three African races, regarded by some authorities as full species. The **chacma baboon** (*P. c. ursinus*) is grey and confined largely to areas south of the Zambezi. The **yellow baboon** (*P. c. cynocephalus*) is the yellow-brown race occurring in Zambia, northern Mozambique, Malawi, southern and eastern Tanzania and eastern Kenya. The **olive** or **anubis baboon** (*P. c. anubis*) is a hairy green-to-brown baboon found in Ethiopia, Uganda, northern Tanzania and Kenya.

Vervet monkey *Cercopithecus aethiops* Length (excluding tail) 40–55cm. Weight 4–6kg.
Also known as the green or grivet monkey, the vervet is probably the world's most numerous monkey and certainly the most common and widespread representative of the *Cercopithecus*

guenons, a taxonomically controversial genus associated with African forests. An atypical guenon in that it inhabits savanna and woodland rather than true forest, the vervet spends a high proportion of its time on the ground. It occurs throughout Zambia, preferring belts of tall trees and thicker vegetation within easy reach of water. The vervet's light grey coat, black face and white forehead band are distinctive – as are the male's garish blue genitals. Vervets live in troops averaging about 25 animals; they are active during the day and roost in trees at night. They eat mainly fruit and vegetables, though are opportunistic and will take insects and young birds, and even raid tents at campsites (usually where ill-informed visitors have previously tempted them into human contact by offering food).

Vervet monkey

Blue monkey *Cercopithecus mitis* Length (excluding tail) 50–60cm. Weight 5–8kg.

The blue monkey is known also as **moloney's monkey** in Zambia, the **samango monkey** throughout southern Africa, the **golden monkey** in southwest Uganda, **Sykes' monkey** in Kenya and the **diademed** or **white-throated** guenon in some field guides. This most variable monkey is divided by some authorities into several species. It is unlikely to be confused with the vervet monkey, as blue monkeys have a dark blue-grey coat, which becomes reddish towards its tail. Its underside is lighter, especially its throat.

These monkeys live in troops of up to ten animals and associate with other primates where their ranges overlap. They live in evergreen forests, and so are most likely to be seen around the Copperbelt and North Western Provinces, or north of Kasanka. However, they occur as far south as the Lower Zambezi National Park and are resident along the Luangwa's Muchinga escarpment.

Blue monkey

Angola black-and-white colobus monkey *Colobus angolensis* Length (excluding tail) 65cm. Weight 12kg.

This beautiful jet black monkey has bold white facial markings, a long white tail and white sides and shoulders. Almost exclusively arboreal, it is capable of jumping up to 30m, a spectacular sight with its white tail streaming behind. Several races have been described, and most authorities recognise this Angolan variety as a distinct species. In Zambia they are very rare, but have been reported from the forests north of Mwinilunga.

Bushbaby *Galago crassicaudatus* Length (excluding tail) 35cm. Weight 1–1.5kg.

The bushbaby is Zambia's commonest member of a group of small and generally indistinguishable nocturnal primates, distantly related to the lemurs of Madagascar. In Zambia they occur throughout the country, though are very seldom seen during the day. At night their wide, endearing eyes are often caught in the spotlight during night drives, Bushbabies are nocturnal and even around safari camps they can sometimes be seen by tracing a cry to a tree and shining a torch into the branches; their eyes reflect as two red dots. These eyes are designed to function in what we would describe as total darkness, and they feed on insects – some of which are caught in the air by jumping – and also by eating sap from trees, especially acacia gum.

They inhabit wooded areas, and prefer acacia trees or riverine forests. I remember once being startled, whilst lighting a barbecue, by a small family of bushbabies. They raced through the trees above

Bushbaby

us, bouncing from branch to branch whilst chattering and screaming out of all proportion to their modest size.

Similar species **Lesser bushbaby** *Galago senegalensis* Length (excluding tail) 17cm. Weight 150g. The lesser bushbaby, or **night ape**, is half the size of the bushbaby and seems to be less common than its larger cousin. Where it is found, it is often amongst acacia or terminalia vegetation, rather than mopane or miombo bush.

LARGE ANTELOPE
Sable antelope *Hippotragus niger* Shoulder height 135cm. Weight 230kg.

The striking male sable is jet black with a distinct white face, underbelly and rump, and long decurved horns – a strong contender for the title of Africa's most beautiful antelope. The female is chestnut brown and has shorter horns, whilst the young are a lighter red-brown colour. Sable are found throughout the wetter areas of southern and east Africa.

Sable antelope

They are not common in Zambia. However, Kafue is probably the best park for sable, with Kasanka also worthy of note. In the Luangwa, they're confined to the foothills of the Muchinga Escarpment, so very rarely seen by visitors. Sumbu has a small population, and there have been reports of sable in Sioma Ngwezi and West Lunga.

Sable are normally seen in small herds: either bachelor herds of males, or breeding herds of females and young which are often accompanied by the dominant male in that territory. The breeding females give birth around February or March; the calves remain hidden, away from the herd, for their first few weeks. Sable are mostly grazers, though will browse, especially when food is scarce. They need to drink at least every other day, and seem especially fond of low-lying dewy vleis in wetter areas.

Roan antelope *Hippotragus equinus* Shoulder height 120–150cm. Weight 250–300kg.

Roan antelope

This handsome horse-like antelope is uniform fawn-grey with a pale belly, short decurved horns and a light mane. It could be mistaken for the female sable antelope, but this has a well-defined white belly, and lacks the roan's distinctive black-and-white facial markings. The roan is a relatively rare antelope; common almost nowhere in Africa (the Nyika Plateau being one obvious exception to this rule). In Zambia small groups of roan are found in South Luangwa, Kafue, Kasanka, Sumbu, Liuwa Plains and (probably) Sioma Ngwezi.

Roan need lots of space if they are to thrive and breed; they don't generally do well where game densities are high. Game farms prize them as one of the most valuable antelope (hence expensive to buy). They need access to drinking water, but are adapted to subsist on relatively high plateaux with poor soils.

Waterbuck *Kobus ellipsiprymnus* Shoulder height 130cm. Weight 250–270kg.

The waterbuck is easily recognised by its shaggy brown coat and the male's large lyre-shaped horns. The **common race** of southern Africa (*K. e. ellipsiprymnus*) and areas east of the Rift Valley has a distinctive white ring around its rump, seen on the left of the sketch. The **defassa race** (known as *K. e. defassa* or *K. e. crawshayi*) of the Rift Valley and areas further west has a full white rump, as indicated on the right.

In Zambia, the common waterbuck populates the Luangwa and Lower Zambezi valleys, whilst the defassa race occurs throughout most of the rest of the country, including Kafue National Park. They need to drink very regularly, so usually stay within a few kilometres of water, where they like to graze on short, nutritious grasses. At night they may take cover in adjacent woodlands. It is often asserted that waterbuck flesh is oily and smelly, which may discourage predators.

Waterbuck

Blue wildebeest
Connochaetes taurinus Shoulder height 130–150cm. Weight 180–250kg.
This ungainly antelope, also called the **brindled gnu**, is easily identified by its dark coat and bovine appearance. The superficially similar buffalo is far more heavily built. When they have enough space, blue wildebeest can form immense herds – as perhaps a million do for

Blue wildebeest

their annual migration from Tanzania's Serengeti Plains into Kenya's Masai Mara. In Zambia, one such gathering occurs on the Liuwa Plains around November, when tens of thousands of animals congregate here as the rains arrive.

Elsewhere, wildebeest naturally occur from around the Kafue National Park area westwards, to Angola. There's also a subspecies, **Cookson's wildebeest**, *Connochaetes taurinus cooksoni*, which is endemic to the Luangwa Valley. It's found commonly on the north side, in North Luangwa, but only rarely further south. It differs from the main species by having cleaner colours including slightly reddish bands and being a little smaller and more compact.

Lichtenstein's hartebeest
Alcelaphus lichtensteini Shoulder height 125cm. Weight 120–150kg.
Hartebeests are awkward antelopes, readily identified by the combination of large shoulders, a sloping back, a smooth coat and smallish horns in both sexes. Numerous subspecies are recognised, all of which are generally seen in small family groups in reasonably open country. Though once hartebeest were found from the Mediterranean to the Cape, only isolated populations still survive. Hartebeests are almost exclusively grazers and they like access to water.

The only one native to Zambia is Lichtenstein's hartebeest, which used to be found throughout the country, except for the extreme south and west. They are seen frequently in Kafue, and also occur in Sumbu and Kasanka. The Luangwa has a good population, but they generally stay away from the river, and so remain out of view for most visitors.

Similar species The **tsessebe** (*Damaliscus lunatus*) is basically a darker version of the hartebeest with striking yellow lower legs. (A closely related subspecies is known as *topi* in east Africa.) These are very sparsely distributed in Zambia, occurring in the Kasanka–Bangweulu area, and to the far west of the Zambezi, in Liuwa and Sioma Ngwezi. Its favourite habitat is open grassland, where it is a selective grazer, eating the younger, more nutritious grasses. The tsessebe is one of the fastest antelope species, and jumps very well.

Kudu
Tragelaphus strepsiceros Shoulder height 140–155cm. Weight 180–250kg.
The kudu (or, more properly, the greater kudu) is the most frequently observed member of the genus *Tragelaphus*. These medium-size to large antelopes are characterised by their grey-brown coats and up to ten stripes on each side. The male has magnificent double-spiralled corkscrew horns. Occurring throughout Mozambique, Zimbabwe, Zambia, Botswana and Namibia, kudu are widespread and common, though not in dense forests or open grasslands. They are normally

associated with well-wooded habitats. These browsers thrive in areas with mixed tree savanna and thickets, and the males will sometimes use their horns to pull down the lower branches of trees to eat, with mahogany, *Trichelia emetica*, being a particular favourite.

In Zambia they occur throughout the country except for the far northern areas. Normally they're seen in small herds, consisting of a couple of females and their offspring, sometimes accompanied by a male. Otherwise the males occur either singly, or in small bachelor groups.

Sitatunga *Tragelaphus spekei* Shoulder height 85–90cm. Weight 105–115kg.

The semi-aquatic antelope is a widespread but infrequently observed inhabitant of west and central African papyrus swamps from the Okavango in Botswana to the Sudd in Sudan. In Zambia sitatunga are very widespread. Good populations are found in Bangweulu, the Busanga Swamps, Sumbu and Kasanka.

Because of its preferred habitat, the sitatunga is very elusive and seldom seen, even in areas where it is relatively common. They are also less easy to hunt/poach than many other species, although they are exceedingly vulnerable to habitat destruction. Kasanka National Park's tree hide is commended, at least to the more agile of visitors, as one of Africa's very best places to see these antelope. It provides a superb vantage point above a small section of papyrus swamp, and sightings are virtually guaranteed in the early morning or late afternoon. Sitatunga are noted for an ability to submerse themselves completely, with just their nostrils showing, when pursued by a predator.

Sitatunga

Eland *Taurotragus oryx* Shoulder height 150–175cm. Weight 450–900kg.

Africa's largest antelope, the eland is light brown in colour, sometimes with a few faint white vertical stripes. Relatively short horns and a large dewlap accentuate its somewhat bovine appearance. It was once widely distributed in east and southern Africa, though the population has now been severely depleted. Small herds of eland frequent grasslands and light woodlands, often fleeing at the slightest provocation. (They have long been hunted for their excellent meat, so perhaps this is not surprising.)

Eland

Eland are opportunist browsers and grazers, eating fruit, berries, seed pods and leaves as well as green grass after the rains, and roots and tubers when times are lean. They run slowly, though can trot for great distances and jump exceedingly well. In Zambia they occur widely but sparsely, and are largely confined to the country's protected areas.

MEDIUM AND SMALL ANTELOPE

Bushbuck *Tragelaphus scriptus* Shoulder height 70–80cm. Weight 30–45kg.

This attractive antelope, a member of the same genus as the kudu, is widespread throughout Africa and shows great regional variation in its colouring. It occurs in forest and riverine woodland, where it is normally seen singly or in pairs. The male is dark brown or chestnut, while the much smaller female is generally a pale reddish brown. The male has relatively small, straight horns and both sexes are marked with white spots and sometimes stripes, though the stripes are often indistinct.

Bushbuck

Bushbuck tend to be secretive and very skittish, except when used to people. They depend on cover and camouflage to avoid predators, and are often found in the thick, herby vegetation around rivers. They will freeze if disturbed, before dashing off into the undergrowth. Bushbuck are both browsers and grazers, choosing the more succulent grass shoots, fruit and flowers. In Zambia they are very widely distributed and fairly common.

Impala *Aepeceros melampus* Shoulder height 90cm. Weight 45kg.

This slender, handsome antelope is superficially similar to the springbok, but in fact belongs to its own separate family. Chestnut in colour, and lighter underneath than above, the impala has diagnostic black-and-white stripes running down its rump and tail, and the male has large lyre-shaped horns. One of the most widespread and successful antelope species in east and southern Africa, the impala is normally seen in large herds in wooded savanna habitats. It is the most common antelope in the Luangwa Valley, and throughout much of the central and southern areas of Zambia. However, in more northerly areas, puku are sometimes more common. As expected of such a successful species, it both grazes and browses, depending on what fodder is available.

Eland

Reedbuck *Redunca arundinum* Shoulder height 80–90cm. Weight 45–65kg.

Sometimes referred to as the **southern reedbuck** (as distinct from mountain and Bohor reedbucks, found further east), these delicate antelope are uniformly fawn or grey in colour, and lighter below than above. They are generally found in reedbeds and tall grasslands, often beside rivers, and are easily identified by their loud, whistling alarm call and distinctive bounding running style. In Zambia they occur widely, though seem absent from the very bottom of the Zambezi and Luangwa valley floors. (They do occur in both Luangwa and Lower Zambezi national parks, but usually on slightly higher ground, away from the rivers.)

Reedbuck

Klipspringer *Oreotragus oreotragus* Shoulder height 60cm. Weight 13kg.

The klipspringer is a strongly built little antelope, normally seen in pairs, and easily identified by its dark, bristly grey-yellow coat, slightly speckled appearance and unique habitat preference. Klipspringer means 'rock jumper' in Afrikaans and it is an apt name for an antelope which occurs exclusively in mountainous areas and rocky outcrops from Cape Town to the Red Sea.

They occur throughout most of Zambia, except for the extreme western areas, but only where rocky hills or kopjes are found. Given Zambia's generally rolling topography, this means only the odd isolated population exists. They are seen occasionally on the escarpments of the main valleys, but usually away from the main game areas. Klipspringers are mainly browsers, though they do eat a little new grass. When spotted they will freeze, or bound at great speed across the steepest of slopes.

Klipspringer

Lechwe *Kobus leche* Shoulder height 90–100cm. Weight 80–100kg.

Lechwe are sturdy, shaggy antelope with beautiful lyre-shaped horns, adapted to favour the seasonal floodplains that border lakes and rivers. They need dry land on which to rest, but otherwise will spend much of their time grazing on grasses and sedges, standing in water if necessary. Their hooves are splayed, adapted to bounding through their muddy environment when fleeing from the lion, hyena and wild dog that hunt them, making them the most aquatic of antelope after sitatunga.

Lechwe are found in DRC, Angola, northern Botswana and Namibia's Caprivi Strip, but their stronghold is Zambia. Wherever they occur, the males are generally larger and darker than the females, and in Zambia there are three subspecies (though none occurs in the Luangwa or Lower Zambezi valleys).

Lechwe

The **red lechwe** (*K. l. leche*) is the most widespread subspecies. It's the only one found outside Zambia and has a chestnut-reddish coat, darker on the back and much lighter (almost white) underneath. Its legs have black markings, as does the tip of its tail. Inside Zambia red lechwe are found in large numbers (about 5,000 probably) on the Busanga Plains, with smaller populations in the Western Province and the Lukanga Swamps.

The **Kafue lechwe** (*K. l. kafuensis*) are slightly larger animals, with bigger horns, and are restricted to the Kafue Flats area, between Lake Itezhi-Tezhi and Lusaka. This race is more light brown than red, with black patches on their shoulders that run into the black on their legs. Most of the 40,000–50,000 that remain are confined to the Lochinvar and Blue Lagoon national parks.

The **black lechwe** (*K. l. smithemani*) used to occur in huge numbers, perhaps as many as half a million animals, centred on the plains to the south of the Bangweulu Swamps. They are now restricted to about 30,000–40,000 animals in the same area, and a small population have been re-introduced into the Nashinga Swamps to the west of Chinsali. Black lechwe are much darker and the older males have almost black backs and brownish undersides.

Puku *Kobus vardoni* Shoulder height 80cm. Weight 60–75kg.

Unless you see them beside each other, puku can be hard to distinguish from red lechwe – though the adults are generally slightly smaller than the lechwe. They are also stocky, orangey-red antelope with shaggy coats. Male pukus have stout, ribbed horns which curve forwards at the tips, though are shorter and spread out less than a lechwe's horns.

Puku are grazers, typically inhabiting open plains adjacent to rivers or marshes, or woodland fringes. They are always found close to water, although are not as fond of completely flooded areas as lechwe. Puku usually feed early or late in the day, and will often lie down in the shade when the sun is at its highest.

They are one of Zambia's most common antelope, found throughout western and northern Zambia, and the Luangwa Valley, although they are noticeably absent from the Lower Zambezi Valley. South of Zambia, puku are exceedingly rare, occurring only in one small corner of northern Chobe; to the north they are native to areas of Malawi and the DRC, and common in Tanzania.

Young males form bachelor groups, from which prime animals break away to form territories. The more dominant the buck, the more attractive are the feeding resources within these territories, into which they attract females. Breeding takes place between April and July and thus calves are born in the green season when food resources are abundant.

Steenbok

Steenbok *Raphicerus cempestris* Shoulder height 50cm. Weight 11kg.

This rather nondescript small antelope has red-brown upper parts and clear white underparts, and the male has short straight horns. It is very common south of the Zambezi, but only occurs in southwestern Zambia (Mazabuka seems to be about the limit of their distribution). They like grasslands and open country with a scattering of cover, and seem to do very well in the drier areas. Like most other small antelopes, the steenbok is normally encountered singly or in pairs and tends to 'freeze' when disturbed, before taking flight.

Similar species Sharpe's grysbok (*Raphicerus sharpei*) is similar in size and appearance, though it has a distinctive white-flecked coat. It occurs widely throughout Zambia, and appears to be absent only from the far northwest (Liuwa/Mwinilunga area). It is almost entirely nocturnal in its habits and so very seldom seen.

The **oribi** (*Ourebia ourebi*) is also a widespread but generally uncommon antelope. It is usually found only in large, open stretches of dry grassland, with the termitaria zones of the Busanga Plains, Lochinvar and Bangweulu area standing out as good places to spot them. It looks much like a steenbok but stands about 10cm higher at the shoulder and has an altogether more upright bearing.

Common duiker *Sylvicapra grimmia* Shoulder height 50cm. Weight 20kg.

This anomalous duiker holds itself more like a steenbok or grysbok and is the only member of its (large) family to occur outside of forests. Generally grey in colour, the common duiker can most easily be separated from other small antelopes by the black tuft of hair that sticks up between its horns. They occur throughout Zambia, and tolerate most habitats except for true forest and very open country. They are even found near human settlements, where shooting and trapping is a problem, and are usually mainly nocturnal. Duikers are opportunist feeders, taking fruit, seeds and leaves, as well as crops, small reptiles and amphibians.

Common duiker

OTHER LARGE HERBIVORES

African elephant *Loxodonta africana* Shoulder height 2.3–3.4m. Weight up to 6,000kg.

The world's largest land animal, the African elephant is intelligent, social and often very entertaining to watch. Female elephants live in close-knit clans in which the eldest female plays matriarch over her sisters, daughters and granddaughters. Their lifespans are comparable to those of humans, and mother–daughter bonds are strong and may last for up to 50 years. Males generally leave the family group at around 12 years to roam singly or form bachelor herds. Under normal circumstances, elephants range widely in search of food and water, but when concentrated populations are forced to live in conservation areas their habit of uprooting trees can cause serious environmental damage.

African elephant

Elephants are widespread and common in habitats ranging from desert to rainforest. In Zambia they were common everywhere except for the Upper Zambezi's floodplains, but have now become more restricted by human expansion. However, individuals often wander widely, turning up in locations from which they have been absent for years.

Zambia's strongest population is in the Luangwa, where there are now about 15,000. As recently as 1973 estimates put the Luangwa's population at more than 100,000, but the late 1970s and '80s saw huge commercial poaching for ivory, which wiped out a large proportion of this. Outside of a small, protected area in South Luangwa National Park, Zambia's elephants fared even worse. The populations in Kafue and even North Luangwa are still small, and the individuals are very nervous and skittish near people. (The exception here is possibly the Lower Zambezi, where the elephants regularly swim between Zimbabwe and Zambia, because the Zimbabwean parks were, on the whole, better protected from poaching than the Zambian parks. Hence the Lower Zambezi's elephant population is also fairly relaxed and numerous.)

Black rhinoceros *Diceros bicornis* Shoulder height 160cm. Weight 1,000kg.
This is the more widespread of Africa's two rhino species, an imposing and rather temperamental creature. (White rhino are not thought to have been native to Zambia.) In the 1960s, the black rhino was recorded in the Kafue, Luangwa, Lower Zambezi and in the far north around Sumbu and Mweru Wantipa. However, by the late 1990s it had probably been poached to extinction in Zambia, whilst becoming highly endangered in many of the other countries within its range. (There were a handful of reports of isolated individual animals existing in very remote areas; none was ever confirmed.) However, in mid 2003 black rhino were re-introduced into a subsection of North Luangwa National Park, and there are plans to bring more in.

Black rhinos exploit a wide range of habitats from dense woodlands and bush, and are generally solitary animals. They can survive without drinking for four to five days. However, their territorial behaviour and regular patterns of movement make them an easy target for poachers. Black rhinos can be very aggressive when disturbed and will charge with minimal provocation. Their hearing and sense of smell are acute, whilst their eyesight is poor (so they often miss if you keep a low profile and don't move).

Black rhinoceros

Hippopotamus *Hippopotamus amphibius* Shoulder height 150cm. Weight 2,000kg.
Characteristic of Africa's large rivers and lakes, this large, lumbering animal spends most of the day submerged but emerges at night to graze. Strongly territorial, herds of ten or more animals are presided over by a dominant male who will readily defend his patriarchy to the death. Hippos are abundant in most protected rivers and water bodies and are still quite common outside of reserves.

Hippos are widely credited with killing more people than any other African mammal, but I know of no statistics to support this. John Coppinger (one of the Luangwa Valley's most experienced guides) suggests that crocodile, elephant and lion all account for more deaths in that area than hippos – despite the valley having one of Africa's highest concentrations of hippos. So whilst undoubtedly dangerous, perhaps they don't quite deserve their reputation.

In Zambia they are exceptionally common in most of the larger rivers, where hunting is not a problem. The Kafue, the Luangwa and the Zambezi all have large hippo populations.

Buffalo *Syncerus caffer* Shoulder height 140cm. Weight 700kg.
Frequently and erroneously referred to as a **water buffalo** (an Asian species), the African, or Cape, buffalo is a distinctive, highly social ox-like animal that lives as part of a herd. It prefers well-watered savanna, though also occurs in forested areas. Common and widespread in sub-Saharan Africa, in Zambia it is widely distributed. The Luangwa, and especially the north park, seems to have some particularly large herds, hundreds of animals strong. Buffalo are primarily grazers and need regular access to water, where they swim readily. They smell and hear well, and it's often claimed that they have poor eyesight. This isn't true, though when encountered during a walking safari, they won't be able to discern your presence if you keep still and the wind is right.

Huge herds are generally fairly peaceful, and experienced guides will often walk straight through them on walking safaris. However, small bachelor herds, or even single old bulls (known in the Luangwa as 'kakuli'), can be very nervous and aggressive. They have a reputation for charging at the slightest provocation, often in the midst of thick bush, and are exceedingly dangerous if wounded. Lion often follow herds of buffalo, their favourite prey.

African buffalo

Giraffe *Giraffa camelopardis* Shoulder height 250–350cm. Weight 1,000–1,400kg.
The world's tallest and longest-necked land animal, a fully grown giraffe can measure up to 5.5m high. Quite unmistakable, giraffe live in loosely structured herds of up to 15, though herd members often disperse, when they may be seen singly or in smaller groups. Formerly distributed throughout east and southern Africa, these great browsers are now found only in the southern side of the Luangwa Valley and the far southwest of Zambia.

About eight subspecies of giraffe have been identified in Africa, and the Luangwa Valley contains one such distinct population, **Thornicroft's giraffe** (*G. c. thornicroftii*). These are generally regarded as having dark body patches and lighter neck patches than the normal 'southern' race of giraffe, and their colour patches don't normally extend below the knees, leaving their lower legs almost white. Their faces are also light or white. The vast majority of these live on the east side of the Luangwa River, in the GMA outside the park. They have been protected from hunting by a local taboo.

Much further west, the pocket of giraffe which are thought to still survive around the Sioma Ngwezi National Park are **Angolan giraffe** (*G. c. angolensis*), although so little is known of what survives in Sioma Ngwezi that their current status there is uncertain.

Plains zebra *Equus quagga* Shoulder height 130cm. Weight 300–340kg.
Also known as common zebra, this attractive striped horse is widespread throughout most of east and southern Africa, where it is often seen in large herds alongside wildebeest. It is common in most conservation areas from northern South Africa all the way up to the southeast of Ethiopia.

Plains zebra

Most southern races, although not those found in Zambia, have paler brownish 'shadow-stripes' between their bold black stripes. In Zambia, the subspecies in the Luangwa Valley is **Crawshay's zebra** (*E. q. crawshaii*), which also occurs on Nyika Plateau and possibly in Malawi's Vwaza Marsh. Norman Carr comments in his book on the Luangwa's wildlife (see *Appendix 3*, page 536) that the zebra found to the west of the Muchinga escarpment belong to the *E. q. zambeziensis* subspecies. In the Kafue's Busanga Plains, the subspecies is known as **Grant's** or **Boehm's zebra** (*Equus q. boehmii*).

Regardless of these minor taxonomic differences, zebra are widely distributed throughout Zambia, though they tend to be restricted by human activity to the more remote or protected areas. They lack the brown shadow-stripes of their cousins further south, but otherwise are very similar.

Warthog

Warthog *Phacochoerus aethiopicus* Shoulder height 60–70cm. Weight up to 100kg.
This widespread and often conspicuously abundant resident of the African savanna is grey in colour with a thin covering of hairs, wart-like bumps on its face, and rather large upward-curving tusks. Africa's only diurnal swine, the warthog is often seen in family groups, trotting around with its tail raised stiffly (a diagnostic trait) and a determinedly nonchalant air. They occur in most areas of Zambia, except in the extreme northwest, and are very common in most of the national parks. They don't usually fare well near settlements, as they are very susceptible to subsistence hunting/poaching. Wherever they occur, you'll often see them grazing beside the road, on bended knee, with their tails held high in the air as soon as they trot away.

Similar species Bulkier, hairier and browner, the **bushpig** (*Potomochoerus larvatus*) is known to occur throughout Zambia, and even in the vicinity of cultivated land where it can do considerable damage to crops. However, it is very rarely seen due to its nocturnal habits and preference for dense vegetation.

SMALL MAMMALS
African civet *Civettictis civetta* Shoulder height 40cm. Weight 10–15kg.
This bulky, long-haired, rather feline creature of the African night is primarily carnivorous, feeding on small animals and carrion, but will also eat fruit. It has a similar-coloured coat to a

African civet

leopard: densely blotched with large black spots becoming stripes towards the head. Civets are widespread and common throughout Zambia in many habitats, and make frequent cameo appearances on night drives. Though occasionally called 'civet cats', this is misleading because they are far more closely related to the mongooses than the felines.

Similar species The smaller, more slender **tree civet** (*Nandinia binotata*) is an arboreal forest animal with a dark brown coat marked with black spots. It is really a resident of the equatorial forests, although is found in a few mountain areas on Zambia's Malawi border (including Nyika) as well as north of Mwinilunga. It is nocturnal, solitary and largely arboreal – and so is very seldom seen.

The **small-spotted genet** (*Genetta genetta*), **large-spotted genet** (*Genetta tigrina*) and **rusty-spotted genet** (*Genetta rubignosa*) are the most widespread members in Zambia of a large group of similar small predators (which even the experts often can't tell apart without examining their skins by hand). All the genets are slender and rather feline in appearance (though they are not cats), with a grey to gold-brown coat marked with black spots (perhaps combining into short bars) and a long ringed tail.

You're most likely to see them on nocturnal game drives or occasionally scavenging around game reserve lodges. They are found all over Zambia, even in urban areas if there is a plentiful supply of rodents. They are excellent climbers and opportunists, eating fruit, small birds, termites and even scorpions.

Banded mongoose *Mungos mungo* Shoulder height 20cm. Weight around 1kg.
The banded mongoose is probably the most commonly observed member of a group of small, slender, terrestrial carnivores. Uniform dark grey-brown except for a dozen black stripes across its back, it is a diurnal mongoose occurring in playful family groups, or troops, in most habitats throughout Zambia. It feeds on insects, scorpions, amphibians, reptiles and even carrion and bird's eggs, and can move through the bush at quite a pace.

Banded mongoose

Similar species Another eight or so mongoose species occur in Zambia; some are social and gather in troops, others are solitary. Several are too scarce and nocturnal to be seen by casual visitors. Of the rest, the **water** or **marsh mongoose** (*Atilax paludinosus*) is large, normally solitary and has a very scruffy brown coat; it's widespread in the wetter areas. The **white-tailed mongoose** (*Ichneumia albicauda*), or white-tailed ichneumon, is a solitary, large brown mongoose with long, coarse, woolly hair. It is nocturnal and easily identified by its bushy white tail if seen crossing roads at night. It's not uncommon in cattle-ranching areas, where it eats the beetle-grubs found in the manure.

The **slender mongoose** (*Galerella sanguinea*) is as widespread and also solitary, but it is very much smaller (shoulder height 10cm) and has a uniform brown or reddish coat and blackish tail tip. Its tail is held up when it runs, and it is common throughout Zambia where there is lots of cover for it. The **dwarf mongoose** (*Helogate parvula*) is a diminutive (shoulder height 7cm), highly sociable light brown mongoose often seen in the vicinity of the termite mounds where it nests. This is Africa's smallest carnivore, occurring in a higher density than any other, and is widespread throughout Zambia. Groups of 20 to 30 are not unknown, consisting of a breeding pair and subordinate others. These inquisitive little animals can be very entertaining to watch.

The **large grey mongoose** (*Herpestes ichneumon*), also called the Egyptian mongoose, is a large mongoose with coarse, grey-speckled body hair, black lower legs and feet, and a black tip to its tail. It's found all over Zambia, but is common nowhere, is generally diurnal and is solitary or lives in pairs. It eats small rodents, reptiles, birds and also snakes – generally killing rather than scavenging. The **bushy-tailed mongoose** (*Bdeogale crassicaude*) is a small, predominantly nocturnal species that looks mainly black, especially its legs and tail. It is found throughout Zambia, though appears relatively uncommon south of the Zambezi.

Meller's mongoose (*Rhynchogale melleri*) is a variable shaggy, grey colour with dark legs and a large muzzle. Its distribution is patchy and somewhat uncertain, but it is thought to occur throughout western Zambia and the Luangwa, but not north of the Serenje–Mbala road. It is solitary and nocturnal, eating a large proportion of termites as well as reptiles, amphibians and fruit. **Selous's mongoose** (*Paracynictis selousi*) is smaller, with fine, speckled grey fur, and a white tip at the end of its tail. It likes open country and woodlands, occurring in many areas of southern and western Zambia, even including the Luangwa. It is nocturnal and solitary, eating mainly insects, grubs, small reptiles and amphibians – it seems especially fond of the larvae of dung beetles, and so is sometime found in cattle country.

Honey badger *Mellivora capensis* Shoulder height 30cm. Weight 12kg.

Also known as the ratel, the honey badger is black with a puppyish face and grey-white back. It is an opportunistic feeder best known for its allegedly symbiotic relationship with a bird called the honeyguide which leads it to a beehive, waits for it to tear it open, then feeds on

the scraps. The honey badger is among the most widespread of African carnivores, and also amongst the most powerful and aggressive for its size; it occurs all over Zambia. However, it is thinly distributed and infrequently seen, except when it has lost its fear of people and started to scavenge from safari camps.

Honey badger

Similar species Several other mustelids occur in the region, including the **striped polecat** (*Ictonyx striatus*), a widely distributed but rarely seen nocturnal creature which has black underparts and a bushy white back, and the similar but much scarcer **striped weasel** (*Poecilogale albincha*). This has been reported from several locations in Zambia, but only rarely.

The **Cape clawless otter** (*Aonyx capensis*) is a brown freshwater mustelid with a white collar, whilst the smaller **spotted-necked otter** (*Lutra maculicollis*) is darker with light white spots on its throat. Both occur fairly commonly throughout the rivers, swamps and lakes of Zambia.

Aardvark (*Orycteropus afer*) Shoulder height 60cm. Weight up to 70kg.

This singularly bizarre nocturnal insectivore is unmistakable with its long snout, huge ears and powerful legs, adapted to dig up the nests of termites, on which it feeds. Aardvarks occur throughout southern Africa, except the driest western areas of the Namib. Though their distinctive three-toed tracks are often seen, and they are not uncommon animals, sightings of them are rare.

Aardvarks prefer areas of grassland and sparse scrub, rather than dense woodlands. They are absent from Zambia's

Aardvark

floodplains and marshes, but otherwise occur throughout the country where termites are found.

Pangolin *Manis temmincki* Total length 70–100cm. Weight 8–15kg.

Sharing the aardvaak's diet of termites and ants, the pangolin is another very unusual nocturnal insectivore – with distinctive armour plating and a tendency to roll up in a ball when disturbed. (Then it can swipe its tail from side to side – inflicting serious damage on its aggressor.) Sometimes known as **Temminck's pangolins**, or **scaly anteaters**, these strange animals walk on their hindlegs, using their tail and front legs for balance. They are both nocturnal and rare – so sightings are exceedingly unusual and their distribution is uncertain. However, they are thought to occur in Kafue National Park and southern Zambia, as well as in the Luangwa Valley. (Evidence of their occurrence in the Luangwa is limited to about two sightings over the last few decades.)

Pangolin

In some areas further south, particularly Zimbabwe, local custom is to make a present of any pangolin found to the paramount chief (often taken to mean the president). This has caused great damage to their population.

Porcupine *Hystrix africaeaustralis* Total length 80–100cm. Weight 15–25kg.

This is the largest rodent found in the region, and occurs throughout Zambia and all over southern Africa. It easily identified by its black-and-white striped quills, generally black hair, and shambling gait. If heard in the dark, then the slight rattle of its quills augments the rustle of its foraging. These quills drop off fairly regularly, and are often found in the bush.

The porcupine's diet is varied, and they are fairly opportunistic when it comes to food. Roots and tubers are favourites, as is the bark of certain trees; they will also eat meat and small reptiles or birds if they have the chance.

Similar species Also spiky, the **southern African hedgehog** (*Erinaceus frontalis*) has been recorded in a few locations in Zambia, including the Lusaka, Mumbwa and Chipata areas. It's likely to occur elsewhere, though is small and nocturnal, so rarely seen even where it does occur. Hedgehogs are about 20cm long (much smaller than porcupines), omnivorous and uncommon.

Yellow-spotted rock hyrax *Heterohyrax brucei* Length 35–50cm. Weight 2.5–3.5kg.

Rodent-like in appearance, hyraxes (also known as **dassies**) are claimed to be the closest living relative of elephants. Yellow-spotted rock hyraxes are often seen sunning themselves in rocky habitats, and become tame when used to people.

They are social animals, living in large groups, and largely herbivores, eating leaves, grasses and fruits. Where you see lots of dassies, watch out for black eagles and other raptors which prey extensively on them.

Rock hyrax

Similar species Very similar, the **tree hyrax** (*Dendrohyrax arboreus*) has been recorded in a few locations on the eastern side of the country, including South Luangwa.

Scrub hare *Lepus saxatilis* Shoulder height 45–60cm. Weight 1–4.5kg.

This is the largest and commonest African hare, occurring throughout Zambia. In some areas a short walk, or drive, at dusk or after nightfall might reveal three or four scrub hares. They tend to freeze when disturbed.

Tree squirrel *Paraxerus cepapi* Total length 35cm. Weight 100–250g.
This common rodent is a uniform grey or buff colour, with a long tail that is furry but not bushy. It's widely distributed all over southern and east Africa, and occurs throughout Zambia in most woodland habitats, although not wet evergreen or montane forests. It's often so common in mopane woodlands that it can be difficult to avoid seeing it, hence its other common name – the mopane squirrel.

Tree squirrels can live alone, in pairs or in small family groups, usually nesting in a drey of dry leaves, in a hole in a tree. They are diurnal and venture down to the ground to feed on seeds, fruit, nuts, vegetable matter and small insects. When alarmed they will usually bolt up the nearest tree, keeping on the side of the trunk away from the threat and so out of sight as much as possible. If they can attain a safe vantage point with a view of the threat, then they'll sometimes make a loud clicking alarm call.

Similar species The **sun squirrel** (*Heliosciurus rufobrachium*) is the largest of Zambia's squirrels, and is found everywhere north of a rough line between Kabwe and Lukulu. It has similar habits to those of the more common tree squirrel, though will lie in the sun more often. Its colour varies considerably between individuals, and seasons, from light fawn to greyish brown, though its long bushy tail is consistently crossed by numerous whitish, longitudinal stripes.

The **red-and-black squirrel** (*Heliosciurus lucifer*) is a very pretty species with flame-red upper parts, a black patch in the middle of its back, and whitish underside. It occurs only in montane forest and in Zambia is thought to be restricted to the Nyika Plateau.

Boehm's squirrel (*Paraxerus boehmi*) has a similar size, shape and greyish colouring to the tree squirrel. However, it has two very distinct white stripes, bordered by black, down the side of its back from nape to tail. It inhabits riverine evergreen forest, and has a limited distribution in Zambia, restricted to the country's far north, around the Sumbu and Lusenga Plain areas.

The **flying squirrel** (*Anomalurus derbianus*) is quite unmistakable as there's a membrane of skin linking the fore and hind legs, and also the base of the tail. It uses this to glide with, when jumping from a higher branch to a lower one. It's a solitary, arboreal species that prefers miombo woodlands. It occurs from the Liuwa area east across Mwinilunga and the Copperbelt, and into the western side of northern Zambia, but is seldom seen.

Appendix 2

LANGUAGES

Zambia's main language groups are briefly outlined in *Chapter 3*, pages 19–23. This section will try to note down just a few useful phrases, and give their local translations in six of the most frequently encountered languages: Nyanja, Bemba, Lozi, Lunda, Tonga and Luvale. The visitor will probably find Nyanja or Bemba the most useful of these: Nyanja is the language that visitors are most likely to hear in the parks, while Bemba is more widely spoken countrywide. However, in the more remote areas – like the Western Province – where Nyanja and Bemba are not spoken, the other languages will prove invaluable.

Space is too short here, and my knowledge too limited, to give a detailed pronunciation guide to these six languages. However, all are basically phonetic and by far the best way to learn the finer nuances of pronouncing these phrases is to find some Zambians to help you as soon as you arrive. Asking a Zambian to help you with a local language is also an excellent way to break the ice with a new local acquaintance, as it involves them talking about a subject that they know well, and in which they are usually confident.

There may be several ways of saying goodbye, depending on the circumstances. In Nyanja, for example, one form may be said by the person leaving, and the other by the person staying behind – translating as 'go well' and 'stay well'. An alternative is to use the more informal 'see you later'.

Note that there is no specific word for 'please'; rather the meaning is incorporated into the word structure, so in Lozi, for example, 'please' is expressed by adding an 'a' to the subjunctive of the verb.

As noted in *Cultural guidelines*, pages 78–81, learning a few simple phrases in the local language will go a long way towards helping the independent traveller to have an easy and enjoyable time in Zambia. Just remember to laugh at yourself, and have fun. Most Zambians will be very impressed and applaud your efforts to speak their language, no matter how hard they may laugh!

	Nyanja	Bemba	Lozi
Good morning;	*Muli bwanji?*	*Mwashibukeni?*	*Muzuhile cwani?*
How are you?	(formal)	(formal)	(formal)
	Muli shani? (informal)	*Muzuhile?* (informal)	*Mucwani?* (informal)
I am fine	*Nile bwino* (formal)	*Eyamukwayi,*	*Lu zuhile hande*
	Bwino (informal)	*Ndifye bwino* (formal)	(formal)
		Bwino (informal)	*Hande* (informal)
Goodbye	*Salani bwino*	*Shaaleenipo*	*Muzamave hande*
See you later (*ciao*)	*Tisau onana*	*Twalaamonana*	*Lukabonana*
yes	*inde*	*eya ye*	*kimona*
no	*iyayi*	*awe*	*baatili*
thank you	*zikomo*	*twa to te la*	*nitumezi*
hey you!	*iwe!*	*iwe!*	*wena!*
I want	*ndifuna*	*ndefwaya*	*nabata*

	Nyanja	**Bemba**	**Lozi**
there	*kunja*	*kulya* (also 'food')	*kwale*
here	*apa*	*hapa* (silent 'h')	*faa*
stop	*imilira*	*yema*	*iminina*
let's go	*tiyeni or tye*	*aluye*	*natuleya*
help me	*niyetizipita*	*ngafweniko*	*nituse kwteni*
how much?	*zingati?*	*shinga?*	*kibukayi?*
it is too much!	*yadula!*	*fingi!*	*kihahulu!*
where can I find … ?	*alikuti…?*	*kwisa…?*	*uinzi kai…?*
the doctor	*sing'ang'a doctoro*	*shinganga*	*mualafi*
the police	*kapokola*	*kapokola*	*mupokola*
the market	*kumusika*	*ekobashita fyakulya*	*kwamusika*
drinking water	*mazi akumwa*	*amenshi ayakunwa*	*mezi a kunwa*
some food	*chakudya*	*ichakulya*	*sakuca*

	Lunda	**Tonga**	**Luvale**
Good morning; How are you?	*Mudi nahi?*	*Mwabuka buti?* *Muli buti?*	*Ngacili?*
I am fine	*Cha chiwahi*	*Kabotu*	*Kanawa*
Goodbye	*Shalenuhu*	*Muchale kabotu*	*Salenuho mwane*
See you later (*ciao*)	*Tuualimona*	*Tulabonana*	*Natulimona*
yes	*ena*	*inzya*	*eawa*
no	*inehi*	*pepe*	*kagute*
thank you	*kusakililaku*	*twalumba*	*gunasakulila*
hey, you!	*enu!*	*yebo!*	*enu!*
I want	*nakukena*	*ndiyanda*	*gikutonda*
there	*kuna*	*okuya*	*haaze*
here	*kunu*	*aano or awa*	*kuno*
stop	*imanaku*	*koyima or ima*	*imana*
let's go	*tuyena*	*atwende*	*tuyenga*
help me	*kwashiku*	*ndigwashe*	*gukafweko*
how much?	*anahi?*	*ongaye?*	*jingayi?*
it is too much!	*yayivulu!*	*chadula! or zinji!*	*yayivulu!*
where can I find…?	*kudihi….?*	*ulikuli…?*	*ali kuli…?*
the doctor	*ndotolu*	*mun'g'anga*	*ndotolo*
the police	*kapokola*	*kappokola*	*kapokola*
the market	*chisakanu*	*musika*	*mushika*
drinking water	*meji akunwa*	*maanzi akunywa*	*meya a kunwa*
some food	*chakuda*	*chakulya*	*kulya*

During your travels you may have the good fortune to meet a Wireless, a Handbrake or an Engine. If you are really lucky, you may encounter a Cabbage. These are names of people I have met in Zambia.

Looking for Fame and Fortune? Look no further than twin boys living in the Western Province. Beware of Temptation though, he is a money-changer known for calculating exchanges solely to his advantage.

Working with Sunday and Friday got rather amusing, 'Sunday, can you work on Saturday with Friday?' Working with Trouble was another matter entirely, as we had frequently to enquire, 'Where can I find Trouble?' Gift, true to his namesake, felt compelled to ask for one, while Lunch took on a whole new meaning and Clever is a friend who is true to his name.

Unusual names aren't limited solely to English. For example, there is Mwana Uta which literally means 'son of a gun', and Saka Tutu meaning 'father of an insect'. Pity the local man named Mwana Ngombe or 'child of a cow'!

Appendix 3

FURTHER INFORMATION

BOOKS
History, politics and economy

Bigland, Eileen *The Lake of the Royal Crocodiles* Hodder and Stoughton, London, 1939.

Clark, John *Zambia: Debt & Poverty* Oxfam, Oxford, 1989. This slim volume looks with clarity at Zambia's international debt, its causes and its consequences.

Hobson, Dick *Tales of Zambia* Zambia Society Trust, London, 1996. This is a lovely book, cataloguing big moments in Zambia's history, as well as some of its quirkier incidents and characters. It has sections on legends, mining and the country's flora and fauna and is very readable. Dick Hobson's knowledge and love of Zambia shine through.

Lamb, Christine *The Africa House* Viking, London, 2nd edition 2004. This fascinating book pieces together the life and times of Sir Stewart Gore-Browne from diaries, correspondence and memories. It's a spellbinding tale, eloquently told. If this can't convey the fascination of Shiwa, and make you want to see it, then nothing can.

Livingstone, David *Missionary Travels and Researches in Southern Africa* 1857. Over a century after it was written, this classic still makes fascinating reading.

Macmillan, Hugh *An African Trading Empire: the story of Susman Brothers & Wulfsohn, 1901–2005* I B Tauris, London, 2005.

Macmillan, Hugh, and Shapiro, Frank *Zion In Africa: the Jews of Zambia* I B Tauris and the Council for Zambia Jewry, London and Lusaka, 1999.

Reader, John *Africa: A Biography of the Continent* Penguin Books, London, 1997. Over 700 pages of highly readable history, interwoven with facts and statistics, make a remarkable overview of Africa's past. Given that Zambia's boundaries were imposed from Europe, its history must be looked at from a pan-African context to be understood. This book can show you that wider view; it is compelling and essential reading. Chapter 47 is largely devoted to the Lozi people.

Roberts, Andrew *A History of Zambia* Africana Publishing, New York, 1976. A detailed and complete history of Zambia, from prehistory to 1974.

Rotberg, Robert I *Black Heart: Gore-Browne and the Politics of Multiracial Zambia* University of California Press, Berkeley, 1977.

Williams, Geoffrey J (ed) *Lusaka and its Environs* ZGA Handbooks, Lusaka.

David Livingstone and the Victorian Encounter with Africa National Portrait Gallery, London, 1996. Six essays on Livingstone's life, concentrating on not only what he did, but also on how he was perceived in the UK.

Zambia: Condemned to Debt World Development Movement (*www.wdm.org.uk*), London, May 2004. The WDM is a charity which researches into global trade and debt trends, and campaigns for policies to reduce injustice and tackle poverty.

Wildlife and natural history Books published by the Wildlife and Environmental Conservation Society of Zambia (WECSZ) and the Zambian Ornithological Society (ZOS), are usually obtainable from bookshops in Lusaka, or direct from the WECSZ office (page 50).

Aspinwall, Dylan, and Beel, Carl *A Field Guide to Zambian Birds not found in Southern Africa* Zambian Ornithological Society, Lusaka, 1998. This excellent small guide is designed to complement a book covering Africa south of the Zambezi, such as Newman's guide, by describing only the birds occurring in Zambia which aren't included in Newman's guide. It's widely available in Zambia, but difficult to find elsewhere.

Bolnick, Doreen *A Guide to the Common Wild Flowers of Zambia and Neighbouring Regions* Macmillan Educational, London, 1995. This is a good small field guide to the more common species. A revised edition was published in 2007 by WECSZ.

Buk, Kenneth (Zoological Museum, University of Copenhagen) 'African Wild Dog Survey in Zambia', *Canid News*, vol 3, 1995. This piece of academic research looked at the distribution of wild dogs in Zambia in 1994, the reasons for their decline, and their possibilities for long-term survival.

Carr, Norman *A Guide to the Wildlife of the Luangwa Valley* Montford Press, Malawi, 3rd edition 1997. This small paperback (70 pages) was written by the valley's most famous guide and conservationist. It's not comprehensive, but is fascinating for the author's personal insights into the Luangwa area and its wildlife.

Coates Palgrave, Keith and Meg (eds) *Trees of Southern Africa* Struik, South Africa, 2003.

Cooray, Gerald, and Lane, Andrew *Minerals of Zambia* Nchanga Consolidated Copper Mines Ltd.

Hide, Phil *Birds of the Luangwa Valley* Zambian Ornithological Society, Lusaka, 2008.

Konings, Ad *Tanganyika Cichlids in their Natural Habitat* Cichlid Press (*www.cichlidpress.com*), El Paso, 1998.

Leonard, Peter *Important Bird Areas in Zambia* Zambian Ornithological Society, Lusaka, 2005. The most comprehensive survey of the country's top birding areas – complete with a lot of other useful detail about Zambia's ecology, flora and fauna.

Newman, Kenneth *Newman's Birds of Southern Africa* Southern Books, South Africa, 1st edition 1988. This has been republished numerous times since its first edition and has become the standard field guide to birds in southern Africa, south of the Kunene and Zambezi rivers. It also covers most species found in Zambia.

Nyerenda, Patrick *A Guide to the Snakes of the Luangwa Valley* WECSZ, reprint 2007.

Sinclair, Ian, and Ryan, Peter *Birds of Africa south of the Sahara* Struik, Cape Town, 2003. The field guide used by many of Zambia's birders as it incorporates both central African and southern African species, though it's a hefty tome to cart around.

Smith, P P *Common Trees, Shrubs and Grasses of the Luangwa Valley* Trendrine Press, Cornwall, 1995. This small, practical field guide has pictures to aid identification at the back, and includes a small section on the value to wildlife of the various plants.

Solomon, Derek *Animals in Action: a guide to the common mammals of South Luangwa National Park* 2005.

van Perlo, Ber *Birds of Southern Africa* Collins Illustrated Checklist, 1999. The only concise field guide that covers both Zambia and the rest of the region.

A Guide to Common Wild Mammals of Zambia WECSZ, 1991. A small field guide to the more common species.

A Guide to Reptiles, Amphibians & Fishes of Zambia Wildlife Conservation Society of Zambia, Lusaka, 1993. Another good guide to the more common species.

Common Birds of Zambia Zambian Ornithological Society, Lusaka, revised 1993. A good small field guide to the more common species.

Art and culture

Jordan, Manuel *Makishi: Mask Characters of Zambia* Fowler Museum of Cultural History, Los Angeles, 2007.

Phillipson, D W, revised by Katanekwa, N M *National Monuments of Zambia* National Heritage Conservation Commission, Livingstone, 1972 (4th printing 1992). Look for this small, green paperback around Lusaka, and buy it if you see one as they're quite scarce. It describes all of Zambia's national monuments, including many historical monuments, archaeological sites and even places of great scenic beauty – with some great old black-and-white photos.

Smith, Benjamin W *Zambia's Ancient Rock Art: The Paintings of Kasama* National Heritage Conservation Commission, Livingstone, 1997.

Coffee-table books

d'Elbée, François *Bush and Eye* Editions de la Martinière, Paris, 2002, and *Busanga: The Northern Plains of the Kafue National Park* 2004. D'Elbée's illuminating photographs focused first on the Lower Zambezi National Park, and then on the northern Kafue – with stunning results.

Travelogues and biography

Carr, Norman *Kakuli: A Story about Wild Animals* CBC Publishing, 1996. A collection of Norman Carr's tales from his time in the Luangwa Valley. Excellent light reading whilst on safari.

Owens, Mark and Delia *Survivor's Song: Life and Death in an African Wilderness* HarperCollins, London, 1993. Published as *The Eye of the Elephant* in the USA. This relates the authors' struggles to protect the wildlife of North Luangwa National Park from poachers, and their efforts to develop viable alternatives to poaching for the local people. It is excellent reading, though insiders complain of sensationalism, and that it ignores valuable contributions made by others.

Palin, Michael *Pole to Pole* BBC Consumer Publishing, London, 1999. This has an excellent section on Zambia, and Shiwa Ng'andu in particular is covered well.

Quarmby, C A *Just Driving Around in the North* Health Rescue International, Zambia.

Siddle, Sheila *Billy The Hippo* Mission Press, Ndola, 2006. A children's book telling the story of an orphaned hippo raised by the author at Chimfunshi.

Siddle, Sheila, with Cress, Doug *In My Family Tree: A Life with Chimpanzees* Grove/Atlantic, New York, 2002, and Double Storey, Cape Town, 2004. Sheila Siddle's story of the establishment of Chimfunshi Wildlife Orphanage makes inspirational – if sometimes shocking – reading.

Guidebooks

Allen, Quentin, Mwanza, Ilse and Chalcraft, Heather *A Guide to Little-Known Waterfalls of Zambia* Published privately, Lusaka, 2005. A mine of useful information, this detailed guide offers an excuse to head off the beaten track as well as detailed information relating to Zambia's innumerable waterfalls. Illustrated with line drawings, paintings and photographs, it also has plenty of practical information, including GPS co-ordinates.

Johnson, Sigrid Anna *A Visitor's Guide to Nyika National Park, Malawi* Mbabazi Book Trust, Blantyre. Length 150 pages. Sadly out of print, but worth buying if you can find a copy, this book provides a detailed historical and ecological background to Nyika, 20 pages of special-interest sites and notes on recommended walks and hikes, as well as complete checklists of all mammals, birds, butterflies and orchids that are known to occur in the park.

Moss, Peter *The Kafue National Park, Zambia – A Visitor's Handbook* The Kafue Trust. Scheduled for publication in 2011, this detailed guide to the national park is written by a biologist but also incorporates visitor information and a species list, with photographs by Ian Murphy.

Rattray, Gordon *Access Africa: Safaris for People with Limited Mobility* Bradt Travel Guides, UK, 2009. Written by Bradt's consultant on disabilities, this is an invaluable guide to taking a safari for travellers with limited mobility, and includes a section on Livingstone.

Atlas of the National Parks of Zambia ZAWA, Chilanga, 2009. Available only at ZAWA's Chilanga HQ, near Lusaka, this useful atlas – priced at Kw50,000 – presents the country's national parks through a series of helpful maps.

Health

Wilson-Howarth, Dr Jane *Bugs, Bites & Bowels* Cadogan Books, London, 2006. An amusing and erudite overview of the hazards of tropical travel which is small enough to take with you.

Wilson-Howarth, Dr Jane, and Ellis, Dr Matthew *Your Child Abroad: A Travel Health Guide* Bradt Travel Guides, Chalfont St Peter, 2nd edition 2005. An invaluable resource for all those travelling with children.

Novels

Banda-Aaku, Ellen *Patchwork* Penguin, South Africa, 2011. Banda-Aaku's award-winning novel of a child growing up in Lusaka gives an insight into Zambian life in the late 1970s. In so doing, it touches on issues as wide ranging as wealth and poverty, cultural evolution and post-independence politics.

Griffiths, Meg *Wonky Tusk* Muddy Boots, Zambia, 2008. A children's story about a naughty elephant whose mother has a wonky tusk. The 'Wonky Tusk' of the title refers to the elephant matriarch who annually leads her family through Mfuwe Lodge in the South Luangwa in search of ripe mangoes.

WEBSITES Website addresses seem to change frequently, especially in Zambia, but some of the more interesting ones include:

Tourist information

www.zambia.co.zm Bills itself as 'The National Homepage of Zambia', and has some useful links.

www.zambiatourism.com The official website of the Zambia National Tourist Board.

Media

www.lowdown.co.zm An electronic version of *The Lowdown*, Lusaka's monthly magazine – although no longer up to date.

www.postzambia.com For an independent view of Zambian affairs, look at this site from *The Post* newspaper. It usually takes a more objective, critical and questioning approach than the rival *Times of Zambia*.

www.times.co.zm The extensive site of the *Times of Zambia*. Featuring the main stories of the day, plus a searchable (but not listed) archive containing selected stories from June 2001 to the present day.

WIN A FREE BRADT GUIDE

READER QUESTIONNAIRE

Send in your completed questionnaire and enter our monthly draw for the chance to win a Bradt guide of your choice.

To take up our special reader offer of 40% off, please visit our website at www.bradtguides.com/freeguide or answer the questions below and return to us with the order form overleaf.

(Forms may be posted or faxed to us.)

Have you used any other Bradt guides? If so, which titles? . . . .
. . . .

What other publishers' travel guides do you use regularly? . . . .
. . . .

Where did you buy this guidebook? . . . .

What was the main purpose of your trip to Zambia (or for what other reason did you read our guide)? eg: holiday/business/charity . . . .
. . . .

How long did you travel for? (circle one)

weekend/long weekend   1–2 weeks   3–4 weeks   4 weeks plus

Which countries did you visit in connection with this trip? . . . .
. . . .

Did you travel with a tour operator?' If so, which one? . . . .
. . . .

What other destinations would you like to see covered by a Bradt guide?
. . . .

If you could make one improvement to this guide, what would it be?
. . . .

Age (circle relevant category) 16–25   26–45   46–60   60+

Male/Female (delete as appropriate)

Home country . . . .

Please send us any comments about this guide (or others on our list).
. . . .
. . . .
. . . .

Bradt Travel Guides

IDC House, The Vale, Chalfont St Peter, Bucks SL9 9RZ, UK
☎ +44 (0)1753 893444 f +44 (0)1753 892333
e info@bradtguides.com
www.bradtguides.com

TAKE 40% OFF YOUR NEXT BRADT GUIDE!

Order Form

To take advantage of this special offer visit www.bradtguides.com/freeguide and enter our monthly giveaway, or fill in the order form below, complete the questionnaire overleaf and send it to Bradt Travel Guides by post or fax.

Please send me one copy of the following guide at 40% off the UK retail price

No	Title	Retail price	40% price
1	. . . .	. . . .	. . . .

Please send the following additional guides at full UK retail price

No	Title	Retail price	Total
. . .	. . . .	. . . .	. . . .
. . .	. . . .	. . . .	. . . .
. . .	. . . .	. . . .	. . . .

Sub total . . . .

Post & packing . . . .

(Free shipping UK, £1 per book Europe, £3 per book rest of world)

Total . . . .

Name . . . .

Address. . . . .

Tel . . . .   Email . . . .

☐ I enclose a cheque for £. . . . . made payable to Bradt Travel Guides Ltd

☐ I would like to pay by credit card. Number: . . . .

Expiry date: . . . / . . . . 3-digit security code (on reverse of card) . . . . .

Issue no (debit cards only) . . . . .

☐ Please sign me up to Bradt's monthly enewsletter, Bradtpackers' News.

☐ I would be happy for you to use my name and comments in Bradt marketing material.

Send your order on this form, with the completed questionnaire, to:

Bradt Travel Guides

IDC House, The Vale, Chalfont St Peter, Bucks SL9 9RZ, UK

☎ +44 (0)1753 893444   f +44 (0)1753 892333

e info@bradtguides.com   www.bradtguides.com

Bradt Travel Guides

www.bradtguides.com

Africa

Access Africa: Safaris for People	
with Limited Mobility	£16.99
Africa Overland	£16.99
Algeria	£15.99
Angola	£17.99
Botswana	£16.99
Burkina Faso	£17.99
Cameroon	£15.99
Cape Verde	£15.99
Congo	£15.99
Eritrea	£15.99
Ethiopia	£16.99
Ghana	£15.99
Kenya Highlights	£15.99
Madagascar	£16.99
Malawi	£15.99
Mali	£14.99
Mauritius, Rodrigues &	
Réunion	£15.99
Mozambique	£15.99
Namibia	£15.99
Niger	£14.99
Nigeria	£17.99
North Africa: Roman Coast	£15.99
Rwanda	£15.99
São Tomé & Príncipe	£14.99
Seychelles	£14.99
Sierra Leone	£16.99
South Africa Highlights	£15.99
Sudan	£15.99
Tanzania, Northern	£14.99
Tanzania	£17.99
Uganda	£16.99
Zambia	£18.99
Zanzibar	£14.99
Zimbabwe	£15.99

The Americas and the Caribbean

Alaska	£15.99
Amazon Highlights	£15.99
Argentina	£16.99
Bahia	£14.99
Cayman Islands	£14.99
Colombia	£17.99
Dominica	£15.99
Grenada, Carriacou &	
Petite Martinique	£14.99
Guyana	£15.99
Nova Scotia	£14.99
Panama	£14.99
Paraguay	£15.99
Turks & Caicos Islands	£14.99
Uruguay	£15.99
USA by Rail	£14.99
Venezuela	£16.99
Yukon	£14.99

British Isles

Britain from the Rails	£14.99
Bus-Pass Britain	£15.99
Eccentric Britain	£15.99
Eccentric Cambrige	£9.99
Eccentric London	£13.99
Eccentric Oxford	£9.99
Sacred Britain	£16.99
Slow: Cotswolds	£14.99
Slow: Devon & Exmoor	£14.99
Slow: Norfolk & Suffolk	£14.99
Slow: North Yorkshire	£14.99
Slow: Sussex & South	
Downs National Park	£14.99

Europe

Abruzzo	£14.99
Albania	£15.99
Azores	£14.99
Baltic Cities	£14.99
Belarus	£15.99
Bosnia & Herzegovina	£14.99
Bratislava	£9.99
Budapest	£9.99
Cork	£6.99
Croatia	£13.99
Cross-Channel France:	
Nord-Pas de Calais	£13.99
Cyprus see North Cyprus	
Dresden	£7.99
Estonia	£14.99
Faroe Islands	£15.99
Georgia	£15.99
Greece: The Peloponnese	£14.99
Helsinki	£7.99
Hungary	£15.99
Iceland	£15.99
Kosovo	£15.99
Lapland	£15.99
Latvia	£13.99
Lille	£9.99
Lithuania	£14.99
Luxembourg	£13.99
Macedonia	£15.99
Malta & Gozo	£12.99
Montenegro	£14.99
North Cyprus	£13.99
Riga	£6.99
Serbia	£15.99
Slovakia	£14.99
Slovenia	£13.99
Spitsbergen	£16.99
Switzerland Without	
a Car	£14.99
Transylvania	£14.99
Ukraine	£15.99
Zagreb	£6.99

Middle East, Asia and Australasia

Armenia	£15.99
Bangladesh	£15.99
Borneo	£17.99
Eastern Turkey	£16.99
Georgia	£15.99
Iran	£15.99
Iraq: Then & Now	£15.99
Israel	£15.99
Kazakhstan	£16.99
Kyrgyzstan	£16.99
Lake Baikal	£15.99
Lebanon	£15.99
Maldives	£15.99
Mongolia	£16.99
North Korea	£14.99
Oman	£15.99
Palestine	£15.99
Shangri-La:	
A Travel Guide to the	
Himalayan Dream	£14.99
Sri Lanka	£15.99
Syria	£15.99
Taiwan	£16.99
Tibet	£13.99
Yemen	£14.99

Wildlife

Antarctica: Guide to the	
Wildlife	£15.99
Arctic: Guide to Coastal	
Wildlife	£15.99
Australian Wildlife	£14.99
Central & Eastern	
European Wildlife	£15.99
Chinese Wildlife	£16.99
East African Wildlife	£19.99
Galápagos Wildlife	£16.99
Madagascar Wildlife	£16.99
New Zealand Wildlife	£14.99
North Atlantic Wildlife	£16.99
Pantanal Wildlife	£16.99
Peruvian Wildlife	£15.99
Southern African Wildlife	£19.99
Sri Lankan Wildlife	£15.99

Pictorials and other guides

100 Alien Invaders	£16.99
100 Animals to See	
Before They Die	£16.99
100 Bizarre Animals	£16.99
Eccentric Australia	£12.99
Northern Lights	£6.99
Tips on Tipping	£6.99
Wildlife and Conservation	
Volunteering: The	
Complete Guide	£13.99

Wanderlust

READERS'
TRAVEL
AWARDS
2011

TOP GUIDEBOOK SERIES

541

Index

Page numbers in **bold** indicate main entries; those in *italics* indicate maps.

INDEX OF ADVERTISERS